Ericksonian Methods

The Essence of the Story

Ericksonian Methods
The Essence of the Story

Edited by
Jeffrey K. Zeig, Ph.D.

Director

The Milton H. Erickson Foundation

Brunner/Mazel *Publishers* • New York

All royalties from this book are the property of The Milton H. Erickson Foundation, Inc., 3606 North 24th Street, Phoenix, Arizona 85016. Royalties will be used to foster educational and scientific efforts that pertain to psychotherapy and hypnosis.

Library of Congress Cataloging-in-Publication Data

Ericksonian methods : the essence of the story/ edited by Jeffrey K. Zeig.
    p.   cm.
    Includes bibliographical references and index.
    ISBN 0-87630-738-1
    1. Erickson, Milton H. — Congresses.   2. Hypnotism — Therapeutic use — Congresses.   3. Psychotherapy — Congresses.   I. Zeig, Jeffrey K.
RC490.5.E75E756   1994
616.89'162 — dc20   93-46938
                                   CIP

Published by
BRUNNER/MAZEL, INC.
19 Union Square West
New York, New York 10003

Manufactured in the United States of America

10 9 8 7 6 5 4 3 2 1

This book is dedicated to

J. Charles Theisen, M.A., M.B.A., J.D.
for years of friendship
and for his contributions to
The Milton H. Erickson Foundation

Contents

Introduction

As Congress organizer and editor of the these proceedings, it is my pleasure to introduce this book. *Ericksonian Methods: The Essence of the Story* contains the proceedings of the Fifth International Congress on Erickson Approaches to Hypnosis and Psychotherapy. It consists of the keynote speeches and invited addresses from the Congress. There have been edited proceedings of each of the previous four Congresses, all published by Brunner/Mazel (for details see pp. 497–498).

The development and evolution of the Erickson Foundation and its Congresses have been a fitting tribute to the landmark contributions of Milton H. Erickson, M.D. Many maintain that what Freud meant to the theory of personality, Erickson meant to the practice of psychotherapy. Yet, Erickson's popularity is a recent development. Erickson's work became mainstream during his last years and then since his death on March 25, 1980. In fact, I believe the term "Ericksonian therapy" initially appeared in a book title in the 1982 published proceedings of the First Congress, which was held in December, 1980.

Erickson's legacy has been developed and advanced by his colleagues and intellectual heirs, many of whom were on the 1992 Congress faculty. The array of Erickson's students is remarkable. It includes exemplary teachers and writers who have made original and important contributions.

ABOUT THE CONGRESSES

The First International Congress on Ericksonian Approaches to Hypnosis and Psychotherapy was held in Phoenix, Arizona, December 4–8, 1980. Milton H. Erickson, M.D., was a member of the organizing committee of that Congress. One of the purposes of the meeting was to give him the opportunity to see the impact of his work. Unfortunately, he died eight and one-half months prior to the meeting. He would have been gratified to see approximately 2,000 professionals who attended that first Congress. When he died, 750 people already had registered.

The purpose of the Second International Congress, also held in Phoenix, November 30–December 4, 1983, was to broaden and advance Ericksonian methodology. More than 2,000 attendees participated in this event, constituting the largest professional meeting held on the topic of hypnosis.

The Third International Congress met in Phoenix, Arizona, December 3–7, 1986, and brought new people to the Erickson movement. Enthusiasm for Dr. Erickson's psychotherapeutic legacy ran high, and there was an attendance of 1,800.

The basis for the Fourth International Congress was expanded to include the theme "Brief Therapy: Myths, Methods, and Metaphors." It attracted more than 2,200 professionals from the United States and 24 countries, to San Francisco, from December 7–11, 1988. Dr. Erickson's development of brief psychotherapy established a foundation for many therapists who follow in that direction today.

The Fifth Congress was held in Phoenix, Arizona, December 2–6, 1992, and was attended by 1,700 professionals from the United States and 21 countries. The theme of the Fifth Congress, "Ericksonian Methods: The Essence of the Story," addressed the essentials of Ericksonian principles and practice as applied to modern health sciences. An additional program, the "Therapist Development Track," was added to this Congress and was well received.

CONGRESS FORMAT

The Fifth Congress featured preeminent practitioners of Ericksonian therapy. It was clinically oriented and was designed to make available a wealth of knowledge and opportunities in order to experience the creative and perceptive psychotherapy developed by the late Milton H. Erickson, M.D.

The faculty consisted of more than 170 professionals, including moderators, copresenters, and special faculty. Registrants chose the format that best suited their needs, whether academic or experiential.

In the academic area, the program consisted of three keynote speeches and 30 invited addresses. The keynote presentations included the following: Jay Haley, who presented "Typically Erickson"; Cloé Madanes's topic was entitled, "Money and the Family"; and Ernest Rossi spoke on "Ericksonian Psychotherapy—Then and Now: New Fundamentals of the Naturalistic-Utilization Approach." It is the academic portion of the Congress that appears in these proceedings.

In the experiential area, there were 65 two-hour workshops and small-group practica, as well as interactive events such as conversation hours, panels, dialogues, and trialogues. Continuing a program initiated in 1983, attendees were able to work in small-group, supervised practica (limited to 12 participants). Here specific experiences in methods and techniques of Ericksonian hypnotherapy were offered, such as induction and the use of metaphor. These were led by faculty members.

The "Therapist Development Track," a new option for training, was offered during the Fifth Congress. Six one-day tracks centered on the personal development of the therapist. Cultivation and empowerment of the therapist's personal process were emphasized. These programs were led by: Stephen Lankton, M.S.W.; Ernest Rossi, Ph.D.; Stephen Gilligan, Ph.D.; Kay Thompson, D.D.S., and Betty Alice Erickson, M.S., L.P.C.; Jeffrey Zeig, Ph.D.; Michael Yapko, Ph.D., and Norma Barretta, Ph.D.

On the third day of the Congress (Friday), a format change allowed attendees an opportunity to participate in interactive events, including one-hour clinical demonstrations, conversation hours, panels, group inductions, dialogues, and trialogues.

An additional training opportunity was provided for the registrants to attend miniworkshops (short courses), symposia, and accepted papers, presented by professionals from around the world who responded to a Call for Proposals.

The evening programs included a welcome reception, an authors' hour, a videotape production entitled *Milton H. Erickson, M.D., Explorer in Hypnosis and Therapy** (produced and edited by Jay Haley, M.A., and Madeleine Richeport, Ph.D.), and an Arizona party.

Ericksonian Methods: The Essence of the Story, presented standards of modern Ericksonian practice. Both faculty and registrants responded enthusiastically. In fact, this Congress was the most highly rated of all previous Erickson Congresses.

Jeffrey K. Zeig, Ph.D.

---

*Editor's Note: To purchase a copy of this videotape, contact Brunner/Mazel, Inc.; 19 Union Square West; New York, NY 10003; Telephone (212) 924-3344.

Acknowledgments

Many persons were involved in making this Congress successful, and I want to thank them.

The following professionals reviewed the abstracts of papers and short courses/symposia submitted for presentation: Yvonne M. Dolan, M.A.; Janet S. Edgette, Psy.D., M.P.H.; Kristina K. Erickson, M.S., M.D.; Betty Alice Erickson, M.S., L.P.C.; Brent B. Geary, Ph.D.; Stephen Gilligan, Ph.D.; Ronald A. Havens, Ph.D.; Lynn Johnson, Ph.D.; Roxanna Erickson Klein, R.N., M.S.; Richard Landis, Ph.D.; Carol Lankton, M.A.; Stephen Lankton, M.S.W.; Herbert S. Lustig, M.D.; Michele Ritterman, Ph.D.; Gary P. Ruelas, Ph.D.; Sandra M. Sylvester, Ph.D.; Kay Thompson, D.D.S.; and Catherine Walters, M.S.W.

The Editorial Review Board is listed in the back of the book. The editors made an important contribution in reviewing papers for publication in this volume. Each paper was read by a minimum of two editors. Members of the Editorial Board also served as moderators at Congress events.

Thanks also to Bernie Mazel and Natalie Gilman for their editorial assistance. Brunner/Mazel Publishers have been a strong supporter of The Milton H. Erickson Foundation through the years.

On behalf of the Board of Directors of The Milton H. Erickson Foundation, I want to thank the distinguished faculty of the Fifth International Congress. Their contributions brought numerous compliments from attendees.

The staff of the Erickson Foundation devoted much time and energy in preparations for the meeting; processing registrations; arranging for faculty and guests; coordinating volunteers; planning publicity, brochures, and the syllabus; and in numerous other administrative tasks. With Linda Carr McThrall, Executive Director, the following staff deserve special recognition: Theresa Germack, administrative assistant; Sylvia Cowen, bookkeeper; Diane Deniger, volunteer coordinator; Greg Deniger, Congress registrar, computer operations manager; Jeannine Elder, faculty coordinator; Alice McAvoy, office assistant; Regina Murua, administrative assistant; Lori Weiers, M.S., editorial assistant.

Appreciation is also due to the volunteers who worked with the staff prior to and at the Congress. Special thanks to Ed Hancock for his video assistance, and to Vicki Tarulis who served as a special administrative assistant and Congress photographer. In addition to these, 65 graduate student volunteers served as monitors and assisted with registration and the processing of continuing education credits.

Special thanks go to Barry Shephard of SHR Communication Planning and Design of Phoenix, who designed the Erickson Foundation logo.

I am grateful to the Maricopa Medical Center, Department of Psychiatry and to Arizona State University, Departments of Psychology and Social Work who cosponsored the Fifth International Congress.

The Board of Directors assisted in all the planning that produced the Congress, and I thank them for this. In addition to myself, the members of the board are Kristina K. Erickson, M.S., M.D.; Elizabeth M. Erickson, B.A., and J. Charles Theisen, M.A., M.B.A., J.D.

I am especially grateful to Linda Carr McThrall, Executive Director of the Foundation, for her extraordinary efforts in administering the Congress.

Jeffrey K. Zeig, Ph.D.

Contributors

Joseph Barber, Ph.D., has a private consulting practice in Seattle. He is Clinical Associate Professor, University of Washington, School of Medicine; Assistant Editor for the *American Journal of Clinical Hypnosis;* a Fellow and President of The Society for Clinical and Experimental Hypnosis; Diplomate of the American Board of Psychological Hypnosis; and a member of the Associate Editorial Board of the *Ericksonian Monographs.* With Cheri Adrian, he coedited *Psychological Approaches to the Management of Pain* (Brunner/Mazel, 1983), and has authored or coauthored more than 30 articles and chapters.

Philip Barker, M.B., B.S., is Professor of Psychiatry and Pediatrics, University of Calgary and Director of the Department of Psychiatry at Alberta Children's Hospital in Calgary. He is Editor of the *Canadian Child Psychiatric Bulletin* and a member of the Editorial Board, *Child Psychiatry and Human Development.* He has authored five books and many papers and chapters.

Shirley E. Bliss, Ph.D., does research in Denton, TX, in the mental health field. She is a professional member of the International Society of Hypnosis, The Society for Clinical and Experimental Hypnosis, The North Texas Society of Hypnosis, and the Texas Counseling Association.

Gene Combs, M.D., is codirector of the Evanston Family Therapy Center and a faculty member of the Chicago Center for Family Health, an affiliate of the University of Chicago, and has a private practice. He has coauthored with Jill Freedman, *Symbols, Story, and Ceremony: Using Metaphor in Individual and Family Therapy* (Norton, 1990).

Steve de Shazer, M.S.S.W., is cofounder of the Brief Family Therapy Center in Milwaukee, WI, and is a Fellow and an Approved Supervisor of the American Association for Marriage and Family Therapy. He is a member of the Editorial Boards of *The Journal of Strategic and Systemic Therapies, Zeitschrift für Systemische Therapie, The American Journal of Family Therapy, Familiendynamik, Journal of Family Therapy,* and *Systeme.* He has authored or coauthored numerous books, articles, and chapters.

Yvonne Dolan, M.A., is a psychotherapist in private practice in Denver, CO. She has published several articles and two books: *Resolving Sexual Abuse* (Norton, 1991) and *A Path with a Heart* (Brunner/Mazel, 1985).

Betty Alice Erickson, M.S., is a psychotherapist in private practice in Dallas, TX. She is coeditor of The Milton H. Erickson Foundation Newsletter and has authored or coauthored several articles and chapters.

Richard Fisch, M.D., organized the Brief Therapy Center of the Mental Research Institute in Palo Alto, CA, in 1966, and is its director and principal investigator. He is a Clinical Associate Professor of Psychiatry at Stanford University, Department of Psychiatry and Behavioral Medicine, and has a private practice in Palo Alto. He is a member of the Associate Editorial Board of the *Ericksonian Monographs,* and has coauthored with Paul Watzlawick and John Weakland, *Change* (Norton, 1974), and coauthored with John Weakland and L. Segal, *The Tactics of Change* (Jossey-Bass, 1982). He also has authored numerous articles and chapters.

Jill Freedman, M.S.W., is codirector of the Evanston Family Therapy Center, and is on the faculty of the Chicago Center for Family Health, an affiliate of the University of Chicago. She coauthored with Gene Combs, *Symbol, Story, and Ceremony: Using Metaphor in Individual and Family Therapy* (Norton, 1990).

Brent B. Geary, Ph.D., is the Coordinator of Training at The Milton H. Erickson Foundation, and has a private practice in Phoenix, AZ. He has authored and coauthored several articles and chapters.

Stephen G. Gilligan, Ph.D., has a private practice in Encinitas, CA. He is a member of the Associate Editorial Board of the *Ericksonian Monographs.* He has authored *Therapeutic Trances: The Cooperation Principle in Ericksonian Hypnotherapy* (Brunner/Mazel, 1986) and edited with Jeffrey K. Zeig, *Brief Therapy: Myths, Methods, and Metaphors* (Brunner/Mazel, 1990); and has authored or coauthored numerous articles and chapters.

Jean Godin, M.D., Ph.D., is president of the Institut Milton H. Erickson de Paris and of the Editorial Board of the Milton Erickson Institute of Paris journal, *Phoenix.* He has authored *The New Hypnosis* [French] (Albin Michel, 1992), and has written numerous articles and chapters.

Jay Haley, M.A., is codirector of the Family Therapy Institute of Washington, DC. He is the former Editor of *Family Process,* and is a member of the Associate Editorial Board of the *Ericksonian Monographs.* He has authored seven books, coauthored two, and edited five. He also has made more than 50 contributions to professional journals and books.

Ronald A. Havens, Ph.D., is Professor of Psychology at Sangamon State University in Springfield, IL; is a member of the Advisory Editorial Board of the *Ericksonian Monographs;* and has a private practice. He has authored *The Wisdom of Milton H. Erickson* (Irvington, 1985), coauthored with Catherine Walters, *Hypnotherapy Scripts* (Brunner/Mazel, 1989), and *Hypnotherapy for Health, Harmony, and Peak Performance* (Brunner/Mazel, 1993), and has authored or coauthored numerous articles and chapters.

Carol J. Kershaw, Ed.D., is codirector of the Milton H. Erickson Institute of Houston; has a private practice; and has membership in seven professional organizations. She has authored one book, *The Couple's Hypnotic Dance* (Brunner/Mazel, 1991), and several chapters.

Alfred Lange, Ph.D., is Professor of Psychology at the University of Amsterdam and Chairman of the Dutch Society of Family and Couple Therapy. He is a member of the Editorial Board of *The Journal of Family Therapy,* the coeditor and founding member of the Board of *Directive Therapie,* and a member of the International Advisory Board of the *Ericksonian Monographs.* He is first author of *Directive Family Therapy* (Brunner/Mazel, 1983), and has published three Dutch-language books.

Carol H. Lankton, M.A., has a private practice in Gulf Breeze, FL, and is a member of the Associate Editorial Board of the *Ericksonian Monographs.* She has coauthored, with Stephen Lankton, three books: *The Answer Within* (Brunner/Mazel, 1983), *Enchantment and Intervention in Family Therapy* (Brunner/Mazel, 1986), and *Tales of Enchantment* (Brunner/Mazel, 1989). She has also authored and coauthored numerous articles and chapters.

Stephen R. Lankton, M.S.W., is founding editor of the *Ericksonian Monographs.* He is an Approved Consultant of the American Society of Clinical Hypnosis; a Fellow, and Approved Supervisor, of the American

Association for Marriage and Family Therapy; a Diplomate in American Hypnosis Board for Clinical Social Work; and a Diplomate in Clinical Social Work. He also has a private practice in Gulf Breeze, FL. With Carol Lankton, he has coauthored three books: *The Answer Within* (Brunner/Mazel, 1983), *Enchantment and Intervention in Family Therapy* (Brunner/Mazel, 1986), and *Tales of Enchantment* (Brunner/Mazel, 1989), and he has authored *Practical Magic* (Meta, 1980), *The Blammo-Surprise Book: A Story to Help Children Overcome Fears* (Brunner/Mazel, 1988), and numerous chapters.

Camillo Loriedo, M.D., is a Professor at the University of Rome, is in private practice, and is President of the Family Therapy Association of Italy. He is Editor of the journal, *Attraverso lo Specchio* and is on the Advisory Editorial Boards of *Terapia Familiare, Revista Italiana di Ipnosi, Ecologia della Mente,* and the *Ericksonian Monographs*. He has authored *Terapia Relazionale* (Italian, 1978) and coauthored, with Gaspare Vella, *Paradox and the Family System* (Brunner/Mazel, 1991).

John D. Lovern, Ph.D., is President, International Association of Eating Disorders Professionals; and President, Orange County Chapter for the Study of Multiple Personality and Dissociation. He has a private practice in Orange, CA, and has authored *Pathways to Reality: Erickson-Inspired Treatment Approaches to Chemical Dependency* (Brunner/Mazel, 1991) and numerous journal articles and chapters.

Cloé Madanes, Lic. Psychol., is codirector of the Family Therapy Institute of Washington, DC, and Adjunct Associate Professor in the Department of Psychiatry at the University of Maryland. She is a member of the Associate Editorial Board of the *Ericksonian Monographs* and has authored *Strategic Family Therapy* (Jossey-Bass, 1981) and *Behind the One-Way Mirror* (Jossey-Bass, 1984) and several chapters.

Jean-Michel Oughourlian, M.D., Ph.D., is a member of the Board of Directors of the Institut Milton H. Erickson de Paris. Currently he is Professor at the Sorbonne University.

Robert E. Pearson, M.D., is past President of the American Society of Clinical Hypnosis, the American Board of Medical Hypnosis, and the Northern Michigan Medical Society. He has served as a member of the Editorial Board of the *American Journal of Clinical Hypnosis,* and is a member of the Associate Editorial Board of the *Ericksonian Monographs*. He has a private practice in Houston, TX, and is the author of numerous articles and chapters.

Madeleine Richeport, Ph.D., is Adjunct Associate Professor, Department of Psychiatry, University of Miami; a mental health consultant; and a member of the Advisory Editorial Board of the *Ericksonian Monographs.* She has published numerous papers and chapters on anthropology.

Michele Klevens Ritterman, Ph.D., has a private practice in Oakland, California, and is a member of the Advisory Editorial Board of the *Ericksonian Monographs.* She is the author of *Using Hypnosis in Family Therapy* (Jossey-Bass, 1983) and *Hope Under Siege: Terror and Family Support* (Ablex, 1990). She is also the author of numerous chapters in books and professional papers in the fields of hypnosis and systemic therapies. She is also a published poet.

Sidney Rosen, M.D., is the founding President of the New York Milton H. Erickson Society for Psychotherapy and Hypnosis. He is an Assistant Clinical Professor of Psychiatry at New York University College of Medicine and University Hospital, as well as a Faculty Member at the American Institute of Psychoanalysis (Karen Horney). He is a member of the Associate Editorial Board of the *Ericksonian Monographs* and *Hypnose und Kognition* in Munich. He has a private practice in New York City and is the editor of *My Voice Will Go With You: The Teaching Tales of Milton H. Erickson, M.D.* (Norton, 1982; paper 1991).

Ernest L. Rossi, Ph.D., is affiliated with the C. J. Jung Institute in Los Angeles and is Editor of *Psychological Perspectives: A Semiannual Review of Jungian Thought.* He is a member of the Editorial Board of the *American Journal of Clinical Hypnosis* and an Associate member of the Editorial Board of the *Ericksonian Monographs.* He has edited or published 17 books including four volumes of Erickson's collected papers (Irvington, 1980).

Sandra M. Sylvester, Ph.D., is on the visiting faculty of the Gestalt Institute of Cleveland and is a clinical instructor in the Department of Anesthesiology at the University of New Mexico. She is an Advisory member of the Editorial Board of the *Ericksonian Monographs,* has a private practice in Cedar Crest, NM, and has authored various articles.

Kay F. Thompson, D.D.S, is a Clinical Associate Professor in the Department of Community Dentistry at West Virginia University, and an Assistant Clinical Professor of Psychiatry in the School of Medicine at West Virginia University. She has served as President of the American Society for Clinical Hypnosis and the Pennsylvania Dental Association, and has a part-time private practice. She has authored numerous chapters, and is currently on the Associate Editorial Board of the *Ericksonian Monographs.*

Bernhard Trenkle, Dipl. Psych., is Director of the Milton Erickson Institut Rottweil, and a member of the Board of Directors of M.E.G. (Milton H. Erickson Gesellschaft). He is founding editor of the M.E.G. Newsletter and is in private practice in Rottweil. He is on the Editorial Board of *Ericksonian Monographs* and *Hypnose und Kognition,* and has authored several articles and chapters.

Gaspare Vella, M.D., is Professor of Psychiatry and Director of the School of Psychiatry and of the Psychiatric Clinic of the University of Rome.

Catherine Walters, M.A., M.S.W., is Adjunct Professor of Psychology at Sangamon State University in Springfield, IL, and is in private practice. She has coauthored, with Ronald Havens, *Hypnotherapy Scripts* (Brunner/ Mazel, 1989) and *Hypnotherapy for Health, Harmony, and Peak Performance* (Brunner/Mazel, 1993).

John H. Weakland, Ch.E., is affiliated with the Mental Research Institute in Palo Alto, CA, and is codirector of the Brief Therapy Center. He is Clinical Associate Professor Emeritus in the Department of Psychiatry and Behavioral Sciences at Stanford Medical School, and is a Fellow of the American Anthropological Association and of the Society for Applied Anthropology. He has coauthored a number of books, including *Change* (Norton, 1974) and *Tactics of Change* (Jossey-Bass, 1982).

André M. Weitzenhoffer, Ph.D., is retired from the University of Oklahoma Health Science Center and is a past member of the Editorial Board of the *American Journal of Clinical Hypnosis.* He has authored and coauthored numerous papers, chapters, and encyclopedia articles, and has authored *Hypnotism: An Objective Study in Suggestibility* (John Wiley, 1953), *General Techniques of Hypnotism* (Grune & Stratton, 1957), and *The Practice of Hypnotism, Vols. I and II* (John Wiley & Sons, 1989).

Michael D. Yapko, Ph.D., is Director of The Milton H. Erickson Institute of San Diego. He is the past editor of the Erickson Foundation's Newsletter, an Advisory Editorial Board member of the *Ericksonian Monographs,* and a Fellow of the American Society of Clinical Hypnosis. He also has a private practice in San Diego. He has authored five books, including *Hypnosis and the Treatment of Depressions* (Brunner/Mazel, 1992) and *Suggestions of Abuse: True and False Memories of Childhood Sexual Trauma* (Simon & Schuster, 1994). He also has authored numerous chapters and articles.

Jeffrey K. Zeig, Ph.D., is the founder and Director of The Milton H. Erickson Foundation in Phoenix, AZ. He organized the five International Congresses on Ericksonian Approaches to Hypnosis and Psychotherapy, as well as the two landmark Evolution of Psychotherapy Conferences and the Brief Therapy Conference. He has a private practice and serves on the Editorial Boards of two foreign and three American journals. He has edited, coedited, or authored 13 books and five monographs.

Convocation

As you prepare to enter into the Congress, I would like to briefly present a personal perspective about Milton H. Erickson. Many of you at this Congress were his colleagues, friends, and students, but some of you did not know him personally. It may be helpful to know some of the characteristics of Erickson's life, work, and thinking processes that made him effective both personally and professionally. Also, I would like the opening remarks of this Congress to include some of Erickson's own words, to initiate a constructive Ericksonian frame of reference.

This Congress is designed to emphasize communication and observational skills which are the very essence of Ericksonian therapy. My hope is to bring you a little closer to Milton Erickson. If you know more about him, you may be better able to use the didactic content of this meeting.

Milton Erickson was born in 1901 to a mining and farming family and was one of 12 children, three of whom died in infancy. Though his parents were emotionally supportive, finances were a serious and constant struggle. Erickson was stricken at the age of 17 with debilitating polio. He worked very hard during his adult lifetime to overcome illness and disability. In reflecting back on his life and health, Erickson said, "I had to learn to reconcile myself to the unfairness of life." In that process of reconciliation, he learned to use and appreciate the abilities that he had. Appreciation was intrinsic to his therapy. He said, "I always find when I can do something, it's pleasurable." Because of his physical limitations, his talents at observation and communication assumed critical importance. Prior to having polio, he was very athletic and, in fact, a champion pole vaulter. Following his illness and residual paralysis, his career options were limited.

Typical of Ericksonian reframing, he credited polio with guiding him into the field of psychiatry. As a busy family man, with physical limitations, eight children, and a demanding professional life, it is not surprising that he was an exceedingly practical therapist. He said, "You must observe ordinary behavior and be perfectly willing to use it. . . . In other words, whatever your patient has, make use of it."

Erickson utilized whatever assets he could, including family, social systems, and environmental resources. He developed his therapies within the context of the cultural and social systems of the particular time. As you read Erickson's cases, recognize that his therapy spanned 50 years. To understand his work, one must refer examples to their temporal and social situations. Socially desirable objectives and outcomes in 1935 differed from social objectives in 1980. A unifying principle is that the therapist must work within the framework of the times.

Erickson had great respect for his fellow man and woman. He understood that solutions lie within the patient. The therapist served as a guide. He said that concepts of advanced psychotherapy should "Rely on the capacity of the individual patient to furnish the cues, the information by which to organize psychotherapy, because the patient can find a way if given an opportunity." It is the objective of the psychotherapist to observe and communicate in such a way that the patient can achieve a positive outcome. Erickson said, "One should look upon patients as possessing understandings that are available if therapists are willing to respect that patient and willing to give the patient the opportunity to function and react to the therapeutic situation."

In speaking and advising on the personal development and skills of a therapist, Erickson recommended openness and personal growth: "And therefore you have to have an open mind; not a critical mind, not a judgmental mind; but a curious, a scientific mind wondering what the real situation is." Contributing to his success was the fact that my father was a very curious man. He loved acquiring knowledge and enjoyed the intellectual challenge of figuring out what a patient really meant.

Erickson said, "You listen to your patient, knowing that he has a personal meaning for his words, and you don't know his personal meaning and he doesn't know your personal meaning for words. You try to understand the patient's words as he understands them." He also said, "I emphasize the importance of understanding the patient's words and really understanding them. You don't interpret your patient's words in your language."

Erickson believed that therapy is very hard work. In describing the process of developing suggestions, he stated, "Years ago, I'd write down about 40 pages of suggestions that I would condense down to 20 pages, and then down to 10. Then I'd carefully reformulate and make good use of every word and phrase until I finally condensed it down to about five pages. Everyone who is serious about learning suggestion needs to go through that process to become truly aware of just what they are saying."

My father was 50 years old when I was born. I knew him as a wise, older man who found great enjoyment in people and in life. He had a terrific sense of humor, a wonderful imagination, and a very strong sense of ethics. He found knowledge and information exciting and told me that he learned something every day of his life. He greatly enjoyed professional meetings that reputably advanced a serious cause. He believed meetings to be a fine forum for the interchange of knowledge. He would have been delighted with this Congress and the variety of topics and information and people this meeting brings together. I believe he also would have found great pleasure in knowing that more than 12 years after his death in 1980, his works carry an active role and influence in the ongoing study of psychotherapy and hypnosis.

The Board of Directors of The Milton H. Erickson Foundation joins me in hoping that you will have an extremely profitable and educational time at this Congress.

Kristina K. Erickson, M.S., M.D.
Board of Directors
The Milton H. Erickson Foundation

"Each person is a unique individual. Hence, psychotherapy should be formulated to meet the uniqueness of the individual's needs, rather than tailoring the person to fit the Procrustean bed of a hypothetical theory of human behavior."

—Milton H. Erickson, M.D.

PART I

Keynote Addresses

CHAPTER 1

Typically Erickson

Jay Haley

As I was planning this paper, I found it difficult to think of something new to write about Milton Erickson. I decided to talk about what is familiar about him—what everyone knows as "typically Erickson." I will present some aspects of his approach and how it differs from others. Some of the cases and ideas will be familiar because I will be repeating published cases. Since, sadly, we will no longer be having new cases by Erickson, we must continue to share and enjoy the finite number we do have.

Many years ago, in the 1950's, Ray Birdwhistell, the authority on body movement, estimated to me that Erickson had 5,000 hard-core fans. He was surprised at the size of that crowd. I was surprised that a psychiatrist would have "fans." Even though he was outside the mainstream of therapy in those days, Erickson was known to a surprising number of people. If someone mentioned him, another person would say, "Did you hear the case of the man who could only pee through a 24-inch wooden tube" (Haley, 1985, p. 154). They would discuss his unique way of solving that problem. When the case was recounted, one realized at once that it was an Erickson case because it was so typical of him. It was also something no other therapist would do.

I once stated that Erickson's cases were as distinctive as a Picasso painting. One knew at once who had created that work of art. The style was bold and unlike that of other artists. To continue the parallel, one must consider the period of time of an artist's work, since styles change over the years. Picasso's early work when he was mastering technique was rather traditional and quite different from his later style. His early work also was influenced by the other artists of his period. What of Erickson's ideas? Did he develop from a more traditional way of thinking about psychiatric classification to a greater appreciation of the social situation in the real world? Or was he always oriented to the real world? What of his therapy approach? Did that change and develop over the years? I think perhaps not. One cannot distinguish an early case of Erickson from a later case with any confidence.

ERICKSON'S MENTORS

Was Erickson influenced in his development by other therapists and teachers of his time? Apparently not.

When we examine the work of Erickson, a question arises. Where did he come from? Who were his predecessors and teachers? What tradition was he working within? He was properly trained in psychiatry, but he did not think like his colleagues who had the same training. When we attempt to place him within some ideological framework, we cannot fit him into the schools of therapy of his time or with the teachers.

Most therapists acknowledge a teacher in their development. Erickson did not refer to a teacher or to the influence of anyone, as I recall. I think he deliberately minimized whoever might have influenced him. He said that he learned about hypnosis as a college student when Clark Hull gave a demonstration at the University of Wisconsin (Erickson to Haley, personal communication). Could one say, therefore, that Hull was his teacher? Erickson would deny that. He said that after that demonstration he took Hull's subject to his room and hypnotized him himself. In the Fall he took a seminar from Hull. Does that mean Hull was his teacher? No, not necessarily. Erickson said that the seminar focused upon the hypnotic techniques that Erickson had developed during the summer. Therefore, he must have been teaching Hull.

A PERSPECTIVE OF CHANGE

When one is talking about therapy, it is helpful to assume there are two types of theory in the field that should not be confused. One is the theory of why people behave as they do and how they got that way. The other is a theory of change, or what to do about it. These two theories may not be related. What was distinctive about Erickson was that even when he shared with the field a theory of how people got the way they are, his ideas about how to change them were different from anyone else's. Who else in the 1940's would help a young man, in the way Erickson did, who could pee only through a wooden tube? He had him change the material, size, and length of the tube until he revealed that his penis itself was a tube. Where did that approach come from?

The case can be dated to the days Erickson served on the draft board in the 1940's; thus, it was not a later development. At that time the only clinical ideas in the field were psychodynamic. Family therapy and behavior therapy had not been born. Any other therapist at that time would have assumed that a person behaved as he did because of repressed unconscious ideas that must be brought into awareness with interpretations. How would they have explained the wooden tube and what therapy would they have done with it? In fact, they would not even have focused on the tube because it was assumed one should not focus on a presenting problem. They would have dwelt on the rich psychopathology behind the tube and its symbolic meaning. Where did Erickson learn to focus his therapy on the presenting problem?

Erickson accepted some psychodynamic ideas and even experimented with them. He tested out the psychopathology of everyday life by using hypnosis to suggest an unconscious idea and then he observed the effect on behavior. At that time, he apparently assumed that some people have symptoms as a result of unconscious ideas built in by their past. What he did to cause change was not like what anyone else did who accepted that hypothesis.

The classic example was the phobia. It was assumed that a phobia was caused by a past trauma that the person had repressed into the unconscious. The orthodox therapy was to bring into awareness that trauma and the feelings around it. Should one describe a therapeutic intervention of that type, one would know it was not typically Erickson. Even though he might accept the premise that a phobia had a past cause, what he did about it was different.

As an example, I would cite the case of an inhibited young woman who was phobic in relation to sex. The assumption was that her mother had frightened her with a lecture warning her against sex; then the mother died. Erickson regressed the young woman back to childhood to a time before the mother had given her the frightening warnings. He talked with her about how mothers give advice that only covers part of a problem, and later they offer a more complete teaching when they know their daughters are mature enough to receive it. He then took the young woman forward in time through Mother's frightening warnings about sex, agreeing with what mother had said. Then he discussed with the young woman what Mother would have said about sex in the future had she lived. The daughter would then be mature enough to use good judgment in relation to sex and her mother would talk about the positive aspects. The unfortunate death prevented her mother from completing the daughter's education. Now, the young woman was ready to accept what Erickson could provide — the more positive view of sex that Mother would have given had she lived.

Erickson's ideas about what to do to change people set him apart in the field. Other people were providing insight into the past. Erickson was setting out to change the past, as in this case, and more fully in the various February Men cases (Haley, 1986, p. 179). It was also typical of Erickson to accept and agree with the negative comments the mother had made and then to change them. He did not condemn the mother or her sexual views when they were so important to the daughter. Erickson's idea that one should use accepting techniques to change people was controversial at the time, and still is. Other therapists argued that you should not approve of a mother's views on sex with which you do not agree. Erickson would argue that not accepting them would have made him unable to communicate adequately with the daughter. Similarly, it was typical of Erickson to be hard on a client who was accustomed to people being hard on him. He considered it necessary for communication. From whom in our kindly profession did he learn such an idea?

Erickson's view of how to change a phobia appears always to have assumed that the phobic situation must be entered with the person distracted and experiencing a new set of emotions and expectations. He would have a person enter a feared elevator while concentrating only on the sensations in the soles of his feet, or he would have a person prepare for the phobic situation by imaging fears on a screen, thus distancing himself from frightening emotions. He would also go out into the world and take action to resolve a phobia. For example, an elderly doctor came to him to recover from a fear of elevators (Haley, 1986, p. 297). He worked in a hospital on the fifth floor, and he had always walked up the five flights of stairs. He was afraid to ride in the elevator even though the elevators were run by competent young women and were safe. He was getting old and frail, and he could not continue to make it up the stairs.

There are different ways a therapist might conceptualize this fear and its cause, and different ways to think about how to induce change. What would one consider a typically Ericksonian approach? Let me list what I believe were a few of his assumptions and observations as they might fit this case.

1. He would not ask about past traumas, but would focus upon a change in action in the present. He apparently assumed the phobia would be relieved if the client used an elevator while not experiencing the fear of elevators.

2. Since he focused upon symptoms, he was interested in the details. He learned that the doctor was able to go in and out of an elevator. It was when the elevator moved that he panicked.

3. As always, he observed his client carefully, and noted that the elderly doctor was a very correct, rigid man who was extremely proper in his behavior.

Given these observations and assumptions, could one guess what Erickson's typical intervention would be?

Erickson went to the hospital with the elderly doctor and observed the elevators with him. Since the doctor could go in and out of the elevator, Erickson chose an elevator and asked the young woman operator to hold it on that floor. He had the doctor walk in and out, which he demonstrated he could do. Erickson asked the doctor to walk in and out one more time. This time when the doctor walked in, the operator shut the doors. She said to him, "I can't help myself, I have this desperate desire to kiss you." The prudish doctor said, "Stay away from me, behave yourself." The young woman said, "I just have to kiss you." The doctor said, "Take this elevator up at once!" She pushed the handle and the elevator started to rise. Between floors she stopped it again and said, "We're between floors, no one can see me kiss you." "Take this elevator up," said the doctor, and she did so. The doctor's fear of rising in an elevator ended with that one intervention.

ERICKSON'S USE OF AUXILIARY PERSONNEL

A typical Erickson assumption was that single-session therapy was quite possible. Erickson also typically used auxiliary personnel to achieve his ends, such as hairdressers and dressmakers and elevator operators. How different that was from the therapists of the time who would not even talk to a relative on the telephone, far less involve someone else in the therapy. Where did he get the idea of using auxiliary personnel when no one did that? In fact, he involved his children in his therapy, which no one would have done then, or perhaps even now. In those days, even if a client inquired whether or not a therapist had children, it would not be revealed. The therapist would say, "I wonder why you ask that?" Erickson's waiting room for years was the family living room.

Erickson thought it important for a therapist to be personally involved with a client. He did not think the therapist should be a blank screen or a neutral observer. It was his personal involvement that often induced the change he was after.

ERICKSON AND INSIGHT

When clarifying the idea that Erickson was not in the psychodynamic school, one should note the difference between insight in psychodynamic therapy and Erickson's educational approach. He never made interpretations in the usual sense. If a therapist says, "Have you noticed that the way you respond to your boss is like you responded to your father," one can be sure the therapist was not Erickson. He never used such phrases as, "Isn't it interesting that . . ." or "Do you realize that . . ." or "I wonder why you defeat yourself in that way." Yet he often educated clients about themselves. He would not help a slim boy realize he was jealous of his strong brother. but he would help the boy discover that he was slim and quick and so more agile than his large and muscular brother. A primary difference between Erickson's educational approach and the insight of psychodynamicists was that he emphasized the discovery of the positive side. But where did he get this idea? In that early period the clinical field explored only the negative.

Erickson did not provide the usual insight, and he demonstrated that change could occur without people having any understanding of why they had the problem or how they got over it. It was his willingness to change someone without teaching them the cause of the problem that was most typical and most opposed by the therapists who believed that only self-knowledge leads to salvation.

Erickson apparently considered insightful interpretations to be rude. A distinctive characteristic of his therapy was that it was often so courteous. If one hears of a therapist accepting the delusion of a patient and working within it, the odds are the therapist was Erickson. For example, a woman said there was a large bear trap in the center of Erickson's small office (Haley, 1985, p. 232). Since no one else could see it, one might assume this was a delusion, if considered in a psychiatric framework. However, Erickson would not violate that bear trap. In the woman's presence he carefully walked around it each time he left the room. That is typically Erickson.

Other therapists would refuse to participate in such a delusion. They would tell her that the trap was not there and discuss how she was misperceiving the world. Some would consider it a sign she was untreatable and could only be medicated. Others would consider it unethical not to correct her delusion. Erickson seemed to assume that the introduction of the bear trap was a way of communicating something to him and he would accept that metaphor.

Let me cite an example that many people know because it has been published (Haley, 1986, p. 197). A mother came to Erickson and said that her teenage daughter had withdrawn from the world and would not leave the house to go to school or anywhere. She had the idea that her feet were too big and she would not show them outside. A therapist in those days was incapacitated by the rule that one should only see clients in the office. The girl would not leave her house.

What was typical of Erickson was that he always did what had to be done, within the limits of his strength. He went to the house for two obvious reasons: one, the girl would not come to him, and two, he would like to see if her feet were normal in size. Erickson typically checked out the truth of supposed misperceptions or delusions. He used as an excuse that the mother was not feeling well and he was a physician making a house call. He examined the mother and asked the daughter to help by standing beside him and handing him towels, or whatever he might need. He observed that the girl's feet were of normal size.

At a certain point Erickson decided what he should do. He maneuvered the girl until she was just behind him, and then he stepped back as hard as he could on her foot. The girl yelled in pain. Erickson turned on her angrily and said, "If you would grow those feet *big* enough for a *man* to see, I wouldn't be in this position." He continued to examine the mother while the daughter looked thoughtful. Later in the afternoon the mother called Erickson and said her daughter had asked if she could go out to the movies and had done so. The next day she went back to school and was over the problem.

Those of us teetering on the edge of eternity had the privilege of knowing Erickson when he was physically active. He could easily drive around town and visit clients or fly to Schenectady and do a workshop. Those who only knew him confined to a wheel chair could not appreciate that a typical Erickson intervention was a home visit, something not considered by properly trained therapists. He seemed to assume a psychiatrist should be like an old-fashioned family doctor in making himself available.

Erickson often brought about change, in this case and others, without anyone understanding what had happened. Not only did he offer change without awareness, but sometimes also without permission. According to the orthodoxy, change without insight or education was impossible, or it was defined as not really change. Not only would psychodynamicists object to this approach, but so would cognitive therapists, or behavioral therapists, or cognitive behavioral therapists, or solution-oriented therapists, or even constructivists.

Let me summarize some of the differences between Erickson and the therapists of his time and raise the question of where he learned to do the opposite of his colleagues. He focused on a presenting problem when they did not. He sought a single-session therapy when he could, and he never argued that long-term therapy was better or deeper. He used auxilliary personnel. He was personally involved. He did not make interpretations or provide insight. Other therapists were helping people remember every miserable moment in their past, and they considered that helping people forget was wrong. Erickson induced amnesia for present and past events. He accepted what the client offered and did not correct their ideas prematurely. He made home visits. Finally, he did not merely offer reflection, but took action and gave directives.

When one attends a large meeting honoring Erickson with a faculty of prominent teachers of the major schools of therapy, one finds that even today most of them are not enthusiasts for this typical Erickson approach. In fact, they are shocked by change without understanding and prefer a more rational approach when dealing with irrational problems. Apparently they had an orthodox source of their ideas. But what was the source of Erickson's ideas?

INFLUENCE WITHOUT AWARENESS

What about the other schools of therapy developing in the 1950's? At that time, new innovations began to appear. One of the few advantages of being older is that one has seen the birth and death of various ideologies and ways of doing therapy. I recall an early instance of the beginnings of a new therapy approach and a serious argument over changing someone outside their awareness. It was in a Veterans Hospital in the 1950's when I was on Gregory Bateson's research project on communication. We were developing a therapy with a family orientation. We shared a building with research psychologists who were developing what was to become behavior therapy.

At one of our lunchtime research presentations, two young psychologists said they wished to present a new idea. The audience was a group of hospital staff, almost all of them psychoanalysts or with a psychodynamic ideology. The leader of that group was the Director of Training. He was an elderly, conservative analyst.

As their presentation, the two young men offered a way to increase the expression of emotions, which was considered important at that time. If you wish a patient to express more emotion, they said, every time he expresses emotion you nod and smile. When he doesn't, you remain impassive. They said if you do that, you'll have a very emotional patient at the end of an hour. The Director of Training and his analytic colleagues reacted with indignation to this presentation. The Director said this was immoral, if not the behavior of a cad. To influence a person without that person being aware of what you are doing is simply improper. One of the young men said, "Well we do this anyhow. If a patient does what we like, we respond positively, and if he doesn't we don't respond." The Director of

Training said, "If you do it and you don't know you're doing it, that's all right!"

Since we had been studying Erickson, we were not shocked by the use of suggestions outside a client's awareness. It was typically Erickson and had been for years. He would say that directives are more difficult to resist if the subject does not know he is receiving them.

Erickson argued that a therapist should know how to influence a client both in and outside awareness by communicating both directly and indirectly through control of the choice of words and vocal inflections. A therapist should also communicate deliberately with his posture and movements. With that control, he could emphasize certain words in a sentence and so be saying one thing while suggesting another, and perhaps offering a third suggestion with his body movement. How different this was from therapists who considered only words to be communication.

There are two issues here that one typically faces with Erickson. One, he was willing to change people outside their awareness. Two, he did not use positive reinforcements in the usual sense. Were his origins in the learning theories of the behaviorist school? I think they were not. He was using behavioral techniques before they were discovered in the learning therapies, but he did not use the typical positive reinforcements that are at the heart of that school. He did not say, "You did that well ..." or "That was excellent ..." or "I like the way you did that ..." Nor did he use M & M's to reinforce a response. One always knew when Erickson was pleased with what one did. Yet I cannot recall him saying, "You did that well."

Erickson and Reinforcement

Erickson once said to me that one should not compliment patients for acting normal. I think of that when I hear one of my students saying to a client, "Oh, how wonderful, you came on time today." I could not generalize from that and say that Erickson did not do the usual positive reinforcement because he assumed the individual should take responsibility for his or her actions. Therefore, if a person did well, Erickson responded as if that contribution belonged to the person, not to him guiding the person. He who reinforces takes the power.

The idea is now built into our culture that behavior can be shaped by positive reinforcements, and so parents and therapists and all guidance people compliment people who are doing what they want. I don't believe Erickson did that. Perhaps others might recall him expressing a positive reinforcement, but I do not. If he did, it was when he had his client in a trance. Then he would emphasize being pleased with certain behavior. Certainly, Erickson shaped behavior and persuaded people to do what he wanted and to even do it more. How did he do that? If he had a child write a sentence a thousand times to improve his handwriting, he would not compliment the child when be brought in the handwriting. He would not say, "Oh, you did wonderfully." Instead, he would say, "That's a clearly written "O" or that "Z" is better than that one. In this way he emphasized the item in the class of positive reinforcements without stating the class.

Even if he did not use positive reinforcement, everyone knew when Erickson was pleased. For example, I struggled for years and finally finished writing the book *Uncommon Therapy*. I sent it to Erickson and received no compliment from him. Yet, I learned that he bought many copies to give out to people. His compliment was in action or in other ways than verbal reinforcement.

Erickson also did not typically offer direct criticism as a way of teaching. To cite a personal example, I was treating a woman with phantom limb pain in her right arm that was no longer there. I hypnotized her by having her levitate the phantom limb. She pointed to where it was as it went up. I thought that was rather clever and might deserve a paper. I told Erickson about the case, and he did not particularly respond. He talked of other things. Sometime later, he talked about how one should not hypnotize a person with a focus on what is painful, but rather with a focus on what is pleasant. He said one should not hypnotize a headache case by focusing upon the headache. That evening, or perhaps the next day, I realized that I probably should not have hypnotized that woman by focusing upon her painful arm.

Without positive reinforcements, one cannot be in the school of behavior therapy. Yet, somehow Erickson seemed to resist them and go his own way. This is not a minor issue. Erickson was one of the great persuaders. People did what he wished them to do. If he did not achieve that end by positively reinforcing the behavior he liked, then how did he do so? I think there is a research project to be done here that might discover a new way of motivating people—the way of Dr. Erickson.

If Erickson was not within the behaviorist ideology, nor in the psychodynamic ideology, what of systems theory? Could we say that his ideas were based on that therapeutic approach?

Before setting out on that profound subject, let me dwell awhile on the idea of changing people outside their awareness. There is a justifiable controversy over this issue, and Erickson is at the heart of it. However, it is more than just an ethical aspect of Erickson's techniques. The nature of therapy is defined by this issue.

I have always thought we should restrain therapists from helping people who do not wish to be helped. However, I was never concerned about Erickson doing that. I knew him as a kindly person who took responsibility for what he did and whose judgment was sound, or at least agreed with mine. However, other therapists who attempt to follow Erickson are not necessarily that kind, nor are they as sound in their judgment of what people need or indirectly request.

Among the many important aspects of influencing someone outside their awareness, besides the ethical issues, there are two that stand out. One is whether or not you can change people without their being aware of it, two is whether or not influence and change in therapy do not always involve collaboration.

Let us consider an example. A couple had a sexual problem and did not wish to discuss it explicitly. Yet they wanted a change in sexual behavior. If Erickson decided they should change, he might influence them indirectly with metaphor. He would discuss a parallel activity, such as having dinner together, in such a way that he influenced their sexual problem. He would ask if they liked appetizers before dinner to stimulate the juices, or if they just dove into the meat and potatoes. In other cases he might make suggestions and give amnesia so that change was kept out of the client's conscious awareness. He was willing to take responsibility for changing what he thought should be changed.

When a therapist influences a client with interventions that are subtle and deliberately kept outside the client's awareness, the therapist is on the treacherous ground of changing people without permission, or a contract, to change them.

There are therapists who argue that one should not change people without an agreement to do so. Erickson was willing to work without such an explicit agreement. As an example, it was typical of Erickson to say that if a patient comes in complaining of headaches, and he has tracks on his arm that indicate he is an intravenous drug user, it is the therapist's obligation to try and cure the drug addiction. He should not necessarily make that explicit with the client. If the man wishes to present headaches as the problem, that should be their therapeutic focus; indirect ways should be found to deal with the addiction. Once again, Erickson's therapy might be called courtesy therapy. He did not force people to concede problems just as he did not force insight on clients by interpreting their body movement to them.

Unlike other therapists in his time, Erickson considered the therapist responsible for the results of therapy. That meant an obligation to use his power to induce change when he could. He was also aware that power is the result of collaboration. It is in the area of collaboration that the nature of influence outside awareness becomes an interesting question. It is an oversimplification to say that one can do therapy by making the client aware of all that you are doing, or that you can do it without the person being aware of your interventions. Those who argue that one should make the client aware of everything one is doing have not thought through this situation. A client can never be fully aware of everything the therapist is doing. In fact, the therapist cannot be fully aware of everything he or she is doing. Even if the therapist tries to reveal all by lecturing the client, if one examines slow motion films of therapy it is obvious the interchange is too complex for conscious awareness. Ray Birdwhistell estimated that two people in a conversation exchange 100,000 bits of information per minute. That seems reasonable if one studies films of therapy frame by frame. For example, suppose a client says something, and the therapist uncomfortably looks away, and the client changes to another subject. The therapist does not even know he exerted influence; far less can he share it with the client.

The other aspect of awareness is even more complex. If a therapist communicates a metaphor that the subject responds to outside awareness, can it really be outside awareness? How could the client respond to the suggestion and be influenced if not aware of the suggestion? The suggestion would not have been received.

Let me cite an example in a typical area of interest and investigation by Erickson. He noted that if one hypnotizes a subject and gives him a negative hallucination for a table in the room, the subject will not see the table. The table will be outside his awareness. However, if asked to walk across the room, the subject will walk around the table. Even though the subject is unconscious of the table, he will walk around it. Erickson described this as "unconscious awareness." I suggested to him that this was a contradiction in terms. If one is aware of something, one cannot be unconscious of it, by definition. It seemed to me, and still does, that the language of "conscious and unconscious" is too primitive to deal with these issues.

How is this relevant to therapy? If one gives directives to a subject outside the subject's awareness, and the subject responds correctly to those directives, at some level the subject's mind is receiving the message and cooperating. The person is not unconscious of the directive. It would seem there is a collaboration involved when one is influencing someone outside his awareness. One offers a metaphor, such as discussing a couple having dinner as an analogy to sexual interchange, and the couple choose within the metaphoric message the ideas relevant to them and their problems. They *choose* to collaborate or not in that sense rather than being robots responding to the therapist's directives. Yet, they are not conscious of receiving the metaphoric message. In fact, Erickson taught that if the couple is becoming conscious of the parallels in the metaphor, one should "drift rapidly" away from the subject and return to it later. Incidentally, I always assumed that when a client became aware that Erickson was suggesting something, he might actually be letting the client focus on that so that he or she would not notice another suggestion, which was the one he wished the client to receive.

Just as the subject must see the table in order not to see it, the subject receiving a metaphoric directive must be aware of the analogy while responding to it without being aware. For example, when he said the couple should really enjoy dinner together, he was assuming the couple would connect his recommendation with enjoying sex since they were aware, even though unconsciously, of the suggestion. All of Erickson's storytelling techniques involve communication through metaphor, with or without awareness by the receiver of messages being sent. Erickson typically told stories as an important part of his therapy, unlike other therapists of his time, many of whom hardly spoke at all, or only said. "Tell me more about that." From whom did he learn to tell stories?

Another aspect of collaboration might be emphasized. It was not simply that Erickson gave a directive and the subject followed it. More typically, he gave a directive and the client did it with modifications. The ultimate task that was carried out was often a collaboration.

In summary, there are some generalizations around this issue that are typically Ericksonian. He would accept a person's indirect communication as an indication of a problem, and he was willing to take responsibility for ways a patient should change. For example, at his hypnotic demonstrations, he was often offered a clue as to how the volunteer subject needed help, and he would indirectly supply that without the audience knowing. He was trustful of his own judgment about what should be done. When he made suggestions to influence a person outside awareness, he did it with an assumption that there was an unconscious awareness which he was guiding to follow his directives. He also assumed that clients would modify his suggestions. Some people fear the idea that a therapist might impose his ideas on a client outside the client's awareness and without permission; they should consider the matter to be a more complex collaboration than is usually thought.

The issue is actually broader and includes one's conception of the healing profession. Many therapists choose to educate clients in the therapist's theories. When that is done, clients become a special élite with a knowledge of psychology not shared by the general population. In contrast, one can have as a goal that the client be like ordinary people who have no special knowledge of psychology. It was typical of Erickson to shift people back to normal without educating them in therapy ideology. Erickson typically chose to consider therapy ideas to be the business of the therapist, not of the client, although if a client wanted to know what he was doing, he would explain — as long as it did not interfere with the therapy. I recall him saying that if you examine a normal sample of successful men and women, they have little or no interest in their childhood or in theories about psychology.

SYSTEMS AND FAMILY THERAPY

Erickson liked to say, particularly to my students when they visited, that he was not a family therapist. Yet, obviously he did therapy with couples and whole families. How can one explain this? One observation is that he also did not call himself a Gestalt Therapist, or a Psychodynamic Therapist, or a Rogerian Therapist, or an Existential Therapist, or a Brief Therapist. He also did not say he was a Group Therapist. I think he did not like to be classified as a type of therapist. Like most good therapists, he wished to maximize his freedom to maneuver. This means seeing clients in a whole range of different ways.

Erickson liked to approach each case in a unique way rather than follow a method. Most therapists in his time wanted a method to fit everyone into. Erickson did not. To have a label, like "Family Therapist," meant that one could not do a variety of interventions without being accused of unorthodoxy within that label. It also meant one was in a camp with colleagues one might not approve of. I have never chosen to be called a Family Therapist because such a label organizes and limits a therapist's approach. Obviously, any therapist with average intelligence deals with the family, and one does not need to be in a therapy category to do that.

Erickson believed that a therapist received what he or she expected from a client. Systems theory is based on the idea of a self-corrective, governed system that prevents change. If a husband goes too far, the wife reacts; if a wife goes too far, the husband reacts. If they both go too far, the child reacts. Erickson did not like to have therapists expecting people not to change because they were stabilizing a system. He considered resistances of various kinds to be important for a therapist to circumvent, but as I understood him he did not like resistance built into a theory.

One might become academic and raise the question of whether Erickson's therapy had its origins in family therapy. To deal with that, one must define family therapy. That is difficult to do. Erickson typically dealt with families, but not as other family therapists did. However, that is true of other family therapists, since there are different schools of family therapy, each dealing with families differently.

In my research on Erickson's therapy, I encouraged him to talk about his conjoint family interviews because that was what was new in the field at the time. However, more typically, he would see family members separately. At the heart of Erickson's theory was the individual. That was the unit he typically focused upon. A therapist is always the agent of someone, and Erickson typically saw himself as the agent of an individual. He was also willing to expand that unit to include two people. These might be husband and wife, mother and child, or therapist and client. He did not typically expand his problem unit to three people, and so he did not think in terms of coalitions, as some family therapists do. Of course, there were exceptions, but I am talking about his typical ways.

As an example, Erickson once presented to John Weakland and me a case of a woman with extreme sexual inhibitions. Erickson changed her into a rather sexy being, even persuading her to dance into her bedroom nude. Erickson did not deal with her husband. We asked him if he was not concerned about the husband suddenly having to react to a sexually enthusiastic wife. We were thinking within a systems view and assuming the wife and husband had a contract that she was inhibited. This could have been her way of saving her husband from having to deliver sexually. When she changed and made demands upon him, the marriage might well be disrupted. Wasn't it the responsibility of the therapist to deal with that risk? Erickson replied that he was not thinking that way. He said that the husband had passively accepted his wife's inhibitions, and now that she had changed he would passively accept that change. He apparently was not assuming that the wife's problem had a function in relation to the husband, nor that he was triangulating by joining the wife and not the husband. He focused on a woman motivated by individual sexual inhibitions.

However, in other cases of couples, that was not necessarily his premise. For example, a wife came to him with the problem that her husband always had an erection when they went to bed (Haley, 1986, p. 159). It was independent of anything she did. Erickson arranged that the man masturbate excessively and then go into the bedroom without an erection. The wife was pleased to arouse the man. The husband was pleased with the wife's reaction. Is that family therapy? I have not seen a case like that in the family therapy journals.

Let me deal with this issue historically. I met Erickson at one of his seminars in 1953, the same year I joined Gregory Bateson's project on communication. We began investigating hypnosis and John Weakland and I went regularly to Phoenix to talk to Erickson or he visited us when he came to San Francisco. This began in 1955 and continued over the years. We began to realize that he had a special approach to therapy and we inquired into that as well as into hypnosis. In 1956, I began to do therapy with a family of a schizophrenic on the Bateson project. I also went into private practice that year as a hypnotherapist and marriage therapist. I spent time in 1957 with Erickson talking about cases because I needed supervision for my practice in brief therapy. Erickson was the only one I knew with a brief therapy approach.

The family I was seeing on the project in 1956 was actually an individual therapy, with the parents brought in because the patient was afraid of them. (This was the patient who sent his mother a Mother's Day card saying, "You've always been like a mother to me"; Haley, 1959, p. 357.) We did not consider it therapy for the family. However, by April of 1957 we were doing therapy with whole families and calling it family therapy. We were beginning to think in terms of systems theory. I consulted with Erickson over the years, and by 1956 or 1957 I had begun therapy with whole families. Was Erickson already doing therapy with families? It depends upon what one calls therapy with families.

By 1959, the Bateson project held a special conference with Erickson, which we labeled as on marriage and family therapy. At that point, we considered him an authority on that subject. There were only one or two others in the country. By then, we were making use of his family therapy ideas, and perhaps he was using ours as well. Yet he had been dealing with couples and families before we discussed these types of cases with him, so we could not have been the only source of his ideas.

To return to his typical approach in therapy, he often presented a case as an individual problem and then we would find out that he had also been dealing with family members around the problem.

Let me cite an example from that period. I was in practice in Palo Alto, and an elderly gentleman came to me and asked me if I would treat his daughter for some problems. He told me that he had another daughter who had been treated successfully by a therapist. I asked him why he didn't take this second daughter to the same therapist, since that had gone well. The gentleman said to me that he did not dare do that. When I asked why, he said it was because when he took his daughter to see that therapist, the therapist put him under house arrest for six months. One might guess who the therapist was. I pointed out that he could go back to Erickson and refuse the house arrest. He looked at me as if surprised at my naivete. Finally, I suggested that he return to Dr. Erickson with this second daughter, which he did. It is interesting that Erickson was on good enough terms with the gentleman so that when he visited Palo Alto he stayed in his house. Could one call this case family therapy? I have not seen house arrest therapy in the family therapy catalogue. Yet he was obviously doing therapy with the family to help a daughter or he would not have involved the father in that way.

Erickson's therapy approach raises the issue not only of whether he did family therapy but of what family therapy is. Let me cite some cases to raise the question:

1. When a man was constantly complaining about his fear of dying of a heart attack, although there was nothing wrong with his heart, Erickson had the man's wife distribute funeral literature around the house whenever he complained about his heart (Haley, 1986, p. 178). The man recovered from his fear. Was this individual or family therapy?

2. Early family therapy was often based upon the theory of repression. Therefore, family members were encouraged to talk and express their hostile feelings while the therapist pointed out how negatively they were dealing with each other. The rule was that all family members could say anything since they were getting out those down deep feelings.

Erickson did not seem to have that view of families or how they should be treated. He was focused upon organizing the family so that specific goals were achieved. When he brought the whole family together, it was in a way that enabled him to control what happened. For example, he had a mother and father and daughter who were yelling complaints at each other. Rather than encourage that, he scheduled them by requiring each of them to complain for 20 minutes. The father, mother, and daughter each had a turn.

In another approach that was typical of him, he prevented free expression in an interview with a whole family. It was a mother, father, and two sons, one of whom was a problem. The mother would not stop talking or allow the others to talk. Erickson asked her if she could hold her thumbs one-quarter of an inch apart. She replied that of course she could. He had her demonstrate. She did so. He said that while she was doing that, he would talk to the others and she should listen so that she could have the last word. He spoke to the son, and the mother answered, but when she did so her thumbs separated more than one-quarter of an inch. He pointed this out to her and she put the thumbs back again. She could not speak without moving her thumbs, and so she was quiet while he talked with the father and sons, then giving her the last word. Would a family therapist organize an interview that way?

Many family therapists at that time would argue that one should not arrange an interview in such an organized way. Preventing a family member from talking was shocking at a time when free expression was the goal. I recall in the early 1960's Don Jackson, a major family therapist who worked with us, was interviewing a mother and father and their 17-year-old daughter diagnosed as schizophrenic who had just dropped out of college. In the interview, Jackson was talking to the mother when the daughter interrupted. Jackson told the daughter to let her mother speak, and he continued talking with the mother. Jackson did not have as a goal free expression, but was organizing the family to get the girl back to school. A number of therapists at that time were shocked by a therapist restraining someone from speaking, particularly a young daughter with problems.

In that same interview, the mother in the family began to cry, the daughter began to cry, and the father started crying. Jackson politely brought them out of it, but he was clearly irritated. Many family therapists would be pleased if a whole family cried because they would be getting in touch with their feelings. Jackson was interested in getting past the weeping to achieve therapeutic ends. Yet no one said Jackson was not a family therapist.

Erickson did not encourage the expression of feelings as a goal of therapy. He was not really interested in getting people to cry. In fact, he once asked me how I would stop a woman from crying if it was going on too long. Oddly enough, I had no procedure. He said that he would stop her by handing her Kleenex and saying, "At Christmas I give out green Kleenex." That would stop anyone from crying.

3. A couple with a drinking problem came to Erickson and mentioned that their weekends sitting at home were miserable. He sent them out on weekends to go boating on a lake and enjoy the fresh air. That could be considered family therapy. One often hears therapists advising couples and families to do enjoyable things together, to find more pleasure, to take trips together, to seek a vacation from the children, and so on.

Erickson's arrangement of the couple to boat together on the lake was not in this family therapy tradition. He typically advised families to do what they did not want to do. He asked this couple to go boating when he found that neither husband nor wife liked to go boating. They both hated boating on a lake. When they followed his orders and went boating, they found it unpleasant and persuaded Erickson to let them go camping. He allowed that, and they were pleased since they enjoyed spending pleasant weekends camping. I do not recall that Erickson often sent people out to simply enjoy themselves or vacation together. It is difficult to think of any family therapy school that does not directly encourage more enjoyable behavior in the family. Is Erickson's approach family therapy?

4. A hospital nurse went for a walk behind a building and met a young male staff member there. Sitting down on a bench and talking, they discovered they shared a common situation—he was gay and she was a lesbian. This was a problem for both of them since there was great prejudice against such a sexual orientation in those days. They would lose their jobs if it was known, and suspicions had already been aroused. After talking together, they became friends and ultimately decided to get married as a cooperative way of concealing their sexual orientation. One might think of this as a fortunate chance encounter of these two people. In fact, Erickson

had arranged it. He had suggested to the nurse that she take a stroll behind that building, not saying why, and he arranged that the young man happen to be there. Could this be called family creation?

5. There was a little girl who couldn't do anything and was failing in school. Erickson went to her house each evening and played jacks with her and jumped rope and played other games (Haley, 1986, p. 205). Her parents looked down on such behavior. Is this family therapy? If not, does it become so if one emphasizes how he antagonized the parents by joining the child in this way?

6. In another example that was typically Erickson, a mother and father had a son who wet the bed (Haley, 1986, p. 206). Erickson reports that the mother was a kindly woman trying to help her child. The father was a loud, arrogant man who said he had wet the bed until he was 16 and why shouldn't the boy do that. Erickson said he interviewed the father alone and listened to him at length. The father spoke to him as if he were about 60 feet away. After having heard the father out, Erickson set the father aside and worked with the mother and child to solve the problem. Clearly, he was thinking that both mother and father as well as the child needed to be involved in this case. He was also pleased with the positive response of the father after the success. That could be called family therapy.

7. Erickson once directed a young man to leave everything and go live alone on a mountain top all alone for one year. Could that be family therapy? Clearly it shows a willingness to disrupt a young man's whole social network.

8. In the 1950's, many women were inhibited about sex and Erickson was one of the first therapists to do explicit sex therapy to help them overcome their fears. There was no sex therapy at that time, and so he appeared extreme. He also dealt with men who had inhibitions. In one case, a young husband and wife came with the complaint by the wife that the husband was prudish and would not enjoy his wife's breasts (Haley, 1991). Erickson required the young man to give a name to the left breast of his wife, or else Erickson would provide a name he would be stuck with. Was that family therapy?

Differences

Let me offer some differences in the ways Erickson and some family therapists viewed problems.

There are two premises that Erickson did not seem to have when dealing with families. He was not thinking of the three-person unit, and so he did not describe a child as caught between mother and father, or expressing a conflict between therapist and parents. He did not think in terms of a triangle, and so did not see that a therapist joining the youth against the parents could increase the youth's problem. He also apparently did not have the theory of motivation that developed in family therapy. One motivation theory is that young people stabilize a family system by having difficulties. They help parents by harming themselves. If a young person shoots heroin, or is delinquent, it can be assumed that it is protective of the family in some way. If a daughter acts up or runs away, it is assumed that it can be a way of helping a depressed mother. If a wife avoids sex, it is hypothesized that she can be protecting her husband from conceding a problem. Erickson did not seem to hold this view of motivation. Not having that view, he did not hypothesize that if a therapist upsets parents, the child can relapse as a way of helping them. One way to upset parents is to side with the child against them.

To put the matter simply, if one assumes a youth is helping parents by failing, there are two approaches. One is to help the parents so the youth does not need to do so. Erickson would, at times, simply tell the young person to leave his parents to him and he would take care of them while the young person went about his business. The other approach is to disengage the youth from the parents and work alone with the child, letting the parents solve their problems on their own. Erickson worked both ways, but I think some of his failures occurred when he joined the child against parents and did not think the parents had to be helped to help the child. He was so fond of children and so irritated with parents who behaved badly that at times he would set out to save children from parents.

Erickson was successful with problem children of all ages, and he particularly enjoyed children. The family view would be that he typically did not take into account the fact that he was triangulating with child and parents, nor did he acknowledge the effect on parents when he succeeded with a child. Parents who have tried and failed to help their child for a long period of time can be upset when a therapist is successful. Erickson would say that they simply needed to adjust to their child becoming normal.

Unlike systems-oriented therapists, Erickson would sometimes tell a young person never to have anything to do with his parents again. He would forbid communication between parents and youth. Just as he would, at times, tell a wife to leave an abusive husband, he would tell young people to leave abusive parents. He believed that at times parental behavior was so obnoxious and unchangeable that the young person should simply break off contact with the parents.

CONCLUSION

In summary, how did Erickson work differently from others doing a more family-oriented therapy? He did not interview family members together and have them express their feelings as many family therapists did in the early days. Instead, he typically saw family members separately and only occasionally together. He did not always try to have family members communicate with each other if they were not speaking, as therapists with a systems view might do. He was quite willing to separate family members and block them off from contact with each other. He did not typically assume that people harm themselves to help others. He did not map a family in triangles, but more often thought in terms of the individual or the dyad.

As I review here aspects of Erickson that I consider typical, I am aware that what was typical to me might not be typical to others who knew him. Others, for example, might be immersed in his ways of working with hypnosis, which I have not particularly emphasized here. One factor is the period when one knew Erickson. I knew him best in the 1950's when he was active and vigorous and doing seminars all over the country while busy with a private practice. Others have known him in his old age in a wheelchair where he continued to be powerful but was more limited in what he could do.

To generalize about Erickson is a special problem since he was different at different times for different people. He tended to speak the language of whomever he was teaching, and he educated with metaphors within which different people could find different meanings. Naturally, when we try to understand him, we try to place him in a category in the field of therapy. Yet, it seems clear he did not operate from any of the standard therapy ideologies of his time. He did not base his ideas on psychodynamic theory or use the basic tool of that approach, the interpretation of the unconscious. He did not accept the basic premises of behavior therapy or use the primary tool, explicit positive reinforcement. He did not accept family systems theory and its basic idea that the behavior of everyone in a system is a product of the behavior of everyone else. Just as he developed his own unique ways of doing hypnosis, he developed his own therapy approach. Now, a decade after his death, we still cannot fit him easily into any of the current or former fashionable schools of therapy.

It is remarkable that a therapist can be so well known and his typical therapy cases so widely reported, while his basic ideology remains in many ways obscure. He was a man who created his own ways. However, I can recall him saying that he was influenced by one particular man. When Erickson was a boy, a kindly doctor cured him of a pain and gave him a nickle. That was when Erickson decided to become a doctor. Perhaps that kindly practitioner not only set him off on his career but provided a model for him. Despite his sophistication, in many ways Erickson worked like a kindly and clever country doctor.

REFERENCES

Haley, J. (1959). The Family of the schizophrenic: A model system. *Amer. J. Ment. and Nerv. Dis., 1129*, 357–374.

Haley, J. (Ed.) (1985). *Conversations with Milton H. Erickson, Vol. 1.* Rockville, MD: Triangle Press.

Haley, J. (1986). *Uncommon therapy.* New York: Norton.

Haley, J. (Ed.) (1991). *Milton H. Erickson. Sex Therapy: The Male.* Audiotape. Rockville, MD: Triangle Press.

CHAPTER 2

Money and the Family
Cloé Madanes

The greatest dilemma of human beings is to what extent we are going to love one another, protect one another, and to what extent we are going to do violence to one another. Violence involves not only physical pain but also intrusiveness, domination, control, and taking advantage of others. Love and violence are part of a continuum where frequently one leads to the other.

At what point does a loving relationship that is possessive and overbearing become intrusive and controlling in a way that is violent? To what extent are people tied to one another in violent ways but so intensely that one could say that the bond is stronger than the bond of love? This dilemma is often aggravated by the struggle for material possessions and its common denominator: money.

This struggle is part of every relationship and is particularly played and replayed in marriage and in family life where money can be offered and accepted as an expression of love, and where it can be withheld or rejected as an expression of violence.

Today, everyone is worried about money. For one reason or another, money is an issue for all of us. There are those who feel that if only they could have more money they could find happiness and their lives would be greatly improved. There are those who have a great deal of money and are constantly worried about losing it for one reason or another. No one seems satisfied with how much money they have and how they use it.

The problems of the poor are very different from the problems of the wealthy, yet the family conflicts caused by how money is used may be quite similar across socioeconomic classes. But the kind of people that I'm going

25

to discuss in this chapter are those where money is so intertwined with their lives that issues about money affect their health, their intimate relationships, their relationships with their children, their parents. Money ruins their digestion. Money is in bed with them when they have sex. It's an ever-present issue. Those are the people I will be talking about here.

What is money? It is not just currency, not just that which allows us to acquire material possessions. With money we also can buy education, health, and safety. We can buy time to enjoy beauty, art, the company of friends, adventure. With money we can help those whom we love and ensure that our children will have better opportunities.

Just as we know all that money can buy, so everyone is familiar with the problems it causes. Husband and wife, parent and child, brother and sister can fight bitterly over money. Wealth sometimes appears to be cursed, bringing with it more misery than joy. I am going to address not only how money can be at the origin of problems, but also how money can be used in therapy as a solution to problems that may not even have originated as money problems and that may, in fact, be totally unrelated to money issues.

Essential to Erickson's approach were his abilities to see that which is obvious and yet difficult for most people to see, his courage in demystifying taboos, and his optimism in the belief that the therapist can utilize the patient's own strengths to solve problems. Money is one of those strengths. It is important to talk about it and it is a resource that can be utilized to solve problems brought to therapy.

There are two broad categories, or dimensions, in terms of how people handle issues of love and its metaphors (such as money and all that money can buy). There are some people who are mainly focused on being loved and have great difficulty in giving love, as opposed to those who are mainly focused on giving their love and have difficulty in receiving it.

THOSE WHO WANT TO BE LOVED

I will first address the issues of those people who are mainly focused on wanting to be loved. There are certain difficulties that are characteristically experienced by those who are focused on wanting to be loved, wanting to receive, wanting to have more. I will describe the problems, explain how they relate to money issues, and offer some practical solutions for the therapist.

Typical problems that occur at this level are self-destructive behaviors including psychosomatic and physical problems, depression, anxiety, phobias, and eating disorders. All these are problems that develop when people are extremely focused on wanting to receive. Depression and anxiety can occur as a reaction to feeling unloved or to the belief that one is not receiving as much love, attention, or material possessions as others in the family or as much as one is entitled to. In turn, depression and anxiety can lead to phobias and to physical illness. Eating disorders are often related to the frustrated wish to punish someone who is not giving and loving. These disorders are the wish for revenge turned inwards.

The main emotion experienced by these people is desire and the frustration that always comes with desire. They talk constantly about the things they want, be it money, food, or what they want from others. A sense of unfulfilled desire is manifest whether they are talking about money, sex, food, or material possessions. They are the kind of people who talk about how their problems would be solved if they had another car, a better house, or another television set.

The problem with desire is that it inevitably leads to total frustration because there is always something more or something better that you could have, that you want. If you have a good husband, you can conceive that somewhere there must be a better husband. If you have a pretty dress, certainly there must be a prettier dress somewhere and you could have it. So no matter what you have, you are always frustrated. This causes a great deal of internal pain that is related to many of the physical problems that appear at this level. The sense of emptiness can become so great that it causes health problems.

Together with desire, the interactions of these people are characterized by excessive demands and criticism that can become quite devastating. Nothing is good enough; they always need more. Even the family therapist finds it painful to listen to the intense criticism, particularly when it is directed to children.

There are some general strategies that are helpful in getting people unstuck from this dilemma. First, it is important to figure out if there are traumas from the past that may be influencing the present. A person may have been the victim of a traumatic event or the trauma may have been suffered by a loved one. Victims of unexpected traumatic events are often left feeling "This shouldn't have happened to me; why me?" And this feeling often leads to a sense of entitlement: "The world should compensate me for what happened." With this sense of entitlement comes a sense of frustration that is at the origin of many of the problems presented in therapy. For this reason, it is important to be aware of the worst things that have happened in a person's life.

In order for past traumas to be overcome they must be remembered. In the same way, one needs to uncover past resentments. Usually there are long-standing resentments between husband and wife, parent and child, towards in-laws and siblings. It is difficult to understand the present situation if one doesn't understand these resentments from the past. Resentment usually comes together with rejection. Family members are excluded, people don't talk to one another, and the repercussions affect everyone.

As traumas and resentments from the past become clarified, one often discovers that they are related to financial issues, the sense of having been taken advantage of, exploited, deprived, or treated unjustly. It becomes necessary to focus on the current financial situation and its origins in the past. The therapist working with a couple or with a family can ask them to bring to a session all their financial information, such as sources of income, debts, properties (and whose name is on them), cash flow, etc. The therapist then helps them to organize this information in a way that makes sense, clarifying what parents have given to children, what promises were made and if they were kept, and what people's expectations are with regard to money. As these issues get clarified, issues of unfairness and betrayal may surface. A husband may have bought a property only in his name and the wife may resent that her name is not on the title. A parent may have given more money to a son than to a daughter. These actions obviously symbolize the way people feel about one another. Every attempt must be made to reorganize the finances fairly in order to prevent further resentments and estrangements.

Other strategies that are helpful in getting people unstuck from problems of desire have to do with changing the way people talk to one another. The subject of an argument between spouses, for example, can be reframed in positive ways. If they are fighting about money, for instance, you can maintain that in fact they are not fighting about money, they are fighting about love. The money symbolizes the love that they want so much from one another. You don't have to actually believe this; in fact, it is probably not true and when you fight about money you are fighting about money, not about love. But the tone of the argument becomes more positive when you talk about love rather than merely about money with its materialistic and somewhat despicable connotations. To argue about who loves whom and how much seems more noble than to argue about money. The general principle is to look for a noble cause and to reframe the source of disagreement in that noble way.

Another principle of therapy to be applied to money issues is that in ongoing relationships people need to apologize to one another for the bad things they have done. When a husband, for example, changes the title of a property to include his wife's name, he also needs to tell her how sorry he is for having offended her. To put her name on the house without the apology is not enough. Together with the apology, there has to be reparation. There has to be some act that indicates that the apology is truly sincere. Not only will there be an apology, but it will be followed by a special invitation, a present, or other action that signifies love and special consideration.

Rituals are particularly helpful in setting aside past traumas and resentments. Going on a second honeymoon to signify the beginning of a "new" marriage, or even having a ceremony of renewal of marital vows, is a ritual that contributes to a fresh start. This ceremony can be performed in church or even by the therapist in a session. Another useful ritual is to send a couple to visit all their relatives and to tell each one how happy they are with one another or how much each appreciates the other. It is important that the ritual prescribed be commensurate with the severity of the presenting problem. If a problem has been going on for many years, for example resentments that date back decades, a renewal of marital vows is best when it happens with the complete ceremonial of the church to signify that this is truly the beginning of a new marriage. If the problem is more minor, going out for a special dinner may be enough of a ritual to signify that the couple is celebrating a solution to a disagreement in which they have been involved for some time.

Another possible intervention is to prescribe symbolic acts. The therapist designs a directive that will symbolize the presenting problem, but in such a way that the symbolic act will replace the problem behavior, and the problem behavior will no longer be necessary. When a wife is bulimic, for example, the therapist can ask the husband for an estimate of how much money is wasted each day because of the bulimia. That is, how much food a day does she consume that she then throws up, and how much does that food cost? Usually, the husband gets indignant when he figures this out, particularly if you ask him how much this adds up to in a week, a month, etc. Then the therapist asks the wife to take that amount of food each day, that is, the amount of food that she and her husband have agreed that she wastes each day, and put that amount of food, untouched, in the garbage. So each day she will throw away, whether or not she has vomited, a certain amount of food—perhaps a cake, a gallon of ice cream, cookies, whatever. When the husband comes home, he is to check the garbage to make sure that she has done it. The idea is that the bulimia represents the wish to waste the money that the couple work so hard to earn. So why not waste it without it going through her body first, why not throw it away directly?

What happens is that the husband usually has not been bothered by the symptoms of the bulimia because his wife does it privately and it does not interfere with his life. Although he may be collaborating with the therapy, he does not really care that much. However, after the discussion about the money wasted on food and when he hears the directive to throw away food, he becomes extremely annoyed at the idea of all this money going into the garbage. Even more annoying is that he is asked to throw away the food if she hasn't done so. Thus, the relationship between the two spouses begins to change; then the whole art of the therapy is how to direct that change in a positive way.

In all the interventions I have described, it is important to involve the extended family and to make generational boundaries. Just as a nuclear family may be focused on desire and on demands and criticism, the same applies to the extended family. The bond between nuclear and extended family may not have been cut. Just as the couple may be demanding and critical of one another, they may behave in the same ways with their families of origin, so the therapist needs to work to make those generational boundaries.

MONEY AND THE YOUNG COUPLE: A 10-STEP PROCEDURE

In working with couples around money problems, I make a distinction as to whether it is a young couple or a middle-aged or older couple. There is a difference between people who have not been married long versus those who have been together for more than 15 years.

I will address first the issues of young couples and the strategies that I like to use with them. A basic issue with young couples is how much each one wants of the other and how little each one is willing to give to the other. Each of the spouses wants love, money, security, self-esteem, success, and friends, and each is focused on his/her own needs.

The typical difficulties they encounter at this stage in their marital life are low self-esteem, feelings of inadequacy, envy of the other spouse, feelings of inferiority in relation to one another, the reluctance to give, and the feeling of emptiness. Also, the feeling that the relationship is more like a competition and a war rather than a collaboration.

There are 10 steps for a therapist to follow in these therapies. Although not all these steps involve dealing directly with money issues, each step represents the preparation that is necessary for dealing with them. Thus, some of the steps are specifically about money and some are not. The order in which I present the steps is somewhat arbitrary and does not need to be followed in precisely the same way.

First, the therapist has to help the couple to make the shift from needing one another because of their inadequacies to needing one another because they have fun together. That is, the therapist has to help them make the shift from wanting to be together because each helps the other with their inadequacies to wanting to be together because they enjoy one another.

The second step is to move the couple from wanting to be cared for, wanting to be loved, to wanting to give their love, to care for the other person. That is, a successful marriage has to be a combination of wanting to be loved, wanting to receive, and of wanting to give love and protection.

The third step is a shift from feelings of emptiness to feelings of self-worth, wealth, and richness. Each spouse needs to change from a focus on what the couple do not have, on what is missing in the relationship, to a focus on what they do have, on the positive aspects of the relationship, on each one's good qualities, on the material and spiritual possessions that they do have.

The fourth step is a change from dealing with provocation by having a battle to dealing with provocation as a signal to play. Young couples may get into fights that can actually lead to violence because they provoke each other. The way they respond to provocation is with war, instead of responding as if it were play. As an example, the following is a controversial directive that I once gave and for which I was much criticized. A young couple came to therapy. They were both lawyers. They were very verbal, attractive, educated, and successful. Yet they had a terrible problem with violence. The wife felt that the husband was always withdrawing from her. They would both come home from work and she would go after him usually talking about their financial difficulties, bills to be paid, how to invest money in the future, asking for his opinion, wanting answers. He would answer briefly and try to get away from her. She would go after him complaining that he wasn't paying attention to her. He would answer something; it would be unsatisfactory. She would then hit him or throw something at him. After a few punches from her, he would hit her back and hurt her. They had decided that they were at the point in their careers where they wanted to have a child; instead, violence had developed. So they were uncertain and didn't want to have children because they thought they shouldn't raise a child in this atmosphere of violence. They also were very ashamed about their behavior. They thought this shouldn't be happening to the kind of people that they were.

I was supervising the therapy and suggested that the therapist say to the husband that he had a solution to the problem but wasn't sure that the husband was brave enough to follow the suggestion that he could give him. The husband said that he thought he was brave enough. So the therapist suggested that the next time his wife provoked him by screaming at him and hitting him, which often happened in the street, at a restaurant, at a movie, at a party, when they were out with friends, anywhere, instead of hitting her back, he should put his hand inside her blouse or under her skirt and fondle her. The wife was always dressed in a power suit. She had wonderful little blue suits with white blouses and she was very proper. Also she was very pretty. She said, "You wouldn't dare do a thing like that!" He said, "I think I would." They left and they came back the next week. The therapist asked the husband, "Did you have occasion to fondle your wife?" He said, "I did but not in the circumstances that you suggested." She had not hit him. After a few weeks, she got pregnant and the therapy ended.

This is an example of turning provocation into play. I haven't used this intervention very much because it's been very rare to find a couple who were violent but nice. With most violent people you would not suggest any kind of touching of one another because it could turn too easily into physical aggression. With this couple, however, you could tell that they were in love and the husband wouldn't turn the fondling into hostile sexual behavior.

What I suggest to couples who are not so nice is that the husband begin to take off his clothes, no matter where they are, when the wife becomes hostile. He will begin by taking off his tie, then he will take off his shirt, and then he'll start unbuttoning his pants—even if they are in a public place. This directive interrupts the interaction and the message becomes "This is play."

I think that what inspired this intervention is a wonderful paper by Bateson (1985), "A Theory of Play and Fantasy," where he describes how dogs, beavers, and other animals exhibit a behavior that humans could easily identify as aggressive, but animals can distinguish whether it is truly aggressive or playful. Dogs and other animals will fight in play without any hostile intent. Humans may have difficulty recognizing the difference while observing the animal behavior, but the dogs know.

Human interaction can be influenced in the same way, so that instead of deteriorating into violence it can shift to humor and play. In fact, I never understood why I was so criticized for this case; after all, I was asking a husband to fondle his wife. It wasn't illegal or with the intent of humiliating— and it solved the problem. So, whenever possible with couples, it is a good idea to change provocation and hostility into provocation to play.

Step number five is to search for the origin of the feelings of inadequacy and emptiness not in the relationship with the spouse but in the childhood of each spouse. It may be necessary to blame somebody, even though it may be stretching the truth a little. You want to ask, "How did you get to feel so unloved or so easily humiliated or mistreated? What happened to you in your childhood?" You discuss early relationships within the family of origin and look to childhood for what intrusiveness there was, whether there was physical abuse or sexual abuse, illnesses, or neglect. That is, you want to explain each spouse to the other in relation to what happened to them in the past.

Step number six is to bring in the family of origin to consult with them about what truly happened in childhood, about the origin of the way each spouse relates to the other one.

Step number seven is to get the parents, the family of origin, to apologize for whatever part they had in the difficulties the young spouse is experiencing today. You bring in, for example, the mother of the wife to confirm the reality of the wife's relationship with her father, and then you have the mother apologize for not having protected her from her father. The idea is not just to bring out the wrong as an endpoint; you have to do something about it. You need some confirmation of the reality of the young spouse and some repentance on the part of the parents for what they did that was wrong.

Step number eight follows logically — to arrange for the parents or the family of origin to give love, money, security as reparation to the young spouse, to enhance their self-esteem. You arrange for the parents in the family of origin to nurture the young spouse, so that she or he, in turn, will be able to give to the other.

This brings to mind another controversial case for which I was criticized and on which I have a recent follow-up. This case was published in my second book, *Behind the One-Way Mirror* (Madanes, 1985), and I called it the "Bachelor Party." I was criticized for the therapy and for the fact of calling it the "Bachelor Party," even though it was clear that I saved this young man's life. It is an example of how to use the family of origin to solve the problem. In this case, we didn't have time to figure out what were the wrongs they had done. We just needed the family of origin to help the young man to heal.

The situation was that a young couple had married because she was pregnant. In fact, they weren't even serious about each other when she got pregnant, but he wanted very much to marry her. The baby was born right after her father died. She was very close to her mother and she and her mother began to raise this baby and totally excluded the young husband. I think that he was only 21 or 22. He was sort of a lost soul who worked at a health spa and didn't do much else. They came to therapy because the wife had filed for divorce and wanted to end the marriage and he didn't want that. The wife felt it was senseless to be married when the husband couldn't support her and the baby.

The therapist said it would be best to try to improve the marriage before taking a drastic action like divorce, particularly considering that they had a baby. The wife said she was willing to work on the marriage, but she was not going to stop the divorce proceedings she had started. In the course of the attempt to improve the marriage, which was not improving, the divorce came through. A couple of days later, the husband went to visit the child, grabbed the baby, took a knife from the kitchen and cut his own wrists. He didn't hurt the baby but, bleeding, he ran off into the street with the baby in his arms. The wife ran after him, dragged him into the car, and took him to the hospital. They came for an emergency session and they were both very distressed.

From the session, we called his father who lived in another state. We had him fly into town that same day and we also brought in an uncle who lived in town. When the therapist met with the three men — the young husband, the father, and the uncle — she sent the wife out of the session. She then said to the father and the uncle that the young man's problem was that the wife and her mother were too strong and he needed another strong, attractive woman on his side to be able to go through the separation from his ex-wife. Their job was to find that woman for him, because he currently was too disturbed to look for another woman.

They wondered how they could possibly do this and talked about all the difficulties. The young man said he didn't want another woman. The therapist said that he really didn't know what he wanted, with which everyone agreed. Finally, the two older men began to come up with ideas about whom they could introduce him to. Pretty soon, in spite of the fact that the young man's arms were bandaged because of the suicide attempt and it was pretty dramatic to just look at him, they were all laughing and making jokes about what kind of woman he should have, where to meet her, what to do with her, and so on.

In the ensuing months, the father frequently stayed in town and together with the uncle took the young man out almost every night, even though he was refusing to have a relationship with anyone. I think it took about three months until he finally began to go out with a woman. He didn't make another suicide attempt, the baby was unharmed, the wife had her divorce, and he eventually moved to California and became a millionaire in real estate.

This therapy happened about 12 years ago and the wife called the institute a few weeks ago and said she wanted to speak with someone in charge. The clinic director answered the call and she said that she wanted to know whether or not we had kept any videotapes of her therapy because she wanted to show the tapes to her son. She wanted to show the boy how his father had been at the time of the therapy. The therapist said that we don't keep tapes that long, but perhaps she could refresh his memory by telling him a little about the problem that she had come to therapy for. So she described what had happened with the husband's suicide attempt and the therapist remembered the case from my book.

I think that probably what happened is that because the husband is now a millionaire, the son wants to know why the mother divorced him. She wants to show him how crazy he was in the sessions when he came in bandaged. It's interesting that she could remember the therapy so well and that it was so significant in her life. She had also remarried. So this is an example of bringing relatives to help at desperate times in the marriage. We don't hesitate to do that and we will fly people in from out of town; we insist that they come and save the life of a young spouse. Similarly, we don't hesitate to ask parents to help their children with financial support, and children to help their parents in the same way.

Step number nine is to find alternatives to the self-destructive behavior. For example, in the therapy just described, the idea was that instead of cutting his wrists and wanting to die, the young man should find some gorgeous woman who would be very demanding and would keep him happy so that he wouldn't want to die.

Step number 10 is to encourage in the couple overt rather than covert requests for love and help. Most of the problem with these couples is that instead of saying overtly, "I need you, help me," they exhibit self-destructive behavior as a way of asking for help. They cannot say, "Help me," because they don't want to acknowledge that the other one has the power to help.

MONEY AND THE MIDDLE-AGED OR OLDER COUPLE

I will turn now to the difficulties of the middle-aged or older couple. Typical problems are old resentments, a mediocre sex life, unfair financial arrangements, a mediocre social life, and what often can be called an emotional divorce. The steps here are quite different from those with younger couples.

The first step is to pick up on the love and passion that they once had for each other and to help them recover some of those feelings. It helps to ask them how they met, what attracted each to the other, what "swept them off their feet," how they fell in love. Just to talk about this sometimes brings back a spark of the old feelings. As they talk, the therapist needs to pay attention to their words to pick up on phrases or expressions that reflect attraction and passion and that later can be used as triggers to bring back those feelings. For example, when a woman described her first date with her husband, she said that he put his arm around her and it was an "electric arm." The therapist remembered those words and used them repeatedly during the therapy. He said to the husband, for instance, "I think that you need to use that electric arm again," and to the wife, "Remember that electric arm." The electric arm became the metaphor for the love and passion they had for one another.

Step two is to handle old resentments by using the statute of limitations, which the therapist explains to the couple is the law of our country. According to the statute of limitations, a person cannot be tried for a crime committed more than seven years ago. When applied to marriage, this means that the spouses cannot bring up, allude to, or express resentments or accusations about things that happened more than seven years ago. This includes misuse of funds, affairs, betrayal, or whatever. The only exception is sexual abuse, where the statute of limitations does not apply (which also coincides with the laws of the country).

Since it is best to phrase things in a positive way, the therapist says to the couple that it is important to focus on the problems of the last seven years, but to set aside those that happened previously. Should one of the spouses forget the rule about the statute of limitations, the other spouse will remind him/her that they cannot talk about that. This forces each spouse, as they begin to express old resentments, to make the effort of remembering what year they are talking about, which can become quite tedious. When a couple has been married for 20 or 30 years, there are an infinite number of old resentments that can be remembered at any time to throw a damper on the therapist's attempts to bring the couple together. The limit of seven years makes a more manageable time frame. It is also better than asking the couple to forget all the past and focus only on the present and the future, which most couples find too extreme. In fact, what often happens is that as they make the effort to remember that they cannot talk about complaints more than seven years old, they propose that it would be easier to make a fresh start and forget the whole past.

The third step is financial planning. The therapist helps the couple to fairly organize their finances as best they can. This is similar to what is done with young couples, but is even more necessary since the financial problems of older people are usually more complicated. It is difficult to succeed at bringing the couple back together if they have unresolved financial issues that make them resentful of one another.

Once financial problems are resolved so that at least there is agreement and collaboration, step number four is to revive the couple's sex life. Here it is useful to see each spouse alone and encourage each on how to approach the other in unusual, fun ways. A wife who has never done this might welcome her husband at the door wearing only a negligee. A husband who has not shown sexual interest for a long time might wake up the wife with affectionate sexual demonstrations. The couple might be encouraged to go to a hotel where they can take a jacuzzi together. The therapist needs to respond to objections and fear of rejection in playful ways and by reminding each spouse of the trust and love they used to have for one another.

Step number five is effected at the same time as the effort to revive their sex life and consists of reminding each spouse of the investment they have made in the relationship and in one another, and the importance of not losing all that they invested over so many years.

Step number six also happens at approximately the same time and consists of using metaphors—about food, for example, and how to have a good meal, or about sports, such as how to enjoy a good game of tennis or golf—to encourage the couple to enjoy each other and to come closer together.

Step number seven usually happens spontaneously and consists of the couple talking to the therapist about good meals together and fun times. This usually means that the relationship is improving, together with their sex life.

Step number eight is for the therapist to bring up again that it is important to discuss the resentments of the last seven years. (It is better when the therapist brings this up rather than one of the spouses.) It is a good idea to ask what is the worst thing that each has done to the other in seven years, and then to give the couple a sense of reality as to how bad this really was. Sometimes, people have really hurt one another and then it is important to recognize it and put it in the context of the good things that were also done. However, people can harbor resentments over truly ridiculous things and it is also important to recognize this. The therapist can list what other husbands and wives do to each other and make a comparison with this couple's situation, taking the opportunity to congratulate them on the minimal ways in which they have hurt each other.

Step nine is for the therapist to talk about the mystery of love that holds a couple together over so many years and how it is not yet understood, encouraging the couple to feel special, particularly in a spiritual way.

Step 10 is to talk about future plans, fun times, vacations, perhaps a renewal of marital vows and a second honeymoon. Here it is important to emphasize that the threat of divorce has to be abandoned once and for all. It is impossible for the couple to have fun when one of them is threatening divorce.

Step 11 is to begin to let the couple go. When a couple has been married for 20 years or more, it is demoralizing to have to see a marital therapist for long. The therapist can say that the couple knows more about marriage than the therapist because they have been married for so long, so they don't need the therapist for too long. They can always come back if a special difficulty arises. Before letting them go, the therapist can give them the following recommendations: to maintain the seven-year rule, to remember that always inside of them is a core of the love and passion that they have had for one another and will carry into the future, and to remember that the expression of resentments on either one's part is really a request for love, so that the appropriate response to resentment is with love. This is similar to the approach with young couples of responding to provocation with humor and play instead of with hostility. Older couples are encouraged to respond to resentment with love instead of by withdrawing.

THOSE WHO WANT TO GIVE LOVE AND PROTECTION

I have talked about people who primarily want to be loved. Now I will address the issues of those who basically want to give their love and protection. Typical problems here are feelings of guilt, obsessive thoughts, and suicide threats and attempts. Guilt and obsessions are characteristically associated with worrying about someone and wanting to give love and care.

Suicide threats and attempts are most frequent in adolescence. The following is a classic situation. A mother becomes depressed and her adolescent daughter worries about her and tries to understand her and help her, but doesn't know how to do it. The mother becomes more and more depressed and the adolescent behaves in disturbing ways as she becomes more and more filled with despair over her concern about her mother. Eventually, the adolescent girl makes a suicide attempt and the mother comes out of her depression to help her daughter and care for her. The daughter improves and eventually the mother becomes depressed again and the cycle repeats itself.

The main emotion in people who are frustrated in not being able to give their love and protection to others is despair. The metaphors they use in their communication are of imprisonment and entrapment because they feel that no matter how they fail they must keep on trying to give their love and protection. These are the adolescents and young adults who feel that they will never be able to leave home, or the spouses who feel they could never divorce no matter how bad the marriage since they are trapped in the relationship. What adds particularly to the despair is that the efforts of these people are usually seen as misguided and they are not appreciated. The adolescent girl is seen as causing trouble, the dedicated spouse is perceived as demanding. The usual response to generosity is not appreciation but resentment, and the more the generosity, the greater the resentment that it elicits, thus adding to the despair of those who are mainly focused on giving.

Appropriate demonstrations of appreciation for those who are offering their love and protection are essential to the therapy. For example, the parents of a 16-year-old girl consulted the institute because they said she was out of control She went out too much, they didn't like her friends, she didn't help with the chores, she didn't help the mother who had a chronic illness — on and on went the list of complaints. At first, the girl refused to come to the sessions. When she finally came, the therapist met with her alone. She said that those people in the waiting room were not her family. Her friends were her family. She didn't want to have anything to do with those people, she didn't want to talk to the therapist, she just wanted to be left alone. She held three jobs and went to school, so she didn't have time for therapy. This girl was the adoptive daughter of the mother and her divorced first husband, who had died recently. The mother's second husband was the girl's stepfather.

The therapist was concerned about the girl's mourning over her father's death and her mother's chronic illness and talked to her alone for a long time. She spoke angrily but tearfully. Slowly the therapist pieced together that she worked three jobs because the family had no money. The stepfather had been out of work for a year and the parents could not provide for her. She paid all her expenses from the money that she herself earned. Moreover, she had inherited some money because of the father's death and had given it all to her parents, who also kept the monthly checks that came to her from her father's pension. She had to work because she was given no allowance and none of her expenses were paid.

The therapist brought the parents into the room and asked them to confirm that all this was true, which they admitted while refusing to give information about specific amounts of money. The stepfather was angry and threatening to the girl for having revealed the situation to the therapist, who assumed all responsibility for being interested in the subject. Several times he had to quiet the girl who was insisting that the subject of money be dropped. The stepfather explained with hostility that he was out of work and that couldn't be helped.

With great clam, the therapist insisted that what was called for was for the parents to thank their daughter for helping them over these difficult times, and to show appreciation for all that she was doing rather than to complain about her. The father responded with anger, but eventually thanked her with tears in his eyes. The mother also thanked her. The therapist talked about how that money should be considered a loan that would be payed back with interest.

A week later the father found a job. He had realized that in these difficult economic times one sometimes needs to come down one level in order to find work and he had given up trying to find a job as a manager and had accepted a regular job instead. Remarkably, all three were getting along. The parents were interested in and encouraging of the girl's activities, and the girl behaved as if they had always been a close, loving family. This is an example of the importance of insisting that the response to generosity be appreciation and not resentment.

Sometimes, the despair of not being able to give one's love and protection to a spouse leads to marital violence. This is common when one of the spouses is controlling and intrusive. One strategy is to arrange for a financial consequence for the violence. This penalty should be commensurate with the financial situation of the violent spouse and should be severe enough to prevent any satisfaction being derived from the violent behavior. The therapist can ask a husband, for example, to deposit a certain amount of money in a special account. Should he ever hit his wife again, the money will go directly to his mother-in-law or to his wife's children from a previous marriage. If the sum of money is large enough, the husband will never hit the wife again. This strategy was inspired by Milton Erickson who would ask a husband to deposit a certain amount of money in a special account in Erickson's name to do with "as I see fit," as Erickson would say (Haley, 1985). He would then proceed to describe the vacations that he would like to take and the things that he would like to buy. I always liked that strategy.

For violent couples there is also the strategy of the Japanese businessman (Keim, 1994). This consists of the following steps or rules that the therapist requires that the couple follow every time they have a discussion or a negotiation about a disagreement. First, the word "No" does not exist; it cannot be used. The closest they can come to saying "No" is to say "I will think about that." Second, each spouse has to participate in the conversation with the understanding that this is only one of hundreds of conversations that will take place about the same or similar subjects. The Japanese businessman wants this to be one of many conversations because he wants to keep his client in an ongoing relationship, just as the spouses want to keep each other. Third, a desirable outcome is a win-win situation, never a win-lose situation because if one person loses, that person will not want to do business again. To arrange for a win-win situation, each spouse must help the other to save face in the discussion.

The fourth principle is that each negotiation must end with a happy social interaction. Because negotiation is painful and both spouses want an amiable relationship, the day cannot end with the memory of an unpleasant conversation. There has to be a pleasant event after the discussion, such as a nice dinner or a walk in the park. These rules are very helpful with volatile, temperamental couples.

HOW MONEY CAN BE USED TO SOLVE PROBLEMS

I often use financial consequences to solve problems with families. Money can be used as punishment and it also can be used to improve relationships. Directives about money and what money represents can be straightforward or paradoxical, and they can involve metaphors and ordeals.

Using Fines in Therapy

Imposing fines for certain behaviors is a useful strategy when people know that they are not doing what they are supposed to do. For example, a man with a heart condition needed to exercise regularly and had to avoid certain foods. He said, however, that he had a chronic state of anxiety, for some mysterious biological reason, that prevented him from resisting the temptation to eat cookies and other goodies and that interfered with his intention to exercise. The wife was tired of nagging him and worrying about him. She threatened and cajoled him to no avail and he complained that she was controlling. She threatened to leave him.

The therapist said that he certainly had the right to do as he pleased, particularly when he lived in such a state of anxiety, and that no one should tell him what to do. However, since his behavior so affected his wife, who had to prepare for becoming a widow in the near future if his behavior continued, something had to be done to calm her anxiety. The solution was that the husband would eat as he pleased and continue to defer exercise if he didn't feel like it, but for each item that he ate outside of his diet, he was to pay his wife a certain amount of money. After a long negotiation, it was agreed that for each cookie that he ate he was to pay her $10, a tablespoon of butter was worth $20, a piece of meat was worth $50, anything with caffeine $25, and so on. For any day he didn't exercise, he had to pay her $200. As they left the session, the wife was already planning what clothes she would buy with all the money she would be making. The husband had to pay her a few times in the next weeks, but soon got his diet and his exercise under control.

I used financial consequences with another couple who had been to therapists for years because of their marital problems. They were successful professional people who came from very different backgrounds. He was Jewish from New York and she was Protestant and very British. They had been stormily married for more than 20 years. They could not have been more different from one another. He loved parties, she hated them; he wanted to travel, she wanted to stay home; he wanted spontaneity, she needed careful planning. He worked long hours and was frequently away on business trips. Her work kept her at home most of the time. What she most resented about him were certain idiosyncracies that she could not understand and could not forgive. For example, he was always late, while she preferred to be always early. If she expected him to come home for dinner, he would inevitably arrive half an hour or an hour late. He would also be late when she was meeting him at a restaurant, the movies, a party, or in the street. She felt desperately at his mercy and threatened divorce again and again. The husband was upset by his own tardiness, but was helpless to change.

I told the husband there was a solution to his problem, but he had to do as I said. He replied that I had to understand that his work was often unpredictable and he was delayed by meetings and urgent phone calls. He couldn't be punctual. I again insisted I had a solution, but he had to do as I said. He agreed. I dictated to him the following contract: If his wife was waiting for him at home, he would pay her a dollar for every minute he was late. If she was waiting at someone else's home, a restaurant, etc., he would pay her two dollars for every minute he was late. If she was out in the street, the price would be three dollars per minute, except if it was raining, cold, or snowing, when the fine was five dollars per minute. He had to always carry cash because the payment would be in cash at the time he was late; there would be no checks and no delayed payments. The money that she made on his tardiness could be spent only on herself, not on the house or the children. She loved the idea. From then on she never again complained about his lateness. When he was late, he paid her every time. I suspect that she began to encourage his tardiness. In fact, I don't even know whether he became more punctual or if it just stopped being an issue.

The same couple had another serious problem. His profession entailed frequent entertaining. He had to take people out to dinner and attend parties and social events. The wife liked to go out with him, and with him only, and hated his social life. She usually refused to participate in events involving his colleagues; if she attended, she was often disagreeable. He felt mistreated and disappointed in her, particularly because he admired her intelligence and it was important for him to show off his wife. They had violent fights about this problem. They had negotiated this issue with other therapists unsuccessfully and I knew my approach would have to be different.

I asked the wife how much she charged per hour in her practice. She said she charged $60 per hour. I suggested the following: Every time the husband wanted her company at a social event, he should pay her her hourly fee, minus a small discount because after all he was her husband. I thought that $50 per hour would be fair. Thus, if she went to a dinner, a party, or any other social occasion where he wanted her presence, he would pay her $50 for every hour she was there. Since she was being paid as a professional, she would behave as such and be interested in the people she met, act polite and engaging, and would talk about interesting things. She was being paid for that. The wife thought this was a good idea and immediately asked whether or not travel time counted. We agreed that for travel she would be paid $30 per hour. The husband accepted this arrangement and from then on their social life was no longer a problem. The husband has subsequently complained that all my solutions involve money and he would like me to come up for once with a strategy that won't cost him anything.

Financial Rewards for Horrible Parents

Financial rewards can be used not only with difficult couples but also with horrible parents. A single mother of a 10-year-old boy beat her son brutally. Her boyfriend also beat him. The boy had been placed in foster homes and hospitalized several times. Previous interventions by therapists and the department of social services had failed. The mother said that when she beat her son she had out-of-body experiences; she could see herself doing it from the ceiling where she was floating in the air, but she could not control her behavior. After several sessions in which the therapist tried unsuccessfully to improve the relationship between mother and child, we decided to try an unusual strategy.

The therapist told the mother that the institute was so concerned about her and her son that we had decided to pay her $10 a day for each day that she or her boyfriend did not hit the boy. She would be paid $70 once a week in the therapy session. But if she had hit the boy even once she would lose all $70 for that week. The therapist said he believed she was an honest person and would take her word as to whether or not she had hit him. The boy's report would also be taken into consideration and he would be examined for obvious marks. In order to take care of the issue of provocation, the son, who was quite misbehaving, would be paid one dollar a day for every day that his mother did not hit him. He would make seven dollars a week, but he also would lose the whole amount if his mother hit him even once during the week. For this boy, seven dollars was a fortune. For the mother, who was on social assistance, $70 a week doubled her income.

The contract was in effect for three months, but then had to be discontinued because of the high cost to the institute. The boy was not abused again. The mother got rid of her boyfriend because she found it was too much trouble to make sure he did not hit the boy. She found a better boyfriend and as she became accustomed to having more money, she began to talk with the therapist about how she could improve her life, get some training, find a job, move to a better neighborhood. The rest of the therapy focused on these issues as she took steps to find a job and improve her life.

Compensating Adult Children

One can never overestimate the financial issues that may be underlying the problems presented to therapy. A young adult woman requested therapy to help her remember whether or not she had been sexually molested by her father. She said she had that suspicion, although she could not remember because of the difficulties that she was experiencing in her life. Because of this suspicion, she had become estranged from her parents and had not talked to them in two years. She explained all this in a first session where she was seen individually. The therapist tried to help her remember and suggested that it would be best to bring in the parents and find out the truth. The parents travelled from another state to come to the next session because they did not understand why their daughter would not visit or talk to them and they wanted to have a relationship with her.

I was the supervisor behind the one-way mirror and the father did not seem to me at all like the type who would have sexually or in any way abused his daughter. However, I am always suspicious in these situations and never trust my first impressions. The therapist encouraged the young woman to speak what was on her mind, but she could not say it and appeared quite angry and upset. So the therapist said that she would speak for her and sent her out to the waiting room. She then explained to the parents that their daughter suspected that she had been sexually molested by her father as a child, although she could not recover any memories, and she wanted to know the truth. The parents were very upset and insisted that no such thing had ever happened. The therapist insisted in every possible way, talking about the importance of helping their daughter to heal, but the parents were shocked and denied anything of the sort.

Finally the therapist called the young woman back into the session and told her that she had reached an impasse. The parents denied any sexual molestation, yet the young woman felt it had happened. What to do? The young woman angrily said she still felt the same. The therapist said that since they had reached this impasse, what was important was for the father to recognize that whatever he actually had done or not done, he must have done something very bad or had a very bad relationship with his daughter for her to have this suspicion. Therefore, what was in order was for him to do reparation, to compensate her in some way for having elicited these thoughts in her. The therapist said that she realized that one cannot truly compensate for sexual abuse, but even symbolically something can be done as reparation. She asked the young woman in what way her father could do reparation for the harm that he had done to her. The young woman screamed and raved that there was no reparation possible, she had been too deeply hurt. The therapist insisted and finally the young woman said that $50,000 would do it.

We then found out that she had a brother to whom the parents had given $50,000 to set him up in business when he graduated from college, whereas they did not do the same for her because she was a girl. The father was very angry and refused to give her the $50,000. We negotiated and he finally accepted that he would pay for her graduate school and all her living expenses for as long as it took her to get a Ph.D. in psychology, which was what she wanted to do with the money. They left the session reconciled and happily went off to dinner together.

CONCLUSION

Money is not only a source of problems in families, but an important resource to be used to improve relationships and to solve problems brought to therapy. If therapists can overcome the idea that it is somehow intrusive or in poor taste to talk about money, they will be able to solve conflicts that have plagued couples and families for ages. If as therapists we can think about money as a repository of good things, we can devise therapy strategies that use money to improve relationships and solve problems. As we approach the end of the century, we can look back and realize how instrumental the field of therapy has been in demystifying sex. Perhaps, before the century ends, we will have also contributed to the demystification of money.

REFERENCES

Bateson, Gregory. (1985). *Steps to an ecology of mind.* New York: Ballantine.

Haley, Jay. (1985). *Conversations with Milton H. Erickson.* Three volumes. New York: Norton.

Keim, James. (1994). Triangulation and the art of negotiation. *Journal of Systemic Therapy, 12*(4), winter (in press).

Madanes, Cloé. (1985). *Behind the one-way mirror.* San Francisco: Jossey-Bass.

CHAPTER 3

Ericksonian Psychotherapy— Then and Now: New Fundamentals of the Naturalistic-Utilization Approach

Ernest L. Rossi

The major theme of this, our Fifth International Congress, *Ericksonian Methods: The Essence of the Story,* presents a heroic but daunting opportunity for all of us to come together to explore our continuing endeavor to understand and further develop Erickson's innovative methods and teaching of psychotherapy. By now, we all recognize that we are a marvelously diverse and widely ranging group, each of us enjoying the pursuit of one aspect or other of Erickson's multifaceted genius. How will it be possible for us to hold together in a common core and still follow our highly individual creative pathways into the future of our science and therapy?

I believe any answer to this question must express our individual quests for personal meaning and development as well as the objective contributions we can make to our profession as a group. Perhaps this is precisely where we can find a common core of agreement about our endeavor: We have all been inspired by Erickson's broad humanity in helping people find and respect their own developing individuality as well as their potentials for helping others.

THE WOUNDED HEALER MODEL

I believe that a broad appraisal of Erickson's life, character, and work provides a profound and persuasive role model about this unique interplay between our individual development and the ideal of contributing to the group that we all share. We recognize that Erickson's destiny as a "wounded healer" who was born with sensory-perceptual handicaps and the tragedy of being crippled by polio are in some way a metaphor for the personal struggles we all experience as our lives unfold. The creative transformation from handicap and outrageous misfortune to the true grit and genius of healing ourselves and others is certainly what we are all about.

I believe there are many sources to what Erickson called his "naturalistic" and/or "utilization" approach to life and psychotherapy in the many fundamental papers he wrote in this area (Erickson, 1958/1980, 1959/1980). There was his deep heritage, of which he was proud, that combined the genes of his Viking ancestors with the Native American Indian; this was certainly a root of his interest in anthropology and his passion to support the disenfranchised of our society as well as native cultures of the Third World. There was his family background as practical farmers in the American West that emphasized a reverence and cooperation with all things natural, from desert ecology of Arizona to the Palo Verde tree in his backyard that he claimed was the largest in the whole state of Arizona.

His personal rediscovery of the ideodynamic approach to hypnotherapeutic healing and his practical, self-designed recovery program from polio certainly contributed to his emphasis on the naturalistic approaches to exploring and accessing each individual's mind and body for their unique patterns of life experiences that could be utilized as hidden resources for facilitating healing. I believe this is the Essence of the Story that became clear to me only when I summarized Erickson's lifetime of personal autohypnotic experiences (Erickson & Rossi, 1974/1980). Erickson's personal development led him to an understanding of the essence of *therapeutic hypnosis* as the accessing and utilization of the patient's own lifetime of experiential learning for problem solving. This is in striking contrast to the diametrically opposite focus of *academic and experimental hypnosis* that conceptualizes hypnosis as a form of suggestion, manipulation, and influence imposed on the patient from the outside.

I believe that the tension between these two opposing points of view—hypnosis with an *inner focus* accessing the inner, personal, and creative that is unique to each individual versus hypnosis with an *outer focus* that uses the individual as a blank slate on which suggestions can be written—is what motivated Erickson to break away from the traditional academic researchers of his day to found the American Society of Clinical Hypnosis

and become the first editor of the *American Journal of Clinical Hypnosis.*
But the Essence of the Story really is not as simple and clear as this because
in his widely ranging exploration of the nature of human behavior as well
as naturalistic healing, Erickson also developed a host of highly directive
and manipulative methods of influencing others. Erickson was a master
with both an inner and outer focus.

THE NEW LANGUAGE OF HUMAN FACILITATION:
THE PHENOMENOLOGICAL LEVEL

The tension between these two apparently opposite approaches to hypnotherapy has been a continuous source of befuddlement to me in most of my
recording and analysis of Erickson's work. Finally, in my most recent
editing of volume four of Erickson's *Seminars, Workshops, and Lectures,*
entitled *Creative Choice in Hypnosis* (Rossi & Ryan, 1992), I try to let the
chips fall where they may by presenting four practical therapeutic method-
ologies on this outer and inner continuum of focus in hypnosis. I make an
effort to continue the legacy of Erickson and Gregory Bateson in their work
on the therapeutic potentials of the double bind.

I illustrated how Haley's analysis of the double bind as a "paradoxical
directive" presented a useful approach to psychotherapy by focusing on the
outer, interpersonal dynamics between people. My own analysis of the
therapeutic double bind as a way of depotentiating a patient's learned
limitations so as to free up the possibility of creative choice placed the focus
on the *inner, intrapersonal* dynamics within the individual. I attempted to
illustrate how David Cheek's ideomotor approach to finger signalling is
actually a unique use of the double bind to facilitate mind-body communication between the physiological and verbal levels of behavior. With my
colleague Patrick Jichaku, who was a Zen monk in training at the time, a
fourth therapeutic use of the double bind in the form of the Zen koan was
explored.

This four-level analysis of the therapeutic uses of the double bind can be
seen as an exercise in how we can all learn to use both the inner and outer
foci of Erickson's indirect approaches to suggestion. I like to call this *The
New Language of Human Facilitation.* I hypothesize that the development
of this new language of human facilitation evolved out of Erickson's own
early handicaps with sensory-perceptual confusions that appeared to be of
a dyslexic nature. Erickson often said that all these approaches to trance
induction involved confusion. What does that mean? I believe it is central
to understanding what is most unique and valuable in his naturalistic and
utilization approach. It is a very deep approach to the eternal issues of
confusion and paradox in human problem solving. It involves many of the

paradoxes of human consciousness that have motivated creativity by our leading thinkers from the ancient philosophers to modern logicians and mathematicians—from Zeno to Isaac Newton and Bertrand Russell—and psychologists from Freud and Jung to the present. It involves the phenomenon of *self-referential* statements that are peculiarly acute, motivating, and confusing in human consciousness. This line of development from Bateson and Haley to Erickson is a profound area for the future development of the new language of human facilitation on the phenomenological level of mind and mental experience in psychotherapy that I can only touch upon here.

THE MIND-BODY IN THE NEW LANGUAGE OF HUMAN FACILITATION

While most of my dozen or so collaborative volumes with and about Erickson's approaches deal with the new language of human facilitation on the phenomenological level of mind and how it may be accessed and utilized by words and meaning, much of this early work has the flavor of "Then—the past, the first stage of my studies with Erickson." The *now* of my interests is to extend the new language of human facilitation into the body right down to the cellular-genetic matrix of life at the molecular level. Here we must recall that Erickson was, after all, a physician. He said he decided to become a medical doctor only after he recovered from his first bout with polio at the age of 18 and decided that although he had experienced a remarkable physical rehabilitation, a certain body strength still was lacking. He just did not feel he was strong enough to become a farmer so he decided to become a doctor as the next best thing.

Throughout his career, Erickson emphasized what he called the "Psycho-Neuro-Physiological" basis of hypnotherapy. It wasn't until the third volume of the *Seminars, Workshops, and Lectures of Milton H. Erickson* series titled *Mind-Body Communication in Hypnosis* (Rossi & Ryan, 1986) that I finally caught up with this aspect of his work. It was in my effort to update his views in this area that led me to my current interest in extending the new language of human facilitation into the body where information, signaling, and communication take place on the molecular level. I realize that this is quite a jump for most of us—to extend our vision and professional competence to encompass the entire mind-body as one vast system of cybernetic communication in psychotherapy.

This profound shift from the phenomenological and behavioral level to the entire mind-body in psychotherapy is a bit disorienting for me. I keep getting the feeling of being a juvenile in the kindergarten of psychotherapy even though I have been in clinical practice for 30 years. Yet, in the last decade of his life one of Erickson's favorite sayings was, "Juvenility is vastly to be preferred to senility." These whimsical words, believe it or not, are what have kept me going during the past 10 years when I went back to take undergraduate and graduate classes at UCLA in the developing fields of molecular biology, physics, mathematics, and computer mathematics. The current revolution of understanding in the theory and practice of the life sciences is changing so rapidly that it is difficult for all of us to stay in touch with the Essence of the Story of Ericksonian methodology.

Therefore, let me tell you about an Essence of the Story of how Erickson allowed his daily work to be guided by subtle mind-body cues whose nature he did not entirely understand himself. I wrote about this in the very first paper I published about Erickson's approach titled "Psychological Shocks and Creative Moments in Psychotherapy" (Rossi, 1973). The basic idea is Erickson's view that we cannot really do good work on a problem unless that patient is actively experiencing it during the psychotherapeutic situation. During those two-hour or longer seemingly leisurely sessions when Erickson was disarmingly pleasant and casually conversational, he was actually hyperalert in observing patients' mind-body behavior for cues about their emotional involvement with the topic being discussed. At the end of our first book, *Hypnotic Realities* (Erickson et al., 1976), I summarized about two dozen of these behavioral cues as Trance Readiness Indicators. In the last eight years of his life when I studied with him, Erickson often used these Trance Readiness Indicators as cues that the patient was ready to enter trance to do some effective therapeutic work.

He reminded me that back in the 1950's he had written a letter to André Weitzenhoffer (in Erickson & Rossi, 1981) about the "common everyday trance": everyone, Erickson believed, just naturally fell into a sort of day-dreamy state at odd times throughout the day when they were a bit tired and needed to take a break for a while or perhaps even a little nap. The Trance Readiness Indicators reminded him of the common everyday trance with its obvious (yawning, staring into space, closing eyes for a few minutes, etc.) and subtle behavioral cues (mild body catalepsies where a person seemed "transfixed"—literally *trance fixed*—and did not move for a moment or two, slowing of sensory-motor coordination, mild states of momentary confusion and memory loss with that "tip of the tongue" feeling, etc.).

I sometimes believe that the most important of my discoveries about the nature of Erickson's work was the day a few years after the publication of *Hypnotic Realities* when I happened to read about biological rhythms in waking fantasy (Kripke & Sonnenschein, 1978; Kripke, 1982). Although the paper was sketchy, it inspired a very broad intuitive leap in my perspective about the general relationship between hypnosis, biology, and psychology that I have been struggling to validate for almost 15 years: *Erickson's Trance Readiness Indicators are identical with many of the behavioral signs characteristic of the rest phase of the major 90-120-minute psychobiological rhythm called the Basic Rest Activity Cycle (BRAC); "The Common Everyday Trance" is Erickson's name for what the chronobiologist called "The Rest Phase of the BRAC."* When I pointed out the similarities between his observations and those of the chronobiologists, Erickson acknowledged that he had never even heard of ultradian rhythms or the BRAC. We both immediately recognized, however, that this possible association could be the psychobiological basis of his naturalistic and utilization approach (Rossi, 1982, 1986a).

Erickson was not simply putting people in trance and using the magic of words to somehow suggest or program them into health, as the conventional view of hypnotherapy would have us believe. Rather, Erickson's genius for observation led him to stumble upon a hidden window into the mind-body when it was carrying out its own natural healing functions every hour and a half or so throughout the day and night. The so-called suggestions administered at this time did not work as some sort of "word magic." I believe Erickson was using his stories, metaphors, and words at just the right time to facilitate the entrainment and utilization of those natural psychobiological healing functions that usually take place during the rest phase of the BRAC.

From this perspective, Erickson's extra-long hypnotherapeutic sessions were no mere idiosyncrasy; they were careful periods of observation searching for the right moment when the patient was going into a naturalistic common everyday trance that could be utilized for therapeutic purposes (Rossi, 1986; Rossi & Cheek, 1988). The words most commonly used by most hypnotherapists to facilitate therapeutic trance, such as "relaxation, comfort, rest, and sleep," are actually "psychosocial cues" that our culture uses to enter (that is to facilitate, evoke, entrain, or synchronize) the healing rest phase of the Basic Rest Activity Cycle.

THE ESSENCE OF THE STORY: HYPNOTHERAPY AND CHRONOBIOLOGY AS SISTER SCIENCES

But most of this is still my intuitive hunch, at best a conjecture about the Essence of the Story, the basic psychobiological process that may account for the efficacy of Ericksonian approaches. How could we prove this hypothesized association between hypnotherapy and chronobiology? And even if we could prove it, of what relevance would it be for our daily therapeutic work? My first formulation of these issues was as follows (Rossi, 1982, p. 26):

> The implications of this association between disruptions of the ultradian cycle by stress and psychosomatic illness are profound. If the major proposal of this section is correct—that therapeutic hypnosis involving physiological processes is actually a utilization of ultradian cycles—then we can finally understand in psychophysiological terms why hypnosis traditionally has been found to be an effective therapeutic approach to psychosomatic problems: *Individuals who override and disrupt their own ultradian cycles (by ignoring their natural periodic needs for rest in any extended performance situation, for example) are thereby setting in motion the basic physiological mechanisms of psychosomatic illness.* Most of this self-induced stress could be conceptualized as left-hemispheric processes overriding their ideal balance with right-hemispheric processes and associated parasympathetic functions. *Naturalistic therapeutic hypnosis provides a comfortable state wherein these ultradian cycles can simply normalize themselves and thus undercut the processes of psychosomatic illnesses at their psychophysiological source.* (Rossi, 1982, p.26)

After my initial observations and hunches about Erickson's work, my first step toward hypothesis testing was to pull together an atlas summarizing more than a hundred papers and books wherein I hoped to demonstrate how the fields of chronobiology and hypnosis have been dealing with many of the same psychosocial, behavioral, psychobiological, and psychopathological processes over the past 200 years quite independently of each other (Rossi, 1986a; Rossi & Cheek, 1988; Rossi & Lippincott, 1992). Chronobiology and hypnosis seemed to be twin sister sciences that were born about two centuries ago in an age when the inner and outer sources of life's movement and behavior were being sorted out. Chronobiology began with the observations of the astronomer De Marian who placed a plant in a dark closet and verified that it had its own endogenous (inner) rhythms of leaf movement every 24 hours that was independent of sunlight. Hypnosis began about the same time with the observations and activities of Mesmer. Mesmer made the same mistake about human behavior, believing it was controlled by outer forces in the heavens, that others made about plant movement behavior before De Marian. It would take hypnosis another hundred years before King Louis XVI set up the first Royal Commission with our very own Benjamin Franklin to determine that healing by hypnosis was due to the endogenous expectations, imagination, and resources of the patient rather than the purported healing powers and magnetism of the therapist.

This analogy between the inner sources of plant movement and the inner sources of hypnotherapeutic behavior may seem farfetched until it is realized that practically all the behaviors of mind and body that we are interested in when we do psychotherapy and hypnosis have natural endogenous or inherent rhythms. What observations of human behavior and relationships are you as a psychotherapist most interested in exploring and facilitating? Emotions, mood, memory, learning, sexuality, all sorts of adaptive and maladaptive behavior and performance in word and deed, psychosomatic symptoms, addictions, aggression, pain, pleasure, sleep, dreams—what have I left out? Human relationships? Yes, all forms of human relating have their own natural rhythms from breast feeding to work, play, sexuality, sleeping, and even getting irritated with each other. Most of the major dynamics of human relating can be conceptualized as patterns whereby we entrain, synchronize, and regulate each other's natural rhythms of being. The only difference is that the psychologist says we *"condition, influence, suggest, direct, etc."* each other instead of using terms like *entrain* or *synchronize* for essentially the same behavioral relationships as described by the chronobiologist.

Einstein is reported to have made the penetrating remark, "It is the theory which decides what can be observed" (Heisenberg, 1983). With this attitude, I made a series of predictions about the time parameters of Erickson's naturalistic/utilization approaches that could never have been asked before the relationship between chronobiology and hypnosis was recognized. This may be a good time to review some of these predictions together with the pilot studies and experimental results generated over the past 10 years.

1. Hypnotic susceptibility has a natural periodicity or chronobiological rhythm during circadian (daily) and ultradian (hourly) time periods throughout the 24-hour day.

While it is regarded as a well-established fact of traditional experimental work that hypnotic susceptibility is a stable trait in longitudinal studies over 20 years (Hilgard, 1982), there were until recently no empirical studies of circadian and ultradian parameters of hypnosis. This first unique prediction of chronobiological theory received its initial experimental verification from Aldrich and Bernstein (1987) who found "time of day" was a statistically significant factor in hypnotic susceptibility. They reported a bimodal distribution of scores on the Harvard Group Scale of Hypnotic Susceptibility (HGSHS) in college students, with a sharp major peak at 12

noon and a secondary, broader plateau around 5 to 6 P.M. Since they
assessed their subjects in large groups, they acknowledged the limitations
of their study as follows: "Research with individuals would also be a better
test of Rossi's (1982) contention that an ultradian rhythm exists in
hypnotizability. These rhythms would have been cancelled out when the
individual rhythms were averaged together when analyzing the data in the
present study" (p. 144).

Naturally I expected that this brilliant confirmation of chronobiological
theory published in one of our leading journals of experimental hypnosis
would lead to a flood tide of research assessing the other "64 Hypotheses in
Search of a Graduate Student" that I had published the year before (Rossi,
1986). But theory is easy, research is difficult. Another five years went by
and no one had published anything else. Finally, one day in a fit of pique
when I could stand it no longer, I suddenly broke off my usually congenial
manner in the middle of a workshop I was teaching and demanded that the
participants keep daily and hourly diaries of their experiences with self-
hypnosis and what I was beginning to call "The Ultradian Healing Response."
After a couple of failures I finally designed a fairly decent pilot study
whereby individual subjects could keep diaries that might identify periodicity in their daily patterns of self-healing, whatever they called it. A
Hypnosis Diary Group made up of individuals with an interest in learning
self-hypnosis were instructed to keep a "Self-Hypnosis Diary" for two
weeks in which they daily recorded three items: (1) the time of day when
they did self-hypnosis, (2) how much time they remained in self-hypnosis,
and (3) a few sentences describing their healing experience of self-hypnosis.
Another group of subjects were encouraged to keep an "Ultradian-Healing
Diary" about rest breaks they took throughout the day. Both groups were
encouraged to do their "inner healing work" and diary recording as many
times a day as they felt a need to.

From a total group of over 100 subjects I was able to select 16 diaries
(with a total of 292 observations that could be analyzed) that complied
with all the instructions of this pilot study. Since I was not familiar with the
necessary time-series techniques of experimental analysis required to deal
with these data, they were analyzed blind with the computer technique
of Multiple Complex Demodulation (MCD) carried out by Helen Sing,
chief statistician of the Behavioral Biology Department of Walter Reed
Army Institute of Research (Sing et al., 1985). The results were a series
of symmetrical curves representing a prominent circadian rhythm with a
peak between noon and 1 P.M. This result was entirely consistent with
Aldrich and Bernstein's initial finding of a peak in hypnotic susceptibility
at noon.

While chronobiological theory (Kleitman, 1969, 1970, 1982) suggested there would be, in addition, a 90–120 Basic Activity Rest Rhythm (BRAC) in the data, the MCD analysis found a 180-minute period as the most prominent ultradian rhythm in both groups of this pilot study. How can we account for the prominence of this longer ultradian rhythm in the "self-hypnosis" and "ultradian healing response" groups? A careful study of the chronobiological literature reveals that the 90–120 BRAC is most clearly evident only under carefully standardized "bed rest" conditions. Virtually all ultradian rhythms are highly adaptive and responsive to environmental demands, particularly psychosocial cues. Since this pilot study was carried out during the subjects' normal everyday pattern of activity rather than during bed rest, it is reasonable to speculate that the ultradian rhythms of these subjects were a bit longer because their typical workday did not usually permit them to take a break or rest period for self-hypnosis or an ultradian healing response whenever they really felt a need to.

Flushed with this initial success (Rossi, 1992a), I continued to explore other predictions of the chronobiological theory of Erickson's naturalist approach within the limitations of my private clinical practice. Here is the next idea I thought I could assess with the data at hand and more to come.

2. There is a natural (typical) trance time of about 20 minutes (plus or minus about 10 minutes), corresponding to the 20-minute rest phase of the Basic Rest Activity Cycle (BRAC), for patients who are permitted to stay in therapeutic hypnosis for as long as they need to for resolving currently experienced personal problems.

A significance observation in the analysis of the diary data was that both groups remained in self-hypnosis or ultradian healing for about 15 or 20 minutes with a range between 5 and 30 minutes. This is consistent with chronobiological observations where Kleitman (1969, p. 37) reports on "The relief obtained by some individuals from brief 10-to-15-minute cat-naps perhaps representing a 'tiding over' the low phase of a BRAC . . ." This apparent correspondence in the natural ultradian rest periods and self-hypnosis suggested further studies to determine whether or not there was a natural therapeutic trance time.

I began to make systematic observation on a group of the next 30 successive patients that I saw in private practice for double-length sessions (90–120-minute therapy sessions). I found that my typical three-step fail-safe hypnotherapuetic trance inductions usually required one to three minutes for eyes to close (Rossi, 1986a/1993; Rossi & Cheek, 1988). I always ended with a permissive suggestion in the form of an implied directive (Erickson & Rossi, 1976; Rossi & Ryan, 1992) phrased as follows: "You will remain in therapeutic trance as long as is necessary for you to resolve the issue you have been dealing with in as satisfactory a manner as is possible at this time. Your unconscious (or "inner mind") will then allow you to awaken entirely on your own, feeling refreshed and alert."

The results of this study (Rossi, 1993) were consistent with the prediction of chronobiological theory: Patients remained in a naturalistic therapeutic trance for about 20 minutes. This naturalistic trance time is reliable in the sense that there was a correlation of .49 (significant at the .02 level, df=28) between time spent in this type of permissive trance on two occasions. There were large standard deviations and wide range of times spent in these naturalistic trance periods (between 2 and 67 minutes), however, so it is easy to understand why this has not been a generally recognized variable in the literature.

Because of the significance of finding that there is a naturalistic therapeutic trance time for a general theory of the relationship between the psychobiology of time and hypnosis, three other independent efforts were made to verify these research results. Brian Lippincott (1990), Carol Sommer (1990, 1992, 1993), and Shirley Sanders (1991a, b) each reported independent replications of the above study with (1) significant modifications of procedure, (2) subjects assessed in different age ranges and parts of the country, and (3) scales for measuring hypnotic susceptibility. All three found essentially similar results. Lippincott reported a mean naturalistic trance time of 18.55 minutes (standard deviation, 14.11) when using the Spiegel Hypnotic Induction Profile with college students. Sommer reported the mean naturalistic trance time with the Wilson Creative Imagination Scale for 32 subjects to be 18.02 minutes (standard deviation, 9.62) when she controlled for a variety of variables such as sex (half her subjects were male and half were female) and amount of previous trance experience.

In a clinically oriented survey conducted by Shirley Sanders (1991a) before she was aware of my interest in chronobiology, further supportive evidence for a natural 20-minute trance time was found. Sanders mailed a self-hypnosis questionnaire of a general nature to 1,000 members of the American Society of Clinical Hypnosis. In the 233 responses she received it was found that a 15-20 minute period was most typical in the use of self-hypnosis. In a more recent study, Sanders and Mann (1992) found an interesting relationship between naturalistic trance time and subjective reports of trance depth. Ninety-five subjects from the University of North Carolina Department of Psychology were administered the Stanford Clinical Scale of Hypnotic Susceptibility individually. Following this induction, subjects were given the non-directive suggestion to "allow themselves to explore the trance state and go as deeply as their unconscious mind would like to go." These subjects reported that their trance depth increased with a negatively accelerating curve that appeared to reach an asymptote at 20 minutes when the experiment was terminated.

In another study, Lippincott (1990) tested a unique hypothesis derived from ultradian theory: If the 20-minute naturalistic trance is, in fact, an important psychobiological period ("marker") for some endogenous psychobiological rhythm, one would expect that after subjects have experienced it, they would no longer have a need to remain in a second naturalistic trance for another 20 minutes within the same 90–120 BRAC ultradian period. This leads to the prediction that subjects (N=30) will remain in a permissive naturalistic trance for much shorter periods if they are asked to experience a second, third, and fourth trance in rapid succession immediately after they have awakened from their first 20-minute naturalistic trance. This prediction was well supported by the results where the first trance had a mean length of 18.55 minutes while the second, third, and fourth experienced in rapid succession were 4.03, 1.96, and 0.98 minutes respectively.

A perceptive peer reviewer of these results noticed that they looked like the typical extinction curve of classical learning theory and, therefore, expressed the view that ultradian dynamics might not be required as an explanatory principle. But this is an important area of study where traditional learning theory may be faulted for ignoring the facts of chronobiology. A chronobiological factor of "spontaneous recovery" is usually associated with every learning and extinction process. This recovery of the learned response is itself an ultradian phenomenon, a chronobiological factor in the classical learning and extinction process that usually has not been recognized as such by experimental psychologists.

Our peer reviewer's point is still an excellent one, however. Further research is now needed to substantiate the chronobiological factor by repeating Lippincott's experiment over the course of an entire day and repeatedly assessing hypnotizability over short intervals in much the same manner as Lavie (1992) has for assessing sleep tendency. If the extinction hypothesis is valid, hypnotizability will go down consistently throughout the day and finally be extinguished altogether by the end of the day. The chronobiological hypothesis would predict, to the contrary, that hypnotizability will recover every 90–180 minutes throughout the day so that the data will follow a sinusoidal pattern as documented by Rossi (1992a).

The existence of a naturalistic 20-minute trance is consistent with a number of earlier reports by clinicians and researchers that documented a 20-minute natural trance time in an incidental manner without recognizing its theoretical significance for chronobiological theory. Erickson, for example, mentions 20 minutes as a typical unit of trance time in a number of his clinical papers and workshops (Erickson 1943b/1980). In one early research report, he outlines how he used approximately 20 minutes for "the development of a deep trance state"; approximately another 20 minutes for "the development of a stuporous trance state"; and yet another 15 minutes for "the development of a somnambulistic state" (Erickson, 1954/1980, p.53).

I have described how most forms of "holistic healing" using a variety of approaches such as meditation, prayer, biofeedback, imagery, music, accupuncture, etc. all use a 20-minute period of healing without realizing how they are thus entraining our natural 20-minute ultradian healing response (Rossi & Nimmons, 1991). The same is true of most experimental studies in this area; they invariably use a 20–30-minute period for assessing whatever healing method they are testing without mentioning how they are thereby entraining the natural healing phase of the Basic Rest Activity Cycle.

A review of the literature of experimental hypnosis turned up a number of studies that could be interpreted as providing further support for a natural 15–20-minute trance time. The earliest reference I have found so far is by the classical hypnosis author Albert Moll (1898, p. 128) who reported, "Brock finds that in a short hypnosis of 20 minutes duration, with partial catalepsy, the sum of the solid constituents and phosphoric acid decreases; as Strubing has described in catalepsy." It will require a scholar of hypnosis with a good command of the German language to go back into these early reports to determine if they could be anticipations of our modern understanding of phosphate (as adenosine triphosphate, ATP) being a central constituent of our natural rhythms of energy dynamics at the cellular-molecular level. On the very next page, Moll, by the way, describes the experiments of Krafft-Ebing and others using hypnosis to change body temperature (which has its own circadian rhythm) "when the subject vividly imagined to himself a rise temperature and feeling of warmth in the hand . . ."

In a methodological study more than a generation ago, Dorcus, Britnall and Case (1941) compared the amount of time a group of 20 deeply hypnotizable subjects remained in trance after the hypnotist left the room with a control group who were told to simply lie down and relax. In both groups, the majority of the subjects got up and left the room within 20 minutes. In two studies using control groups of subjects simulating hypnosis, it was found that highly hypnotizable subjects remained in trance for 10.7 and 16.5 minutes (Orne & Evans, 1966; Evans & Orne, 1971) when they believed they were left unobserved, while the simulating low hypnotizable subjects acted as if they were in trance for 25.2 minutes.

It is interesting that while none of these researchers set out to test the ultradian prediction that there is a natural 15–30-minute trance time, all their data support it. Since there is no other theory of hypnosis that would make such a prediction, the consistent observation of a 15–20-minute natural trance time in a great variety of clinical and experimental situations by many researchers working independently of each other with different theoretical perspectives provides considerable support for a chronobiological theory of hypnosis that may have important implications for therapeutic suggestion.

3. There is an inverse relationship between hypnotizability and naturalistic trance length.

This was an accidental discovery by Lippincott. I initially expected that there would be no relationship between hypnotizability and naturalistic trance length. Lippincott and Sommer noticed that there was a tendency for highly hypnotizable patients as measured by the Barber-Wilson Creative Imagination Scale to experience somewhat shorter naturalistic trance. This inverse relationship between hypnotizability and naturalistic trance length was not statistically significant in any of our clinically oriented pilot studies, however. In what was a better controlled experimental study with college subjects, however, Rossi and Lippincott (1992) found a statistically significant inverse relationship between hypnotizability as measured by the Hypnotic Induction Profile and naturalistic trance length.

One way of interpreting these results is to say that whatever the psychobiological basis of the naturalistic trance length relationship may be, the more highly susceptible hypnotic subjects are more efficient in their experience of it since they require less time to do it. This makes clinical sense when we recall that the subjects were asked to resolve a real-life problem during their naturalistic trance. Presumably, highly hypnotizable subjects are more highly focused and, therefore, more efficient at their therapeutic task. Verification of these findings with a broader range of subjects, tasks, and measures of hypnotic suggestibility are required before we can accept their implications for a chronobiological theory of hypnotherapeutic suggestion.

4. The classical phenomena of hypnosis are entrained utilizations of natural patterns of chronobiological behavior that are characteristic of certain phases of circadian and ultradian rhythms.

As discussed earlier, Erickson taught that all the classical phenomena of hypnosis were manifestations of natural human behavior during the "common everyday trance." While there has been a great deal of controversy about the nature of hypnotic phenomena, most modern theorists agree that the "feats of hypnosis" are all within the normal range of human behavior (Wagstaff, 1986). These researchers openly acknowledge, however, that they have no adequate theory about the source and parameters of hypnotic performance. Naish (1986), for example, has recently summarized the situation as follows: "As [hypnotic] susceptibility is normally assessed, a high scorer is one who *produces* the behavior, the *reason* for its production remains unknown . . . the claim was frequently made that cognitive processes are involved in the production of 'hypnotic' effects. However, the exact nature of these processes generally remained obscure" (165–166).

The chronobiological hypothesis is consistent with Erickson's clinical findings as well as with those experimental conclusions summarized by Wagstaff and Naish above: *The source and parameters of hypnotherapeutic responsiveness may be found in that class of circadian (daily) and ultradian (more than once a day) psychobiological rhythms that are modulated by psychosocial cues.* This hypothesis initially was assessed in a qualitative manner by careful examination of the written diary reports of the subjects and patients in the author's two studies reported above (Rossi, 1992a, b) and was replicated by Lippincott (1990), Sommer (1993), and Sanders (1991a). Sommer and Lippincott both determined that while there were the typically wide variations in the nature of what each subject reported about the subjective aspects of their naturalistic trance experience, within their total groups virtually all the classical phenomena of hypnosis were experienced by implication as described above even though they were not directly suggested.

While the contingencies of the ongoing therapeutic situations limited most of these studies to the qualitative level, Sanders (1991a) took the first step toward quantifying these findings by simply counting the frequencies of commonly reported hypnotic phenomena in naturalistic trance. She found the following frequencies of classical hypnotic phenomena, for example, in her group of 95 college-age subjects: 69, relaxation; 39, dissociation; 18, imagery, dream, and fantasy; 12, amnesia. Erickson's basic premise that patients in therapeutic trance tend to experience many of the classical phenomena of hypnosis spontaneously even when they are not suggested in any way is supported by these studies as well as by the more specific test of the predictions of chronobiological theory about age regression and analgesia to be reported in the next section on owls and larks.

5. There are differences in the hypnotic susceptibility of owls and larks throughout the day.

Aldrich and Bernstein's (1987) finding of bimodal peaks in hypnotic susceptibility in the morning and evening led me to hypothesize that from a chronobiological perspective such results could be a reflection of the different optimal periods of hypnotic susceptibility in a mixed population of larks (people who claim to be more alert in the morning) and owls (people who claim to be more alert in the evening). Accordingly, Lippincott (1992a) designed an experiment to test three hypotheses: (1) larks would have higher hypnotic susceptibility in the late afternoon (4 P.M. to 6 P.M.), (2) owls would have a higher susceptibility in the morning (8 A.M. to 10 A.M.), and (3) there would be no difference in hypnotizability between midnight and 2 A.M. when both groups would normally be asleep.

All three hypotheses were confirmed. Since Wallace (1993) independently replicated the finding that owls and larks have different periods of optimal hypnotic susceptibility throughout the day, there will be profound implications for future theory, research, and practice. It is important to realize, for example, that if the owls and larks had not been separated in these studies there would have been no significant differences in apparent hypnotic susceptibility over time because the inverse patterns of owls and larks would have canceled each other out. If future studies confirm such ultradian and circadian performance shifts in owls and larks it will require a profound reevaluation of many previous studies on psychobiological variables in general as well as in hypnoses in particular. These results challenge previous conceptions of hypnotic susceptibility as a relatively fixed, unvarying trait of the individual (Hilgard, 1982, 1992).

A careful comparison of the hypnotic and chronobiological literature revealed that all but two of the classical phenomenon hypnoses, age regression and analgesia, were reported as characteristic of the low or near sleep or napping phases of our natural rest periods (Rossi, 1986, 1990a; Rossi & Lippincott, 1992). This allowed me to make the prediction that age regression and analgesia would be found as a natural behavioral manifestation of biological rhythms; the confirmation of this unique prediction (that would not be made by any other theory of hypnotic phenomena) could be regarded as further evidence for an association between chronobiology and hypnosis.

Lippincott (1992b, 1993) tested this prediction by administering the Stanford Hypnotic Susceptibility Scale, Form C age regression subset and the Cold Pressor test of hypnotic analgesia to 60 graduate students at 8 to 10 A.M. and 8 to 10 P.M. in a rolling Latin square format. Colman's Owl and Lark Questionnaire as well as oral temperature (body temperature is one of the classical measures of the circadian rhythm in chronobiology) was used to identify the subjects using a median split. These predictions of chronobiological theory were confirmed when it was found that larks (identified by both questionnaire and body temperature) were significantly higher in age regression and analgesia in the evening. Subjects identified as owls, by contrast, had significantly higher age regression and analgesia scores in the morning.

In a more recent study to replicate Lippincott's original findings on owls and larks with a different population and set of controls, Sanders and Mann (1992) reported what initially seemed to be contradictory results. They found that owls reported a significantly greater subjective sense of trance depth in the afternoon and evening, whereas the larks reported greater subjective depth in the morning. There were a number of important differences in the experimental procedures that could account for the differences between Lippincott and the Sanders and Mann study: (1) Lippincott used objective measures of hypnotic susceptibility (HGSHS:A), while Sanders and Mann used subjective measures of trance depth (which are positively correlated with the HGSHS:A, however); (2) Lippincott's use of a longer hypnotic induction period with the HGSHS:A may have generated a more relaxed state in his owls in the morning and thus induced them to relapse more easily back into a passive state of hypnotic susceptibility in the morning, when they are more vulnerable to relaxation and sleep than the larks. The Sanders and Mann study, by contrast, used the shorter and more challenging induction from the Stanford Clinical Scale, which may have generated a more cognitively focused alert state in larks in the morning and thus accounted for their superior performance relative to the owls.

Another pair of papers by Wallance and his colleagues contributes to the issue of hypnotic susceptibility and the vividness of imagery and time of day. Initially Wallace et al. (1992) found that the Vividness of Visual Imagery Questionnaire was related to time-of-administration (every half hour over a three-hour period). This in itself was a neat confirmation of the one aspect of the natural alterations of awareness that take place over the ultradian time domain that I have called the "the wave nature of consciousness" (Rossi, 1991, 1992c). In a second paper, Wallace (1993) found that day persons (larks) exhibited peak hypnotic susceptibility at 10 A.M. and 2 P.M., while for night persons (owls) the peak was at 1 P.M. and 6 P.M. These results held for the assessment by the Harvard Group Scale of Hypnotic Susceptibility, Form A, as well as the Stanford Hypnotic Susceptibility Scale, Form C. The category of day and night persons was assessed by a novel Alertness Questionnaire, however, so it is difficult to compare these results with those of the Lippincott and the Sanders and Mann studies discussed above. Wallace (1993) reports that his data tend to falsify the hypothesis that differences in hypnotic susceptibility over time of day is related to changes in the body temperature rhythm, but it may be related to periods of food intake.

The significance of such contextual psychosocial and experimental variables in producing apparently opposite responses with owls and larks reminds us of the subtlety of hypnosis research and how easy it is to be misled. The owl-lark variable remains to be clarified by further research on the nature and significance of hypnotic processes. Failing to take this variable into account could be responsible for many type 2 errors in hypnosis research — failing to reject the null hypothesis when it should be. When the responses of owls and larks are averaged together, as they have been in all previous research in hypnosis, they may cancel each other out so that the researcher reports that the null hypothesis has been accepted when it should be rejected. This means that many research reports that reject hypnosis as a significant variable may be in error. At the very least, ignoring the owl-lark variable could account for many inconsistent findings in the clinical and experimental literature in hypnosis.

6. There an ultradian association between the nasal brain-breath rhythm and hypnosis.

One of the most intriguing areas of recent research exploring the association between hypnosis and psychobiological rhythms is the so-called nasal breath-brain connection. The German rhinologist Kayser (1895) is credited with recognizing and measuring the widely varying ultradian shifts in the degree to which air is inhaled in the left or right chamber of the nose. In humans, the left and right chambers of the nose alternate in their size and shape to change the degree of air flow through each every few hours.

Recently, Werntz (1981) reported a contralateral relationship between cerebral hemispheric activity (EEG) and the ultradian rhythm of the nasal cycle. She found that relatively greater integrated EEG values in the right hemisphere are positively correlated with a predominant air flow in the left nostril and vice versa. In a wide-ranging series of studies, Werntz et al. (1982a, b) found that subjects could voluntarily shift their nasal dominance by forced uninostril breathing through the closed nostril. Further, this shift in nasal dominance was associated with an accompanying shift in cerebral dominance to the contralateral hemisphere and autonomic nervous system balance throughout the body (Shannahoff-Khalsa, 1991).

The ultradian nasal cycle not only is a marker for cerebral hemispheric activity, but could also be used to voluntarily change the loci of activity in the highest centers of the brain and autonomic system that are involved in cybernetic loops of communication with most organ systems, tissues, and cells of the body. Some of these investigators hypothesize that this nasal-brain-mind link may be the essential path by which the ancient practice of breath regulation in yoga led to the voluntary control of many autonomic nervous system functions for which the Eastern adepts are noted (Brown, 1991a, b; Rossi, 1990b, 1991a).

These relationships inspired a recent Ph.D. dissertation by Darlene

Osowiec (1992), who assessed hypothesized associations between the nasal ultradian rhythm, anxiety, symptoms of stress, and the personality process of self-actualization. She found that: "(1) there is a significant positive correlation between self-actualizing individuals having low trait anxiety and stress-related symptoms and a regular nasal cycle . . . and (2) nonself-actualizing individuals with high levels of trait anxiety and stress-related symptoms exhibit significantly greater irregularity in the nasal cycle . . ." These results are reminiscent of the ancient texts that emphasize that an irregular nasal cycle, particularly one in which the person remains dominant in one nostril or the other for an excessively long period of time, is associated with illness and mental disorder (Rama et al., 1976).

In a more recent 12-week follow-up study, Osowiec (personal communication) is finding that highly hypnotizable subjects evidence more regularity in their ultradian nasal rhythms when they practice self-hypnosis, but low hypnotizable subjects do not. Osowiec tentatively concludes that her findings with the ultradian nasal rhythm are similar to the general types of association that are found between stress, symptoms, personality, and responsiveness to therapeutic hypnosis.

To further assess the hypothesis of an association between hypnosis and the nasal breath-brain link, Lippincott (1992c) studied the effect of two forms of hypnotic induction: (1) a traditional form of hypnosis via the Harvard Group Scale of Hypnotic Susceptibility and (2) a naturalistic form of hypnosis, via my Ultradian Accessing Formula (Rossi, 1986a), on the nasal rhythm. He hypothesized that since hypnosis has been associated with shifts in cerebral hemispheric dominance (Erickson & Rossi, 1979) one would expect that hypnotic induction would be associated with a shift in nasal dominance. He found that both groups of subjects experienced more nasal dominance shifts than a resting control group and, further, the group that experienced a naturalistic hypnotic induction exhibited significantly more nasal shifts than the traditional hypnotic induction group.

7. There are mathematical relationships in the Ericksonian approaches to facilitating the chronobiological parameters of all psychosocially entrainable parameters of our natural psychobiological rhythms.

It is truly dismaying to realize that in its entire 200-year history hypnosis has yet to come up with any mathematical model. How can hypnosis be a science if it lacks the defining parameters of mathematics? The chronobiological approach immediately suggests how we might introduce mathematics into hypnosis. I will here outline how some of the basic parameters of hypnosis might operate with a simple harmonic (periodic or oscillatory) model of motion as illustrated in Figure 1. The recent research of Winfree

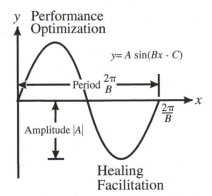

Fig. 1. Parameters of a mathematical model of how hypnotherapeutic suggestion may entrain and utilize psychobiological rhythms.

Amplitude refers to the absolute value of the height or depth of a cycle or rhythm of responsive behavior; it measures how far a rhythm deviates from its mean level. The amplitude may correspond to a "hypnotic constant" that refers to the hypnotizability of a subject or the degree to which hypnotherapeutic suggestion may optimize performance variables or healing parameters.

Period is the time required for one complete cycle of a rhythm; the length of time after which one cycle recurs. The period is frequently a highly variable parameter of psychobiological rhythms that may be contracted or stretched by hypnotherapeutic suggestion. The *frequency* is the reciprocal of the period.

Phase is that part of the cycle that is associated with behaviors of interest; it is the instantaneous state of a cycle within its period. The crest or peak phase of chronobiological behavior is often associated with activation (sympathetic system) while the low or troth phase is often associated with relaxation (parasympathetic system) behaviors. The number C/B, called the *phase shift*, is a measure of the degree to which certain portions of chronobiological behavior can be modulated or entrained with hypnotic suggestion.

Entrainment or synchronization refers to the interaction of psychobiological rhythms (x and y below) with a psychosocial cue such as hypnotherapeutic suggestion (H below) that leads to the phase resetting (phase perseveration, locking or trapping) of certain parts of a chronobiological cycle. Many hypnotherapeutic responses may be conceptualized as phase locked portions of the Basic Rest Activity Cycle (BRAC) that are utilized for facilitating healing. A mathematical model of the hypnotherapeutic entrainment of a Van der Pol oscillation of psychobiological rhythms (adapted from Kronauer, 1984) is illustrated below where H is the "influence coefficient;" ω_x and ω_y are the natural frequencies of individual or systems of psychobiological rhythms x and y; k may be a constant associated with the intrinsic entrainability of a particular psychobiological rhythm by psychosocial cues.

$$k^2\ddot{x} + k\mu_x(-1 + x^2)\dot{x} + \omega_x^2 x + F_{yx}k\dot{y} = 0$$
$$(k = \pi/12)$$
$$k^2\ddot{y} + k\mu_y(-1 + y^2)\dot{y} + \omega_y^2 y + F_{xy}k\dot{x} = F_y$$
$$H = F_{zy}\cos(k\omega_z + \theta_z)$$

(1991) and Jewett et al. (1991), discussed in Rossi and Lippincott (1992), however, indicates that this model is certainly too simple to account for the nonlinear dynamics of most ultradian-circadian processes in humans. Figure 1 is only a didactic lesson to introduce one view of how some of the major parameters of chronobiology are related to the familiar concepts of hypnosis.

The four parameters of interest in this mathematical model are the *amplitude, period, phase,* and *entrainment* of hypnotic behavior. A broad approach to the relationship between these parameters of our natural psychobiological rhythms and hypnosis leads to many basic questions. To what degree does hypnosis modulate (synchronize or entrain) the amplitude, phase or period, and frequency of psychobiological rhythms? From Figure 1 we can infer that the entrainment of the high and low *phases* of psychobiological rhythms is of paramount interest in hypnotherapy. The basic problem of hypnotherapy from this point of view may be stated as one basic question: *How does hypnotherapeutic suggestion synchronize, entrain, or "phase lock" the high and low phases of our natural psychobiogical rhythms for therapeutic purposes?*

What specific research areas in current hypnosis could assess these parameters of a chronobiological theory of hypnotherapeutic suggestion? Here are just a few such areas.

Hypnotizability and Control of Chronobiological Rhythms. Experimental studies have documented how highly hypnotizable subjects have a greater cognitive flexibility and capacity for absorption and dissociation. Evans (1991) reviewed studies indicating that highly hypnotizable subjects have a greater capacity to take naps when they want to, for example. From a chronobiological perspective, this suggests that highly hypnotizable subjects have a greater degree of control over the parameters of their ultradian and circadian rhythms. Which parameters of Figure 1 are more easily controlled by such subjects—the phase, period, amplitude, the capacity for entrainment, or all of them?

Does this question have relevance for practical issues such as jet lag and shift workers? We know that some shift workers adapt easily to changes in their scheduled work periods, while others suffer a proneness to psychosomatic problems and accidents (Naitoh, 1982). If the highly hypnotizable are more easily able to shift important parameters of their psychobiological rhythms, then we would predict that they would adapt more easily and successfully to jet lag (Graeber, 1982) and shift work.

Hypnosis, Aging, and the Amplitude of Psychobiological Rhythms. A number of independent studies have reported that hypnotizability decreases with age (Higard, 1965). Likewise, chronobiologists have reported that certain parameters of biological rhythms, such as their amplitude, decrease with age (Moore-Ede et al., 1982; Wever, 1988). This suggests the easily testable prediction that there would be a significant correlation between the changing parameters of biological rhythms and hypnotizability over a wide age range. Would this data also provide parameters for the differential equations of the hypnotic process proposed in Figure 1?

Hypnosis and Clinical Diagnosis. Likewise, we would predict that some diagnostic groups that have been found to have altered hypnotic susceptibility, such as phobic and bulimic patients (Evans, 1991) and those with dissociative disorders, would have corresponding changes in their biological rhythms. In general, we would predict that any variable or pattern of individual differences that modulates hypnotic susceptibility would also modify chronobiological rhythms (their amplitude, phase, period, frequency, reliability, etc.) in a similar direction and vice versa. These clinical associations would have obvious therapeutic as well as theoretical implications for hypnotherapy.

Hypnosis, Pain, and Periodicity. What clinical phenomena would be most easily assessed in a quantitative manner to explore the mathematical parameters of Figure 1? The closest thing we have in clinical and experimental research may be Hilgard's classical studies of analgesia (Hilgard & Hilgard, 1983). Will pain associated with the various clinical conditions that are experienced periodically, for example, be more amenable to hypnotherapeutic suggestion than pain that is not periodic? That is certainly one prediction of our developing chronobiological theory of naturalistic hypnotherapy that could be easily assessed with a variety of medical conditions. We know, for example, that Erickson had striking success with the periodic pain of cancer (Erickson, 1964, p.284). How about the pain of surgery that is not periodic and the pain of childbirth that is?

RESEARCH PROPOSALS FOR THE ESSENCE OF THE STORY

Why are we doing all this chronobiologically oriented research into Erickson's naturalistic-utilization approaches anyway? We all know today that the essence of the healing process, whatever the problem, is in some way or other related to the molecular-genetic level as the bottom line of all life's informational and communication processes (Rossi, 1986a, 1990b). All of these psychobiological processes operate within circadian and ultradian rhythms and time parameters. If we can find a relationship between these rhythms and hypnosis, we will have a key to predicting and accessing a whole new class of mind-body processes for facilitating healing with hypnosis. All the research reviewed above is consistent with the chronobiological theory of Erickson's naturalistic-utilization approach, but more direct evidence is needed.

The major motivation for my recent editing of a research volume on *Ultradian Rhythms in Life Processes* (Lloyd & Rossi, 1992) was to bring together the latest data documenting how ultradian rhythms on the molecular-genetic, neuroendocrinological, and psychosocial (including hypnosis) levels are all related in one vast cybernetic mind-body process of communication that we call "The Unification Hypothesis of Chronobiology." I would therefore like to take this opportunity to focus your attention on just three fundamental research proposals that will be critical for establishing this new chronobiological mind-body link for healing in hypnosis in the future.

1. Does a shift in the circadian rhythm lead to a shift in hypnotic susceptibility?

The most interesting leading-edge chronobiological research has developed a methodology for shifting the human circadian pacemaker and attenuating endogenous circadian amplitude (Jewett et al., 1991). Since the Aldrich and Bernstein (1987) and the Rossi and Lippincott studies reviewed in this paper found hypnotic susceptibility to be a function of ultradian/circadian rhythms, we would expect that shifting and/or temporarily attenuating a subject's circadian amplitude would be a way of temporarily shifting the peak period and/or modifying the subject's hypnotic susceptibility. A double-blind study utilizing the well-controlled Jewett methodology for modulating human biological rhythms would be the most direct and convincing documentation of an association between hypnosis and chronobiology.

A related but as yet unpublished study by Sanders and Mann (1992) took a preliminary step in this direction by examining the effects of two important chronobiological variables, light and temperature, on hypnotic susceptibility. The range over which they used light (room illumination of 60 versus 400 watts) and temperature (surface room temperature of 68 degrees versus 78 degrees farenheit) in the morning and evening did not affect hypnotic susceptibility as they measured it. These negative results are readily explained by recent chronobiological research that reports how the effects of light on the endogenous circadian rhythms of core body temperature and cortisol are most evident when administered two or three hours before awakening, when body temperature is at its daily minimum (Jewett et al., 1991) rather than during the morning and evening hours of the Sanders/Mann study. The really crucial test of the chronobiological theory of hypnotic susceptibility therefore remains to be done.

2. Can Erickson's naturalistic-utilization hypnotherapeutic approaches shift the natural circadian and/or ultradian periods, pulses, or phases of the endocrine system?

Erickson believed that one of his key contributions to an understanding of the psycho-neuro-physiological basis of hypnosis was his clinical demonstrations of the hypnotherapeutic alteration of breast development (Erickson, 1960/1980a) and menstrual functioning (Erickson, 1960/1980b). Since then, a host of other researchers have documented these and other findings in gynecology and obstetrics that suggest hypnosis may modulate many hormonal and neuroendocrinological processes (Hammond, 1990, p. 269ff.). Still, the critical research measuring the actual ultradian pulses and rates of hormone flow remains to be done.

I believe this would be an excellent opportunity to assess the relative merits of the different degrees of directiveness in the use of the therapeutic bind in facilitating creative choice proposed by Haley, Cheek, and myself and described earlier (Rossi & Ryan, 1992). Recent research on the circadian/ultradian pulses of virtually all hormonal systems that have been measured provides very clear guidelines and experimental models about how such research could be conducted.

3. Can Erickson's naturalistic-ultradian approaches modulate the molecular-genetic level of mind-body communication?

Here we come right down to the bottom line of the most intriguing developments of current mind-body research: Can mind methods be used to modulate the expression of our genes (Rossi, 1986, 1992)?

This is a relatively easy research project, since a practical laboratory model has already been published (Glaser et al., 1990). The research of Glaser's team is the clearest example of what I have been calling "The Mind-Gene Connection" (Rossi, 1990b). An abstract of their initial study, which they claim is the first evidence of the mind-gene loop of information transduction, tells the whole story.

> We explored the expression of the interleukin 2 receptor (IL-2R) and the synthesis of IL-2R messenger RNA by peripheral blood leukocytes obtained from medical students experiencing examination stress in three independent studies. The peripheral blood leukocytes obtained at low-stress baseline periods had significantly higher percentages of IL-2R positive cells when compared with cells obtained from the same individuals during examinations. In additional, IL2-R messenger RNA in peripheral blood leukocytes decreased significantly during examination periods in a subset of 13 subjects. In one study, we found an increase in the accumulation of interleukin 2 in cultures of cells showing down regulation of IL-2R expression and IL-2R messenger RNA levels. While there are ample data demonstrating stress-associated dec-

rements in the immune response in humans and animals, these data provide the first evidence that this interaction may be observed at the level of gene expression. The data suggest one mechanism whereby the central nervous system modulates the immune response during psychological stress. (*Arch Gen Psychiatry*, 1990;47:707-712)

Those who are familiar with the messenger molecule interleukin 2 will recognize that it is one of the crucial links that the psychoimmunological system has in its fight against cancer (Rosenberg & Barry, 1992). Establishing this mind-gene link may therefore be a dramatic step in establishing the actual mind-molecular pathway for the continuing reports of the amelioration of cancer by psychotherapeutic methods (Hammond, 1990; Spiegel et al., 1989).

SUMMARY

The traditional significance of time, rhythm, and psychophysiology in the naturalistic-utilization dynamics of Ericksonian approaches to hypnosis and psychotherapy finds a new conceptual foundation in the 10 years of research on the chronobiological theory of therapeutic suggestion as reviewed in this chapter. The chronobiological theory proposes that the source and parameters of hypnotherapeutic responsiveness may be found in that class of circadian (daily) and ultradian (more than once a day) psychobiological rhythms that are modulated by psychosocial cues. Recent research comes to the surprising insight that most of the known psychological and psychobiological processes on the cognitive-behavioral, neuroendocrinological and cellular-genetic levels that manifest a natural variability during ultradian and circadian rhythms are also modifiable by psychosocial cues such as hypnosis.

These recent findings lead to the hypothesis that what has been traditionally called "therapeutic suggestion" may be, in essence, the accessing, entrainment, and utilization of the natural variability of ultradian and circadian processes that respond to psychosocial cues. Within this framework, the classical phenomena of hypnosis may be conceptualized as the entrainment of extreme manifestations and/or perseverations of time-dependent psychobiological processes that are responsive to psychosocial cues. The natural psychobiological rhythms associated with memory, learning, emotions, dissociation, and psychopathology may be understood as mediating variables between the words and suggestions of the hypnotherapist and the psychophysiological processes that are the essence of mind-body communication and healing at the molecular level. I fully expect that the host of new research approaches for exploring the "mind-body problem" via the further exploration of the chronobiological theory of Erickson's naturalistic approaches will lead us all ever closer to the Essence of the Story.

REFERENCES

Aldrich, K., & Bernstein, D. (1987). The effect of time of day on hypnotizability. *International Journal of Clinical and Experimental Hypnosis, 35*(3), 141-145.

Brown, F., & Graeber, R. (Eds.) (1982). *Rhythmic Aspects of Behavior.* Hillsdale, NJ: Lawrence Erlbaum.

Brown, P. (1991a). Ultradian rhythms of cerebral function and hypnosis. *Contemporary Hypnosis, 8*(1), 17-24.

Brown, P. (1991b). *The Hypnotic Brain: Hypnotherapy and Social Communication.* New Haven: Yale University Press.

Dorcus, R., Britnall, A., & Case, H. (1941). Control experiments and their relation to theories of hypnotism. *Journal of General Psychology, 24,* 217-221.

Erickson, M. (1943a/1980). Experimentally elicited salivary and related responses to hypnotic visual hallucinations confirmed by personality reactions. In E. Rossi (Ed.), *The Collected Papers of Milton H. Erickson on Hypnosis. II. Hypnotic Alteration of Sensory, Perceptual, and Psychophysical Processes* (pp. 175-178). New York: Irvington.

Erickson, M. (1943b/1980). Hypnotic investigation of psychosomatic phenomena: A controlled experimental use of hypnotic regression in the therapy of an acquired food intolerance. In E. Rossi (Ed.), *The Collected Papers of Milton H. Erickson on Hypnosis. II. Hypnotic Alteration of Sensory, Perceptual, and Psychophysical Processes* (pp. 169-174). New York: Irvington.

Erickson, M. (1943c/1980). Hypnotic investigation of psychosomatic phenomena: Psychosomatic interrelationships studied by experimental hypnosis. In E. Rossi (Ed.), *The Collected Papers of Milton H. Erickson on Hypnosis. II. Hypnotic Alteration of Sensory, Perceptual, and Psychophysical Processes* (pp. 145-156). New York: Irvington.

Erickson, M. (1943d/1980). Hypnotic investigation of psychosomatic phenomena: The development of aphasia-like reactions from hypnotically induced amnesia. In E. Rossi (Ed.), *The Collected Papers of Milton E. Erickson on Hypnosis. II. Hypnotic Alteration of Sensory, Perceptual, and Psychophysical Processes* (pp. 157-168). New York: Irvington.

Erickson, M. (1954/1980). The development of an acute limited obsessional hysterical state in a normal hypnotic subject. In E. Rossi (Ed.), *The Collected Papers of Milton E. Erickson on Hypnosis. II. Hypnotic Alteration of Sensory, Perceptual, and Psychophysical Processes* (pp. 51-80). New York: Irvington.

Erickson, M. (1958/1980). Naturalistic techniques of hypnosis. In E. Rossi (Ed.), *The Collected Papers of Milton H. Erickson on Hypnosis. I. The Nature of Hypnosis and Suggestion* (pp. 168-176). New York: Irvington.

Erickson, M. (1959/1980). Further clinical techniques of hypnosis: Utilization techniques. In E. Rossi (Ed.), *The Collected Papers of Milton H. Erickson on Hypnosis. I. The Nature of Hypnosis and Suggestion* (pp. 177-205). New York: Irvington.

Erickson, M. (1960a/1980). Breast development possibly influenced by hypnosis: Two instances and the psychotherapeutic results. In E. Rossi (Ed.), *The Collected Papers of Milton H. Erickson on Hypnosis. II. Hypnotic Investigation of Sensory, Perceptual, and Psychophysical Processes* (pp. 203-206). New York: Irvington.

Erickson, M. (1960b/1980). Psychogenic alteration of menstrual functioning: Three instances. In E. Rossi (Ed.), *The Collected Papers of Milton H. Erickson on Hypnosis. II. Hypnotic Investigation of Sensory, Perceptual, and Psychophysical Processes* (pp. 207-212). New York: Irvington.

Erickson, M., & Rossi, E. (1974/1980). The autohypnotic experiences of Milton H. Erickson. In E. Rossi (Ed.), *The Collected Papers of Milton H. Erickson on Hypnosis. I. The Nature of Hypnosis and Suggestion* (pp. 360-365). New York: Irvington.

Erickson, M., & Rossi, E. (1979). *Hypnotherapy: An Exploratory Casebook.* New York: Irvington.

Erickson, M., & Rossi, E. (1981). *Experiencing Hypnosis: Therapeutic Approaches to Altered States.* New York: Irvington.

Erickson, M., Rossi, E., & Rossi, S. (1976). *Hypnotic Realities.* New York: Irvington.

Evans, F. (1991). Hypnotizability: Individual differences in dissociation and the flexible control of psychological processes. In S. Lynn & J. Rhue (Eds.), *Theories of Hypnosis: current models and perspectives.* New York: Guilford.

Evans, F., & Orne, M. (1971). The disappearing hypnotist: the use of simulating subjects to evaluate how subjects perceive experimental procedures. *International Journal of Clinical and Experimental Hypnosis, 19,* 277-296.

Glass, L., & Mackey, M. (1988). *From Clocks to Chaos: The Rhythms of Life.* Princeton: Princeton University Press.

Glaser, R., Kennedy, S., Lafuse, W., Bonneau, R., Speicher, C., Hillhouse, J., & Kiecolt-Glaser, J. (1990). Psychological stress-induced modulation of interleukin 2 receptor gene expression and interleukin 2 production in peripheral blood leukocytes. *Archives of General Psychiatry, 47,* 707-712.

Gorton, B. (1957). The physiology of hypnosis, I. *Journal of the Society of Psychosomatic Dentistry, 4*(3), 86-103.

Gorton, B. (1958). The physiology of hypnosis: Vasomotor activity in hypnosis. *Journal of the American Society of Psychosomatic Dentistry, 5*(1), 20-28.

Graeber, R. (1982). Alterations in performance following rapid transmeridian flight. In F. Brown & R. Graeber (Eds.), *Rhythmic Aspects of Behavior* (pp. 173-212). Hillsdale, NJ: Lawrence Erlbaum.

Hammond, D. (1990). *Handbook of Hypnotic Suggestions and Metaphors.* New York: Norton.

Heisenberg, W. (1983). *Encounters with Einstein.* Princeton: Princeton University Press.

Hilgard, E. (1965). *Hypnotic Susceptibility.* New York: Harcourt, Brace & World.

Hilgard, E. (1981). Hypnotic susceptibility scales under attack: An examination of Weitzenhoffer's criticisms. *International Journal of Clinical and Experimental Hypnosis, 24,* 24-41.

Hilgard, E. (1982). Hypnotic susceptibility and implications for measurement. *International Journal of Clinical and Experimental Hypnosis., 30*(4), 394-403.

Hilgard, E. (1992). Dissociation and theories of hypnosis. In E. Fromm, & M. Nash (Eds.), *Contemporary Hypnosis Research* (pp. 69-101). New York: Guilford.

Hilgard, E., & Hilgard, J. (1983). *Hypnosis in the Relief of Pain*. Los Altos, CA: William Kaufmann.

Jewett, J., Kronauer, R., & Czeisler, A. (1991). Light-induced suppression of endogenous circadian amplitude in humans. *Nature, 350,* 59-62.

Kayser, R. (1895). Die exacte Messung der Luftdurchgangigkeit der Nasa. *Archi fuer Laryngologie und Rhinologie, 3,* 101-120.

Kirschbaum, C., & Hellhammer, D. (1989). Salivary cortisol in psychobiological research: An overview. *Biological/Pharmacopsychology, 22,* 150-169.

Kleitman, N. (1969). Basic rest-activity cycle in relation to sleep and wakefulness. In A. Kales (Ed.), *Sleep: Physiology & Pathology* (pp. 33-38). Philadelphia: Lippincott.

Kleitman, N. (1970). Implications of the rest-activity cycle: Implications for organizing activity. In E. Hartmann (Ed.), *Sleep and Dreaming*. Boston: Little, Brown.

Kleitman, N. (1982). Basic rest-activity cycle — 22 years later. *Sleep, 5,* 311-315.

Kripke, D. (1982). Ultradian rhythms in behavior and physiology. In F. Brown & R. Graeber (Eds.), *Rhythmic Aspects of Behavior* (pp. 313-344). Hillsdale, NJ: Lawrence Erlbaum.

Kripke, D., & Sonnenschein, D. (1978). A biologic rhythm in waking fantasy. In K. Pope & J. Stringer (Eds.), *The Stream of Consciousness* (pp. 321-332). New York: Plenum.

Kronauer, R. (1984). Modeling principles for human circadian rhythms. In M. Moore-Ede & C. Czeisler (Eds.), *Mathematical Models of the Circadian Sleep-Wake Cycle* (pp. 105-128). New York: Raven.

Kupfer, D., Monk, T., & Barchas, J. (1988). *Biological Rhythms and Mental Disorders*. New York: Guilford.

Lavie, P. (1992). Ultradian rhythms in sleep propensity: Kleitman's BRAC revisited. In D. Lloyd & E. Rossi (Eds.), *Ultradian Rhythms in Life Processes: A Fundamental Inquiry into Chronobiology and Psychobiology* (pp. 283-302). New York: Springer-Verlag.

Lippincott, B. (1990). Testing two predictions of the ultradian theory of therapeutic hypnosis. Paper presented at the 32nd Annual Scientific Meeting and Workshops on Clinical Hypnosis, March 24-28, Orlando, Florida.

Lippincott, B. (1992a). Owls and larks in hypnosis: Individual differences in hypnotic susceptibility relating to biological rhythms. *American Journal of Clinical Hypnosis, 34,* 185-192.

Lippincott, B. (1992b). Owls and larks in hypnosis: Age regression and analgesia. (In preparation)

Lippincott, B. (1992c). The nasal cycle and hypnosis: A brief communication. (In preparation)

Lippincott, B. (1993). Temperature, rhythm and hypnotizability. *Contemporary Hypnosis, 10,* 155-158.

Lloyd, D., & Rossi, E. (1992). *Ultradian Rhythms in Life Processes: A Fundamental Inquiry into Chronobiology and Psychobiology*. New York: Springer-Verlag.

Lloyd, D., & Rossi, E. (1993). Biological rhythms as organization and information. *Biological Review,* 1-15.

Moll, A. (1898). *Hypnotism.* New York: Scribner's Sons.

Moore-Ede, M., Sulzman, F., & Fuller, C. (1982). *The clocks that time us.* Cambridge: Harvard University Press.

Naish, P. (Ed.) (1986). *What Is Hypnosis? Current Theories and Research.* Philadelphia: Open University Press, Milton Keynes.

Naitoh, P. (1982). Chronobiological approach for optimizing human performance. In F. Brown & R. Graeber (Eds.), *Rhythmic Aspects of Behavior* (pp. 41-103). Hillsdale, NJ: Lawrence Erlbaum.

Orne, M., & Evans, F. (1966). Inadvertent termination of hypnosis with hypnotized and simulating subjects. *International Journal of Clinical and Experimental Hypnosis, 14,* 61-78.

Osowiec, D. (1992). Ultradian rhythms in self-actualization, anxiety, and stress-related somatic symptoms. Unpublished doctoral dissertation, California Institute of Integral Studies, San Francisco.

Rama, S., Ballentine, R., & Ajaya, S. (1976). *Yoga and Psychotherapy: The Evolution of Consciousness.* Honesdale, PA: Himalayan International Institute of Yoga Science and Philosophy.

Rapp, P. (1979). An atlas of cellular oscillators. *Journal of Experimental Biology, 81,* 281-306.

Rapp, P. (1987). Why are so many biological systems periodic? *Progress in Neurobiology, 29,* 261-273.

Rosenberg, S., & Barry, J. (1992). *The Transformed Cell: Unlocking the Mysteries of Cancer.* New York: Putnam/Chapmans.

Rossi, E. (1973). Psychological shocks and creative moments in psychotherapy. *The American Journal of Clinical Hypnosis, 16,* 9-22.

Rossi, E. (1982). Hypnosis and ultradian cycles: A new state(s) theory of hypnosis? *American Journal of Clinical Hypnosis, 25*(1), 21-32.

Rossi, E. (1986a/1993) *The Psychobiology of Mind-Body Healing,* Revised Edition. New York: Norton.

Rossi, E. (1986b). Altered states of consciousness in everyday life: The ultradian rhythms. In B. Wolman & M. Ullman (Eds.), *Handbook of Altered States of Consciousness* (pp. 97-132). New York: Van Nostrand Reinhold.

Rossi, E. (1986c). Hypnosis and ultradian rhythms. In B. Zilbergeld, M. Edelstien, & D. Araoz (Eds.), *Hypnosis: Questions and Answers* (pp. 17-21). New York: Norton.

Rossi, E. (1986d). The Indirect Trance Assessment Scale (ITAS): A preliminary outline and learning tool. In M. Yapko (Ed.), *Hypnotic and Strategic Interventions: Principles and Practice* (pp. 1-29). New York: Irvington.

Rossi, E. (1987). From mind to molecule: A state-dependent memory, learning, and behavior theory of mind-body healing. *Advances, 4*(2), 46-60.

Rossi, E. (1989). Mind-body healing, not suggestion, is the essence of hypnosis. *American Journal of Clinical Hypnosis, 32,* 14-15.

Rossi, E. (1990a). The new yoga of the west: Natural rhythms of mind-body healing. *Psychological Perspectives, 22,* 146-161.

Rossi, E. (1990b). Mind-molecular communication: Can we really talk to our genes? *Hypnos, 17*(1), 3-14.

Rossi, E. (1990c). From mind to molecule: More than a metaphor. In J. Zeig & S. Gilligan (Eds.), *Brief Therapy: Myths, Methods and Metaphors.* New York: Brunner/Mazel.

Rossi, E. (1990d). A clinical-experimental exploration of Erickson's naturalistic approach: A pilot study of ultradian time and trance phenomena. *Hypnos, 20,* 10-20.

Rossi, E., (1991). The wave nature of consciousness. *Psychological Perspectives, 24,* 1-10.

Rossi, E. (1992a). Periodicity in self-hypnosis and the ultradian healing response: A pilot study. *Hypnos, 19,* 413.

Rossi, E. (1992b). A clinical-experimental exploration of Erickson's naturalistic approach: Ultradian time and trance phenomena. *Hypnos, 20,* 10-20.

Rossi, E., (1992c). The wave nature of consciousness: A new direction for the evolution of psychotherapy. In J. Zieg (Ed.), *The Evolution of Psychotherapy: The Second Conference* (pp. 216-235). New York: Brunner/Mazel.

Rossi, E., & Cheek, D. (1988). *Mind-Body Therapy: Ideodynamic Healing in Hypnosis.* New York: Norton.

Rossi, E., & Lippincott, B. (1992). The wave nature of being: Ultradian rhythms and mind-body communication. In D. Lloyd & E. Rossi (Eds.), *Ultradian Rhythms in Life Processes: A Fundamental Inquiry into Chronobiology and Psychobiology* (pp. 371-402). New York: Springer-Verlag.

Rossi, E., & Lippincott, B., (1993). A clinical-experimental exporation of Erickson's naturalistic approach: A pilot study of ultradian time and trance phenomena. *Hypnos.*

Rossi, E., & Nimmons, D. (1991). *The 20-Minute Break: Using the New Science of Ultradian Rhythms.* Los Angeles: Tarcher.

Rossi, E., & Ryan, M. (Eds.) (1986). *Mind-Body Communication in Hypnosis. Vol. 3. The Seminars, Workshops, and Lectures of Milton H. Erickson.* New York: Irvington.

Rossi, E., & Ryan, M. (Eds.) (1992). *Creative Choice in Hypnosis. Vol. 4. The Seminars, Workshops, and Lectures of Milton H. Erickson.* New York: Irvington.

Sanders, S. (1991a). Self-hypnosis and ultradian states: Are they related? Paper presented at the 33rd Annual Scientific Meeting of the American Society of Clinical Hypnosis. April 14-18, St. Louis, Missouri.

Sanders, S. (1991b). *Clinical Self-Hypnosis: The Power of Words and Images.* New York: Guilford.

Sanders, S., & Barton, J. (1992). The effects of light, temperature and trance length on hypnotic trance depth. Paper presented at the 34th Annual Scientific Meeting of the American Society of Clinical Hypnosis. April 4-8, Las Vegas, Nevada.

Sanders, S., & Mann, B. (1992). Hypnotic susceptibility in owls and larks. Paper presented by the 33rd Annual Scientific Meeting of the American Society of Clinical Hypnosis. April 14-18, St. Louis, Missouri.

Schulz, H., & Lavie, P. (1985). *Ultradian Rhythms in Physiology and Behavior.* New York: Springer-Verlag.

Sing, H., Thorne, D., Hegge, F., & Babkoff, H. (1985). Trend and rhythm analysis of time-series data using complex demodulation. *Behavior Research Methods, Instruments and Computers, 17*(6), 623-629.

Shannahoff-Khalsa, D. (1991). Lateralized rhythms of the central and autonomic nervous systems. *International Journal of Psychophysiology, 11*, 225-251.

Sommer, C. (1990). The ultradian rhythm and the common everyday trance. Paper presented at the 32nd Annual Scientific Meeting on Clinical Hypnosis, March 24-28, Orlando, Florida.

Sommer, C. (1992). Ultradian rhythms and the common everyday trance. *Bulletin of the Delaware County Medical Society.* January, 6-7.

Sommer, C. (1993). Ultradian Rhythms and the Common Everyday Trance. *Hypnos, 20,* 135-144.

Spiegel, D., Bloom, J., Kraemer, H., & Gottheil, E. (1989). Effect of psychosocial treatment on survival of patients with metastatic breast cancer. *Lancet,* October 14, 2, 888-891.

Veldhuis, J. (1992). A parsimonious model of amplitude and frequency modulation of episodic hormone secretory bursts as a mechanism for ultradian signalling by endocrine glands. In D. Lloyd & E. Rossi (Eds.), *Ultradian Rhythms in Life Processes* (pp. 139-172). New York: Springer-Verlag.

Wagstaff, G. (1986). Hypnosis as compliance and belief: A socio-cognitive view. In P. Naish (Ed.), *What Is Hypnosis? Current Theories and Research* (pp. 57-84). Philadelphia: Open University Press, Milton Keynes.

Wallace, B. (1993). Day persons, night persons, and variability in hypnotic suscep- tibility. *Journal of Personality and Social Psychology, 64*, 827-833.

Wallance, B., Turosky, D., & Koloszka, A., (1992). Variability in the assessment of imagery vividness, *Journal of Mental Imagery, 16*, 221-230.

Werntz, D. (1981). Cerebral hemispheric activity and autonomic nervous function. Unpublished doctoral dissertation, University of Califiornia, San Diego.

Werntz, D., Bickford, R., Bloom, F., & Shannahoff-Khalsa, D. (1982a). Alternating cerebral hemispheric activity and lateralization of autonomic nervous function. *Human Neurobiology, 2*, 225-229.

Werntz, D., Bickford, R., & Shannahoff-Khalsa, D. (1982b). Selective hemispheric stimulation by unilateral forced nostril breathing. *Human Neurobiology, 6*, 165-171.

Winfree, A. (1991). Resetting the human clock. *Nature, 13*(7), 18.

Wever, R. (1988). Order and disorder in human circadian rhythmicity: Possible relations to mental illness. In D. Kupfer, T. Monk, & J. Barchas (Eds.), *Biological Rhythms and Mental Disorders* (pp. 253-346). New York: Guilford.

PART II

Reflections: The Ericksonian Approach

CHAPTER 4

The Fight Against Fundamentalism: Searching for Soul in Erickson's Legacy

Stephen G. Gilligan

"I'm certainly glad I'm not a Jungian."
—Carl Jung

"I would never belong to a club that would have me as a member."
—Groucho Marx

One of the most interesting things that could be said about Milton Erickson is that he did not practice Ericksonian psychotherapy. He rejected theory, frameworks, and set techniques. His writings usually emphasized a few generative principles, then concentrated on describing specific cases where these principles were creatively applied. The effectiveness of his work inspired many, though few of us seemed to take his atheoretical claims at face value. Instead, we proceeded on the assumption that *of course* there was a theory or a framework, it was just hidden or unstated. This assumption conveniently allowed many of his students, myself included, to "helpfully" explain what Erickson was "really" doing. A whole new field of Ericksonian psychotherapy was born, as the intricacies of Erickson's patterns were written about and promulgated at a dizzying rate. Twelve years after Erickson's death, this "field" is gathered here in Phoenix, ostensibly around the theme of addressing "the essence of the story."

I would like to suggest that the essence of Erickson had to with things like soul and aesthetics, and that this essence is becoming increasingly obscured by the ever increasing "stories" or models purporting to reveal what Erickson was "really" about. I don't think this has anything to do with the myth-makers, of which I have been one. I agree with Jeff Zeig's insightful observation that one of Erickson's great gifts was attracting and mentoring bright and dedicated students. Rather, my suggestion is that the way Erickson operated was so nontraditional that attempts to describe him in traditional terms, such as a particular framework or set of techniques, are woefully inadequate and misleading.

If you read the various "stories" or books about Erickson, it seems that they are not talking about the same person, but about many different persons. Therein I believe is an extraordinary essence of Erickson: He operated within the ancient and venerable tradition of the Magician Healer, a master shapeshifter who adapted at deep levels to whomever he was addressing—patients and students alike. He was like an aikido master in his centered presence, accepting and using whatever patterns were presented in order to reconnect persons with their own centers. He drew upon his extraordinary skills and experience uniquely in each case, changing not only the patterns of the patient or student but also his own form simultaneously. In other words, he operated flexibly on two levels simultaneously—the level of communication patterns and the deeper level of the personality applying the communication pattern.

This extraordinary skill is, I must admit, somewhat difficult to address in written form. However, I would like to try to do so, in hopes that it may open new ways to sense the essence and the story (or stories) of Erickson's legacy. I'll begin by suggesting the figure/field (or figure/ground) distinction as a generative principle for psychotherapy. This distinction will be used to draw a difference between therapy approaches based on fundamentalist philosophies and those organized around aesthetic principles. A case from Erickson will be used to illustrate an aesthetic approach. Finally, four generative principles for practicing such an approach will be elaborated.

THE FIGURE/FIELD DISTINCTION

When you took your first psychology course in college, you probably learned about the figure/ground concept, represented in Figure 1. The idea is that you perceive something only against a background different from that something. Thus, if you see something moving, it's because the movement is in relationship to a field (including yourself as an observer)

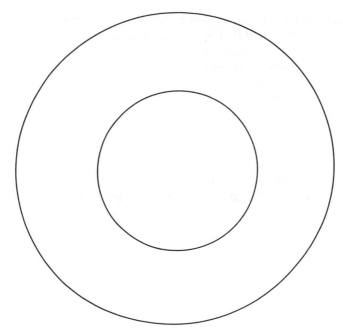

Fig. 1. The figure/field distinction.

that it is not moving in that way. Similarly, you hear a sound only because it's different from that which preceded and that which follows it. (Interestingly, if the same sound is presented continuously, your brain habituates to it and you don't hear it anymore.) As Bateson (1979) put it, we sense "differences" only insofar as that something is different from something else.

This basic idea is a generative principle for therapy. We might call it the "little circle/big circle" approach to life. The "little circle" is what we focus on (what's in our "conscious mind"), while the "big circle" is the larger context in which it is held (what's in our "unconscious mind"). There are a number of different examples of this figure/field relationship. If the little circle is the "text" — the story or description of things — the big circle is the "con-text" (all the values, experiences, intentions of the writer/reader). If the little circle is the conscious mind, the big circle is the unconscious mind. The little circle might be an individual, while the big circle is the social system within which that person is in relationship. If the little circle is a single experience — say, a trauma — the big circle is the entire life experiences of the person. If the little circle is a diagnostic category, ego-state, or frame of reference — such as depression or anxiety — the big circle is the larger context of all the person's ego states and frames of reference.

A central idea in this approach is that an awareness of both circles in the figure/field distinction is crucial. (In fact, I will be suggesting that the Self is the integration of these two domains.) As individuals, we feel empowered and competent when we have a sense of both our individuality and our connectedness or a sense of belonging to something bigger. Similarly, we feel more able to deal with a difficult experience when we maintain a sense of connectedness to what Erickson called the vast array of (other) experiential learnings.

At the same time, if our experience of the "little circle" becomes disconnected from the "big circle," bad things happen. As the Spanish poet Antonio Machado (1983, p.147) remarked:

> In my solitude
> I have seen things very clearly
> That were not true.*

One striking example of the effects of figure/field disconnection is the experience of trauma. Here an event occurs that knocks a person from connectedness to his or her body, community, and other experiences. The victim often feels isolated, disempowered, and out of relationship to both inner and outer worlds. When one is in such a state, it seems that no other possibilities exist: The traumatic event *is* the person's identity.

I call this a fundamentalist approach to life: The text is "read" as the one true description of reality. That is, there is objective truth and it is singular. No other possibilities are contemplated. The world breaks into some version of the inside "us" against the outside "them." A primary premise is that there is "original sin," that is, there is something wrong with one's core essence. Control and violence become dominant means of dealing with the world.

As Erickson repeatedly stressed, we therapists traditionally operate as fundamentalists. We start with the premise that something "out there" in the client is wrong; we use our model or theory as the fundamentalist text to "diagnose" or tell us what exactly the person is doing wrong (and what he/she should be doing as signs of "true" mental health); and we try to control the relationship with the intention of "converting" the client (or "sinner") to the light of mental health. The point, to echo Erickson, is that we try to reduce the person into the Procrustean confines of our "little circle" and lose connectedness to the "bigger circle" of the Self and its

---

*Reprinted from *Times Alone: Selected Poems of Antonio Machado,* Wesleyan University Press, Middletown, CT, 1983. Translation copyright 1983 by Robert Bly. Reprinted with his permission.

unique values, experiences, and interests. When this happens, attempts to solve the problem actually have the unintended effect of creating new and bigger problems (cf. Watzlawick, Weakland & Fisch, 1974).* The suggestion here is that recurrent problems indicate a disconnection between whatever is being referenced in the little circle—whether it be a person, a body pain, an undesirable behavior, etc.—and the rest of the experience in the big circle.

An alternative to fundamentalism is what Bateson (1972, 1979; Keeney, 1983) called aesthetics. Aesthetics focuses on neither the figure nor the field, but rather regards them as the warp and woof of a single relationship pattern. Bateson (1979) called this "the pattern that connects." He asserted that neither the conscious nor the unconscious was capable of producing wise or artistic expression: The "pattern that connects" the "little circle" (ego) and the "big circle" is the key.

As an aside, I would like to suggest that while this view is consistent with how Erickson acted, it is different from how he talked. Erickson emphasized that the goal of hypnotherapy was to move consciousness from the limitations of the conscious mind ("the little circle") to the creativity of the unconscious ("the big circle"). However, I think Erickson's description did not always fit his actions. He certainly saw how by talking to what he called a person's "unconscious mind" some extraordinary changes would result. However, I think that Erickson, operating as a quintessential participant, committed the predictable error of not including himself in the description. In other words, the generative pattern was neither the patient's nor Erickson's unconscious mind in isolation; it was the aesthetic fit between Erickson and his patients that made the difference.

Gregory Bateson, who sent a number of people (including myself) Erickson's way, suggested something of what I'm trying to get at when talking about Erickson and his students during an interview with Brad Keeney (1977):

KEENEY: You're saying that people who go see Erickson come away with a craving for power?

BATESON: Yes! They all want power.

KEENEY: Is there something about seeing {Erickson} that induces this power hungriness?

BATESON: Well, it's the skill which he has of manipulating the other person which really in the long run does not separate him as an ego dominant to the other person. He works in the weave of the total complex and they come away with a trick which is separate from the total complex,

---

*The idea that conscious purpose distorts consciousness and thus leads to faulty adaption was central to Gregory Bateson's (1972) thinking.

therefore, goeth counter to it and becomes a sort of power. I think it's
something like that. (p. 49)

This "weave of the total complex" is the aesthetic field of which I speak.
In contrast to a fundamentalist focus, aesthetics is not tied to a model,
theory, or set of techniques. The relationship itself is the text, and its
organicity means that it is forever changing. Working effectively within
this field requires rigorous training in a tradition (such as hypnotic therapy),
but the specific techniques arise from this ever shifting ground; thus, their
form and meaning are also constantly changing. Obvious examples of
working in this way are playing jazz or writing novels. When such an
approach is used in therapy, curiosity and fit predominate as organizing
principles, rather than control and manipulation.

Technique is thus seen quite differently in an aesthetic context. In a
fundamentalist approach, for instance, metaphor comes to be regarded as
a clever technique for manipulating a person's "unconscious mind" to
change its ways in a manner presumed by the therapist to be superior. It is
an error-correction device performed by a privileged expert from the
outside in. It usually deteriorates rapidly into an approach where you are
thinking, "What stories do I tell for depression or for anxiety?" rather than,
"How do I cooperate with and empower *this* unique person at *this* unique
moment?

In contrast, an aesthetic approach works from the outside in and the
inside out simultaneously. In joining a person rather than filling a conceptual framework, the therapist shifts from manipulating someone "out
there" to cooperating with someone with whom a connection is felt.
Patterns and values are felt not only in terms of their symbolic values but
also in kinesthetic terms such as contour, texture, and numinosity. (As
someone once remarked, aesthetics is born as a discourse of the body.)
Stories arise from an interest in validating and expanding these patterns,
so their expression can be more variable and more connected to a sense of
well-being. A metaphor is thus not a causal vehicle for change but rather a
possibility for expanding the ways a person can, as Bill O'Hanlon says, "do
and view" what they're already "up to."

Other differences between aesthetic and fundamentalist approaches
are equally startling. Take, for example, Erickson's suggestion to "trust the
unconscious." A fundamentalist would hear that as saying the "unconscious" is a sort of Savior or Messiah, the All-Knowing and All-loving
Father or Mother or Inner Child who, if we give ourselves over to it
completely, will lead us to the Promised Land where we will live happily
ever after. One's self would presumably be seen as passive and on the
sidelines, taking in the drooling mouth or full body levitations of one's

amazingly hypnotized body. Of course, some people, therapists and clients alike, are drawn to this fantasy, and see hypnosis or stories or indirect suggestion as the magical wand that heals. Others adopt a cynical, senescent attitude, criticizing "trust in one's unconscious" as a dangerously irresponsible challenge to the monolith of control-driven thinking. Each response would be sharing the same literal, reductionistic understanding of "trust the unconscious."

Trusting the unconscious means something quite different within an aesthetic approach. It suggests an artistic process of becoming a part of something bigger than your ego while maintaining your individual center in the process. In the case of therapy, it means letting go of fixed scripts to join a field where you have connectedness to your self *and* to your client(s) *and* to some shared purpose or intent. You are constrained, in the best sense of the word, to feel and follow the ever shifting fit between people having a conversation about creating a future that works for the client(s). While this requires tremendous letting go and being guided by something "bigger" than one's conscious mind, it also requires considerably more concentration, rigor, and compassion than fundamentalist approaches. Thus, the aesthetic understanding of "trusting the unconscious" is more like a saxophonist playing jazz, a dancer feeling the music, or Magic Johnson leading a fast break.

THE AFRICAN VIOLET QUEEN:
WORKING WITH A PERSON, NOT A PERSONA

Having brushed in broad strokes the outlines of an aesthetic approach to therapy, I'd like to turn now to some of the ways it might play out in psychotherapy. Let me begin by offering a beautiful case example which is especially helpful in illustrating the figure/field distinction. This is Erickson's case (reported in Zeig, 1980) of the African Violet Queen of Milwaukee. The woman's nephew, a Detroit physician, had been seeing Erickson as a psychiatry patient. He mentioned to Erickson his concerns about his aunt, a 52-year-old wealthy woman who lived alone in her large house in Milwaukee. The woman had never been married and was not very socially active. She ventured out of her house only to attend church services, and her family grew increasingly concerned that she was depressed and suicidal. She apparently had refused to seek help and the nephew, upon hearing that Erickson would be in Milwaukee on a speaking engagement, asked Erickson if he might pay the woman a visit. Erickson agreed to do so.

As traditional therapists, we would probably form an immediate answer to the underlying question of, "Who is this woman?" From a fundamentalist view, this response probably would be organized in terms of a "depression" that needed "treatment," whether in the form of medication or metaphors. Depression would be the name of the little circle, and the big circle of the rest of the person's life space would probably be ignored or dealt with as secondary at best.

Forever a nonfundamentalist, Erickson approached the situation in a different way. He arranged to meet the woman in her home and got her to give him a tour. He observed that (1) she was socially isolated and emotionally flat, with a passive and obedient response style, (2) she expressed a deep sense of commitment to her church community (she attended services regularly, though she never talked or made contact with others), and (3) she grew some beautiful African violet plants in the sunroom of her house. Appreciating these and other descriptions as equally valid, he became curious about how this "big circle" of distinctions might increase the woman's participation in the community.

He got the woman to raise many more African violets. He then directed her to give one of these plants to individuals or families in her church community each time one of them experienced an important transition event, such as a marriage, death, birth, leaving home, illness, or job change. You can imagine what happened both to her inner and outer worlds. As Erickson noted, she became "too busy to be depressed." At the same time, others began to respond to her in warm and affectionate ways. She became quite active in the community and earned the appreciation and attention of many people. When she died some 20 years later, many mourned the loss of the woman who had come to be known as the "African Violet Queen of Milwaukee."

What's remarkable to me about this case is how Erickson worked with a person rather than treating a problem. Instead of reducing her to some "little circle" of mental diagnosis or metaphorical description, he approached her as a unique person with a variety of identities, values, and interests. He demonstrated that while persons stuck in "problems" typically restrict their attention to a single "little circle" or frame, therapists looking to empower widen their lens to include the big circle of multiple distinctions. Therapy thus becomes a conversation that uses distinctions of both the little and big circles, especially the shifting relationship between them, to empower solutions that are already developing.

SOME GUIDELINES FOR AESTHETIC PRACTICE

An obvious question at this point is how one learns this type of therapy. Unfortunately, this is a little like asking how one learns to live life: There is no set way. Each person must find his or her own way, informed in part by different traditions that suggest different possibilities. To see what possibilities arise from an aesthetic tradition, let us return to our figure/field distinction. Four aspects of this relationship are relevant. The first is the little circle, which in hypnotic terms is known as the conscious mind. It contains the dominant focus of attention. We will refer to this as the dominant story or persona with which the client identifies and/or by which the therapist describes the client. For example, the dominant story might be that the client is depressed or a trauma survivor or a borderline personality.

A second aspect of the figure/field relationship is the big circle, which in hypnosis is the unconscious mind. It represents all that is a part of the person but not presently consciously attended to. In the case of the African Violet Queen, this included the African violets and her commitments as a church member.

The third aspect is the combination of the little circle and big circle, which might be called the Self. This aspect often goes unnoticed, since it is not connected to doing or having, but rather with being. Erickson (1980) referred to it as the "vital beingness of the self that is often overlooked" (p. 345).

The fourth aspect is the life energies pulsating through the person. These are the experiential learnings that are challenging the person at a given time. To paraphrase Bly (1981), someone inside tries to teach us only one or two things each day. As we will see, these teachings include loving, fighting, healing, blessing, dying, and all the other great nonanalytical forces in the world.

These four aspects of the figure/field relationship translate into four intervention principles:

1. Sense the Self;
2. Make room for the dominant story/persona;
3. Include nondominant stories/personae;
4. Get that the person is "up to something big."

Let's look at each of these principles in turn.

1. Sense the Self

The Spanish writer Ortega y Gasset once was talking with a friend about why he loved a particular woman. He remarked that from a psychological point of view, one might suggest that he loved the woman because she reminded him of his mother (or perhaps *didn't* remind him of his mother);

or because she fulfilled some need in him; or because they were polar opposites, and so on. Ortega y Gasset rejected such conjecture as wholly irrelevant, saying instead that he loved this woman precisely because she was *this* woman and no other. She was who she was and no one else. Is was *her* that he loved, not her story or her psychology or her differences or similarities.

Connecting with a person at this level is possible in many contexts, and I think it is a central organizing principle for working, in Bateson's words, in the weave of the total complex. It is about seeing a person not in terms of a historical past or a problem or even a solution. It is about sensing and aligning with the soul of a person who doesn't think in terms of "change" and doesn't need mental constructs or your latest epistemologies, but rather is felt as a sense of being in community. When such a being "shows up," good things happen.

In an aesthetic tradition, feeling and relationship connectedness, not mental precision, are the primary guides in such an endeavor. These are not emotional feelings, but rather something less personal and ego-driven. It is the feeling an athlete or musician or any other artist must sense in order to let things happen with controlled spontaneity. It is not a feeling of an inner state or an outer state, but of a relationship field that includes both self and other and perhaps something else.

Usually, we are so busy trying to manipulate each other and avoid our anxiety that such a connection is not sensed as a possibility. However, it shows up clearly at special times in each of our lives. You may have experienced it when holding a new baby in your arms, or when sitting with a dying person. In such moments, the masks and the stories fall away and you are left experiencing the incredible uniqueness and humanness of the persons involved. This may also happen when you experience great art, at special moments in a friendship, in a hypnotic trance, when gardening, or perhaps when walking in the woods. These activities constitute what I call "traditions of the aesthetic," for they move one from a state of doing to an aesthetic state of being. Of course, one may still be active during such events; it's just that it feels like it's all happening without conscious dominance. You may gently steer at times, but you cannot aggressively control. It is at this "intersection of the timeless with time," as Eliot (1963, p.198) called it, where you "fall in love" with life and with the beingness of the person or the vision of the artist.

I am suggesting that this "falling in love" process is central to an aesthetic approach. It provides a centering context where the therapist can "not know" and "not do," to use Erickson and Rossi's (1979) idea. This releases the therapist from the compulsiveness of "trying to help" or "trying to change" the person and allows him or her to experientially "get" that the client doesn't need to do anything in order to be OK. This aesthetic connection allows one to sense the client's wholeness, center, and experiential vitality. This connectedness *is* the ever shifting "creative unconscious" that one feels and follows in aesthetic psychotherapy. At this level, people are not seen as *having* problems or *doing* inappropriate things; rather, they are experienced as *being* unique and extraordinary, "up to something big." They may wish to express themselves differently in the world, and you may support and challenge them to get the details of their life in order, but they don't need to *do* anything to be OK. They already are and always will be.

2. Make Room for the Dominant Story

Once this contextual connection is developed, the therapist is able to make room for the dominant story. This is what's inside the little circle, what the client is often exclusively focused on. It may also be referred to as the dominant persona, the presenting problem, the presenting self, or the ego-state from which a person is operating. In psychotherapy interviews, it typically is organized around a single identity theme, such as:

1. I am depression
2. I am a helpless victim
3. I am trauma

Like any story, this identity will have a beginning (that is, what happened to cause the present state); other characters involved (especially antagonists, such as parents, perpetrators, or a symptom such as anxiety); dominant actions (symptomatic behaviors); an emotional tone (e.g., tragedy); and an implied future ("Things will always be like this").

This dominant story is the fixed frame that gets imposed upon an experience, so that whatever comes up continues to be viewed and interacted with in predictable, fixed ways. Thus, while a dominant story contains essential experiences vital to a person, it also prevents the person from freely discovering effective ways to interact with these experiences. Therefore, an essential goal of aesthetic psychotherapy is to deconstruct a story, so a person can experience what's inside of it without being bound by fixed ways of understanding or responding to it. This "deconstruction" or "deframing" is the same process that a hypnotic induction seeks to accomplish in psychotherapy: freeing a person from frames and reconnecting him or her to life without story. Thus, this aesthetic approach is somewhat "anti-narrative"; it sees narrative descriptions as ultimately secondary to the primacy of the person who cannot be reduced to any story.

It is easy for therapists and clients alike to get caught in the story. In a psychotherapy conversation, the therapist is often implicitly invited into the story as a heroic rescuer who will help the traumatized client in some noble way to overcome some bad processes. Once inside the story, however, the therapist will lose any sense that the person is much more than the story, and conversation will be limited to trying to fix a persona rather than talking with a person who is capable in many, many ways.

There are a variety of ways to know one is lost in the story. Perhaps the easiest is when you feel caught in the undertow. Every therapist has had the experience of looking at the appointment calendar and getting that terrible feeling of "Guess who's coming to therapy?!" Similarly, when you find yourself thinking of a client primarily in terms of a traditional diagnosis — "This patient *is* a borderline," or "This guy *is* chronically depressed" — you are in danger of losing a vital connection to the person and his or her multiple identities. The challenge is to make room for these dominant stories, knowing that sometimes they need to be heard, sometimes they can be utilized, but always they represent only one description of a person. Many others exist, and the task of psychotherapy is to make room for some of these others as well. Again, the story of the African Violet Queen is instructive. Erickson made room for the depression story and worked in the bigger field of the person at the same time.

When one is talking with a client, it is helpful to note when the story is beginning. Cues include explanations ("I am this way because of the past"), feelings that have a scripted quality, disconnection from the relationship connectedness, and feelings in the client or therapist of helplessness. At such points, it may be helpful to stop listening to the story and reconnect with the person via nonverbal channels.

When I first started studying with Erickson, he advised me to work with schizophrenics. I secured a couple of volunteer positions, one in a locked ward of a large mental hospital and the other in a halfway house for adolescent schizophrenics. I thought I would practice hypnosis with these patients, but it turned out that their inductions and stories were much more hypnotically potent then mine! In other words, I would end up much more "tranced" in such conversations. When I related this to Erickson, who worked extensively with schizophrenics, he laughed and advised me to develop a meaningful relationship with the patient's left ear. I asked him to elaborate, because after all I needed a big solution for my big problem. When he refused, I felt I had no alternative except to develop the most meaningful relationship with a left ear that had ever been developed.

I went back to the halfway house, where the schizophrenics were lined up, waiting for my return, ready to practice all their latest hypnotic techniques. As I sat down with the first person, he wound up for the delivery and began his schizophrenic "pitch." I found myself deeply absorbed with his left ear, an experiential connection that grew as he continued his story. What was amazing was that I was no longer listening to the content, I was staying with the relationship! A wonderful feeling of calm elation filled me, as I realized that no matter where the story went, I was just sitting in the room with this person. I could make room for the story, without losing my center or connectedness to the relationship!

As I practiced developing this sort of connection with other clients, it was a wonderful thing to discover that such a two-level relationship allowed me to sense that the person was not the persona, but much, much more. This appreciation allows conversations to include important information from the little circle while continuing to blend it with resources and other possibilities from the big circle, all in the service of moving consciousness from an identification with a position or story to a centering within a person. Again, this is what a hypnotic induction looks to accomplish in therapy. It frees the person from the learned limitations of a frame and connects him or her with the generativity needed to show up and deal with the "now" of a given situation.

3. Include Nondominant Stories/Personae

The third principle of an aesthetic approach involves expanding the conversation to make room for the many other possible descriptions and resources of the person. Steve de Shazer (1985, 1988, 1991) has contributed immensely in this area, with his suggestions for psychotherapy conversations based on what a person is doing when the problem isn't happening ("exceptions") or what the person might be doing if the problem were solved ("miracle questions"). Indeed, the whole emerging emphasis on solution-focused and solution-oriented questions looks to shift the conversation from the little circle to the big circle.

In my own practice, I often move to the big circle by holding what I call "contemplative questions" about the client. For example, I might wonder what he looked like when he was born or what he will look like at the moment of his death; or what he looked like before the problem became a dominant story or will look like after the problem is solved. I especially like to wonder what the opposite persona to his dominant story looks like. For example, if the person presents as a selfish and uncaring persona, I look for his extraordinary compassion and vulnerability. Once I experientially sense this "other self" by both seeing it and feeling it, I look to speak to it. For example, I might compliment the person on his extraordinary compassion, adding that probably he receives such compliments regularly. If he says he doesn't, I might gently chide him for being so shy, adding that surely his extraordinary vulnerability and loving nature is obvious to others. Delivered in the proper way (usually involving a blend of what we will describe below as Lover energy with Trickster presence), it usually accesses curiosity as well as vulnerability, and sometimes sadness. Now, both the dominant persona (which might be reframed as "caring about one's self") and the complementary nondominant persona (which might be called "the incredible longing to connect with others") are both in the aesthetic field. Of course, the person is neither of these personae, so the conversation now becomes how the Self can be responsible for both of these needs in the service of something bigger. This leads us to our fourth principle, namely:

4. Get That the Person Is "Up to Something Big"

In aesthetic terms, this is an inevitable, normative learning that would have to be faced regardless of history or circumstances. In other words, over the course of your life, whether or not you like it, you will need to master challenges that come from someplace much deeper than your conscious mind. You cannot control such experiences, but you can cooperate and learn from them. Trauma or other crises may precipitate them and shape and color their meaning, but such learnings will challenge each person in various ways throughout life.

Examples include forming and transforming a self-image, a social identity, a sexual identity, a community, and so forth. Many skills are important in these and other tasks; the point here is that people are constantly engaged in such primary, normative learnings. Both therapist and client often focus on the "mistakes" incurred during such times, thereby committing what Pearce (1981) has called the "error-correction error," which is akin to primarily focusing on the falls incurred during the process of learning to walk. Such focus to secondary processes disconnects consciousness from what Pribram (1971) has called the deeper "image of achievement" that relentlessly calls us to "walk, walk, walk." It's easy to lose awareness of this primary level—in hypnotic terms, we would say that we lose touch with the unconscious and become overly identified with the error-correction, control-driven orientation of the conscious mind. Therapeutic conversations in the aesthetic tradition thus look to dissolve the storied frameworks of the conscious mind and return persons to an experientially felt sense of their own inner voices, their own inner images, and their own feelings. With these connections, it is possible to navigate the important learnings of life.

One way I've been working with this process in recent years is through what might be called "archetypal traditions of learning." The basic idea, developed by Jung (1964) and addressed more recently by Pearson (1989) and Moore and Gillette (1990), is that we have stored in our unconscious different patterns of learning, developed over thousands of years of experience. Each of these traditions has a positive side and a negative side, depending on whether they are grounded or ungrounded within the Self. The central idea is that you need to come to terms with these energies, or they will come to terms with you in the forms of their dark sides.

The four archetypes I've been working with are the King/Queen, the Lover, the Warrior, and the Magician (see Figure 2). The King/Queen provides blessings and a sense of one's place(s) in the social world; its dark side is tyranny and curses. It is the inner voice that tells you in the best way that you belong in the world, that you are special and have something important to contribute; or that you have no right to exist or no abilities or competencies or future.

The Lover deals with passion and communion; when unintegrated or

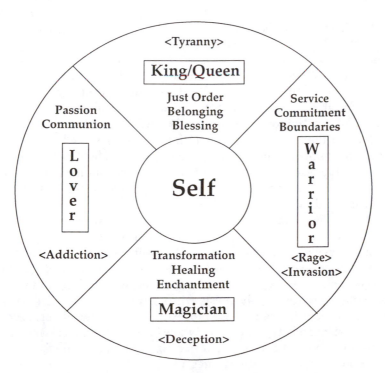

Fig. 2. Some great traditions of learning: King/Queen, Warrior, Lover, and Magician (adapted from Moore and Gillette, 1990).

abused, its dark side is addiction. So its energies draw you to connect and join and surrender to something bigger than yourself. When not grounded within the Self, it is expressed as addictive communion with drugs, food, people, or some other pseudo Lover.

The Warrior energies are concerned with boundaries, commitment, and service. They help you to declare your values, your interests, your sense of Self. They keep you focused and committed in relationships. They detect bullshit, reflect attacks, and help you to fight for integrity and for your voice to be heard and respected. When unintegrated, Warrior energies are expressed as rage and invasion of others.

The Magician energies focus on transformation (the death of one identity and the birth of another), enchantment, and healing; the dark side is deception and trickery, and the dark spells of symptomology. You encounter these energies especially at times of identity shifts, or during traumas, or in trance. Magicians know the paradoxical, image-symbolic, storytelling language of the underworld. Erickson was a beautiful example of the Magician archetype, all the way down to his physical wound due to polio, purple outfits, storytelling, and hypnotic language. In its dark form, the Magician is into deception of self and other; it is a bullshitter, chameleon, distracter, seducer, and cheap reframer.

The important thing is that *none of these archetypes is you.* As Jung repeatedly emphasized, the most important archetype is the Self, which is the unique *you* that is waiting to be claimed and developed. When the Self is sensed, the different archetypal learnings coalesce as unique expressions of you. You continue to integrate the powers of love into your life. You develop the Warrior skills of setting boundaries, declaring values, making commitments, cutting through deception, and fighting for integrity. You learn the Magician skills of persuasion, enchantment, reframing, storytelling, and navigating developmental transitions. You cultivate the inner King and/or Queen that give blessings to self and other, and you sense how people and patterns fit and belong in a just order.

When these archetypal energies are not connected with the Self, they continue to challenge you nonetheless. However, now you are left mired in their dark forms—addiction and anxiety, self-denigration, rage and boundary-breaking, and the dark trances of symptomology. Thinking in terms of these archetypes can help therapists sense how even (or especially) when clients are caught in any of these processes, they are deeply engaged in some important archetypal process. By sensing what this process might be, the therapist may support a person in claiming it and expressing it with more variety, responsibility, and integrity.

To accomplish this, I have been using what might be called "listening questions" for each tradition. These are not questions to be answered cognitively; they are internally held in a focused, contemplative way while one is talking with the client, in the same way that a hypnotic subject is encouraged to allow ideas or associations to develop with relaxed concentration, experientially felt connectedness, and curiosity. As the poet Antonio Machado (1983, p. 143) suggested:

> To talk with someone,
> ask a question first
> then—listen.

For the tradition of the Lover, the listening questions are:

1. For whom/where is this person's passion or love connected?
2. For whom/where is love being withdrawn?
3. As this person connects with his inner Lover, what might his future look like?

From the Warrior tradition, the questions are:

1. This person is fighting for something important—what is it?
2. Where are more boundaries needed?
3. As this person connects with her inner Warrior(s), what might her future look like?

The questions for the Magician archetype are:

1. What major shift in identity is occurring? From what to what?
2. Where are the unattended wounds that need to be addressed?
3. As this person connects with the Magician energies, what might his future look like?

And the King/Queen questions are:

1. What is this person's place(s) in the world—personally, socially, professionally? (That is, where is she special?)
2. What blessings are needed?
3. As this person connects to the inner King or Queen, how might his or her future be different?

As the therapist reflects on these questions, any responses arising are not taken as truth, but as suggestions about how the symptom may be seen as a solution. The value of a description is entirely in the client's response: If the person stays cognitive and intellectual, it won't make a difference. If the therapist's response accesses some deeper experiential response in the client — a trance, an emotional feeling, a disruption — it's a keeper. Further conversations then look to keep a person engaged at this experiential level — again, cognitive discussions will make a mockery of the archetypal traditions — with the intent of encouraging the person to claim the power so that it may be developed in responsible, satisfying ways.

The three questions asked for each tradition enable three intervention ideas central to Erickson's legacy:

1. You're up to something big! *(Compliment)*
2. You can do it even "more and better." *(Expand)*
3. As you continue to do it, many possible learnings will develop. *(Suggest possibilities/open imagination).*

Thus, for example, a male perpetrator of violence might be acknowledged as having big-time involvement in the Warrior archetype, albeit in its dark, immature forms. Invitations to responsibility, as Jenkins (1990) has called them, are then developed that encourage and challenge the person to identify and expand his images of an inner Warrior. (Many may be initially imaged as rageful fathers or Rambo-like sociopaths.) As more responsible, integrated Warrior energies are connected, they can be blended with those of the King (who is in charge of directing the Warrior) and the Lover (who softens and balances the Warrior). Again, the person is none of these archetypes, so you continue to talk directly and encourage him or her to "show up" in a responsible way.

Similarly, a person with suicidal thoughts might be seen as engaged in the death and rebirth cycle of the Magician tradition. In this way, the voice that says "I don't want to live this life anymore" may be regarded as having great integrity. It is, of course, a highly dangerous situation, since the person (and the culture) usually stories such ideas in terms of images of suicide. The challenge is, therefore, to develop a ritual space that contains the person from physically acting while making room for the deeper psychic process of death and rebirth. In terms of the latter, I might say to the suicidal client something like, "There's something inside of you that says a death is needed. I hear that voice and believe that voice . . . I think it speaks with great integrity . . . something may indeed need to die inside of you." When delivered in an experientially sensitive way, such a message typically absorbs and relaxes a suicidal person, as it is often the first time someone has spoken directly to the relentless death-seeking voice and validated it as vital to Self-development. Further conversations seek to develop ways to allow this inner voice to help in a self-affirming though difficult psychic death process. Since the Magician energies are especially familiar with altered states, ritual and trance are common features of this conversation.

As with any therapeutic process, the therapist works at each step of the process to ensure adequate safety and maintain experiential participation. The client's inner processes guide the action, but the therapist is responsible for creating a therapeutic context where new meanings and possibilities arise. Of course, many other techniques are used along with the archetypal processes. The goal in therapy is not to develop archetypes; it is to help a person live life in a more satisfying fashion.

SUMMARY

What I have tried to do is suggest how therapy might be conducted within an aesthetic approach. Central to this approach is the figure/field distinction that recognizes not only the little circle of a person's conscious mind and the big circle of the unconscious, but also the Self that permeates both and the human processes of learning that move through the entire system. We have seen that when consciousness is reduced to a position or a story, fundamentalism follows and bad things happen. When consciousness spreads both inside and outside whatever circle of distinction has been drawn, the art of living one's life well is possible.

In closing, I want to return to the main theme of the Congress, namely the essence and story of Erickson's legacy. I am suggesting that the essence is *not* a story; it's something more organic and much less describable. Stories are the "sweet nothings" that we whisper into each other's ears as we go about the bigger business of showing up in life in a direct way. They may help us to make meaning and focus attention, but once we identify with them, we become rigid fundamentalists.

I believe Erickson's legacy was one of freeing therapists and clients alike from fundamentalism. I have suggested various ideas about how fundamentalism might be discarded in favor of an aesthetic approach. Of course, all these suggestions are more "sweet nothings" waiting to create the next generation of fundamentalists. The challenge remains as before: how to enjoy the stories while still sensing that the essence is something else altogether. Thus, I would like to leave you with the exhortation of the poet Antonio Machado (1983, p. 149), who said:

Wake up, you poets:
let echoes end,
and voices begin.*

---

*Reprinted from *Times Alone: Selected Poems of Antonio Machado*, Wesleyan University Press, Middletown, CT, 1983. Translation copyright 1983 by Robert Bly. Reprinted with his permission.

REFERENCES

Bateson, G. (1972) *Steps to an ecology of mind.* New York: Ballantine Books.

Bateson, G. (1979) *Mind and nature: A necessary unity.* New York: Dutton.

Bly, R. (1981) Four ways of knowledge. In *The man in the black coat turns: Poems by Robert Bly.* New York: Doubleday.

de Shazer, S. (1985) *Keys to solution in brief therapy.* New York: Norton.

de Shazer, S. (1988) *Clues: Investigating solutions in brief therapy.* New York: Norton.

de Shazer, S. (1991) *Putting difference to work.* New York: Norton.

Eliot, T.S. (1963) *Collected poems: 1909-1962* (Centenary edition). New York: Harcourt, Brace, Jovanovich.

Erickson, M.H. (1980) Basic psychological problems in hypnotic research. In E.L. Rossi (ed.), *The collected papers of M.H. Erickson, Vol. II.* New York: Irvington Press.

Erickson, M.H., and Rossi, E. (1979) *Hypnotherapy: An exploratory casebook.* New York: Irvington Press.

Jenkins, A. (1990) *Invitations to responsibility: The therapeutic engagement of men who are violent and abusive.* Adelaide, South Australia: Dulwich Centre Publication.

Jung, C.G. (1964) *Man and his symbols.* New York: Doubleday.

Keeney, B. (1977) On paradigmatic change: Conversations with Gregory Bateson. Unpublished manuscript.

Keeney, B. (1983) *Aesthetics of change.* New York: Guilford.

Machado, A. (1983) *Times alone: Selected poems of Antonio Machado* (R. Bly, trans.) Middletown, CT: Wesleyan University Press.

Moore, R., and Gillette, D. (1990) *King, warrior, magician, lover: Rediscovering the archetypes of the mature masculine.* New York: HarperCollins.

Pearce, J.C. (1981) *The bond of power.* New York: E.P. Dutton.

Pearson, C.S. (1989) *The hero within: Six archetypes we live by.* New York: Harper and Row.

Pribram, K. (1971) *Languages of the brain: Experimental paradoxes and principles in neuropsychology.* Englewood Cliffs, NJ: Prentice-Hall.

Watzlawick, P., Weakland, J., and Fisch, R. (1974) *Change: Principles of problem formation and problem resolution.* New York: Norton.

Zeig, J.K. (1980) *A teaching seminar with Milton Erickson.* New York: Brunner/Mazel.

CHAPTER 5

Everything Is Problem Solving: The Essence of the Story

Stephen R. Lankton

INTRODUCTION

My thesis is that all human conduct, especially that which we encounter in the therapy offices in the form of a "problem," is problem-solving behavior. Specifically, it is problem solving related to developmental demands (these are in most cases socially and biologically stimulated). In saying this, I immediately wonder if I have said anything significant. After all, haven't we, since Freud, thought that people adhere to the "pleasure principle" and isn't this frame some sort of "bottom line" that states that all behavior is to solve problems? Yes, I think the answer is affirmative. In fact, solving problems is the single fundamental activity underlying the avoidance of pain or the pursuit of pleasure.

However, I am still going to develop my thesis because I repeatedly notice that client behavior is not necessarily seen in a positive light despite this fundamental dictum. In fact, despite this core belief about individuals, we have developed layers of theory that obscure the very point I wish to emphasize. Finally, I think it is this aspect of belief that is fundamental to the more skeletal idea of "positive framing" derived from the work of Erickson and that is the essence of his epistemology and, hence, at the basis of his interventions.

There are at least five fundamental reasons for my taking the view that all of human conduct is problem-solving behavior: 1) aesthetic, 2) scientific parsimony, 3) phenomenological, 4) pragmatic, and 5) ethical. I will elaborate each of these reasons and provide case examples to help clarify my position about the phenomenological and pragmatic areas.

1. THE AESTHETIC REASON FOR TAKING THIS VIEW

My aesthetic reason is that taking this view feels better to me and it feels better to my clients than other alternatives. To illustrate: There was the man who informed me that he was less distressed after hearing on TV that mental illness was genetic and that he was not to blame for his daughter's illness; also the man who came to me to be reevaluated in an attempt to eschew the "manic-depressive" label he had received from a psychiatrist; and the numerous clients who considered their stress and wondered, "Does this mean I am crazy?" In other words, clients usually don't appreciate the labels, or the inference behind the labels, about their behavior.

Research has shown that a major source of stress for a client is a lack of understanding about the disorder (Falloon, 1988). The positive developmental frame I suggest not only removes that stress by providing an understanding, but does so without using the framework of "disease," "pathology," and "disorder" in the first place. While, I fully support the concept known as "adaptive mechanism" (Hartman, 1958), it seems that those who insist upon the normative, linear, traditional paradigm for mental health do a disservice to Hartman by whitewashing their emphasis on pathology. In that view, "adaptive" becomes nothing more than a "pretty smart way to cope while being crazy."

If one views my suggestions from a psychoanalytic framework, what I am doing is using and strengthening the adaptive mechanisms of the ego. This helps the client resolve pathological conflicts from a creative framework of adaptive mechanisms. This explanation falls short by current standards of understanding. My goal in helping people is to avoid that framework and that dichotomy entirely. This results in a paradigm shift that I have discussed at length elsewhere (Lankton, Lankton & Matthews, 1992).

2. THE SCIENTIFIC PARSIMONY REASON FOR TAKING THIS VIEW

Parsimony refers to how sparing a theory is. As I recall it, that theory that most simply explains the event under discussion is the most highly valued. It is simple if it needs fewer invented and reified concepts and is most immediate, direct, and ultimately useful. That thrifty explanation, then, is called the parsimonious one. The position that everything is problem solving may well be the most parsimonious. It seems fundamental, as well as in league with "the pleasure principle" and the "law of survival of the fittest." There is little need to reify internal constructs or to ascribe metaphors of warfare (conflict, defiance, attack, resistance, oppression, etc.). What is needed, instead, is experiential contact with and a dialogue between the client and the therapist and an understanding of the client's life-context.

3. THE PHENOMENOLOGICAL REASON FOR TAKING THIS VIEW

I can best understand the motive of clients and assist them to arrive at helpful interventions when I set out to identify with the dilemmas they face and have faced. In other words, it makes more sense when I project myself into the client's world for rapport, empathy, and understanding. I would not want to "get into" the world of my clients' and try to feel *abnormality* in my identified experience. But, I have little hesitation entering the world of my clients in order to inspire *attempts to resolve* difficulties related to self-development and family development.

The following case illustrates how clients shape my experience and also shows how my sense of their experience leads me to interventions. This case deals with treatment of a 44-year-old woman with severe migraine headaches. She is married and the mother of two children, 12 and 14 years old. Her headaches existed since childhood and became migraine type at the birth of her first child. She sought medical help for the headaches prior to the birth of the first child, including extensive testing, from blood tests to CAT scans and MRIs. She has seen neurologists, osteopaths, chiropractors, ENT specialists, nutritionists, and other specialists potentially related to this problem. She has tried a number of medications prescribed by her neurologist over the course of 20 years. At the time I first saw her, the headaches were very frequent, yet she did not let discussion of them occupy much of her social or work time. Nor did she often talk about them other than at her doctor's offices. They were, however, used as the reason for not accompanying her husband on the weekends to the country farm (which used to belong to her parents before their death).

As she continued to work outside of her home, her children needed less home care than they did as infants. When she came for therapy, she was having more time for herself and her work than in the years past. She was also experiencing an increase in headaches. She appeared well groomed, alert, and pleasant except for the contorted tension in her forehead. She suffered her headaches silently except in those instances where the migraine attack became so severe that she had to lie down and retreat from all other stimuli. Her situation was unchanging and she did not aggressively seek therapy. Actually, the only reason she had sought me for assistance was her dissatisfaction with the medication the family doctor and her neurologist had prescribed. The neurologist referred her for psychiatric evaluation and the psychiatrist suggested she contact me for several sessions of hypnotherapy, since it might be possible to ameliorate or entirely reduce her awareness of the pain.

I found her to be articulate, with a sense of humor and well oriented to people, place, and time. Her level of social engagement was well developed within a range of conduct: She made moderate attempts to provide leadership and was socially responsive to the needs of others. Surprisingly, I found that her ability to be oppositional was inhibited. It became increasingly apparent that she was uncomfortable engaging in any type of behavior that she thought others might construe as cold or unfriendly. This even included getting rid of invasive telephone solicitors at mealtime hours. She found it hard to simply say, "No." She found it hard to quarrel and argue. Instead, she pushed herself to discover what it was she was feeling but did not understand. She was quicker to criticize herself for not understanding another than she was to criticize the speaker for being unclear. She presented the picture of someone who intended to make no mistakes, but would take responsibility for anyone else's mistakes, someone who intends to never intimidate another, someone who intends to display herself as always meeting you on your terms and, if you are friendly, having no terms of her own. This was especially true in her posture toward her husband.

This is a lengthy social picture I have tried to draw because, as you might imagine, I am going to attempt to relate this interpersonal posturing to how she and I solved the headache problem decisively. What I would like to emphasize is the *pattern* that this client communicated to me—how she had come to know that headaches were a form of acceptable and useful behavior for her and how at that point in her life she came to believe (in some way) that the conduct she used to create these headaches would actually solve an interpersonal dilemma.

I could look at two methods for using this case in illustration of the thesis of this chapter. One method would be to look at the therapy I provided and how that was remarkable for not seeing this client as resistive, not seeing this client as someone who was out to demonstrate that all professionals would fail to help her. Actually, when the dynamic living process that gave rise to these headaches is examined, it will be clear how possible it is to construe explanations consisting of accidentally demanding concepts. The point is not that those constructs are incorrect, but rather that employing those constructs leads the therapy in a direction I don't need to pursue in my desire for parsimony. I need not label this process. Instead, I can perceive directly and be led to treatments for those experiences, which I empathically understand.

Again, using those constructs to understand the client gives rise to a potential limiting posture for the therapist. Rather, we could listen to the way the client creates a conversation with me and how she relates the way she converses with others over time both about her problem and about her general posture with others in her social world. By listening to the key elements that are inadvertently emphasized or the presuppositions that are shared unquestioned (as if they were consensus reality), one can hear, in her delivery, the key features. We can organize these features in order to construct therapeutic interventions.

The second way in which this case is illustrative is in showing my method of inquiry and empathy. It shows how I discovered that the client came to know herself as "a person with headaches." This case is useful because it involved an articulate person who was capable of introspection. Still, this inquiry brings with it the potential for distortion created by memory. It brings with it large gaps of knowledge where human experience was used but was unknown to the user (changes in breathing, passing thoughts not articulated, unexpressed fantasies, moods that may have affected perception but were undetected, unnoticed, and unreported, emotional residue from events of the day, and so on). I want to interact with the client during this type of introspection that results from my questions.

While the client's information can be useful, my empathic understanding of the circumstance is often crucial. More often than not, introspection alone does not provide the same complexity of information that I am able to acquire by experiencing the client in the "here and now" but interacting with the client and with the historical material brought to the session and presented as the story of his or her life. In this case, my emphasis is on that methodology of how this particular client shaped my behavior to be helpful to her. Let's call this client Paula so we can bring her to life a bit.

The Therapist's Mind Set

As I continue the discussion of Paula, I'd like to emphasize my understanding of my mental set as I listen to the client. You might say I suffer from a certain malady called "dyslexic clairvoyance" — I can see very clearly, but only into the past. Seriously, though, there is a certain aspect of my approach with clients that I think is related to my ability to "see." This has to do with an ability to not consciously organize and to suspend thinking and internal dialogue as I experience the client. I attempt to create a neutral mind set where I am not disposed to pull away or to move toward the client. While my metacommunication and metasituation are moving toward the client, my actual communication is uncommitted. I observe the client and attempt to actually experience what the client is telling me "as-if" I were the client having the experiences. I attempt to take two experiences of the client's at once and to take the position of sensing the things the client is reporting to have sensed. As I do this, I also try to get a sense of how the client is feeling being in the room speaking to me. I attempt to get a sense, by bringing an "as-if" model into my mind, of what it would be like to be that person who had the experience he or she is speaking about.

When Paula tells me that her father never listened to her and frequently walked away, I put myself in her shoes as if I had been there. For a moment I let my experience be shaped by what she has communicated to me as she shares the story of the life that she lived. This "as-if" experience of the world is akin, I believe, to what Erickson repeatedly conveyed to us, his students, as he would emphasize that we ought to put one foot inside the client's world and leave one foot inside our own world.

Recall Carl Rogers. In *On Becoming a Person* (1961), he summarized five elements necessary for learning from a therapeutic context. His explanation of empathic understanding in his description of the therapist created an "as-if" mind set. The other elements are facing a problem, congruence, positive regard, and — the fifth element expressed by Rogers — that none of these elements was very helpful in the therapeutic relationship without it being a transaction of genuineness (Rogers, 1961, p. 284).

Thus, part of my experience as I put one foot in the client's world is to sense from time to time whether or not the story I am hearing from the client answers all the questions I have — not intellectual questions, because I am not really having any, but all the experiential questions. In my "as-if" world, I realize I am talking to a father who is turning away coldly, I am having a difficult emotion to deal with, something like rejection and sadness and even supressed joy and frustration. Possibly, I could feel anger as a secondary reaction. Questions arise: "What do I do with my sadness? What do I do with my joy that I intended to express? And if I haven't been able to express my joy and if I haven't been able to express my sadness, what is my experience as a child? How do I explain it to myself?"

She reported that *that* is when the headaches began in childhood. In my sensing, I wonder: How do I get from this feeling to a headache of which I am aware? Is the headache just because I am trying to figure out why Dad does not act as I wish or expect him to do? Or is it more than that? That thought doesn't give me a headache. But, I can do it. I can get the headache in my experience. I can tighten up my forehead and when I do I can forget about my loneliness and sadness. But to do so I have to tighten up my forehead a great deal. Of course, I got the idea of tightening up my forehead from watching this client. When I did, I stopped myself from asking any unanswerable questions, and it sure solved my problem of what I was going to do with my joy and my sadness. This solution never asks me (as it did Paula) to compromise these values, values that say it is bad to push others away with anger, values that say, "Don't be like Dad; we don't like the way he is cold." I really wanted to understand that man when I imagined being her with those feelings. Back here in the office, this client really wants to understand me. So, the gestalt comes together.

Dad put up a wall. It was a barrier. If I imagine such a barrier, a cold wall, I am just milliseconds away from having tension in my head that will be strong enough to stop my loneliness and sadness. Sitting there trying to understand how to solve the problem of my desire to show feelings—this existing wall—and beginning to get a headache, I said, "Do you think your father felt that children were a headache?" (It seemed as if I would have thought this as a child in her shoes.) She said, "Yes," and became tearful with increased head tension.

Then, I had so many pieces. I had the etiology, the explanation, and an historical learning with a reinforcement history. It did not fully explain the migraines, but it helped me to understand the origin of these headaches. The headaches began after she had children, so we could surmise that her attempts to identify with her father caused her to redouble her headache pain when she had real headaches (that is, children) of her own. Nevertheless, I would like to see if we could unravel her headaches (even without fully pretesting and preconfirming our hypothesis) by providing a different means of problem solving than that which we just played out. Was it possible that whenever she happened to feel sad or alone she continued to feel that she was speaking to that brick wall and used this same problem-solving method? Is it possible that her current husband gives her sufficient information about being a "brick wall" himself that she can easily use this same problem solving from the past (the head tension) with him?

Let me tell you that her husband did not want his wife to have credit cards or to use his credit cards. He was invited to therapy and informed that if he chose not to participate, changes his wife might make could go in directions other than those he had input about. The best use of the energy that becomes available in therapy would occur if he were present to help shape it toward their mutually satisfying marital goals. However, he declined the invitation. I asked her to lead me through the answers to each of those experiential questions that arose, in the same way as I did for the tension and headaches.

Formation of the Decisive Intervention

This client was extremely attentive to trying to reduce stress and bring joy to the people around her. It occurred to me that, in her shoes, as soon as I made another person happy and was responsive to her joy, I would feel a great deal of joy and relief myself. Part of my experience, "as if" her, was an attempt to create joy. Experimenting, while being in her shoes, I found that if I experienced joy my mounting headache stopped. I checked with her and she agreed that her use of these mechanisms of tension was and is an attempt to create joy. So I asked her to do what I felt like doing: employing this urge and these motives and imagining or anticipating herself in the future, in a marriage, where she felt that she "counted." She could imagine herself with this husband she loved or a fantasy husband if she liked. While she was doing so, I wanted her to imagine herself in a marriage she will have one day in which the kind of chauvinism she had experienced was not present and there was a responsiveness to her needs. (Notice that I did not say, "might happen someday" or "could happen someday," but I said the sort of situation that she "*will* be in someday.") I don't want this fantasy she is having and this joy she is feeling to have a negative presupposition attached: Furthermore, I think she *will* accomplish this because I am quite optimistic and hopeful about what we are doing together in therapy.

As she did this for a few minutes, it was quite clear that she was beginning to feel joy and she was smiling. I asked her then if she would retain that feeling of joy and begin to visually imagine that little girl who she once was, that sad little girl who experienced the cold wall of her father. I had her create a visual fantasy of what that little girl in front of her looked like and imagine a communication where she, as the joyful woman from the future, communicated a sense of that joy to the lonely and sad frustrated little girl from the past.

Now, in her fantasy, some sort of process began to unfold. As it did, I saw an increase in the vertical line of tension in forehead as she simultaneously thought of being the sad little girl. She began to have tears in her eyes as she experienced the present joy interact with the memory of the little girl who was without that joy. Beginning to bring sadness, sensitive to what she wants as a little girl, a huge and alarming vertical line formed from her nose to her hair line. It split her cortex in half and made a dent in her forehead that was approximately a quarter inch in depth. This was a remarkable and painful event to witness. It almost gave me a horrible headache observing her, and it was an event so far outside my range of comfort that I refused to have a headache to that degree. I only watched her at this point.

Let us examine this moment before we go further. One of the characteristics of this intervention is that it is a type of cognitive behavior therapy, as well as a type of dissociation and association. However, we can also see that this explanation is not really accurate for the reality of the event; it is simply a convenient way to discuss the reality of the event, but it is not the truth of the matter. If might be better to say that calling it a dissociation/association or calling it an internal dialogue is merely using a metaphor to discuss the event. As with any metaphor, it creates a context. At that moment in therapy, Paula and I had created a context in which some new problem-solving strategy was occurring, and that something was entirely new: It was the simultaneous occurrence of an experience of joy with the memory of her childhood. She had never solved problems before with her thoughts of childhood paired with joy.

We created a context that gave Paula permission to imagine herself, even when she remembered her childhood, as joyous. This was a context in which she was thinking about the child having needs, a context in which she was not put off by the needs of the child. This was a context in which she had not identified with her father as a person without joy but had formed an experience and identity of herself as a person with joy. In doing so, she was sensitive to the little girl she once was. In her memory she resurrected the attitudes, beliefs, and feelings of that little girl in the context of considering and accepting those thoughts, rather than turning a cold shoulder to them as her father had. There was no therapist trying to explain what she was doing wrong in trying to please others, as she usually does. Her context associated the feeling of joy with the child's behavior and thoughts. Based on my own sense of standing in the past in the shoes she once wore, I sensed that I wanted to feel some joy and that I wanted to convey joy to her father and I wanted to know that the joy I had to share was conveyed to him and that he recognized that I had joy, which I wanted to share. That is what I felt when I empathized.

The point of this digression is to underscore the concept that it may be somewhat misleading to oversimplify this as an internal dialogue of a dissociation/association. It may be best simply to say that in the conversation that has taken place she has helped me form sufficient understanding so that I could bring an additional piece which, in turn, created a new context. And in that context she could test a new way to solve problems. That was a context that had not existed before and it seemed to solve some personal problems better than getting a headache. The personal problem being solved concerned the recognition for her joy and her unique contribution to the family. It had been created around the almost singular experience provided by her, but paralleling her posture in my office. The "joy" had been my contribution—the framework I provided by identifying with what she provided.

Follow-up and Conclusion

Paula's headache was gone. I asked her to retain her experience of comfort and acceptance while recalling the funeral of her father. I suggested she do a number of things in fantasy: Say goodbye to him and explain that she was not going to carry his coldness around, not going to carry the wall around, not going to carry his tension with his family. He could have it all back—she didn't want it anymore.

She did this entire drama with no tension visible on her face and head. And as she reoriented herself from the fantasy we had created, she continued to feel no further tension in her forehead. This was startling for her because her headache had gone away as a result of "simple" mental imagining. Very "simple" mental gymnastics had occurred where no drugs were involved, nor any medical treatments. The headache tension that had begun increasing as she began the session had not only stopped increasing but had actually gone away.

I followed this case for several months afterwards to help the client give shape to how she would interact with her husband now that she realized that she had been unrealistically putting limits on the joy she was entitled to feel. She had to decide whether or not she could live in a marriage where she could continue to modify the husband somewhat by her interaction (since he would not come to therapy). This is what she decided to do. She had great relief from the headaches that had once plagued her. An interesting incident in the retraining of her husband later occurred when she cut up her husband's credit cards, got her own, and kept them from him!

In this case example, we see many, if not all of the elements that led me to conclude that we have a different epistemology here. By understanding how I might help a client create a context for change, I notice that all the things that are occurring are problem-solving events. The client had been attempting to solve problems. If I can understand the problem the client is trying to solve, *experientially* understand that problem (put one foot in the client's world and leave one foot in my own), and help create a context in which that problem could be better solved using some of my ideas and resources, we may come up with new ways to use "the self" to solve problems. I offer my experience as a way for clients to get from themselves what they were asking for or what they have been afraid to ask for. I offer them their experience of themselves in a context that is largely of their own (safe) creation. This is what I mean by interventions; I hope you can see they are in no way mechanical.

Everything is problem solving, and the epistemology that was at the foundation of this is based upon the sense that clients communicate problem solving again and again, second after second, during human interaction in the therapy process, during the time with their spouses, school teachers, family members, family of origin members, and so on. I am not under any impression that my rendition is ultimately the most accurate—just that it was translatable into Paula's world so that what she took was accurate for her. I did not arrive at these interventions in any sort of labored way. I let Paula lead me to them by my experiencing, as I indicated. I didn't stand at a distance as an observer to make thoughts or judgments of any pathology this client had so that I could learn to treat it. I want to point out that it is easy to look back on this case and see a well-formed psychoanalytic explanation for the problem. The unfolding process, the unfolding conversation of the therapy would not have progressed as it did if I had progressed with a linearly based psychoanalytic epistemology.

Understanding Versus Using Information in Therapy

To conclude the phenomenological reason for using this approach, I should point out that our goal of doing something effective in therapy may hinge upon a decision we need to make: whether we want to analyze and understand as our goal for gathering information or whether we wish to create a context for change. If we are trying to use the information in therapy to help the client, we ought not go through a process of information gathering that presupposes a distance from the client. This is because the unfolding nature of that conversation leads us to a posture where we are the experts, making conclusions drawn from intellectual hypotheses that are removed from experience and based upon reification and directing the behavior of a passive client.

Such derived conclusions about this client's anger with her husband and her father run the risk of being irrelevant to the next step the client needs to follow. These might be conclusions about how she wishes to show that all authority figures are wrong, that she wishes to show her father to be wrong. Yet, this client would find all these sorts of "easy" conclusions to be reprehensible because her personality really is based upon trying to cooperate and get along with others. And, yes, she would resist those ideas, especially at this stage of her life. The fact that she resists them should not reinforce our notion that the ideas are correct. The situation is this: Do we wish to analyze and be "correct" or do we wish to create a context for change for a client? This implementation of a different epistemology, which is Erickson's contribution, seems built upon the phenomenological viewpoint presented in this section.

4. THE PRAGMATIC REASON FOR TAKING THIS VIEW

This view helps create a more reasonable "straight line" between the current and the desired state in the client. Perhaps the best way to illustrate this point is with the pragmatics of some cases. One such case concerns a referral originally made for pain control for a man's injured back. This case was successfully concluded after brief marriage therapy, hypnotherapy with his wife, and self-hypnosis training for him. What I want to show in this example is the impact of unresolved trauma and marital problems on readiness for pain control. I want to speculate on how things might have gone if we had not dealt with those marriage problems, including his wife's post-traumatic stress from childhood incest-rape. In that speculation, I want to show what aversive impacts conventional therapy might have had on him. Overall, the goal here is to illustrate that "everything is problem solving." That is, what might have appeared to be resistance (or secondary gain) on the part of the failure of the husband to learn to reduce his pain was the prioritizing of goals, perhaps at an unconscious level. Failing to recognize so-called resistance as problem solving would have resulted in a long and difficult set of sessions which may have failed at even the relatively easy pain reduction.

The individuals in question are primarily the marital dyad. The husband, McGyver, and the wife, Farrah. McGyver was referred to me for aid with his back pain, which left him disabled and unable, in the opinion of his former employer, to return to work. He had performed moderately well in secondary school courses except for mathematics, in which he excelled, and English, in which he did below average work. He married his high school girlfriend before his graduation. He felt that his home life as a child was mostly uneventful. He became employed as a skilled laborer and performed various jobs well over the years and received a few well-earned promotions. In his spare time, he worked as a volunteer fireman. It was on this job in 1990, while performing a rescue by carrying a victim, that he injured his back so badly that he became disabled. Surgery improved his ability to move somewhat but left him with a great deal of pain.

Initially, he sought treatment for chronic pain syndrome and for an evaluation of his degree of impairment, the latter at the request of the insurance company. The evaluating psychiatrist referred him to me for therapy. It was the opinion of the previous doctor that he was malingering and resistive to rehabilitation. McGyver sat in my office on his first visit and explained his situation with two emphases. His initial intent had been to overcome his pain so that he might be reemployable. After all, a job had been promised to him by his former employer. This job, which would not require lifting, would be available if and when he was able to pass various criteria for range of motion and pain reduction and had received a bill of health from other exams, including the psychiatric exam. However, this initial intention had to be modified in light of his recent discovery that his wife had became extremely dissatisfied and wanted to divorce him. This was related to me somewhat parenthetically by the client when he realized from my diplomas that I was a marriage and family therapist as well as a hypnotherapist. When he had told his physician that his marriage needed help, the doctor replied that this was another diversion from his rehabilitation.

We can quickly see in this case that the priority of problems experienced by the client could have a bearing on the development of the case. I reassured him that he might benefit from therapy for marital problems and that I would, in fact, prefer to meet his wife in the therapy. He vowed to try and bring her for the next session, and we used the remainder of time in the first session to discuss the history of his accident, his pain problems, and how he could expect hypnosis to help in that area.

In the next session, I met his wife. She seemed to be as in love with him as he was with her, and was equally concerned with the possible failure of the marriage. She was a student, primarily, and a waitress by necessity. She was motivated to extricate herself from the economic trap she felt the family was in both before the accident and especially now that the accident had replaced his income with the meager income from workmen's compensation. As the dissatisfaction of the marriage became the focus of conversation, the point of her anger finally emerged. She believed that her husband had had sexual affairs with three of her former girlfriends.

His attitude toward his wife's concern was interesting. When she began to tell me about these affairs, he nondefensively nodded his willingness for her to publicize this "old" argument. He, very believably, and rather quietly, told me that what she thought was not true, but that he had, regrettably, kissed one of these women when he had been drinking and they were with a group of acquaintances. He added that the woman had encouraged the kiss. Nevertheless, he felt he was in error and regretted it. Still, his wife was sure another incident had taken place involving sexual intercourse. At that moment, the session had to come to a rather abrupt close. I want to add that in most cases I tend to agree with the woman's account of these adulterous activities and perhaps err in favor of the woman's account. Over the years, I have gotten rather skillful at reading lies in the face of a denying husband. That said, it was interesting that McGyver did not seem to be lying. I was not convinced by her version as they left, but all I could do was note how she began to feel hurt and pulled away from his modest attempts to touch her neck tenderly in support.

I received an emergency call from McGyver that evening. He was in the midst of an argument with his wife. She was beside herself with anger because he had denied the affairs in my presence. She had called his parents to their home for some unclear (to me) reason and was shouting and screaming loudly. I asked him to calm her down by telling her repeatedly that he was sorry for how she felt, and I spoke with her and asked her to hear him. This got them through the crisis and I scheduled them for my next available session. She did not attend as she was not motivated to save the marriage at that time. However, his account of the incident and my attempt to understand his wife's experience brought me to a hypothesis that she had been the victim of early family sexual abuse. I asked McGyver about it and he vaguely recalled that she had mentioned something about that once when she was intoxicated. Since I could sense how this might be relevant to her feelings about him, I urged him to tell her what I had said and to invite her to come for the next session.

In the third session, I voiced my concerns to her. Proceeding from the little I knew of them, I wondered if her conclusions about not trusting him may have been entwined with some preconceived expectations about not trusting him. I asked her if this was true and if it might still be a problem for her. She admitted it was true, but added that she thought it was behind her. So I asked that she think it over and make another appointment. I also explained briefly how she might be able to use therapy to deal with this problem.

The following day she kept her appointment. She stated that she had been teetering "for and against" keeping the appointment 20 times in one day and she didn't want to do that for an entire week! Farrah told me of her past and I will summarize it here:

She had been raised, with her sister, by her father after the death of her mother at age three. Her father was a musician and a drug addict who would frequently inject her with heroin and force her to have sexual intercourse. This happened on repeated occasions from age nine to 13. Finally, she awoke in a motel in Alabama to discover that her father had abandoned her and left a hundred-dollar bill and a note explaining that the money was for her to "get by" with and that he had returned to Florida. She was on her own at 14.

Incredibly, this woman survived by taking waitressing jobs, lying about her age, and eventually hitchhiked home to Florida over the course of the next four months! She didn't like it at home, but she had nowhere else to go. She was able to fight off, refuse, and threaten the father successfully from then on to prevent any further incest. In high school a couple of years later, she met and married McGyver and soon she became pregnant and dropped out of school. Before meeting me, she had completed her GED while waitressing and was taking accounting classes in junior college.

She was successful in overcoming the helpless feelings about the incest in two intense therapy sessions. I'll briefly convey some of the gains made by this client regarding how she saw and handled memories of the past. (Keep in mind, events in her marriage did seem to be analogous to things she had experienced and tried to solve in the past—sexual betrayal, being used and unloved, potential abandonment—so any reminder of the past put her in touch with the limits and resources of the past.) Before the sessions, she tried to avoid thinking about how terribly helpless, frightened, and abandoned she felt. She would feel bad even if she accidentally began thinking about even a portion of those early events. She tried to avoid feeling needy and asking for care and tenderness (both then and now) as one way to avoid recalling how she had been raped and denied care.

Why did she get suspicious and confused and imagine such things about her marriage? As I see it, she had, as we all do, only a limited range of skills to use to solve her distress related to intimacy. Those tools were used by her as a child and they worked to a certain degree. So if her husband offered her tenderness, she would claim she did not want it. If he offered any explanation about sexual conduct, she would be suspicious and feel some-what violated. To her conscious mind, she was perfectly justified and could even offer examples of how his conduct warranted her conclusions. She never once saw that her expectations, in large part, shaped *his* conduct. Whatever unpleasant experiences she had with her husband, she had "double" when she thought about her father, the child she once was, her feelings of the past.

After two sessions of therapy, she could think about the child she once was and feel safe and proud of herself. She could think and realize that she was lovable and that she did not create the shame she had felt. She could be tender with the memory of herself instead of hard and harsh. She could imagine protecting herself and seemed to deeply realize that she had escaped the abuse she had always wished to escape. It was as if she could, in many ways, if not all ways, finally stop running from the past, from the need for love, from the desire for comfort, from the idea that she deserves better, from the urge to escape. Therapy allowed her to dissociate from the automatic bad feelings of the past and associate to many of the resources of strength and safety she had accumulated over the years and that she felt in certain situations (such as in my office and in her academic life).

Following these sessions, she and her husband were seen together once. He was doing a remarkable job of being understanding and loving. She, in turn, was not pulling away (as she had done in the first session) when he caressed her neck in response to her sadness. She was surprised to hear that she felt she was "with him" even though she had been thinking that she was taking from him. It was a touching moment. She went on to interact with and depend upon him and others even more.

Now, let us turn back to the husband's improvement before we summa-rize the point of using this case. After this short "detour" with his wife, his willingness and readiness to learn hypnosis for pain control was keen. Within four weeks, he learned to keep his pain reduced at any time. He had some additional help from me when he prepared to be reexamined for range of movement and job readiness. He used a visual self-rehearsal and became so well prepared that he surprised his rehabilitation therapists.

I am excited about the success of this case, since a family considered to have multiple problems and to be resistive instead became an inspiration for others. It began with a referral for teaching pain control to a man considered to be suffering chronic pain syndrome. It soon turned into a marital therapy case even though the marital disharmony had been viewed by the physician as a complaint made to further malinger. The referral source thought the man's complaints about marital problems were made to avoid rehabilitation from the pain-inflicting accident. When I saw his wife in therapy, she was suspicious and seemingly over-reactive. She pulled away from the comforting he offered her. Finally, she was a very likable person who seemed to be under a good deal of stress, getting no comfort.

She did not wish to avoid intimacy, as one therapist has suggested — at least not as I saw it. In fact, she was eager for it. She was just busy solving a problem regarding herself and her independence and sexuality by using suspicion, doubt, and quarreling. Paying no attention to sexual matters, she failed to hear her husband's complaints about "come ons" from her friends. Yet, she was predisposed to hear that she had been "messed over" by the sexual desires of a man.

He had been labeled as a man with secondary gain who was resistant to rehabilitation from the pain of his accident. Yet, he was more than willing to turn his full attention to overcoming his depression and learning self-hypnosis for pain after his marital tension was eased. He was one of my fastest learners for pain control. It should be noted that he also worked extremely hard in the face of a cold bureaucracy to become employable in his original company. They refused him at every turn and insisted upon his completing and passing various tests on repeated occasions. In each case he succeeded in passing the tests with earnest preparation. Finally, even though he was flatly refused employment, he still refused to give up, enrolled in school, and managed to secure reimbursement for his tuition. He and his wife are now working together in junior college where they are both students. She hopes to have full-time employment soon and go to school in the evening while he completes his course work for an associate degree. They are truly hardworking and deserving people. But I am sure that this brief therapy would not have been successful if I had been unwilling to look at *all* of their behavior as problem solving instead of resistant and malingering.

A Case of "Intimacy Melt-down"

I want to end with a recent case involving a man who suffered from a problem of severe jealousy. He was 42 years old when I saw him, and he had seen several therapists intermittently over a number of years. His problem was one that he personally understood from these previous therapists. He had gained a sense of shame for his conduct, but he had not stopped it. Incidentally, I don't think these other therapists had intended that he learn to be ashamed. It was just that his conduct was unpleasant and of his own doing, and he had come to see it as such. For instance, on a recent occasion he walked his lady friend to her car and saw a map on the front seat with call letters of a local radio station penciled on it. He began at that moment to fight thoughts that she might be keeping a secret. He covered these thoughts sufficiently to say an adequate good-bye to her and then went back into his house. At that point, he began to elaborate on the thoughts about the map and the call letters. He wondered if she was having an affair with someone at the radio station, if the map was to help navigate there, if she really was going to work on the weekend, and so on. While he realized these thoughts were part of his obsession, he couldn't or wouldn't stop them as therapists had recommended; hence, he was additionally ashamed. He was in my office still looking for a cure. My therapy with him became very brief, in most part because of my position: "Everything is problem solving."

My investigation was along the lines of what in the world he could possibly be trying to solve that was still unresolved? I should emphasize that there are no simple linear answers in a pursuit like this. He surely solves the traditional psychodynamic concerns of defending against emotions that are a perceived threat. He certainly solves the problem of not outdoing his father, if you want to get Oedipal about it. He certainly got the problem solved of collecting a "game-payoff" and a "stamp" to advance his life script, if you want to observe the so-called objective reality of his life-script analysis. He certainly is "setting up" women to fight with them, if you want to get more judgmental about it. None of these answers are particularly wrong. However, the framework from which each is taken could certainly lead to a solution; they have for many clients in the past.

But I saw none of those answers doing more than clogging up my thinking about what this man was trying to accomplish by charging into such an obsession upon seeing a map. I inquired about how, where, why, and when he had learned to get so creative about such odds and ends (the maps and call letters) that he could start inventing such fantastic story lines from them. I asked him, somewhat facetiously, if he was genetically related to some famous playwright or something? He said he was, in a manner of speaking. He further explained how his father had forced him to torturous betrayal of his mother over many years. For example, when he was a boy, his father would often come into his bedroom when his mother was out of the house and demand that he reveal just what he had seen the mother doing with other men when the father was out. I will quote here: "He [the father] said, 'Your mother was really fucking the gardener while I was at work, wasn't she? You don't have to say the word *fucking* if you don't want to, you can just say she was screwing him.'" He said that his father would not take "no" for an answer and that he was terribly upset by what he has now come to realize was a bind. This bind his father placed him in was, "Tell the truth, but you must tell me she was having sex with other men." If he denied that she was, the father became more insistent and more threatening until the boy finally lied and said that his mother had been adulterous.

I pointed out that my eight-year-old son does not understand the meaning of these words and I wondered if the father used other words or if he himself had understood the meaning at that age. He said he sort of knew the meaning and that the father would give him the choice of saying "screwing" if he was uncomfortable with the term "fucking." This seemed like a reasonable answer to me. Of course, I inquired about his understanding of his father's motive. "What do you suppose possessed your father that he was so unfeeling about your distress?" He explained that he did not fully understand, but he knew that his father had seen his own mother (the client's grandmother) having sexual relations in their barn when he (the client's father) was age eight. (Apparently, this woman was divorced at that time.) In any event, it understandably shocked the boy, who became my client's father.

Looking at this answer, I pointed out to my client that it appeared he was going to be the first man in his lineage to solve problems of how to be intimate. At his request, I briefly elaborated that his father pestering him so about possible confusion regarding his wife was no doubt due to his father still working on solving something related to his sense of confusion from witnessing his own mother in childhood. It even seemed that he was putting my client into a sort of psychodrama, with my client replacing his father and his father in turn replacing his own father (the father he had not spoken to). Then, he somehow demanded that this alter ego (my client) figure out how to tell the truth about seeing a sexual event. Perhaps it was because this man had never told his own father and had much guilt and other confusing feelings about it. If so, he was trying to work it out through a drama with his son (my client).

In any event, my client was confused by his father's behavior and agreed with me that he had been distanced from his own mother by the lies he was forced to tell and the secrets about them he had kept. I told him that, in his shoes, I believe I would feel that I knew very little about how to maintain intimacy! After all, his father had a trauma concerning it. His mother was not allowed as close to him as he might have wished due to the barrier of the secrets and the shame of his own lies and alliance with his father. And, finally, he had never developed beyond those barriers erected by his obsessive jealousy. In his shoes, I imagined that he would feel like an eight-year-old for whom a relationship with a woman was a real mystery, at least in one area—how to trust continued intimacy with someone for whom he cared. He seemed to have learned from his father that it had to do with disappointing fantasies he could construct and obsess upon. He agreed and said that he really didn't know how to be intimate. But, I added that the real trick was to figure out how to insure intimacy, and that seemed to be what he was trying to solve. I suspected that this was the motive behind the urges that called him to obsess about the maps and call letters of the radio station.

As soon as I said that, he froze in his chair and listened motionless for a few sentences until, at last, he said, "Wait, go back! What was that you said about my urges?" I repeated that he was probably trying to insure intimacy when his unconscious fixated on the maps and radio call letters and that his subsequent behavior of obsessing was his best attempt to insure continued intimacy. At this point he became a caricature of Archimedes, calling out "Eureka" upon making a scientific breakthrough. Then he fell somewhat sad. I asked about this, pointing out that one is expected to say "Aha" and not "Aha, Jeez!" He said he had just realized that his father was trying to insure intimacy too and that was the reason for his father's craziness. I pointed out that he could stop trying to figure his father out now and get on with more suitable behaviors for insuring intimacy. Then we discussed what those would be like.

We spent another 25 minutes going over what one does in one's mind to insure, build, promote, and plan intimacy in a relationship, especially when the other person is not present. When he has urges to fantasize about possibilities, he should do so. But he should fantasize about what sort of experience he would like to organize, plan it, think about how he will enjoy it, how he will invite her, what options he will leave open if his original plan is not possible, and so on. This, I emphasized, is how one can use time to help insure continued intimacy into the future. These were ideas that he had never learned and that had never occurred to him before.

5. THE ETHICAL REASON FOR TAKING THIS VIEW

It seems to me that if we assume any orientation other than problem solving, we run the risk of attributing a certain malice to client conduct (resistance, pathology, hidden motive, evil, etc.). Perhaps with the exception of behavior modification dealing strictly with behavior and reinforcements, most theories presuppose a certain malice on the part of the client. This happens by accident and not by design in most cases. I hesitate to give examples because I doubt that the architects of any particular theory intended for negative motivations to apply in such a way that they degrade, shame, or alienate clients. It is interesting to note that most of our meta-phors of internal events in therapy are rooted in our warlike past. Thus, we must explain people as oppressing, suppressing, defending, attacking, conflicing, denying, and so on. We have developed a language that, despite our better wishes, begets an adversarial definition of client behavior more easily than it creates a problem-solving definition.

I am not so naive as to assume that all people are kind, but I do assume that conditions of living give shape to these impulses for kindness or harm-fulness. All human problems are not "pathology" and all psychodynamic and interpersonal problems are not deserving of the implicit or accidental blame that comes from such combative metaphors.

SUMMARY

I have provided three case examples to illustrate that all therapy is problem solving. One longer example was used to convey the phenomenological reason for taking the view and two cases were used to show the pragmatic reasons and how interventions flow easily from this view of human conduct. In addition, I spoke of the aesthetic and parsimonious reasons. I believe that the particular emphasis on problem solving in Erickson's work is difficult to teach and express clearly, and yet it is "the Essence of the Story."

REFERENCES

Falloon, I. (1988). Behavioral family management in coping with functional psychosis. *International Journal of Mental Health, 17* (1), 35-47.

Hartman, H. (1958). Ego psychology and the problem of adaptation. New York: International Universities Press.

Lankton, S., Lankton, C., & Mathews, W. (1992) Ericksonian family therapy. *Handbook of Family Therapy, Vol. II.* Gurman & Kniskern (Eds.), New York: Brunner/Mazel.

Rogers, C. (1961). *On becoming a person.* Boston: Houghton Mifflin.

Rosegrant, J. (1988). A dynamic/expressive approach to brief inpatient group psychotherapy. *Group, 12* (2), 103-112.

CHAPTER 6

"Have You Done Anything Ericksonian Today?" Co-Creating Positive Self-Fulfilling Prophecy

Carol H. Lankton

INTRODUCTION

Despite wide differences in Ericksonian methods, at the heart of the approach are assumptions of client resources, health-seeking intentions, and the possibility of creating better solutions. From these beliefs there naturally emerge a genuine positive framing and utilization of anything offered, even of those behaviors that might be perceived as problems or evidence of "resistance." This chapter describes several strategies for helping clients to see purpose and options within their behavior and to presuppose eventual success at relevant goals.

The presupposition of eventual success is a key element of Ericksonian work in which the client and therapist may be thought of as co-creating a positive self-fulfilling prophecy. "Self-fulfilling prophecy" is a term often used to mean that negative expectations lead to dreaded outcomes, which, in turn, reinforce the original pessimistic beliefs. This chapter expands upon this concept of self-fulfilling prophecy to include and focus on the role of positive expectations as contributors to positive outcomes, which reinforce optimistic beliefs.

AN ERICKSONIAN ORIENTATION

Occasionally, clients who have perused the biographical sketch on display where I work will notice reference to something called the "Ericksonian approach," and ask me what that is, and whether or not I did anything "Ericksonian" to them in the session we have just completed. I tell them that I generally expected the best from them in terms of cooperation and potential and didn't attribute any pathological motivations or labels to them. I add that I didn't and won't do anything "to" them, but will work *with* them to stimulate their own ideas and solutions. This co-creation acknowledges the influence of my expectancies and various interventions, while recognizing that power ultimately rests with clients to make conclusions and generate relevant solutions to developmental challenges. These ideas are the essence of an Ericksonian approach, rather than any predetermined set of interventions.

Ericksonian therapy involves relating to clients as individuals, so as to understand the unique constellation of resources, challenges, obstacles, and desired outcomes each presents. It avoids stereotypic diagnostic problem categories and "canned" cures. It deemphasizes dysfunction and emphasizes symptoms as manifestations of clients' positive intention of dealing with situations as they access what they believe to be the best choices available. Too often in our "look and feel good at all costs" society, symptoms are viewed as suspicious, pathological things that should be "fixed" as quickly as possible, regardless of the situation, circumstances, and developmental demands to which the individual may be reacting and attempting adjustment. Often, psychiatric drugs are requested or prescribed, even in situations where acceptance, tolerance, expression, and processing of natural, healthy feelings such as sadness, anxiety, or anger might be preferable in the long run. An added benefit of this Ericksonian diagnostic viewpoint is that the client avoids pejorative labels widely associated with those who "break down" or request medication.

Challenging Negative Expectations

The powerful effect of expectation is well known in contemporary psychology and medicine. We recognize the influence of expectations about ourselves and about our performance as it affects actual outcomes. We also are increasingly aware of the power of our expectations about others that influence their beliefs about themselves and their futures. National awareness of these ideas has been heightened by such historically important research as the oft-cited Rosenthal studies (1968) of teacher expectation on student performance, which countered the previous assumption that internal traits are the primary determinants of behavior.

Nevertheless, we seem less aware, as a society, of the similar effect of culturally induced expectations regarding adequate response to the variety of challenges we encounter in the life cycle. There is often an implicit or even explicit demand that we be strong, please others, be perfect, do it right the first time, make no mistakes, know everything without having to learn it, or even have no "problems" or times when emotional discomfort shows. And when we respond in strong, adequate ways, without much emotional distress, we create a cycle of expectations in ourselves and others that our future responses will be similarly adequate.

This may or may not be true. When we respond by feeling distraught and making roundabout or poor choices, we create expectations that further these negative cycles of expectation, and their fulfillment or unfulfillment complicate and pathologize many responses to crisis. Like other practitioners of Ericksonian therapies, I believe that the creation and execution of an adequate response to life's challenges often is preceded by or punctuated with an adjustment period during which individuals and groups look weak, make mistakes, have problems, and suffer emotionally. I believe that such a period of adjustment is a reasonable and logical component of health, rather than a response that should be feared, looked down upon, or artificially attenuated.

When clients come to therapy thus "pathologized" by social conditioning and possibly by physicians consulted for related physical ailments such as sleeplessness or indigestion, the way in which we respond to them can reinforce or break the negative cycle of expectation and self-devaluation. If we operate from a traditional epistemology that defines the individual as sick and looks for evidence of pathology or resistance, we do clients a disservice. At times of transition, they are likely to be especially vulnerable to external expectations, especially by a mental health professional perceived as the "expert" in such matters. Conversely, communications that disrupt negative expectations often are welcomed as reassuring, refreshing, and encouraging. Such communication is equally important in all phases of therapy whether it be brief or long term. In fact, therapy often turns out to be much briefer than originally expected. Perhaps this is because a shifting of the lenses through which reality is perceived facilitates a generative change throughout the client's system. "Problems" are rightly integrated as opportunities for learning, and the inevitability of creative adjustment is conveyed.

The expectations and beliefs we convey as we meet clients and gather information, the questions we ask and how we ask them, what we respond to, show interest in, take notes on and emphasize is just as important as whatever else we do, if not more so, when we officially begin "treating" the conditions we have diagnosed. The essence of this approach is depathologizing people (Fisch, 1990). If we view any so-called resistance as the person's best effort at cooperation, though it might be so convoluted as to appear "upside down and backward," then we are genuinely expecting the best of people, believing in innate resources and potentials, as well as health-seeking intentions, despite vast differences in interpersonal style, presenting problems, tangled patterns, and feelings of helplessness. Positive expectations challenge pathological and oppressive stereotypes and rigid beliefs, focusing instead on the healthy adjustments people are striving to accomplish, the available resources, and the current interpersonal context. Therapy is a process of developing a context in which positive expectancies can be initiated or reinforced.

To this end, the first step in the Ericksonian approach to therapy is usually to connect with the client by empathizing, accepting, and understanding the validity of feelings of pain, desperation, and helplessness that often are presented. In the Ericksonian model, these "problems" will, moreover, be framed positively and utilized as a heretofore unrecognized means to desired goals. This approach subverts traditional cycles of expectation and allows for feelings of adequacy while in the midst of a problem state.

In my experience, this type of therapist response results, most often, in an immediate sense of stunned relief and hopefulness in clients. It replaces fears of "going crazy," "breaking down," or being in other serious mental trouble with a sense of being accepted and already "in the process" of solving their problems. It makes sense for people to experience the feelings they have as legitimate. As Erickson said to a client (in Lustig, 1975), "You have a right to have all of your feelings, simply by virtue of being alive." This would seem to apply, especially, in times when we are stressed by severe developmental and circumstantial challenges. Unfortunately, the assumptions to the contrary are so ingrained in our culture that we expect a judmental response from others, particularly those in authority. A newscaster might report, matter-of-factly on a rape trial, describing how the victim "broke down and cried uncontrollably several times during the testimony." The implication is that she is weak and perhaps uncertain. Viewers would be surprised to hear, instead, that the rape survivor who stopped several times to cry was courageously expressing the pain she suffered during this incident.

THIS MATTER OF BEING ERICKSONIAN . . .

An indicator of effective therapy is that clients feel respected, inspired, empowered, capable, and free to outgrow symptoms and solve problems. They identify themselves with their positive intentions and give up notions of inherent pathology or irreparable damage. But what makes therapy Ericksonian? There is some controversy and confusion about what "Ericksonian therapy" means. It is obvious that Erickson did not invent or have a monopoly on many techniques that have become associated with or attributed to him. But more importantly, he could not be confined to *any* set of techniques, regardless of whether or not he invented them. Unfailingly characteristic of Erickson and underlying his method and techniques was a staunch belief in the special needs and potential of each person. Perhaps his most consistent characteristic was his committment to flexibility in generating unique ways of proceeding with each client so as to unleash potentials and establish positive expectancy for their continued unfolding. These beliefs, like the techniques, were not held exclusively by Erickson, but his work repeatedly exemplified and emphasized them.

PERCEIVING NEW OPTIONS

The experience in the therapy context, though just a moment in time, becomes an exciting opportunity to "come to one's senses" and perceive new options. Clients examine and challenge previously unchallenged, unconscious aspects of expectancy operating in the form of "life scripts" (Berne, 1961). They can review early decisions that were based on erroneous information. Discovery of these adaptive mechanisms can be promoted as evidence of a creative, protective "part" of the person that worked in the best interest of the entire client system. When people realize that it is possible to view the same situation in an entirely different way such that its meaning is changed, it is as if an exciting awareness literally "dawns on" them.

Self-talk reflects the view of reality one consciously and unconsciously chooses. This internal dialogue is an important force that guides evaluations of self and others. Favored beliefs are often transformed into rigid rules and a sense of pressure. A person can complain that they "have to" do something and subsequently feel depressed and victimized as opposed to recognizing and emphasizing the view that they "get to" do the same thing, with resulting feelings of enthusiasm and power.

I recently spoke to a man who was feeling angry at his wife for the affair she had revealed to him several months earlier. Prior to this revelation, the couple had separated and a divorce to which he was opposed seemed imminent. She had been feeling so guilty about the affair that she was choosing a divorce she didn't really want to avoid confessing to her husband. She eventually risked confession, however, and they moved back together immediately. Though he suffered great pain, humiliation, and anger, he was enormously relieved that the marriage was not being dissolved. The husband chose to accept his wife back. As a symbol of their recommitment to each other, they even decided to have another child.

However, when I spoke to him, he was obsessed with the recurring thought, "I shouldn't have to put up with this [her affair]." He completely forgot that he didn't have to at all, but that he had chosen to reunite and was glad for the opportunity to do so. When he remembered that nothing prevented him from leaving, he could realize the power he had in the relationship. He was not a helpless victim. He still had to put up with the imperfection and breach of faith of his wife, but he also could engage in the loving and otherwise supportive relationship that he had nearly lost. And he could give up illusions about having a perfect marriage. Instead, he had the opportunity to do some hard work to develop the real relationship that can exist between two nonperfect partners. I remembered Dr. Erickson warning my husband and me when we were newlyweds not to give up any of our faults because we were going to need them to understand and accept the faults of our partner (personal communication, 1979).

The recognition that another view of reality is possible need not happen only in therapy, of course. We are able to make such discoveries throughout life. I remember one day when my five-year-old daughter was swinging in the sunshine, laughing as she attempted to touch the clouds with her toes. She suddenly announced to me that she had decided not to ever have babies because the birth would hurt too much. This was quite surprising coming from a little girl who never saw a baby doll she didn't desperately need and who had collected more than she could count. Several moments later, she shared a different conclusion. She would have babies, she decided, and when the birth happened she was going to think about swinging in the sunshine and laughing in the clouds. I think this view of reality she has chosen will be more enjoyable than her previous one.

As therapists, we are all too familiar with the unfortunate examples of adults who, as children, were taught to expect and find the worst in people and situations. One of my adult clients suffered enormous self-image damage in the process of growing up with a critically abusive mother. One day, my client was discussing her three-week-old infant and how she could tell when the child's crying signaled that she was hungry or wet versus when she was "just throwing a fit." It was a striking example of just how early the process of unexamined negative interpretation and attribution can begin. I felt an urgency to invite the mother to disrupt this pattern before it was established. Ironically, the woman followed this "casual" statement with a request to work on her own self-image during the next session, seemingly unaware of her potential for negative and positive participation in the development of the still untarnished self-image of her baby. She would need to exchange inherited explanations about herself and her baby's spiteful or problem-making motives in favor of more pragmatic, health-seeking motives. It would be a forgiving new option to expect that all people make their best effort to adjust to moment-by-moment demands from the time of conception and just as congruently after birth.

Of course, nearly all children are failed in some way by well-meaning but less-than-perfect parents. To adjust, survive, make sense of, and deal with circumstances, we consciously and unconsciously construct expectations or "decisions" about ourselves, others, and reality. These internal maps guide subsequent feelings and behavior in the form of "life scripts" (Berne, 1961), potent versions of post-hypnotic suggestion. These scripts influence long after they are relegated to the unconscious and they are difficult to recognize, examine, and challenge. As a child, I remember being excited, amazed, and somewhat skeptical when my mother shared a discovery from an article she was reading about the power of positive thinking. It forwarded the notion that there are measurable physiological correlates of self-statements such as "That really burns me up" or "This is a pain in the neck." This was a bold concept in the 50's. There are many who choose to diminish their responsibility and power over the experiences they help create, both negative and positive. We prefer explanations that emphasize "luck," genetics, or privilege as pivotal determinants.

I once was engaged in cross-country skiing with a friend of equal experience and skill (adequate to shaky) on a mostly flat course with occasional hills. I noticed an interesting phenomenon each time we encountered a hill. At the top, he exclaimed, "Whooaah!" and fell at about the midpoint of the hill. By slight but significant contrast, at the top of each hill, I uttered a different word, "Wheeeee!" I proceeded smoothly (and rapidly) to the bottom, feeling a sense of exhilaration. Since we tend to be somewhat unaware of what we believe, fear, or expect, it seems reasonable to attribute responsibility for various outcomes to chance or fate. We usually underrate how influential our expectations are.

The Right to Select Goals

We are active participants in shaping outcomes. This recognition is an important aspect of perceiving and creating new options. In therapy, focusing on goals helps to specify which options are desired and implies that the client has the right and power to proceed in a sometimes vastly different manner. Asking clients what is desired now and in the future alerts them to the possibility of constructive change. It also validates wanting to do something as a "good enough" reason to do it (assuming that it is legal and doesn't hurt or infringe on anyone else's rights or safety). Clients often seem only to want not to suffer from anxiety, discomfort, or other symptoms. It might be far more productive to focus on what they do want. Sometimes, of course, having a problem can result in awareness about what is wanted. Recognizing what they don't want can result in knowledge about what would be better or different. Perceiving a problem as an information-gathering device to clarify goals is definitely a new option for many people.

Even when clients are unable to initially answer the question, "What do you want to accomplish," I find that simply asking the question as though it is extremely important to the process of therapy serves to communicate an expectancy about the power and the right of the person to be an independent agent. For example, a client of mine presented symptoms of excessive anxiety, episodes of "lost time," nightmares, and flashbacks to Vietnam, prompting a probable diagnosis of post-traumatic stress disorder. He was frightened that he would hurt his family while he was "out of his mind" and he feared "going crazy." These were severe problems.

This man was overweight, rigid, and stiff in his bearing. In his late 40's, he was recently forced to retire from a high-ranking military position in which his identity had been invested for 20 years. He had received numerous awards for exemplary performance. The anxiety symptoms began almost immediately after his retirement. For 20 years, he had manifested no "post-traumatic stress" symptoms. As I listened to him, I wondered what positive function these symptoms were attempting to accomplish.

Upon encountering the "open-endedness" of retirement, this man, who had always had his time structured, suddenly found himself without a mission or meaning in life. It appeared that his unconscious, searching for some kind of "mission" to fill this void, had returned (via flashbacks of Vietnam) to a set of circumstances that held "life or death" meaning for him. I suggested that he could recognize the motivation evidenced by his "problem" and select a different mission. This alternative mission could provide the meaning and direction he sought without the anxiety associated with that earlier mission. "So, what do you want to do?" I asked him, adding that he had an opportunity to really give this question the consideration it deserved.

He listened intently and agreed enthusiastically with my hypotheses that he wasn't going crazy and that he was not a victim of true post-traumatic stress. Instead, I posited, he was seeking a healthy solution to this important challenge of regaining meaning and purpose in his life. However, he seemed dismayed by the idea he could actively participate in choosing his own meaning. In fact, he looked so deflated when I posed the question that I was doubtful it would generate a significant response from him. However, asking the question disrupted his other-directed focus. He was shocked to realize that no one had ever asked him that question before. He had always done what others had told him to do without question. He joined the Marines before he finished high school, completed several tours of duty in Vietnam, and then continued his military career as a cost analyst. In all of these areas, he was told what to do and was reinforced for compliance. Now there was no reinforcement, no direction. His wife was dissatisfied regarding their loss of status, income, and routine. He felt guilty for letting his family down. He didn't know how to interact with his teenaged children who were accustomed to living without him. He was feeling displaced and frustrated by unsuccessful attempts to secure employment.

When he returned the next session, I barely recognized him. He was relaxed, dressed casually, moved energetically, and proceeded to explain a variety of goals he had considered during the week. These included courses he wanted to take, trips he wanted to make, exercise and nutrition programs, "dating" his wife, externalizing his war traumas into written memoirs, cars he wanted to refurbish, and "odd" jobs he thought would be satisfying for various reasons. He also wanted to communicate the old frightened, vulnerable feelings to his family. All of these goals seemed to hold meaning for him and contributed to his relaxed yet enthusiastic demeanor. He had internalized a basic freedom — the permission and right to pursue happiness in a moment-by-moment focus on what he wanted. His symptoms had become obsolete as he perceived new options.

STRATEGIES FOR CO-CREATING POSITIVE EXPECTANCY

There are five strategies for co-creating positive expectancy: Congruence, Positive framing, Implication of success, Defining and expanding expectations, and Building Self-image. Each is discussed below.

Congruence

The attitude of "compelling expectancy" (Erickson & Rossi, 1980) is very important in psychotherapy. In experiments in which hypnotists were told that subjects were "able" to accomplish all trance phenomenon except one, this result was repeatedly found (Erickson & Rossi, 1980). What we look for is what we find. An attitude of compelling expectancy that a client will accomplish selected goals is consistent with an indirect and permissive, nonauthoritarian approach. It is characterized by a congruent belief in abilities rather than a demand to do something in a way the "expert" decrees. If we believe that people are able and resourceful, they look for related evidence and find it. If we suggest hypnosis with a voice tone that suggests we are fearful of it, clients will naturally show reluctance and caution to engage in the process. If we give an assignment as though we don't really believe the person can or will do it, chances are high that the assignment won't get done. People come to therapy doubting their own power and wisdom. They look to experts to tell them what is wrong with them and what to do. Therapy can be designed to draw upon their own power and to find what they need to solve their own problems. In this way, clients can take credit for the solutions they generate.

Positive Framing

The belief that every behavior is an attempt to solve some problem or accomplish a legitimate goal appears to be a common denominator among Ericksonian therapists. It makes it possible to convincingly frame experiences positively and to utilize whatever is being presented to generate goals, retrieve resources, and presuppose eventual success at accomplishing relevant goals.

While many interventions rest upon this foundation belief, one technique I particularly favor facilitates my ability to positively frame and utilize whatever behavior occurs. It is the indirect suggestion form referred to by Erickson and Rossi (1980) as "apposition of opposites." My personal use of it is often guided by the formula: "The more you are *able* to do 'X' (the 'problem' behavior), then the more you are going to be able to do 'Y' (the goal, solution, or opposite behavior). Sometimes, I do not know when I begin such a sentence how I am going to complete it, but the act of using this sentence structure initiates a search for possible relevant opposites that will be welcomed and recognized as desirable. It is a simple device to activate utilization. The presented "problem" behavior is accepted as valid and the inevitability of the desired behavior is presupposed, precisely by means of the client being able to display what had been considered the problem.

A genuine belief in the interconnectedness of apparent opposites is essential. I can congruently congratulate a person on his ability to experience his inadequacy and vulnerability because in doing so he is more able to discover his true confidence and power. The more he can recognize what he doesn't like, the more he is able to understand what he wants and needs. Or, as Victor Frankl (1967) said regarding the search for meaning, the occurrence of thirst proves the existence of something called water. In this fashion, I am able to prescribe almost any personality orientation, symptom, or concern by framing it as an ability that leads in some requisite way to its desired opposite. It is a matter of accepting clients and validating the presence of strength even in what they had considered a weakness, fault, or problem.

Implication of Success

Contracting about client goals is preceded by an understanding of what clients want to happen. Sometimes, this involves an understanding of what the apparent here-and-now function of a symptom represents. Success can develop as a result of our asking clients to imagine themselves in a future in which the presenting problem has been solved in a most satisfactory and comprehensive manner. In speculating about what they "see" in this future, I can stimulate their thinking. As I describe relevant details of new interpersonal relating, I observe signs of the acceptance or rejection of these options. Implication of success occurs with a presupposition of their capacity and right to make this image a reality. To the extent that they agree on the relevance and desirability of these options (via head nods, smiles, and other signals), therapy has been authorized to proceed. This is now an "unconscious" contract that has been co-created and agreed upon as a relevant direction. It is simultaneously a phase of assessment as well as a powerful expectancy shaping intervention.

Defining and Expanding Expectations

A marital couple may come to therapy entangled in some immediate conflict that was continually exacerbated by their negative interpretations and beliefs, which limited their use of interpersonal options. They often are able to expand into a novel arena of interactions when beliefs change and they take responsibility for getting needs met. It is also helpful for each to believe that he/she can depend on the other to cooperate. It is unfortunate when one person manufactures "evidence" that the spouse is stingy and insensitive based solely on internal expectations when, in fact, the spouse is eager to cooperate.

Negative expectations need to be exchanged for positive expectations. Frequently, this means deciding that the other person can be trusted to care, be sensitive to expressed needs and feelings, be able to survive and even benefit from the expression of negative feelings, and tell the truth as he/she comes to know it about needs, feelings, likes, and dislikes. I assess with couples where each spouse rates on the deserving/demanding continuum. The best prognosis is when each person feels deserving enough and trusting enough of the other that he or she is willing to express feelings, wishes, needs to the other.

Contrast this perspective with a trouble-causing sense of entitlement at the other end of the continuum wherein both persons believe it is their right to have their way and make demands on the other to comply, often failing to ever actually state specifically the underlying need. These people rely generously upon the language of "You should" rather than "I want and feel." Furthermore, they perceive themselves to be the expert on what the other feels and wants and they negate feedback to the contrary from the actual person in question. If the other person fails to comply with a demand or need that was stated, or simply assumed or expected, then additional negative expectations about that person's lack of caring, dependability, honesty, etc. are generated, usually without the client explicitly checking these out for accuracy with that other person. Or one may begin a familiar tirade detailing the other's character flaws, thus fulfilling an internally generated prophecy of what disappointment can be expected from the other and inviting the other to respond compatibly with the prophecy, justified by the idea that "I'm going to be accused of it anyway, so I may as well do it."

I challenge such couples to examine what it is they hope to accomplish staying in a relationship where they congruently believe that the other doesn't care or can't be trusted to be honest, actually thinking the other intends harm or hurt. I also wonder what exactly they feel that marriage entitles them to. Does each assume automatic happiness and gratification if truly "in love" with the "right" person? Is the other person responsible for one's happiness now, and if one isn't happy, is one justified in blaming the spouse who doesn't "love enough" or may be guilty of having his or her own needs?

This kind of questioning sometimes results in uncomfortable recognition or reluctant admissions that, in fact, one or both were holding these unexamined notions and judging the other in related terms. They also admit that they really have no basis for such ideas and they are invited to consider alternative beliefs, if only experimentally at first. "Think of your spouse 'as if' he/she is your best friend and partner on the same team and that you both want the best, both for yourself and for the other." When there is a conflict between best friends, it isn't a matter of who is right or wrong, good or bad, but a question of how to proceed so both sets of feelings and needs are weighed and taken into account in reaching whatever compromise or solution the two can agree upon.

In order for this kind of workable conflict to even arise, both partners must be operating on the deserving and trusting principle enough to express to the other what is wanted and felt. Bumping into the "I shouldn't have to ask" obstacle frequently occurs in this arena (with related proof that the other person who didn't know or act in the desired manner simply doesn't care—which results in more withholding, withdrawing, blame, and distancing). It becomes a matter of "getting to" increase the chances of needs being met by feeling deserving enough to clarify them and providing a courtesy to the other who is seen as motivated (even honored) to be trusted, included, allowed to participate in helping the loved one get needs met. It is comforting and feels safe to interact with someone who can be depended upon to clarify his or her needs, thus minimizing the need for haphazard second guessing and assumptions about what is needed. Such people are sometimes seen as "selfish" from a certain view, and the positive intention behind refraining from stating preferences and needs is usually based on a desire to avoid such selfishness. This is unfortunate because the illusion is fostered that it is somehow possible not to have needs and to be concerned only with others. Chronic reliance on this interpersonal style results in an accumulation of resentment, hurt, and even illness and other symptoms over time.

I recently worked with a couple who had been married for 30 years. The wife was energetically challenging her traditional sex-role inheritance. As the oldest sister in an Italian family, she was indoctrinated to care for others. She had recently revealed to her husband the long-kept secret of chronic incestuous abuse by her elder brother. She was experiencing newly found power, relief, self-respect, and trust in her husband. She was also setting some limits and making her needs known for the first time in her life. We sat together in the session, supposedly focused on what each wanted. However, she persisted in insisting that her husband needed to make more friends and play more golf. He maintained that he was quite happy with his current level of social contact and recreational activities. Finally, she was able to assert that what she really wanted was space without him hovering over her. She feared the consequences of making such a selfish, "antisocial" request for herself. He, however, was much more receptive to this idea than he was to her earlier indirect proposal for getting her needs met. She realized that she was not doing him a favor by concealing her needs and thereby making him guess them. She had expanded her expectations to realize that her husband didn't need to be protected from the truth of her feelings, good or bad. She could protect him from the demoralizing implication that he couldn't or wouldn't be able to handle the truth or be sensitive to her feelings.

I encourage people to look ahead to the time when they will be able to interact in a way that reflects their new beliefs. For example, they can start by seeing themselves as deserving and trustworthy. They then can imagine how they will have created new levels of intimacy, sharing, and mutual support with others. Perhaps they see themselves modeling for their children options for respectful and trusting interaction. They can be proud that they have chosen, practiced, and become accomplished at this kind of interaction even though they were not fortunate enough to have received such modeling and permission when they were children. This includes setting limits and boundaries, taking responsibility for choices, creating opportunities for connecting and sharing, with no one acting as anyone else's jailor, boss, or informant on what he/she "should" be doing. Most people agree that such pictures look good to them. Even if conscious doubts persist about whether or not it is an attainable reality, an unconscious prophecy is taking shape. After all, they can see, agree, and be. Or, as Erickson said, "You can pretend anything and master it" (in Lustig, 1975). Self-fulfilling prophecies are unconscious wishes that motivate outside of consciousness by "haunting" one until the dream is made a reality.

Building Self-Image

Updating one's self-image nurtures and validates unconscious wishes. Desired characteristics and options replace limited self-images. Earlier I mentioned contracting to presuppose the inevitability of success in negotiating demands at upcoming developmental stages. With self-image building, we seek to stabilize interpersonal tools, resources, and skills and to focus awareness upon component parts of day-to-day situations and events. Thinking is stimulated about how the person will accomplish larger goals by means of specific transactions and interactions that reflect desired characteristics. The goal is for persons "reviewing" potential scenarios to value and approve their own behavior. It is not necessary to picture the "right" behaviors that guarantee that other people are satisfied. Others may complain, criticize, threaten, or refuse, and still the person can value self-approved interactions.

The self-image building process employs aspects of dissociation, positive hallucination, age-progression, and selection of verb tense to facilitate the development of positive self-fulfilling prophecies. The person dissociates from the anxiety typically associated with difficult situations that arise from negative self-fulfilling prophecies. Dissociation is facilitated by the systematic retrieval of positive resource experiences and by "addition" of visual indicators of these qualities to the original picture of the self in the mind's eye. Then, the person watches the psychologically embellished image of the self take center stage and cope more effectively with situations that previously elicited anxiety. The unfolding scenario is a series of words and pictures "out there" somewhere that the person is able to watch from a comfortable and fortified distance. The conscious mind need not believe that this fantasy could actually become real in order for the unconscious to project the desired interaction.

Initially, seeing need not mean believing. However, I do encourage people to keep the fantasies within realistic dimensions so that they later can actually enact these thoughtfully constructed interpersonal options. I urge them to watch fantasy rehearsals for as many situations and events as they can imagine, seeing themselves with a wide range of other people. In each case, the central self-image is reviewed interacting in such a way that the person approves of his or her actions. While expecting the best from involved others, no specific response or outcome is required to define the interaction as successful. In this way, desired psychological characteristics are associated to events and people from the person's social environment. Triggers that were formerly anxiety producing now can be expected to prompt a range of more desired feelings and behaviors.

Finally, I ask clients to picture the central self-image in a time farther in the future (five or 10 years) when larger goals have been accomplished. This image might be similar to the picture initially developed during earlier contracting. This time, it will hopefully be even more detailed due to the focus on goals during the course of therapy. I ask the person to "merge" with that self in the future and enjoy the feelings of success, pride, confidence, etc. when they will have made fond dreams a reality. Erickson enjoined us to "look ahead to the days when you can look back" (personal communication, 1979). I similarly suggest that clients take time to "look back over the steps you took to make your dream come true." As they respond to this suggestion, I encourage them also to review times when they made valuable mistakes. I remind them of obstacles that alerted them to the discovery of new options and difficulties that became opportunities. In this way, positive, self-fulfilling expectations are associated to inevitable mistakes, obstacles, and hardships.

As they reorient from the future image to the present time, there is often the lingering sense that they are on the path to making this dream a reality. Though the entire experience might be stored unconsciously at various points as "fate" unfolds, they might have fleeting glimpses or brief memories that this occurrence is something they dreamed about or knew would happen.

EXPECTING HAPPINESS NOW

People have a right to expect the best from and for themselves. It's never too late to change one's mind. The future options for interacting in a deserving and trusting manner are available to all despite the past that has been survived. There were learnings and opportunities in even the most horribly oppressive past. Co-creating the expectancy that it is possible to be "happy" right now is at the heart of good therapy. It seems tragic to me that so many people do not enjoy life now, but wait for some future event. It is as if they are living their lives on the deferred payment plan. It sounds like a positive self-fulfilling prophecy to plan to be happy when some future arrives, but not if it is at the expense of being happy now. Happiness is a mental habit, a mental attitude of positive expectancy. If it is not learned and practiced in the present, it is rarely experienced in the future, no matter what occurs.

Everyone is familiar with the kind of external events typically expected to "bring" happiness: getting married, getting a better job, getting a bigger house, getting the children through college, retiring, getting rich, losing weight, finally getting a parent's approval and love. Obviously, these external things reflect what that person doesn't have and what he or she imagines to make everyone else happy. "The grass is always greener on the other side of the fence" phenomenon seems responsible for a widespread failure to appreciate current reality in favor of longing for something else. The arbitrary aspect of this expectation is never more obvious than in consecutive sessions in which the first client attributes all her unhappiness to not having children, while the next complains that she can't possibly be happy until she gets some space from her children. They both fail to see that happiness is a decision that is not necessarily contingent on external circumstances. The inspiring example of people such as Viktor Frankl shows that we can maintain serenity, purpose, meaning, even happiness in even the worst situation, such as a concentration camp.

People have unmet goals and problems in all areas of life; when one problem is solved, another appears to take its place. A chronic pattern of putting off happiness "until" or "when" creates a sad situation because perfect conditions never arrive. Others are not necessarily happy just because they enjoy the trappings (such as money, fame, good looks, relationships, etc.) believed to guarantee happiness. As Paul Simon sang, "The only time love is an easy game is when two other people are playing it." If I can help people expect to be happy now as well as later, this becomes a valuable, self-fulfilling prophecy or mental habit. When I hear people wishing they could hurry up and get through their current life in favor of some dimly fantasized future, I remind them of their potential to be happy here and now. If we expect that we can live fully now, we attune ourselves to the fleeting present and its rich opportunities. I teach people to tell themselves, "I am completely relaxed at the present time, both mentally and physically." They needn't put off relaxing until all work is done, all pressures are gone, and they are on vacation. Neither do they have to actually be relaxed to create the self-fulfilling prophecy that they intend to relax. We find what we look for and expect to find. To perceive is to make choices in interpretation.

I'm reminded of the poem by Markham about the prophet who stood on a crossroad near a particular village. A passerby inquired what the people were like in the town. The old prophet first asked what people in his home were like. When the passerby bitterly complained about their inconsiderate, rude, and selfish ways, the prophet suggested he keep traveling, as he would no doubt find the people here to be equally disappointing. When another traveler in search of a new home asked the same question, the prophet similarly inquired about the people of his previous home. The traveler described them as generous, loving, honest, and fair. The prophet welcomed him to his new home, assuring him that the people of this town were exactly the same way.

We do find what we look for, including happiness and opportunity. Milton Erickson embodied this attitude of embracing life's opportunities with curiosity, hope, and the expectancy of learning. He sustained more than his share of hardships. He could have complained or used his disabilities as reasons for not participating fully in life, but he chose not to use those excuses and he challenged his clients to similarly abandon theirs. He told others, "Don't worry about me, I'm just in a wheelchair!" We don't have to be in wheelchairs to model this same attitude with our clients and in our own living. At many points of choice each day, we are free to make excuses to explain away our dissatisfaction, or we can discover possibilities and options in living each moment. Stimulating the growth and development of positive expectancy is truly the essence of the story.

REFERENCES

Berne, E. (1961). *Transactional analysis in psychotherapy.* New York: Grove Press.

Erickson, M.H., & Rossi, E.L. (Eds.) (1980). *The collected papers of Milton H. Erickson on hypnosis: Vol. 2. Expectancy and minimal sensory cues in hypnosis.* New York: Irvington.

Erickson, M.H., & Rossi, E.L. (Eds.) (1980). *The collected papers of Milton H. Erickson on hypnosis: Vol. 1 The variety of indirect suggestion.* New York: Irvington.

Fisch, R. (1990). "The broader implications of Milton H. Ericskon's work." In S. Lankton (Ed.), *The broader implications of Ericksonian therapy* (pp. 1-5). New York: Brunner Mazel.

Frankl, V. (1967). *Psychotherapy and existentialism.* New York: Simon and Schuster.

Lustig, H. (1975). "The artistry of Milton H. Ericksin, M.D." A videotape.

Rosenthal, R., & Jacobson, L. (1968). *Pygmalion in the classroom.* New York: Holt, Rinehart and Winston.

CHAPTER 7

Whose Story Is This, Anyway?
A History of His-Story

Kay F. Thompson

This is a story about an exceptional man and his impact on an extended, self-selected family.

But it is also a story about all those people in that self-selected family who want to be like him.

But the end, yet the beginning, of the story is about the people who will benefit from his teaching as it filters down and is filtered down through all the ones who follow him.

His story is like a cascading waterfall on a powerful river. There is the main torrent of water, which, after it falls, continues to flow on as the river. But there are also drops and little streams and fallout from the waterfall that spray/stray far away, while others fall close to the mainstream, and others dry up before they ever land. Then there are others that start their own stream instead of rejoining the existing river.

But this particular story can only be my story of how I perceived his-story.

So it is a story of how I use what I think I learned from Erickson to help those who have special needs that must be met before they are able to learn trance. It will also speak to my two primary beliefs, that of motivation and the need for inexhaustible and unending practice of basic skills with hypnosis! I will address basic techniques in utilizing hypnosis and trance.

The essence of these stories is the distillate: the result of straining the original product repeatedly until it is reduced to a potent potion, a portion

136

of which can be applied sparingly as we learn how to mix it with our own ingredients to produce a product that is particularly personal and pleasing.

In this way, each of us takes the essence of what we saw in the substance of Erickson and each of us strains it through the sieve of our own perspective, thereby creating a new product. But in our insecure, needy, greedy way, we prefer for a while to interpret it as the original, and so the essence takes on many different extractions or configurations, none of which are the original, each continuing a filtered distillate of the original, until we forget that it is not the same as the original.

I wonder what it is that is in the molecular distillate that I absorbed from Erickson. I reflected on how I use what I think I learned. I am sure that my view is influenced by my clinical utilization, which requires a reorientation of the patient's physiology, not just psychology. And I don't always have a lot of time to accomplish this change "within their heads" before I go in to change some physical thing in their heads.

The intensity of my physical intervention utilizing trance requires development of a belief in the physiological alterations that can be activated and achieved during the hypnotic trance. We physicians and dentists do not have much time to work through the bonding and transference that occur with the use of hypnosis, directly, but they need to occur, indirectly, with the guidance of the doctor. About the time I get comfortable with just having to talk to people, I get a patient who is scheduled for surgery, and often I am also doing the surgery, so there is a different level of need and urgency and a deeper sense of commitment on my part.

There are a number of general opportunities I utilize to help this particular population with their special needs. Most of these patients have tried hypnosis before without success.

I believe that the work I do with hypnosis is grounded in: 1) my learned focus on the foundation of motivation for change within the patient; 2) my learned willingness and perceived obligation to employ every means to enhance and restructure, reinforce, and build on that motivation; and 3) the conviction that there is the potential for change.

In looking for commonalities in what takes place, I find a consistency in my acknowledgment and appreciation of individual differences. I cannot utilize others' predetermined approaches like frozen entrées, or even canned recipes, although I may start with the same cookbook. Nor must I rely on theories in those cookbooks. I must work with the ingredients on hand and I must have a taste for what is simmering with this one patient, different from any other I have seen, demanding a new adaptation of any recipe.

I find a constancy, in that all patients have within them the power to change, given the appropriate motivation and relearning. The change must fit their belief systems. We, as therapists, cannot do it for them. Accepting the patients' potential and the multiple variations in that potential makes it possible to work with those needs and motivations. The more the therapist can speak the true language of the patient, the better the patient is able to understand.

It is difficult to determine the "across-situations" incidence of consistency. It is the mixing and shifting back and forth from one approach to another, as required, that makes Ericksonian trance so difficult to analyze. He had the skill to be able to do the complex, simply.

But always, enhancement of motivation is the key I use to open the options the patient has locked out. Erickson understood and used these motivational differences. He was exceptionally smooth at slipping back and forth unnoticed, using his master keys on any locked door that presented itself. He would also combine and confuse what was behind the doors by using additional communicative tools. Neither the burglar nor the locksmith cares what combination of tools gets him in to the valuables. I am not concerned about where that lock came from in the past. I am concerned only that the patient is ready to change the future.

Motivation can come from different motivating factors, and a motivating factor can have multiple origins. One door can be opened with many keys, and one key can open many doors.

Since much of what occurs takes place in the unconscious, it is difficult to track. One constant is that trance is tracked by movement toward the future, as determined by the key motivation of the client.

SET ONE

How do I determine which key to use for the door that I am to help open? My first task is to determine the type of door and lock. The initial meeting is an inventory of the problem doors, so the patient is encouraged to talk, while I take scrupulous notes. Much can be learned without asking. I do ask what is being asked of me. The objective is to listen actively and observe carefully for the nonverbal communication as well as for the words. Then it is time to make a judgment, based on the perceived motivation.

The first personal skill, then, is in deciding what approach the patient needs, so that you can affect the effect by a change in your behavior and an offering of trance. The offering must vary, so you must know how your key fits each door, and this requires practice.

Each of us must practice to acquire the skills and techniques to express the appropriate aspect of our personality for that person in the personal way it is needed. One of the things that always was impressed on me in

Erickson his-story was to note his rigorous practice and self-discipline. He wrote out verbalizations and monitored his own behavior, ready to shift immediately as he observed minute changes in the patient. Because of his care and compassion for each person who came to him, he did all this to enrich his ability to reach the patient. He would listen intently for the tumbler to fall and act quickly when it did.

Practice, patience, creativity, and commitment—and always to work hard—these provide the rosin that smoothes the key for teaching trance. After you master basic direct, indirect, permissive, authoritarian, and confusion approaches—only then focus on storytelling and metaphor.

There are still those who say they just open their mouths and let their unconscious speak. It is OK to trust in and rely on the spontaneous unconscious, but only after there is an abundance of knowledge and experience in the spontaneous unconscious to rely on. If you are contemplating using a combination keyless lock, make sure you can remember the combination.

SET TWO

Once you know the many master keys you have available, how do you decide which key to begin with? Formal, informal, direct, indirect?

If hypnosis is the last hope for the client, formal trance is essential. I cannot just talk to that patient, because he has tried that and everything else. He talks to himself all the time and has learned how not to listen. My job is to teach him to listen again.

Two A

With formal trance I am rigid and I am structured, but I am also very permissive about things that don't matter, such as feet flat on the floor or eyes closed. I do not want to overload and distract the patient with things that are irrelevant to the trance.

The traditional approach sometimes involves asking the patient to do things that may seem a little silly. The key here is to identify them first as ridiculous, before asking that they be done, which takes away the excuse and embarrassment. I may say, "Look, I'm going to ask you to do something silly, but that's OK, do it anyway. Hold both arms out in front of you, like this . . ." The safe, traditional approach provides you with invaluable feedback and lets the patient know that something is happening outside of his conscious control. This is reassuring. You both know the combination has the potential to be effective on that lock.

Two B

Indirectly approaching the formal technique reduces the stage hypnosis attitude. One way I might do this is to put on my sincerely curious attitude and get the patient involved in questions and factual observations that lead gently into trance. By pointing out the obvious, one defuses the defenses and resistances and lets the key work more easily.

The "Have you ever . . ." and "Did you notice . . ." questions narrow from generalities to specifics and utilize the specifics of different physiological attentions, abilities, and inabilities. This gentle, slow development of logical attention to facts mixed with memories lends itself to an awareness of the different state that is developed. Gently turning the key can slowly bring it around.

Sometimes locks that won't open can be oiled more easily than forced. When you acknowledge facts in a way that demands looking at the facts differently, it also demands looking at the faces differently.

SET THREE

"You can't make that key work. It can't be done. It isn't the proper way." That challenge becomes the induction technique.

"See if you can" is a very effective system for defusing resistance, as well as removing the belief that the therapist/doctor must be in control. "See if you can balance your fingers exactly evenly on your knees. Of course, you know you can't, but try anyway." The published Erickson case of "See if you can pace a little more slowly" includes that type of challenge.*

If the challenge is an acceptable one, the individual not only goes into trance, but learns that it was pure personal skill that provided that opportunity.

SET FOUR

Teach hypnosis separately from the problem and from utilization of trance. There are at least two doors into different parts of that house, and we will go in using a key for a different door in a different way.

Patients may perceive a threat to their symptom inherent in going into trance. It is almost as if there were a contract stating, "If I go into trance, then I am obligated to use hypnosis for my problem." If the patient is not

*Erickson, M.H. (1967). Further techniques of hypnosis—utilization techniques. In Jay Haley (Ed.), *Advanced Techniques of Hypnosis and Therapy: Selected Papers of Milton H. Erickson, M.D.* New York: Grune & Stratton, 34-35.

yet certain that is her goal, then the easiest way to address it is simply to resist going into trance. The therapist, therefore, not approaching the issue directly but approaching it nevertheless, says, "All right, today we are going to teach you about hypnosis. That is all. Next time you come in we can discuss whether or not you want to use it to help you with your problem." In that way the patient is free to learn trance. Once it has been learned, it probably will become an appealing system for unlocking the possibilities within the problem.

SET FIVE

Another belief in my locksmith system is that I am glad if the door doesn't open easily, as if it were already unlocked.

It takes an intelligent person to want a second opinion, and to get it by testing me. It makes sense for the referred patient to be skeptical. I express my admiration for the person who comes in critical and suspicious, asking many appropriate questions. The patient who gives me a difficult time during the initial appointment is reassured that I respect his hesitation and recognize that he is not "gullible." As the patient continues to challenge me during the induction, he demonstrates his wisdom. After all, once I pass the test the patient is then free to trust me to be responsible in dealing with the real reason for which he was referred.

This acceptance on my part permits me to see through the more abrasive patient to the scared yet hopeful person within, the person I want to help.

SET SIX

"This key used to work. I'm sure it still will."

With all patients I maintain a "Yes, but" philosophy. It follows the principles of reframing and is an important part of defusing the importance of the symptom for the patient. "Yes, but" can be portrayed in a number of ways, all of which indicate that you agree with patients, but then by adding consequences or getting them to look at things from a different perspective, you get them to see the advantage of change.

SET SEVEN

"It may be important that you keep this key, even though it doesn't fit very well anymore" is the next step beyond "Yes, but."

No matter what patients say in a negative fashion about the symptom, I can defend the symptom. This validates their integrity in having the symptom, removing the need for them to feel guilty for not giving it up, and unconsciously supports their own esteem. In this interaction I permit patients to point out to me all the bad, negative things about their symptom, while I emphasize all the positive things about it.

I also express my serious concern about what can ever take the place of the symptom, and I must be convinced by patients that they can live quite nicely without that impediment. I may voice my concern about having them give up the symptom, and I become quite resistant to the idea of change. They become committed to convincing me that they can, should, and must give up the symptom and change! Reluctantly I can then agree to continue to work with them to get the new key.

SET EIGHT

One key technique I have used for years involves pointing out to the patient how the symptom might have actually been needed and useful at the time it was acquired. Then I become curious about how it got "sidetracked." Somehow the training never progressed beyond that sidetrack. We wonder about how to get that sidetracked train car out onto the main line so we can change the destination to a positive one. I remain very respectful of the patient's right to have and have had the symptom.

I wonder aloud about the mechanism, determination, and persistence that let the symptom continue to sidetrack the patient and what it was that blocked the tracks. Did no one bother to let him know the schedule had changed, so he could make arrangements to hook up with a new train? This lets the rest of the world go by every day, riding in shiny new trains, looking disdainfully at that old car off on the side, getting ever more dusty and rusty and out of date.

But then a train aficionado comes along who recognizes value in that old car. It had a good strong structural foundation, with a frame constructed of top-quality metal and wood, better than many builders of today use. First it is necessary to clean and restore the inside, and that is quite a job! We have to throw away the moth-eaten upholstery and get rid of the mildew smell. Eliminate the musty, mold-infected velvet and change to smooth, fresh leather. Clean the dirt and soot off the windows so one can see through the panes again. Clean the darkened interior until the light wood paneling glows richly. Scrub and wax those hardwood floors until they shine, too.

Once the inside is clean and resilient, it's time to renew the function of the car. The electrical system must be sandblasted and wires checked to eliminate short circuits, and the power of the generators increased. The mechanical system must be overhauled and lubricated and any necessary parts replaced. Then the shell of the train car can be cleaned and dents removed. Finally it is painted, waxed, and polished. There is no resemblance to that rusty, dirty, old car that sat stalled on that sidetrack for so long. Now, with small, gentle moves at first, it can begin to approach the main track. Its function has been restored, and it is ready to be attached to the newer, faster cars that come by.

It selects the train and track with the destination that pleases it, and goes on its way, leaving behind the residue of the renovation, ready to rejoin the main line. It can look back on what it once was, proud to know it learned to know what it needed to do to become what it is going to be.

SET NINE

"This key just doesn't work."

Acknowledging the patient's strong willpower by formally and directly trying to hypnotize him and succeeding in failing will satisfy the patient's need to resist and to know that he retains control. He can also take pride in countering my best efforts, and that pride permits him to feel sorry for me and conciliatory toward me. That allows us to go on and just be curious about the problem, asking a few questions about it and wondering about the facts of it related to life. An indirect trance induction can be utilized. Since he has already demonstrated that I cannot hypnotize him, there is no longer any need to resist, which he knows he could always do if he chose to.

SET TEN

"Let's give up on this key."

After you have worked diligently and unsuccessfully with patients who succeed in failing to go into trance, what else can you do? You explain that in a minute you are going to ask them to complete this experience. As you say that, you can see the clients take a deep breath and heave a sigh of relief at having successfully resisted all your efforts. Right then they drop their guard and their resistance, and you have about fifteen seconds to make one or two powerfully worded suggestions about the next visit, including the enhanced trance-ability they may discover.

SET ELEVEN

What of the door that appears locked, but is ready to go to pieces when touched in the right place?

Once I have made my paradigm shift and set aside my assumption that I knew anything at all about how the world worked, I have broadened my options. Now I can demonstrate to patients that the usual way is not my way, which encourages them to respond more spontaneously.

Each meeting is a unique encounter. As we tailor the therapy to each person's patterns, we must be ready with quick on-site alterations when the unexpected fit presents itself.

Sometimes the therapist introduces the concept of confusion in order to help patients be receptive to change by disrupting the normal impulse pattern of the thinking channel and opening new lines of communication. Trying a newer, more suitable lock may lead to the discovery that the fit is much more secure than the old way that seemed so safe.

Make quantum leaps in diagnosis and pull the rigid rug out from under patients. This requires risk. Go further than strict theory might, but leave the interpretation open to patients to resolve.

Little words can be contract words: Hook the unconscious, which hears them in ways the conscious mind does not. When you think back, remember that you were asked to do regression, to go into trance at other times, in other places. Regression is what I asked you to do with the remark, "When you think back, you remember when." It was done so simply that you did not need to realize it was a request for a regression. *When* you pay attention to the little contract words, *then* you begin to understand their power, and you can *try* them out. Have you done that *yet?* We must pay attention to the word's power, since words do possess power. Be possessive about the power of words, those symbols for experience and power for change.

In summary, language and motivation are the combination of keys I work with to open these doors long rusted shut.

The language of trance can be the therapeutic tool for change. Language reflects back on all the things Erickson taught me to learn. The intricacy of the simple words provides the opportunity for multilevel messages and manages to manipulate the mood of the moment to maintain the method by which we mean to maneuver the change.

All of these methods cross barriers from one theory to another, just as Erickson combined and utilized all types of intervention, not bound by anyone's rules to stay within any one parameter. Today this is an acceptable and desirable approach. Just as times change, so can people change.

This basic piece of my story as unlocked from his story can add to your repertoire for health and growth, a synonym for change, the essence of Erickson's life and his-story.

PART III

Overviews

CHAPTER 8

Ericksonian Therapy Demystified: A Straightforward Approach

Betty Alice Erickson

INTRODUCTION

Milton H. Erickson, M.D., is widely regarded as the one of most innovative and creative therapists who ever lived. His accomplishments were legendary—he reestablished hypnosis as a legitimate therapeutic tool, published more than 100 scholarly articles primarily on the use of hypnosis, founded the American Society of Clinical Hypnosis, and was its founding journal editor for 10 years. He is also widely regarded as the originator of brief and strategic therapy and spent the last several years of his life teaching mental health professionals.

I have the good fortune of being Erickson's daughter and was lucky enough to participate in a great deal of his teaching. More people than I can count have practiced learning hypnosis with me as a teaching and demonstration subject. As you know, hypnosis is an extraordinarily effective way of teaching and communicating, so I was able to learn a great deal working with Erickson and hypnosis.

I have a vested interest in making sure that what people understand as Ericksonian approaches is true to my father's philosophy. An Ericksonian approach to psychotherapy is respectful, effective, creative, and helps the patient achieve legitimate goals in the most productive and wholesome ways possible. I have also have a vested interest in helping people under-

stand an Ericksonian approach in ways that will encourage them to practice and hone their abilities. While Erickson is impossible to duplicate, his
methods of therapy are eminently replicable.

In this chapter, I am not discussing psychotherapy for psychotic or
severely mentally ill persons. This population has special needs, although
they can be treated with Ericksonian psychotherapy.

Ericksonian psychotherapy is deceptively simple. Like peeling an onion,
one can begin with the top, the easiest, the most obvious issue. If a patient
presents with any number of problems—"I had a miserable childhood, I
was beaten by my mother, I can't hold a job, I have no friends, and
furthermore, I suck my thumb whenever I feel insecure"—Erickson would
start with getting that thumb out of the patient's mouth. This is also the
most respectful approach—maybe, just maybe, teaching the patient how
to cope without public thumbsucking, will be enough to start a snowball
effect. People will respond to the patient differently when thumbsucking is
not an issue; because of this different treatment, the patient will behave
differently.

Each patient deserves the opportunity to build productively upon his
own changes without the interference of the therapist. Sometimes, when a
car is stuck at a bump in the parking lot, only a small push is needed so that
the car can begin to drive away. Sometimes, more is needed. Erickson used
the example of a chicken hatching out of its egg. One little piece of shell
removed might be enough to make the crack large enough so that the chick
can emerge.

The second part of that metaphorical example also applies to an
Ericksonian style. Each chick must crack the egg and emerge by itself. If
too much help is given, the chick is weakened and won't survive. Erickson
knew that the only way a patient can build strength for independence is
through self and industriously utilizing the strengths that are already
within the person.

COMMUNICATION

Erickson understood communication. Words are not only vehicles for our
thoughts, they structure our thinking. Additionally, there are clearly understood rules of communication that we know we know without knowing
how we know or even exactly what we know, but we know we know. For
example, if I say, "Let's do it your way this time," I am clearly saying that
next time we'll do it my way.

Words have precise meanings. A deliberate and precise vocabulary is
one hallmark of an effective Ericksonian therapist. Mauve means something different than pink, and rose is different than either mauve or pink.

Even when we can't clearly verbally describe the difference, we know there is one.

In order to communicate effectively, there must be common understanding of the meanings of words. We all like to believe that words have specific meanings and that these meanings are the ones that we have. We are reinforced in that belief because most of the time, we do communicate with each other. But there are many times when the same words have completely different meanings.

Erickson loved to illustrate these differences by telling a story. I have a cousin who was born the same day as I was. Once, when he and I were both about three years old, there was a gathering of relatives at my grandparents' farm. My cousin and I came downstairs ready for bed. We were the same size, both of us had blond curls and big blue eyes with little round glasses, and we were identically dressed in long white nightgowns. Our assorted aunts marveled that, dressed as we were, it was hard to tell the country boy from the city girl. My father announced that it was easy to tell the country boy from the city girl. He looked intently at us and said, "Kids, look at the piggies!" My country cousin rushed to the window and looked out. I sat down, lifted my foot, and looked at my toes. The message of this teaching tale is obvious.

There are also rules for nonverbal communication that are just as clear and specific and that we learn without knowing that we've learned and know without knowing we know. There is only one area on your body that can be touched by a stranger, the rules say, at any time and with impunity. That's your upper arm or shoulder. Even those areas are limited to the side and back of your upper arm and the top or back of your shoulder. We all know that without knowing we know unless we stop to think about what we know.

OBSERVATION

Observation is the key to effective communication. Observation of the world around us enables us to build a framework of usual and ordinary behavior that gives the ability to see and understand differences. The therapist also must know the world of the patient in order to use that world as a means of instituting change. The use of the patient's world as one mechanism of change enables avoidance of resistance.

Erickson was interested in learning about the behavior of others his whole life. I have always been amused by one story of his curiosity about people. When he was a boy, he often got up early on schooldays to make paths in new snow. Then he would hide and observe his schoolmates as they walked to school. If the path Erickson had made was straight and direct, everyone followed it. That's common sense. What intrigued Erickson, however, was that he could make the path curved and indirect and still people would follow it. That piece of information was one he kept his whole life.

Part of his ability to observe clearly and objectively came from his life experiences. He spent a year bedfast with infantile paralysis, and he also had certain physical handicaps. Those parts of his life are well known. Fortunately, most of us will never have the opportunity to develop those observational learnings. The philosophy contained in that last sentence is a metaphor for Ericksonian therapy; obstacles, problems, handicaps, failures, all the vicissitudes of life can be handicaps and obstacles or, flipped, they are opportunities to expand knowledge because one never knows when such learning will be useful.

Erickson also served as an examiner for the Draft Board during World War II and evaluated thousands of military inductees. While these were a limited segment of American society—physically healthy young men—this exposure provided him with a vast amount of information about human behavior, thought, action, and reaction. Fortunately, again, probably none of us will have that opportunity either. We do have the opportunity, however, to exercise the curiosity and delight in learning that were an instrumental part of Erickson's abilities.

HYPNOSIS

Another tactic to sharpen observational skills is the use of hypnosis. Erickson emphasized the use of hypnosis and the principles of hypnotic communication. He often said that he couldn't define exactly where hypnosis began and other communication ended. Expertise in the use of hypnosis can be developed by learning and practicing formal trance work. Becoming aware of the naturalistic trance states that we are all expert in slipping into and in producing in others is another path.

Part of a trance state is accessing unconscious resources. The wisdom that each of us has gained from living and experiencing life that is stored in the unconscious can be elicited with self-hypnosis.

All of us have had flashes of intuitive understanding or insight. That is knowledge we have but don't fully realize that we have. Trances help access it. When Erickson said, "Trust your unconscious," he was referring to using that vast storehouse of experiences and knowledge from life experiences. He was suggesting that we learn to access these abilities as an addition to the thought and hard work that is necessary in planning therapy. Learning to use self-hypnosis skillfully enough so that one can slip in and out of a trance easily enables one to access these abilities and resources. People generally tell us a great deal about themselves and what they want and the tasks of truly seeing, hearing, and understanding are made easier by a trance state.

One of the least discussed and most important parts of Erickson's work was his ability to join in a healthy way with his patients. Erickson practiced in a different time and era and, in some ways, parts of his interactions with his patients cannot be duplicated. Other parts can be. Erickson had respect, appreciation, and genuine liking for his students and patients. This free-will offering was given without constraints and could therefore be accepted. This sense of value and appreciation was a part of his therapy as surely as were his creative interventions. Hypnosis can help build this sense of appreciation and respect.

REALITY

Another important part of Ericksonian therapy is a firm adherence to reality. No matter what reality is, every person must learn to recognize and accept it. The only way to meet goals, to satisfy needs, and reach peace and contentment is to build upon reality and to focus capabilities on coping with reality.

Reality itself is unchanging, but perceptions of reality and reactions to it vary with both circumstances and time. Not being one of the first people chosen to be on a sports team in grade school is an unchangeable reality. As result, a person might have felt rejected and incompetent. If, however, that person was in a wheelchair and happy to be scorekeeper, the perception of not being chosen would be markedly different.

On a timeline, looking back, there is a realization that being chosen first for a fifth-grade volleyball team really doesn't have much to do with a productive adult life, and there may even be amusement at how important that really unimportant event once seemed.

Separation of hard reality from an easy and pleasant fantasy in ways that invite or even allow recognition and acceptance can be difficult and perplexing at best. But without effective coping with reality, patients are not able to have the experiences that teach them to manage their lives appropriately and productively.

Recognizing and separating reality from fantasy, wishes, idealism, and hopes is basic. Being able to offer alternatives, options, and other perspectives in such an intriguing, appealing, and appetizing way that the patient is enabled to expand perceptions and reach legitimate goals more effectively is therapy. Hypnosis enhances therapy because trances allow bypassing of automatic conscious defenses and accesses unconscious resources.

METAPHORS

Metaphorical and indirect interventions are probably the most widely recognized part of Ericksonian psychotherapy. Many therapists regard teaching tales and metaphors as the most difficult and complex part of an Ericksonian framework. Formulating an elegant, multilevel, indirect, complicated yet understandable therapeutic metaphor is definitely a skilled art. The effective building and use of metaphors, however, is a learnable skill. Erickson spent the last years of his life teaching professionals that the creation of therapeutic metaphors is a learnable skill and the use of those metaphors can be a very effective part of the whole framework of therapy.

Metaphors delivered in a naturalistic trance state are even more effective. A trance state allows accessing of unconscious understanding on multiple levels. Trance states allow clients freedom to tailor the message within the metaphor to the most helpful and personalized therapeutic form. Because the clients have drawn their own conclusion, they have created their own interventions from raw material. Resistance is avoided and independence nurtured.

I am going to illustrate building of metaphors, first using a common issue as the problem and then with case examples. The case examples also illustrate the use of naturalistic trance states as a part of communicative interactions.

Inability to set reasonable requirements on the behaviors of others is a frequent client complaint. Clients who have difficulty in setting limits comfortably in their personal lives can develop new perspective on their strengths when they focus on their work roles. I help them understand that learning to set limits comfortably is already part of them; they already know how to do it. All they have to do is learn different ways to do what they already do so well. This gives a framework of already successful behavior upon which to build.

We all know what credit limits are. Credit cards and banks have made us quite aware of them. We all know we have credit limits at the bank. We also have credit limits with friends and co-workers but without knowing that we have them. I frequently use myself as a part of therapeutic examples. There is a joining and a modeling that takes place. I point out that if the client and I were co-workers and we went on our coffee break and I had forgotten my money, my client would have no hesitation in paying for my coffee.

If this occurred the next day, the client would probably still pay, but would note it in the internal tally-book in her head. If, on the third day, I still had no money, the client would probably say something but might still pay. I doubted, however, if this situation would continue on for the rest of the week. A co-worker's credit limit is three or four coffees and that is perfectly acceptable.

The next truism solidifies the acceptance of this reality. I point out that everyone has a credit limit. The problem is not one of recognizing that piece of reality, but the skill of discerning the limits of each person's credit. It is clear that people we care about have a higher credit limit than do co-workers.

It is also clear that people who run their credit up to the limit need to have the opportunity to pay back some of their obligation. It certainly wouldn't be acceptable if a credit card company kept our spending limit a secret from us. It then becomes obligatory for the client to let the debtor know ways in which to manage reciprocation. This description reframes powerlessness to personal power.

This discussion also has changed the presenting problem from lack of boundaries and powerlessness to a more manageable problem of learning a skill. Additionally, it gives clients a verbal peg upon which to hang new behaviors. This new verbal description can elicit and enable new thinking patterns.

Occasionally, a client will insist that a loved one has no credit limit— that this loved one can ask for anything anytime and it is the client's duty and obligation to provide. That doesn't happen often because the boundaries can be drawn to the limits of ridiculousness. Whether or not the client's loved one would actually ask for a particular response is immaterial. You, as the therapist, are merely trying to understand the client's position.

If the client is unwilling to acknowledge any limits on willingness to give, recognition must be given to the truism that what is tolerated provides markers for what is received. In the work world, for example, if a supervisor tolerates tardiness, most people will be late far more often than they would be for a supervisor who docked their pay for every minute of tardiness.

There must also be a concurrent acceptance that the client is abdicating responsibility. It is the responsibility of those who know and who give to insist on limitations. That's why children have parents and banks have collection departments.

An acceptance of the abdication of responsibility is a paradox and provides a foothold for the building of acceptance of more responsibility. In this way, the therapist can use whatever the client offers as a place for growth. Even maladaptive behavior can provide a foothold for more appropriate learnings.

Case Number One

Tom was an architect who had hit and killed a pedestrian while driving. It was truly an unavoidable accident. The pedestrian had been running across a four-lane highway at night and Tom saw him only an instant before the impact. Tom was well within the speed limit; no citation was issued.

Tom wrote an apology to the family and contributed to a charity in the name of the victim. He drew a number of charts and diagrams to convince himself in black and white that he was not to blame; there was no possible way he could have seen the victim, and even if he had, it would not have been physically possible to stop the car. However, he was still consumed by guilt and "what-if's." His guilt was complicated because he also was angry at himself for not accepting that the accident was not his fault and that he had been completely unable to avoid it. He knew the accident was entirely the victim's fault. That increased his guilt because he was angry at the victim who had died for being at fault in the accident.

Tom was intellectually oriented. His world was one of logic, sensible conclusions, and charts. Paradoxically, his world of logic was exactly what was blocking him because he didn't know how to use his tools of logic and common sense to make himself feel better. One goal was to expand his world of responses and help him tap into other ways of understanding and accepting.

Tom already had the experiential learnings that sometimes logic and common sense aren't necessary or even useful. There is no logical or commonsense reason to like vanilla ice cream better than chocolate. However, he was consciously fully committed to his logical approach. A naturalistic trance state induced by concentration on a metaphor would allow him to receive information on multiple levels.

I told him I wanted him to concentrate because I wanted to explain something to him. Overtly asking for his attention was the beginning of the induction. I asked him to picture a graph. I drew a right angle in the air with the vertical line to my right. This enabled him to visualize the graph from the more familiar perspective. As he looked at the imaginary lines, I put a question mark in my voice as I labeled them. "The 'y' axis goes up and down and the 'x' axis is horizontal?"

His nod combined with his fixed gaze indicated that he was in a light naturalistic trance. I continued. "The 'y' axis is our intellectual processes. We work with this most of the time. Most of our problems are solved in this way."

I gave examples that brought up memories of successful learnings in his past. As he looked within to remember, his focused attention was continued and reinforced. "When you first tried to tie your shoes, it was hard. But you practiced and learned. You didn't know your multiplication tables, but you studied hard. When you got your first computer, you practiced and read the instructions and asked people and figured it out. All that was on the 'y' axis, the intellectual thinking axis.

"The 'x' axis is the nonlogical part of you." I moved my hand to trace the horizontal bar. "You wouldn't trade your dog for a valuable purebred. There is no rhyme or reason to your liking for jam on cottage cheese, and you can't even explain why the sound of bagpipes is pleasant to you."

He smiled as he agreed because, logically, all those things were illogical but true. I explained that sometimes when an issue was on the 'x' axis, the nonlogical one, we attempted to resolve it by moving up the 'y' axis. We were most familiar and comfortable with that method and we certainly received reinforcement because problems were usually solved logically. "When the issue is nonlogical," I continued, "we can work on the 'y' axis forever and only get farther away from the issue."

He nodded thoughtfully as I demonstrated with my hands, and the concentrated focus of the naturalistic trance was broken. It is important to let preparation be absorbed by the client; ways of thinking have to be shifted and expanded. Later, I elicited the memory of that naturalistic trance by reminding him of the time we had talked about how things sometimes aren't logical.

I told him that conversation had reminded me about the time my guinea pig died. Wheetie was a dear little pet who whistled for lettuce every time we opened the refrigerator. We'd whistle back and he'd whistle louder. We really loved him. My son, who was only five years old, put him in the back yard to eat grass one day. The sun was too hot and Wheetie died. We were terribly sad. We wrapped him in red velvet and buried him by the railroad tracks so he could hear the whistle of the train.

That evening, my son went to a neighbor's house and invited the 15-year-old to go in the alley and light matches. Of course, the neighbor boy brought my son home. My son stood there waiting for his punishment. I knew that something out of the ordinary was happening—my son didn't light matches and if he did, he certainly would not invite a 15-year-old to observe. So I called my father, who was a very wise man. My father told me to put my son on my lap and explain to him that accidents happen and that he had already been punished by that accident far more than anyone else could ever punish him, and that was enough punishment because punishment is not always needed.

When I reminded Tom of the graph of intellectual and nonlogical thinking, I signaled that there were going to be multiple meanings to the story I was about to tell. The detail of burying the guinea pig by the railroad track so he could hear the whistle of the train reinforced that what we do isn't always logical. Sometimes logic does not help.

The rest of the story continued to pace. The suggestion, "already been punished by the accident and that was enough," followed in a somewhat circular and confusing fashion, which enhanced the development of a naturalistic trance state.

Tom listened to the story and agreed that my son had been punished more than enough by the accident. It was clear that he was also thinking about himself. The next visit, Tom carefully explained to me that accidents don't require punishment—that is why they are called accidents. He said he felt only pity for the victim because he had paid such a huge price for an error in judgment.

A metaphor allows listeners to draw their own conclusions. Resistance is circumvented because the conclusions belong to them. Further, each person draws upon previous self-learnings and puts this old knowledge into an expanded format.

Case Number Two

The following is another example of helping a client define and accept reality by using ordinary life as a model. Often the definition of words forms our thinking. This can be used as a therapeutic tool.

Frequently, abuse survivors want to forgive their abusers and are unable to accomplish this. They then feel even more shame and guilt because of this perceived failure.

Liz came to therapy with a number of problems, including some questions about parenting. The problem she most wanted resolved, however, stemmed back to her sexual abuse by her stepfather. She had been in therapy previously and felt that she had handled most of the issues around the abuse. She had even confronted her stepfather, and while he didn't deny the abuse, he had told her it wasn't that important because it had lasted only a few years and it had occurred a long time ago. He told her that, if she wanted, he would tell her he was sorry. She did and he did. Now she felt guilty because she hadn't forgiven him and was still angry at him even though he had apologized.

After several sessions where we discussed many issues and worked on parenting techniques, I felt we had developed a close and friendly relationship. I asked her to imagine crashing into me in the doorway of my office, knocking my appointment book out of my hands, and making me stumble against the wall. At first she was horrified at the thought. I insisted, so she tried.

When she could imagine walking into me and making me fall against the wall, I asked her to play out the entire scenario in her mind and to tell me what she saw. It took quite some time for her to be able to imagine the whole episode. She trusted me enough, however, to realize that I must have a good reason to ask her to do something so uncomfortable for her.

Finally, she was able to tell me what she could imagine. She pictured walking into me, my book flying out of my hand, the papers that are in it scattering on the floor, and me hitting the wall. She continued with the story. She would stop, tell me she was sorry and that she hadn't seen me. She would probably apologize more than once. Then she would make sure I was all right. Next, she would stoop down and pick up my book, gather the papers, put them back in the book, and hand it to me. She said she would probably apologize again for messing up the papers and she might even ask me if I wanted a glass of water.

I asked her to continue and imagine my reaction. She said she was sure I would forgive her because she was sorry and had done what she could to make up. I asked her what she would do if I didn't accept her apology. She said there was nothing she could do; she had done all she could do.

I helped her examine this imagined event. I told her that an apology has four parts: 1) I am sorry; 2) please forgive me; 3) I won't do it again; and 4) some sort of atonement. Liz had done this in her imagined episode even though she hadn't said the exact words of each part. She had said she was sorry more than once. That could be heard as asking for forgiveness. Telling me she hadn't seen me indicated that she wouldn't do it again. Picking up my papers and book and asking me if I wanted a glass of water was doing what she could to make amends.

She agreed with this analysis. I asked her if she would expect me to forgive her if she had done none of those parts. She was shocked and assured me that if she didn't apologize properly, she wouldn't deserve my forgiveness. I agreed. Why would I forgive her if she hadn't apologized?

Liz didn't ask me why I had wanted her to imagine walking into me in the doorway of my office and I didn't tell her. We didn't discuss that portion of the session again. We continued talking about parenting and marital concerns.

Two sessions later, Liz told me that she had suddenly understood why I had insisted she picture walking into me. She said she had been in her car driving to her mother and stepfather's home for a visit and anticipating the guilt she would feel when she saw her stepfather. Suddenly, she said, she had pictured him crashing into her in the door of my office and then telling her that if she wanted him to say he was sorry for hurting her, he would.

Liz told me she now knew forgiving her father wasn't really an issue for her. He hadn't apologized so why would she forgive him?

Case Number Three

Another way of helping a client to accept and deal with the realities of life situations is to teach them to step out of the situation and view it from a different perspective and with different eyes. Trance, formal or naturalistic, is a powerful tool here.

Patty was a 20-year-old college student who was completing the developmental task of separating from her parents. One of the issues she had not yet resolved was her anger at her mother for not parenting in a supportive way. Her description fell into the vague category of "she was never there for me." It was clear, however, that she wanted to let go of the hurt and anger that had developed from her recollection that her mother hadn't parented correctly.

Patty was willing to accept that her mother was a product of her own raising. She understood the metaphor of her mother pulling her own past behind her and being so focused on the load behind that she had no strength or ability to look forward. She had come to loving acceptance of her mother's flaws and knew beyond a doubt that her mother loved her a great deal.

She was still angry, however, that her mother had not shown her much support. She also felt a great deal of pain over some of the times that her mother had not supported her emotionally even though she knew these feelings were irrational. She felt stuck in letting go of that hurt.

I asked for her most vivid memory of a time when her mother had not cared for her appropriately. She told me of a time when she was eight years old and a neighbor boy had beaten her up. She had run home and had a distinct memory of standing in the living room screaming at her mother to go out and tell the boy to get out of their yard. Her mother had stood there weeping, unable to confront the 10-year-old neighbor child. Her mother had then begged her not to tell her father that the mother had not gone out to scold the boy.

Patty still remembered her feelings of fury and betrayal as her mother had stood motionless while the boy called taunts through the screen door. She cried as she told me about it.

I listened to her story with a great deal of sympathy. Then I asked her if she knew whom I felt the most compassion for? She looked at me expectantly, waiting for verbalization of my sympathy.

I did not answer the question I had asked; I waited until I had her focused attention. Then I told her that I wanted her to do some homework. I wanted her to come back and describe this scene from her mother's eyes. Then she would have the answer to my question.

She returned the next week and told me that she had been angry at me because she had not received the emotional support she felt she deserved from me. Nonetheless, she decided to do her homework. Lying in bed, she had replayed the scene over and over in her mind trying to step into her mother's shoes.

Finally, she said she had seen the pathos of a grown woman standing there helplessly wringing her hands, too afraid to protect her little girl who had been physically injured. She couldn't imagine the pain her mother must have felt when she realized that she couldn't confront a 10-year-old even when her eight-year-old daughter was telling her how to do it. She felt pity for her mother, knowing that she had been so fearful that she had to beg an eight-year-old not to tell her father about the mother's inadequacies.

Patty cried again as she talked about the pain her mother must have felt. She told me she knew the answer to the question I had asked the previous week: Her mother deserved the most sympathy, she said. Raising a daughter was her mother's most important task and she knew she was failing.

There was careful planning with this case. I had thoroughly investigated Patty's feelings about her family and herself and I knew that she was confident in her knowledge of her mother's genuine love. But she was stuck using the eyes of a hurt little girl when she remembered that scene, which symbolized much of the neglect she had felt in her childhood. I wanted her to interweave the pain of that little girl with her more current and adult learnings.

As an adult, Patty knew one of the most important tasks of a parent is protecting that parent's child. In this instance, her mother had failed painfully. She also knew her mother had shown her love and caring many times over the years.

Maturity and adulthood give us the ability to accept weaknesses in those we love if we decide to do so. That was the realization Patty needed to reach and in a way which would allow her to divest herself of childhood interpretations of adult behavior. With a new perception of her mother's failure and pain, her conclusion was inescapable. Her mother's inability to care for Patty in the way Patty wanted was sad, not anger-provoking.

TRUST

Trust is a vital part of therapy but clients often have difficulty trusting. The lack of trust is not limited to their therapists; it permeates their life and is generally because they have been used and abused as a matter of course.

Although most interactions are benign and trustworthy, people with a history of abuse tend to mistrust even when they want to trust. Learning to control their automatic mistrust allows them to have more options in life. Circumventing habitual mistrust in order to teach trust can be effectively done with a planned naturalistic trance. The trance bypasses resistance and helps clients elicit useful information from stored life experiences.

Let me illustrate using a naturalistic trance to help develop a trusting relationship with a client. When working with a client who has difficulty with trust, we discuss that. Then I ask the client, "Do you know why I am one of the most trustworthy people you'll ever meet?" This is an unusual question, which focuses the client's attention with an expectant receptivity. This can be the beginning of a naturalistic trance.

I enhance the development of that trance by asking the client to pay close attention because I'm going to be talking on two levels. "One level is conceptual," and I lift my hands to my head to indicate the intellectual understanding of concepts. "The other level is a personal level." I put my hands over my heart to symbolize that. Then I tell my client that I like him and add that I like all my clients, thereby ensuring that this admission of caring is heard on a professional basis. My clients all do know I like them and we look at each other and enjoy that moment of pleasure.

I move my hands to my head when I am speaking on a conceptual level and to my heart every time I speak about my personal feelings. The movement of my hands continues to focus their attention and emphasize that I am speaking on multiple levels.

I then tell my client, "On a conceptual level, which is very different than a personal level, conceptually speaking, I don't care. Win some, lose some. So, on a conceptual level, which is very different than a personal level, I really don't care what happens. It doesn't matter, even though, on a personal level, I do care because I do like you."

This is delivered in a trance-inducing verbal style. The confusing construction adds to the focus and the induction of a naturalistic trance, which allows the accessing of the unconscious.

"Because I don't care, even though I do care because I like you," I continue, "I am one of the few people you will ever meet, who wants nothing *from* you. I want things *for* you, and I want things *with* you. But I want nothing *from* you."

Then I shift positions and wait for the clients to absorb this. They usually smile as they integrate this with their experiential knowledge. Trust becomes easier for them. Often, they refer to this during later therapy and mention that they know that all I really want is the best possible life for them.

The problem of clients wondering if I am trustworthy merely because I am their therapist creates a struggle. They seek to reconcile the intellectual knowledge that I probably am trustworthy with their life experiences with people who used and abused them. The trance state allows them to draw upon their knowledge that most of life consists of benign, predictable, and trustworthy interactions with people; most life experiences are overt and open.

Clients also can remember the users and abusers in their lives. They easily realize that each of the abusers wanted something *from* them and was not concerned with their well-being.

The obvious conclusion is reached by the individual. Therefore, the resistance of conscious fears and reluctances is avoided; there is nothing to resist. There is also a paradox. While I want them to decide that I am trustworthy, I really don't care whether or not they reach that conclusion. But obviously I do care because I am making a concentrated effort to give them information. And they know I like them; part of my definition of therapy is that I like my clients, so while I can't care on one level, I do care on another.

I had one client who supposed his presenting problem was unique and special. He remarked that I wanted knowledge and expansion of my experience from him. I responded that if he weren't in my office that hour someone else would be and I learned and grew from all my clients.

The obvious and open issue of payment is something that has been agreed upon by both of us freely. Therefore, it doesn't fit in the category of wanting something from them.

SUMMARY

Milton Erickson was a remarkable and extraordinarily creative psychotherapist. His genius and exceptional abilities can't be taught. But Ericksonian psychotherapy is teachable, learnable, and replicable.

Ericksonian psychotherapy is known for the belief that therapy should always be designed to fit the patient. Each of us is unique. Therapy should access and use one's personal resources. There is no Ericksonian theory of psychotherapy because the infinite variety and uniqueness of people are too vast for any one theory to encompass. This type of therapy is pragmatic, respectful, and forward-looking.

Often it is seen as deceptively simplistic, but its clean elegance carries with it careful plans and thoughtfulness. Observation and utilization of the patient's own resources is vital. Understanding and using hypnosis to increase the receptivity of both the therapist and the patient is part of the overall approach. Unconscious resources can be accessed through both formal trances and naturalistic trances for both the patient and the therapist.

Resources patients have in their conscious and unconscious are fully adequate to construct and conduct a productive and worthy life. Part of the therapist's job is to teach the patient the accessing of these resources so that the resources and abilities can be used appropriately. Hypnosis is one way to do that.

Ericksonian psychotherapy emphasizes understanding of the patient's world gained from careful observation of the patient, from a knowledge of normal ranges of behavior and developmental tasks, and from study and comprehension of communicative rules and styles. This world can then be used as a means of productive change for the patient.

A central theme of Ericksonian psychotherapy is the acceptance and use of reality. People must experience and accept the realities of their lives. Only then can they cope successfully with their lives and the problems that are an unavoidable part of living. Acceptance of unpleasant reality, however, sometimes meets with resistance, and Ericksonian psychotherapy often uses an indirect approach in order to circumvent this.

Ericksonian psychotherapy recognizes that people generally know much more than they realize they know and that their unconscious is a vast storehouse of previously learned coping abilities. Therapy is a way to help patients to access these resources and hypnosis, with its access to the unconscious mind, gives people the ability to utilize previous learnings.

The use of metaphors, one of the most easily identifiable facets of Ericksonian psychotherapy, is a learnable skill. Therapeutic metaphors are one way of inducing a fixated focus of attention, which accesses the unconscious in a light or naturalistic trance. Metaphors can be created to help a person step into another's world so that offered information and alternatives can be easily accepted.

Reduction of issues to the bottom line of reality often helps the therapist construct a teaching tale. A story can be told that offers an understanding of the reality in the patient's world from an alternative perspective. Grief can be part of the patient's world. That is the reality. It can be seen, from a different perspective, as a loss of hope. It also can be understood, from yet another perspective, as reluctance to accept an ending.

Ericksonian psychotherapy is built on the vast potential of the unconscious, and consequently has unlimited potential. Sometimes therapists lack confidence to rely on these potentials. With careful planning and objective observation and an appreciation of the benign wisdom of the unconscious, along with constant practice and objective monitoring of the processes, therapeutic abilities are enhanced and an Ericksonian perspective refined.

CHAPTER 9

Good News for a Change: Optimism, Altruism, and Hardiness as the Basis for Erickson's Approach

Catherine Walters & Ronald A. Havens

Several months ago an editor who published Ericksonian texts informed a colleague that interest in Ericksonian approaches is on the wane and that, consequently, she is reluctant to support the publication of any new texts on the subject. From her point of view, Erickson's uncommon techniques have been incorporated into the established therapeutic schools and his work now has little new to offer.

These perceptions about what is happening to the Ericksonian movement are chilling because they may turn out to be right. Over the years, numerous efforts have been made to minimize the conflicts or differences between Erickson's approach and the approaches used by those within the psychiatric, psychotherapeutic, and hypnotherapeutic mainstreams. To make Ericksonian therapy more palatable (and marketable?), emphasis has been placed on his innovative techniques while his conceptual disagreements with other schools of therapy have been downplayed. Ericksonian therapists have sought to belong, to be accepted by, and to contribute to the establishment rather than to challenge or change it, and now we risk being absorbed by it.

Blurring the boundaries between Ericksonian psychotherapy and more traditional models may have served a good purpose originally; it introduced Erickson's novel approach to the broader field with a comforting emphasis on commonalities rather than differences. However, Erickson *was* different. His work represents a completely new therapeutic paradigm, a dramatic redefinition of the basic nature and purpose of therapy itself, not merely a fascinating collection of technically impressive hypnotic and therapeutic techniques. Erickson's underlying assumptions, his fundamental views regarding people and life, are essentially different from other forms of therapy. Thus far, the therapy field has missed this point. A few of his techniques and some of his observations regarding the unconscious mind have been borrowed, but the monumental paradigmatic shift that his work represents has gone unrecognized and unacknowledged.

This brings us to the good news. We believe that there is an important chapter yet to be written in the Ericksonian saga. This chapter has its foundation in the new "science of well-being" (Myers, 1992, p. 19) and in the slow, but decisive paradigmatic shift that this science is creating in the health and helping professions. The emerging paradigm—labeled *the wellness paradigm*—is slowly moving medicine and psychology away from an analysis of illness and negative emotions. Instead, these fields, like Erickson, are moving toward an understanding of how people stay healthy and happy.

Just as Erickson's legacy seems about to be lost, medical and psychological research is finally beginning to demonstrate the validity of his unique underlying assumptions—that people have all the resources they need to be healthy and happy, and that wellness, not illness, is the appropriate focus of psychotherapy.

This may be one of the most important chapters in the Ericksonian story because the new wellness research offers direct empirical support for Erickson's therapeutic goals and observations about people. Specifically, we propose that the essence of Erickson's genius was his knowledge that a healthy human being is: 1) optimistic, 2) future-oriented, 3) connected to people, and 4) convinced of his or her own capacity to influence life events. These understandings grew from Erickson's personal experiences and his finely honed observations. They also directed his actions as a therapist. We believe that Erickson knew something the rest of the field has tended to overlook, and we suggest it was *how to be well.* If this is the case, the more we can learn about the factors responsible for our physical and mental well-being, the more we should be able to understand and replicate his work. That would be very good news indeed.

It has been suggested that Erickson's complex approach is not well suited to the reductionistic scientific method because he rarely did the same thing twice and refused to present his working hypotheses in testable form. Nonetheless, we maintain that Erickson's clinical writings and his actual work with patients reflect a coherent, consistent set of fundamental observations about people. Further, we submit that these observations are testable and, in fact, are currently being tested by those involved in wellness research.

The empirical process of sifting and sorting the factors associated with wellness is only just beginning. Still, we believe that the weight of current evidence already clearly links Erickson's pioneering work and the wellness paradigm. Our goal here is to direct your attention to these connections. We hope to demonstrate that things like optimism, altruism, and hardiness — all critical components of wellness — are also critical elements of an Ericksonian approach. We also hope to demonstrate that Erickson saw something akin to wellness as a basic goal for his patients and that a majority of his interventions were specifically designed to create wellness. These are the premises of the Ericksonian chapter we present here.

Accordingly, we will begin with a discussion of the fundamental differences in content and purpose between the traditional therapeutic paradigm and the paradigm used by both Erickson and the wellness movement. Next, we will introduce three of the central features of wellness — optimism, altruism, and hardiness — and discuss the relevance of these qualities to Erickson's personal style and therapeutic work. We also will describe cases wherein Erickson accomplished a therapeutic outcome by encouraging or utilizing one or more of these qualities with his patients.

ILLNESS OR WELLNESS

Noted psychiatrist Thomas Szasz once said, "Happiness is an imaginary condition, formerly attributed by the living to the dead, now usually attributed by adults to children and children to adults" (Myers, 1992, p. 8). This vision of happiness as an unattainable figment of the imagination captures the general pessimism therapists have been saddled with for the past century. Indeed, as we survey the current landscapes of psychology and medicine, we cannot fail to notice the lack of a certain *joie de vivre*. Countless books and articles are written each year outlining the actual and potential sources of human misery. Studies of negative emotions, such as depression and anxiety, are numerous, while experiments exploring positive emotions, such as happiness or satisfaction, have, until quite recently, been few and far between.

This lack of interest in the kinder and gentler aspects of human welfare may be ascribed in great part to the fact that medicine and psychology are dominated by a conceptual concern with illness or pathology. Indeed, a pathology paradigm has been the consensual model in these fields for over 100 years. The pathology model has directed the questions researchers have asked and the issues they have studied. It also has suggested, in an indirect way, what conclusions and actions are clinically appropriate. Consequently, all orthodox theories of physical and mental functioning have assumed that health is the absence of illness and that the elimination of illness is the overriding goal.

As a framework for organizing data and explaining events, the pathology model, like virtually any conceptual model, does have some utility. However, as we shall see, this model's central assumptions regarding the nature of healing are limited and flawed (cf. Peterson & Bossio, 1991). Spence (1982) has speculated that any long-lived theory survives not merely because it has some historical truth value, but because it provides a compelling narrative metaphor for practitioners. The abiding narrative metaphor within the pathology model traditionally has been a metaphor of war. This can be demonstrated simply by examining the descriptive language of our professions. We battle physical and mental illnesses. Bacteria and viruses are the common enemies on the medical front. On the psychological front, the theories of the profession often place people in a battle against themselves. In the past, many wars were waged against an unruly id or a rigid superego. Currently, people fight depressive cognitions, struggle with a host of addictive behaviors, or resist the misfortunes of faulty parenting. In each of these struggles, clinicians have devised strategies to locate, identify, and eliminate the causes of the so-called mental diseases. This "search and destroy" mentality is deeply embedded in the helping professions, as well as in the popular mind. As such, it constricts our clinical actions and constrains our clinical goals.

When war is the defining metaphor, people may "survive," they may even "recover." But questions of happiness or pleasure do not take precedence on a battleground. Happiness or the capacity for joy seems irrelevant or unattainable under these conditions.

The pathology model, with its narrative of struggle and conflict, stands in stark contrast to the work and writings of Erickson, for whom happiness was both a personal and a therapeutic goal. Erickson clearly had some very definitive ideas about what is required to live life happily, and he obviously believed that the attainment of happiness is a legitimate and focal goal of therapy. There are countless references to happiness in his writings and his conversations. In speaking of his work with patients, Erickson once stated, ". . . they come into the room to disclose their unhappiness. I send them out to establish their happiness" (Haley, 1985, Vol. 2, p. 111). He defined his therapeutic role as, ". . . presenting to patients their way of living happily in a world of reality" (Haley, 1985, Vol. 2, p. 87). In short, Erickson was concerned with creating happiness and well-being, rather than with eradicating illness.

It is impossible to comprehend Erickson's work if we view it through the prism of pathology. There simply is no way to integrate his therapeutic approach into such a framework. The questions of interest to Erickson, his basic frame of reference, and the narrative metaphors that describe his work are completely incompatible with a disease or illness orientation. His approach represents a completely different paradigm.

Erickson flatly rejected the disease emphasis of the traditional theoretical schools. In fact, he rejected all attempts to explain the nature and purposes of various psychopathological symptoms on the grounds that, "No person can really understand the individual patterns of learning and response of another" (Erickson, 1980, Vol. 1, p. 154). Consequently, it is tempting to assume that Erickson operated solely on an intuitive basis. Just because Erickson was atheoretical and was disinterested in using psychopathology as a reference point in speculating about clients, however, does not necessarily imply that he operated without a conceptual compass of any sort.

Although Erickson rejected the "Procrustean bed" of theory, he certainly maintained a definable set of observations regarding human behavior. These observations, in turn, can and have been reduced to a describable set of values or a definable point of view that informed his writing, his therapy, and his teaching (Rosen, 1982b). His overall point of view, including his emphasis on the attainment of happiness, bears little resemblance to the pathology paradigm, but it does bear a remarkable resemblance to the fresh research findings pertaining to wellness. As the wellness literature continues to flower and grow, it becomes increasingly apparent that Erickson was a man ahead of the times.

Erickson accomplished therapy by living well and by promoting the ingredients of wellness long before the wellness movement began. He recognized that optimism, altruism, and self-efficacy are among the most fundamental ingredients of well-being and of healing, the essence of a life worth living, and he used these recognitions to guide his interventions.

Many metaphors capture the flavor of Erickson's underlying paradigm; the healthy garden, the resourceful farmer, and ecology metaphors that describe nature's evolving patterns of change and growth. He tapped into the classic American narrative: life, liberty, and the pursuit of happiness. These metaphors capture the essential elements of Erickson's approach, and they reflect his therapeutic goals for his clients. Erickson represents the quintessential all-American optimist absorbed by the search for happiness in a profession dominated by a pessimistic preoccupation with pathology.

ERICKSON AND OPTIMISM

In her paper at the Third International Congress on Ericksonian Approaches to Hypnosis and Psychotherapy in 1986, Kristina K. Erickson, M.D., Erickson's youngest daughter, described her father like this: "He was future-oriented, optimistic and practical. He encouraged productivity and enjoyment of life" (Erickson, K., 1988, p. 379). It is hard to formulate a more straightforward and knowledgeable description of the essence of his life and work.

It also is hard to conceive of a better definition of what researchers Epstein and Meier (1989) refer to as "effective optimism." By effective optimism, social scientists do not mean Pollyanna-like vague notions that things will turn out for the best. Healthy optimism is a frame of mind or conscious set that includes a positive view of the self and others, a positive future orientation that minimizes negative expectations and negative emotions (like worry), the absence of categorical thinking, and a belief that one can exert some control over one's life (Epstein & Meier, 1989).

Erickson, by these criteria, was a magnificent optimist. He came by it quite naturally, it seems, since optimism apparently "ran in his family." Witness, for example, Erickson's story of his mother who broke her hip when she was 93 years old. She said, "This is a ridiculous thing for a woman my age to do. I'll get over it" (Rosen, 1982a, p. 169). She did get over it. The following year, however, she broke her other hip. Her resources had been much depleted during her previous recovery and she wasn't sure she could recover again, but she declared, "Nobody will ever say I didn't try" (p. 169).

Erickson's positive orientation toward the future also had its roots in his farm background. He frequently discussed the future orientation of the farmer with his clients and his students. When the crops are lush and plentiful, you enjoy that. If the vagaries of nature interfere and the crop is lost, you look forward to next year (cf. Rosen, 1982a; Zeig, 1980).

Countless examples from Erickson's life affirm his healthy optimism. In speaking of his ability for keen observation, Erickson said, "You see, I had a terrific advantage over others. I had polio, and I was totally paralyzed . . ." (Rosen, 1982a, p. 47). A true optimist, he took a seeming disadvantage and parlayed it into an opportunity to learn. When Erickson was scheduled to give an important convocation on less than a day's notice and his commitments left him with minimal prep time, his confident reaction also reflects his optimism at work. Recalling the situation, he said, "I was not concerned, however, because I knew I could talk, and I knew I could think, and I knew that I'd learned much in the course of the years" (Rosen, 1982a, p. 57). This example of Erickson's optimistic trust in his own unconscious is balanced by his optimistic trust in the unconscious reserves of his clients. Such optimism about the unconscious abilities of others was one of the cornerstones of his approach.

Erickson's personal optimism about others is also contained in his generous vision of their motives and intentions. In a 1956 conversation with Jay Haley, Erickson described work he had recently completed with a married couple. Both Haley and his colleague, John Weakland, attempted to assign negative meaning to each partner's behaviors, suggesting that their continuing quarrels were manifestations of hidden resentments or passive anger. Erickson kept reiterating that this was not the case, that the problem was, instead, a "lack of understanding" (Haley, 1985, Vol 2, p. 39). Haley, seemingly recognizing that Erickson would not put a negative label on his patient's behavior, finally stated, "I think you tend, Milton, to interpret people's being mean to one another as a lack of understanding," to which Erickson laughingly replied, "There usually is" (p. 41). Or consider Erickson's response to Haley's request for him to explain his "set of premises about what's a good marriage and what's a bad marriage" (Haley, 1985, Vol. 2, p. 6). Erickson's response is optimistically straightforward. He explains: "The major premise is this: that there is such a thing as a good marriage. . . . that there is a good marriage possible for each and every one of us" (p. 6). He goes on to say that all marriages can be successful if the partners appreciate what is there instead of lamenting what is not there. From his optimistic perspective, marriage (like life) is what we make of it. Erickson was being completely candid when he said: "Why not live and enjoy life because you can wake up dead" (Zeig, 1980, p. 269).

It is important that Erickson's optimism be acknowledged as a sophisticated component in a groundbreaking paradigm for understanding human behavior, rather than viewed as simply a charming personal quality or homey philosophy of life. Doing so gives us the opportunity to examine Erickson's work from a completely different vantage point and provides useful guidance for those of us desiring to become more "Ericksonian."

Of course, optimistic themes may be initially illusory for clinicians. Many professionals, having been schooled in the pessimism of Freud, the skepticism or objectivism of the sciences, or the psychiatric concerns with pathology, may find it a struggle to accept optimism as the basis of a new psychological, psychotherapeutic paradigm. Somehow, adopting a more optimistic world view seems intellectually suspect. Fortunately for skeptics, a host of rigorous new studies suggest that optimism is associated with better physical and mental health. More importantly, perhaps, social scientists now indicate that human beings may actually have an innate predisposition to process information in an optimistic fashion (Taylor, 1989).

In the past decade, three distinct lines of research have clarified the nature of optimism. Clinical psychologists like Seligman (1990) offer evidence that optimism may act as a buffer against emotional distress. The optimistic person is less likely than his or her pessimistic counterparts to suffer from depression or anxiety because the optimist sees misfortune as limited in time, specific to the situation, and ultimately changeable (Seligman, 1990).

A second line of research, from medicine and health psychology, suggests that optimism about one's health actually enhances health, and may enhance immune system function as well (Kiecolt-Glaser & Glaser, 1988). In fact, believing our physical health to be good or excellent when it actually is only fair to poor may promote a return to good health. On the other hand, stoically resigning ourselves to bad news about our health may actually make us worse (Kaplan & Comacho, 1983; Lazarus, 1979). Believing we have some control over our health, even when actual control seems impossible to outside observers, assists in recovery from illness (Schier & Carver, 1985; Peterson & Bossio, 1991).

As this suggests, an optimistic view does not necessarily need to be the most realistic perspective on an event. Research by Roth and Ingram (1985) indicates that mildly depressed people may, in fact, see themselves and their futures more accurately than do their happier fellows. This "depressive realism" (Abramson & Alloy, 1981) is not the result of too much negative thinking, but seems to spring instead from a lack of positive thinking (cf. Taylor, 1989). In other words, positive beliefs and attitudes will enhance happiness (and, conversely, guard against depression) even when such beliefs are not entirely accurate (cf. Lockard & Paulhus, 1988). Thus, if optimism, even unrealistic optimism, provides protection against emotional distress, the therapist's role becomes one of showing the client how to think like an optimist. The therapist can teach a client how to focus on the positive now and to have hopeful expectations for the future.

Apparently, this ability to be an optimist is a natural one. This brings us to a third area of research, one that reveals some surprising facets of optimism. Studies of human information processing indicate that the human mind appears to have an innate predisposition to attend to positive information and to screen out negative information (Taylor, 1989). There may even be an evolutionary basis for this tendency, given that it appears to be the typical cognitive style of children (Taylor & Brown, 1988). In other words, it is quite natural for us to see ourselves and our potentials through a slightly rosy filter. Apparently, this predisposition is normal, inherent, and adaptive.

These findings are novel and surprising. Psychology has long viewed the brain as a producer of rational thought (Ornstein & Sobel, 1987). Theorists have imagined that in some area of the brain a "social perceiver monitors and interacts with the world like a naive scientist" (Taylor & Brown, 1988). This supposed inner scientist collects data, organizes it in a logical fashion, and employs it in decision making. One assumption here is that people can perceive reality accurately and base their inferences on these accurate perceptions. A corollary assumption is that the psychologically healthy person is the one who accurately perceives reality (Taylor, 1989).

The actual ways in which people process information, however, do not conform to this "brain-as-scientist" model. Rather, people tend to process information about themselves and their environment in ways that are not always accurate, but are consistently self-enhancing.

Normal human thought is not notable for its evenhanded self-evaluations and cautious future predictions. Rather, the average person on the street processes information about her or himself and the environment using a mild positive bias. Taylor (1989) labels this bias "positive illusions." She suggests that three specific illusions are most common: a favorable self-evaluation in comparison to others, a belief that one can exert control in one's life, and an optimistic future orientation that includes pleasant expectations for one's personal future. Why are these cognitive stances called illusions? Because they contradict statistical reality. For example, people tend to believe themselves to be luckier than chance would predict (Langer & Roth, 1975). They tend to believe that their futures will hold far more happy events than negative ones (Taylor & Brown, 1988; Perloff & Fetzer, 1986). And people continue to rate themselves as excellent drivers, even after having been at fault in one or more accidents (Svenson, 1981). In short, most people think of themselves as better-than-the-mean in comparison to their fellows, yet everyone cannot be better than average!

Positive illusions, then, represent a way of giving ourselves the "benefit of a doubt" by viewing ourselves and our lives from a maximally positive perspective. Such findings contradict a conventional criterion of mental health. They contradict the position that an accurate view of reality, including knowing one's faults as well as one's virtues, is a necessary hallmark of mental health.

From a traditional clinical perspective, these optimistic biases are usu-ally viewed as defense mechanisms, ways of distorting reality to keep us from feeling anxious (Greenwald, 1980; Taylor, 1989). But optimistic illusions do not distort reality any more than any other point of view — a direct, objective perception of reality is not available to any of us (cf. Ornstein & Sobel, 1989). Optimistic illusions simply allow the reality we create for ourselves to be a happier one. As Erickson said about one of his patients, "He's placed a bad interpretation on a loss of erection. Why should he keep that forever and ever?" (Erickson & Rossi, 1979, p. 266).

This is not to say that negative world views and devaluing self-talk have no basis in experience. Several conditions can challenge and, in some cases, eliminate this natural optimistic bias. Victimizing events, especially those that occur in childhood, lessen the ability to view the world as safe, or one's self as good. Tragedy and trauma can shatter a belief in personal control and instill a mistrust of self and others. Many people who seek psychotherapy have had such optimism-shattering experiences. When one considers all the research on positive illusions and their relationship to mental health, it would certainly seem sensible for therapists to consider treatment that eschews self-analytic attempts to "uncover" negative emotion. Shifting clients' beliefs toward their lost optimism may be more useful.

Certainly, this is what Erickson did in his work. He had little patience for therapy that focused on insight or sought to discover the negative influences of a client's past. When Haley (1985, Vol. 2, p. 11) probed Erickson's obvious disinterest in seeking an answer to "why" patients behave in particular ways, Erickson replied:

> Well, look over the lives of a lot of happy, successful, well-adjusted people and ask them why. It's so nonsensical. They're happy, they're well-adjusted, they like their work, they have got a joy of living. Why should we analyze their childhood, parental relationships. They've never bothered and they are never going to bother.

The reason Erickson gave for not asking "why" is simply that normal, happy people are not interested in that question. This implies that helping patients requires knowing how happy people feel and behave, and then encouraging patients to act in the same way. It can be demonstrated that many of Erickson's interventions were designed to tap such natural, positive ways of being, to utilize them, to strengthen them, and, in some cases, to recreate them.

Erickson accomplished this goal with his patients in many different ways, but it would seem that he particularly enjoyed introducing positive or optimistic points of view to his clients after inducing a trance. For example, he often first induced trance by asking the patient to return to a happy time in childhood (the seat of positive illusions) and then used the absorbed attention of that trance state as an opportunity to instruct the client in some positive or optimistic perspective that the client lacked. During one demonstration, he painstakingly instructed a hypnotized student, who had a phobia about vomiting, in the positive, adaptive aspects of regurgitation for birds, animals, and humans (Rosen, 1982a, p. 91).

In another case, he treated a woman who was deeply afraid of sexual intimacy by teaching her the positive qualities of sex. This woman had explained to him that her mother, who died when she was very young, had warned her of the dangers of men and sex. Erickson used trance to create more optimistic attitudes and expectations for this woman. He did so by constructing a new reality for her, one in which the client's mother could tell her daughter all the positive things she would have wanted to say about sexuality had she lived (Haley, 1973, pp. 79-80).

Erickson also created positive illusions for his clients without formal trance. He once sent a lonesome, phobic man into the Arizona desert with the instruction to walk "until you find a reason for being glad you went down there" (Haley, 1985, Vol. I, p. 116). The man returned to Erickson to describe with wonder the beauty of a saguaro cactus and a blooming palo verde he had seen. Erickson also taught a man being fed through a tube how to enjoy a "good" burp, and showed a paraplegic woman how to have orgasms in her ear lobes (Haley, 1985, Vol 1). He even helped an insecure little girl learn to see her freckles, which she had loathed, as an asset (Rosen, 1982a).

Erickson's emphasis on optimism reflects his understanding that it is a vital aspect of our internal health maintenance system. He apparently recognized that much of the emotional unhappiness and suffering he saw in his clients came from their loss or distortion of this natural, adaptive human ability, the ability to highlight and cherish positive feelings and experiences. As the wellness experts now recommend, he gave them back this ability.

ERICKSON AND ALTRUISM

Another parallel between the wellness research and the work of Erickson may be found in studies on the beneficial effects of altruism and interpersonal connection. Researchers have found that helping others and maintaining strong social ties contribute a great deal to our health and happiness (House, Landis & Umberson, 1988). Good friends and good deeds are good medicine.

Erickson was an altruist. Zeig (1980) described Erickson as "kind, considerate and compassionate" (p. xxi). Erickson's genuine interest in others and his generosity are readily apparent. He demonstrated respect for his students and patients even before some had earned it, correcting problem behaviors with humor and tolerance (Rosen, 1982a). He shared his time and his personal resources with them, often with little or no financial reimbursement. At times, he even included them in the life of his family. He took them out to dinner, cooked meals for them, and sometimes invited them to be guests in his home (Haley, 1973, 1985; Lankton & Lankton, 1985; Rosen, 1982a; Zeig, 1980). He occasionally arranged dates for them, and he often contacted friends or acquaintances and asked them to "help out" a patient (Zeig, 1980). Obviously, Erickson often crossed over the conventional boundaries of psychotherapeutic practice to help his patients, perhaps because he had an unconventional idea of what psychotherapy is about.

Ornstein and Sobel (1987) reviewed research results that would suggest that Erickson's generous and charitable spirit probably greatly aided him in his own struggles with ill health. The more he did for others and the more he interacted with others, the healthier he was likely to become. In fact, today the bond between social support and health is so well documented that social scientists have coined the term "psychosocial risk" (Smilkstein, 1988) to describe the negative effects of social isolation. Loneliness is hazardous to the health of mind and body. Continual self-involvement and self-centeredness are correlated with heart disease, cancer, and depression (cf. Ornstein & Sobel, 1987). The factor most highly associated with early death is not smoking, nor drinking, nor a family history of disease, it is the death of a spouse (Ornstein & Sobel, 1989). People who have the comfort of friends and family live longer, get sick less often, and recover from illness more rapidly and with fewer complications (House, Landis & Umberson, 1988). People who give their time and energy to those in need have greater life expectancys and fewer emotional problems when compared to their more selfish counterparts (Luks, 1988).

Erickson apparently recognized the connection between altruism and feeling good. He often instructed his clients to behave altruistically and/or to reconnect with others. In one case, a construction worker was completely paralyzed except for the use of his arms. He was obviously in both physical and emotional pain. Erickson told the worker to ask his friends to bring him cartoons, comic books, and funny sayings. The injured man was instructed to make scrap books from these comics and "every time one of your fellow workmen lands in the hospital, send him a scrap book" (Rosen, 1982a, p. 177). Thus, in one swift move, Erickson enabled this man to reach out to friends and family, and gave his life an altruistic purpose.

This emphasis on purposeful altruism is also clear in the story of the "African Violet Queen." In this case, Erickson agreed to visit the home of a very depressed and reclusive woman who would leave her house only to go to church. During his visit he noticed that she grew African violets.

Erickson instructed her to take cuttings from her African violet plants and to grow 200 more violets. Once she got them growing, she was told to give them as gifts to people in her church. She was to send them for weddings, for christenings, for sickness, and for funerals. She was told to contribute them by the dozen to her church bazaar. For the next 20 years, this woman grew violets and gave them away. She died happy and with many friends, in Erickson's words, "too busy to be depressed" (Zeig, 1980, p. 286).

Erickson demonstrated his skill at helping others reconnect, as well as his sense of humor, in a story about one of his medical students. This particular student had been outgoing and popular until he lost a leg in an accident. After the accident, he withdrew and cut himself off from others. Erickson arranged for one of the other students to block the elevator doors on a high floor, so the elevator call button could not bring the elevator down. He then stood with his students at the elevator, making small talk and wondering where the elevator was. Finally, he turned to the injured student and said, "Let's us cripples hobble upstairs and leave the elevator to the ablebodied" (Rosen, 1982a, p. 227). By allowing the student to identify with him, Erickson bestowed a new social status on this boy and reconnected him to his peers. Erickson tells us, "he was socializing at the end of the hour" (p. 227).

Erickson often modeled a more empathic reality for his clients, giving them lessons in how to be supportive or tolerant or generous. In one case, a woman complained her husband never complimented her. Her spouse, conversely, maintained that since there were, in fact, other women more charming and beautiful than she was, he could not give her the sort of compliment she wanted. Erickson told this husband he would demonstrate how to compliment his wife. He turned to her and said, "You know, unquestionably there are many women more beautiful than you are, but not for me" (Haley, 1985, Vol. 2, p. 107). He subsequently explained that "the reality of the interpersonal relationship world" calls for certain skills and behaviors not required by "the hard, harsh reality of the world in general" (p. 107).

Clearly, Erickson understood the healing powers of altruism and the necessity of interpersonal connection for well-being. He often used trance to strengthen his empathic connection with his clients (Gilligan, 1987) and during hypnotherapy often gave the client a chance to explore the benefits of cooperation, mutuality, and connectedness (Gilligan, 1987; Walters & Havens, in press). Erickson's wisdom regarding the beneficial effects of altruism and interpersonal behavior has been overlooked, at times, because of an emphasis on technique. Thus, interventions such as those above sometimes get reduced to a formula such as, "get the patient to do something." What Erickson actually told us, however, was to "get the patient to do things that are very, very good for him" (Zeig, 1980, p. 195). Erickson's recurrent altruistic emphasis reflects his uncanny understanding that altruism, like optimism, is very, very good for people. He also recognized that a positive sense of self-efficacy is good for us, and so he had his patients engage in self-efficacious acts as well.

ERICKSON AND HARDINESS

When people believe in their own self-efficacy, they are confident in their ability to act in ways that will result in success (Bandura, 1982). Self-efficacious people believe they can "make things happen." Self-efficacy combined with two other qualities—commitment and an openness to challenge—are components of a personal style that wellness researchers (e.g., Kobasa, Maddi & Kahn, 1982; Maddi & Kobasa, 1984) have labeled "psychological hardiness." Psychologically hardy individuals welcome change and challenge, seeing all aspects of life as possibilities for learning. They are self-valuing as well as committed to others, drawing strength from loved ones, their work, and a strong personal value system. Hardy people are action oriented. They set goals and they achieve them. The psychologically hardy individual is flexible, and flexible people appear to be more resistant to the negative effects of stress than are their more rigid, hence fragile, counterparts (cf. Ornstein & Sobel, 1989; Peterson & Bossio, 1991). Thus, hardy people are better able to cope and are less prone to illness. These hardy qualities have been labeled "resistance resources" (Antonovsky, 1979), and they have been identified as factors that determine whether a person moves toward health or tends toward physical or mental illness.

Less hardy, more fragile individuals, on the other hand, are rigid in thought and behavior. They avoid risk and seek to minimize change. Their sense of self-efficacy is low. Fragile people use fewer and less complex coping strategies, often putting most of their energy into trying to manage their emotional responses to events.

Inarguably, Erickson possessed a marvelous psychological hardiness. Probably the best anecdotal evidence for this is found in his well-known story of his first bout with polio. Lying in bed, Erickson overheard three doctors tell his mother, "The boy will be dead by morning" (Rosen, 1982a, p. 52). He responded to this "ultimate" challenge with characteristic feistiness, angered that anyone would have the nerve to tell a mother something so heartless. He vowed to prove the doctor wrong, to live to see the sun rise the next morning. He had his mother move the furniture around the room until he had a clear view through his bedroom window, and he did see the sun rise, even though he later noticed that the only thing one could see out that window was the side of a barn.

Erickson also is remembered for his highly positive beliefs about his own abilities. He taught his students to meet their clients the way he did, with an attitude of positive expectancy and a confident belief in themselves as catalysts for change (cf. Haley, 1985; Lankton & Lankton, 1985; Zeig, 1980). And if there is any one quality that Erickson viewed as vital for a happy life, it certainly is flexibility. Erickson considered "rigid" patterns of thought and behavior to be highly detrimental to one's chances for successful living (cf. Havens, 1985; O'Hanlon, 1987).

When Erickson worked with a patient, one of his characteristic aims was to get the person to break down rigid patterns and to behave in an efficacious manner. Often, before he would agree to recommend a treatment, he would secure a commitment from the patient to follow any prescription given. Erickson's "prescription" would then challenge the client to take charge of some aspect of his or her behavior heretofore believed to be out of the realm of personal control, and would offer the person the means to do just that. Thus, an alcoholic who believed he could not pass a tavern without stopping for a drink was instructed to walk to work on a route that took him six miles out of his way, but avoided all bars (Rosen, 1982a). Or, in another instance, an aphasic woman who refused to try to talk was instructed to sit silently with her husband each evening staring at tropical fish in an aquarium; as a result, she was soon bursting to speak.

Hundreds of Erickson's cases follow this familiar pattern. First get a commitment and then introduce elements of challenge and control into the situation. Ericksonian therapy consistently introduces the components of psychological hardiness (commitment, self-efficacy, and challenge) into a client's life. Obviously, Erickson knew what wellness researchers have just recently figured out, that these qualities help keep people happy, healthy, and stress-free.

We also must wonder if it is simply serendipitous that Erickson's hardy prescriptions for wellness so often included opportunities for his clients to experience pleasure as well. Ornstein and Sobel (1989) have outlined the healing benefits of pleasure, and Erickson often encouraged "healthy pleasures." He told his clients to enjoy a good meal, exercise, experience the beauty of nature, even "fuck for fun" (Haley, 1985, Vol. 2, p. 125). Erickson taught people to be hardy and to have a good time — and these are important ingredients of good health.

CONCLUSIONS

Milton Erickson was an optimist when pessimism was the psychological vogue. He prescribed action for clients when the most popular psychotherapies concerned themselves with self-analysis. And Erickson recognized the healing powers of social connection when theories of existential alienation were capturing the post-war imagination. Erickson was in the unenviable position of attempting to focus professional attention on the goal of happiness, and on the therapeutic value of qualities like optimism, altruism, and efficacy, without the benefit of an empirical research base. His techniques fascinated others, but his guiding goals of happiness, optimism, and altruism, seemed like quaint homilies. Today, the wellness literature not only offers scientific corroboration of Erickson's unique understandings and intentions, it clearly establishes him as a forerunner and original author of this new paradigm. What exactly did Erickson know that social and medical science has just recently discovered?

First, and most importantly, Erickson considered happiness or wellness to be the *appropriate* therapeutic outcome. Second, he recognized that optimism is one of the paths to this goal. He understood that the human mind is predisposed toward optimism and that effective therapy will utilize this optimistic bent if it is present and revitalize it if trauma or tragedy has weakened it. Erickson also understood that another way to feel good is to do some good, for ourselves and for others, and he prescribed this for clients as well. Finally, Erickson was aware that challenge, change, and self-efficacy, the ingredients of psychological hardiness, also contribute to well-being and happiness.

Erickson was a master at structuring situations that enabled or encouraged his clients to experience such things first hand! But Erickson's psychotherapy was uncommonly effective not just because his techniques were masterful but because his goals were uncommon and his appreciation of the conditions that led to those goals differed from the prevailing norms. Today, the "Ericksonian Therapeutic Paradigm" can stand on its own, buttressed by the new research on wellness that supports his keen observations and therapeutic insights.

If, as Ericksonians, we begin to pay more attention to the wellness aspects inherent in Erickson's approach, we reap a double benefit. First, Erickson's interventions, which can sometimes seem baffling or mysterious when considered from within a traditional pathology paradigm, are quite understandable when viewed from the vantage point of wellness. For example, metaphorical anecdotes, so-called paradoxical prescriptions, and "ordeals" no longer look like mystical koans or clever manipulations of symptoms from the wellness perspective. Rather, they appear to be straightforward requests for normal, healthy behaviors. Most of his interventions, in fact, begin to look like simple, direct attempts to instill healthy attitudes or behavior. In addition, establishing an Ericksonian/wellness paradigm linkage eliminates the possibility that Erickson's wisdom eventually will be reduced to a collection of interesting techniques. It establishes Erickson as the founder of a new way of *thinking* about therapy, not merely a new way of doing it. The efforts of Ernest Rossi (1986) to establish an Ericksonian link to mind-body healing are a major step in this direction. The next step is to connect Erickson's basic therapeutic philosophy and goals to the entire wellness movement. That is our intention here.

We began this chapter with some bad news about the future of Ericksonian techniques, but are happy to report that there truly is some good news to report. The good news is that Erickson's therapeutic approach and the new and exciting research findings on health and happiness share an intimate and integrative connection. The change promised by this good news will come when we Ericksonians, and other therapists as well, recognize that the essence of Erickson's wisdom is the focus on actions and beliefs that build health. Erickson's rejection of a pathological emphasis, his joy of life, and his health prescriptions for his clients were far from mainstream ideas at the time. Erickson's wisdom was visionary then. It is still visionary: it shows us *how* to be well.

REFERENCES

Abramson, L.Y., & Alloy, L.B. (1981). Depression, non-depression and cognitive "illusions": A reply to Schwartz. *Journal of Experimental Psychology, 110,* 436-437.

Antonovsky, A. (1979). *Health, stress and coping.* San Francisco: Jossey-Bass.

Bandura, A. (1982). Self-efficacy mechanism is human agency. *American Psychologist, 37,* 122-147.

Epstein, S., & Meier, P. (1989). Constructive thinking: A broad coping variable with distinctive components. *Journal of Personality and Social Psychology, 57,* 332-350.

Erickson, K.K. (1988). One method for designing short-term intervention-oriented Ericksonian therapy. In J. Zeig & S. Lankton (Eds.), *Developing Ericksonian therapy: State of the art* (pp. 379-398) New York: Brunner/Mazel.

Erickson, M.H. (1980). *The collected papers of Milton H. Erickson on hypnosis,* E. Rossi (Ed.). New York: Irvington.

Erickson, M.H., & Rossi, E.L. (1979). *Hypnotherapy: An exploratory casebook.* New York: Irvington.

Gilligan, S. (1987). *Therapeutic trances: The cooperation principle in Ericksonian hypnotherapy.* New York: Brunner/Mazel.

Greenwald, A.G. (1980). The totalitarian ego: Fabrication and revision of personal history. *American Psychologist, 35,* 603-618.

Haley, J. (1973). *Uncommon therapy.* New York: Norton.

Haley, J. (1985). *Conversations with Milton H. Erickson,* Vols 1 & 2. Rockville, MD: Triangle Press.

Havens, R.A. (1985). *The wisdom of Milton H. Erickson.* New York: Irvington.

Havens, R.A., & Walters, C. (1989). *Hypnotherapy scripts: A Neo-Ericksonian approach to persuasive healing.* New York: Brunner/Mazel.

Hayano, D.M. (1988). Dealing with chance: Self-deception and fantasy among gamblers. In J.S. Lockard & D.L. Paulhus (Eds.), *Self-deception: An adaptive mechanism?* (pp. 186–199). Englewood Cliffs, NJ: Prentice-Hall.

House, J.S., Landis, K.R., & Umberson, A. (1988). Social relationships and health. *Science, 241,* 540–545.

Kaplan, G.A., & Comacho, T. (1983). Perceived health and mortality: A nine-year follow-up of the human population laboratory cohort. *American Journal of Epidemiology, 11,* 292–304.

Kiecolt-Glaser, J.K., & Glaser, R. (1988). Behavioral influences on immune function: Evidence for the interplay between stress and health. In T. Field, P. McCabe & N. Schneiderman (Eds.), *Stress and coping, Vol. 2* (105–139). Hillsdale, NJ: Erlbaum.

Kobasa, S.C., Maddi, S.R., & Kahn, S. (1982). Hardiness and health: A prospective study. *Journal of Personality and Social Psychology, 42,* 168–177.

Langer, E.J., & Roth, J. (1975). Heads I win, tails it's chance: The illusion of control and function of outcomes in a purely chance task. *Journal of Personality and Social Psychology, 34,* 191–198.

Lankton, S., & Lankton, C. (1985). The answer within: A clinical framework of Ericksonian hypnotherapy. New York: Brunner/Mazel.

Lazarus, R. (1979). Positive denial: The case for not facing reality. *Psychology Today, 13*(6), 44–60.

Lockard, J.S., & Paulhus, D.L. (Eds.). (1988). *Self-deception: An adaptive mechanism.* Englewood Cliffs, NJ: Prentice-Hall.

Luks, A. (1988). Helper's high. *Psychology Today, 22*(10), 39–42.

Maddi, S.R., & Kobasa, S.C. (1984). *The hardy executive: Health under stress.* Homewood, IL: Dow Jones-Irwin.

Myers, D. (1992). *The pursuit of happiness: Who is happy and why.* New York: William Morrow.

O'Hanlon, W.H. (1987). *Taproots: Underlying principles of Milton Erickson's therapy and hypnosis.* New York: Norton.

Ornstein, R., & Sobel, D. (1987). *The healing brain.* New York: Simon and Schuster.

Ornstein, R., & Sobel, D. (1989). *Healthy pleasures.* Reading, MA: Addison-Wesley.

Perloff, L.S., & Fetzer, B.K. (1986). Self-other judgements and perceived vulnerability of victimization. *Journal of Personality and Social Psychology, 50,* 502–510.

Peterson, C., & Bossio, L.M. (1991). *Health and optimism.* New York: Macmillan.

Rosen, S. (1982a). *My voice will go with you: The teaching tales of Milton H. Erickson.* New York: Norton.

Rosen, S. (1982b). The values and philosophy of Milton H. Erickson. In J. Zeig (Ed.), *Ericksonian approaches to hypnosis and psychotherapy* (pp.462–476). New York: Brunner/Mazel.

Rossi, E. (1986). *The psychobiology of mind-body healing: New concepts in therapeutic hypnosis.* New York: Norton.

Roth, D.L., & Ingram, R.E. (1985). Factors on the self-deception questionnaire: Associations with depression. *Journal of Personality and Social Psychology, 48,* 243–251.

Schier, M.F., & Carver, C.S. (1985). Optimism, coping and health: Assessment and implications of generalized outcome expectancies. *Journal of Personality, 55,* 169-210.

Seligman, M.E.P. (1990). *Learned optimism.* New York: Knopf.

Smilkstein, G. (1988). Health benefits of helping patients cope. *Consultant, 6,* 56-67.

Spence, D. (1982). *Narrative truth and historical truth.* New York: Norton.

Svenson, O. (1981). Are we all less risky and more skillful than our fellow drivers? *Acta Psychologica, 47,* 143-148.

Taylor, S.E. (1989). *Positive illusions.* New York: Basic Books.

Taylor, S.E., & Brown, J.A. (1988). Illusion and well-being: A social psychological perspective on mental health. *Psychological Bulletin, 2,* 193-210.

Walters, C., & Havens, R.A. (in press). *Hypnotherapy for health, harmony and peak performance.* New York: Brunner/Mazel.

Zeig, J.K. (1980). *A teaching seminar with Milton H. Erickson.* New York: Brunner/Mazel.

CHAPTER 10

The Transitional Gap in Metaphor and Therapy: The Essence of the Story

Jean Godin &
Jean-Michel Oughourlian

The words "Essence of the Story" may be understood in many different ways.

The "Story" is what is being told. This story might be real, but we are just as interested when the story is fictional. By "Essence" we mean what really matters in a phenomenon. Therefore, the essence of the story is what makes the story important. We will explain how important a story can be in affecting the human psyche and show how and in which perspective a story can be psychologically active.

THE FRAMEWORK OF OUR STUDY

The Framework of the Psychological Language

We use simple concepts, after having defined them. Comprehensive and extensive definitions of the concepts we need in our theory and in our practice have recently been published (Godin, 1992). Let us stress here that when we refer to conscious and unconscious psychological levels we refer to Milton Erickson's way of thinking—that the term *unconscious processes* is just a handy way to refer to those processes that the human being develops unwittingly and of whose functioning he is unaware.

The Framework of Psychotherapy

Of course, we are interested in those effects that can be useful to a patient during the psychotherapeutic process. Our concern is to avoid "intrusion." It is of paramount importance to respect the person in front of us, to avoid cultivating his or her dependence, and to refuse to impose our own point of view (no matter how legitimate it might seem to us).

In developing a framework of a general conception of human "interdividual rapport," this mimetic conception that one of us has developed also will be helpful in our work. This theory unfolds a new anthropology based on the hypothesis that desire is mimetic. Essentially, desire produces what is known as a self (Oughourlian, 1991).

The basic principle in that theory is that the psychological rapport between two people is composed of two vectors of the same intensity but of opposite directions: suggestion and imitation. In everyday relationships, those vectors constantly change directions. Individual 1 and Individual 2 exchange suggestions and imitations. Those two vectors are two aspects of one and the same reality, since we cannot say that 1 has suggested anything to 2 as long as 2 has not actually imitated it. Conversely, if we say 2 has imitated 1 it is obvious that the move he has imitated has been suggested by 1.

In everyday life, those vectors come and go incessantly with incredible speed between 1 and 2 and among a lot of others. The traditional hypnotic relationship may be defined, in this perspective, as a temporary immobilization of those two vectors.

For many centuries, authors have thought about hypnosis in terms of power and about the hypnotic relation in terms of an imposed relationship. A caricature of that type of thinking is seen in the idea of one brain taking over another. Our work and research, along the lines of Milton Erickson, show that something completely different is occurring.

THE STORY

We want to find out how and why a story can activate the psyche of the one who listens to it. We have considered several possibilities, all of which reveal an "essential" relationship with that which is called "hypnosis."

The Direct Influence of the Story

A story told may carry beliefs that orient our psychological functioning. Let us take the example of traditional hypnosis where there is a story, tacit or explicit, whereby the hypnotizer has some kind of power that will trigger certain effects in the subject. That story works as a suggestion and induces certain effects independently of the patient's consciousness. It is that particular belief that is cultivated and it is in this context that sequences of suggestions will be effective. This story is fictitious but active. One of us has developed that point of view in a communication at the last Ericksonian Congress (Godin, 1988). In this way, traditional hypnosis can produce aberrant behavior in people, which we refer to as "the coercion of hypnosis."

We no longer believe in this power of hypnosis. As Milton Erickson's work indicates, it is clear that hypnosis does not allow one to control people (Erickson & Rossi, 1976, p. 41). However, we believe that if some subjects are fundamentaly convinced that they will be under control it is likely that this will happen to a certain extent, in what could be called a "self-fulfilling prophecy."

These phenomena, which are exaggerated in the practice of traditional hypnosis, do exist to a lesser degree in everyday life, meaning that beliefs carried by stories do influence our way of thinking. In the case of traditional hypnosis, therefore, the essence of the story is a "fictitious prediction."

The fact that the subject cannot remember what he has been told during certain hypnotic trances gives a peculiar character to that story. To a certain extent, the subject is deprived of his own story. This is not a value judgment but an observation. In this context, it might be legitimate to use traditional hypnosis in order to amplify a direct action of the body or to facilitate the emergence of certain behaviors within the framework of an intelligent strategy.

The Story as a Basis for the Psychotherapeutic Action

Any story told can be used by the hypnotist to generate psychological action. "The one who is the object of a communication ignores to what extent his associative processes have been activated in multiple directions" (Erickson & Rossi, 1981).

The subtle and precise use of language, the art of transitions, careful attention to the echo of the words, knowledge of literality, etc. will allow the hypnotist to mobilize unconscious processes in a subject even when the subject may be consciously aware that he is listening to an apparently banal story.

This science of unconscious mechanisms, as explained by Erickson, is so important that it may be used to facilitate (in a cooperative subject) the emergence of that particular mode of psychological functioning we call hypnosis.

Those same techniques may be used within the framework of a hypnotic trance or independently of any hypnotic reference in order to orient certain processes of thought in a given individual. The words used then have value as psychological switches. They are chosen for their own semantic value or for the echoes they might trigger. Moreover, the nonverbal and body communication and the tone of voice will be used to complement the story to produce the desired effect.

Erickson has shown that "specific" modes of communication can be used in banal conversations about everyday life. The knowledge of those communication modes has produced new types of psychotherapy. For example, Erickson's therapeutic approach tends to evoke and to use the personal repertoire of positive answers in a subject to obtain therapeutic responses that would have otherwise been beyond his reach (Erickson & Rossi, 1981).

In the literature, those subtle actions are usually labelled "suggestions," but the psychotherapeutic action is not simply to use suggestions hidden in banal talk. We have to think more deeply about this.

It is difficult to imagine how truly direct suggestion could be included in a soothing story for pain relief. That is why in those stories the hypnotist uses indirect suggestions, that by definition are not identified by the subject.

Let us review several formulations of indirect suggestions:

1. The *Yes-Set* is probably the most binding form of indirect suggestion. The formulation of several statements to which the subject cannot avoid agreeing increases his tendency to accept the real suggestion that follows.
2. *Implication* refers to what the hypnotist wants to suggest as a given fact in order to make the unconscious admit a proposition that the critical mind of the subject would have probably questioned.
3. *Paradoxical Intention* is another way to orient thought processes. This consists of referring to something in a negative way, e.g., "I'm *not* asking you to think this," or "You *don't* need to think this," or "I *don't* know if. . . ." These are propositions the subject cannot elude. Quite obviously, his brain will not be able to help evoking the very thing he was consciously or unconsciously avoiding thinking about.
4. *Open-ended Suggestion* is so different from other indirect suggestions that we wonder whether it should be called a suggestion at

all. Nothing is suggested except that something is going to happen. Open-ended suggestion is simply a mobilizing suggestion. An open-ended suggestion may be included in a simple pause of speech, e.g., "This will enable you to benefit from. . . ." In such a sentence, what is important is the pause after "benefit from." The unconscious of the subject will try to finish the sentence and will wonder what he could possibly benefit from. In fact, this type of suggestion consists of activating useful chains of associations without influencing the response.

In all those examples, the essence of the story is a useful distraction that captivates the attention of the subject while simultaneously the words used by the therapist stimulate action in the subject at an unconscious level. In one of Erickson's cases called "Ann's Inhibition," he talks about apparently irrelevant matters, for instance the furniture or the temperature of the water in the tub, in order to allow the patient to reframe her attitudes and to confront her own sexuality.

The Influence of the Story Itself

The story told is active by its very nature. We shall first consider the intentionally told story. Erickson was gifted at telling stories. His stories are extremely subtle and those who listened to them still wonder about the "Maestro's" intentions. It is the story in itself that is supposed to act at the psychological level. If the story has enough similarities to the structure of the patient's problem, it will be able to influence the sequence of events. A story that symbolically represents certain problems or difficulties of the patient can help him overcome them by activating previously rigid structures.

The similarity between the story and the problem may be unveiled to the patient, and it is then an "analogy." Sometimes the relationship between the story and the problem is just implied, and it is then a metaphor or a metaphoric suggestion.

Since Aristotle, "metaphor" has signified a word or a sentence that describes something but suggests something else by analogy. A common example is "the boat that ploughs the sea."

Erickson cleverly widened that concept by using its etymology; "Metaphor is then a means to bring new significance to consciousness" (Erickson & Rossi, 1979, p. 50). A word or a sentence may evoke memories or may have several meanings. We are now used to talking of metaphor to refer to a mode of expression that includes several possible meanings.

The use of double-level language was one of Erickson's favorite methods. The metaphor is addressed only to the unconscious of the patient, who is supposed to do the work of seeing the similarities between the metaphor and his own situation (Erickson & Rossi, 1976, p. 204). Erickson also used analogy as an efficient tool inasmuch as it called on the conscious as well as the unconscious. In both instances, just like in humor, a first reading is readily comprehended. A second meaning works its way underground on its own. That second meaning is the essence of the process of humor when it becomes conscious.

In our therapeutic approach, a first meaning is immediately obvious. It is there to distract the attention. A second meaning, which is related to the patient's problem, works its way underground and triggers the developing processes that will come to mature and produce the desired effect. That second meaning can indeed help develop future insights, but most often it will be the starting point of psychological rearrangements.

The comparison with humor seems a good way to understand how the new hypnosis is not just simple manipulation. Laughter and hypnosis alike develop away from willpower. One of us (Godin, 1988) has suggested that hypnosis is a phenomenon that the patient cannot accomplish alone. It is mostly a "let-go," a personal reaction that can in no way be imposed.

Metaphoric language activates a series of psychological associations and starts working at the unconscious level without the paralyzing interference of conscious thought. Therefore we believe we should no longer speak of "indirect suggestions," but rather of "activating suggestions" or even of "activating stimulations."

That stimulation will bring to the patient's unconscious some material with which to work and will be all the more efficient if not recognized as such. A metaphoric suggestion may contain an explicit solution to one type of problem or an allusion to a possible happy ending. More frequently, an open metaphor may not suggest anything. In all instances, the metaphor avoids any rivalry with the patient and activates reappraisals. Certain metaphors speak for themselves, such as those examples taken from our journal *Phoenix*: The Great Spring-Cleaning (Turner, 1989, p. 22), The Can Opening (Adrian, 1991, p. 5), the Gardener and the Blade (Garnier, 1990, p. 70), The Princess with a Cold (aimed at enuretic children) (Courtial, 1989, p. 24), The Travelling of a River Boat (told to a patient with vaginismus) (Ribes, 1989, p. 32), The Story of an Acorn (invented for a neurotic teenager) (Touret, 1989, p. 22), The Story of Mythridates and the Moon (Jousselin, 1990, p. 24).

When telling these stories, we recognize similarities with an hypnotic approach. For instance, as the sequence unfolds, there is fixation of the attention, confusion, and then the beginning of unconscious processes. All of that does not include any typical trance, and the Ericksonians periodically wonder if the word "hypnosis" should still be used. That, in fact, is of little importance inasmuch as we can speak of "hypnosis" in the broader sense of the word and also keep the word "hypnosis" itself for a more systematic action.

Erickson often used his knowledge of human psyche in a more sophisticated way. For instance, he would tell several stories having a common denominator, such as stories pointing to the fact that training can eliminate undesirable sensory phenomena (Erickson & Rossi, 1989, p. 103). The patients in that case, a woman suffering from tinnitus and her husband suffering from a phantom limb, listen to those stories without paying much attention, but their brains were influenced unwittingly. A new attitude or a new idea may then emerge, which the patients may claim as their own.

Among the stories, a special reference must be made to folk tales and especially to fairy tales. Any reference to the world of childhood is of consequence to the adult, because the rigid patterns that need to be activated and changed often date back to childhood.

Listening to a fairy tale makes adults and children travel back into their imaginary world. Listening to a fairy tale may become with the conscious or unconscious cooperation of the patient, the beginning of the induction of a real trance.

Bettelheim has made us understand that fairy tales have a therapeutic value, as they allow the patient to meditate about what the story reveals about himself and about his internal conflicts at a given time of his life (Bettelheim, 1976, p. 38).

A fairy tale might be rewritten and programmed to induce sleep or to convey metaphoric communications. For instance, one day when a direct intervention was not possible in a severely motor-handicapped child after an accident, one of us made an audiocassette with a specially prepared story of the Sleeping Beauty (Godin, 1989). This cassette has since been used for many blocked or insomniac children.

Let us return to the metaphor, which appears to have more meaning than that of a simple suggestion. Adrian (1991) has developed the idea that the metaphor would be a transitional space in the sense used by Winnicott (1971).

The metaphor, on one hand, produces comprehension by the patient, i.e., the metaphor must trigger identification of the patient with the hero of the story. But the metaphor is also the healing space provided by the therapist, since the patient will find in the metaphor whatever the therapist puts in it: new knowledge and new meaning, which was previously unknown to the patient. That meeting place, therefore, has the capacity to be at the same time "self" and "non-self."

In hypnosis, the way Erickson has taught us to understand it, the metaphor might have a special value just because it represents the language of the right hemisphere (Erickson & Rossi, 1979, p.144). Metaphor would then allow patients to go beyond "acquired limitations" (p. 50).

Used in that way, the metaphor is the meeting place between two human beings: the first one provides the second with propositions made at such a level that the latter is unable to identify an outside intervention. If the proposition does not suit him, the patient will just forget about it. If, on the contrary, the proposition is in harmony with the patient's being, he will adopt that proposition without realizing that anything has been imposed upon him.

The essence of the metaphoric story is as a transition within the framework of a psychological work done by the patient. The metaphor is a place, a transitional space, in which two human beings communicate in a common search that aims at furthering the psychological evolution of the patient.

The therapist bears in mind all along that he's trying to reach the unconscious resources of the patient—forgotten learnings, unaccomplished programs, or gifts not yet exploited.

The story aims at evoking and utilizing the patient's personal repertoire of positive understanding in order to obtain therapeutic responses that would have otherwise been beyond the patient's reach (Erickson & Rossi, 1981). Such stories give way to reframings and they result in "Type two" change (Watzlawick, Weakland & Fisch, 1974, p. 116).

Hypnosis, when present, facilitates concentration on the above resources and allows useful psychological associations to emerge more easily. As Garnier (1990) puts it, "In traditional hypnosis the unconscious was programmed like a machine; in the new hypnosis the unconscious is called upon as a reservoir of possible programs."

The Value of the Story Told without Any Specific Intention

Erickson and Rossi (1979) believe that a metaphor may be "deterministic" when the therapist's intention is to activate psychological processes in a given direction. But they claim it also can be "non-deterministic" when the essence of the story has a transcendental function, i.e., when neither the patient nor the therapist are able to anticipate the effects that will appear, which are, in any event, the patient's doings.

How Does a Therapist Manage to Find Such Stories?

We think that in the way we practice hypnosis the operator finds himself "de facto" in a quasi-hypnotic state. That is how he perceives the smallest clues given by the patient and is able to respond to them in a way that his reasoning could not have anticipated. He therefore becomes particularly creative and sensitive to unconscious messages. Inasmuch as he is in an atuned relationship with the patient, we think that the story or the metaphor will be naturally adapted to the patient, who has, in fact, suggested it. That is how a story spontaneously emerges in the mind of the therapist.

"Subliminal communication" is the correct concept that describes this relationship with all its subconscious elements. Freud's definition of psychoanalysis, "Communication from an unconscious to an unconscious" (Freud, 1912), is a good example of this subliminal of communication.

In this way, the therapist does not speak to the patient's hypnotic place as in traditional hypnosis, nor does he speak for the patient as in the new (Ericksonian) hypnosis. One further step has been taken: The therapist speaks by putting himself unconsciously "in the place of the patient." The patient speaks through the mouth of the therapist, and the dialogue becomes a dialogue of the patient with himself!

It is, therefore, the psychological work of the patient that is verbalized by use of all the stories and all the symbols that belong to him.

The speech then becomes that of the patient in words and understandings he was never able to formulate himself. The operator has truly been a catalyst. A well-known French psychoanalyst, Jacques Palaci, said after watching a videotape of one of our therapies: "This is not just suggestion. You have lent your psyche to the patient to enable him to do a job he couldn't do alone."

Thus, the essence of the story would reflect the opportunity offered to the two psyches to establish quasi-fusional communication.

CONCLUSION

We are led to think that there is no single "Essence of the Story" as such. When we tell stories to our patients, we must bear in mind that numerous psychological mechanisms are at play. In other words, there is no "Essence of the Story" that could be defined as such. There are, depending on the case, several possible "essences" that are important for us to know about. We have here briefly reviewed some of these that we have tested in our practice.

What is remarkable is that all these modes of action are connected to what we call hypnosis or, at least, to the processes that hypnosis has taught us to use. The most banal stories might be related to the modalities of psychological functioning that we call hypnosis. The study of those processes allows us to better understand what takes place when a story is told;

most of all, it gives us a clearer understanding of and a better control over our psychotherapeutic effectiveness.

REFERENCES

Adrian, J. (1991). La metaphore au long cours. *Phoenix, 4,* (13), 3-6.

Bettelheim, B. (1976). *The use of changement.* New York: Knopf.

Courtial, M. (1989). Il etait une fois une Jeune fille enuretique. *Phoenix, 2,* (5), 24-25.

Erickson, M. H., & Rossi, R. (1976). *Hypnotic realities.* New York: Irvington.

Erickson, M. H., & Rossi, E. (1979) *Hypnotherapy.* New York: Irvington.

Erickson, M. H., & Rossi, E. (1981). *Experiencing hypnosis.* New York: Irvington.

Freud, S. (1912). Conseils aux medecins sur le traitement psychanalytique. *G.W., 12,* 375-387.

Garnier, S. (1990). La jardinier en herbe. *Phoenix, 2,* (7), 25-26.

Godin, J. (1988). Hypnose, manipulation et humour, dans l'esprit de Milton Erickson. Congress International. Den Hagen.

Godin, J. (1989). Sleeping beauty. *Bulletin de la societe Francaise d' Hypnose, 1,* 25-28.

Godin, J. (1992). *La nouvelle hypnose, vocabulaire, principes et methode.* Paris: Albin Michel.

Haley, J. (1985). *Conversations with Milton H. Erickson.* Rockville, MD: Triangle Press.

Jousselin, C. (1990). Mythridate et la lune. *Phoenix, 2,* (7), 24.

Oughourlian, J-M. (1991). *The puppet of desire.* Stanford, CA: Stanford University Press.

Ribes, G. (1989). Histoire de peniche et d'ecluse. *Phoenix, 2,* (5), 32.

Thouret, J-L. (1989). L'Histoire du gland. *Phoenix,* (4), 22-23.

Turner, J. (1989). Utilisation des metaphores du patient. *Phoenix, 5,* 22-23.

Watzlawick, P., Weakland J., Fisch R. (1974). *Change: Principles of problem formation, and problem resolution.* New York: W.W. Norton.

Winnicott, D. W. (1971). *Playing and reality.* London: Tavistock.

CHAPTER 11

Restorying the Mind: Using Therapeutic Narrative in Psychotherapy

Carol J. Kershaw

INTRODUCTION

We live in the body of our conscious and unconscious stories. The stories are hypnotic narratives about attachment to others, identity, personality, and the experience of the world. The stories are told by our culture, family, generation, and those in power. Stories induce the ways of the cultural world and the social context by virtue of what is related and the way it is told. We learn values, perspectives, and the essence of experience through oral and written narratives.

Many of these narratives become unconscious directives that influence choices, attitudes, emotions, and behaviors. They contain themes, plots, mythic characters, roles, and story lines that suggest a particular way to live, what and whom to value, how to spend time, what to avoid, whom to model, what future to imagine. We "story" our lives to give them meaning, understand the past, and predict the future. Sometimes, the story offers medicine (Estes, 1992) for what was lost or never found when we were young. Sometimes, the story offers a wasteland of pain and suffering, a narrative without hope that points toward future alienation.

The author gratefully acknowledges Bill Wade, M.Div., LPC, LMFT, Co-Director of The Milton H. Erickson Institute of Houston, Texas, who offered valuable editorial comments.

In any case, an experience may affect the individual at a psychophysiological dimension and influence the systems in which the individual is involved. The stories about these experiences describe our family values and consensual reality that each generation alters by its perceptual and experiential contributions. Our clients' stories tell us where healing is needed. Therapeutic stories offer a path toward healing.

Healing begins with a narrative told by the patient to the therapist. Healing change is stimulated at an unconscious level when an hypnotic meta-narrative is told by the therapist—a story about a patient's story, dreams, or body memories that inspire in the patient the evolution of a new life story. The focus of this chapter is the healing conversation that utilizes a positive and nurturing attachment to the therapist through the "healing trance" for new learning. Conversational hypnotic strategies can intervene in a symptom and co-author a new story that integrates experience and creates generative learning in the patient.

FAMILY STORES

Family stories often describe the family system dynamics. All systems in which we operate and by which we are influenced have various characteristics: associative, connected, dynamic, and networked. Families are self-organizing, dynamic processes. If they allow flexibility, freedom, and interdependence, the families' atmospheres are warm and nurturing, and they support growth and exploration. If the family system is closed and rigid, new possibilities are blocked. The stories told by family members reflect the system that evolved along the way.

Hypnotic implications are continuously communicated in family stories. They limit roles, influence physical and emotional health, and suggest definite futures while eliminating others. We are shaped by our stories, by who narrates them, how the narrative is structured, and how we enact them. Each story describes some different aspect of experience and serves to provide some understanding of that experience.

Living Narratives, Hypnotic Narratives, Frozen Narratives

The task for the psychotherapist is to participate with the patient to mutually create new living narratives. Each story contains hypnotic elements that persuade the listener toward a perspective and set of beliefs. These new stories may lead the patient to evolve a new role or behavior in the family. Co-evolving from the relationship of patient and therapist, a new story develops that holds new meaning, has more flexibility, and is generative. Anderson and Goolishian (1990) commented that "meaning, understanding, and language never remain static in dialogue. They are always becoming history on the way to change" (p. 162). We become with our patients co-authors in writing a new story that offers several descriptions of an event.

It is difficult for people to stand outside their own stories. Mair (1988) says, "the story is greater than individuals" (p. 129) The culture and the family as culture lead its members to enact a drama so as to become the kind of member that can belong. The story lives on beyond its first narrators as it is told by others. The telling of our storied experience allows others to take us in and gives us a future beyond ourselves. The story ultimately takes on a life of its own. As Mair suggests, "As we live out the stories of our place and time . . . we are crisscrossed by words and sentences. We are articulated by the story, permeated and formed into relevant beings in the image of the story. We are made in the image of the masterstory that we serve" (p. 127–128).

Most lives contain hypnotic narratives told by their families, influenced by the social context, and massaged by the cultural milieu. These hypnotic narratives tell the listener which categories of joy, pain, problems, and solutions are available. When stories lose flexibility and become rigid in their descriptions, they may fail to account for much of the complexity of life, making it more likely that our stories will clash in an either/or or an all-or-nothing fashion. Thus, the way is paved for conflict and symptomatic behavior.

A family who has an adolescent daughter may push the girl to make straight A's. Even though she makes A's and B's and allows herself to have a reasonable social life, her parents may suggest to her that she falls short, and they continue to push. The continual pressure can lead to resentment and anger in the girl and hidden questioning of her own worth. The story the parents tell may be that their daughter is irresponsible. The story the daughter tells may be that she feels peer pressure and has different needs than do her parents. She can experience her parents as uncaring. The more the girl fails to follow the parents' requests, the more the parents believe their story is true. The more the parents believe their story is true and behave toward their daughter as if she were irresponsible, the more their daughter believes her story is true. The storytellers may become frozen in their version of an experience and pressure others in the system to tell the same story. The more these conflicting stories are told and acted out, the more possible is the escalating conflict that becomes symptomatic.

Symptoms could be thought of as frozen narratives that have lost the ability to describe and motivate new learning and behavior. They have become bogged down in one description only. Thus, the pain increases in all story participants, and the narrators become more wedded to their story. The frozen story only makes it more likely that its narrator cannot find a way out.

A colleague of mine told the story of the horror at watching his family being forced to the gas chambers in Nazi Germany. He suffered from depression for years. As a boy, he had been imprisoned in a concentration camp and kept a diary to record his experiences. As an adult, he became an artist as well as a psychotherapist. Painting called upon him to express his soul in creative art. He related that finally one day he painted the diary into a montage on a canvas, framed it, and hung it on his wall. That action helped contain his anger and depression.

As he looked at the painting, he noticed that he also potentially possessed the emotions of hate, racism, rage, murderous desire, and greed, as well as other characteristics of the people who had victimized him. When he realized this, he was able to free himself from the obsession of thinking about being victimized and needing to seek revenge. He realized that later, as he could fully accept the "Nazi" in himself, he could move on beyond the trauma. He would never forget the horror, but he could focus his attention on other aspects of his life. My colleague had been committed to moving beyond the past, and he was able to work through the trauma by his own creative art, a hypnotic healing endeavor. Most people are extremely vulnerable to the hypnotic influence of a painful experience and the story that evolves about the experience.

THERAPIST GOALS

When a patient enters therapy, the therapist has two goals. First, the therapist can offer a new and healthy attachment figure through nurturing, caring, gazing, attending, and warm voice tones and body posture. Attachment in adults reflects earlier bonding as children. The bonding process is influenced by responsiveness of the therapist and how amenable the patient is to his influence. When bonding has occurred, the patient can remember phrases the therapist may have said or the face of the therapist, and the therapist's caring stance. The therapist's influence may become greater than the original parent.

Second, the therapist can induce emotional arousal to create uncertainty about an existing belief or behavior. The therapist needs to raise the patient's anxiety enough to create disorganization of a rigidly held belief. Each real-life story told to a therapist describes that which was lost or never found. The tale has a protagonist, antagonist, conflict, struggle, and some attempted resolution of a problem. The story itself may reveal whether or not the person has experienced a secure, anxious, or avoidant attachment to caretakers. Those adults who feel secure remember their caregivers as dependable; those adults who feel anxious remember care-takers as having both positive and negative traits; while those who avoid relationships have memories of caretakers as overbearing and remote (Roberts, 1992, pp. 357–364). A new belief and behavior can then be formed that may be more functional.

In the beginning of therapy, the use of deep empathy and rapport is important in the maintenance of trust when later emotional arousal is stim-ulated. When a client feels genuinely cared for, anxiety can more likely be tolerated and channeled toward change. Heightened arousal and cognitive disorganization has been shown to be a precursor for receptivity to sugges-tion and attitude change (Hoehn-Saric, 1978, p. 103–104). Emotional arousal can be further heightened through therapeutic stories that can develop from the patient's adventures to alter beliefs and behavior and seed ideas for new generative stories. The essence of therapeutic stories is in their multidimensional healing qualities that can offer new solutions. The conscious mind can be bypassed through the telling of the story, and if the story is important to the listener, it will be remembered or activate unconscious processes.

The story told by the therapist is healing because it causes an altered state of consciousness, seeds ideas at multiple levels, and creates a medici-nal silence for inner work to take place. Memory organizes experiences into certain categories, and some experiences are remembered in story form (Schank, 1990). The act of telling a story about an event results in the event and accompanying feelings being remembered. If a person has amnesia for the feelings that occurred during an event but remembers the incident, the affective experience may be locked in the body. Telling the story of that incident may not evoke feelings, whereas the experience of a touch may. The recognition of a symbol of an experience may bring back a memory. When the memory is told, a story is recounted. When a therapist tells a story to a patient for therapeutic reasons, the story will evoke a healing trance, categorize learning, and become a resource to the patient.

To one couple in the throes of disappointment over the marriage, I sug-gested they listen to a musical production. They returned and began to laugh at some of their complaints, a change that stimulated greater change in the system as we worked. In the London production, "Into the Woods," several fairy tale characters (Cinderella, the Prince, Little Red Riding Hood, the Witch) discover life is different after "happily ever after." The happy ending is stolen by the Giant who destroys part of the woods. Cinderella is a courageous tomboy, her Prince is a coward, and one of the characters laments, "I'm in the wrong story." The Witch struggles with how to stay connected to her daughter without locking her in a tower, how to capture her own beauty and power, and how to stop the future from becoming the present (Ratcliffe, 1991). These old familiar fairy tales collapsed into one are told in a new and sometimes shocking way to break the trance the old stories created. The themes with which the characters struggle are similar to our patients' themes and to our themes as well.

Each person in the family has a different story that she or he believes is the true story of the family. All of the family's characters revolve around basic themes and plots that contain hypnotic elements. Stories told by family members speak of how people belong to the family and offer indirect suggestions to direct the future of their lives.

CASE STUDY

One woman, 56, entered therapy for several reasons. She had disturbing dreams and anxiety-provoking fragments of memories, and was hypervigilant. She described her family of origin as a poor southern family where strange and secret events occurred. The patient always noticed that she was the only redhead in the family and had a recurring memory of being taken away from a red-haired woman. Her mother denied that she was adopted, but this woman always knew she did not belong to the family. Intense fear would overcome her, and "it seems like a monster is going to get me." Several physical symptoms were troublesome, such as asthma, high blood pressure, and heart palpitations. The anxiety came in waves and in order to manage it, this woman would doodle the same figure a hundred times. The doodle resembled the back of a hooded cape. I suggested she draw the doodle several times in the office. She became so fearful that her hand began to shake.

Before further memory retrieval, safety resources were elicited (Kershaw, 1992). She was able to find some experiences in her childhood where she felt secure. I suggested to her:

> You are sitting here in this room with me. Your feet are flat on the floor. You and I are here together now. The story you are telling me is about another place and time. And perhaps you have noticed that old tree in the back of my office. It is over 80 years old. It has seen many people come and go, many changes in the neighborhood. This old tree has survived many storms— knowing how to go with the wind. What stories it could tell! When we moved here, the owner laid asphalt for parking behind the house. A few weeks later, some of the limbs began to drop from the trees. John called a tree expert to examine the old tree. The consultant told him that he needed to break up some of the concrete around the tree so it could breathe properly. So John

broke up the concrete around the tree. The expert told him that
the roots of the tree go deep into the soil, and there would always
be enough moisture and nourishment. The tree seemed to drop
those branches it did not need and keep those it did. After a few
weeks, new growth could be spotted.

Several suggestions were given metaphorically to this patient to experience safety, notice there would be enough nourishment and "water" for
life, and she could breathe easier when some of the memory fragments
were filled in.

  After several sessions, this patient called to say that she had an overwhelming feeling that she wanted to take an ice pick and puncture
something. She selected a phone book and stabbed it repeatedly until
exhaustion overtook her. Finally, when her husband was massaging her
neck, the memory surfaced. She began to share with me:

> I am very young; maybe four. Men are stuffing me into a bag and
> taking me somewhere. I look out of the bag and see a black man
> tied up. Other people are standing around. They are dressed in
> white robes and hoods. One of them is poking the black man with
> a knife. To my left is a burning cross. The same man who looks so
> mean takes me and forces me to touch the genitals of the black
> man. Finally, a woman dressed in the same hooded robe takes me
> away. Now I know it was the Ku Klux Klan.

Remarkably, as she shared the memory, a red mark appeared on her neck
in the shape of a cross. The woman began to weep and feel ashamed. I
responded by saying, "This was a terrible experience that was forced upon
you. You were a child with no responsibility for what happened." She
agreed that the black man, the intended victim, felt sympathy for the child
even in his terrible situation.

  After the memory came to her, she reported feeling lighter and more
associated. She realized that her doodles were a way of attempting to
control the unknown horror hidden in the depths of her mind. For further
healing, she traveled to the state in which her family lived when this event
occurred. She read old newspaper accounts, talked with some of the
townspeople, and found her way to the place where the trauma had taken
place. Finally, she was able to work through the terrible memory. She
continued searching for relatives whom she believed her mother had kept
from her. Additionally, her physical symptoms greatly improved.

  Anderson and Goolishian (1988) suggested that "we are narrative artists
co-creating with our clients new coherent meaning from the fragments of

memory, fantasy, and story we are told. As therapists, we are co-authors of narrative that has not been told" (p. 5). Whether the narrative that has not been told has been known and kept secret or whether therapist and client rewrite the story by telling it and retelling it, the actual telling is therapeutic. As a client recounts a story to one who is caring and non-judgmental, healing occurs in the process of relating and creating a new story. This process could be considered "restorying the mind."

RESTORYING THE MIND

There are four stages in the process of restorying the mind.

Stage One

The client's story must be heard and respectfully accepted by the therapist. First, the therapist may ask the diagnostic question: "What does the client need to learn that may be represented by the problem the patient describes?" The therapist can listen for the psychological system in which the patient believes she is embedded, and which supports her. The context in which the patient lives may be maintaining or contributing to the difficulty. The "problem" is renamed as a new task that needs to be learned.

As the patient tells the story, the therapist may want to ask: "What is interfering with the flow of the story or achieving a solution or goal? Does this story lack solutions to problems that have been described in the patient's recounting of a situation or are the solutions old and inflexible? What is the major life theme that this patient lives by and through?" A colleague told me that the tenet he now lives by is "Everything is interesting and nothing is important" (Robert Elliott, personal communication). Are there mythic elements or developmental conflicts or denial of terrible abuse that keep mothers and sons, fathers and daughters, daughters and mothers, and sons and fathers from reconciling relationships? Are people more loyal to the story of the family than to their own development? Are there secret traumas that have never been told? What are the painful events that have been left unintegrated into one's life? Each individual and family has an organizing metaphor (story) in life with various characters, themes, subplots, and story lines. The organizing metaphor can be the door to open new possibilities of change. As the patient recounts her story, these can become clear.

The organizing metaphor is the expression of a central belief that may result in conflict or emotional pain on the one hand and, on the other, serve as a life story that protects its narrator. One patient who was sexually abused and tortured by her grandmother's boyfriends when she was eight years old began to develop a fantasy country with several characters. She would practice going into the story while she was with the abusers. "I just step out of time and place and go away," she would recount.

After many sessions of rapport and trust building, she was willing to introduce me to the characters in her story. This ongoing novel that she had written in her mind over a period of 30 years had been an actual story containing many chapters in which she would participate when she felt stress or unacceptable anger. The dissociative process had helped her survive the terrible abuse from which no parent had protected her. The problem she presented was that she would dissociate at times when she preferred to stay connected, experiencing the symptom as out of her control. The central belief was "to be alive you must go away." I suggested that "Your ability to step out of time into another place has been an important resource and one that you really want to keep. You have said that you want to be able to manage when you step away and decide when to return." Because she could work with the characters, bring them into the psychotherapy sessions, and speak through them, the characters themselves revealed how they assisted the patient in her everyday actions.

This client obsessively fantasized scenes that portrayed sexual torture and wanted relief from her association of pain with the sexual response. She felt terrible shame whenever she engaged in these fantasies. I suggested to her that the fantasies were a way she had devised to master the terrible events that had been forced upon her as a child. She wanted to learn a new way to separate the torture experiences and her own sexual response as a human being.

Her assignment was to purchase one of Georgia O'Keefe's art books and "to really notice the expression of wonderful feminine sexuality in the many colorful flowers." She reported having had a positive experience of looking at the paintings and feeling their "juiciness" in a way that lacked any shame. I asked her to bring the book to the next session. Reviewing the paintings in a therapy atmosphere of support, acceptance, and new perspective allowed her to expand her view of sexuality into one aspect of beautiful, acceptable sensuality. The assignment had provided a safe structure for her to experience sexual feelings in the safety of her home, and to interpret them in a positive frame. She became so enchanted with the learning that she began studying more of Georgia O'Keefe's paintings. Each positive experience built on the last.

Through more hypnotic therapy, this client eventually reduced the frequency of torture fantasies, began to enjoy her own sexual response, and had more pleasant sexual experiences with her husband. I suggested she could allow her sensual, artistic self to sit next to herself sitting next to her husband. This self could tell her a story about how to enjoy touch and pressure. She preferred to tell the story to herself and smiled when she was finished. She worked through the rage she had carried toward her grandmother and learned she could move beyond the experience.

Stage Two

A second stage in restorying the mind occurs when the therapist can assist the patient in facing his or her personal history, mastering it, and looking to several possible positive futures. As the patient tells the life narrative and the therapist listens, the experience of the story and the story itself can begin to change. In a reconciliation session with a father and an 18-year-old daughter, the father asked, "I'd just like some gratitude for all the things I've tried to provide Sally." Sally looked away with tears of guilt and rage. She said, "You don't like any of my friends and you want to control me. I see our family as distant, and I don't want to be around here." I said, "You both feel hurt and unsure of one thing. I think you both are asking each other the same question: 'Do you love me?'" Both showed tears and softened. Each looked at the other and said, "Of course I love you."

I said, "Sometimes it is hard to remember those special feelings when there are different needs between you. You, Sally, notice that you feel confused about when you want to be close and when you want to be distant. As your dad tries to support your independence, he remembers you as that little baby he held in his arms. It is so difficult for him to remember with such sentiment and love but move from that image to see you as an adult woman. Sometimes I feel at home like I'm shrinking in size because my youngest stepdaughter, who is 13 years old is 5'7", and I remember when she was very small." Dad then addressed his daughter, "I really like how you are trying to negotiate with your mom and me." And she said, "It's so much better than arguing." I interjected, "So when you are negotiating, that is a time to notice that you are feeling closer." The daughter and her dad began to develop a new collaborative story that was more positive and generative of new attitudes and behavior.

Stage Three

A third stage for restorying the mind is to begin to create the healing trance in the session with the patient. The healing trance is a state of shared health between therapist and patient. The healing quality of the trance state experienced with the therapist is marked by a shift in consciousness and change in a belief, perspective, self-narrative, and role in the family system. This positive altered state of consciousness can be fostered in the beginning of therapy by the therapist responding to the level of need in the patient by acceptance of boundaries and hypnotic alliance. Before she was willing to enter a pleasant trance state, one patient asked me three times to push my bangs aside so that she could see my eyes. They were in no danger of covering my eyes, but the patient demonstrated a strong need to be in control and a fear that I might pull something over her eyes literally and metaphorically. I moved my hair gently from left to right, gazed into her eyes, and said, "Is this just right for you? Can you see clearly into my eyes and breathe comfortably now?" then I offered a suggestion to relax and begin a new learning in her own way and time. She relaxed and began to experience a positive trance, learning about letting go of such tight control.

Within the healing trance, the therapist may develop a metaphor that is so synchronous with the patient's experience, that the deep communication between the two stands out. One client asked for assistance in managing her tendency to overwork. She had difficulty relaxing even when she created space in her schedule. Besides the "hypnotic" imperatives from her family that work meant she was valuable, she pushed herself into activity to avoid anxiety. I began to narrate a hypnotic story.

> The city of Houston is beginning to develop zoning. Certain areas of the city in the future will have more structure. The city began as a boom town and, consequently, residences sprang up with businesses next to them. There was little concern for the ecology. The focus was on getting things done and establishing the most the quickest. Now, people are beginning to realize that it is important to have new zones, areas where there are only homes and areas where there is only business. People in our area, in fact, want a rezoning, a new zone of comfort between business and living. It can be nice to enjoy that new zone of comfort. Of course, there are those who don't support this revolutionary idea. They long for absolute freedom, and you know where that has gotten us: no order, little space reserved for the aesthetic. It is nice to have comforting space between what you do and where you live.

The client came out of trance and said she had conflict a long time ago with her father over the same topic. The story had been remarkably synchronous with her experience so that it captured her attention. The idea of a zone of comfort was quite interesting to her. She began to think about taking time off in a new way. To have comforting space between what you do and where you live was a suggestion to reorganize those internal aspects as well as external ones that are necessary to growth.

Stage Four

The fourth stage for restorying the mind is the use of strategic methods that include 1) meta-narrative enactment, a story about the patient's story that is active and dynamic in the present; 2) hypnotic conversation that is patient-centered and suggests an expectation of healing; 3) hypnotic questions that use implication and suggestion; and 4) the therapist's use of healing silence or quieting trance to impact the dynamics in the session. Various techniques to accomplish the preceding aspects of the fourth stage are described in the following case.

The meta-narrative enactment may be a therapeutic metaphor (Lankton & Lankton, 1983; Kershaw, 1992), an actual story about the patient's story, or an active dialogue about an imagery assignment, such as an abstract drawing of a relationship. A creative drama unfolds between therapist and client in an enactment that brings the story into the present moment.

CASE STUDY

A woman in her late 30's suffered from constant waking in the night during which she saw someone trying to watch her or conspire against her. She described her family history as abusive and frightening. Her father would come home drunk and rage at the family. Her mother would disappear into another room, and she and her brother were left to be whipped with a belt. Much of her history was a blur, but she did remember her brother touching her genitals in the middle of the night several times. Her grandfather lived in the house, and on several occasions, he fondled her. She never told anyone about either of these traumas.

I used hypnotic questioning and implied expectations of healing with her and asked: "How did you manage to survive those terrible experiences? How did you go on to marry, to be a successful professional woman? And can you, perhaps, wonder just how those resources that have sustained you in the past can be used in the future?" Through her therapy this patient called her brother and told him she wanted to speak to him about his abuse of her. She had hated him for years and refused to talk to him. He apologized in tears, asked her forgiveness, and told her he wanted a relationship with her. She began to heal the hurt and pain of betrayal with her brother, but said she could never be close to him. However, she began to have other healing conversations with him.

The expression of feelings was difficult for this woman. She could not find her own voice. It had been so punishing to speak the truth in her family that she had stopped allowing herself to feel. Her descriptions of the abusive events were intellectualized. Her eyes would glaze over and she would dissociate when speaking about the past. She told me dispassionately that her baby had died at birth when she was 18, and her mother told her to speak no more of the child. I asked about her sadness at losing her only child. She could not feel it, she said, but her eyes became moist with feeling. I told her this story:

> A colleague of mine went to an abbey in the north for a silent retreat. He met a priest there who during the short social time each day told my colleague about his experience in New Guinea. The priest recounted that the tribes in New Guinea are close communities and work to support each family. One day, he said, a young boy had a tragic accident and died. His family was overwhelmed with grief. The rest of the tribe gathered coconuts, took the family, and went into the forest to dance. They entered a trance dance and continued into the early hours of the morning until the tribe as a community hallucinated the young boy who reassured the tribe and family that he was happy, and they could let go of him. He could remain alive in their memories. The community then returned to their lives.

The young woman began to cry and told me her son would be 19 now. "Tell me what he would look like and what kind of person he would be," I asked. She responded by looking out in front of her and describing her son. "I never thought of myself as a mother, but I am," she said. She began to allow herself to grieve over the next few months. I suggested that she visit his grave and have a conversation with him. She went to the grave, talked with him, and came back to tell me that it was the first time she had ever been there. Her child had been buried while she was still in the hospital. Healing over this profound loss finally began. Since she had such difficulty allowing herself to feel, I explored another avenue.

As a hobby, she painted and sculpted. I requested that she paint an abstract of her feelings. She responded that the exercise would be risky. "Could you paint a risky abstract?" I requested. She agreed to complete the assignment. She brought in an abstract pastel painting. I suggested she allow herself to go into the painting and become each of the colored forms, a meta-narrative enactment. She went into trance and began to say, "I am cold, lonely, isolated. If I could get rid of this wall (referring to an abstract wall in the painting), the light would be brighter. I'm trying to protect myself from the dark side." I asked about a small blue dot in the painting. She said, "I am the soul." My instructions were for her to go inside the soul and paint another abstract from that perspective. She returned with a painting of a human figure in yellow that was bent over. The patient reported, "I feel full of wisdom and power but cannot stand up yet."

She spoke more about her father and her anger toward him. I suggested she continue the therapeutic work by doing a painting of her relationship with her father. She began to have the feeling that her father had abused her as well and recounted a dream that had prompted her to seek therapy. She dreamed she was sleeping naked next to her father, and he began to touch her sexually.

The next session she brought in the painting. She described it: "I pounded red with my fingers around the part that represents Dad. The red is my anger. When I started, I could see Dad's eyes—devil eyes that were green and gold." I suggested that the pounding of the red was carefully done around the part that was her father. She responded, "Why did I have to protect him? I know. Because I wasn't beaten like my brother." She stared for a long time at her painting and said, "There are several penises in this painting. Oh my God! I didn't want us to touch, but I couldn't keep the figures from touching. I'm afraid of the phallus touching me because that would mean he abused me . . . he abused me," she said after a long wait. I responded, "And if he could have been the father he most wanted to be, that would have never happened. But it did and you survived. Healing can continue now at a very deep level. Your unconscious mind can help you place many things in perspective, and you can remember what you need to, and what you want to forget can stay forgotten. You only need to tell a story once for healing unless your unconscious directs in a different way."

After several sessions of processing this awareness, the patient painted herself as the many feelings coming together with a flower blooming from them. I sat quietly in an externally oriented trance, a state of externally focused attention, feeling a sense of calm. The patient sat quietly looking at the painting. Her eyes remained fixed and staring. It seemed that something important was occurring. She then said that the painting was an expression of some new integration that was happening inside her that she had no words to describe. I suggested to her: "You can have a partial understanding now of something that can be more complete in the future. A new understanding can occur; a new feeling, a new thought or idea that continues the healing process inside you."

During the course of therapy, these healing silences occurred frequently. It is in the healing silence that change can be fostered. This healing trance might be considered a state of healing consciousness that the therapist enters and shares with the patient. As the therapist maintains the healing trance, the dynamics of the patient may change. The healing quality of the trance state experienced with the therapist is marked by a shift in consciousness, evidenced by a change in the patient's self-narrative, behavior, and affect. The hypnosis literature is replete with studies where altered states of consciousness influence psychological and physiological health (Barber, 1961, 1984). The healing trance and conversation create new images, new feelings that continue to generate new learnings on their own. The experiential aspects of hypnotic psychotherapy help change the rigid repetitive patterns that diminish one's experience of the fullness of life. Then a new story can be told—a story of healing change.

REFERENCES

Anderson, H., and H. Goolishian. (1988). Human systems as linguistic systems: Evolving ideas about the implications for theory and practice. *Journal of Strategic and Systemic Therapies, 7*:54-70.

Anderson, H., and H. Goolishian. (1990). Beyond cybernetics: Comment on Atkinson's and Heath's "Future thoughts on second-order family therapy." *Family Process, 29:*157-163.

Barber, T. X. (1961). Psychological aspects of hypnosis. *Psychological Bulletin, 58,* 390-419.

Barber, T. X. (1984). Changing unchangeable bodily processes by hypnotic suggestions: A new look at hypnosis, cognitions, imagining, and the mind-body problem. *Advances, 1(2),* 7-40.

Estes, C. P. (1992). Women who run with the wolves: Myths and stories of the wild woman archetype. New York: Ballantine Books.

Hoehn-Saric, R. (1978). Emotional arousal, attitude change, and psychotherapy. In *Effective Ingredients of Successful Psychotherapy,* edited by J. Frank, et al., 73-106. New York: Brunner/Mazel.

Kershaw, C. (1992). The couple's hypnotic dance: Creating Ericksonian strategies in marital therapy. New York: Brunner/Mazel.

Lankton, S., and C. Lankton. (1983). The answer within. New York: Brunner/Mazel.

Mair, M. (1988). Psychology as storytelling. *Journal of Personal Construct Psychology, 1:*125-137.

Ratcliffe, M. (1991). Into the woods (Musical Production). New York: BMG Music.

Roberts, T. (1992). Sexual attraction and romantic love: Forgotten variables in marital therapy. *Journal of Marital and Family Therapy, 18*(4), 357-364.

Sarbin, T. (Ed.) (1986). Narrative psychology. New York: Praeger.

Schank, R. (1990). Tell me a story: A new look at real and artificial memory. New York: Charles Scribner's Sons.

CHAPTER 12

The Essence of Ericksonian Methods: Up for Grabs

Richard Fisch

If you have been wondering what the title of this chapter means, you can forget it. It really has nothing to do with what I will be saying. When I was first asked to give an address and was told it should revolve around the theme of "Erickson: The Essence of the Story," I said, "Sure." But when I started to think about how to pinpoint the essence of his work, work so sweeping and so revolutionary in its scope, I was in a quandary. Therefore, the title really refers to the uncertainty of my approach to this most challenging of tasks.

At best, my attempts are groping. I've written and rewritten this a number of times and I'm still not happy with it. I'd like to blame that on Erickson himself; if he had ever made explicit the model he had developed, we wouldn't have to bother with trying to figure out the essentials of his work. However, it is probably better that he didn't; it keeps so many of us busy trying to figure out what he was really doing or believing. My own attempts will, unavoidably, reflect my biases. It really does seem that "Seeing is believing ," is less the case than "Believing is seeing." As part of my bias, I decided that instead of focusing on what in Erickson's work made it so effective, I would focus on what in his work was most significant in reordering ideas about people and their problems.

First, I think it important to keep in mind the clinical climate existing during the time he was developing his own directions, a climate that has not changed all that much. For the most part, people seeking help with their distress were offered few basic options: They could enter into a mysterious relationship with a therapist, one that involved a peculiar, one-sided conversation that went on for years and at great expense. This was most often called "analysis" or, equally impressive, "individual psychodynamic psychotherapy." Or, if they didn't have the proclivity for that kind of endeavor or, more importantly, the money for it, and, worst of all, if they just wanted to get over their problems as quickly as possible, then they were offered "supportive" treatment. This was a euphemism for, "They don't have enough brains or sophistication for real therapy, so let's not waste a lot of time on them. We'll have to shoot from the hip, maybe use a little TLC or some condescending practical advice, and see if there are any appropriate groups we can park them in for the foreseeable future." Or, they could be offered drugs (the more respectable term is "medication"). Of course, if they were behaving in a way that was significantly troublesome enough to someone else, such as family members, the neighbors, or agents of social control, they would be placed in psychiatric warehouses to languish, comfortably enough (if one could afford private mental hospitalization) or austerely (in public facilities). There they were given, usually involuntarily, the benefits of contemporary psychiatric science: electric shock, psychosurgery, insulin coma, metrazol convulsive treatment, and, for a quiet change of pace, seclusion rooms. Later, the psychotropic drugs made their appearance and, since they didn't seem so brutal, became more popular. It's somehow less disturbing to see inpatients just quietly shuffling along the halls than to see them manhandled into a straightjacket.

Now, there was one unifying theme behind all these approaches, whether inpatient or outpatient. It was the idea, borrowed from traditional medicine, that people in distress, certainly those acting in deviant or troublesome ways, were suffering from an illness, a malady, a disorder. Since one couldn't X-ray it, find blood, or see other bodily changes on postmortem, not even cellular changes that would hold up in any decent scientific lab, then, of course, it had to be a "disease of the mind," a "mental illness" for which appropriate diagnostic labels could be invented; thus the beginnings of DSM-I, the winner of the Hugo Award* of its time.

This idea that the complaint, whatever its nature, merely represented the "tip of the iceberg" and that beneath lay a web of rather mysterious intertwinings, possibly originating in the dim past, is, in itself, a pessimistic notion to proceed on. But this was the accepted notion of the time and to a

---

*Ed. Note: The Hugo Award honors accomplishments in science fiction.

significant degree remains so. Based on that "norm," "long-term therapy" was the standard. Attempts by some innovators, Erickson among them, to focalize treatment and thereby shorten it were held in disrepute. "Problem-focused" treatment was discounted as "superficial." It was "band-aid therapy" at best, applicable to only a few patients. Even people within the field of brief treatment supported the notion that it was of limited application; "What are the indications for brief psychotherapy ?" is a phrase still in current use, implying that "long-term treatment" was the standard and preferred mode.

What I believe was unique to Erickson and most compelling and intriguing in his work was that he didn't seem to deal with people as if they were sick. It was this factor that was a major inspiration for the Brief Therapy project at the Mental Research Institute (MRI). Whether the complaint was about child rearing, marital problems, odd compulsions or obsessions, or even psychosis, he steadfastly focused on the stated complaint. He was not intimidated by "craziness" and, in fact, might even use the very "craziness" of the patient to steer things in a productive path. One cannot be overly impressed with the notion of psychopathology if one begins a dialogue with a hospitalized patient claiming to be Jesus Christ with the opener, "I understand you have some experience with carpentry."

We stand in great respect, probably awe, at Erickson's creativity in honing communication to such a finely precise and influential instrument; wording, phrasing, emphasis, timing, the predominant use of implication, even the use of his body — all of these were deliberate tools in his efforts to beneficially influence his patient. But of equal, if not greater, importance was what he focused on as the fundamental task of that influence. It was that kind of focus that most distinguished his work. He opened up a different pathway along which treatment could proceed and grow. In a nutshell, he demolished the dichotomy of "long-term" versus "brief" therapies into a continuum I would best describe as, "How much time do you want to spend getting down to business?"

What he said to patients, what he told them to do, both explicitly and implicitly, and, equally, what he didn't bother with, suggest that he just did not see people as sick—foolish, maybe, but not sick. Often, it seemed that he saw their complaints, their distress, as misplaced efforts to achieve goals eminently human and understandable, and he would induce them to go about their efforts in some different and eminently more workable way. One of his well-known cases was that of the young man who claimed he could urinate only by holding a hollow tube at the end of his penis. This had become a problem for him because he was facing military induction and did not want to be disqualified. Erickson did not take time to "explore" with him this unusual practice. He "simply" prescribed that the young man continue the practice, but cut off a small length of the tube a bit at a time over a period of some weeks until he was able to dispense with the last vestige of the tube and urinate "normally."

This case, like so many of his cases, is an example of Erickson's interest in *using* what the patient presents, not in challenging it. This calls to mind the man who sought help from Erickson, but warned him that he would be unable to be hypnotized because his very complaint precluded hypnosis. He had a compulsion to pace the floor ceaselessly. Erickson accepted that limitation, but asked the man to pace in directions Erickson suggested, the suggestions becoming more tenuous and confusing until the patient responded to the simple and reasonably direct command to ". . . just sit in that chair and let yourself go into a trance." Using what the patient offered was a hallmark of his work, whether in a hypnotic or nonhypnotic context. I would see that as an enormously useful technique in the service of viewing patients' problems as unfortunate but understandable efforts needing to be redirected.

Ironically, then, I would see as the essence of his technique the very extensiveness with which he applied the technical aspects of his work; it opened the door, freeing therapy to pass beyond the search for better ways of treating this or that to being able to look at problems differently. I believe this was neccessary to enable brief therapy to become the standard; one of these days, we'll be able to do away with the word "brief" altogether. I don't think any of us will ever match Erickson; among other things, it takes enormous courage to persevere in the directions he did. But, we don't have to match him, even if that were possible, because his work opened up options and tools upon which we can build.

CHAPTER 13

Reframing:
The Essence of Psychotherapy?

Philip Barker

INTRODUCTION

In this chapter I want to address the somewhat daunting question of how psychotherapy works. My thoughts on the subject have been inspired largely by my study of Milton Erickson's work. What has struck me about his therapy has been the enormous variety of things he did to help his patients. Jay Haley has raised the intriguing question of how Erickson came by the methods he used (see Chapter 1). Who were his teachers? What were his models? How was it that he developed approaches that were so different from those of his contemporaries?

I cannot answer these questions, but I suggest that Erickson approached each therapeutic challenge by considering how the situation with which he was presented, or some aspect of it, might be reframed. Was reframing really the essence of his work? Is it, perhaps, the core of all successful psychotherapy, whatever its ostensible theoretical basis?

At least two books have addressed the question, "What Is Psychotherapy?" (Bloch, 1982; Zeig & Munion, 1990). The more recent of these is remarkable in that it brings together the perspectives of 81 contemporary psychotherapists and presents a very wide range of therapies. It also offers 81 definitions of psychotherapy and raises the question of whether or not there is any one thing we can call "psychotherapy?" Indeed, Bloch (1988) suggests that we should use the term "psychotherapies" rather than trying to make one thing out of psychotherapy.

What do these diverse approaches have in common apart from the broad objective of producing some sort of change? Just how do they promote change? This seems to be unclear, even in that most long-established of therapeutic approaches, psychoanalysis (Meissner, 1991). And what about "supportive psychotherapy"? Can providing "support," which, according to some definitions at least, seeks to support the person while he or she copes with stress or distress of some sort, legitimately be called psychotherapy? Of course, it all depends what you mean by supportive. Crown (1988) suggests that "supportive psychotherapy" is a contradiction in terms. If it is supportive — rather than change-promoting, presumably — it cannot be psychotherapy; and if it is psychotherapy, it cannot be supportive. (Some authors, however, use the term "supportive psychotherapy" in a different sense [see Chessick, 1990; Holmes, 1988].)

I want to suggest here that the process of "reframing" may be the one common denominator in psychotherapy. If a "therapy" does not do this, I contend, it should not qualify as psychotherapy. Whether reframing is the actual *mechanism* of change is a different question, one that I will address later in this chapter.

According to Coyne (1985), reframing is "a basic tool of strategic therapists." I agree with this, but what I suggest is that it is also a basic tool of all effective psychotherapy. While strategic therapists may be those who make the most conscious use of the process, I believe that reframing, whether consciously intended by the therapist or not, occurs in all forms of psychotherapy, when they are successful.

The many ingenious "strategic" interventions reported, for example, in *Change* (Watzlawick, Weakland & Fisch, 1974) are all examples of reframing. Perhaps the same can be said of the entire reported psychotherapeutic work of Milton Erickson. *My Voice Will Go With You* (Rosen, 1982) has a chapter entitled "Reframing," but I believe a case can be made that every therapeutic maneuver used by Erickson had the effect of reframing something. But I will return to Erickson's work later.

REFRAMING DEFINED

So, what is reframing? The term, though much used, is not easily defined. Perhaps the simplest definition, and therefore maybe the best, is just, "changing the perceived meaning of something." This may be a bit of an oversimplification because the process seems to involve both a change in perception and a change in cognition, as well as, very often, an affective change. Any of these three changes may come first.

The analogy of changing the frame of a picture has been used to explain therapeutic reframing, but it does not seem to be adequate. There is one form of reframing—"context reframing," described by Bandler and Grinder (1982)—that is quite similar to changing a picture frame. There is no doubt that the meaning of a behavior experienced in a different context, may change, but reframing is not confined to changing context. Bandler and Grinder (1982) also refer to "content reframing." This is the creation of a different sense of meaning to the "thing" itself, rather than simply changing the context in which it is viewed or experienced. A child's behavior may be seen as a reaction to the child's situation, and indeed children's behaviors do commonly vary greatly from one context to another, but the actual meaning of the behavior ("He's just upset," "He's a real bad kid," "He's going through a difficult phase," "I was just like that as a kid," or "He's going to kill someone one of these days") will depend on the cognitions of whoever is considering it. Any of the above meanings—and many others—may be given to one set of behaviors. But the behaviors are the same whatever view one takes of them. Beating up another child is beating up another child, no matter how it is understood.

If the meaning attributed to the behavior by those who must deal with it does not lead to a resolution of the problem, that is to say, to certain changes in behavior, the therapeutic task is to give it a new meaning, in other words, to reframe it.

Coyne (1985) has provided one of the most thoughtful discussions of reframing, though he concentrates on its use as a key feature of "strategic" therapy. Yet, in a sense, all therapies are strategic in that they inevitably employ a strategy designed to bring about change. As Coyne points out, Bateson (1955, p. 338) is credited with proposing the use of the term "frame" for "the organization of interaction such that at any given time certain events are more likely to occur and certain interpretations of what is going on are more likely to be made."

THE CONSTRUCTIONIST PERSPECTIVE

This brings us to the matter of constructionism: Reality is what we make it. Watzlawick (1978) has pointed out that "the most dangerous delusion of all is that there is only one reality (p. xi)," and he goes on to write that "there are many different versions of reality, some of which are contradictory, but all of which are the results of communication, and not reflections of eternal, objective truth (p. xi)." If we accept this thesis, and I believe there are good reasons for doing so, there can be no single explanation of the symptoms or problems our clients bring to us. Their problems are real enough, but how they are to be understood depends on the point of view of the person considering them. This may explain why so many different approaches to psychotherapy seem to be successful, at least in certain cases.

The constructionist point of view is that we organize our experiences according to our concept of the world. One person regards a child's misbehavior as the responsibility or "fault" of the child, another sees it as due to a failure of the parents to take proper control of the child; another may regard it as an attempt to engage the parents' attention. One may see it as indicating a serious defect of character, while another regards it as a transient developmental phenomenon. Yet, all are considering the same set of behaviors. It is from such premises that strategic therapists derive their interventions.

Thus, is reframing any different from changing our constructs, that is, our understanding of the world, at least insofar as they are relevant to the matters being dealt with? Maybe not.

WHY IS THE CONCEPT OF REFRAMING IMPORTANT?

Before going on to consider how various psychotherapies reframe things, I should like to explain why I believe this is an issue of practical importance. If psychotherapy is a process during which something useful happens, we need, in order to assess its value, to be able to demonstrate both that something relevant has happened and that this has had beneficial results—that is to say, the desired results have been achieved, at least in some measure.

To use an analogy, it is the opinion of many that one's risk of getting cardiovascular disease is lessened if one's blood cholesterol is kept below a certain level. Various treatments, dietary and otherwise, are advocated to help people achieve this goal. There remains, however, the central question of whether lowering blood cholesterol is the essential mechanism that contributes to the success of all methods of reducing the risk of heart disease. The importance of knowing the answer to this question is obvious. I suggest that the importance of knowing whether or not reframing is central to all successful psychotherapy is of comparable importance.

REFRAMING IN PSYCHOTHERAPY

Let us now consider some psychotherapy approaches as reframing procedures. Space constraints make it impossible for me to consider here all forms of psychotherapy, so I will confine myself to a few examples. I have chosen to consider some of the categories discussed in *What Is Psychotherapy?* (Zeig & Munion, 1990). (It may be worth pointing out, however, that the term "reframing" does not even appear in the index to this book.)

I will start with "psychoanalysis." While this term covers a variety of ways of proceeding, it seems to aim to achieve the most radical reframing of any form of psychotherapy. The successfully psychoanalyzed subject emerges with a greatly changed view of himself or herself. As Zeig and Munion (1990, p. 17) put it:

> The therapist takes the position of promoting understanding and bringing hidden aspects into consciousness. These are the lenses for both therapist and patient. There is a commitment to charting the murky recesses of the unconscious and understanding its evolution.

To the dynamic therapist, therefore, the task is to reframe the patient's symptoms in terms of past experiences, especially the emotions related to those experiences. These are considered to be repressed and out of conscious awareness. Part of the role of the psychoanalyst is the interpretation of these issues in the context of the transference relationship. If the patient does not emerge from the therapy with a fundamentally changed view of his or her original symptoms, which are now understood as representing the consequences of experiences earlier in life, the treatment has failed.

Let us turn next to what is often considered the other extreme of the therapeutic spectrum, behavior therapy. A strength of behavioral approaches is their empirical nature. Our behavior is conceived of as a set of learned responses, cognitions, and emotions that are regarded as learned behaviors.

The newer, cognitive forms of behavior therapy clearly aim to reframe subjects' cognitions. In *Cognitive Therapy of Depression*, Beck and his colleagues (1979, p. 3) state that:

> . . . an individual's affect and behavior are largely determined by the way he structures the world. . . . His cognitions (verbal or pictorial "events" in the stream of consciousness) are based on attitudes or assumptions (schemas), developed from previous experiences.

In other words, our learned "attitudes and assumptions" are the problem. Therapy becomes the task of teaching new attitudes. This is nothing if not reframing.

But what about other forms of behavior therapy, such as classical and operant conditioning and modelling? It is not difficult to understand modelling as reframing. The subject sees someone achieving something in a particular way, or using a particular method, and observes that this achieves success. If this is different from the subject's previous behavior, it reframes the task as one to be carried out in a different way. Put more simply, you see me taking a shortcut to somewhere or something, and your idea of how to get there quickly is changed—or reframed.

Then there is classical conditioning. Consider Pavlov's dogs. I suggest that Pavlov just carried out a simple process of content reframing, changing for the dogs the meaning of the sound of the bell. Operant conditioning does the same thing by giving the "reward" or "punishment" after the event rather than before it. Thus, the significance, or meaning, of a lever that, when pressed, yields nothing becomes reframed when it starts to yield M & M's, or whatever. If extinction occurs, as it will if pressing the lever fails to elicit the expected reward over a certain period of time, the reframing has been lost—or perhaps one should say that the meaning of the lever has become re-reframed.

Let us consider now client-centered therapy. Sanford (1990, p. 81), in her chapter on this treatment modality, describes the reframing process beautifully. She says that psychotherapy is:

> . . . a process in which two persons enter into a relationship for the purpose of assisting the client to make positive changes in attitudes towards self and others and to find increasingly satisfying ways of coping with life situations.

Interestingly, Sanford goes on to question whether or not it is possible to define psychotherapy as a whole. She suggests that the value of the exercise in definition is "for each of us to define what psychotherapy means for us" (p. 81). She may be right, but how confusing such a situation is bound to be for anyone wanting to study the subject and, perhaps most of all, for the client seeking the treatment that will best meet his or her needs.

Describing the process of client-centered therapy, Sanford says that this is "a way of being with a client based on the premise that within each human organism there are vast resources for . . . change in ways of being and behaving" (p. 8). It is easy to see this as a reframing process.

ERICKSON'S WORK

Instead of going through a whole list of other psychotherapies and telling you how I believe their success can be explained as caused by the process of reframing, I will turn to the work of Milton Erickson and his enormously rich heritage of therapeutic ideas.

One of the most striking things about Erickson's work is its apparent diversity. He differed from so many other founders of "schools" of psychotherapy in saying little about theory and instead demonstrating what could be done by various means. I would not presume to speculate on just how he thought up the many therapeutic interventions he used, but they all seem to involve the process of reframing. I suspect, however, that understanding problems in a new way, which is the essence of the reframing process, was at the heart of his work

My first introduction to Erickson was reading Haley's (1973) book *Uncommon Therapy*. This is an extraordinary collage of original approaches. As I see it, Erickson approached every one of the clinical problems reported in this book by thinking about it in a new way — a way in which no one who had previously tried to solve the problem had done.

Perhaps this is the hallmark of psychotherapy as distinct from "counselling." I have noticed that these terms are nowadays often used in ways that are almost indistinguishable. But, to me, counselling is essentially the giving of advice, or counsel, while psychotherapy refers to a more sophisticated approach to resolving human dilemmas that do not yield to straightforward advice.

O'Hanlon and Hexum (1990) have done us a great service in gathering together in one book summaries of all of Erickson's reported cases. These are neatly outlined, with the main clinical features mentioned, followed by a brief description of the treatment Erickson used, and then a listing of the techniques used in the therapy. As one would expect, reframing is mentioned many times, but I suggest that it played a part, probably a key part, in every case reported.

As good a place to start as any is probably the beginning. I would draw your attention to the first two cases summarized in O'Hanlon and Hexum's book. These are cases of thumb sucking. In both, Erickson used symptom prescription. A 16-year-old girl sucked her thumb and a variety of approaches, especially religious ones, had failed to solve the problem. The parents requested that Erickson take a religious approach, but Erickson declined to do this. This is the first "reframe." It quickly becomes apparent to anyone entering the field of psychotherapy that trying more of the same things that have already been tried unsuccessfully seldom works. So it is not surprising that Erickson declined to do this. By choosing not to regard the problem as being a religious one or a moral issue, he immediately gave it a new meaning.

The symptom had been labelled an aggressive behavior by a school psychologist. Looked at conventionally, this might lead to therapy designed to explore the origins of the patient's aggressive feelings and to resolve them. That would likely be a long process and success would not be assured, if only because the idea that the symptom was an aggressive behavior was just an hypothesis. Nevertheless, Erickson decided to start with the "aggressive" hypothesis. He builds his treatment approach by reframing the hypothesis. If the symptom is aggressive in nature, let's use it but reframe it. Expressing aggression in this way is not bad, it's good. Let's get the girl to suck her thumb noisily and aggressively in certain situations. (Incidentally, this is not just symptom prescription, it is symptom magnification.) For the patient, the symptom becomes reframed in just about the most radical way possible. It becomes a chore that has to be done at certain prescribed times. After a while the girl got tired of sucking her thumb as prescribed and quit sucking her thumb altogether. At follow-up a year later she had not returned to thumb sucking.

The other case of thumb sucking summarized by O'Hanlon and Hexum (1990) is that of a six-year-old boy who also bit his nails. Punishments and dire warnings of the ill effects of thumb sucking had proved ineffective. Erickson again used paradox, or what I prefer to call magnification, telling his patient that little boys need to suck their thumbs and bite their nails, but that he was being unfair to his other fingers and he should suck them too, and as much as he wanted. The symptom was reframed as something age-appropriate. That, of course, meant that it would not be appropriate at a later time. Erickson then pointed out that, while six-year-old boys need to suck their thumbs, he didn't know of any seven-year-old boys who did this; and he suggested that the boy should get all his thumb sucking done in the next two weeks, since he would soon be a seven-year-old boy and would want to join the other big boys. The thumb sucking and nail biting ceased shortly before the boy's seventh birthday. This is a clear case, but quite a sophisticated one, of developmental reframing, as described by Coppersmith (1981).

It is perhaps a reflection of the sway that psychoanalysis held in North America during Erickson's lifetime that many patients came to him with problems that psychoanalysis had failed to resolve. In such cases, Erickson invariably reframed the problem. Usually by implication rather than overtly, he suggested that the problem was due to something other than the effects of the repressed conflicts that psychoanalysis hypothesizes as the cause. Erickson's genius is particularly evident in some of these cases.

One of his reported cases is that of a 50-year-old smoker with Buerger's disease, diabetes, heart disease, and hypertension, whose medical condition had deteriorated during eight months of psychoanalytic treatment, his smoking having increased from one and a half packs a day to four packs a day. He had also gained 40 pounds and his blood pressure had risen 35 points. As is so often the case with Erickson's treatments, the prescription Erickson gave his patient was quite simple. He induced trance and then had the patient tell him what he thought would be the proper therapy for his problem. The patient came up with a clear treatment plan, and Erickson had him repeat it four times and then feel a compulsion to follow it, since it came from within him (O'Hanlon & Hexum, 1990). The result was that the man changed his habits and became fit.

It seems likely that this man had some awareness of the concept of the unconscious. After all, he had had eight months of psychoanalysis. Erickson built on this, but reframed it. He didn't deny the existence of the unconscious, but he reframed it — as was so typical of him — as a resource to be used rather than as the container of a burden to be lifted. Implicit in his treatment was the assumption, which he seemed to make in all of his work, that his subjects had within them the resources they needed for recovery. In a sense, this is a truism. If we do not have the potential for healthy functioning somewhere within us, what hope is there of recovery?

Let's look at one more of Erickson's cases. This one is selected completely at random. I simply opened O'Hanlon and Hexum's book with my eyes closed. The book opened at page 272. Here we have the story of a bright but rebellious, destructive, angry eight-year-old boy who was apparently reacting to his single mother starting to date men. This is a situation commonly seen in child psychiatric practice, that of a parent who cannot control a child. In my experience, this is a problem often encountered when it is a single mother and a boy who are involved in the conflict.

What Erickson did in this case was really quite simple. He empowered the mother and thus enabled her to take control of her son. He was faced with a child who was in control of his mother; she was presumably feeling defeated and impotent. The situation had to be changed so that the mother was in control of the boy. Erickson gave instructions to the mother in the boy's absence. He decided to stage a showdown between mother and son. He had the mother send the other children to her parents' so that she had only the rebellious child to deal with. When the boy started to rebel — which he started do at breakfast time — his mother sat on him, something that Erickson had assured her it was safe to do. She did this for most of the day, continuing to do so until the boy came up with an acceptable plan of how to control his behavior. Rather than expressing her determination to control him, she told the boy that she could not think of a way to do so and didn't think she would come up with anything. So probably he would have to be the one to come up with a plan. He produced several plans, which the mother rejected as insincere, but eventually came up with a plan to control his behavior that she found convincing. Although there was a bit of a relapse — dealt with effectively by Erickson — several months later, the response was good and after two years the boy even accepted the man his mother decided to marry, once he discovered that Erickson approved of this man.

So where is the reframing here? In fact, this case report is rich with reframes. Most basic is the empowering of the mother. No doubt the situation was initially framed by both mother and child as one in which the boy was in control and the mother was impotent. By the end of the therapy, which, incidentally, involved only two sessions, the situation was reframed as one in which the mother was in charge and had the power to control the boy. Along the way, there were a number of other reframes. Erickson manipulated things so that it became the task not of the mother to devise control strategies, but of the boy to come up with a plan. The previous frame was one in which the mother had to come up with a plan, but this became the boy's task. (In reality the whole thing was Erickson's plan, of course.)

After the boy had come up with an acceptable plan, the mother went out of her way to offer the boy things he didn't like. Thus, the next morning she gave him oatmeal for breakfast, this being one of his least favorite foods. One may surmise that in the past the mother had tried to achieve her son's compliance by offering him rewards and generally indulging him in the hope of currying his favor and thus getting him to do what she wanted. This tactic invariably fails in situations such as this one. When the mother reversed the procedure and took control of the eating situation, the relationship was radically reframed.

THE SIGNIFICANCE OF REFRAMING

At first sight, it may seem as though calling the essence of psychotherapy "reframing" is just an exercise in semantics. However I don't believe it is. I would propose that it is the feature that distinguishes *psychotherapy* from *counselling,* or the giving of advice. If you like, it is a sophistication of the counselling process, in that sometimes advice is given that leads to a reframing, as in the case mentioned above.

Counselling, as I suggest the term be used, is a matter of weighing the relative merits of alternative courses of action, or giving the person being advised the benefit of one's greater knowledge of a subject (for example, which school may best suit the needs of a particular child). It is a valuable service that friends as well as those working in the helping professions may provide. It requires wisdom and a sound knowledge of the area in which advice is being sought.

Psychotherapy involves looking at and thinking about the "problem" in a different way. "Bad" behavior is reframed as "childish." Lying is reframed as the creative use of one's imagination, to be applied in appropriate rather than inappropriate situations. Marital conflict may be reframed as a sign that the couple care deeply about each other, or about their children, or whatever the focus of their conflict is . . . and so on.

What distinguishes a master therapist from a journeyman is the former's greater skill at reframing things. The "strategic" therapists have labelled this process more clearly than most other therapists have, but I believe all successful psychotherapy must involve the reframing process.

When confronted with a psychotherapy client, we should not think, in the first place, about the technique to use. We need not even formulate according to any particular psychotherapy school, be that psychodynamic, structural, "strategic," behavioral, or whatever. The concepts and techniques of all schools can be used to reframe things. We need to consider how to reframe the problem or situation with which we are confronted in a way that will be therapeutically helpful. The reframing starts in the therapist's mind, or in the collective mind of a team, and our "therapy techniques," whatever they may be, are then used to accomplish the reframing process.

WHY IS BRIEF THERAPY BRIEF?

I'd like to add something about "brief therapy." Much has been written during the last decade or two about brief methods of psychotherapy. Being brief is in itself not a method, but it is instructive to look at what therapists are referring to when they describe "brief" methods. De Shazer (1982) describes the development of the approach used at the Brief Family Therapy Center at Milwaukee, Wisconsin. An important feature was the use of a "consulting team," which became an integral part of the therapy. De Shazer's book also contains an interesting section entitled "Frames" (pp. 22-24) and then one on "Reframing" (pp. 24-26). In the latter the author suggests that:

> "Brief family therapy" can be described as an attempt to help people change the frames that cause them trouble and give them reason to complain. (p. 25)

Indeed, de Shazer goes on to offer us another definition of reframing, quoted from the book *Change* (Watzlawick et al., 1974):

> ... to change the conceptual and/or emotional setting or viewpoint in relation to which a situation is experienced and to place it in another frame which fits the "facts" of the same concrete situation equally well or even better, and thereby changes its entire meaning. (p. 95)

A perusal of de Shazer's work and other literature on brief therapy suggests that what makes this treatment brief is its concentration on the reframing process. It is interesting to note that, as de Shazer (1982) himself points out, the Milan group of therapists had—unknown to him—been using a similar approach, employing an observing and assisting team, in its time-limited, quite brief work with severely disturbed families (Palazzoli et al., 1973). It is often easier for a team to come up with new and better frames than it is for an individual therapist. Several perspectives become possible and one result can be the use of a "split" opinion offered to the family. Offering this is itself a reframe because it implicitly suggests that there is more than one way of understanding the problem.

ACHIEVING THE REFRAME

Space does not permit me to discuss the many ways in which reframing may be achieved. Each psychotherapy school has its own methods, including all the "strategic" methods I have discussed elsewhere (Barker, 1992). What I am suggesting is that we should approach therapy as an endeavor that aims essentially to reframe, rather than to resolve, unconscious conflicts, or to apply "scientifically evaluated procedures that enable people to change their maladaptive behaviors, emotions, and cognitions themselves" (Emmelkamp, 1990), or to provide "professional foster parenting with the deliberate function of facilitating the patient's efforts to be more himself or herself" (Whitaker, 1990), or to do any of the myriad other things therapists of different schools have described. All these procedures are basically just means of achieving reframing. I suggest that the universality of the reframing process is nowhere better illustrated than in the work of Milton Erickson.

In conclusion, I would like to quote a few lines from Meissner's (1991) book, *What Is Effective in Psychoanalytic Therapy?* After saying that "we are still in search of a theory of therapeutic change" (p. 178), Meissner later (p. 179) quotes Weiss and Samson (1986), who argue:

> . . . that what changes in the course of therapy are pathogenic belief systems, often false and misguided, that influence the patient's interaction with the world. These beliefs are complex forms of unconscious mentation that derive from traumatic experiences . . . Testing and correcting of these false beliefs within the safe confines of the analytic situation leads to gradual change, especially by disconfirmation regarding the transference.

This would appear to be a description of the process of reframing. Perhaps this is the "theory of therapeutic change" that Meissner says we need.

REFERENCES

Bandler, R., and Grinder, J. (1982). *Reframing: Neuro-Linguistic Programming and the Transformation of Meaning.* Moab, UT: Real People Press.

Barker. P. (1992). *Basic Family Therapy,* 3rd ed. Oxford: Blackwell.

Bateson, G. (1955). "A theory of play and fantasy." *Psychiatric Research Reports, 2,* 177-193.

Beck, A.T., Rush, A.J., Shaw, B.F., and Emery, C. (1979). *Cognitive Therapy of Depression.* New York: Guilford.

Bloch, S. (1982). *What Is Psychotherapy?* Oxford: Oxford University Press.

Bloch, S. (1988). (Letter). *British Journal of Psychiatry, 153,* 119.

Chessick, R.D. (1990). "Dynamic psychotherapy." In *What Is Psychotherapy?* Ed. J.K. Zeig and W.M. Munion. San Francisco: Jossey-Bass.

Coppersmith, E. J. (1981). "Developmental reframing." *Journal of Strategic and Systemic Therapies, 1,* 1-8.

Coyne, J.C. (1985). "Toward a theory of frames and reframing: The social nature of frames." *Journal of Marital and Family Therapy, 11,* 337-344.

Crown, S. (1988). "Supportive psychotherapy: A contradiction in terms?" *British Journal of Psychiatry, 152,* 266-269.

de Shazer, S. (1982). *Patterns of Brief Family Therapy: An Ecosystemic Approach.* New York: Norton.

Emmelkamp, P.M.G. (1990). "An experimental clinical approach." In *What Is Psychotherapy?* Ed. J.K. Zeig and W.M. Munion. San Francisco: Jossey-Bass.

Haley, J. (1973). *Uncommon Therapy: The Psychiatric Techniques of Milton H. Erickson, M.D.* New York: Norton.

Holmes, J. (1988). ""Supportive analytical psychotherapy: An account of two cases." *British Journal of Psychiatry, 152,* 824-829.

Meissner, W.W. (1991). *What Is Effective in Psychoanalytic Therapy?* Northvale, NJ: Jason Aronson.

O'Hanlon, W.H., and Hexum, A.L. (1990). *An Uncommon Casebook: The Complete Clinical Work of Milton H. Erickson, M.D.* New York: Norton.

Palazzoli, M.S., Boscolo, L., Cecchin, G., and Prata, G. (1973). *Paradox and Counterparadox.* New York: Jason Aronson.

Rosen, S. (1982). *My Voice Will Go With You: The Teaching Tales of Milton H. Erickson.* New York: Norton.

Sanford, R. (1990). "Client-centered psychotherapy." In *What Is Psychotherapy?* Ed. J.K. Zeig and W.M. Munion. San Francisco: Jossey-Bass.

Watzlawick, P. (1976). *How Real Is Real?* New York: Vintage.

Watzlawick, P., Weakland, J.H., and Fisch, R. (1974). *Change: Principles of Problem Formulation and Problem Resolution.* New York: Norton.

Weiss, J., and Samson, H. (1986). *The Psychoanalytic Process: Theory, Clinical Observations, and Empirical Research.* New York: Guilford.

Whitaker, C.A. (1990). "Symbolic experiential therapy." In *What Is Psychotherapy?* Ed. J.K. Zeig and W.M. Munion. San Francisco: Jossey-Bass.

Zeig, J.K., and Munion, W.M. (Eds.) (1990). *What Is Psychotherapy?* San Francisco: Jossey-Bass.

PART IV

Conceptual Issues

CHAPTER 14

Ericksonian Myths
André M. Weitzenhoffer

PART I: SOME OF THE MYTHS

According to *The Random House College Dictionary* (1988) as well as other dictionaries, the term "myth" can be used to denote as many as four different things. The one meaning that I will discuss in this chapter is that of "myth" denoting

> *a belief or a subject of belief whose truth*
> *or reality is accepted uncritically.*

I will also take the expression *uncritical acceptance* to be synonymous with the acceptance of something being true, or a reality, in the absence of any verification of this being so and, as it frequently happens, *in spite of its even being contrary to actual facts.*

Over the years I have found the Ericksonian literature to contain many such myths. These have usually been mentioned, often quite authoritatively, as characterizing, if not defining, so-called "traditional hypnosis." This is hypnotism as it was presumably understood and practiced before Erickson's teachings and ways of operating in the hypnotic context became widely taught and adopted. I would like to dispel some of the more prominent of these myths. For one thing, I cannot see that they serve any worthwhile purpose. But I also think that doing so is important because one cannot obtain a full picture of the essence of the Ericksonian story unless Erickson's contributions are viewed in the context of realities and not of myths.

I do not think that Erickson would have wanted it to be otherwise. Most of us know Milton Erickson as the fine psychotherapist that he was, but I wonder how many know that he also was a fine scientist. Sadly, this aspect of Erickson has been largely forgotten or ignored. He was very interested in the scientific development of hypnotism and, directly and indirectly, made significant contributions to it. I believe the last thing he would have wanted to see is the incorporation of myths into his teachings. So, as a tribute to Erickson the scientist, if for no other reason, I shall try to do what I think he would have wanted to do, had he been given this opportunity: clear up these myths.

I will not try to cover all the myths in question. Merely providing an exhaustive list of these myths could easily fill this chapter. This would leave no space for discussing why they are myths, and I would end up essentially begging the question by asserting they are so. I shall, therefore, be selective and limit myself to three authoritative sources in this regard: Yapko, Zeig, and Gilligan. By doing so, I think I am in a better position to make the claim that I am talking about an accepted Ericksonian position and not that of poorly informed individuals claiming to be Ericksonians.

The first group of myths comes from a major work of Yapko (1984):

Myth #1. "Many traditional textbooks on hypnotism" claim that "retarded, psychotics and senile individuals are unhypnotizable" (p. 34).

Exactly what textbooks have stated this? Exactly how many? I think we can safely assume that these were books written prior to the publication of works dealing with Erickson's contributions.

I have gone through some 20 authoritative texts in English on hypnotism published between 1900 and 1975 and found *only two* that specifically stated psychotics could not be hypnotized! A number of these books clearly presented evidence to the contrary. In fact, by 1953 it had been clearly established that psychotics were hypnotizable (Weitzenhoffer, 1953). Summarizing the consensus of the time, I will admit to having said in 1953, although with some *qualifications,* that "feeble-minded" individuals were not considered hypnotizable. At most, then, we are looking at one or two books out of some 20. This hardly constitutes a foundation for speaking of "many." Insofar as 20th-century textbooks are concerned, Yapko's assertion is pure myth!

Myth #2. Traditional hypnotism is associated with the popular notion that "anyone who can be hypnotized must be weak minded."

"This particular misconception," Yapko continues, "refers back to the all-powerful Svengali image of the hypnotist and is based on the belief that in order for a hypnotist to control a subject, the subject must have little or no will of her own" (p. 37).

Now I must grant that Yapko does not specifically use the term "traditional" in making this statement. This may be more of a reference to what he sees to be a widespread *popular* misconception about hypnotism in general. Unfortunately, his assertion is made in an overall context that strongly implies, at least for me, that this has been a view also held by past, "traditional" hypnotists. Be it as it may, let me say that I do not know of any modern so-called "traditional" recognized authority who has proclaimed this idea.

Yapko also intimates that this notion is a widespread one. But what are the facts here? No figures are available. Yapko may have frequently encountered this belief among his patients but, speaking for myself, I cannot recall any subjects or patients in more than 40 years of research and clinical practice who have intimated to me having such a belief!

But to the extent there might be such a belief, from whence would it have come? Yapko takes it back to the novel *Trilby* (du Maurier, 1895). I must say this is the first time I have seen this attribution made. I am puzzled by it because there is little evidence that *Trilby* has been widely read in modern times, although it was popular when it was published. Furthermore, there are few, if any, references to it in 20th-century texts dealing with hypnotism. In any event, the story of *Trilby* does not actually depict Svengali as an "all-powerful" hypnotist taking over control of a "weak-minded" individual!

I would add that I cannot recall any of my past subjects mentioning the name of Svengali!

Myth #3. Having just referred to Svengali, Yapko adds, "Modern 'scare stories' about evil hypnotists who control their subjects and force them into doing terrible things play on this misconception" (p. 37).

Just what scare stories about "traditional hypnotism" does Yapko have in mind? Does he mean "stories" in the sense of fiction, such as the film *The Manchurian Candidate,* or in the colloquial sense of rumors? Again, few of my subjects or patients have ever made allusions to anything of the sort! Over the years, I have occasionally come across brief references to hypnotism in newspapers, magazines, and television, but not in the context of anything "scary." It certainly is a fact that, in the somewhat more than 200 years of the combined existence of animal magnetism and hypnotism, there have been a *relatively small* number of notorious cases of their alleged criminal use. However, they were never highly publicized in America in this century and, in any case, the details are to be found only in books not likely to have been read by the average person.

The next group of myths I will consider were specifically referred to in a workshop lecture given by Zeig in Montreal in 1990.

Myth #4. Traditional clinical hypnotists take a historical approach to the diagnosis of the patient's problem.

I will simply point out that taking or not taking a historical approach to diagnosis has nothing to do with one's view of, understanding of, or approach to hypnosis, hence with "traditional" hypnotism.

Myth #5. Referring to the use of suggestibility tests *prior* to an induction, which he claims to be an act characteristic of "traditional" hypnotists, Zeig states, "These suggestibility tests are done with an underlying purpose — to demonstrate to the patient that the patient will respond." The aim, he adds, is to put the patient into a "state of readiness to respond."

I think the time has come to ask who do Yapko, Gilligan, and particularly Zeig specifically have in mind when they refer to "traditional" clinical hypnotists? The work titled *The Practical Application of Medical and Dental Hypnosis* by Erickson, Hershman, and Secter (New York: Julian Press, 1961) shows that, in the seminars he led up to 1961, Erickson was pretty much following "traditional" lines in his teachings, although one does see some typical Ericksonian ideas and methods starting to appear. For this reason I feel it is safe to assume that the majority of accredited clinicians using hypnosis prior to 1961 were "traditional" in their approach. Since source material on pre-1900 clinical hypnotism is largely in German and French and is not readily available, it seems unlikely it has served as a source of information for Yapko, Gilligan, and Zeig. Furthermore, it is my feeling that they are largely talking about 20th-century clinical hypnotism as practiced in the U.S. before Erickson's influence became evident. I believe one can then safely consider that the "traditional" clinicians they have in mind include the majority of clinicians using hypnosis between 1900 and 1961. But which among these are to serve, or should serve, as reliable, authoritative sources of information regarding the clinical practices of that period? Let me ask the reader this: Given a choice, should I go to just anyone claiming to be an Ericksonian hypnotherapist or therapist to find what it is all about, or should I go to Erickson, Zeig, Rossi, Yapko, Gilligan, Lankton, and other recognized experts in that field as sources of information?

I have no idea to whom Zeig turned to get his information. I do know that if I wanted to have authoritative answers and facts regarding so-called "traditional" hypnotism I would go to such experts as Wolberg, Lindner, Schneck, Watkins, H. Rosen, Gill, Brenman, Heron, Aston, Secter, Hershman, Marmer, LeCron, Biddle, Kline, Frankel, E. Fromm, Brown, Crassilneck, Kroger, J. A. Hall, and Hartland, to name some of the principal ones. Let me point out that none of these practitioners has advocated any kind of routine extensive suggestibility testing prior to doing an induction and, with the exception of Wolberg, the only reason they had for doing a prior test of suggestibility, when they did, was to have a preliminary idea of the subject's potentialities in this regard.

Wolberg (1948, p. 102) is one of the few who mentions, as additional reasons for using such tests, that "they often get a patient into a suitable frame of mind, developing in him confidence in his ability to respond to suggestions that will lead to a trance." As for the concept of "readiness to respond" as applied to hypnotic behavior, this appears to have been strictly a contribution of Erickson.

My feeling is that here Zeig is presenting his interpretation, *as an Ericksonian,* of why *he* might use pre-induction suggestibility tests, were he to do so, and projects these reasons upon the "traditionalists."

Myth #6. Zeig also asserts that the use of suggestibility tests *following* an induction is part of the usual traditional approach and is for the purpose of demonstrating to the subject/patient that there has been a change in the locus of control. For instance, he says in reference to this, "The metaphor of hypnosis is that from the period of induction start to the period of termination control is different." To this he adds that, irrespective of where control actually is, "the induction is to induce a different feeling of control, a different experience of control which is validated when the person can respond to the challenge, to the test suggestion."

Here again, I believe that Zeig is giving his interpretation, *as an Ericksonian,* of why one might use suggestibility tests thus. This is not supported by the existing "traditional" literature. Those so-called "traditional" hypnotists who proceed thus do so mainly to get an idea of what degree of suggestibility the subject/patient *now* has. Then they erroneously use the results as a measure of the "depth of hypnosis" they presume the subject/patient has attained (Weitzenhoffer, 1953, 1957, 1989). Few, if any, view this as a way of convincing or otherwise showing the patient there has been a change in control that demonstrates he must be hypnotized.

Myth #7. Zeig also states, "In traditional hypnosis you ask a practitioner, 'How long should I do an induction?' The expert says 20 minutes — so you watch your watch for 20 minutes. In Ericksonian hypnosis, you judge on the basis of getting responses to minimal cues. This determines when the induction is over. This may take two seconds or two hours or more."

To begin with, I do not know of any experienced traditional hypnotist, and this includes stage hypnotists, who ever maintained an induction should take a specific amount of time. Most have known better than that and, in their practice, just like Ericksonians, allowed various indices of the presence of hypnosis to determine when to end the induction, adjusting the induction accordingly.

True, books written in this century by so-called "traditional" hypnotists have frequently provided sample inductions that, at times, may have required 20 minutes to go through, the writer saying nothing regarding what to do should the subject show signs of having become hypnotized before the end of the text had been reached. These authors probably knew this could happen and should probably have said something in this regard. Some may have unreasonably assumed the reader would understand these were model inductions *to be modified as needed.* Others may have overlooked the need to include a note in this regard.

It is true there are some well-known cases of inductions published by traditional hypnotists that specifically and deliberately do demand the hypnotist follow a rigid schedule. Possibly, these are the ones Zeig has in mind here. But these are special cases in which adhering to this schedule of induction is a requirement of the fact they are part of standardized psychometric instruments designed for specialized uses. Fixed-length inductions used in this context cannot be taken as being typical of so-called "traditional hypnotism." They are compatible with this approach, *but they are not required by it.*

Myth #8. The traditional induction of hypnosis "makes use of the principle of fascination."

Such a reference to "fascination" is archaic and obsolete. Offhand, I cannot think of any 20th-century authoritative text on hypnotism that makes reference to such a principle or even to the term "fascination." This is certainly not to be found in any of Bernheim's writings, which have served as foundation for 20th-century hypnotism. Historically, there was a brief period during the latter part of the 19th century when the term "fascination" was used by a very small group of researchers and practitioners *to denote a very special form* of hypnosis and hypnotic behavior they believed to exist. There is outwardly little that is common between past productions of so-called "fascination" and 20th-century formal inductions of hypnosis.

The last group of myths I will consider comes out of some of Gilligan's (1987) writings.

Myth #9. "The authoritarian conception derives partly from the writings of historical figures such as Mesmer, Bernheim, Charcot and Freud" (p. 5).

In contrast to other Ericksonian authorities, such as Zeig and Yapko, Gilligan does not use the term "traditional." He speaks instead of three "approaches" to hypnotism: the authoritarian, the standardized, and the cooperative. Regarding the first of these, he states (p. 4), "The extreme version of this approach involves some 'powerful' individual (the hypnotist) with special mental abilities (e.g., the 'hypnotic eye', 'a strong will') who *causes* another individual (the subject) to enter a relatively passive state wherein he or she is 'susceptible' to the hypnotist's 'suggestions.'" These suggestions, he adds, "can 'force' subjects to perform various behaviors." A little further he continues with, "Notions of 'mind over matter,' 'loss of control,' 'implanting suggestions,' and 'susceptibility' abound within this viewpoint, themselves 'implanted' by books, movies, and folklore." Since there can be little question that this is also a description of Zeig's and Yapko's "traditional" hypnotist as he/she is discussed by them, I feel justified in taking it up in the present context.

Again I would ask with some skepticism, how widely and frequently has this particular picture of past hypnotists been presented in books and movies? I must admit I do not watch the late late and early morning shows on television, nor B-grade movies, so that I may have missed something here. Those movies I have seen in recent years in which hypnosis was used have not depicted the hypnotist and hypnotism as Gilligan would have us believe.

In any case, insofar as Freud, Charcot, and Bernheim are concerned, this perception of hypnotists, really more correctly of *magnetizers,* existed *before these men came onto the scene.* Furthermore, there is little, if any, evidence to be found in their writings to support their having held to any such notions or having acted accordingly. Indeed, the writings of Charcot and Bernheim can be said to have immensely contributed *to correcting* this picture. As for Freud, let me point out that he cannot be, nor ever was considered to be, an authority on hypnotism, so if he had perceived hypnotism as described above, *which he did not,* this perception would not likely have had much impact on his contemporaries, his successors, and, particularly, the public.

This leaves Mesmer. I will agree that his ideas regarding animal magnetism did serve as a foundation *for other, later* practitioners of animal magnetism and some hypnotists to think along lines such as described by Gilligan. But insofar as Mesmer is concerned, these notions cannot be directly ascribed to him, as is well shown by his main writings (Mesmer, 1971; Tinterow, 1970; Podmore, 1963).

Myth #10. Having stated the defining features of the "authoritarian approach," Gilligan then states, "These conceptions are often held openly by lay persons, but many therapists who use hypnosis also believe them implicitly" (p. 4).

Again, in all of my years of research and clinical practice, I have encountered few lay individuals who held such beliefs, but I am willing to consider that Gilligan's experience with lay individuals may have been appreciably different than mine. Still, his and mine combined might raise a question about how "often" is "often." But what about therapists themselves? Who are these therapists who have provided Gilligan with material upon which to base his assertion? He does not say, which is unfortunate. I can assert, however, that *there is nothing in the writings of the 22 "traditional" authorities I mentioned earlier that supports Gilligan's claim inso-*

far as they are concerned. I am not going to maintain that there have not been or still are not licensed therapists using hypnotic techniques holding to such ideas as Gilligan refers to. But they are not to be found among the leaders and experts on hypnotism, be they Ericksonian or not, and I think it is to these experts that one should turn if one wants to know what is and what is not true of hypnotism.

Myth #11. "The most influential advocates of the standardized approach have been the academicians seeking to legitimize hypnosis by subjecting it to rigorous tests of experimental psychology" (p. 6).

I somewhat question the validity of creating a special class of hypnotists on the basis of the use of a "standardized approach," especially where clinicians are concerned. Yapko seems to agree with Gilligan in this regard, but Zeig clearly considers such hypnotists, and I think with some justification if one is going to talk about "traditional" hypnotists, under this broader heading.

However, this is not the reason why I have placed the above statement under the heading of a myth. I have done so specifically in regard to Gilligan's reference to "legitimization." Standardization is a "legitimization" if he means by "legitimization" what I understand it to mean, namely, to make something acceptable. Certainly, the use of the scientific method in any form has a legitimizing effect. On the other hand, speaking for myself and, I think, also for a number of other researchers, the reason for using rigorous methods of testing and other features of the scientific method has been as much, if not more, *simply for the sake of finding out just what are the facts of hypnotism, with no thought about legitimacy in the above sense.* The writings of Charcot and his associates and those of Bernheim show as much, but I think this can be particularly said about research from 1953 on, because by then it had been pretty well established that hypnotism was a legitimate subject matter, at least in scientific circles. This is not to say that since then there have not been questions about the legitimacy, meaning by this the correctness or appropriatness of speaking of "hypnosis" and of "hypnotic" phenomena, for everyone agrees that the term "hypnosis" is etymologically wrong, and there are some who still question the existence of this class of behaviors.

Myth #12. Gilligan (pp. 4–6) indirectly but strongly asserts that Bernheim's hypnotherapy was limited to suggesting symptoms away. He particularly does this by quoting Cheek and LeCron (1968), who do not say what the basis for their statement is.

The fact of the matter, however, is that what Bernheim did or did not do with suggestions in his clinical practice cannot be readily documented. Rather unfortunately, most of the time, when describing the treatment of a case, he limits himself to saying that "suggestions were given" (Bernheim, 1886/1947). So suggestions were given. Indirect, direct, authoritarian, permissive, or other? There is no telling. Was hypnosis first induced, and if so, how? No details are available. However, in describing how he hypnotized and produced hypnotic effects, Bernheim distinctly indicated that sometimes one must be authoritarian and at other times permissive. It is also clear from his own writings as well as from other accounts, such as that of Barrucand (1967), that Bernheim frequently used suggestion, with hypnosis presumably absent. There is no question that Bernheim frequently suggested the disappearance of symptoms with direct suggestions, but some of the cases he discusses in his writings indicate this was not always true. Some of the things he describes himself as doing were, in fact, rather like what Erickson might have done.

PART II. THE GREATER MYTH

If the statements I have quoted and paraphrased were uniquely those of one individual, it would be one thing. But this is by no means the case. These are repeated and alluded to over and over in one form or another in the Ericksonian literature and in Ericksonian workshops and seminars to the point, I feel, of falling under the heading of general Ericksonian myths. I am not going to try to speculate how or why these various myths and others I have not touched upon came about or what possible purposes they may serve. This is not germane to this presentation.

There is no question that many of the myths I have discussed *do* represent *popular* conceptions and misconceptions that have existed at one time or another and probably are still encountered, and that may have been shared by certain "practicing" hypnotists. *But they are not the basic tenets that were held by the majority of leading authorities* on hypnotism during more or less the first two-thirds of this century. *This, I think, needs to be recognized by Ericksonians once and for all!* In fact, these myths do not even represent the majority view of earlier experts (Bramwell, 1903/1930; Moll, 1909). If there is a *fundamental* distinction to be made between what might better be spoken of as a "pre-Ericksonian" and an "Ericksonian" (and a "post-Ericksonian") *hypnosis,* it must be sought elsewhere. However, I do not believe that at this time a good foundation exists elsewhere for such a distinction. That is to say, then, that the Ericksonian idea of the existence of a "traditional" hypnosis *is itself a myth* to which all the other myths converge. *It is the greater myth.*

In support of this last statement let me first point out that hypnotism, as it was known and practiced after 1890 and through at least the first two-thirds of this century, *is founded* upon the "suggestion doctrine" formulated by Bernheim in 1884. In it, among other things, he posited the primacy of suggestion, that is, that all so-called "hypnotic phenomena," including hypnosis, are *the products of suggestion.* He also made the important observation that clinical hypnotism is to be seen as *the methodical, systematic and reasoned application of suggestion for the purpose of producing therapeutic changes.* How this is to be implemented was left by Bernheim to the therapist to decide on the basis of his understanding of the nature of the symptomatology and of the therapeutic processes and, to some extent, on the surrounding circumstances. As I have explained in some detail elsewhere (Weitzenhoffer, 1992), the writings of those 20th-century experts I referred to earlier show that their approach to using suggestions and hypnosis was largely *shaped* by these elements *and not by their blindly and compulsively subscribing to some so-called "traditional" model or approach.*

Furthermore, even though I am not aware that Erickson ever made any mention of Bernheim in his writings, it seems most likely that he must have been acquainted with Bernheim's views and been influenced by them. Erickson's writings certainly suggest such an influence. In any case, for whatever reasons this may have been, it is clear that the two men shared a number of fundamental ideas regarding hypnotic phenomena and their use. The parallel or similarity that has existed between the two men's thinking and approaches can be best seen by concurrently reading their various writings. But even a limited reading of Bernheim's 1886 work (the only one available in English) and of *Hypnotic Realities* (1976), the first of Erickson's work co-authored with Rossi, allows one to see the essential similarities. For both men, suggestion was a central element in the production of hypnotic effects. For both, ideo-dynamic action was a fundamental mechanism behind these effects. Both viewed "hypnosis" or "trance" as an important adjunct but not as an essential one. Both men advocated flexibility and creativity in the use of suggestion. They both were authoritarian and permissive, as called for by the situations encountered. Erickson emphasized the role of the "unconscious" and so did Berhneim under the heading of "le psychisme inférieure." This is not to say that there were not differences between Erickson and Bernheim. This is most evident, for instance, in Erickson's preference for indirect suggestions and informal inductions contrasted to Bernheim's preference for direct suggestions and formal inductions. And again, Bernheim saw hypnotic depth and suggestibility as being related, whereas in his later years, Erickson did not. But, these are minor differences and, as I see it, I feel one can reasonably assert that Erickson was fundamentally Bernheimian, just as were his early colleagues. From this standpoint there seems to be little ground on which to make, at a conceptual level, a fundamental distinction between a "traditional" and an "Ericksonian" hypnosis.

Insofar as hypnotic phenomenology is concerned, there is no sound basis for believing that there are fundamental differences between the phenomenology Erickson produced and used under the heading of "hypnosis" and that which so-called "traditional" hypnotists have produced and used in the laboratory and in the clinical setting under this same heading. At best, one can speak here only of observably distinct approaches to or ways of producing and using this phenomenology. But whether or not they are effectively different *remains yet to be clearly demonstrated.*

I would further point out that "traditional," according to dictionaries, denotes beliefs and practices that have been handed down by word of mouth and by example from generation to generation and acted upon, presumably without concern about their reliability or truth value. Much of pre-Ericksonian hypnotic practices can certainly be said to have contained traditional features in the above sense, for what else have workshops and teaching seminars on hypnotism done in the past but transmit, by word of mouth and by examples, the lore, the practices, and a few verified facts, the whole being accepted without question by the neophytes. By the same token, the same can be said of today's Ericksonian practices! To be "traditional" in this sense is no special distinction.

Finally, I would point out that in Erickson's work as a clinician — and this is the part of his work upon which the Ericksonian movement has centered — there has been a great deal of confounding of what is psychotherapy proper with that which is hypnotism proper (Weitzenhoffer, 1989, 1992). Having examined this problem pretty carefully, I have been led (Weitzenhoffer, 1992) to conclude that what particularly distinguishes Erickson *as a hypnotherapist* is much less his view of hypnotic phenomena *than his view of psychotherapy proper.* This perspective, in particular, *shaped* his approach to the production of hypnotic effects. That which stands out most for me in Erickson's work is not so much anything that can specifically be called "Ericksonian hypnosis" in distinction to a so-called "traditional hypnosis," but instead something that can clearly be spoken of as an *Ericksonian psychotherapy.*

To conclude, I believe *it is high time Ericksonians stop confusing popular beliefs with those held by the scientifically oriented community.* It is also time for them to relinquish these pejorative myths about "traditional" hypnotism, the presumed differences between "Ericksonian" and "traditional" hypnotism, and to focus, instead, upon Erickson's real contribution, *his psychotherapy model,* realizing that hypnotism was ancillary to it as it has usually been for other hypnotherapists of repute.

REFERENCES

Barrucand, D. (1967) *Histoire de l'hypnose en France.* Paris: Presses Universitaires de France.

Bernheim, H. (1886/1947) *Suggestive therapeutics. A treatise on the nature and uses of hypnotism.* Translated from the French by C. Herter. New York: London Book Company.

Bramwell, J.M. (1903/1930) *Hypnòtism. Its history, practice and theory.* Philadelphia: J.B. Lippincott.

Cheek, D., and Le Cron, L.M. (1968) *Clinical hypnotism.* New York: Grune and Stratton.

du Maurier, G. (1895) *Trilby.* London: Osgood, McIlvain.

Erickson, M.H. et al. *The practical application of medical and dental hypnosis.* New York: Julian Press.

Erickson, M.H. et al. (1976) *Hypnotic realities: The induction of clinical hypnosis and forms of indirect suggestion.* New York: Irvington.

Gilligan, S.G. (1987) *Therapeutic trance: The cooperative principle in Ericksonian hypnotherapy.* New York: Brunner/Mazel.

Mesmer, F.-A. (1971) *Le magnetisme animal.* Collected writings edited by R. Amadou. Paris: Payot.

Moll, A. (1909) *Hypnotism: Including a study of the chief points of psychotherapeutics and occultism* (4th ed.). London: Walter Scott Publishing.

Podmore, F. (1963) *From Mesmer to Christian Science.* New York: University Books.

Tinterow, M.M. (1970) *Foundations of hypnosis from Mesmer to Freud.* Springfield, Ill.: Charles C. Thomas Publisher.

Weitzenhoffer, A.M. (1953) *Hypnotism: An objective study in suggestibility.* New York: John Wiley and Sons.

———— (1957) *General techniques of hypnotism.* New York: Grune and Stratton.

———— (1989) *The practice of hypnotism. Vol.II.* New York: John Wiley and Sons.

———— (1992) "Erickson and the unity of hypnotism." Keynote address given at the Pre-Congress to the 12th International Congress of Hypnosis and sponsored by the Milton Erickson Society of Clinical Hypnosis of Germany, Jerusalem.

Yapko, M.D. (1984) *Trancework: An introduction to the practice of clinical hypnosis.* New York: Irvington.

Zeig, J.K. (1990) Taken from a videotape of a workshop given in Montreal and hosted by the Institut quebecois de therapie et d'hypnose ericksoniennes inc. Videotape available from the Institut.

BIBLIOGRAPHIC APPENDIX

For the benefit of those readers who might wish to further verify the mythical nature of the quoted statements discussed in the main text, I have included a list of authoritative texts on so-called "traditional" hypnotism. I have primarily selected works published before 1961 to ensure the majority of these would be free of any influence by Milton Erickson's teachings and thus would be truly "traditional." There are, however, more recent works that are equally representative of the so-called "traditional" approach.

Brenman, M., and Gill, M. (1947) *Hypnotherapy.* New York: International Universities Press.

Estabrooks, G.H. (1959) *Hypnotism.* New York: E.P. Dutton.

Heron, W.T. *Clinical applications of suggestion and hypnosis.* Springfield, Ill.: Charles C. Thomas Publisher.

Kline, M.V. (1967) *Psychodynamics and hypnosis.* Springfield, Ill.: Charles C. Thomas Publisher.

Kuhn, L., and Russo, S. (1947) *Modern hypnosis.* New York: Psychological Library.

LeCron, L.M., and Bordeaux, J. (1947) *Hypnotism today.* New York: Grune and Stratton.

Lindner, R.M. (1944) *Rebel without a cause.* New York: Grove Press.

Marcus, F.L. (1959) *Hypnosis: Fact and fiction.* Middlesex, England: Penguin Books.

Marmer, M.J. (1954) *Hypnosis in anesthesiology.* Springfield, Ill.: Charles C. Thomas Publisher.

Rosen, H. (1953) *Hypnotherapy in clinical psychiatry.* New York: Julian Press.

Schneck, J.M. (1965) *The principle and practice of hypnoanalysis.* Springfield, Ill: Charles C. Thomas Publisher.

Shaw, S.I. (1958) *Clinical applications of hypnosis in dentistry.* Philadelphia: W.B. Saunders.

Watkins, J.G. (1949) *Hypnotherapy of the war neuroses.* New York: Ronald Press.

Wolberg, L.R. (1948) *Medical hypnosis.* New York: Grune and Stratton.

Wolfe, B., and Rosenthal, R. (1948) *Hypnotism comes of age.* New York: Garden City Blue Ribbon Books.

CHAPTER 15

Essential, Non-Essential: Vive la Différence

Steve de Shazer

INTRODUCTION

Talking about "the essence" of Erickson's work immediately sets up a polarity with "essence" on one side and everything else, marginalized and trivialized, on the other side — which might accidentally lead us to miss something useful. Therefore, I will talk about neither "essentials" nor "non-essentials" but rather some other more useful view.

A woman brought her husband from California to see Erickson. One year before, the man had had a stroke and since then had been lying helpless in bed. During this time, he had been unable to talk, to feed himself, or to wash himself. While telling Erickson about her husband, she mentioned that he was a Prussian.

Erickson told her not to interfere while he talked to her husband, and he sat down in front of the man and said:

> So, you're a Prussian German. The stupid, God damn Nazis! How incredibly stupid, conceited, ignorant, and animal-like Prussian Germans are. They thought they owned the world, they destroyed their own country! What kind of epithets can you apply to those horrible animals. They're really not fit to live. The

The author wishes to thank his colleagues Insoo Kim Berg, Larry Hopwood, and Scott Miller for their contributions to this essay.

world would be better off if they were used for fertilizer . . . You've been lying around on charity, being fed, dressed, cared for, bathed, toenails clipped. Who are you to merit anything? You aren't even the equal of a mentally retarded criminal Jew! (Haley, 1973, p. 311–312)

Erickson carried on like this for quite some time and ended with this statement: "And you're going to come back tomorrow, aren't you!" The man came right back with an explosive "No" (Haley, p. 312), his first word in over a year. The man did come back the following day after walking — unsteadily and with great effort — angrily out of Erickson's office.

❁　　　　❁　　　　❁

The world is in all its parts a cryptogram to be constituted or reconstituted through . . . deciphering.
　　　　　　　　　—Jacques Derrida (1978, p. 76)

The theme of this conference, the "essence of Erickson's work," is for me, as the popular saying puts it, déjà vu all over again. Searching for the "essence of Erickson's approach" was, after all, where I began my trek into and around the world of doing therapy.

To provide us with some context, it might be advantageous to look in Webster's New 20th-Century Unabridged Dictionary, 2nd edition, where "essence" is defined in this fashion:

essence, 2. that which makes something what it is; intrinsic, fundamental nature (of something); essential being...6. in philosophy, that which constitutes the inward nature of anything, underlying its manifestation; true substance.

Thus, when searching for the "essence" of anything, one looks for a fixed, stable center or foundation that is determined both ahead of time and for all time. From this perspective, the "essence" is in the clinical work itself and has been put into the written descriptions of his work by Erickson himself. It becomes the reader's job to *discover* it and to pull it out (i.e., to surgically remove it, so to speak) so that we can properly interpret it. The quest involves looking for an "underlying, fundamental theory" upon which Erickson's approach was built. Once one starts reading Erickson's work, it becomes obvious that this is not a simple task.

Of course, in this sort of endeavor, the more complex the subject matter, the more puzzling the meanings involved. Simple structures combine into highly elaborate structures, which, in turn, potentially increase the depth of the interpretation—*a program that privileges complexity over simplicity.* Erickson's work was an obvious and classic choice, a gold mine, for such an approach. (Almost as good as scripture, Shakespeare, or Milton.) Although I knew that these assumptions did not necessarily hold for literature (such as poetry), nonetheless I believed they held in the "scientific," "objective world." In short, borrowing a term from literary criticism, Erickson's papers, read in the usual "scientific" way, become "verbal icons" or containers of truth. In hindsight, now I can see that it was both an impossible task and an indispensable one.

*   *   *

When I first began learning how to do brief therapy with my clients (in the late 60s and early 70s), I was fascinated with Milton Erickson's work, particularly with the ways Erickson and Jay Haley wrote about this unique approach to clinical practice. It was certainly not standard psychotherapy; that much was clear to me. Each case was apparently unique and there seemed to be no unifying theme or theory—that is to say, the essence was hidden away. Erickson's papers seemed to be reports about the work of a shaman or wizard. As Haley put it, "Part of the problem when examining Erickson's therapeutic technique is the fact that there *is* no adequate theoretical framework available for describing it . . . When one examines what he actually does with a patient, traditional views do not seem appropriate" (Haley, 1967, p. 532) (emphasis added). Perhaps mistakenly, I read Haley as at least implying that no theory was even possible.

I agreed with Haley that at that time there was no adequate theory available; however, I was not convinced that Erickson did not have a theory, since Erickson said, "I know what I do, but to explain how I do it is much too difficult for me" (Erickson, 1975, p. viii). That is, if Erickson *knew* what to do, then he also knew what *not* to do. Therefore, a theory, a set of rules, could be described by an observer even if Erickson himself could not do it.

Both by inclination and training, I thought that Erickson's cases could be studied, and from these cases an essence could be abstracted and then a theory could be constructed that included rules—rules explicit enough so that at some point when working with a client, a therapist could say to herself, "Now, I can go on!" with some confidence that she was following Erickson's rules. That is, he* would "know" what to do and be able to do it.

---

*The pronouns "he" and "she," etc. will be used alternately unless in reference to a particular person.

A writes a series of numbers down; B watches him and tries to find a law for the sequence of numbers. If he succeeds, he exclaims: "Now I can go on!"

—Ludwig Wittgenstein (1968, #151)*

Take any series of numbers, say: 1, 2, 3, 4, 5, etc., or 1, 3, 5, 7, etc., or 2, 4, 6, 8, etc., or even 1, 3, 4, 7, 11, 18, 29, 47, 76, 123, etc.** The sequences each follow a rule or rules. Once we figure out a rule that seems to work*** or, as we put it in everyday life, once we "know what the rule is," we can carry on. In this world of numbers, certain signs are used to tell us what to do: add, subtract, multiply, divide. Rules help us decide which operations (addition, subtraction, multiplication, division) are appropriate. And when we get the right answers, we can say that we "know" the rule; we can say we "understand." The rules for how we decide whether or not to add, subtract, multiply, or divide are the essence of the sequence of numbers games. But, as Wittgenstein (1975) points out,

> If I now assume there could be a random series, then that is a series about which, by its very nature, nothing can be known apart from the fact that I can't know it. Or better, that it can't be known. (#145)

That is, if we cannot figure out a rule for a particular series of numbers, if the numbers were picked arbitrarily, then we can never figure out how to carry on because the "essence" of number sequences is missing; it is unknown and unknowable. Of course, since only four operations are used in arithmetic, figuring out the rules for number sequences is relatively simple when compared with figuring out the rules of doing therapy.

Clearly, when we watch a client and a therapist at work through a see-through mirror or on videotape, the therapist's activities seem purposeful and rule-bound. These rules may be more similar to the rules of grammar or soccer than to the rules of arithmetic, but they are rules nonetheless.

THE STRUGGLE

In the early 70s, my colleagues**** and I read and analyzed hundreds of cases that Erickson had written up, and we used various tools to attempt to

---

*References to Wittgenstein's work are by section number rather than page number.
**The Lucas Sequence's rule: 29 + 47 = 76
***The rule we come up with may or may not be the rule of the sequence's inventor.
****Joseph Berger and Jerry Tally.

figure out some of his rules. Sorting the cases into "individuals" and "couples" did not help, nor did attempts to sort the cases into problem types or symptom categories or use or non-use of hypnosis. After much trial and a lot of errors, things naturally evolved toward more simplicity once we decided that Heider's balance theory seemed a useful tool (de Shazer, 1978, 1979).

We developed five distinct sequences or maps, each of which had several cases that fit the rules. That is, if a new case fit the parameters of any of the five sequences, we then knew how to carry on. From the degree of fit, we were quite encouraged that we could carry on from that point. However, we also had a sixth pile of miscellaneous cases that did not fit either with each other or with any of the five.*

We knew our project was in real trouble when we found out that not only did this motley pile contain the most cases, it also was larger than the other five piles combined. Of course, like Cinderella's stepmother, we tried to force these weird cases into our five sequences, but our shoehorn did not work: We would have had to mutilate the weird cases beyond recognition.

We then got the idea that Erickson's approach was similar to the variations on a theme in music when the theme is both unknown and unstated. That is, just by listening to a single variation by itself you can have no idea how close or how far it is from the unstated theme. We had lots of variations, but had not as yet been able to describe the theme itself.

However, at this point, two things were clear about all these cases:

1) clients' problems somehow maintain themselves, and
2) all of the cases were in some way goal-directed;
   a) some seemed to involve the client's goals,
   b) some seemed to involve the therapist's goal, and
   c) some others involved implicit goals brought into the story by the reader's interpretation.

Although Erickson said he *knew* what to do, it seemed to us that:

1) either much of what he did was extremely arbitrary and Haley was right that there is no theory and no theory is possible, or
2) we had the wrong tools of analysis, or
3) we just were not clever enough.

---

*Whether or not Erickson mentions using trance and, if so, whether it is "deep" or "light" has nothing to do with placing a case in either the patterned piles or the miscellaneous pile.

We tried other tools of analysis but all of these only made matters worse. Simply stated, there was just too much variety and too much diversity within the variety.

OTHER APPROACHES

At about this time, I ran into John H. Weakland and his partners Richard Fisch and Paul Watzlawick who were also developing a simple and elegant goal-driven model (Weakland, Fisch, Watzlawick & Bodin, 1974), which was based, at least in part, on Erickson's approach and which fit snugly onto one or two of our maps. What is really interesting about their model is the idea that the very efforts the client makes to solve the problem can be seen as accidentally maintaining it. The fact that their model fit with mine reinforced the idea that I was on the right track in my search for a way to describe the essence of Erickson's work.

Somewhat later, Bandler and Grinder (1975) described certain patterns they developed from Erickson's work that involved a microlevel of analysis different from our more macrolevel descriptions and involving some hypothetical, structuralist assumptions we were not willing to make. Like all structuralism, their model makes an interpretation more important, more relevant (more "true"?) than what it is an interpretation of, i.e., looking at the "deep structure" is meant to get at what a person *really* meant by what he or she said (the "surface structure") much in the same way that Freud's dream analysis is meant to get at what the dream *really* meant. In fact, we thought Bandler and Grinder's patterns actually led away from being able to generalize Erickson's approach or to construct a viable theory and that their work therefore resulted in further mystification.

At this point, my team and I came to a parting of ways over the question: Were we trying to *discover* Erickson's theory, which was hidden away and therefore discoverable, or were we trying to *invent* or construct a theory based on Erickson's work? In this regard, I chose the latter and followed Wittgenstein's idea that "there must not be anything hypothetical in our considerations. We must do away with all explanation, and description alone must take its place" (1968, p. 109).

ARBITRARINESS AS AN ESSENCE?

The aspects of things that are most important for us are hidden because of their simplicity and familiarity. (One is unable to notice something — because it is always before one's eyes.)
— Wittgenstein (1968, #129)

Meanwhile, as I continued to practice, I saw that the majority of my cases could be described using just one of the patterns (de Shazer, 1979). I was, of course, deliberately trying to use all five patterns, but despite my efforts, I also continued to add to that damn miscellaneous pile.

The wide spectrum of Erickson's cases and mine that did not fit into the rules suggests that something was going on here that we were not able to figure out. Could it be that the essence of Erickson's approach was a simple rule like: If you do not know what to do (which might even be the majority of times!), then do something totally unexpected, something arbitrary, something perhaps absurd? If so, then Erickson's approach would turn out to be uniquely Erickson's and thus unlearnable. We could know little or nothing about the cases, and thus Erickson's approach would turn out to be an evolutionary dead end, beyond theory or even rigorous description. As far as I am concerned, that is a totally unacceptable outcome.

Therefore, I once again almost felt pressed to *want* to look "behind and beneath" for this elusive "essence" upon which a viable theory could be constructed. However, this urge to look "behind and beneath" I then saw as a sign saying: *Danger! Here come speculation and muddle.*

My weird "data" from this entire project and my own practice led me farther and farther away from my starting point of "positivistic science" and reinforced my developing rejection of "structuralism." All of which led me closer and closer to a position now called "post-structuralism" (a topic well beyond this presentation), which is loosely related to a position in the family therapy world that is inadequately called "constructivism" (de Shazer, 1991).

Seduced by Haley's, Erickson's, and my own readings of these cases (and my own cases) into seeing these reports about doing therapy as a construction of the therapist's rather than a scientific (positivistic) report about the therapy, I was led to continue my search for the "essence" of Erickson's construction of Erickson's approach. I now saw this primarily as fitting under the rubric of "therapist-ingeniousness," a totally inadequate frame from a teaching and researching point of view, but one I saw forced upon me. (Of course I did not mind seeing myself and having others see me as clever—but how does one teach "being clever"? Additionally, I noted with regret that failure from this point of view must be seen as due to lack of therapist ingeniousness.) But now it was clear that whatever the rules looked like, they were more similar to the rules of soccer than to the rules of arithmetic. Clearly the rules I was searching for were descriptive rather than prescriptive.

But the arbitrariness of the "do something different" rule appalled me. Yes, John Weakland narrowed down the arbitrariness by focusing on the problem-maintaining features of the problem (i.e., patterns), but I found it difficult to teach therapists how to figure out which part of the problem-maintaining features should be the focus of intervention even though it usually seemed obvious to me. It turns out that it can be difficult for some people to tell patterns from randomness because "pattern recognition" is not a simple skill and can be difficult to learn. Perhaps some people are "pattern-blind" as some are color-blind.

FLUKES OR ANOMALIES?

For many years, our attempts to construct a theory based on Erickson's approach led me and my colleagues* to treat that damn "miscellaneous cases" pile as aberrations or flukes and thus set them aside. We were certain that a rule-based approach, our approach to theory construction, was the way to go. And certainly it has proved fruitful. Since then, my colleagues and I have been able to construct a rather elegant and strikingly simple yet comprehensive model using this approach to theory construction and model building (de Shazer, 1985, 1988).

About 10 years ago, as part of our project, we learned that *exceptions* are at least as important as, if not more important than, the rules to which they are exceptions. Even if these exceptions are accidents (of course, accidents are always possible), then these exceptions—even if only potential exceptions—necessarily need to be included within the theory. It was no longer possible to view the cases in the troubling miscellaneous stack as flukes. These cases involving seemingly arbitrary therapist activity *must* be included within the theory and not left outside as examples of Erickson's idiosyncratic genius. That is, this apparent arbitrariness must necessarily be covered by the rules of a theory for doing therapy that includes and is, in part, based on Erickson's approach. To me, this whole project now seemed hopeless.

I began to wonder if I had been missing the point all along. Perhaps, the secret or conundrum was that there was nothing hidden away and that the variety and diversity were the "essence" of Erickson's approach. Therefore, just accepting things as they are was the only option available to me. This would mean that my theory of Erickson's approach had many branches, but no center whatsoever. Furthermore, this would mean that there was no Theory, no "grand design." Instead, they were just local, rather idiosyncratic activities that were primarily situationally dependent.

To escape this situation, I decided again to follow Wittgenstein (1968)

---

*On this project, they were primarily Insoo Kim Berg and Wallace Gingerich. Other members of the BFTC team were also involved in various ways.

and renounce all Theory: "To put all this indefiniteness, correctly and unfalsified, into words" (#227). And this is what I decided to do. However, "the difficulty of renouncing all theory [is that] one has to regard what appears so obviously incomplete, as something complete" (Wittgenstein, 1980, #723).

REREADING ERICKSON

In order to reread Erickson's case examples as though for the first time, I needed to adopt a reading strategy that would allow me to not drag along all of my previous readings that involved the pursuit of a Theory. Somehow, I had to take the words at face value, to keep my reading on the surface, to avoid any and all reading between the lines, and to somehow overcome the urge to look behind and beneath. This is not an easy job.

To aid me in this rereading, I decided to interpret these case examples as stories—not as exemplary lessons, but as pure stories. Thus, I read them as if they were fiction, which meant that I was no longer taking the distinction between "literature" and "science" very seriously at all. It was no longer appropriate for me to search for the author's intention, or what he really meant, while ignoring my role as reader. That is, the unit of investigation had switched from Erickson and his papers to Erickson, his papers, and me.

These are good stories, with plots and subplots, beginnings, middles, and endings, strong characterizations, and frequent, unexpected twists and turns. Erickson-the-author has a definite style and command of language, everything a reader could want. As I read story after story, I came to see Erickson-the-therapist in these stories as the persona developed by Erickson-the-author; this persona I came to call "Erickson-the-clever."

As I continued to read using this strategy, I started to see myself and Haley and even Erickson-the-author in much the same relationship to these tales as the Baker Street Irregulars have to the Sherlock Holmes adventures.* That is, we were all seduced by Erickson-the-author into believing in the reality of Erickson-the-clever much as the Baker Street Irregulars were seduced into believing, or at least pretending to believe, that Sherlock Holmes was indeed a real human being who existed as you and I exist. Then I started to see Haley's writing about Erickson-the-clever as somewhat similar to Doctor Watson's role in the Sherlock Holmes stories. I started to see Haley-the-author as an invention of Erickson-the-

---

*I have often wondered if Erickson read and reread the Sherlock Holmes stories as avidly as I do. Long before I wanted to emulate Erickson's approach to problems, I wanted to emulate Holmes' approach. Is there or is there not a strong similarity between the character "Sherlock Holmes" and the persona "Erickson-the-clever"?

author, which Erickson-the-author used to strengthen the reader's sense of Erickson-the-clever as clever. Importantly, like Watson, Haley helped to point the reader in a certain direction by always seeing things clearly from a direction that is "wrong" but not as "wrong" as the official psychiatric view. Sherlock Holmes and Doctor Watson's view of Holmes and of his view of the various events depicted (in contrast to Holmes' view or the views of the official police) are exactly what make the Holmes stories something special. Viewed from this angle, these stories would be boring indeed without the persona of Erickson-the-clever. All of which helps to make an ordinary story into a good story.

It then dawned on me that the Erickson-the-clever stories, like the Sherlock Holmes stories, actually underdevelop or underrealize all the other characters that appear in the stories, particularly the clients. Often, these other characters, like inspector Lestrade, no matter how important to the story itself, are just cardboard cutouts. We have little or no idea about their contributions to the therapeutic endeavor.

However, as you and I know, and as Erickson and Haley also know, in order to have a therapeutic enterprise, there needs to be both therapist and client. As I reread my own cases from this point of view, I came to realize what clever clients I have had. Most of the ideas for "unusual interventions" in the miscellaneous pile in fact came from the clients themselves! Fortunately, we were cleverly listening when they told us what to do.

To reread my own case stories using the persona of clever-clients unfortunately forces the therapist-in-the-story to appear to be incredibly stupid. Undoubtedly, we therapists could not learn as much from de Shazer-the-stupid* as we did from Erickson-the-clever. Maybe we all need to remember systems theory here and reread all these stories with an interactional focus, which would lead us to the idea that clever therapy depends on having clients and therapists cleverly working together in clever ways.

❊   ❊   ❊

At this point, in our practice at Brief Family Therapy Center, we see that about 83% of our cases fit within the constraints of our maps, i.e., at some point early on in the therapy the therapist (and/or team) recognizes the plot the client and therapist are constructing together, so that it becomes clear that the therapist can say, "Now I can go on!" (Just because we know how to carry on does not mean that carrying on will be easy or successful.)

---

*Actually, I should have seen all this long ago, since the two major influences on my interviewing style have been John Weakland's persona "Weakland-the-dense" and Insoo Kim Berg's persona "Insoo-the-incredulous."

As I see it, the range of plots is constrained by how clients and therapists talk about what they talk about. In the other 17%, the team and the therapist do not arrive at the point where they can say, "Now I can go on" with any confidence whatsoever until much later in the therapy, if at all. The client and the therapist are not developing one of the usual plots because they are talking about things in a different way.

Case Illustration

Some years ago, I was seeing a father and mother who complained about everything their 12-year-old son did. Even if he smiled and was obedient, they would complain about it since they figured, "He must be up to something." I asked a lot of questions about this, but I could not find a single exception. No matter what the son did, the parents could find a way to complain about it. Throughout all this, he just sat there like a bump on a log, sometimes grunting in response to my infrequent questions and comments to and about him. Then I asked our miracle question (de Shazer, 1985):

> Let me ask you this. You may find this a strange and difficult question: Suppose that tonight you go to bed and while you're asleep, a miracle happens and the problems that brought you here today are solved, just like that. Since this happens while you are sleeping, you cannot know that this miracle has happened. Once you wake up the next morning, how will you begin to discover that this miracle has happened? What would be different in the morning? How would other people know?

Father and Mother described seeing a complete change in their son's attitude, which meant, it turned out, that they would not have anything to complain about. He would be doing many of the same things, but his attitude would be different and, somehow, they would know it. The son's miracle picture involved the parents not complaining all the time. However, reasonably enough, the boy could not describe what they would be doing instead because, as he said, that had never happened. As a team, we did not have any confidence that we knew how to go on, so we just used our fallback task for vague situations and asked the family to observe what happens that they want to keep happening.

When the family returned for the next session, the father and mother reported that the boy's attitude had changed completely! Everything that had happened they wanted to see continue and, therefore, they had no complaints.

Every once in a while clients tell us about sudden, complete, and unexplainable changes, so I started to wonder to myself if there had indeed been a (real) miracle. I decided I had better investigate it, so I asked, "How did this happen?" Mother and Father said that they did not know and they wondered aloud if there had been a miracle. The son then said that, following the previous session, he had decided that he "would simply pretend that a miracle had happened." He was amazed that his parents suddenly stopped complaining. And I was amazed that they did not complain about his only pretending. At this point, I knew how to go on since we have a general rule that says, "Once you know what works, do more of it."

We pay a lot of attention to an exceptional plot like this and we have found that "pretending the miracle has happened" is a useful task for a rather large number of clients, particularly those who are able to describe a miracle picture in great detail.

If I had told you about any one of the hundreds of subsequent cases where we have given "pretend the miracle has happened" as a homework task and the client did pretend and found it useful without my first having told you about this young man's having invented it, then you might read "clever therapist" into the story regardless of whether or not that was part of my intention.

CONCLUSION

I have come to recognize that the miscellaneous-cases pile, the exceptional cases that do not follow the typical plots, is one of the "essential" sources of clinical and theoretical innovation. Although the majority of cases essentially follow the rules, the exceptions are essential for developing new rules that serve to increase our flexibility and to increase the clients' options. And yet, no matter how rigorous, comprehensive, and content-free* our rules have become, it still seems that 17% of our cases continue to be exceptional. Thus, we can have some confidence that we can continue to learn how to do therapy.

Although the search for the "essence" of Erickson's approach turned out to be frustrating and incomplete, it was nonetheless useful. In fact, although such searches may all turn out the same way, figuring out that there is no such thing as an essence may be useful in itself. And, in some senses, such

---

*For instance, one of our "rules" is stated like this: "Is there a goal? Yes or no." If "Yes," then one type of therapist activity is suggested; if "No," some other activity is suggested. The question the rule addresses is not, "What is the goal?" because simply knowing *whether or not* there is a goal can be seen as quite enough to help a therapist decide what to do next.

searches may be necessary and not only unavoidable but desirable because the process can lead to simplification as a result of disciplined observation. Importantly, it is necessary to throw out all theory along the way so that not a single example is discarded from the study.

❃   ❃   ❃

O'Hanlon (1990) tells this story:

> A 20-year-old man came to see Erickson about his stunted growth. Erickson found out that the man saw everything as if he were looking at it from the same level as his navel. Erickson got him to hallucinate his world as if he were standing halfway up a staircase. The man grew 12 inches in the following year. Erickson never wrote about this case since he knew that nobody would believe it. (p. 48)

We need to keep in mind that, as Wittgenstein might say, "You've got what you've got and that's all there is."

REFERENCES

Bandler, R., & Grinder, J. (1975) *Patterns of the hypnotic techniques of Milton H. Erickson, M.D.* Cupertino, CA: Meta Publications.

Derrida, J. (1978) *Writing and difference* (A. Bass, Trans.). Chicago: University of Chicago Press.

de Shazer, S. (1978) Brief hypnotherapy of two sexual dysfunctions: The crystal ball technique. *American Journal of Clinical Hypnosis, 20:*203-208.

de Shazer, S. (1979) On transforming symptoms: An approach to an Erickson procedure. *American Journal of Clinical Hypnosis, 22:*17-28.

de Shazer, S. (1985) *Keys to solution in brief therapy.* New York: Norton.

de Shazer, S. (1988) *Clues: Investigating solutions in brief therapy.* New York: Norton.

de Shazer, S. (1991) *Putting difference to work.* New York: Norton.

Erickson, M. H. (1975) Preface in Bandler, R., & Grinder, J. *Patterns of the hypnotic techniques of Milton H. Erickson, M.D.* Cupertino, CA: Meta Publications.

Haley, J. (1967) Commentary on the writing of Milton H. Erickson, M.D. in Haley, J. (Ed.), *Advanced techniques of hypnosis and therapy.* New York: Grune & Stratton.

Haley, J. (1973) *Uncommon therapy: The psychiatric techniques of Milton H. Erickson, M.D.* New York: Norton.

Heider, F. (1946) Attitudes and cognitive organization. *Journal of Psychology, 21,* 107-112.

O'Hanlon, W. (1990) *An uncommon casebook.* New York: Norton.

Weakland, J.H., Fisch, R., Watzlawick, P., & Bodin, A. (1974) Brief therapy: Focused problem resolution. *Family Process, 13:*141-168.

Wittgenstein, L. (1968) *Philosophical investigations* (G.E.M. Anscombe, Trans.) (3rd ed.). New York: Macmillan.

Wittgenstein, L. (1975) *Philosophical remarks* (Hargreaves & White, Trans.). Chicago: University of Chicago Press.

Wittgenstein, L. (1980) *Remarks on the philosophy of psychology.* G. Anscombe & G. von Wright (Eds.). Oxford: Blackwell.

CHAPTER 16

The Locksmith Model

Joseph Barber

INTRODUCTION

Among the stories told repeatedly by Milton Erickson were those about patients who could not be hypnotized by other clinicians, but whom Erickson was able to hypnotize. It was apparently a matter of great importance to Erickson that he be able to hypnotize anyone. Erickson was legendary for the energy and creativity with which he tried to hypnotize "difficult" subjects. He seemed to be able to do whatever was necessary to hypnotize virtually anyone. One conclusion we draw from these writings is that we can learn about Erickson's hypnotic mastery by discovering and identifying the underlying principles that he used intuitively.

A further conclusion we may draw from Erickson's stories is that a person's capacity for experiencing hypnosis may be accessible under some circumstances and not others. Though he did not discuss the issue of hypnotic responsiveness directly, Erickson seemed to acknowledge that there were individual differences in what Ernest Hilgard has called "hypnotic talent." Erickson might describe one person as a "good subject," and another he might not. (I am not aware that he ever told stories about people whom he could not hypnotize, although I personally do know two such persons.)

Erickson's writings focused upon describing the techniques he employed,

This chapter is developed from The Locksmith Model (Barber, 1991), a chapter in *Theories of Hypnosis: Current Models and Perspectives,* edited by S. Lynn and J. Rhue (Guilford, 1991).

almost to the exclusion of all else in the interaction between himself and a patient. Consequently, among psychotherapists interested in understanding Erickson's work, there naturally has evolved an emphasis on particular hypnotic strategies. What was so compelling about Ericksonian technique was the strange and wonderful way he used language to engage and entrance.

What I wish to discuss now, however, is what was not so obvious about Erickson's work, and what may be not so obvious about hypnotic treatment. My own view (and that of many others who have written about the psychotherapeutic relationship) is that it is primarily the relationship that develops, sometimes instantaneously, which makes possible either hypnotic responsiveness or therapeutic responsiveness that may only *seem* to be hypnotic in nature.

ABOUT HYPNOSIS

First, let me denote what I mean by hypnosis, since this term means different things for different people. Hypnosis is an altered state of consciousness in which the individual's imagination creates vivid reality from suggestions offered either by someone else, by suggestions inferred from environmental cues, or by suggestions initiated by the individual her/him self. This condition allows individuals to be inordinately responsive to such suggestions, so that they are able to alter perception, memory, and physiological processes, which, under ordinary conditions, are not susceptible to conscious control. Hypnosis is a special condition that, for most people, is not a common, everyday occurrence. It might be related to, but is not the same as, reverie or inattentiveness.

What is it about the experience of hypnosis that is curative? It is widely believed that the suggestions themselves are what is effective. This belief is particularly characteristic among those who call themselves "Ericksonians," and whose work is so energetically focused on the creative development of therapeutic suggestions. But I have a different view. To account for the effect of suggestions, we need to attend to two other features of the hypnotic experience: 1) The salutary effect of the subjective experience of the hypnotic state or condition, and 2) the healing power of the hypnotherapeutic relationship. By understanding the interaction between these factors, we may understand the phenomenon of hypnosis and its nature as a healing influence. In this chapter, I suggest that the natural variations in the ways people experience hypnosis require the therapist to undertake a "locksmith" approach to engaging both hypnotic and curative capacities. I will explain this approach in more detail later.

THE LOCKSMITH MODEL

The Locksmith Model incorporates the following assumptions:

1. Psychotherapeutic cures involve alterations in both cognitive and affective processes. Such alterations require shifts in one's ability to attend to experience that is not within a person's ordinary awareness, and to capacities for change that are not within volitional control.

2. Hypnosis allows access to not-conscious (not necessarily only unconscious) experience.

3. In an altered state in which one can both be conscious and simultaneously have access to not-conscious processes, one can alter assumptions, meanings, perceptions, memories, and learned associations. In this way, one can bring about change in behavior and experience.

4. As a process, hypnosis seems to attenuate ordinary defensive processes. Hypnosis also seems to by-pass normal nondefensive cognitive structures that serve the healthy function of keeping out-of-conscious material or automated cognitive connections out of awareness, thereby facilitating a patient's attention to material that is meaningful in the context of treatment.

5. The therapeutic relationship that develops within the experience of hypnosis is an essential element in this process of diminished defense. The therapeutic relationship creates a place of safety that allows a patient to experience him or herself in a different, hopefully more benevolent way, making internal change more likely.

6. Having such an altered experience itself changes one's assumptions and expectations of the possibilities for new affect and behavior. The therapeutic relationship facilitates the development of the altered consciousness, which, in a positive feedback loop, facilitates the further development of the relationship, and so on.

7. People vary in their abilities and in their readiness to develop an altered state. This is what Hilgard meant by "hypnotic talent," and what Erickson meant when he described someone as being a "good subject." The hypnotic process and the relationship must be varied idiosyncratically to unlock the naturally occurring capacities for dissociative and other curative unconscious processes.

INVESTIGATING HYPNOTIC RESPONSIVENESS

As investigators or clinicians interested in hypnotic phenomena, we are faced with this question: Is hypnotic responsiveness an unvarying trait of the individual, or is it a variable trait that sometimes cannot be accessed, and at other times it can be, although perhaps with great difficulty? If hypnotic capacities can be variably accessed, what are the factors we need to understand to access them? What features of the hypnotic experience need we attend to? How can we access these variable hypnotic capacities?

The answer I offer here to these questions is two-fold: The capacity for imaginative involvement, up to and including dissociation, is crucial for development of the hypnotic experience, and the hypnotic relationship is the means by which we can engage that capacity in patients.

Focusing on qualities of the patient, such as hypnotic responsiveness or defensiveness, is essential to our inquiry about hypnosis; still, a narrow focus on the patient distracts us from attending to the essentially interactive nature of the phenomenon of hypnosis. Hypnosis is not simply the transmission of suggestions made by one person and received by another. Both Diamond (1984) and Banyai (1985) have demonstrated that the personal qualities of the hypnotist are critical components of the hypnotic process. Banyai's experimental work demonstrates the two-way interaction quite elegantly, illustrating that the experience and behavior of the hypnotized subject affects the experience and behavior of the hypnotist-researcher, creating a feedback of interaction. The relationship, both real and transferential, between clinician and patient, is crucial to the power and effect of suggestion.

Clinicians certainly are familiar with the experience of rapidly developed affect on the part of the patient with whom he or she has done hypnotic treatment. However, we might be less clearly conscious about the effect of such treatment on the experience of our own affect — particularly our feelings toward the patient. The same forces that determine how psychotherapist and patient relate in a nonhypnotic context continue to exert themselves, although often in a more rapid and intense manner, when hypnosis is involved. The sometimes sudden, seemingly magical change that can occur in the context of hypnotic treatment may be due, at least partly, to the experience of this powerful alliance between psychotherapist and patient.

RESPONSIVENESS AND CONTEXT

Although hypnotic responsiveness plays a significant role in determining the likelihood and degree of clinical hypnotic effect, and in the ease with which it may be obtained, it also may be that such responsiveness can be idiosyncratically activated by certain factors in the clinical context. A measurably low hypnotic responsiveness may predict, in a given case, the low probability of obtaining a hypnotic effect. However, if it is important to the patient that she or he experience a significant hypnotic effect, perhaps there are ways, however rare and unlikely, that this can be accomplished.

Such a circumstance more clearly and more often emerges in the emergency or hospital setting, where suffering is acute and profound, and where a patient's deepest adaptive resources can be summoned for action. When a seriously burned worker arrives in the hospital emergency room, suffering the agony of pain and fear of death, he may be more likely to respond to a physician's reassuring suggestions for comfort and well-being than he would be in other, less dire circumstances. If it is true that there are no atheists in foxholes, where one's ordinary intellectual defenses are irrelevant, perhaps it is also true that there are no unhypnotizable patients in emergency rooms, where acute suffering can render customary intellectual defenses irrelevant.

This phenomenon, however, is not usually a simple one. If a patient's suffering renders him panicked and out of control, or if the patient is highly disorganized and defensive, then the physician must be particularly adept to make suggestions effective. In such a circumstance, the clinician can establish a relationship by communicating an effective concern (i.e., "You are in the hospital. Lie still while I take care of you.").

If the patient is suffering, but total panic has not occurred, then there is an excellent opportunity (if the clinician knows how to use it) for rapidly developing a relationship supported by the patient's regressive needs and the clinician's authoritatively helpful (and, perhaps, lifesaving) actions.

Motivation for change and the effect of the psychotherapeutic relationship are two obvious elements that can create change. Perhaps these and other elements present in the hypnotherapeutic setting can liberate or unlock a capacity for hypnotic responsiveness that remains otherwise inaccessible and dormant, just as nonhypnotic capacities for response to psychotherapeutic treatment can be unlocked. This is one explanation for the findings of lack of relationship between measured responsiveness and apparent hypnotic effect, so often documented in the literature.

A LOCKSMITH METAPHOR

A locksmith is skilled at opening locks. Some locks have very simple, straightforward mechanisms requiring very simple, straightforward keys. After assessing what kind of key is needed, the locksmith can fashion such a simple key with ease. Some locks, however, involve more subtle and intricate mechanisms requiring very subtle, very intricate keys. The locksmith also can fashion such a complex key, but with more effort and care, perhaps with more difficulty, and perhaps with failed attempts along the way.

By comparison with a mechanical lock, a human's consciousness-altering mechanisms are ludicrously complex, involving not only intrapsychic locking mechanisms, but mechanisms of interactive feedback with the locksmith, as well. But this comparison between the task of a clinician and the task of a locksmith does illuminate the similar process of assessing characteristics to determine what kind of key will be successful. If we do not take it too literally, the metaphor of the locksmith may guide our thinking about the clinician's assessment of an individual patient's consciousness-altering mechanisms, and what needs must be met in order to unlock them. This metaphor can inspire us to continue working with the lock even when our first attempts fail.

When relating to a patient whose hypnotic responsiveness is not high, or when confronted with a patient whose hypnotic responsiveness is high, but whose hypnotic experience is unsatisfying or inconsequential, we might hypothesize that the patient is defending against the experience of hypnosis, for any of a variety of possible reasons. For instance, the fear of losing control is a common motivator for a patient to defend against the hypnotic experience. Or, if a patient experiences only a fragile sense of autonomy, then the fear of increased dependence on the clinician may be another. If a patient realizes, however vaguely, that he or she is holding significant repressed emotion, then the fear of liberating—and experiencing—that emotion may be yet another reason to defend against the experience of hypnosis. These hypotheses represent potential approaches—keys, if you will—to meeting patient's needs, so that they may be more readily receptive to the hypnotic experience. For example, if I think a patient is defending against a hypnotic experience because he or she is afraid of feeling too much emotional pain, I might incorporate suggestions for maintaining emotional control within the hypnotic induction.

The psychotherapist encountering these situations is confronted with the necessity of judging whether it is beneficial or harmful for the patient to risk loss of control or autonomy, or risk facing emotional pain. One might argue that in certain cases the use of hypnosis—at least, at that point in the therapeutic process—may be inappropriate. And unnecessary. It may be that just discussing the possibility of hypnotic treatment can raise such issues (e.g., the patient's fears) more quickly and more clearly, and, for that reason alone, can accelerate the pace of psychotherapy.

If, for instance, I judge that hypnotic treatment is appropriate, and, further, if I determine that it is both safe and beneficial to either confront or circumvent the patient's defenses toward the experience of hypnotic treatment, then I imagine myself a psychological locksmith whose goal is to avoid the patient's defensive maneuvers (and nondefensive inhibitions, as well) and unlock the hypnotic capacities that can activate a change in the patient's experience. We will then utilize that change to create therapeutic change.

HYPNOTIC RESPONSIVENESS AND CLINICAL OUTCOME

Although the early experimental literature on modifiability of hypnotic responsiveness, for example that of Diamond (1974, 1977) and Sachs (1971) reported that the changes in responsiveness were relatively modest, there is more recent evidence to support a more optimistic attitude toward such modification (Gfeller, Lynn & Pribble, 1987; Spanos, Brett, Menary & Cross, 1987; Spanos, Robertson, Menary & Brett, 1986). These more recent investigations demonstrate that hypnotic responding is closely related to, if not determined by, imaginal abilities, the capacity to relinquish reality-bound thinking, and the capacity for relating to the hypnotist (the same characteristics that I referred to earlier as essential to the development of a hypnotic experience). Further, these investigations illuminate the complexity of the hypnotic response, and lend experimental support to the view that hypnotic responsiveness is mutable, and, more particularly, that such mutability is dependent upon alterations in an individual's attitudes toward hypnosis and in her or his characteristic ways of relating to the hypnotist.

Adding to the complexity of understanding the relationship between hypnotic responsiveness and clinical outcome, however, is the fact that in a clinical context it is difficult to determine with certainty if a patient is, in fact, hypnotized. And perhaps it is the case that when a clinician believes that he or she, through thoughtful circumvention of defenses and other inhibitions, has accessed a low responder's hypnotic capacities and evoked responses from the patient that appear to be hypnotic in character and quality — perhaps — these responses are not actually hypnotic in nature, after all, but merely mimic hypnosis. Perhaps the psychotherapist has inadvertently taught the patient, in effect, how to simulate hypnosis. And perhaps the therapeutic change that occurs is not a function of the patient having been hypnotized at all. Perhaps there is a nonhypnotic effect that can best be produced in unhypnotizable patients in the context of trying to produce hypnotic effects. It would be ironic if the best — or the only — way to produce such effects in patients who are unable to experience hypnosis is to behave as if they are able to do so. However, I think this is the strategy actually employed, perhaps unwittingly, by many clinicians who use hypnosis.

Suppose, though, that "real" hypnotic effects are needed for treatment. How can we obtain them? Imagine for a moment that the seriously burned worker referred to earlier had been the subject of a hypnosis experiment the day before the accident and that he had been generally unresponsive to hypnotic suggestion. No experiment can generate the degree and kind of comforting and life-sustaining motivation that would be generated by his trauma on the following day. So the same unresponsive experimental subject may, a day later, be a highly responsive clinical patient. The circumstances necessary to "unlock" hypnotic capacities were not present in the experimental context, but were in the clinical situation. While, on the one hand, we have to adjust our theories to accommodate experimental findings, we must, on the other, recognize that such experimental findings cannot represent the full picture of the subject. Experimental findings can be excellent and necessary guides, but they do not necessarily represent therapeutic limits, because experiments are themselves limited in the degree to which they can replicate meaningful human experience in the laboratory.

The extreme circumstances of the emergency medical setting may represent the most likely ones in which to observe rare and unlikely responsiveness to hypnotic suggestion. Consequently, clinicians who work in other, less dramatic settings are less likely to obtain hypnotic response from hypnotically unresponsive patients. However, if the above assumptions bear any resemblance to reality, then we can expect that clinicians may be more effective in obtaining such responses when they are better able to engage the processes that underlie response in emergency settings. What might those processes be? How can we better engage them in such prosaic settings as the psychotherapist's office?

One feature that can characterize the hypnotic experience is that of a sense of profundity, solemnity, and depth: Nothing in the world matters at that moment except the experience of the patient. That is one of the characteristics of an emergency situation, as well. Consequently, when endeavoring to engage a patient in a hypnotic experience, I often try to convey the deeply important, even crucial, nature of that moment with the patient, and to join with the patient in the experience. While at the same time trying to understand the patient's internal world at that moment, and to empathize with the patient's experience at that moment, one can simultaneously communicate one's attention to the importance of that moment to the patient.

While one's experiences as a clinician need to be carefully evaluated to identify possibly confounding elements, such experiences are nonetheless valid bases for reasoning. Diamond (1987) relates clinical anecdotes, familiar to many psychotherapists using hypnosis, about low responders who ultimately achieve hypnotic effect following certain meaningful experiences in relation to the psychotherapist. Such clinical experience inspires the optimism of the would-be locksmith. It may be difficult, in any single case, to determine if an effect is hypnotic in nature, or is a function of contextual factors. Such difficulty does not, however, mean that the effect is not hypnotic. We may not be able to determine in any given case, if the effect is hypnotic.

I do not want to overemphasize the importance or relevance of any particular attitude toward or communication to a patient in this context. The profundity of the experience need not necessarily be borne by an air of solemnity. With children, for instance, and even occasionally with adults, humor may be a salient feature of the interaction, with the profundity of the circumstance conveyed by the *intensity* of the therapist's involvement. There may be a variety of attitudes that will help a patient to be responsive. The operating principle, I believe, for engaging the patient and accessing the potential for therapeutic response involves an empathic communication of hopefulness—and a nearly limitless quantity of patience.

UNLOCKING POTENTIALS

Magic may be invoked as an "explanation" when a clinician happens to find the right key (especially if it is on the first attempt at treatment). From the perspective of the locksmith, lack of treatment success means that one has not yet found (or fashioned) the right key—not that there is no lock and no key. Some patients' locks are so incredibly intricate, so rusty and stiff from disuse, and may be so ingeniously booby-trapped, that it may not be prudent to attempt to find the right key. Unlike a competent locksmith, a competent psychotherapist cannot expect to open every lock.

On the other hand, it may be tempting to relent too soon in one's efforts. A clinician may perform a procedure (e.g., a hypnotic induction), find a lack of response from the patient, and feel frustrated. Defending against the frustration, he may then conclude that the patient does not have the capacity to respond, and move on to other treatments (or other patients). Making peace with one's lack of effect and trying again (and, perhaps, again and again) may be vitally important, not only because a renewed attempt may be more appropriate for that patient, but because such persistence communicates to the patient that the clinician is optimistic and confident and committed to helping—and is not yielding to discouragement. (Perhaps one reason for the unexpected effectiveness of Rapid Induction Analgesia [Barber, 1977], the technique I developed while I was in graduate school, was that, in each subject or patient, several different forms of each suggestion were given. Further, several attempts were made in the event that the first did not succeed, with the implication that yielding to failure was not expected.)

The language and the tone with which we speak to our patients are important in conveying information and therapeutic suggestions. However,

I believe these variables are important only insofar as they aid in the development of the relationship between clinician and patient. Our interest in and respect for that relationship will, I believe, go far in facilitating therapeutic success.

REFERENCES

Banyai, E. I. (1991). Toward a social-psychobiological model of hypnosis. In S. J. Lynn & J. W. Rhue (Eds.), *Theories of hypnosis: Current models and perspectives.* New York: Guilford Press.

Barber, J. (1977). Rapid induction analgesia: A clinical report. *American Journal of Clinical Hypnosis, 19,* 138-147.

Barber, J. (1991). The Locksmith Model. In S. J. Lynn & J. W. Rhue (Eds.), *Theories of hypnosis: Current models and perspectives.* New York: Guilford Press.

Diamond, M. J. (1974). Modification of hypnotizability: A review. *Psychological Bulletin, 81,* 180-198.

Diamond, M. J. (1977). Hypnotizability is modifiable: An alternative approach. *International Journal of Clinical and Experimental Hypnosis, 25,* 147-166.

Diamond, M. J. (1984). It takes two to tango: The neglected importance of the hypnotic relationship. *American Journal of Clinical Hypnosis, 26,* 1-13.

Diamond, M. J. (1987). The interactional basis of hypnotic experience: On the relational dimensions of hypnosis. *International Journal of Clinical and Experimental Hypnosis, 35,* 95-115.

Gfeller, J. D., Lynn S. J., & Pribble, W. E. (1987). Enhancing hypnotic susceptibility: Interpersonal and rapport factors. *Journal of Personality and Social Psychology, 52,* 586-595.

Sachs, L. B. (1971). Construing hypnosis as modifiable behavior. In A. B. Jacobs & L. B. Sachs (Eds.), *Psychology of private events.* New York: Academic Press.

Spanos, N. P., Brett, P. J., Menary, E. P., & Cross, W. P. (1987). A measure of attitudes toward hypnosis: Relationships with absorption and hypnotic susceptibility. *American Journal of Clinical Hypnosis, 30,* 39-150.

Spanos, N. P., Robertson, L., Menary, E. P., & Brett, P. J. (1986). Component analysis of a cognitive skill training package for the enhancement of hypnotic suggestibility. *Journal of Abnormal Psychology, 95,* 350-357.

PART V

About Milton Erickson

CHAPTER 17

Milton Erickson: Early Postmodernist

*Gene Combs &
Jill Freedman*

A couple of years ago our friends and colleagues, Melissa and Griff Griffith, were putting together an exam for the psychiatric residents they supervise in Mississippi. It was to cover some of the ideas and ways of working that constitute what we would call "postmodern psychotherapy." This is not an easy feat. When you have a body of knowledge that includes ideas such as "There are no essential truths" and "There are multiple possibilities for how to describe and classify the 'reality' of any situation," a true and false test is clearly out of the question. A multiple choice test would be possible to give, but impossible to grade. Melissa and Griff settled on putting together an essay test that they believed would allow each resident to write about his or her own ideas in this arena.

Right about that time, Tom Andersen (1987), who, along with his team in the North of Norway, developed the idea of the reflecting team, and who is very interested in postmodern ideas, came to teach and consult in Mississippi at the Griffith's invitation. Melissa and Griff had been uneasy all along about having an exam, but the medical school required one. As Tom's visit grew nearer, Melissa became more and more uneasy, so much so that she buried the exam under some papers on her desk where it wouldn't come to light during Tom's visit.

But it did come to light. Somehow the test resurrected itself, and when

Tom borrowed Melissa's desk to use her phone, there it was. This led to a long conversation about the exam, about Griff and Melissa's desires to be nonevaluative and collegial in their teaching, their awareness that tests of any kind in this culture don't fit with being nonevaluative and collegial, that postmodern ideas are awfully hard to test, and that there are conflicting demands in the university system. Finally, Tom said, "When you give this test, I would ask only one thing. Could you put, at the top of the first page, 'Remember as you take this exam that there are many, many, many, right answers, and only a very few wrong ones'?"

That got us to musing about our education and what it would have been like to have had such a message on an exam. In medical school and social work school we both had the impression there were right answers—and only one per question. But our continuing education, which for many years for both of us was primarily in Ericksonian approaches, was different.

I (JF) remember being at a teaching seminar in the Erickson's guest-house some years ago. Milton Erickson primarily presented cases and told stories. Many times, although he was talking about a particular case from many years before, everyone in the room *knew* Erickson was really talking directly and specifically to him or her. We each found new associations, new thoughts, new possibilities for ourselves woven through the story Erickson was telling, although it was ostensibly about someone else. Sometimes, Erickson would work explicitly with one person, while the rest of us concentrated on learning how to do therapy as Erickson did. Simultaneously, we would have our own personal associations to, and applications of, the work he was doing. At other times, Erickson would finish presenting a case and then ask, "What would you do?" smiling expectantly. We would banish thoughts of our personal stories as best we could and one by one suggest ways of proceeding. Then Erickson would say, "Here's what I did," and go on to tell one of his now famous stories.

POSTMODERNISM

A central tenet of postmodernism is that, at the social level, there is no single, essential, "true" body of knowledge about how people, families, or societies should function. Erickson's teaching fit this idea. Here, for instance, are his (1965/1980, p. 223) words from 1965:

> The therapist's task should not be a proselytizing of the patient with his own beliefs and understandings. No patient can really understand the understandings of his therapist nor does he need them. What is needed is the development of a therapeutic situation permitting the patient to use his own thinking, his own

understandings, his own emotions in the way that best fits him in his scheme of life.

In order to describe more specifically what we mean by postmodernism, we will start by defining *modernism*. We think Roger Lowe's (1991) definition is clear and succinct:

> [modernism] . . . is used interchangeably with Enlightenment or Western thought. This form of thought insists that knowledge can be founded upon, or grounded in, absolute truth. It assumes that knowledge is "about" something external to the knower, and can present itself objectively to the knower.

Modernist thinkers tend to consider the scientific method as the one best way of advancing knowledge. They assume that the history of knowledge is a story of progress, of coming closer and closer to essential, foundational, generally applicable facts about the nature of a concrete and knowable universe. They tend to use metaphors based in Newtonian physics: force-counterforce, cause-effect, balance, measurement, impact, etc. DSM-III-R, with its aims of classifying all possible deviations from the norm of human mental functioning into 17 major categories and 250 or so subcategories, with the ultimate goal of finding a single specifiable cure for each distinct entity, is a paradigmatic modernist enterprise.

It seems that any modernist enterprise, when extensively pursued, begins to (if we may use a postmodernist buzzword here) deconstruct itself. Physicists, those paragons of pure science, encountered this effect during the first two decades of this century. Their quest for the fundamental building blocks of physical reality led to the description and naming of smaller and ever more numerous particles, and eventually to entities whose essential nature was unspecifiable, changing from particle to wave and back again depending on how they were measured. We all have encountered one or another reference to the relativism, uncertainty, and even metaphysical musings that surround physicists' current inquires into quarks, black holes, cold fusion, and the like.

Modernism has been slower to deconstruct itself in the field of social science, philosophy, and psychotherapy, but as our present century draws to a close, more and more psychotherapists are questioning the applicability of modernist, machine-age metaphors to our work. We are turning to *postmodernism* in one form or another for our guiding metaphors.

Postmodernism is not exactly antimodernism. Most postmodern thinkers would see the modernist worldview as one of many possible stories, one that is quite useful in pursuing criteria of predictability and control, but no more fundamentally "true" or "real" than many other stories about the nature of the universe. Postmodernist scholars are more interested in difference than they are in similarity. They are more interested in specific, contextualized details than they are in grand generalizations. Exceptions interest them more than rules. Clifford Geertz, a prominent postmodern voice in anthropology, has written on the importance of focusing on "local knowledge" instead of seeking universally applicable general knowledge when trying to understand ourselves in relation to the rest of humanity. In a typical quote (1983, p. 234) he says.

> . . . the world is a various place, various between lawyers and anthropologists, various between Muslims and Hindus, various between little traditions and great, various between colonial thens and nationalist nows; and much is to be gained . . . by confronting that grand actuality rather than wishing it away in a haze of forceless generalities and false comforts.

Another way of contrasting modern with postmodern thought is to say that while modernist thinkers are concerned with fact, postmodernists are concerned with meaning. In their search for and examination of meaning, postmodernists find metaphors from the humanities more useful than the modernist metaphors of physical science. "Narrative," "history," "language," and "text" are words that appear frequently in the writing of postmodernist thinkers.

As the world moves into a postmodern era (Anderson, 1990; Gergen, 1991), new ideas about how to do psychotherapy have begun to appear in the literature (Anderson & Goolishian, 1988; Gergen, 1985; Hoffman, 1990; White & Epston, 1990). We have been excited and energized by these ideas; they seem to fit easily with our own.

We have been surprised that many of our non-Ericksonian colleagues are not so stimulated, and even more surprised when people who are interested in postmodern ideas have difficulty applying them in therapy. We have come to believe that our background in Ericksonian ideas accounts for much of the ease and familiarity we feel in applying a postmodern worldview to psychotherapy. We think that Milton Erickson was a postmodernist before the word existed.

In the remainder of this chapter, we will consider six interrelated ideas that we believe characterize postmodern thought as it applies to psychotherapy:

1. Realities are socially constructed.
2. There are multiple possibilities for how to describe and classify the "reality" of any situation.

3. Knowledge is *performed,* not found.
4. Knowledge is constituted through language.
5. Realities are organized and maintained through narrative.
6. There are no "essential" truths.

There is abundant evidence that Erickson performed these knowledges long before people were talking and writing about them under the rubric of postmodernism. Let's take the ideas one at a time and see how they are exemplified in Erickson's work.

REALITIES ARE SOCIALLY CONSTRUCTED

As the world grows smaller, people find themselves in closer contact with an increasing number of diverse cultures, and it becomes more and more obvious that "reality isn't what it used to be."*

We live a block and a half north of Devon Avenue in Chicago. The stretch of Devon due south of us is lined with Indian restaurants and stores selling saris and gold jewelry from India and Pakistan. As you proceed west on Devon, you see Jewish bakeries, kosher butcher shops, Hebrew book stores, delis, and what used to be our favorite Jewish restaurant. Also within walking distance on Devon, you can find an Islamic book store, Muslim butchers, a Thai restaurant, a Greek restaurant, a Korean restaurant, several Chinese restaurants, the Chicago Croatian Social Club, and video stores catering to Arabic and Indian clienteles. Interspersed among these stores one can find a Walgreens, a Gap clothing store, an American diner, an ice cream parlor, and various other kinds of shops that you would find most any place in North America. On Saturdays, the street is jammed with Indian families doing their weekly shopping, Hasidic men and boys on their way to and from religious services, and other people we notice less, because they look more like us.

We don't believe we should wear saris or cover our heads when we frequent Devon Avenue, but many of the people we encounter there believe that they should do one or the other. And the differences in our taken-for-granted realities don't stop at how we dress. Some of the differences that societies have constructed among themselves are so great that wars are being fought over them in other parts of the world at this very moment.

If you don't have a Devon Avenue near you, you do have a television set, and it brings you into contact with even more cultures and systems of belief. It is harder and harder to believe that the folkways that have been

---

*This is the title of W.T. Anderson's (1990) popular book about postmodern culture.

constructed by one's own culture are the only right and proper ways to live and believe.

We each grew up in towns largely inhabited by people of our own socio-cultural-economic groups (which for each of us would not have included the other) and for each of us, the rather uniform cultures we grew up in comprised the world. But in the world we now inhabit, difference is the norm. It becomes harder and harder to deny that social realities are different in different cultures. Postmodernists believe that laws, institutions, social customs, hairstyles, and all the other things that make up the fabric of "reality" arise through social interaction over time. In other words, we, together, construct our realities as we live them.

Erickson seems to have known about the social construction of reality from a very young age. He used to tell the story of how, when the first snowfall of the year came, he would rise especially early so that he could be the first one to school. He would take a meandering path through the fresh snow and delight in watching how the people who followed him took the same path. In later years, as we all know, he interacted socially with people to invite them into "hypnotic realities."* And on many occasions he expanded the social sphere through which new realities might be created for a particular client by engaging others to participate.

For example, he tells of Ralph, a physician he saw who had multiple problems. Erickson referred to one of the problems as his "peculiar behavior about restaurants." Ralph never stayed in restaurants long enough to eat a full meal, and he only frequented those with male waiters. Erickson arranged for himself and Mrs. Erickson to accompany Ralph and his wife to a restaurant for a prime rib dinner. The waitress, an old friend of the Erickson family, seated the four. The realm of social interaction through which realities could be created now included not only Ralph and Erickson, but both of their wives and the waitress. Erickson reports (Zeig, 1980, p. 275):

> The waitress left us, and Ralph suddenly found that there was a clock on the wall that he could see. We waited and waited. Half an hour later the waitress showed up with four trays of salad. The waitress was very concerned. Ralph looked away and said, "I'll take that one." (Erickson looks away and points.)
>
> She said, "You haven't even looked at it." She used the tongs and she picked up each constituent of the salad and explained what it was. Ralph said, "I'll take it." She said, "But you haven't

---

*See the book of the same title by Erickson, Rossi, & Rossi (1976).

looked at the other three salads." So she had him examine all four salads twice before she let him choose his salad.

Then she said, "I have four different dressings."

The meal continued in a drawn-out fashion, with the waitress telling jokes and eventually making Ralph clean his plate.

The next night Ralph, his wife, and daughter went back to the same restaurant and were waited on by the same well-coached waitress who was completely professional this time. From then on, Ralph was comfortable going to restaurants.

Erickson told many stories like this in which he expanded the social system to facilitate the construction of new experiential realities for the people who came to see him.

MULTIPLE POSSIBILITIES

Last summer, we had brunch at the home of some friends. When the conversation turned to the Olympics, five-year-old Ben asked us if we were rooting for the Americans. We assured him that we were and he nodded knowingly. "That's because you're Jewish," he explained.

We think Milton Erickson would have enjoyed that moment and understood Ben's description and classification. Erickson knew a lot about the difficulties classifications can get you into and he avoided them assiduously.

We think of Ben's confusion (and he *was* confused by the laughter following his statement) as a kind of postmodern dilemma: Absolute classifications just don't seem to fit in the postmodern context of so many possibilities. Ben knew his family was Jewish. They were rooting for the Americans. He drew the conclusion that Jewish people root for the Americans. Some do, but so do many African-Americans, Catholics, and other groups. There are Jews who don't root for the American teams. The possibilities are endless, and confusing—not just to five-year-olds, but to anyone trying to live by modern criteria in a postmodern world.

Erickson valued multiple possibilities. He wrote, "There are plenty of alternatives in any situation . . . When you attend a session of group therapy, what on earth are you going to see? That is what you go there for" (Erickson and Rossi, 1981, p. 206).

Erickson utilized the world's multiple possibilities in his therapy and teaching. He told stories of the Tarahumara Indians, the Balinese people, and other people in other places to suggest (among others) the idea that one need not be limited by the belief system that one is born into. He said, "I had always been interested in anthropology, and I think anthropology should be something all psychotherapists should read and know about, because different ethnic groups have different ways of thinking about things" (Zeig, 1980, p. 119).

KNOWLEDGE IS PERFORMED

Along with his celebration of multiple possibilities, the postmodern idea most clearly characterized in Erickson's work is that knowledge is *performed,* not found. It is an activity or process that we *do.*

Modernists tend to treat knowledge as if it were a commodity, something that can be uncovered, stored away, and passed intact and unchanged on to succeeding generations. Postmodernists stress the interactive and communicative aspects of knowledge. For them, it exists only in social interaction. Granted, the interaction is sometimes a conversation with oneself; but books, institutions, or traditions have meaning only when people use them. Each interaction is a new performance.

While some therapists talked with clients about their history in attempts to get to "the root of the problem" and others hypothesized and shared those hypotheses with clients, Erickson got people to do something. He once said, "The thing to do is to get your patient, any way you wish, any way you can, to do something" (Zeig, 1980, p. 143). In the act of doing, people performed knowledge.

Erickson even seems to have been able to get people to perform knowledge after his physical presence had left us. The year after Erickson died, we each climbed Squaw Peak and went to the Botanical Gardens. At every Erickson Conference, we've met others who continue to do the same.

Erickson's stories and case reports are peppered with suggestions that people should "perform knowledge" by doing something. The following is a short example from *My Voice Will Go with You* (Rosen, 1982, p. 127):

> Another woman called me up and said, "I'm ashamed to come in to see you. For the last two years I've neglected my husband, my family, my children. I've sat in the kitchen and eaten everything I could lay my hands on. My husband takes the children to school and brings them back. He does all the shopping and I cook and eat things. I'm grossly overweight. I don't even want you to be able to see me."
>
> I said, "You want to lose the weight. You've neglected your children and your husband for two years. In that case why don't you take your children out of school; put them in the station wagon and sightsee all over Arizona, New Mexico, Utah, California, and every other cotton-pickin' place you can think of. And make

your kids read brochures, historical and geographical brochures, on your sight-seeing trip. Stay in motels where you can't take charge of the kitchen. You'll be too busy looking after your kids to eat. On your husband's present income, he can join you every weekend. The family can really enjoy a vacation for a year."

A year later she called up and said, "I'm back to normal weight. I'm interested in my kids. I love my husband and I want to return to household duties. Do I have to do any more sight-seeing?"

I said, "Not until you gain weight."

KNOWLEDGE IS CONSTITUTED THROUGH LANGUAGE

Language is the medium through which we socially construct reality. By "language" we refer to more than words. We refer to words, pictures, gestures, and the like—all the signs we use to convey meaning. In the modernist worldview, the signs of language correspond to objects and events in the "the real world"; they are passive carriers of fixed meaning. Postmodernists believe differently. They focus on how the language that we use *constitutes* our world and beliefs. Rorty (1989, p. 5) puts it this way: "Truth cannot be out there—cannot exist independently of the human mind—because sentences cannot so exist, or be out there."

To postmodernists, the only worlds that we can know are the worlds we describe to each other in language, and description is an active process. In agreeing on a description, we draw a distinction, and that distinction shapes subsequent distinctions, which in turn shape still other distinctions.

Here is a simple example: When I (GC) was growing up, my Uncle T. A. delighted in taking me on long walks in the woods where he would point out, name, and tell stories about the various plants and flowers we saw. Although Jill's grandparents often took her brother and her to formal gardens, they would never name flowers, but only comment on their beauty. Consequently, when we walk through the neighborhoods and parks of Chicago each spring, I see daffodils and azaleas and redbuds and bleeding hearts, and note (each and every year as if it were the first) that they bloom all at once rather than in the slow and stately progression they enjoyed in Kentucky where I grew up. Jill sees beautiful flowers. The different linguistic distinctions our families brought forth in our youth continue to constitute different knowledges of spring in our middle age.

Erickson was very aware of the constitutive power of language. Much of his work was built on the presupposition that particular language can lead to particularly altered states of consciousness. He often talked about the importance of choosing particular language in suggesting a more workable reality to a person who came to see him.

For example, when asked about seeing a couple in which the husband is an alcoholic, he said,

> I ask him to define the problem situation for me. He'll say something like, "I don't think I'd be an alcoholic if my wife didn't nag me all the time." My comment to the wife is, "I doubt if you really nag him; I expect you express your legitimate regret that he drinks excessively. And that has used a lot of your energy in the past. As he improves, what are you going to use that energy for?"
>
> I persuade her to wonder about that. But by putting it that way, I give the husband an opportunity to watch her to see that she uses her energy in those other areas. And he has to stop drinking so that she can have that energy to use in other areas. You always tie the two in together, but you never tell them that. When you commit her to use her time and energy elsewhere, you're committing him to give her the opportunity. (Haley, 1973, p. 240)

This kind of explanation is typical of Erickson's writing and teaching and demonstrates how important he considered language to be in suggesting alternative realities.

REALITIES ARE MAINTAINED THROUGH NARRATIVE

If the distinctions that bring forth different realities are made in language, those distinctions are then circulated and remembered in stories. The central role of narrative in organizing, maintaining, and circulating knowledge of ourselves and our worlds has been stressed by many postmodern writers. (e.g. Bruner, 1986; Geertz, 1986; Rorty, 1991) Our understanding of these ideas as they apply to therapy is that people make sense of their lives through the meaning they perform on certain events. Each remembered performance constitutes a story, and the stories of individual events are strung together through time to constitute a life narrative. When life narratives offer little choice, they can be changed in therapy by the highlighting of different events or by the performing of new meaning on events, thereby constituting new narratives.

Erickson's use of stories in his teaching and psychotherapy shows that he understood the power of narrative in shaping lives. He is almost as renowned for his skilled use of stories as he is for his contributions to hypnotherapy. His well-known "February Man" (Erickson & Rossi, 1979) approach clearly illustrates how he worked actively and strategically as co-author of people's life narratives. But the most impressive illustration of

Erickson's understanding of narrative's importance in shaping reality is the way that he wrote and rewrote his own life story as he lived it, performing positive meanings on what others might have experienced as adversity.

Born color blind, he took one color and made it his own. Each new purple gift from a student, colleague, or client became another incident in the complex and fascinating story of the "Purple Sage" and all the happy associations he had involving that color. He used the knowledge he gained in his struggles with dyslexia, tone deafness, and the inability to appreciate musical rhythms to inform the inspirational and instructive stories he told others about how to persist, how to learn, and the possibility of breaking free of limiting mental sets. His nearly lifelong struggle with polio and its aftereffects was a recurring theme in his "teaching tales," and instead of framing the effects of the polio as deficits, he storied them as assets.

For instance, Rosen (1982) documents a story Erickson told about his days as a medical school professor. There was a student who became "very withdrawn and oversensitive" after losing a leg in an auto accident. Erickson arranged for a few other students to help him stall the elevator one morning, and here's what happened:

On that Monday, with Jerry holding the elevator doors open and Tommy stationed at the head of the stairwell, I found the class all on the ground floor waiting for me at seven-thirty. . . . I said, "What's the matter with your thumb, Sam? Is it weak? Push that elevator button."
He said, "I have been."
I said, "Maybe your thumb is so weak, you ought to use two thumbs."
He said, "I tried that too, but that damn janitor is so worried about getting his pail and mops down, he's probably holding the elevator doors open."
. . . Finally, at five minutes of eight I turned to the student with the artificial leg and said, "Let's us cripples hobble upstairs and leave the elevator for the able-bodied."
"Us cripples" started hobbling upstairs. Tommy signaled to Jerry; Sam pushed the button. The able-bodied waited for the elevator. Us cripples hobbled upstairs. At the end of the hour, that student was socializing again — with a new identity. He belonged to the professorial group: "Us cripples." I was a professor; I had a bad leg; he identified with me; I identified with him. (pp. 226-227)

It strikes us that, in identifying with the medical student, Erickson was writing a new chapter in his own personal narrative. He was constructing a society of professionally competent, outgoing, well-liked physicians who had the further distinction of being "crippled," and he was placing himself squarely in the middle of that society. Later in his life, when he was confined to a wheelchair, he told his life story in such a way that it let him experience himself as an Olympic Medal winner. He told Sid Rosen (1982, p. 102), "Out of a wheelchair I win the Olympic championships all the time," and went on to recount how he had worked patiently over a number of years with Donald Lawrence to help him win two gold medals in the shot put, how he had taught the coach at Texas A & M his approach to training Lawrence, and how that coach had used his methods to train Masterson to set the first world record of 70 feet or more. It seems obvious in the telling that Erickson *had* won gold medals from his wheelchair. He was saying that if he could, so could others.

Toward the end of his life, when students began to worry aloud about Erickson's impending death, instead of joining them in their potentially pessimistic narratives, he told stories of the longevity and optimism of his parents. We believe that these stories served an inspirational purpose for Erickson's students and for Erickson himself, advancing the social construction of the mindset that led him to say, "I have no intention of dying. In fact, that will be the last thing I do!" (Rosen, 1982, p. 167)

THERE ARE NO ESSENTIAL TRUTHS

If realities are socially constructed, and if knowledge is performed and constituted through language, it follows that, at least at the social level, truth is somewhat fluid and negotiable; there are no essential truths. For instance, the modernist idea of norms, such as criteria for mental health or developmental stages, is still dominant in our culture. Many people compare themselves to norms with the belief that in so doing they will discover some essential truth about themselves. Looking through a postmodernist lens, we see such concepts as stories about ways of being, not as descriptions of essential truth.

While modernists speak as if they believe in a deep, real, or essential self, postmodernists believe that self-knowledge is performed and constituted through language and maintained through narrative. There are multiple possibilities for how people constitute themselves through social interaction. Certainly, particular possibilities are preferred by particular people and particular cultures, but none represent essences.

This does not mean that "anything goes." Tradition, personal history, and "common sense" constrain us, blinding us to certain possibilities and leading us to see others as desirable. Saying that values are socially constructed does not mean that all values should be tossed out the window or that all societies construct equally useful values. However, it does mean that we can strive for an awareness of the subjectivity of our worldviews and cultivate humility in the face of beliefs that conflict with our own.

Even before we encountered the essential/constructed distinction and distinguished ourselves as constructionists, our immersion in Erickson's teachings led us to agree with Erickson's words (Erickson & Rossi, 1979, pp. 233-234):

> Psychotherapists cannot depend upon general routines or standardized procedures to be applied indiscriminately to all their patients. Psychotherapy is not the mere application of truths and principles supposedly discovered by academicians in controlled laboratory experiments. Each psychotherapeutic encounter is unique and requires fresh creative effort on the part of both therapist and patient to discover the principles and means of achieving a therapeutic outcome.

As early as the 30's Erickson (1930/1980, p. 482) was writing:

> Properly, it [therapy] is not a matter of advancing particular schools of thought or of attempting to substantiate interpretative psychological theories, but simply a task of appraising a patient's problem or problems in terms of the reality in which the patient lives and in the terms of the realities of the patient's continuing future as he or she may reasonably hope for it to be.

Because they don't believe in essential truths, postmodernists prefer qualitative research—ethnography, narrative descriptions, case histories, and the like—over quantitative research. Erickson (1953, p. 2), always ahead of his time, had this to say back in 1953:

> . . . single instances often illustrate clearly and vividly aspects and facts of general configurations, trends and patterns. Rather than proof of specific ideas, an illustration or portrayal of possibilities is often the proper goal of experimental work.

We believe that Erickson was intensely curious about the "local knowledge" of each new person he met, and he knew that such knowledge had to be, must be, different in many ways from anyone else's knowledge. He celebrated that difference and built his way of working around it. He wrote about cases, about specific people at specific moments in their lives, not about theory and not about essential, overarching truth—which brings us to the title of this volume, "Ericksonian Methods: The Essence of the Story."

Is there an essence to his story? Many people, ourselves (Combs & Freedman, 1990) included, having studied Erickson's work through our own filters, have drawn distinctions that we thought captured some essence or other of Erickson's work. These methods, patterns, techniques, guidelines, approaches, or whatever we called them have been useful in developing our psychotherapeutic skills. But none of us has ever captured the essence of Erickson's story. Margaret Mead (1977) may have come close when she wrote, "It can be firmly said that Milton Erickson never solves a problem in an old way if he can think of a new way—and he usually can" (pp. 4-5). We believe the essence of the story is that there is no essence.*

Each one of us, each community of us as we strive to apply Ericksonian ideas in our daily work, constitutes a particular local knowledge, an embodied enactment, of Erickson's story. And each embodied enactment is unique. Personally, we are glad to have Erickson's examples to emulate. But our every attempt at copying his methods turns out different. As Geertz (1986, p. 380) puts it, "It is the copying that originates."

Try as we might, we cannot replicate Erickson's work, nor, we believe, would he want us to. He celebrated the uniqueness of his students as well as that of his clients, urging them to do things their own way. Remember what Tom Andersen said, "There are many, many, many right answers and only a very few wrong ones."

REFERENCES

Andersen, T. (1987). The reflecting team: Dialogue and meta-dialogue in clinical work. *Family Process*, 26:415-428.

Anderson, H., & Goolishian, H.A. (1988). Human systems as linguistic systems: Preliminary and evolving ideas about the implications of clinical theory. *Family Process*, 27(4):371-393.

Anderson, W. T. (1990). *Reality isn't what it used to be: Theatrical politics, ready-to-wear religion, global myths, primitive chic, and other wonders of the postmodern world.* San Francisco: Harper & Row.

Bruner, J. (1986). *Actual minds, possible worlds.* Cambridge: Harvard University Press.

---

*In the discussion following our presentation of this paper, Michael Rousell Ph.D., from Alberta, Canada, made a comment that we found intriguing. He said that if "realities are organized and maintained through narrative, which is what we appear to do, ever since we've been talking about Erickson we've been talking about his story and maintaining him through story. So maybe the essence of the story is the story of his essence."

Combs, G., & Freedman, J. (1990). *Symbol, story, and ceremony: Using metaphor in individual and family therapy.* New York: Norton.

Erickson, M. H. (c.1930/1980). Shock and surprise facilitating a new self-image. In E. L. Rossi (Ed.), *The collected papers of Milton H. Erickson on hypnosis. IV. Innovative hypnotherapy* (pp. 482–490). New York: Irvington.

Erickson, M. H. (1953). The therapy of a psychosomatic headache. *Journal of Clinical and Experimental Hypnosis,* (4):2–6.

Erickson, M. H. (1965/1980). The use of symptoms as an integral part of hypnotherapy. In E. L. Rossi (Ed.), *The collected papers of Milton H. Erickson on hypnosis. IV. Innovative hypnotherapy* (pp. 212–223). New York: Irvington.

Erickson, M. H., & Rossi, E. L. (1979). *Hypnotherapy: An exploratory case book.* New York: Irvington.

Erickson, M. H., & Rossi, E. L. (1981). *Experiencing hypnosis: Therapeutic approaches to altered states.* New York: Irvington.

Erickson, M. H., Rossi, E., & Rossi, S. (1976). *Hypnotic realities: The induction of clinical hypnosis and forms of indirect suggestion.* New York: Irvington.

Geertz, C. (1983). *Local knowledge.* New York: Basic Books.

Geertz, C. (1986). Making experiences, authoring selves. In V. Turner & E. Bruner (Eds.), *The anthropology of experience.* Champaign: University of Illinois Press.

Gergen, K.J. (1985). The social constructionist movement in modern psychology. *American Psychologist,* 40(3):266–275.

Gergen, K. J. (1991) *The saturated self: Dilemmas of identity in contemporary life.* New York: Basic Books.

Haley, J. (1973). *Uncommon therapy: The psychiatric techniques of Milton H. Erickson, M.D.* New York: Norton.

Hoffman, L. (1990). Constructing realities: An art of lenses. *Family Process,* 29(1):1–12.

Lowe, R. (1991). Postmodern themes and therapeutic practices: Notes towards the definition of 'Family Therapy: Part 2.' *Dulwich Centre Newsletter* (3):41–52.

Mead, M. (1977). The originality of Milton Erickson. *American Journal of Clinical Hypnosis,* 20(1):4–5.

Rorty, R. (1989). *Contingency, irony, and solidarity.* New York: Cambridge University Press.

Rorty, R. (1991). *Essays on Heidegger and others: Philosophical papers, volume 2.* New York: Cambridge University Press.

Rosen, S. (1982). *My voice will go with you: The teaching tales of Milton H. Erickson.* New York: Norton.

White, M., & Epston, D. (1990). *Narrative means to therapeutic ends.* New York: Norton.

Zeig, J. (1980). *A teaching seminar with Milton H. Erickson.* New York: Brunner/Mazel.

Zeig, J. (1985). *Experiencing Erickson: An introduction to the man and his work.* New York: Brunner/Mazel.

CHAPTER 18

Milton H. Erickson, M.D.: The Wounded Physician as Healer

Sandra M. Sylvester

INTRODUCTION

Probably each one of us who has chosen medicine, psychology, dentistry, nursing, or counseling as our profession wants to be able to intervene in another's life in a therapeutic manner, to be a healer. As a prelude to a discussion of Erickson, the Wounded Physician as Healer, I would like to tell you about a conversation I had with Milton Erickson shortly before he died, as an example of his ability to become totally focused on and immersed in something of interest, to the exclusion of all else.

I left a tide-pooling trip in Rocky Point, Mexico, to go directly to Cleveland to teach some hypnosis workshops. The trip in Mexico had been so spectacular that I wanted to share it with Milton, thinking he would have liked to have been there, so I called him on the phone to tell him about it. I told him about the marvel I had seen the previous nights in the Gulf of California: bioluminescence. We talked about the spring bloom of dinoflagellates, billions of tiny microscopic organisms that live in the ocean and biolumi-nesce when they are disturbed. The ocean is transformed. When each wave rolls over on itself, it bursts with a blue-green light. When a fish swims, it leaves a wake of a blue-green brilliance where it has been. If you plunge your hand and arm into the water and swirl it, you leave a trail of light. If you take a bucket of water and pour it into another bucket, it is as if you are pouring light from one bucket into the other.

I told Milton how we spent most of the night reveling in this magical world. Milton joined in an animated conversation in which he related two times in his life when he, too, had seen bioluminescence. We talked on and on, sharing our experiences with each other. When I told him that I would bring some pictures to Phoenix when I got home, Milton asked when I would be home, and I told him, the following Monday. He was silent for what seemed to be a long time, and then said, "Oh, . . . OK."

I got home Monday morning at about 1:30 A.M. At 9:30, I got a call from Kristi Erickson saying "Sandy, can you come to Phoenix? Daddy's dying." Milton was in a coma; the above conversation was the last one we had.

As I reflect back on our conversation, I realize that Milton was probably in great discomfort at that time. Yet, when we spoke, he talked in an animated, interested manner for more than 20 minutes, obviously enjoying the conversation, and in no hurry to end it. This from a man whose telephone conversations were usually brief and sometimes abrupt. Was this a window of comfort in a wall of pain? In our conversation, both Milton and I were transformed and captivated by the wonder of the experience of bioluminescence. For me it was the previous week, for him it was many years before.

How did Erickson learn about different ways of managing pain and recovering from illness? How do his methods work? And how can we experience these same phenomena and begin to use them in our own lives? These are the topics I want to discuss.

Erickson's life has taken on such great importance because of his contributions to the healing professions. In fact, Erickson saw himself as a physician and psychologist primarily involved with the task of healing and helping in his unique way based on his lifetime of experience.

As we discuss the underpinnings of Erickson's natural, self-evident, incremental approach to pain management and recovery, it will become evident that this is not a spooky illustration of someone doing some magical incantation, paradox, or double-bind, and then "presto-chang-o," a person who was once sick is now healthy. Erickson's approach is rooted in his own process of small, just noticeable, incremental changes, as he himself learned how to tap into his own physiological memory.

The concept of the "Wounded Physician as Healer" as used here, is a

Jungian archetype having certain characteristics and requirements. One of these requirements, and a significant one in Erickson's life, is that one has had a serious illness early in life, an unusual illness in which the individual's life order is disturbed and, to be cured, the individual has to cure himself.

When Milton Erickson was 17 years old, he was stricken with one of the three strains of polio. Literally overnight, he was changed from an athlete into a young man critically close to death. His doctors told his mother that he probably would not live until the next morning. The strong-willed Milton vowed that he would not die without seeing one more sunset. So he asked his mother to position the dresser with its attached mirror and tilt the mirror so that he had a clear view out the west window of the house. He saw his sunset. It filled his whole visual sphere. It seemed to fill his total awareness. There was nothing but the sunset. Then he collapsed into unconsciousness for three days.

When he awoke, he asked, "Where was the fence, the boulder, and the tree?" His family didn't know what he was talking about and thought he was delirious, but he was recalling his last memory before the period of unconsciousness when he was looking at the sunset. He was aware that he saw only the sunset. He did not see the fence, the boulder, and the tree through the window, which always had blocked his complete view of the sunset. When he reflected on this event, almost 70 years later, he reported that he was in an altered state of consciousness then, with focused and intense attention, seeing and experiencing only the sunset to the exclusion of all else.

The long tedious process of recuperation followed. Perhaps the most memorable aspect of this was the time his family forgot to move his chair to a window, and Milton was stuck for half of the day inside the farmhouse looking at a closed door. He said that his family had a daily routine. They would work most of the day in the fields, coming back to the house for meals. For the paralyzed Milton, they had taken a rocking chair, pounded out the seat, and put a potty under the chair. Milton's mother or another family member would tie him to the chair so that he would not fall out, then they would leave for a time and work the fields or do chores. Usually, they would position him by a window so that he could look outside. However, one day they forgot to do this. Milton said he wanted to look out or go out so badly that he began looking intently at the door and remembering how it used to feel to put pressure from his hands on the arms of the chair and his feet on the floor boards, lean his head and shoulders forward, increase the pressure on his hands and feet and rise from the chair and walk to the door and go outside. He did this as precisely as his memory would allow. He recalled each muscular movement that would allow him to rise from the chair and walk. Then he noticed that the rocking chair began to rock ever so slightly. Somehow his paralyzed body was able to make small twitches and get the chair to rock. Milton was accessing and activating old physiological patterns for movement. It was at this moment that Milton Erickson began to realize that if he was capable of making random twitches that could cause the chair to move, he could learn how to make these twitches deliberate and someday move, if not walk, again.

His external teacher became his toddler sister, Edith Carol. He watched her crawl, pull herself up on pieces of furniture, and eventually balance herself on her own and take her first steps. While Milton watched her, he did the same movements as his sister in his mind, remembering how it felt for his muscles to do these same movements. He also recalled other movements: walking the furrows of a newly plowed field, climbing his favorite tree, hanging from his arms and swinging—all familiar movements from days gone by, movements stored in neurological memory.

Throughout his life Milton paid attention to the variations in his own physical perceptions of pain, fatigue, enjoyment, and pleasure. He learned that by concentrating on his pain and by dissecting it into its various attributes—piercing, lancinating, burning, throbbing, etc.—and by precisely pinpointing its foci, noting where the pain was most intense and contrasting this with areas of lesser intensity and still other areas of no pain, he could diminish his perception of that pain. He learned that if he could exhaust himself, he could collapse into an exhausted sleep, which was better than no sleep at all. He learned that he could cause himself pain, and that this pain, which he caused and therefore could control, could become more intense and focused than the pain he could not control, thereby lessening his perception of the uncontrollable pain. He also learned that rapture enabled him to ignore pain, as did regression.

Milton also sharpened his observational skills, for which he was well noted, during this recuperative period. He spent time listening to and identifying the sounds around him. By listening to the sound of the manner in which the barn door closed, how long it took the footsteps to reach the house, how the door to the house was opened and closed, and the consequent activity in the house, he assessed which family member it was and what kind of mood he or she was in. He delighted in testing and refining his observational skills throughout his life. By watching a stranger walk, he could tell whether that person grew up in a rural or urban environment, noting that people in a rural environment "felt" the ground with their feet before they stepped, whereas a person who had grown up in an urban environment walked with the expectation that the "ground" (cement or black top) was regular underfoot, leading to subtle differences in walking. He shocked a nurse with whom he worked by congratulating her before she had told anyone that she had just learned she was pregnant; when she asked him how he knew, he replied that the color of her forehead was different. Because he took the time to notice, he saw things most of us would overlook.

In translating his personal strategies for learning about his own process of illness and recovery to his patients, Erickson worked with the real-life experiences of the patient stored in that individual's physiological memory of smells, tastes, sounds, muscle movements, angles of visual perception, sensations, and emotions which manifest themselves in the patient's interests. This became the core of Erickson's method, an approach rooted in the natural order of things, based on the real-life experiences of the individual patient, working within the personality and personal orientation of that individual. Erickson used the patient's own frame of reference, the patient's own concepts and language, observed and listened to that patient, and then accessed the natural therapeutic processes and strengths within that individual.

In adopting Erickson's techniques and applying them to our patients, it is well to remember that we cannot apply Erickson's experiences to our patients, only the experiences we have personally absorbed. It is only when we ask ourselves, as Milton Erickson did, "What is possible from this experience? What is interesting about this experience? How can I play with the boundaries of this experience?" that we discover our own unconscious learnings. In truth, Milton Erickson is the Ericksonian. The rest of us are who we are.

CHAPTER 19

Erickson's Essence:
A Personal View

John H. Weakland

Instead of "Ericksonian Methods," I want here to outline what I see as the essence of Erickson's *approach* to doing therapy; that is, I hope to sketch a view of what was very general and basic in his work. I have two main reasons for making this shift of focus. In the first place, I believe that in recent years discussion in our field has to a considerable extent moved from an emphasis on theory or principles toward an emphasis on techniques. For the most part, this has been a positive and productive change, especially since much of the theory prevalent in past years gave little guidance for practice or, at worst, even steered therapists in directions that hindered their efforts toward helping clients to resolve their problems. But now we are concerned with what was essential in Erickson's work, what legacy he bequeathed to us that is important in guiding our own work in the present — and, perhaps even more central, what will remain important for guiding the work of others in the future. Since that future, including the problems that will arise or be most prominent in its context, will necessarily be different from the present, I believe we should now look for what is most basic and general, and therefore apt to be most lasting, in Erickson's work. There is always some danger in getting lost in the specifics of method and technique, especially when dealing with techniques as fascinating and varied as Milton's were.

Second, the desirability of a shift of focus from the "methods" to "approach" is also suggested by consideration of a different aspect of this meeting embodied in the question "Why are we asking about the essence of Erickson *again?"* After all, this kind of question has already been addressed at some length and by a number of people, starting with Erickson himself — in part explicitly and, being Milton, even more by implication. This was continued by Haley (1973, 1981), Rossi (Erickson, Rossi & Rossi, 1976; Erickson & Rossi, 1979, 1981), O'Hanlon (1987), and Zeig (1985), among others. What they have written has varied considerably in emphasis, in level, in terminology, but they all were concerned not only with methods but also, in varying degree, with Erickson's approach more broadly.

So, is there really anything left to say? I believe there is. The clue to what it is lies in the very fact that such a diverse group of therapists have felt it important to grapple with this question and that in doing so they have come up with quite different answers, though largely complementary rather than contradictory ones. Clearly, Erickson's work has meant important but different things to many different people. How can we account for this remarkable range of interpretation and influence, since these interpreters also practice in quite different ways, as if emphasizing different aspects of Erickson's own range and variety? This problem again leads one to wonder if some identity, some common factors, can be found at the deepest and most general level of Erickson's approach to human behavior and the treatment of human problems.

It would be nice if I could claim that I am now going to reveal the *real* essence of Erickson's approach, the basic schema that underlies and unifies all the prior viewings, but I am not quite that presumptuous or that daring in public. The most I can claim is that by presenting my own view of what was basic to Milton's work, based on my experience both with the man and his therapy, I may shed some additional light on this question.

I believe that one major clue is contained in the very observation that presents the problem — that Erickson and his work had quite different importance for different followers. Why has this been so? Partly, of course, it is an expectable consequence of the richness and variety of his work; it is a lode that can be mined in many different ways. There is also something else that to me appears even more fundamental, and that may also be basic to this variety and richness itself. What I have in mind is not any new discovery; rather, it is evident both in Erickson's therapy and in his teaching. Yet, I think its importance and implications still have not been adequately recognized. Most simply, in a world, perhaps especially a professional world full of the search for fixed answers, Erickson was a lifelong opponent of dogma at any level. That is, he was opposed to the construction of or adherence to grand theories. Over and over, when asked general questions, he would respond instead with another concrete example. Equally, however, although he was a very practical man, he rejected the limiting premises implicit in accepting the received popular wisdom uncritically. He was continually saying and doing things that appeared contrary to "common sense." It is perhaps especially significant—for this is where many opponents of dogma make a large exception—that he clearly was not eager even to establish a new dogma of his own.

However, it is equally clear that he did not simply reject out of hand the knowledge or beliefs of others. And certainly, he did not believe that good treatment could be based simply on some personal inspiration of a therapist. On the contrary, he emphasized the importance of professional education and training, and clearly relied on his own in his work, especially his medical training. Similarly, he often explicitly utilized commonsense material—old adages, clichés, and so on—in his therapy. It was, rather, that he opposed unquestioning reliance on the weight of either professional or popular authority.

All this poses two problems. First, can such apparent contradiction be reconciled in some way? Second, in a world and, especially, a professional field full of ambiguity, uncertainty, and strangeness, what alternative to such sources of authority might there be? Even if there is no certainty to be found, everyone needs some kind of guidelines to deal with difficult situations, and it is clear that Milton had some. Still, even though he was unusually willing to experiment and to shift tack in his work if one way was not going well, it is evident that he did not cast about at random. He made plans, some of which he reported in considerable detail. On what was his planning based?

In my judgment, the key to all this is Erickson's emphasis on *observation.* Again, this is nothing new. Everyone who knew Erickson or has read his works has encountered the stress he placed on close observation. Even so, the full significance of this has perhaps been overlooked. This emphasis was pervasive. It did not apply only to clients; it applied equally to his students and to his approaches to teaching them. He saw them as unique and different individuals, and varied his approach to them accordingly— which may largely account for their learning different things, in different ways, from him.

Also, from this vantage point, the apparent contradiction noted above disappears. Erickson looked at and listened to others (and also himself) carefully. Then he made his own judgments about what to believe and do, based primarily on his distillation of such firsthand experience. But he was ready, secondarily, to listen to "authorities" in the same way—that is, not as sources of truth but as also expressing views, whose value and relevance he would judge for himself. I see his stance as a profoundly individualistic one, yet that of an individual in contact with, not in isolation from, others. Moreover, and perhaps even rarer and more difficult, he proposed that his patients and students do likewise—examine things more widely and deeply, then decide for themselves. We might see this as his one dogmatic principle.

Two basic features of Erickson's approach to his clients appear closely related to this fundamental stance. In a time when the professional authorities "knew" that many if not most, patients needed extended treatment to make any significant change, and also "knew" that such change was not even possible in many really severe cases, Erickson believed from his own observations and experience that useful change was, barring a few specific exceptions, *always* possible and often could be rapid.

Closely connected to this was his largely implicit, yet clear and pervasive, view, in spite of his conventional training toward separating off the "pathological" from the "normal," that all his patients were *people*. This not only fits with the optimistic view of the possibility of change just noted, but also makes the therapist's own life experience relevant to understanding and helping patients, which separating them into a separate "pathological" box inhibits. For example, Erickson's office was full of personal mementos, including a stuffed badger,* and he frequently told illustrative stories from his own life experience for therapeutic ends. All of this is a far cry from the analytic ideal of the therapist as a blank screen.

Of course, and we may be grateful for this, his life experience was unusual in many ways, especially in the severe physical problems he had to overcome. But the principles involved, that difficulties can be dealt with and that our personal experience can be relevant and useful for our therapeutic work, remain the same. Indeed, the second point could be stated as, "Use what you have" as a counterpart to Erickson's "Accept and use what the patient offers." This is a different position from, "Use your own strengths," since your weaknesses also may be useful — for example, in promoting empathy — and certainly it is very different from the idea that "The therapist has to have therapy until all his or her problems are resolved, before he or she can help others."

Again, there might appear to be a contradiction between two aspects of Erickson sketched here — that he was able to understand and accept others on their own terms, and yet was a man who judged things in his own way, often against prevailing opinion, and clearly had a very firm set of personal views and values. Certainly, this is unusual. It is more common to seek certainty for oneself, whether the certainty of a particular dogma or that of relativism, and to support it with the belief that anyone holding a different view is simply wrong. Rather than a contradiction, however, I would see this as demonstrating Erickson's capacity to accept the complexities of life,

---

*Ed. note: Erickson was an alumnus of the University of Wisconsin, whose football team were "Badgers."

even to including apparent opposites: People get stuck but they can change; they act "crazy" but are still understandable as human; human problems are serious but they may also be ludicrous.

In the end, I think the essence of Milton Erickson's work is based on his personal qualities. So I would like to conclude by pointing to three such qualities that I see as fundamental to all he did. This requires going beyond the usual bounds of professional discussion. However, I hope we might follow his example somehow, even though I cannot say how these qualities might be taught to others, nor even how he acquired these qualities himself.

First, Erickson was and remained a man with a great curiosity about life; he wanted to look at and reflect on everything that came into his view. Second, he had a wide and deep sense of humor, which I see as central for his ability to combine engagement and detachment even in very difficult and distressing situations. Finally, and I believe most important of all, a point that needs no documentation: In both his professional and personal life, Milton Erickson was a man of great courage.

REFERENCES

Erickson, M.H., & Rossi, E.L. (1979). *Hypnotherapy: An exploratory casebook.* New York: Irvington.

Erickson, M.H., & Rossi, E.L. (1981). *Experiencing hypnosis: Therapeutic approaches to altered states.* New York: Irvington.

Erickson, M.H., Rossi, E.L., & Rossi, S. (1976). *Hypnotic realities: The induction of clinical hypnosis and forms of indirect suggestion.* New York: Irvington.

Haley, J. (1973). *Uncommon therapy: The psychiatric techniques of Milton H. Erickson.* New York: W.W. Norton.

Haley, J. (1981). The contribution to therapy of Milton H. Erickson. In J. Haley (Ed.), *Reflections on therapy.* Washington, DC: The Family Therapy Institute of Washington, DC.

O'Hanlon, W.H. (1987). *Taproots: Underlying principles of Milton Erickson's therapy and hypnosis.* New York: W.W. Norton.

Zeig, J. (1985). *Experiencing Erickson: An introduction to the man and his work.* New York: Brunner/Mazel.

PART VI

Therapy Techniques

Advanced Techniques of Utilization: An Intervention Metamodel and the Use of Sequences, Symptom Words, and Figures of Speech

Jeffrey K. Zeig

INDUCTIONS*

It's a pleasure to proceed from this platform, can't it be now? And, proceeding to personally discover some of the mysteries of hypnosis can be a departure from your present track. And tracking the process . . . down . . . inside . . . you can experience many things with minimal effort now. For example, you may effortlessly . . . straighten out your head . . . so you're . . . looking forward . . . too . . . learning more. And, your eyes can be opened and you can be still here. . . .

Because today is Wednesday. And how do you conceive "Wednesday"? Can it be an assemblage of separate letters in your mind's eye? Can you envision those letters vividly? Can there now seem to be a comfortable process of coming together . . . of the letters? Can you simultaneously

---

Editor's Note: This initial section is a transcript of the actual presentation on Wednesday, December 2, 1992.

*notice your posture? Are you sitting with open arms? And deeper still, can
you modify the letters easily? Can you make them colorful? For example,
letters can seem red . . . and then you know the kind of day it is. Fascinating.*

And as I have been talking with you, certain changes occur:

Your breathing rate slows down;

The pulse of your experience is different;

You're not swallowing things wholly as you were before;

*You may notice that your head seems farther away from your feet (which
means that your feet are nowhere near your mouth);*

*You may notice that your right shoulder seems farther away from the left
shoulder;*

You may notice that your head seems larger . . . not too large.

*And these experiences can be a platform from which it is a pleasure to
proceed, can they not?*

Obviously, the preceding passage is an induction of hypnosis. The
components that make it an induction could be described. For purposes of
this chapter, however, I would like to suggest that the reader consider a
particular aspect of the induction: What was one of its primary linguistic
vehicles?

Before answering that question, I will offer two more inductions of
hypnosis using different linguistic vehicles. (The following section is a
description and further transcript of the actual presentation.)

One: Zeig asks an audience member to describe a current symptom.

Two: Zeig asks a second audience member to describe the process of
walking into the lecture hall. The ensuing dialogues follow:

One

Susie: I have a headache.

Zeig: This headache that you have, where do you experience it?

Susie: Behind the eyes.

Zeig: Behind the eyes.

    You can close your eyes for a minute, get in touch with that headache
    that you have behind your eyes, and then describe it to me in a different
    way. What's that headache like?

Susie: Like a cloud.

Zeig: Like a cloud. How is it like a cloud?

Susie: It is pressing down and covering.

Zeig: Pressing down and covering. And is there a color to that cloud
    pressing down and covering?

Susie: Gray and red.

Zeig: Okay. Thanks.

Two

Zeig: Now I need someone else who can describe to me what was it like to come into this room? I need a linearly organized person.

Evie: I was upstairs. I sat down with a gentleman. I asked if I was in the right place. He said, "No." I found a helper and then I learned where to come to.

Zeig: Now I would like to personalize brief inductions for Susie and Evie. I will start with Evie.

Evie, I would like you to just put things aside and then to just sit comfortably with your feet on the floor and your hands on your lap so that your thumbs are not touching in any way. And realize, Evie, that as you do those things, there is a certain order that you can follow. An order that can become yours, your order in developing this state of trance . . . in developing this state of comfort.

And I'd like you to understand that as you go inside, there also can be an order. Perhaps you can start out upstairs somewhere in your head, and the reality can be upstairs . . . in your head. But you can realize that you're sitting down and that I can be a gentle man in guiding you to go inside and discover other realities. And you can be wondering upstairs if you are in the right place. And you can think now, "It's nice to just take that easy breath and go down inside." And it's as if you can find upstairs in the back of your mind, your unconscious mind, which may serve you as a helper. And your unconscious mind may say, "No, not right to stay upstairs. Much better to go down inside."

And then Susie, you can orient yourself similarly, in your way . . . comfortably. And recognize that some part of you can hold back. And Susie, realize that some part of you can refuse to go too deeply into the experience. Some part of you can be in reserve, so that you notice that this trance doesn't have to be black or white. It doesn't have to be completely in or completely out. Rather there can be some gray areas of going inside. And you can realize that part of you, perhaps your inner mind, is pressing to go down deeper into trance. But the experience can be cloudy in some way. And all along, behind your eyes, there can be images developing, interesting, following images. So that you can notice the way in which those images may be covering and recovering from some of the blackness, new colors, new shapes, like the kaleidoscope of images that you can notice before your eyes.

All along staying a bit reserved, a bit resistant, holding back so that trance can be more, neither black nor white, but just interesting and comfortable, watching those colorful changes behind your eyes.

And then now, each of you, perhaps recovering something interesting from the experience, can be here, here now fully, take one or two or three easy breaths, and then Susie and Evie, stretch, reorient yourself, completely rested and refreshed, wide awake. Thank you.

Let's consider these three different inductions. There is something about those offerings that makes them hypnosis. Yet, each one of the inductions emphasizes a different linguistic vehicle. What are the linguistic vehicles used for the first induction? For the induction with Evie? Susie? How do those linguistic vehicles differ? And moreover, what therapeutic principle is used to generate those linguistic vehicles? This chapter will address these issues.

INTRODUCTION

The three inductions presented above are extensions of the principle of utilization, championed by Milton H. Erickson, M.D. They represent three special techniques of utilization; namely, the use of *figures of speech,* such as idioms and proverbs, the use of *sequences,* and the use of *symptom words.*

In this chapter, the concept of utilization will be defined and presented within the context of a metamodel of psychotherapy. The three special techniques of utilization will be described and developed. Although the text of the chapter primarily concerns the use of utilization techniques in hypnotic induction, indications will be presented for their use in nonhypnotic psychotherapy, including family therapy.

UTILIZATION

Utilization has been defined as the "readiness of the therapist to respond strategically to any and all aspects of the patient or the environment" (Zeig, 1992, p. 256). Any aspect of the psychotherapy experience can be utilized, including the patient's style, dress, mannerisms, history, and family. The therapist also can utilize the symptom, the symptom pattern, and the resistances. Moreover, the clinician can use the patient's social system and environment (Zeig, 1992).

The literature on Ericksonian therapy is replete with examples of utilization. It is not hyperbole to state that utilization was a central facet of all of Erickson's interventions.

Here are two simple illustrations:

Case Example One

A female patient consulted Erickson due to moderate to severe alcoholism. Her pattern of imbibing was rebellious and covert. When her husband came home from the office, she was already drunk, and that led to many battles. All weekend long she pursued her "little hobby" of gardening, during which time she took sips from a hidden bottle of whiskey.

Her husband also had a "little hobby." All weekend long he sat in his living room chair reading "dusty old books, dusty old newspapers, and dusty old magazines" from cover to cover. The wife confronted the husband about his withdrawal but her efforts were to no avail.

Erickson discovered two additional pieces of information about the couple: Both of them hated fishing. Also, they enjoyed camping, but didn't do it often.

Erickson met jointly with the couple and gave the following instructions: The wife was to hide a bottle of whiskey in the house. When the husband came home, he had a specified amount of time to discover where she had hidden the bottle. If he didn't find it, she could drink with impunity.

For a few days, the wife took decided glee in finding hiding places that no man could easily discover. After a while, however, the task lost some of its pleasure.

When the couple returned for the next session, Erickson insisted that they go fishing. Nothing else would do, only fishing. Why? Well, if they were on a small boat in the middle of the lake, the wife couldn't possibly hide a bottle of whiskey; the husband couldn't possibly bring dusty old books, dusty old newspapers. Therefore, fishing was the only task that was satisfactory.

The couple rebelled against Erickson's prohibition and went camping. Subsequently, they continued to go camping and voluntarily gave up their symptomatic patterns (Haley, 1985).

In this case, Erickson utilized an aspect of the symptom, the patient's sneaky behavior; he turned it into a game, thereby changing the emotional valence of the behavior from negative to positive. Erickson also used the stubbornness of each member of the couple. They could rebel against his task of fishing by choosing their own activity. In the process, they could modify their symptomatic behavior, and they could do so to their own credit.

Case Example Two

I met Erickson for the first time in December 1973. A transcript of our initial three-day visit appears in *Experiencing Erickson* (Zeig, 1985). At the time, my financial resources were limited; I had just completed my master's degree, and I was working at my first professional job as a therapist for acute psychiatric patients in a residential treatment center.

Erickson and I did not have a clear financial arrangement about my visit. However, during the course of our sessions, it became clear that he was not going to charge me for his time.

I asked his daughter, Roxanna, to take me shopping for a thank-you gift.

Because Erickson treasured woodcarvings, I bought him a carving of a duck. The base was unfinished driftwood that abstractly looked like a duck's body. The head and neck were shaped and stained to look more realistically like a duck.

I gave Erickson the gift just prior to departing Phoenix, not knowing whether or not I would ever see him again. Erickson received the carving graciously. He held it and eyed it pregnantly: He looked at me; he looked at the duck. He looked at me; he looked at the duck. He looked at me; he looked at the duck. Then he pointedly said, "Emerging" (Zeig, 1985, p. 54).

At the time, I was emerging both as a therapist and as a person. Erickson's style of thanking me for the gift included a splendid example of multilevel utilization.*

So wedded was Erickson to the idea of utilization that it was an integral part of his persona. Utilization was a life-style, not merely a technique.

In summary, utilization is a "state" that the therapist enters in order to provide effective treatment. Utilization can be considered an aspect of the therapist's "trance": The therapist enters a state of response readiness and thereby becomes a model for the patient to access a similar state. The patient is encouraged to enter into a state of constructively responding, culling kernels of wheat from his life situation, rather than focusing on the chaff. Problems represent a "state" of insufficiency in which patients believe they do not have resources to cope or change; utilization models sufficiency back to the patient.

Although utilization as a technique is used to some extent in other methods of therapy, it is central in the Ericksonian approach. In fact, it can be said that utilization is to Ericksonian therapy as interpretation is to psychodynamic therapy; as desensitization is to behavior therapy. (For more information on utilization, see Zeig, 1992.)

The value of utilization per se can be readily understood; however, one cannot merely effect utilization without considering two questions: 1) Utilization to what end? and 2) What might the clinician select to utilize?

Utilization to What End: A Metamodel of Psychotherapy

Utilization is a goal-directed philosophy of the therapist. As the therapist assumes the posture of utilization, she must think ahead toward actualizing a specific target. There are numerous targets that a therapist can have in mind. To better understand targets and the place of utilization in therapy, I will offer a metamodel of psychotherapeutic intervention, which I recently published, based on five pivotal "choice points" (Zeig, 1992), which are indicated in the following figure:

---

*Erickson placed the carving on the desk in his office, where it remains to this day.

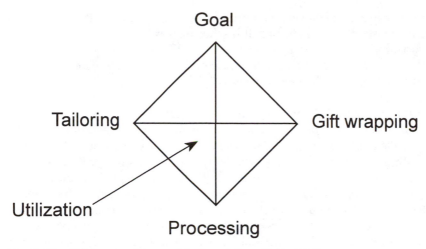

Fig. 1. The Ericksonian Diamond (adapted from Zeig, 1992).

A guiding question is the basis of each facet of the diamond. The facets are "choice points" because if the therapist gets stuck, or encounters resistance, a change can be made in one or a combination of facets. Each of the choice points will be discussed in turn.

GOALS   The goal question that the clinician must answer is *"What do I want to communicate?"* A therapist working toward an induction goal might want to communicate to the patient, "Relax!" In promoting therapy with a depressed patient, the therapist might want to communicate, "Be more actively involved in the world, rather than withdrawing."

Another point about goals is that they can vary, depending on the stage of therapy. Induction goals may differ from therapy goals. Also, goals may be formulated by dividing a goal into subparts. The therapy goal of happiness can be divided into: being self-aware, having a constructive social role, having a social network, etc. During treatment, each subgoal can be addressed independently. Utilization methods can be directed to effect these subgoals.

When therapists utilize, they orient immediately to intended goals. Utilization is directed to some predetermined end. Typically, in Ericksonian therapy, there are both induction goals and therapy goals. In Ericksonian methods, some generic patient goals are the *R & R* of Ericksonian therapy: The induction is effected in order to elicit *responsiveness,* and the therapy goals are focused to develop *resources.* Of course, there are additional induction and therapy goals. Induction goals can include modifying attention, increasing intensity, and promoting dissociation (Zeig, 1988). Therapy goals can include providing new information to the patient that the patient previously may not have had at his/her disposal.

Utilization is primarily concerned with treatment goals. However, to a lesser extent, utilization can be a part of the other facets (choice points) in the metamodel. The second facet is "gift wrapping."

GIFT WRAPPING   After formulating the goal, the therapist must decide *"How do I want to present the goal?"* The method for "packaging" the goal is called "gift wrapping." For example, the goal could be gift wrapped within a story, symbol, or anecdote. It can be presented within an interpretation, a confrontation, a Gestalt dialogue, or a systematic desensitization. Techniques in psychotherapy are merely ways of gift wrapping therapeutic objectives; techniques do not cure. This is an important point: *Techniques are merely formats for presenting therapeutic objectives. It is a philosophical error to think that techniques cure.* Similarly, hypnosis does not cure patients; structurally, hypnosis is merely a way of gift wrapping information.

There are two additional points that should be made about gift wrapping: One, gift wrapping should be recursive: The goal is not presented merely once. Rather, the goal can be presented repetitively in an augmented fashion similar to the way that a theme is presented and developed in a piece of music. For example, the goal can be presented as a direct suggestion within an indirect suggestion within a story within an hypnosis. Each one of the gift-wrapping techniques can offer the thematic goal in a slightly altered form.

A second point about gift wrapping is that communication is judged by the response and not by the cleverness of its structure. Clever gift-wrapping techniques are valuable only if they elicit desirable and constructive responses.

Gift wrapping is related to utilization as follows: The patient "gift wraps" his/her problem in a symptom. The therapist can gift wrap a solution within a technique. The method that the patient uses to gift wrap the problem can be utilized to gift wrap a solution. For example, a schizophrenic patient can talk crazy to create social distance. A therapist can deliberately talk crazy as a way of getting close. For example, I have had "crazy talking contests" with patients, thereby making "crazy" communication into a game (see Zeig, 1987). When using such methods, it is important to be empathic and genuine; the patient should not feel ridiculed in any way.

TAILORING   Concomitant with pondering the goals and gift wrapping, the therapist must decide how to individualize or tailor the treatment to the unique aspects of the patient. In order to effect tailoring, the therapist asks,

"What is the position that the patient takes?" (Fisch, Weakland & Segal, 1982). The therapist needs to know what the patient values. It can be readily understood that therapy (or hypnosis) for a shy person should be different from therapy for an extrovert. Gift-wrapped goals are best effected if they are properly tailored, taking into account the position of the patient, which also includes the environment and social system.

The therapist utilizes the patient position to tailor goals. For a simple example, Erickson autographed a book to me, "To Jeff Zeig, just another book to curl your hair" (Zeig, 1985, pp. 55-56). This personalized message acknowledged my hairstyle, a feature in which I take pride.

PROCESSING   Having decided the first three choice points, therapists must ask themselves, *"How do I present the tailored and gift-wrapped goal?"* I call this method *processing*. Processing occurs in three stages: Setup, Intervene, and Follow Through (SIFT) (Zeig, 1985). By using the SIFT method, the therapist establishes drama and makes the therapy into a significant, emotional experience. The *setup* includes maneuvers referred to as "prehypnotic suggestions," including seeding (Zeig, 1990) and eliciting motivation. Hypnotic induction itself can be considered a prehypnotic maneuver, especially when it is used to elicit the intrapsychic and interpersonal responsiveness that empower future suggestions.

After the *main intervention* is presented, be it an anecdote, reframe, symptom prescription, change history, etc., then the therapist must *follow through*. Follow-through techniques include ratifying changes, induced amnesia, and homework assignments. In short, the intervention is sandwiched between the setup and the follow through. It is not presented in isolation; rather it is dramatically presented over time.

The therapist can utilize a patient *process* to foster treatment. As will be seen, a patient's naturally occurring sequence of having a symptom (or being effective) can be fashioned into an induction of hypnosis.

It can now be understood that utilization is a method directed to establishing any single or combination of choice points. The therapist's utilization philosophy is directed to establishing and effecting goals, to gift wrapping them, to tailoring them, and to processing them. For example, if the patient complains of being "depressed," the therapist can discuss the need for *deep rest* as a stage of problem solving and as a necessary step in the process of achieving goals. If confusion is an aspect of the patient's depression, the therapist can gift wrap an intervention within a confusion technique (Erickson, 1964). If the patient is curious, a confusion intervention can be tailored in that direction. For example, "Curiously, I don't know if you know that developing constructive curiosity is not the kind of task you won't find easy, is it not?" As was previously mentioned, utilization also can be harnessed to effect a dramatic therapeutic process by using the symptom process.

Utilization can be a central philosophy of the therapist. It is one of a number of therapist postures.

POSITION OF THE THERAPIST   Prior to and during assessment and intervention, the clinician must wonder, *"What position do I, the therapist, take?"* The position of the therapist may be more influential in determining the outcome of the treatment than any of the technical maneuvers that the therapist prescribes. Therapists can take the position of being kind, confronting, curious, intellectual, etc. Each therapist has a "lens" (perceptual set), "heart" (emotional set), "muscles" (action patterns), and "hat" (social role). The lens, heart, muscles, and hat are of two varieties, personal and professional, and sometimes there might be considerable discrepancies between the professional and the personal characteristics. Seasoned therapists utilize their position on behalf of their patients.

Utilization is a professional stance that Erickson championed. It was also a philosophy that he lived day to day. Erickson had many other aspects to his professional position, including communicating indirectly and being experiential, rather than didactic. Other clinicians have other professional sets (e.g., being directly confrontational or oriented to history).

The position of the therapist determines to a great extent the goals, the gift wrapping, the tailoring, and the processing. Therapists with a humanistic bent may have more general goals (e.g., growth). Behavioral and strategic therapists may have specific goals.

Therapists often prefer certain styles of gift wrapping. Analysts will use interpretation, clarification, and confrontation. Strategic therapists may use symptom prescription and reframing and may never consider the idea of using interpretation.

In relationship to tailoring, therapists who are body-oriented may notice aspects of posture unrecognized by the family therapists who focus on interactional patterns and determine the position of the patient in relationship to the social system. In regard to process, clinicians who are dramatic will present interventions differently from clinicians who are more staid in their approach.

There are a few additional points to consider in relationship to the five aspects of the metamodel:

1) It should be understood that the metamodel is just a skeleton; it is not meant to proscribe psychotherapeutic intervention into a linear process. Therapy requires both discipline and spontaneity on the part of the clinician. Proscribing choices limits effectiveness.

2) The intervention metamodel presented above is in an attenuated form; it will be developed further in future publications.

3) As was previously mentioned, the five aspects of the metamodel are choice points. If the therapy becomes problematic, the clinician can change the goal, gift-wrapping method, tailoring, and/or the presentation process. Moreover, the clinician can change the position of the therapist; for example, by being more firm, more nurturing, more curious, or more experiential.

As has been indicated, the position of the therapist is an important determinant in both assessment and intervention. If the therapist takes the position of utilization, assessment and intervention will change. The utilizing therapist who practices hypnosis may develop intervention strategies, such as sequences, symptom words, and idioms. Assessment and intervention are an interaction between the position of the therapist and the position of the patient; once the therapist takes a position of utilization, goal setting, gift wrapping, tailoring, and processing will be modified accordingly.

SELECTING WHAT ONE MIGHT UTILIZE

Therapists wedded to the doctrine of utilization will naturally assume certain postures: 1) Such therapists will orient immediately toward goals because utilization is effected toward a particular end; 2) They will orient toward resources and strengths because utilization itself is a method of bringing out the positive side of any given situation; 3) They will be oriented toward multilevel communication. They will realize that multiple positive and negative aspects exist in given situations and that these aspects can be addressed simultaneously.

As the therapist assumes the philosophy of utilization, the assessment phase of psychotherapy will be modified. Assessment will no longer be seen as an operation separate from therapy. Rather, intervention will happen within the context of assessment because the therapist will be set to utilize therapeutically the patient's situation from the very beginning of the therapy process.

When adopting a position of utilization, the therapist has a multiplicity of perspectives from which to conduct an assessment. It is here that we can examine the question, "What might the clinician select to utilize?" What to utilize is dependent on how the therapist views the patient and the presenting complaint. The clinician's perspective is idiosyncratic and depends on his/her personal and professional postures. For example, the therapist can assess and utilize the biology of the problem, family hierarchies, or belief systems underlying the problem. Different therapists have different predilections and tend to impose their predilection on therapeutic situations.

Assessment is too broad a topic to discuss in this chapter. Issues in assessment will be developed in a future publication. But it should be noted that even if the therapist is wedded to the concept of utilization, the therapist still has many choices about what to utilize, and these choices will depend upon the idiosyncratic way in which the therapist examines the problem.

A purpose of this chapter is to describe three aspects of the patient's world that can be assessed and utilized: sequences, symptom words, and figures of speech, including proverbs and idioms. In writing this chapter, I reviewed demonstrations that I conducted at congresses and conferences sponsored by The Milton H. Erickson Foundation during the past 10 years. During that time, I have tried to develop in myself a commitment to the doctrine of utilization. I reviewed the assessment and intervention portions of these demonstrations, especially centering on techniques that I effected early in the induction. I found that the utilization philosophy had led me to especially develop these three gift-wrapping techniques: using sequences, reframing symptom words to solution words, and utilizing figures of speech. Each of these methods will be presented in turn.

Sequences

When assessing problems, clinicians can look for sequences. Problems do not exist as static entities. They are best considered as dynamic processes. If a problem is viewed as a dynamic process, it can be considered a sequence, even though it is perceived as a discrete event. For example, a handshake is considered a single event, but on closer examination, a handshake is a sequence of behaviors, perhaps beginning with eye contact and proceeding through a series of steps that may include a smile, an uttered hello, a step forward, an extension of the hand, etc., until the hands are withdrawn. Similarly, a psychotherapy problem can be considered a sequence that begins with a trigger and proceeds through a series of behaviors, perceptions, internal dialogue, emotions, attitudes, relationship patterns, etc.

However, patients perceive problems as static entities and talk about their problems as such—for example, "My depression," or "My bad habit." Therapists can perceive problems as a dynamic series of events, and orient to the mechanism of the problem, the steps that the person uses to maintain the problem.* The clinician can wonder, "How does this patient

---

*Note that dividing the problem into a sequence is simultaneously an *intervention* and an assessment. Sequencing a problem can create a pattern disruption that in itself is therapeutic.

do the problem?" It can be conceptualized that the problem state is a negative trance (Araoz, 1985) that is maintained by certain steps (cf. Ritterman, 1983, who describes symptom induction in families).

Let us take a simple problem; for example, smoking, and provide a hypothetical example of how it can be seen as a sequence. Smoking could be triggered by the sight of a cigarette. Subsequently, there can be an urge, recognized consciously or preconsciously by a particular "taste" in the mouth. Subsequently, there can be a thought, "I think I'll have a cigarette," followed by a behavioral chain of events, from reaching for a cigarette to seeking fellow smokers to putting it out. This can be followed by a new series of thoughts and feelings, such as disgust and recrimination, "Why did I do that to myself?" Problem sequences customarily end with negative emotions.

During the assessment phase of treatment, the therapist disposed in this direction can look for a sequence to the problem. Depending on the therapist's predilection (lens), the sequence might emphasize behavior, mood, cognition, or systemic interactions. If the therapist conceives the problem as a sequence of events, opportunities for intervention emerge. Once the therapist determines the sequence, which may or may not be done in collaboration with the patient, the therapist has to decide, *"How will I utilize this sequence?"* The sequence can be used to foster both induction goals and therapy goals.

Case Example Three

I first presented the idea of sequences in a workshop at the 1988 Fourth International Congress on Ericksonian Approaches to Hypnosis and Psychotherapy. I conducted a demonstration with one of the attendees who described chronic anxiety, which, at my request, she named "the train." She was able to stop the "train" by using progressive relaxation. But as soon as she relinquished concentration on relaxation, the "train" (anxiety) returned. In the assessment phase, we practiced relaxing and bringing back the train twice, and as she brought back the train, we teased out the sequence that she used, which I determined had six steps:
1) Breathing faster;
2) Defocusing and becoming diffuse in perception;
3) Making movements (e.g., agitated movements in her legs);
4) Noticing that there were people who could be perceived as intimidating;
5) Feeling the train (anxiety); and
6) Racing and doing things to eliminate the train.

This sequence was noticeably devoid of internal dialogue, even though the patient was encouraged during the interview to indicate what her thoughts might be during the process.

As part of the treatment, a six-step process of induction was created, using the patient's sequence. To effect induction, I sequentially did the following:

1) I asked the patient to close her eyes very easily and very *quickly* and notice something about the way in which her eyes closed *"fast."*

2) I asked her to not pay attention (*defocus*) to sensations, especially weight and pressure, e.g., the sensation of pressure of the microphone and the weight around her neck; the way her hands were still; the backrest of the chair.

3) I asked the patient "to *move* inside" into a different state.

4) I suggested to her that her conscious mind could continue to notice the room lights that were *bearing down* on her.

5) I suggested she could follow the "train" of my thoughts and the *"train"* of her own feelings of developing comfort.

6) I suggested, "As your inner mind can continue to *race* from one idea to the next, the sensation of pressure, and the lights . . . your unconscious mind can develop a certain sense of ease."

In this way, I utilized her problem sequence to create an induction sequence. Figures 2 and 3 illustrate:

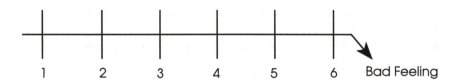

Fig. 2. Symptom Induction.

Fig. 3. Trance Induction.

If the problem can be conceived as having six steps that lead to a negative state, the induction can consist of six steps that lead to a positive state. Hence, the problem sequence is not discarded (or analyzed); it is utilized.

In order to conduct a sequence induction, the therapist must realize one of the experiential parameters of trance. The sequence induction (for that matter, any induction) is created to elicit certain experiences in the recipient. These experiences are induction goals.

Patients customarily report that during trance there is a decided change in *absorption*. Therefore, customarily therapists initiate trance by offering an absorption ritual to the patient. Patients can be absorbed in a *sensation* (e.g., the feeling of warmth in one's hand); a *perception* (e.g., patients can be told to fixate on a spot on the wall); an *hypnotic phenomenon* (patients can be absorbed in the process of arm levitation); a *fantasy* (patients can be absorbed in a scene of being at the beach); a *memory* (Erickson often absorbed patients in the memory of learning to write the letters of the alphabet). Moreover, patients can be absorbed in *sequences,* even the sequence of their own symptoms. In this way, sequences are utilized as absorption devices.

There are decided advantages to using sequences. When one uses sequence inductions, therapy automatically becomes tailored. Therapists do not impose a preset induction script upon the patient, so the therapist does not need to memorize an induction method. The therapist merely extracts the patient's symptom sequence and develops it as an absorption device. Moreover, by using the symptom sequence, the therapist subtly "reframes" a negative process and elicits constructive elements from the problem. The therapist demonstrates that a solution is inherently available — that solutions may even exist within the problem.

Clinicians are not limited to using a symptom sequence. The therapist can use a positive sequence as well as a negative sequence. For example, if a patient had an anxiety problem, the therapist could ask the patient to describe a time of comfort. Subsequently, the therapist could extract the sequence of establishing comfort and elicit the steps that are precursors and that follow comfort. Then the solution sequence can be used to create the induction. Neutral sequences also can be used, as I did in the introductory induction with Evie, whom I asked to describe the process of entering the lecture hall.

Extension for using sequences are numerous. For example, I have innocuously asked patients to remember certain experiences. I noted the behavioral process that the patient effected in order to remember. For example, the patient might take a deep breath, look, up, furrow his/her brow, clear his/her throat, report the memory, and then sigh. On a subsequent occasion I have hypnotically cycled the patient through the sequence of memory behaviors and successfully and indirectly elicited memories.

When working with a couple, the therapist can notice systemic sequences (i.e., sequences that happen between individuals). Subsequently, these sequences can be woven into an induction for the couple. Again, these sequences could be problem sequences or solution sequences. (See Ritterman, 1983, for information on symptom-inductive patterns in families.)

If the therapist is especially clever, the therapist could take any sequence and weave the sequence into a story. The steps of the sequence would form the backbone of the story.

Although I customarily use sequences for inductions, sequences also can be used to effect therapy. For example, the therapist can work to change some of the sequence, and promote pattern disruption by deleting, adding, or modifying aspects of the sequence. These techniques can be effected directly or indirectly (e.g., through anecdotes).

Possibilities for utilizing sequences are endless, and it is not my purpose to be comprehensive about the use of sequences. Rather, I want to emphasize that once the therapist adopts the stance of utilization, effectively using sequences can be a natural consequence.

Symptom Words

Another assessment device for a therapist is to discern and utilize symptom words. During the interview, patients commonly use idiosyncratic terms to describe their problem. For example, an obese patient may describe hunger as "emptiness." Patients often become habituated to their problem and to its description and, subsequently, the problem becomes calcified. Once the therapist determines the patient's "symptom words," the therapist can utilize these terms as solution words. In the process, a negative descriptor is reframed and given a positive meaning. The demonstration induction with Susie, who described her headache, was an example of this method.

Case Example Four

At a recent demonstration, I worked with a patient who complained of sciatica. At my request, she described her pain as a "gnawing" that was "deeply penetrating."

At the end of the five-minute interview, I segued into a conversational induction, suggesting,

> As you concentrate on your breathing, you can take an easy breath. And then perhaps you pick something on which to focus

your attention. And you begin to orient your eyes, and your blink
rate is slowly changing. And there's a tendency to just take an
easy breath, make yourself comfortable, and close your eyes. And
as you close your eyes, there's a question that you may have—a
gnawing question in your mind, and it can be as if your inner
mind begins to push up certain ideas into your consciousness.

And you can wonder, "Just how deeply into a trance can I go
right now?" And it's an interesting process to allow that *penetrating* question to somehow permeate your consciousness, and to
allow that question to consume you. And I'd be interested in your
understanding the transformation of that question, "Just how
deeply can I go . . . ?" "How much can I *penetrate* some of the
mysteries of my own inner mind . . . ?"

This technique of converting symptom words to solution words is often
more effective when the induction does not immediately follow the interview because there is less opportunity for conscious scrutiny of the technique.
Often, my induction, using symptom words, occurs a number of sessions
after the initial interview in which the descriptive words were used.

The use of symptom words as solution words is another utilization
technique. As with sequences, symptom words can be turned into solution
words to accomplish induction and/or therapy goals. Changing symptom
words into solution words is normally one of the minor methods of gift
wrapping. It is not a main intervention, but it is one way of recursively
presenting the main intervention: If the goal for a pain patient is to modify
the experience of pain, changing symptom words into solution words can
be a way of suggesting that process. This idea can be developed in
subsequent forms of recursive gift wrapping.

By using sequences and symptom words to elicit trance, one utilizes
induction as a context for therapy. Traditionally, induction is a *means* of
getting the patient from the normal waking state into a trance. Once the
therapist becomes wedded to the idea of utilization, the induction itself
can be utilized as a *method* for promoting therapy. The idea of using
induction as a method, as well as a means, was customarily effected in
Erickson's inductions.

Figures of Speech

In conducting an assessment, a clinician can be aware of figures of
speech that are relevant to the patient and to the culture and socioeconomic group in which the client was reared. Similar to symptom words,

figures of speech, such as proverbs and idioms, are recursive, microdynamic, gift-wrapping forms for presenting induction and therapy goals. However, figures of speech are different from sequences and symptom words in that they are derived from the patient's linguistic history and may not be derived from immediate experience.

Spoken language is filled with idioms, and native speakers of a language rarely recognize the profusion of idioms in their speech. Also, proverbs become part of the culture and are frequently used in ordinary conversations. For example, in the realm of idioms, one might talk about "being in hot water," or "taking a bull by the horns," or being "up in the air." Proverbs may be emphasized in families. Parents can teach their children a customary admonition of "Don't look a gift horse in the mouth," or "All work and no play makes Jack a dull boy."

Idioms and proverbs are culturally determined, although some may be similar across cultures. For example, one could talk about changing roles by saying, "I wear a different hat." In Mexico, one would communicate the same concept by saying, "I wear a different cap." For another example, in Japan, one might say, "Even monkeys fall from trees." "Anyone can make a mistake" would be the Western version of that proverb.

In the United States, the color yellow might be associated with cowardice, but that would not be true in Germany. Therefore, in order to effectively use symbols and idioms, one must have knowledge of the culture in which the patient has developed.

Erickson often used symbols and idioms in effecting hypnosis and therapy. For example, during the early phase of a regression induction in which the patient became a latency-aged child, Erickson asked her, "Would you like your favorite candy to eat right now (Zeig, 1980, p. 87). This was a symbol of trust. Almost every little girl in every culture is admonished, "Don't take candy from strangers." Once the patient had taken the candy, Erickson could feel more confident that he had established trust.

In another induction, using a similar method, Erickson asked a woman to develop coldness in her left hand, and subsequently develop coldness in her right hand (Zeig, 1981). A popular proverb in many cultures is "cold hands, warm heart." As the woman followed Erickson's prescription on the behavioral level, she would indicate her ability to hypnotically change the sensation. However, on the symbolic level, she could simultaneously experience more rapport (warmth) toward Erickson. Also, in hypnosis, patients are often more literal and fluidly move between the literal and figurative meanings of suggestions.

Remember the initial induction in this chapter? The primary linguistic vehicle that was used was figure of speech. It would be uncommon to use figures of speech as the main method of induction, but it is common to find figures of speech in the inductions I conduct for my patients.

Figures of speech and symbols also can be used as markers in therapy. For example, in working with one hypnotized man in the context of couples therapy, Erickson suggested that he could discover that he "could not stand up." This symbol could have two meanings: It could refer to a lack of assertiveness (e.g., not being able to stand up on one's own feet). Alternately, the symbolic meaning could be sexual, referring to erectile issues. Subsequently, Erickson conducted some therapy with the patient, in which the patient accessed some resourceful feelings. Then Erickson changed the symbol, suggesting to the patient that he could now stand up and still maintain the good feelings that had just been established. In this case, the change in the symbol (standing up) marked out and reinforced the fact that the man responded to the therapy and accomplished significant change.

Techniques of using symbols and idioms require the therapist to understand the patient's associative process, again remembering that the communication is judged by its effectiveness, not by the cleverness of the structure. Symbolic communications are ambiguous, and the therapist must strive to understand the patient's response to the intended symbol.

The technique of using symbols and idioms can be used for both induction and therapy goals. For induction goals, the technique can be used to capture attention, elicit absorption, increase responsiveness, and promote rapport. For therapy goals, figures of speech can be microdynamic gift-wrapping methods used to seed or build toward larger therapeutic goals.

CONCLUSION

Once the therapist assumes the posture of utilization, the therapist will naturally develop techniques such as sequences, symptom words, and idioms. These gift-wrapping techniques can be harnessed to elicit induction and therapy goals. Why would a therapist go to this extra effort? The answer is that the therapist is interested in creating dynamic experiences (Zeig, 1992) through which patient-initiated change can be effected.

REFERENCES

Araoz, D. (1985). *The new hypnosis.* New York: Brunner/Mazel.
Erickson, M. H. (1964). The confusion technique in hypnosis. *American Journal of Clinical Hypnosis, 6:* 183-207.

Fisch, P., Weakland, J., & Segal, L. (1982). *The tactics of change: Doing therapy briefly.* San Francisco: Jossey-Bass.

Haley, J. (Ed.) (1985). *Conversations with Milton H. Erickson, M.D., Volume II, Changing couples.* Rockville, MD: Triangle.

Ritterman, M. K. (1983). *Using hypnosis in family therapy.* San Francisco: Jossey-Bass.

Zeig, J. K. (Ed.) (1980). *A teaching seminar with Milton H. Erickson.* New York: Brunner/Mazel.

Zeig, J. K. (Ed.) (1981). *Symbolic hypnotherapy.* (Videotape showing segments of hypnotherapy conducted by Milton Erickson in 1978.) Phoenix: The Milton H. Erickson Foundation.

Zeig, J. K. (1985). *Experiencing Erickson: An introduction to the man and his work.* New York: Brunner/Mazel.

Zeig, J. K. (1987). Therapeutic patterns of Ericksonian influence communication. In J. K. Zeig (Ed.), *The evolution of psychotherapy* (pp. 392-409). New York: Brunner/Mazel.

Zeig, J. K. (1988). An Ericksonian phenomenological approach to therapeutic hypnotic induction and symptom utilization. In J. K. Zeig & S. R. Lankton (Eds.), *Developing Ericksonian therapy: State of the art* (pp. 353-375). New York: Brunner/Mazel.

Zeig, J. K. (1990). Seeding. In J. K. Zeig & S. G. Gilligan (Eds.), *Brief therapy: Myths, methods, and metaphors* (pp. 221-246). New York: Brunner/Mazel.

Zeig, J. K. (1992). The virtues of our faults: A key concept of Ericksonian psychotherapy. In J. K. Zeig (Ed.), *The evolution of psychotherapy: The second conference* (pp. 252-269). New York: Brunner/Mazel.

CHAPTER 21

Seeding Responsiveness to Hypnotic Processes

Brent B. Geary

INTRODUCTION

To the reader: I hope you will bear with me. Seeding is a concept that has only recently found its way into print, and some of my language and examples might prove rather clumsy. I hope you will bear with me, glean what is useful for you, and forgive any awkwardness you detect in the exposition of the concept.

First, I would like you to use your imagination. Please read the following three scenarios:

(1) Imagine yourself relaxing at home watching television. Take a moment and imagine how cable television will provide you with broader entertainment and informational services. When you use it properly, you will be able to plan in advance which of the programs you wish to enjoy. Take a moment and think of how, instead of spending money on the babysitter and gas, and then having to put up with the hassles of "going out," you will have more time to spend at home, with your family, alone, or with your friends (from Gregory, Cialdini & Carpenter, 1982).

(2) Following the devastation of Hurricane Andrew (in 1992), a number of acts of selflessness, courage, and heroism were noted. One municipality in Florida honored a citizen for his outstanding deeds in helping several families in the flooding after Andrew passed. He saved the lives of several pets that were attempting to find refuge. His small boat carried food and water to many who were stranded without provisions. The man trans-

ported a number of injured people to hospitals. He was honored for his bravery and for the help he offered to others in a time of great need (from Associated Press wire reports).

(3) A friend of mine spent a month one summer in Vienna. He enjoyed himself a great deal, immersing himself in the culture, viewing fine art, and hearing beautiful music. But he said that the highlight of his trip occurred one afternoon while he was sitting in a sidewalk cafe enjoying a cup of Viennese coffee. At a table nearby, he spotted a young woman sitting alone, reading an English language newspaper, and watching pedestrians on the street. My friend was struck by the attractiveness of the woman and he felt the urge to make her acquaintance. But he had always thought of himself as a rather shy fellow and he was unsure how to approach her. He didn't want to appear fresh or look as though, in his words, he was "hustling" her. Finally, he mustered sufficient courage to tell her he was from the United States and interested in reading some news in his native language. My friend discovered that the young woman was also from the United States and was in Vienna studying art at a university summer course. As the conversation proceeded, he wondered how to interest this new acquaintance in spending more time with him. She told him she had an afternoon class to attend. He wanted to get to know her better, but he was still fearful of being seen as overly aggressive.

After some internal conflict, my friend awkwardly blurted his request that the woman "take the afternoon off" and guide him through "the most artistic places in the city." The woman replied that she "really shouldn't," that she was in Vienna on scholarship and wanted to learn as much as she could in the short time she had. My friend persisted, asking her, "What better way is there to learn than to teach a novice such as me? Besides, you might see something new, something you hadn't previously discovered." He later admitted to me that he felt his heart racing and was quite flushed while he argued his case. He had been alone while in Europe and he was anxious for some companionship. The lady considered his entreaties with a subtle smile, looking off into the distance for what seemed to my friend an eternity. At last, she turned to him, looked "deeply" (his word) into his eyes, and rejoined, "No [hesitation] class is so important as to deprive me of the opportunity to spend the afternoon walking with you through this wonderful city."

It might interest you to know that after reading the foregoing accounts, you are more than twice as likely to subscribe to cable television service than someone who did not read the imaginal scenario. Second, you are more likely to respond to other people in a cooperative manner, having been exposed to the prosocial news story. And third, if you are a male, it is significantly more probable that you will behave in a "friendly" manner toward an attractive member of the opposite gender. You will smile more often, have more eye contact with her, will lean forward toward her more if you are seated, and you will talk to her more (Wilson & Capitman, 1982). But hurry to take advantage . . . the effect lasts only four minutes!

The above examples are illustrations of consequences of priming. Maneuvers encompassed under the conceptual umbrella of priming are shown to influence behaviors ranging from the mundane to the complex. The purpose of this chapter is to explore ways in which therapists can utilize priming procedures, through the clinical process of seeding, to enhance patients' responsiveness to hypnotic and psychotherapeutic interventions. Milton Erickson utilized seeding extensively in his clinical work (Zeig, 1990), and there is much in his method that we can cull and apply to enhance our therapeutic effectiveness.

In this chapter, varieties and applications of seeding in clinical hypnosis will be examined. First, an overview of the priming and seeding literature will be offered and seeding and suggestion will be differentiated. Then, applications of seeding at various points in the hypnotherapeutic process will be discussed. The final section explores factors that are relevant in the therapeutic utilization of seeding.

One more thing before I begin. I would like to again stimulate and utilize your imagination. Suppose you have a client who complains of being "awkward." He or she feels "clumsy" in some way, perhaps socially, maybe physically. Your task is to develop a metaphor involving an animal that could be used therapeutically to help this client with his or her feelings of "awkwardness" and "clumsiness." Write enough about this metaphor (e.g., which animal, the gist of the story) to allow you to remember it. We will return to your invention later.

PRIMING IN THE LITERATURE

Sherman (1988) defined priming as "the activation or change in accessibility of a concept by an earlier presentation of the same or a closely related concept" (p. 65). Priming techniques are extensively employed in cognitive and experimental psychological research. Experimental tasks such as lexical decisions (Meyer & Schvaneveldt, 1971; Schachter, 1987), word completion (Tulving, Schachter & Stark, 1982), and free recall (Roediger, 1990) yield consistent priming effects. Problem-solving efficiency seems to be enhanced by priming (Higgins & Chaires, 1980; Maier, 1931), and word association also is influenced (Nisbett & Wilson, 1977). Priming effects can be extremely subtle. Kunst-Wilson and Zajonc (1980) found that although their subjects performed no better than chance at recognizing primed geometric shapes, they showed a clear preference for them when asked which of two shapes (one primed, one a new shape) they liked better. This result was obtained even though the tachistoscopic exposure to the geometric figures, one millisecond, was arguably too brief to permit conscious perception. Semantic network models, such as the spreading activation (Collins & Loftus, 1975) and compound cue (Ratcliff & McKoon, 1988) theories, identify priming effects as evidence of cognitive structures and processes. Studies of memory utilize priming as a central experimental procedure, contributing to the demarcation of implicit and explicit memory processes (Roediger, 1990; Schachter, 1987) and speculation that different forms of priming affect different perceptual representation systems (Schachter, 1991).

Research in social psychology demonstrates priming influences on social cognition and behavior. Measures of moral development (LaRue & Olejnick, 1980), attitudes (Lewicki, 1985), and impression formation (Bargh & Pietromonaco, 1982; Kelley, 1950) were all influenced in primed groups when compared with others. Subjects in two separate studies by Gregory, Cialdini, and Carpenter (1982) rated themselves more likely to be arrested and more likely to win a vacation to Hawaii, respectively, after being exposed to scripts (one taperecorded, one printed) that facilitated imagination of these events. A priming study that holds notable relevance to the clinical context was conducted by Sherman and Anderson (1987). These investigators asked first-time therapy clients to imagine themselves remaining in treatment for four sessions and to explain what allowed them to accomplish this. A substantially smaller percentage of premature termination was found in this group than in a control group of clients.

Whether or not priming can occur at a subliminal level is an issue of considerable debate. Elaborate research procedures have yielded mixed results that suggest semantic activation without conscious identification and preconscious processing are either bona fide phenomena or ambiguous concepts not yet conclusively demonstrated (Holender, 1986; Marcel, 1983). Kihlstrom (1987) summarized the current theoretical state regarding subliminal priming:

> Priming occurs automatically regardless of whether the prime is accessible to conscious awareness, but the automatic effects of consciously perceptible stimuli may be obviated by whatever processing strategies are deliberately deployed to analyze and respond to them. . . . Preconscious processing *can influence the ease with which certain ideas are brought to mind, and the manner in which objects and events are perceived and interpreted* [italics added]. Finally, in order for preconscious processing to affect action it is necessary that relevant goal structures be activated in procedural memory. (pp. 1448–1449)

Seeding is the clinical application of priming, the manner by which this powerful technology can be harnessed and directed to therapeutic ends.

Seeding "sets the table" for psychotherapy. After priming facilitates certain ideas being brought to mind, therapy aims to change the manner in which objects and events are perceived and interpreted. These complementary processes work in tandem. Indeed, Zeig (1990) forwarded the proposition that "any important therapeutic intervention is best presented when there has been prior seeding" (p. 233).

SEEDING IN THE LITERATURE

Haley, in *Uncommon Therapy* (1973), first identified "seeding ideas" as a tactic employed by Erickson in his hypnosis and therapy. Zeig (1990) defined seeding as "activating an intended target by presenting an earlier hint" (p. 222). He also outlined uses of seeding in "chaining" steps in hypnotic processes (Zeig, 1980), for promoting therapeutic amnesia (Zeig, 1985), as an aspect of influence communication that builds responsiveness (Zeig, 1987), and as an integral strategy in symptom utilization (Zeig, 1988). Geary (1989) noted the importance of seeding in group processes and the treatment of depression. Sherman (1988) first linked seeding with the priming literature and advocated the generalization of priming strategies to the clinical domain, stating:

> The possible uses of priming techniques for altering clients' thoughts and behavior have only begun to be appreciated. Understanding both the techniques for priming concepts as well as the likely consequences of priming should be of great value for psychotherapists. (p. 67)

In 1992, I conducted the first empirical investigation of seeding in the hypnotic context. I utilized height of arm levitation as the dependent measure, yielded by the Stanford Hypnotic Arm Levitation and Induction Test (SHALIT) (Hilgard, Crawford & Wert, 1979). Three groups were compared: A direct seeding condition in which subjects memorized four word pairs (Hand-Light, Fingers-Lift, Arm-Float, Elbow-Rise) composed of operative nouns and verbs from the SHALIT, and an indirect seeding group, which read the following passage of prose that contained some of the same words from the SHALIT:

> For me, it's really an uplifting experience when you can arise early, just as the sun comes up, and watch the day begin. I especially like to go up to a high place, with the birds lifting their voices in song, and watch the sun slowly rise in the sky. One particular morning, as I looked across the horizon, I saw a hot-air balloon drifting upward. It just floated in the sky, appearing

weightless as the air elevated it higher and higher. As the balloon hovered, I felt a real lightness in my body. My spirits are raised every time I think of that morning.

The third group comprised the control condition in which subjects merely passed time without an experimental activity. Results demonstrated a distinct indirect seeding effect. Subjects in this group showed nearly three times more arm levitation (35 centimeters) than control group subjects (12 centimeters), significant at the p ≤ .028 level. While the difference was nearly as great when the indirect and direct (16 centimeters) seeding groups were compared, the number of subjects in each cell (18) limited the significance (p ≤ .077) of this comparison. Power analysis suggested that 27 subjects per cell would have produced significant results at the .05 level. Generalization from these results should be cautious, and additional research is needed to further define the parameters of seeding. But these promising initial findings add weight to the clinical lore regarding the efficacy of this approach.

SEEDING AND SUGGESTION

It is useful at this point to clarify similarities and differences between seeding and suggestion. Both can increase the frequency of behaviors. Both can be direct or indirect. The cue (or hint) in seeding can be a suggestion that has therapeutic value in and of itself. The essential distinction is whether or not there is follow-up. In seeding, the cue is always elaborated or developed in some manner. A suggestion is a self-contained therapeutic device. So, suggestion can be a form of seeding. The purpose of the seed (i.e., the cue or hint) is to activate associational processes within the client. Enhanced responsiveness is thereby engendered so the person is more "response ready" for the subsequent intervention(s).

Consider the following example: An anxious patient walks into your office for therapy. You could give this patient the direct suggestion, "Settle down" and it might work. Or, you could use hypnosis and relate the suggestion indirectly: "You might want to settle down into a comfortable, relaxed state in which you feel yourself easily let go of tension." Or, you could present the concept as a hint. For instance, the client could be told, "You want relief and there are a number of things for you to learn. So, I think it's best to settle down to business right away." Later, this intimation could be developed. You might tell a story about a frisky puppy and how wild she was for awhile. But then, as she learned things, she was able to settle down. Within the story, themes of learning, development, and relief could be fashioned to therapeutically address the client's anxiety.

APPLICATIONS OF SEEDING

There are five phases in a session of clinical hypnosis. The prehypnotic phase is typically devoted to gathering information that is germane to the ensuing therapy. But this is also "prime time" for seeding, as will be illustrated below. Induction of hypnosis is the second phase in which responsiveness to hypnotic communication is elicited. Utilization is the third phase, the segment of the hypnosis during which the majority of the hypnotherapy is accomplished. Termination, the fourth phase, effects the transition from the hypnotic back to the waking state. The fifth, posthypnotic, stage is the time that spans termination to the next hypnotic experience (and even can subsume subsequent hypnotic sessions). These phases of hypnosis are much more distinct on paper than in practice. In actuality, there is often overlap and the stages are not necessarily traversed in a set order. But for organizational purposes, these are useful components for the following conceptualization.

In the hypnotic context, there are at least five junctures at which seeding can be utilized, as Figure 1 illustrates:

DIAGRAM ONE: APPLICATIONS OF SEEDING
Phases of the Hypnotic Process

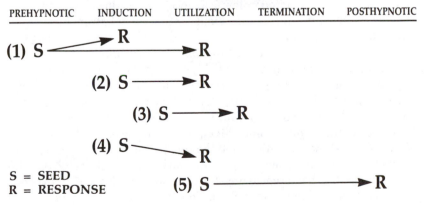

Fig. 1. Applications of Seeding.

A rationale for each phase follows with examples provided to demonstrate the varieties of seeding available during each stage:

(1) Prehypnotic Phase

The set that a client takes into the hypnotic experience is one of the most potent determinants of the eventual nature of that experience. Prehypnotic communication between therapist and client can be designed to promote a facilitative frame for the hypnotherapy. "Laying the groundwork" for comfort, safety, generative associations, and the like should be given careful consideration in this prehypnotic phase. Schneck (1986) discussed prehypnotic suggestion as a means to permissively allow patients to derive insights in hypnosis. Zeig (1990) likened the use of prehypnotic suggestion to providing a "fertilized bed" in which subsequent therapeutic directives have a better opportunity to flourish.

CASE ONE   In a clinical demonstration before a training group, a volunteer client told me that he was bothered by attending to "every" sensation in his chest after open heart surgery several months earlier. After extensively interviewing him about this hypervigilance, I excused myself to consult with the group (in another room behind a viewing mirror) for several minutes. Besieged by questions and suggestions during this time, I returned to the therapy suite somewhat overwhelmed. I told the client about my experience: "I was really deluged with information in there . . . There's so much to pay attention to . . . You know, it's really vital to sort out that to which it's important to attend and just let the rest go. I need to find that *balance* for myself."

Hypnosis then was elicited utilizing a process of "paying close attention" to feelings of relaxation and comfort and "letting go" of extraneous considerations (e.g., sounds outside, the color of the wall behind him, and a need to direct his thoughts), "establishing that *balance* that's conducive to deriving the most benefit that you possibly can derive from this experience." I capitalized on the seeding that was cultivated prehypnotically. In the utilization phase, the hypnotic process itself was used as an example of how the body and mind cooperate to naturalistically provide a natural *balance* for optimal functioning. Metaphors were developed around the *balance* of birds' bodies in flight and the separation of "signal from noise" that ham radio operators must accomplish. An internal "ticker tape parade" was then suggested that he could enjoy as a celebration of his life. Prehypnotic communication seeded the induction. The induction, in turn, seeded the use of indirection in the hypnotic utilization phase.

CASE TWO   Another example illustrates prehypnotic seeding of primary interventions. Tom complained of "workaholism," and during the initial interview, he exemplified a tendency to "race ahead," providing information faster than I could register it. At one point, I interjected, "Whoa! You're like a wild stallion with bountiful energy that needs to be reined in." Tom identified with this symbol, later depicting his behavior as "just like the horse."

In the hypnotic utiization phase, the importance of deriving benefit from "horsing around" as a balance to task orientation was developed. Tom was told he could "kick up his heels" when appropriate and "corral" old critical thoughts about his former inability to find a balance of self-care and work. The central intervention was an anecdote in which I related my memory of the 1973 Belmont Stakes and the way that Secretariat put "greater and greater distance between himself and his competitors." This was likened to the manner in which Tom could "leave behind" old ways and "stay on track" in incorporating new patterns and "saddling up" the fun-loving aspects of himself. The analogies, metaphor, and plays on words were all seeded prehypnotically, during the interview.

CASE THREE   A cogent example of prehypnotic seeding is found in the videotape of Erickson conducting the "Reverse Set Induction" (Erickson & Rossi, 1981). Prior to the demonstration, the following exchange occurred between Erickson and the subject, Ruth:

ERICKSON: "Do you mind if I call you Ruth?"
RUTH: "No, I'd like you to call me Ruth."
ERICKSON: "Does that light feel all right?"
RUTH: "Yes, it does."
ERICKSON: "I understand you've never been hypnotized . . ."
RUTH: "No."
ERICKSON: (*Quickly*) "But that you are interested?"
RUTH: "Yes."
ERICKSON: "And I think the best thing to do is to get right down to work . . . (*looking away and down, his voice falling and his shoulders relaxing*). And how much are "you willing to learn?"
RUTH: "I'm very willing . . . I'm a little nervous, though."
ERICKSON: "A little nervous? Really, I ought to be the one who is nervous. Because I've got to do the work and all you have to do is let things happen . . . and they will happen. . . . Are you forgetting about the light?"
RUTH: "No, I'm not. Am I supposed to look at it?"
ERICKSON: "You *can* forget about it, you know."

The subsequent demonstration allowed Ruth to learn a number of things about her hypnotic capacities. Erickson seeded the ease with which she could experience hand levitation ("all you have to do is let things happen"), dissociation, and responsiveness to his suggestions (i.e., while he did the work). Ruth subsequently was able to dissociate and temporarily deny her name, that she was sitting down, and that she was female. The short time Erickson took in the prehypnotic interchange seemed to pay dividends in the success of the demonstration.

(2) Seeding the Utilization Phase During the Induction Phase

A question for the induction phase is, "How can the induction seed the target intervention?" The answer determines the substance and form of the way absorption is effected in the hypnotic induction. If one is going to utilize age regression during the utilization phase, one can absorb a memory during induction. If one is going to alter the experience of pain through analgesia, absorption as an induction device can be in a sensation (e.g., feelings of numbness in the hands). Focusing on an hallucination during induction can "set up" visualization processes within the hypnotic state. Zeig (1990) discussed this process of seeding interventions as building "toward the desired goal in small steps. A central idea behind 'seeding' is to build therapeutic momentum by starting slowly and then building up steam en route to a goal" (p. 237).

(3) Seeding within the Utilization Phase

While this stage of the hypnotic process often is geared toward embellishing previous seeding, cues can be offered that are developed within the context of interventions themselves. For instance, the acquisition or refinement of behavior (e.g., delivering an effective speech, eating in a controlled and healthy fashion, or sitting on an airplane in a calm manner) is often facilitated by allowing clients to hypnotically review several personal vignettes of learning (e.g., tying a shoe, learning to drive, mastering a mathematical concept, or becoming skilled at a facet of their job). In this manner, the goal of imagining and then implementing a desired ability is primed by a "set" of attainment from the individual's own experience. The possibility of change is thereby made more plausible.

Alternately, a number of anecdotes or metaphors can be "chained" together, each providing an incremental element to a larger message. Discrete stories about a target concept (e.g., success, growth, or control) can have an additive effect in promoting heightened impact of the therapeutic theme.

(4) Seeding for Greater Width/ Depth of Trance

The depth analogy of hypnosis (i.e., light, medium, deep, somnambulistic levels of trance) has been with us for a long time. In counterpoint, Gilligan (1987) noted that "the Ericksonian practitioner is more interested in the *breadth* than the *depth* of trance" (p. 44). The latter conceptualization seems more consistent with recent formulations of consciousness in cognitive psychology (Kihlstrom, 1987) and with models of human semantic processing (Collins & Loftus, 1975; Ratcliff & McKoon, 1988; Schachter, 1991) that hypothesize "spread activation" and lateral accessibility of concepts in consciousness. That is, it might be more useful to think in terms of the associational "flow" that hypnotic subjects experience as a matter of ranging "far and wide" in trance rather than descending to greater depths of consciousness. It has long been noted (Erickson, Hershman & Secter, 1961, 1990) — and I believe it is a familiar phenomenon to hypnotherapists — that many (if not most) of our patients derive as much benefit in trances traditionally labelled "light" as in those designated "deep." The Y-axis (ordinate) of hypnosis has been well developed. Perhaps it is time to similarly elaborate qualities of the X-axis (abscissa) of the trance state.

Whichever representation one favors, seeding is a useful technique in encouraging movement along these planes of experience. In one case, I employed a hobby as seeding with a client who wished to experience "deep states of hypnosis." The process of developing trance was likened to his passion for scuba diving. The alterations of his subjective experience during induction were paralleled with preparations taken before plunging into the sea. Then, the changes that occur with increasing depth of the dive (e.g., lessening of light, differences in sea life, and the ways of moving in water) were used symbolically to establish an expectation of further modification of his experience.

In another case, the vacation upon which a patient was prepared to embark immediately following her session became the grist for seeding. Aspects of the trip ("seeing new sights, letting go of routine, and replenishing oneself") were interspersed as indirect seeds for the "broader experience" she could enjoy in hypnosis. In essence, stories and metaphors can seed the associations that accompany broader and deeper experiences in patients.

(5) Seeding Posthypnotic Experience

Clinical hypnosis is undertaken to effect changes in people's lives. The goal is to extend hypnotic insights, learnings, and associations into active transformation of everyday experience. The posthypnotic context is where the responsiveness of therapy is enlivened. Seeding facilitates this activation.

Posthypnotic suggestion is one of the classic hypnotic phenomena. Seeding from the hypnotic context to everyday life can take the form of posthypnotic suggestion. Specific skills learned in hypnosis (e.g., relaxation, pain management, and hallucination) can be linked to problem situations by marking these situations as cues for learned responses (Barber, 1982). For example, a hypnotized client can be offered the suggestion: "Every time you feel that 'flutter' in your stomach, that can signal you to take those easy breaths and focus on your personal symbol of capability, just as you are doing now." Posthypnotic seeding can also be offered in a nonspecific manner: "And it's nice to know that a variety of discoveries await you . . . as you find ways to put the learnings of this experience to work for you . . . trusting your capacity to apply the resources that you know exist within."

Therapy itself is more potent and enduring when interventions of one session are seeded on earlier occasions. Themes can be developed that are initially set up (e.g., through a metaphor, a symbol, a suggestion) and subsequently reprised and elaborated. This provides momentum and continuity to the therapeutic process.

The foregoing discussed the "wheres" of seeding. Before looking at the "hows" of seeding, let's return to the metaphor you developed for the "clumsy" client. What animal did you employ in your story? Was it a bear? If so, this is a low frequency response that was seeded in the first three sentences of this chapter. Whether or not you chose a bear says nothing about the adequacy of your metaphor. This little experiment illustrates a truism of seeding: Some seeds will grow and flourish, others will not. This highlights the importance of attending to the manner in which one therapeutically utilizes seeding. Let's turn our attention, then, to factors that can influence the effectiveness of seeding.

FACTORS IN SEEDING

The development of seeding as a therapeutic approach is in its infancy. Therefore, little empirical data exist to guide the application of this technique. Fortunately, the wealth of findings in the priming literature is available and clinical experience can provide direction for the deployment of seeding in therapy. The following six variables are offered as guidelines for your thinking and strategizing about ways to enhance patients' responsiveness through seeding:

(1) Self-Relevance

People seem more likely to believe that events will befall them after they imagine personal involvement in such occurrences (Gregory, Cialdini &

Carpenter, 1982). A "heightened expectancy" of conduct apparently results from immersing oneself in the possibility of performing suggested behaviors. I speculated that self-relevance could partially account for the greater arm levitation in the indirect seeding group in my study. Reading a passage about a beautiful morning with birds singing and spotting a hot air balloon is certainly more engaging than memorizing a word pair list.

Therapists have leverage in this regard because patients bring self-relevant matters to the clinical context. Utilization of patient values, aspirations, and experiential backgrounds in seeding, then, can intensify personal involvement and thereby elevate motivation, responsiveness, and compliance. Zeig (1980, 1985, 1990) has stressed the importance of utilizing patient values on a number of occasions. Seeding seems to have more potency when it is tied to an individual's phenomenology.

It is an unfortunate fact that hypnotherapists are frequently forced to battle "negative" seeding. Referrals for hypnosis by other professionals often are effected in a grudging manner. We all too often hear clients report, for instance, that their physician said something like, "Well, go ahead and try hypnosis if you must, but it's not going to work." Or we are asked to assist patients who have supposedly "failed" at hypnosis previously because they are not "good hypnotic subjects." It is wise to bear in mind the power and persistence that inaccurate beliefs foisted upon one can exert (Lepper, Ross & Lau, 1986). Sometimes, "deseeding" must be accomplished in order for therapy to proceed.

(2) Imaginal Rehearsal

When people imagine an event occurring, they are more likely to believe that the event will take place (Carroll, 1978; Sherman, Skov, Hervitz & Stock, 1981). Hence, "a requester may be more successful in gaining compliance with a request if the target person has first imagined a scenario of himself or herself performing the requested behavior" (Gregory, Cialdini & Carpenter, 1982, p. 89). This is a rather direct route to increasing responsiveness: Imagine it to be so and it is more likely to be. But the potential is far-reaching. In order to maintain a consistent self-perception, clients might be more favorably disposed to imagined behaviors that they believe they will perform (Gregory, Cialdini & Carpenter, 1982). Behavioral patterns can be beneficially modified to be more congruent with the new attitudes and perceptions of the self that are fostered by imaginal involvement.

(3) Direct versus Indirect Seeding

Reliable experimental effects are demonstrated with both direct and indirect forms of priming (Richardson-Klavehn & Bjork, 1988). Clinicians can advantageously employ both direct and indirect forms of seeding, depending on their therapeutic styles, values and goals of the patient, degree of perceived resistance, stage of the therapy, and other germane issues. Zeig (1990) indicated that macro- and microdynamic aspects of therapy can be seeded both directly and indirectly.

Erickson exemplified artful and pragmatic utilization: When direct techniques worked, he used them; when indirection was more likely to produce desired changes, he plied these methods. Clinical judgment, willingness to benignly experiment, and continual vigilance for what works are the guiding principles for the varieties of seeding that therapists exercise.

(4) Timing

In experimental conditions, it appears that the effects of priming are at times temporally restricted (Roediger, 1990; Wilson & Capitman, 1982). But, as Zeig (1990) noted, clinicians are not bound by most of the restraints of experimental designs. The persistence of seeding is a multifactorial phenomenon, much like the durability of posthypnotic suggestion. How many of us look both ways before crossing the street and take care in dotting our i's and crossing our t's? When one works strategically, piecing together small steps toward a larger goal, the pacing of seeding becomes a consideration. The key is responsiveness of the patient. Whether it is the appearance of a hypnotic phenomenon during a single hypnotic session or behavioral change during the course of therapy, the observant therapist coordinates delivery with reaction of the patient.

(5) Awareness

The regrettable myth has grown around Ericksonian psychotherapy that the best intervention is the one that obviates conscious recognition. Erickson himself was a champion of greater cooperation among conscious and unconscious processes. Therapists need not engage in self-beratement if a client smiles and says, "I really like the way you set up that suggestion." I take it as a compliment when a hypnotized client smiles in response to a play on words or juxtaposition of one of their beliefs that I offer. To me, it is more likely that reframes, suggestions, directives, and other therapeutic methods will have an effect if they are processed consciously at some point. The hypnotic context allows greater associational elaboration of the recognized communication. On the other hand, I don't feel compelled to provide an explanation if a patient remarks, "I don't know why" as a preface to an insight or shift in perception or change in behavior. When one operates from a "both-and" set, seeding with conscious identification is both useful in itself and complementary to unconscious elicitation.

(6) Supplementary Considerations in Seeding

Building responsiveness is a mutual process of imparting verbal content within a medium of communication. Zeig (1992) refers to the "gift wrapping" that a therapist chooses to convey a message. I allude to the "vehicle" that transports the communication. Seeding occurs on multiple levels, with pauses, inflections, gestures, plays on words, syntactical maneuvers, voice tone and volume shifts, postural changes, and other nuances available to therapists for heightened effect.

A client once told me that my utterance, "What goes down must come up," was meaningful to her in her battle with depression. She thought for months that I had made a mistake in citing the gravitational truism (I hadn't) and this "error really stuck with me." The themes of "lifting mood," "lightness of spirit," and others that were utilized in the therapy were activated by the associations spurred from this simple phrase. Drama, suspense, surprise, and all the other elements of good storytelling can be brought to bear in effective seeding.

CONCLUSION

This chapter has concentrated on applications of seeding in hypnosis. This technique can be (and is) utilized in all forms of psychotherapy. At a metalevel, the work of therapy is seeding for the conduct of life. Being more aware of one's emotional processes while talking to "mother" in an empty chair seeds more constructive interactions with the real person. Imagining successful negotiation of a problematic situation while relaxed primes one for enhanced performance *in vivo*. Within particular therapy sessions, the microdynamics of seeding can be employed by practitioners of all orientations. All that is needed is a forward-looking set and a desire to augment therapeutic effectiveness and creativity.

The effects of seeding can be life-changing. My father was a student of Dr. Erickson's in the 1950s and '60s and to this day he advocates Ericksonian approaches. I have a clear recollection, though I don't remember how old I was, of my father once suggesting to me, "You ought to learn something about Milton H. Erickson." I still am.

REFERENCES

Barber, J. (1982). Managing acute pain. In J. Barber & C. Adrian (Eds.), *Psychological approaches to the management of pain*, 168-179. New York: Brunner/Mazel.

Bargh, J.A., & Pietromonaco, P. (1982). Automatic information processing and social perception: The influence of trait information presented outside of conscious awareness on impression formation. *Journal of Personality and Social Psychology, 43,* 437-449.

Carroll, J.S. (1978). The effect of imagining an event on expectations for the event: An interpretation in terms of the availability heuristic. *Journal of Experimental Social Psychology, 14,* 88-96.

Collins, A.M., & Loftus, E.F. (1975). A spreading activation theory of semantic processing. *Psychological Review, 82,* 407-428.

Erickson, M.H., Hershman, S., & Secter, I. (1961). *The practical application of medical and dental hypnosis.* New York: Julian Press. (Reprinted by Brunner, Mazel, New York, 1990)

Erickson, M.H., & Rossi, E.L. (1981). *Experiencing hypnosis: Therapeutic approaches to altered states.* New York: Irvington.

Geary, B.B. (1989). Integrating Ericksonian strategies into structured groups for depression. In M.D. Yapko (Ed.), *Brief therapy approaches to treating anxiety and depression,* 184-204. New York: Brunner/Mazel.

Geary, B.B. (1992). *Seeding in hypnosis.* Unpublished doctoral dissertation, Arizona State University, Tempe.

Gilligan, S.G. (1987). *Therapeutic trances: The cooperation principle in Ericksonian hypnotherapy.* New York: Brunner/Mazel.

Gregory, W.L., Cialdini, R.B., & Carpenter, K.M. (1982). Self-relevant scenarios as mediators of likelihood estimates and compliance: Does imagining it make it so? *Journal of Personality and Social Psychology, 43,* 89-99.

Haley, J. (1973). *Uncommon therapy: The psychiatric techniques of Milton H. Erickson, M.D..* New York: W.W. Norton.

Higgins, E.T., & Chaires, W.M. (1980). Accessibility of interrelational constructs: Implications for stimulus encoding and creativity. *Journal of Experimental Social Psychology, 16,* 348-361.

Hilgard, E.R., Crawford, H.J., & Wert, A. (1979). The Stanford hypnotic arm levitation induction and test (SHALIT): A six-minute hypnotic induction and measurement scale. *International Journal of Clinical and Experimental Hypnosis, 27,* 111-124.

Holender, D. (1986). Semantic activation without conscious identification and dichotic listening, parafoveal vision, and visual masking: A survey and appraisal. *Behavioral and Brain Sciences, 9,* 1-66.

Kelley, H.H. (1950). The warm-cold variable in first impressions of persons. *Journal of Personality, 18,* 431-439.

Kihlstrom, J.F. (1987). The cognitive unconscious. *Science, 237* (4821), 1445-1452.

Kunst-Wilson, W.R., & Zajonc, R.B. (1980). Affective discrimination of stimuli that cannot be recognized. *Science, 207,* 537-558.

LaRue, A., & Olejnick, A.B. (1980). Cognitive priming of principled moral thought. *Personality and Social Psychology Bulletin, 6,* 413-416.

Lepper, M.R., Ross, L., & Lau, R.R. (1986). Persistence of inaccurate beliefs about the self. *Journal of Personality and Social Psychology, 41,* 258-290.

Lewicki, P. (1985). Nonconscious biasing effects of single instances on subsequent judgments. *Journal of Personality and Social Psychology, 48,* 563-574.

Maier, N.R.F. (1931). Reasoning in humans: II. The solution of a problem and its appearance in consciousness. *Journal of Comparative Psychology, 12,* 181-194.

Marcel, A.J. (1983). Conscious and unconscious perception: An approach to the relation between phenomenal experience and perceptual processes, *Cognitive Psychology, 15,* 238-300.

Meyer, D.E., & Schvaneveldt, R.W. (1971). Facilitation in recognizing pairs of words: Evidence of a dependence between retrieval operations. *Journal of Experimental Psychology, 90,* 227-234.

Nisbett, R.E., & Wilson, T.D. (1977). Telling more than we know: Verbal reports on mental processes. *Psychological Review, 84,* 231-259.

Ratcliff, R., & McKoon, G. (1988). Priming in item recognition: Evidence for the prepositional structure of sentences. *Journal of Verbal Learning and Verbal Behavior, 17,* 403-417.

Richardson-Klavehn, A., & Bjork, R.A. (1988). Measures of memory. *Annual Review of Psychology, 39,* 475-553.

Roediger, H.L. (1990). Implicit memory: Retention without remembering. *American Psychologist, 45,* 1043-1056.

Schachter, D.L. (1987). Implicit memory: History and current status. *Journal of Experimental Psychology: Learning, Memory, and Cognition, 13,* 501-518.

Schachter, D.L. (1991). Perceptual representation systems and implicit memory: Toward a resolution of the multiple memory systems debate. In A. Diamond (Ed.), *The developmental and neural basis of higher cognitive function.* New York: New York Academy of Sciences.

Schneck, J.M. (1986). Integrating hypnosis with insight-oriented psychotherapy. In B. Zilbergeld, M.G. Edelstein, & D.L. Araoz (Eds.), *Hypnosis: Questions and answers.* New York: W.W. Norton.

Sherman, R.T., & Anderson, C.A. (1987). Decreasing premature termination from psychotherapy. *Journal of Social and Clinical Psychology, 5,* 298-312.

Sherman, S.J. (1988). Ericksonian psychotherapy and social psychology. In J.K. Zeig & S.R. Lankton (Eds.), *Developing Ericksonian therapy: State of the art.* New York: Brunner/Mazel.

Sherman, S.J., Skov, R.B. Hervitz, E.F., & Stock, C.B. (1981). Effects of explaining hypothetical future events: From possibility to probability to actuality and beyond. *Journal of Experimental Social Psychology, 17,* 142-158.

Tulving, E., Schachter, D.L., & Stark, H.A. (1982). Priming effects in word-fragment completion are independent of recognition memory. *Journal of Experimental Psychology: Learning, Memory, and Cognition, 8,* 336-342.

Wilson, T.D., & Capitman, J.A. (1982). Effects of script availability on social behavior. *Personality and Social Psychology Bulletin, 8,* 11-19.

Zeig, J.K. (1980). *A teaching seminar with Milton H. Erickson.* New York: Brunner/Mazel.

Zeig, J.K. (1985). The clinical use of amnesia: Ericksonian methods. In J.K. Zeig (Ed.), *Ericksonian psychotherapy, Volume I: Structures.* New York: Brunner/Mazel.

Zeig, J.K. (1987). Therapeutic patterns of Ericksonian influence communication. In J.K. Zeig (Ed.), *The evolution of psychotherapy.* New York: Brunner/Mazel.

Zeig, J.K. (1988). An Ericksonian phenomenological approach to therapeutic hypnotic induction and symptom utilization. In J.K. Zeig & S.R. Lankton (Eds.), *Developing Ericksonian therapy: State of the art*. New York: Brunner/Mazel.

Zeig, J.K. (1990). Seeding. In J.K. Zeig & S.G. Gilligan (Eds.), *Brief therapy: Myths, methods, and metaphors*. New York: Brunner/Mazel.

Zeig, J.K. (1992). The virtue of our faults: A key concept in Ericksonian psychotherapy. In J.K. Zeig (Ed.), *The evolution of psychotherapy: The second conference*. New York: Brunner/Mazel.

CHAPTER 22

One Thousand Induction Techniques and Their Application to Therapy and Thinking

Sidney Rosen

THE NATURE OF A HYPNOTIC TRANCE

I do not need to stress that a trance is not a state of being asleep, un-conscious, or "under." It need not involve relaxation, even though most of us use it at some time or other to help elicit relaxation.

Trance is a state of hypersuggestibility. A person in hypnosis tends to be more responsive than usual to suggestions or influence from a hypnotist or, with self-hypnosis, from himself or herself. The latter includes expecta-tions and "self-talk." If the suggestions are designed to focus attention, it will then tend to be focused on a designated object or mode of experienc-ing or thinking. And, of course, in a trance one can be more in touch than usual with what we call the Unconscious Mind. In fact, Erickson's last definition of hypnosis was that "hypnosis is the evocation and utilization of unconscious learnings" (personal communication, 1978).

Hypnosis can make possible intense communication between people, communication on more levels than usual. Many have had the experience, when in a trance while working therapeutically, of responding to our patient's mood and thoughts even before they were verbalized. It seemed like mind reading, but undoubtedly came from increased sensitivity and increased recollection of past patterns of thinking, as well as an increased awareness of minimal sensory and bodily cues. And the patient, of course, was then most responsive to our suggestions and influence. Increased responsiveness occurs when attention is directed almost exclusively toward the patient, not when we are in a more self-centered state of mind.

People are not more hypnotizable because they are more suggestible. They become more suggestible when they are in a trance. About 25 years ago, I heard Lawrence Kubie, the well-known psychoanalyst who wrote three papers with Erickson, discuss hypnosis at a meeting of the American Psychoanalytic Association. He pointed out that people will go into trance under many conditions, without any suggestions having been given — watching the line on the highway, listening to a repeated tone, being stroked repeatedly on the forehead or on the back. Kubie noted that after the person goes into a trance, the barrier between the hypnotist and the subject is dissolved and the subject hears the hypnotist's voice as if it were coming from inside his or her own head. That is why the hypnotized subject is more suggestible and also why he does not necessarily follow all suggestions that are given, just as he does not act on all of his own thoughts.

How, then, can we enter, or help someone else enter, into a trance? From the examples I have mentioned, we know that we can do this by utilizing a repeated stimulus — visual, auditory, or tactile. For many years, hypnotists relied on repetition, but one of the early contributions that Erickson made to hypnotherapy was his demonstrating that it was unnecessary to repeat suggestions. In fact, casual seeding of a suggestion may be most effective.

In contemplating this question a few years ago, I made a rather large leap. I have always thought that it came from reading a comment by John Beahrs in Erickson's 75th birthday issue of the *American Journal of Clinical Hypnosis* (Vol. 20, 1977). I clearly remembered that Beahrs had written, "Anytime a person focuses attention on one thing he will go into a trance." I have credited Dr. Beahrs with this insight. In preparing this chapter, however, all efforts to find this quotation failed. In desperation, I called John and asked where he had made this statement. He could not remember ever having said exactly that. The closest he could recall was a comment in an article he wrote with Humiston in which he stated:

> It is our experience that whenever a patient is successfully held to vivid experience of whatever is happening anyway, the patient invariably goes into a hypnotic trance . . . This is evidenced by vivid real-life imagery, profound body image experiences, and time distortion, all recognized by Hilgard (1968) as bona-fide criteria of hypnosis. (Beahrs & Humiston, 1972, p. 2)

It appears, then, that I had either extrapolated and expanded on this observation, simply misinterpreted it, or read something somewhere else. In any case, I had concluded, from my own experience, that *anytime a person focuses attention on one thing he or she will go into a trance.*

I have tested this hypothesis in many different settings—in my office with patients, in seminars with therapists, and, of course, with myself—and it seems to be supported. For example, I may suggest to a group of people that they touch something and focus on the sensation of touch, that they look at something and focus on the image, that they recall a smell, such as the smell of cut lemon or apple, that they make a sound and focus on listening to the sound, that they visualize the number 637, a color, or their own first name. Within 30 seconds, almost everyone in the group shows signs that we recognize as indicating the presence of a trance state, e.g., facial lines smooth out, the body becomes immobile, eyelids close, or the eyes assume a staring condition. When, at this point I suggest, "Now you can go into as deep a trance as you want and utilize your trance—for some useful purpose," or ". . . utilize your trance to recall a long-forgotten childhood memory," or ". . . utilize your trance to feel more relaxed than you have felt for a long time," a large number of participants are able to follow the suggestion I have presented. In other words, they go into a trance and become more suggestible or more responsive than usual.

I have divided an audience into four groups:

Group One was instructed to fix their eyes on any point or object. When, within 30 seconds, most of them gave evidence of being in a trance—flattened facial expressions, eyes closed or staring, immobility, with or without relaxed musculature, slowing in breathing—they were told, "Now, you can go into as deep a trance as you like and take yourself to a beautiful vacation spot."

Group Two was invited to take objects from their pockets or purses and to concentrate on feeling the texture and shape of the objects. When they appeared to be in a trance, they were told, "Now, you can go into as deep a trance as you want—and enjoy a feeling of deep calm and peace."

Group Three was advised to listen to an imagined or recalled sound. It was suggested to them that they could then smell and taste a freshly sliced apple.

Group Four were directed to visualize and think of the number "637." They were told to bring back an early memory that they had not thought of for a long time.

When asked for a show of hands afterward to indicate that they had felt themselves to be in a trance, 60 to 75% of each group responded positively. Approximately the same percentages indicated that they had successfully experienced the suggested phenomena.

Of course, once we had demonstrated the effectiveness of the "637" induction technique, we had paved the way for the "638" technique, the "5,294" technique, and so on. If we include the objects of all of our senses—tactile, olfactory, hearing, and vision—the number of objects of focus is truly limitless.

Question: What do the following activities have in common? Acupuncture, shiatsu, zone therapy, crystal healing, psychoanalysis, meditation, the "awareness continuum exercise" of Gestalt therapy, Eye Movement Desensitization and Reprocessing (EMDR), Benson's "Relaxation Response," and hypnosis.

Answer: They are all modalities in which, by focusing attention on one thing at a time, a person can move into a receptive state in which he or she is most open to suggestions of healing and learning (perhaps to other suggestions, as well). As I have indicated, I call this a trance state.

In acupuncture and shiatsu, the attention is drawn to points that are touched. In zone therapy, the attention is drawn to pressure sensations on the bottom of the foot. With crystal healing, it is directed toward seeing the sparkling or colored crystal and feeling the kinesthetic sensations that one becomes aware of when paying attention to the parts of the body that are touched or approached by the crystal. In psychoanalysis the attention is drawn to the subject's thoughts and feelings; these inner mental experiences constitute the "one thing" upon which attention is focused. In meditation practices, the attention is focused on a mantra, vocalized as the sound "OM." It may be focused on a visual pattern, called a "yantra" in Tantric practices, or it may be focused on breathing or on the thinking processes themselves. In Eye Movement Desensitization and Reprocessing (EMDR), it is directed toward the feelings in the eye muscles that accompany lateral eye movements. And, in order to evoke the "Relaxation Response," one need only concentrate on one thing, the number "one."

I do not mean to imply that any of the practices I have mentioned or that any of the other New Age healing approaches are "just hypnosis." I am simply pointing out that they all involve the evocation and utilization of a receptive state, which can be designated as a trance or a hypnotic state. The nature and quality of that state depends to a great extent on the input presented to the subject. This input may come from the outside, as from "demand characteristics of the situation" (Orne, 1962) and from verbal and nonverbal suggestions. It may come from another person or even from a computer screen. Or it may come from the subject's own mind, in the form of self-suggestions and expectations. For example, if the subject is seeking a state of transcendence, she is likely to identify trance experiences of dissociation as being transcendental. If the suggestion is made, or the expectation (self-suggestion) exists, that healing will occur, it is more likely to happen. If the suggestion is made that the subject will be in touch with his "unconscious mind," he will respond with appropriate images, memories, and behaviors.

To summarize: The receptive state is initiated by the subjects being directed and aided toward focusing attention on one thing—such as the sensations on the bottom of the foot, eye movements, "free associations," or a mantra. In this state, suggestions will be followed so long as they are ego syntonic, that is, in keeping with the subject's values and goals.

EARLY LEARNING SET INDUCTION

Focusing is clearly illustrated in Erickson's Early Learning Set Induction, (personal communication, 1978). In this, as in other inductions, every step involves focusing on one thing at a time. Following Erickson, I begin with, "I'd like to remind you that many of the things you now do automatically once required conscious mental effort. For example, you don't remember how you first learned to read and write, but just to tell the difference between the letter 'a' and the letter 'o' was a difficult task . . . and how do you put together a straight line and a little circle to form a 'b' or a 'd' or a 'p' or a 'q', and are there two bumps on the 'm' and three on the 'n' or are there two bumps on the 'n' and three on the 'm'?" (Wondering whether or not these statements are true and trying to visualize all of these suggested letters, even if unsuccessfully, leads to a focusing of attention—on the lines, circles, and resulting letters, on the concept of putting together the lines and circles, or even on the failure to see letters.)

The induction continues: "Do you dot the 't' and cross the 'i' or do you dot the 'i' and cross the 't'? . . . And what made it even more difficult was that there were small letters and capital letters. There were written letters and printed letters."

After the subject has entered into a trance by focusing attention on the suggested items, he or she is more "suggestible" than usual and is therefore more likely to respond to subsequent suggestions. First he is given the reinforcing and reassuring reminder, "And you learned to write all of those letters . . . you learned to write them automatically. And there are so many things you do automatically. You walk automatically. You talk automatically. You count four fingers, two thumbs automatically." Then comes the suggestion, "And you can go into a trance automatically . . . simply by letting your eyelids close . . . the next time I way the word, 'now.'"

I will usually continue with further direction to focus on one thing at a time. For example, "And with your eyes closed, you can examine your eyelids. You may see shadows. You may see some light here or there. You may see patterns and lines. You may see some colors . . . But it really

doesn't matter whether or not you see anything at all. Because the important thing is that you are again focusing attention on one thing . . . on your
eyelids."

For deepening of the trance I may suggest, "If you would like to go
deeper into your trance, keep close track of any phenomenon that interests
you, anything that is in the forefront of your consciousness, and your
curiosity will draw you deeper and deeper into your trance." Obviously
that last direction, similar to the Awareness Continuum Exercise of Gestalt
therapy, again directs the subject to continue focusing on one thing at a
time and it is certainly most easy to focus on a phenomenon that interests
you, isn't it?

By this time you may be wondering, as I have, whether or not it might be
useful to define our experiences so as to state that we are frequently in
some kind of trance. We can talk about being in a "Lovemaking Trance," a
"Working Trance," an "Instrument-playing Trance," a "Therapist Trance,"
a "Problem-solving Trance." We can be in a "Bird-watching Trance," a
"Tennis-playing Trance," or a "Reading Trance." Whenever we are concentrating our attention and energies in one area of functioning, we could
define our state as being a trance.

However, since there has been a tradition of associating the word
"trance" with *unusual* states of consciousness, it would probably be best
for me to substitute a term such as "state of mind" for trance. For the rest
of this chapter, I will use the terms "trance" and "state of mind" or "state"
interchangeably.

IMAGINATION AND IMAGERY

Erickson suggested to me one day that "therapy consists of substituting a
good idea for a bad idea." The ability to do this would obviously be helpful
not only for therapy but also for better thinking. Let us consider therapy
first. It is a bad idea to anticipate panic and pain. It is a good idea to expect
comfort and pleasure while flying in a plane or while eating in a restaurant.
But how can one change a negative or symptomatic response to a positive
or comfortable one? The answer to that question can be found by a review
of the literature of the healing arts, including the approaches and techniques devised and used by those who practice hypnotherapy. I cannot
summarize this vast amount of information, but I can point out a basic
principle. It is expressed by the dictum of Paracelsus, the physician and
alchemist of the early 16th century: "Even as man imagines himself to be,
such he is, and he is also that which he imagines" (Damon, 1971).

This same power of imagery and imagination was inadvertently confirmed by the French commission that examined the work of Mesmer and reported, after observing his follower, D'Eslon, that they could find no evidence of magnetism, but that many of the patients appeared to benefit from the ministrations. This benefit, they postulated, was merely due to their imagination.

While they, like most modern-day thinkers, used the term "imagination" with negative connotations, others, following William Blake, who was himself influenced by Paracelsus, have been able to recognize the central importance of imagination and imagery in our experiencing and responding. Blake, in fact, placed the imagination above our ordinary life and existence in our world, which he called the "Vegetable Universe." "In your own Bosom you bear your Heaven and Earth and all you behold; tho' it appears Without, it is Within, in your Imagination, of which this World of Mortality is but a Shadow" (Keynes, 1969, p. 709).

Imagery and imagination are most obviously utilized by shamans and psychotherapists. We have psychotherapeutic approaches that are aimed at altering the general images that patients hold of themselves. These include approaches aimed at freeing the "hero" or the "child" within and those that center around projections into the future. Other psychotherapeutic approaches may be focused on changing a discrete area of a person's functioning—eliminating a specific symptom or area of dysfunction, such as a phobia.

SWITCHES

Images, like other mental inputs such as colors and words, tone of voice, spatial perceptions, smells, or touch sensations, can be utilized as "switches," so that focusing attention on them will evoke a particular state of mind. If this state is a desired one, we could call it a positive state, and the switch could be called a positive switch. For example, I had a patient who was suffering from excruciating, intractable lower back pain with a condition that neurosurgeons had determined was inoperable. We discovered that when she could enter into a trance and recall the feeling of holding her newborn infant, a child who was now over 40 years old, her pain would disappear. The visual and tactile memories could be called positive switches.

If the state is not desired, e.g. a negative state, such as a phobic panic state, we can identify the negative switch or switches that evoke it. The most obvious and direct switches are the phobic objects or situations themselves—mice or small spaces, for example. Or the thought, "I shouldn't smoke" or "I shouldn't eat dessert" will evoke the compulsive need to smoke or overeat. Negative switches are often easy to identify in phobias, anxiety reactions, and depressive reactions as well as in the bodily responses that we call "psychosomatic."

A switch need not include an entire scene or sentence. Often one element or one word can evoke a desired response. Colors, tactile memories, or memories of body positions associated with successful performances have been used successfully with athletes, for example.

To change negative responses we can use different switches; e.g., with flying phobia, we can teach a person to focus attention on his eyelids or on the weight of his hands. This practice can become associated with feelings of comfort, even of pleasure, and this response can supersede the previous panic reaction. Or we can change the response to existing switches; e.g., change panic response to a needle to a comfort response. We have many approaches for doing this, including desensitization and the introduction of other associations. These can result in the substitution of a positive trance for a negative trance. Thus, instead of, "Whenever I think of food, I am compelled to eat," one can substitute, "Whenever I think of food, I can remind myself that I have had enough. I can remind myself that my mind needs feeding and then can seek some way to feed my mind."

Instead of the panic state that is switched on with inner suggestions such as, "Whenever I move more than one block away from home I will go into a panic," one can substitute, "I can thank my body for letting me know that I am anxious, that I am moving too quickly, too slowly, or whatever. And I can move at my own pace."

These latter directions could be thought of as post-hypnotic suggestions that will be evoked by the switch of "Whenever . . ."

FIRST CONSCIOUS THEN AUTOMATIC

While we can determine or control our entry into certain states of mind, simply, with self-hypnotic exercises, we may require more complex preparations for others. They may require an "entry process." For example, in order to enter into a "lovemaking state," many people must first proceed through some initiatory procedures or even rituals. In order to enter into some states—a speech-making state, for example—some people will go through weeks of preparation: thinking, gathering notes, writing out the speech, practicing its delivery, composing cue cards, going through a period of anticipatory anxiety or stage fright, and finally entering into the optimal state for delivery of the speech.

In order to be able to go into a "doctor state," "a healer state," or a "therapist state," all of us had to go through years of schooling, training, and experience. Otherwise, we could probably, like actors, play the role but not be "the genuine article." We would know it and some of the people we tried to fool would also know it. But even after developing the skills, we are not always in the "therapist state," naive cocktail party acquaintances' expectations to the contrary. We enter the "state" only under particular circumstances—in our offices, when we are asked for help. Outside circumstances or requests of others, therefore, play a large part in evoking the "state."

I am interested in the relationship between outside stimuli and response states. As therapists, we consciously and often unconsciously use words, tone of voice, body posture, and other nonverbal communications as switches—to evoke feelings of security and comfort in our patients, for example. We can also help them and ourselves to find and discover the environments that are most conducive to their healthy functioning. But I am even more interested in helping people to determine their own inner responses—emotionally, cognitively, and even behaviorally—independently of outside stimuli. It has been said that we cannot always control or determine what happens in our lives, but we can determine our responses, our way of looking at what happens, our emotional reactions. I know that most of the time we do not make any effort to do this. In fact, most of the time we react in some habitual or even conditioned way. But we *can* determine our responses. And you will naturally ask, "How?"

My answer is: By entering into the kind of state that we choose. Not, necessarily the one that we learned to enter into during our long period of childhood hypnosis. Then we can ask our unconscious for direction. This direction will come from our "inner learnings."

For example, if our feelings are hurt by someone's slight or omission, we can learn to follow Erickson's suggestion, "Don't hold on to hurt feelings. Throw them into the nearest garbage can and take a bath" (personal communication, 1980). Now, for some of us, perhaps those who had direct contact with Erickson and especially those who were told this by him, just the recollection of his words may be enough to take us out of our "hurt feelings state" and enable us to move to the "cleansed post-bath state." Others might need to go through a short or longer period of self-hypnosis during which they would eliminate the hurt feeling, perhaps by utilizing imagery in which those feelings are sent into the stratosphere via a helium-filled balloon. Then, still in a self-induced trance, they could suggest to themselves that they can find another, nonhurting way of framing or filtering the situation that led to the hurt or angry feelings. I am not suggesting that this process is always easy, but if we recall Erickson's observation, "Most of the things that we now do automatically once required conscious mental effort," then we will do the mental practicing that is required to develop needed abilities.

I will remind you that we can always enter into a receptive trance state by focusing attention on any one thing at a time. But how do we get others, or ourself, to focus attention on one thing? We may simply ask them to do so or we may order them, challenge them, intrigue them, or even suggest that they try not to do so, e.g., "Try not to think of the word 'elephant.'" We may utilize shock, humor, confusion, questions—all the elements that Erickson and Rossi have listed in *Hypnotherapy: An Exploratory Casebook* (Erickson & Rossi, 1979). But, as I have already mentioned, one of the best ways is to instruct them to keep close track of any phenomenon that interests them.

TRANCE IN PSYCHOTHERAPY

As I have noted, all the interventions in all forms of psychotherapy (and in many healing approaches that are not universally considered to be psychotherapy) are most effective when the patient is in trance, which we might call a "receptiveness-to-healing state." Even though this is not the only element in psychotherapy, it seems to be an essential one.

In *psychoanalytic therapies,* the state is evoked when the focus is on specific details, especially of memories and emotions. In other words, the focus is on one thing at a time. Questions and directions, such as "What comes?" and "Feel your feelings," will heighten it. It's the specificity that counts. Having a patient describe the details in a memory scene—colors, shapes, textures, exact locations of objects—leads, of course, to her focusing on one thing at a time and deepens the trance. When the patient is in this receptive state, often when the analyst has been silent for a long time, a comment by the analyst such as "Yes!" can have great impact.

In *cognitive therapies,* the receptive state is evoked when the focus is on cognitive processes, such as inner dialogue. Either with or without some "relaxation" preamble, the patient may learn to redirect his own thought processes. As I have noted, the substitution of a good idea for a bad idea takes place most effectively when the patient is in a receptive state.

In *behavioral therapies,* the receptive state is evoked in the interactions between therapist and patient as they seek and explore the value of various tasks. The focus may be on the precise method for carrying out a behavioral prescription. The linking of learned imagery-evoked comfort with images of being in the symptom-evoking situation also occurs most easily when the patient is in a receptive state.

In *solution-oriented therapies,* the trance state is evoked when the patient is directed to focus on inner processes, mostly imagery, with questions such as, "If your problems were solved magically, how would your life be different?" Even better, "When your problems or symptoms are resolved, how is your life different?"

Relaxation therapies involve a direct application of familiar trance-evoking suggestions—focusing attention on one part of the body at a time, for example, as in progressive relaxation. Then the use of the post-hypnotic cues, which I have called "switches," will bring back the relaxed state.

THINKING

The last time I saw Erickson, he explained to me the reasons for the establishment of his teaching seminars:

> I had to spend too much time on one patient. I would rather teach a lot of people how to think, how to handle problems. I have dozens and dozens of letters saying, "You have completely changed my way of treating patients." I get a lot of patients, but I see them less. I see more patients and I see them for shorter times. When I asked him, "And this is the result of . . . ?" he answered, "Their coming here and letting me tell them stories. Then they go home and alter their practice." (Rosen, 1982, p. 25)

I believe that Erickson applied the same approaches to teaching therapists how to think as he did to treating patients. In both situations, the goal was to teach us how to handle problems and how to think. In order to do this, he indicated, "First you model the patient's world. Then you role-model the patient's world" (Rosen, 1982, p. 35). Frequently the modeling and role-modeling were done through the medium of storytelling, through the use of teaching tales.

When Erickson told his stories, we, his audience, in the manner of Indian children listening to an elder telling tribal tales, were enchanted, enthralled—hypnotized, in fact. He felt, and the results confirmed, that people are most open to learning when in a trance state. Thus, he would put us into a trance and provide himself as a role-model of someone who knew how to think and how to handle problems. When I once asked him what he would do when he ran into a problem that he could not solve, he role-modeled there, too, answering, "I turn it over to my unconscious mind." In other words, when he could not handle a problem in his usual state of consciousness, he would enter into a trance and find his answers there.

It seems that Erickson applied the same process to thinking as did my son, when, at age four, I once asked him what he wanted to do and he answered, "I'll have to ask my mind."

Obviously, just going into a trance by itself will not necessarily lead to solution of problems. When I am teaching automatic writing and direct students to simply go into a trance and write whatever comes, they frequently come up with very global statements, such as "LOVE EVERY-THING."

There are different kinds of thinking: There is the thinking that enables us to approach tasks and causes us to feel interested in or motivated toward the accomplishment of these tasks. There is the thinking that constitutes a kind of inner entertainment that is satisfying in itself, as an activity in itself. Like the thinking about thinking that I did as I was writing this article.

How then, did Erickson instruct us to think effectively and usefully? "Take a good book," he suggested, "by an author you like and respect, and read the last chapter first. Then speculate about what is in the chapter before that. Then read that chapter and speculate about what was in the chapter before that . . . ," (personal communication, 1977) and so on. In other words, think of your goal first. Subordinate everything else to that. When you go into trance, indicate your goal to your unconscious mind and then work backward until you reach your first steps.

"Learn from experience, not from books" (personal communication, 1977), Erickson told me. The study of philosophy may be interesting but it does not teach anyone how to think. We must discover the modes and ways of thinking that work for us — that is, that enable us to function best, to feel good about ourselves, that make us feel that we are ourselves.

In order to think about a particular issue or to think in a certain way, we need to enter into the state in which we can best do the appropriate kind of thinking. In other words, we need to access the learnings that are associated with the required state. We may enter into a general hypnotic state by utilizing one or more of the inductions that I have alluded to, and then we may focus on a switch or several switches that evoke more specific learnings.

For example, if I want to enter into an article-writing state, I may first sit at a particular desk or table that I have associated with this task. This alone may act as a "switch" to evoke the state. If not, I may go through some preparatory ritual — e.g., clearing the desk, having pens and paper available, perhaps in a special place. I will then enter into a trance simply by focusing attention on the paper, the pen tip, or the computer screen. I do not have to spell out for my unconscious mind the request: "I would like to come up with and record the most relevant, comprehensive material and do it in the clearest, best organized, most easily comprehended form." My unconscious mind is already aware that I want these things.

I remember the advice that Elie Wiesel once gave me about writing: "The problem is not that you do not have enough to say but you have too much to say. And if you edit yourself you block yourself. So write out everything that comes to you, without judgment, put it aside for awhile, and then edit it the way you would edit the work of a stranger."

Or putting the above into the language that I have been discussing, "Go into a free-associating state, with the understanding that whatever emerges will relate to the topic you are addressing. Record what comes. Later enter into an editing state."

If I were not able to enter into the desired state, I might add some conscious suggestions or requests to my unconscious mind. For example, I might remind myself of the suggestion that Erickson gave himself when he was asked, at the last minute, to speak at a college commencement: "I know how to speak." I could change this to: "I know to write." I also could add other suggestions such as: "You have all the time that you need to think about this subject, in this case the subject of thinking itself, and to come up with some ideas that may be helpful to others also."

You will note that I am careful to avoid making too heavy demands on my unconscious, as I might have when I was younger, demands that were connected with trying to be brilliant or even to have the last word to say on this, or any other subject. My life experience has taught me that this is not likely to happen and that even if it were possible it would not be desirable. At the same time, I have learned to value my unconscious mind sufficiently to know and expect that it can and will fulfill the modest request for "some useful ideas," "ideas that may be helpful to others."

Hopefully, the ideas that I have already mentioned will fulfill this request.

How about applying my model to other objects of thinking? How would we apply this model to solving a problem in treatment of a patient? We could enter into a trance by focusing on our memory of the patient's face or his way of breathing, or by focusing on our feeling of confusion or blockage. If we want to or need to go through a more formalized series of steps, we might ask our unconscious mind if it is ready and able to come up with possible solutions. If we have already worked out a way in which our unconscious is able to signal "Yes" or "No," with ideomotor signaling, for example, we would await a "Yes" response (e.g., upward movement of the right thumb). After the "Yes" response, we could notice sensations, mental images, and thoughts, assuming that they are providing the answers.

For example, with a patient who was blocked in dealing with his feelings of having been humiliated by an officer during World War II, I found myself coming up with the image of him shooting the officer. I shared this with the patient, and he began a new profession, that of shooting pictures of objects that are generally ignored—manhole covers, cracked walls, and so on. As he gave value to these objects, his self-esteem rose, especially as his photos were valued by others.

STEPS FOR THINKING ABOUT WHAT TO DO NEXT

1. *Enter into a trance by focusing on any one thing inside or out* — e.g., by focusing on an issue that needs to be decided.

2. *Note what comes to you.* It could be some simple sensation, like the tingling sensations I noticed in my fingers once, when I was experiencing a writing block. It could be a story. Or it could be something as simple as a command, such as, "Do it now."

3. *Ask yourself what the story or the sensations are trying to tell you.* For example, the tingling sensations were present in the spots that would be touched if I were holding a pen.

4. *Act on that command.* Or *utilize the new information.* After writing a few sentences with a pen, I was able to go back to using a typewriter.

We limit ourselves so much. Erickson said, "Most of your life is unconsciously determined" (Rosen, 1982, p. 25). These unconscious self-limitations prevent us from "thinking big," for example. Yet there are some people who think big automatically. "Think and grow rich." It does not take only thinking big. One must also develop one's abilities and skills and be willing and able to make the effort required. But, if one does not dare to think about thinking big, even with effort, one will stop short of really "growing rich." One will be frightened by the prospect of success and will subsequently stop short, often far short, of achieving it.

One way of going beyond learned limitations is to play, to make-believe, to tell ourselves that whatever we do or say is not serious and that we won't be held to account for it. This, by the way, is generally a good way to think creatively. And why should we not think creatively all the time? We won't wear out our ability to think. In fact, we will sharpen it.

You may well ask, "How do I go about doing this?" Or, as a therapist, "How can I help my patients do this?"

One way is to go back to the beginnings of your learning. Apply the principle that is mentioned in the Early Learning Set Induction. "Many of the things that you now do automatically once required conscious mental effort." Therefore, to change a pattern of indecisiveness, go into a light trance when you need to make a decision — e.g., ordering in a restaurant, or deciding what movie you want to see. You can do this simply by focusing attention on the question itself: "What would I like to order?" This constitutes focusing attention on one thing. You may have to do this a dozen times, on a dozen different occasions, before the process becomes automatic, but when you discover that it is, you will experience a wonderful feeling of delight. The conscious mental effort of putting yourself into a trance and querying your unconscious mind will have been well rewarded.

In general, Erickson gave us many guides that can help us to think more flexibly, with more openness. We can stretch our minds by solving puzzles, by thinking of as many ways as is possible of accomplishing different tasks, by using certain words. For example, one can think about how many different ways we could use the word "No," or how many ways we could go from one room to another. Or we can try to solve one of Erickson's favorite puzzles: How would you plant 10 trees in 5 rows, 4 in a row? (Answer: A 5-pointed star.)

We can look at things from different perspectives. Betty Erickson gave me an old book that Erickson liked to give out. It is titled, "Topsys and Turvys" and is made up of pictures, with subtexts. When turned upside down, the pictures change and the subtexts complete a two-line poem. For example, one caption reads, "The Malay pirate eyed his foes in hopeless fierce despair." When turned upside down, the picture is different and is described by a caption reading, "Till — bang! — his magazine blew up, and hurled the crew in air" (Newell, 1964).

Looking at optical illusions can help us to loosen up our mental processes. Practicing the exercises in books such as Reid J. Daitzman's *Mental Jogging* (New York: Marek, 1980) may be helpful.

All the exercises and approaches I have mentioned are best done, I have found, when you enter into a trance. As usual, the trance can be attained by focusing attention on one thing, which could be some aspect of the puzzle, or on the illusion itself.

So — Read good books. Listen to good music. Associate with good people.

I say the above with the realization that each of us will have his or her idea of what is good. The principle that I am emphasizing is: "Positive input is important."

We don't really know much about thinking, just as we don't know much about hypnosis. Forty years ago I concluded that if I could understand hypnosis, I would be able to understand thinking. Since then I — and you — have learned something about both. I suppose that hypnosis can be thought of as some form or way of thinking. We have learned more about the neurological underpinnings of thinking. For example, we know something about left and right brain functioning. We are learning about neurotransmitters. But, I'm afraid that I still feel the same way. I'm still hoping that some real understanding will be attained in my lifetime. Meanwhile, I'm enjoying applying the bit of understanding I have achieved — for the enrichment of my life and that of others.

REFERENCES

Beahrs, J. O., and Humiston, K. E. (1972) Dynamics of experiential therapy. *American Journal of Clinical Hypnosis, 17*(1):2.

Damon S.F. (1971) *A Blake dictionary.* New York: Dutton.

Erickson, M.H., and Rossi, E.L. (1979) *Hypnotherapy: An exploratory casebook.* New York: Irvington.

Hilgard, E.R. (1968) *The experience of hypnosis.* New York: Harcourt Brace Jovanovich.

Keynes, G. (ed.) (1969) *Complete writings of William Blake, with variant readings.* Oxford: Oxford University Press.

Newell, P. (1964) *Topsys and turvys.* New York: Dover.

Orne, M. (1962) On the social psychology of the psychological experiment: With particular reference to demand characteristics and their implications. *American Psychologist, 17:*776–783.

Rosen, S. (1982) *My voice will go with you:* The teaching tales of Milton Erickson. New York: Norton.

CHAPTER 23

How to Deal with Resistance to Induction by Refusing to Identify It

Robert E. Pearson

Although almost all of the ideas presented in this chapter stem from Milton Erickson and were elaborated by me, I do not mean to imply that other therapists should copy Erickson, me, or anyone else; they must find out what works for them. Over the years I have refined those that work best for me, and so must others. I found very early that I could not get results by copying verbatim what I had heard Milton say. At least once, on hearing me report one of my successes, he smiled and said that he wasn't sure that he could "get away" with what I had done. And that is what Milton wanted—that each of us should develop our own ways of handling the variety of problems presented to us. I will not apologize for my use of the first person singular in this chapter, but these are the things that work for *me*.

At the Seminars on Hypnosis and American Society of Clinical Hypnosis (ASCH) workshops of the 1950's and 1960's, Milton demonstrated the phenomena of deep hypnosis and how to deal with resistance to induction. The demonstrations were displays of brilliance, seeming to border on the magical and obviously well beyond any of our poor capabilities. Most of us were reluctant to ask for explanation in public, probably for fear of appearing to be stupid, but some of us did ask in private afterward. He seemed to be mystified when we said that the demonstrations were not clarity personified (a most reasonable presumption, since few attendees had asked questions), but then he did answer questions with great patience.

My solution to learning more was to tape the sessions (audio only in those days), then spend hour after hour at home listening for clues to explain what I had seen and heard. When a possible explanation occurred to me, I would write to him, speculating that he had said "A" in order to elicit "B" because ——. I received polite answers saying that I was not quite correct, but he would welcome my trying again. He must have recognized the bulldog in me. I wouldn't quit. I became a pest. But I did slowly begin to learn. And I began to learn to learn, particularly by really watching and really listening to my patients, and gained enough confidence to demonstrate dealing with resistance at workshops.

Some patients *consciously* resist the induction of hypnosis. Their behavior seems to say, "You can't make me go into a trance," or, "I dare you to try to make me do something." I call this a *defiant* patient, not a resistant one.

If a defiant patient tells me, through any of the many ways of communicating, that I can't make him/her go into a trance, I immediately agree, and add that I can't *make* him/her do anything; in fact, I would strongly resist being given such power. Sometimes, I even add that if I ever had had the delusion that I could control others, raising six children had thoroughly disabused me of that notion long ago.

Even if I could make a patient go into a trance, I wouldn't. I have no right to intrude on any patient's wishes, or even to decide what is best for that person. I may make a strong plea for change, but it is the patient's decision to do so.

If I suspect that a patient is being defiant, even though that person says he wants to learn trance, I offer to go back over how I see the relationship between the operator/facilitator/therapist and the subject/patient/client, explaining that it is something he learns to do, not something done *to* him. Most will listen and ask more questions, then settle down and learn, but a very interesting small number, even after another detailed explanation, will still refuse to go on. This is, of course, their perfect right.

So I leave the defiant patient to those who believe that hypnotize is an active verb.

I think of the *resistant* patient as one who *wants* to learn trance and seems to have reasonable motivation to do so, but something has been "getting in the way" of reaching that goal.

Often these are people who have tried a number of times before, and can't seem to get the hang of it. Now, they expect to fail again. In these cases, my orientation is that it is *our* task (the patient and the therapist, working together) to allow the trance to happen.

Please note that the last sentence contains a basic idea that I use repeatedly — that trance is a natural state that will happen if neither the patient nor the therapist "gets in the way." One of my frequent phrases is, "Let it happen. Don't interfere with it." A person can't *go into* a trance any more than she can *go to* sleep, in the active sense of that verb. In both cases, we create a milieu in which the goal is likely to happen, and then just expect that behavior will follow.

I don't believe that, or act as if, difficulty in going into trance is the result of resistance in the psychoanalytic sense. I'm reasonably certain that we are all of the products of everything that has ever happened to us, plus our reactions to those events and others' reactions to our reactions, etc. But I don't find that concept useful in dealing with *this* problem.

INDUCTION PROBLEMS AND MY SOLUTIONS TO THEM

First, you and the patient must decide whether or not you should invest more time and money in learning/teaching trance. At least in psychotherapy, if using hypnosis is the only way you know how to handle a problem, you shouldn't be treating that person.

The following problems are listed in approximate order of occurrence, although that order seems to change from time to time:

1. Patients resistant to induction often have confused induction and utilization of trance. For example, people seeking help in quitting smoking or losing weight may have the mistaken notion that if they learn to go into trance they will then have no choice but to quit smoking or lose weight. In my experience, people are ambivalent about changing; if they were completely convinced that they should do something, they wouldn't need therapists. The facts are that smokers get enjoyment from smoking and all healthy people like to eat. If the patient comes to the therapist believing that induction leads to utilization, and then learns trance, compliance is likely. Therefore, this type of resistance should not be overtly identified as a problem until there is difficulty in induction and the induction/utilization bind is known to be the cause.

If I have identified this as a problem, my customary verbalization goes something like, "It seems to me that you believe that if you learn hypnosis you will then *have to* quit smoking. Let me assure you that even if you learn hypnosis, you will still have to decide whether or not you really want to quit." At this point, many patients go on to learn trance; some utilize it well, some don't.

2. Be sure that the patient understands your ideas about the patient/therapist relationship, e.g., that trance is something they learn to do, not something that is done to them. There is a great deal of misunderstanding about hypnosis. Be sure you're both singing from the same hymnal. Rein-

force the idea that it is a mutual problem that requires a cooperative solution.

3. If the patient's previous failure was with another therapist, ask for details about the experience (who, when, why, etc.). Also ask what seemed to go wrong. Often the patient will tell you astonishing things that happened. Often you will get clues about things you should avoid.

One patient told me that a well-known therapist had spent several sessions insisting that she visualize certain things. She told him she didn't have a visual imagination and could not do what he seemed to demand. I asked her to call my attention to anything I said that seemed to demand "seeing" anything and I proceeded to speak of auditory and tactile sensations only. She quickly entered a deep trance and learned to use it. In a way, the previous therapist did me a favor; the patient was able to tell me what *not* to do.

4. If the patient's previous experience was with you, ask what *did* happen during your verbalization. Ask what seemed to help, what didn't seem to make any difference, and particularly what seemed to interfere with what you both wanted to happen.

One of my first patients had a great deal of difficulty learning trance, in spite of high motivation to do so. After several sessions in which nothing seemed to happen, I taped my verbalization and played it back to her at the next session, asking that she pay particular attention to what happened each time I said something. About five minutes into the tape, she signaled me to stop the tape and said, "The first time you asked me to feel the chair supporting my back, I felt a slight tingling in my back. I just noticed that the tingling came back when you said that again on the tape. Is that important?" Within a very few minutes, she was moving the tingling to her fingers, toes, mouth, etc., learned profound anesthesia, and delivered her first baby a few weeks later, using only hypnosis as analgesia.

Ask the patient to critique your technique! It is amazing what helpful hints the patient can give you (even ideas that apply to other patients).

Erickson (1960, p. 7), "after several hours of intensive effort" to teach a subject to go into trance, asked if she could comment on his technique. He said that the offer was "gladly accepted," and she said: "You're talking too fast on *that* point. You should say *that* very slowly and emphatically and keep repeating it. Say *that* very rapidly and wait a while and then repeat it slowly. And please, pause now and then and let me have a rest. And please don't split your infinitives." When he followed these instructions, the patient went into a deep trance.

Milton was capable of doing absolutely terrible inductions and then innocently asking the patient what he was doing wrong. If you ask the patient to critique your verbalization and the patient responds, he/she is really telling you, "If you do *this* and refrain from doing *that,* I will go into a trance." Who could ask for anything more?

5. Be versatile. Be able to switch smoothly from one technique to another. If the patient has not responded to a particular type of induction, either with you or with others, be sure to avoid that technique; it is already associated with failure in that person's mind.

6. Use the double bind freely. Don't ask the patient to wonder whether or not a hand will levitate, but rather *which* hand will.

As strange as this may seem, remember that if you predict something will happen, and it happens, the patient will believe that it happened *because* you predicted it! During the last 10 minutes of an ASCH workshop, a young doctor reminded me that I had told him I would give him special attention because he needed to learn hypnoanesthesia for a procedure to be done the following week, and that I had not done so. I had an airplane to catch, but was well acquainted with techniques to use when you don't have the luxury of taking your time. My verbalization went about like this: "Doctor, please hold your arm out in front of you. Don't think about levitation or anything else you learned here in the past three days. All I want you to do is wonder what that hand is going to do. Is it going to rise? Is it going to drift downward? Is it going to rotate clockwise? Or counterclockwise? Is it going to move to the left? Or to the right? Are the fingers going to extend? Or flex? Is the hand going to combine several of these movements? Or is it *just going to stay where it is?*" Within a few moments, the hand began to move upward, to the patient's right, and to twist clockwise. The doctor smiled broadly and said, "I have an anesthesia in that arm. I can move the numbness to wherever I want it to be. I must be in a deep trance!" And so he was. But he and many other members of the audience also missed the fact that I had named every movement that the hand could make, including not moving at all!

7. Certain induction methods, such as the coin technique and others like it, create situations in which something will happen if you wait long enough. Again, you predict it. It happens, and it is as if it happened because you predicted it.

8. For some patients, group techniques work best. In the days of the Seminars on Hypnosis workshops, inductions were demonstrated with four or five volunteers at a time. After they were seated, they were told that this was to be a demonstration of a certain verbalization, and it was not expected that all of the volunteers would go into trance. Presented with permission to *not* go into trance, all of them usually did.

9. The "My friend John" (Erickson, 1964) technique involves asking the

subject to watch an excellent subject (real or imagined) demonstrate various phenomena of hypnosis. The patient can go along with the demonstration if he/she wishes.

10. One of Milton's continuing admonitions was that students learn to use everything they saw and heard to enhance the induction. One can even use the resistances themselves. One can teach hypnoanesthesia by asking that the patient feel how bad the pain really is, in exquisite detail if necessary, and then giving the patient permission to go back to the previous amount of pain and to allow the pain to be progressively less. Pointing out areas that don't hurt can be helpful. Anxious patients can be asked to show how tense they can really be, then asked to let go of the extra tenseness they have just so nicely demonstrated.

11. Many facilitators think they have to have very deep trances to utilize the phenomena of hypnosis. Often, light trances will do nicely. There is a strong tendency for patients to go deep enough to elicit the phenomena important to them.

12. Comment positively whenever possible. Those of us who saw Milton function over the years heard him say to a subject, "That's right!" so often that we didn't pay attention to it any more. Then, one day, I heard him ask a patient in a trance what color the flowers she was visualizing were. When she named two colors, he said, "That's right!" It suddenly dawned on me that it was highly unlikely that he would be seeing the same colors she was seeing, since he was color blind. That is when I realized that, "That's right" really meant, "You're doing fine. Just as I hoped you would."

About a week before he died, Milton told me that he believed a large factor in his success as an operator was that he learned early to tell patients how fortunate he was to have a patient who learned so easily and well. He wasn't putting them on. They *did* learn easily.

13. If you get bored or discouraged during an induction, STOP! Your voice will give away your feelings.

14. Within reason, be careful what you say; people in a trance can be very literal. About 10 percent of the population do not like to ride elevators, so be sure to ask about closed spaces if you are using imagery involving elevators. At the first sign of discomfort, change to another technique. Some people have been known to "fall through" clouds the operator has asked them to float on. No harm will be done if something like that happens, but it does disrupt an otherwise smooth induction.

15. Milton once described what I have come to think of as the Milton H. Erickson, M.D., bind. He suggested that you could go through any induction procedure and then give the "post-hypnotic" suggestion that when the patient comes out of the trance he will be absolutely convinced

he was not in a trance! Of course, if he does insist that he was not in a trance, he was responding to a post-hypnotic suggestion, so he must have been in a trance. I have never tried that because I'm convinced that I could never carry it off without giggling.

16. You can even ask the patient to resist your attempts to teach him the trance. Then, when he has become really expert at not going into trance, you can ask him to let go of all that new learning and to just let it happen.

I once led a weekly class of psychologists learning about hypnosis. One of them was slightly slower than the others in developing some of the phenomena, and he seemed embarrassed by that. I asked him if he would be my resistant subject since the whole class had not had a chance to work with resistance, and I said that I would appreciate it if he would, until I asked him to change, resist any induction technique he heard from me or the other members of the class. He seemed relieved and readily agreed. Several weeks later, when he began to express regret that he had promised to stay out of trance, I finally said, "OK, Ed, please catch up." It took him only a few moments.

17. Finally, one more possibility: Hans Eysenck (1958, p. 59), in *Sense and Nonsense in Psychology*, recounts the following:

A very determined hypnotist spent several hours on a given subject without inducing any kind of hypnotic reaction whatsoever. Finally, at the end of a three-hour session, he completely lost his temper and shouted at the subject, "For ----'s sake, go to sleep, you -----." The subject immediately fell into a deep trance and was an exemplary subject ever after.

REFERENCES

Erickson, M. H. (1964). The "surprise" and "my-friend-John" techniques of hypnosis: Minimal cues and natural field experimentation. *American Journal of Clinical Hypnosis, 6,* 293–307. (Also found in Rossi, E. (Ed.), *The Collected Papers of Milton H. Erickson on Hypnosis,* Vol. 1 (pp. 340–59). New York: Irvington.

Erickson, M. H. (1960). Transcript from a lecture delivered at an American Society of Clinical Hypnosis Workshop.

Eyseneck, H. (1958). *Sense and Nonsense in Psychology.* Baltimore: Penguin Press.

CHAPTER 24

Ericksonian Applications in the Use of Art in Therapy

Shirley E. Bliss

This chapter explores some effective ways of utilizing Ericksonian applications in the use of art in therapy. Within this framework, a working model has been constructed based on key principles in Erickson's work, which have been adapted to the drawing process in therapy. This model is designed for use in a clinical setting without the induction of formal trance.

Although Erickson is best known for his innovative strategies in hypnotherapy, a significant part of his therapy was done without the induction of trance. Many of the techniques Erickson developed in his work with hypnosis can also be used effectively with or without formal trance states. Beahrs (1971), for example, noted that Erickson used "formal trance induction in less than ten percent of his work. Yet principles of hypnosis and suggestion permeate most of his therapy ..." (p. 73).

AN ERICKSONIAN PARADIGM

This model explores ways of applying some of Erickson's fundamental principles in the special field of therapeutic drawing. The model is designed to be used either as an adjunct to other ongoing therapy or as a therapy in itself. In both cases, the model can be employed without structured inductions of formal or even informal trance. This paradigm thus provides an accessible framework for those therapists who are interested in working with Ericksonian principles and choose for one reason or another not to employ formal trance inductions when using drawing as a tool in therapy.

This model is structured primarily on Erickson's naturalistic and utilization techniques, which Rossi (Rossi & Ryan, 1985) noted "are considered to be the essence of his [Erickson's] approach" (p. xiii) to hypnosis and psychotherapy. To the naturalistic and utilization base, I have added two other hallmarks of Erickson's work: indirect forms of suggestion and everyday trance phenomena. The unconscious aspects of indirect suggestion and everyday trance blend well with the permissiveness of the naturalistic and utilization concepts. Together, they make a potentially effective combination of strategies in therapy.

To make certain that there is a common understanding of these terms as they are employed in this model, they are discussed briefly below. First, the naturalistic approach was described in part by Erickson (1932a/1980) as "the acceptance and utilization of the situation encountered without endeavoring to psychologically restructure it" (p. 168). The permissiveness of this approach allows the subject a wide range of freedom in habitual self-expression. Second, the utilization concept, which is in keeping with a permissive attitude, was defined by Erickson (1932b/1980) as requiring "a willing acceptance of, and cooperation with, an externally suggested or imposed form of behavior which may be either active or passive" (p. 177).

The third group is the indirect forms of suggestion, which are among Erickson's most insightful interventions. Erickson and Rossi (1932e/1980) defined an indirect suggestion

> as one that initiates . . . unconscious processes within subjects so that they are usually somewhat surprised by their own response when they recognize it. More often than not, however, subjects do not even recognize the indirect suggestion as such and how their behavior was initiated and partially structured by it. (p. 455)

Erickson used both indirect and direct suggestion in his work, depending on the needs of the circumstance and the subject. Over the years, however, Erickson developed the concept of indirection into an art in itself, and indirection is now generally regarded as the more effective modality for accessing the subject's unconscious resources.

The question of what constitutes a suggestion and how it might affect mental processing remains an unresolved issue in scientific hypnotic literature. That issue will not be directly addressed here except to recognize its importance and the impact it could have on this model when that question is more definitively resolved. For our purposes, the findings of Erickson will be accepted as working concepts until other scientific data become available.

The fourth category is everyday trance, which is also known as naturalistic trance. Everyday trance can be characterized by seeming withdrawal when the person may be quietly looking off at a distance, or staring at something, or is being absorbed in inner reflection. During such times, the eye blink may slow and the body may tend toward immobility. Everyday trance occurs in a myriad of different forms in normal life situations, which involve focused, concentrated attention. As one example of many, Erickson (Erickson, Rossi & Rossi, 1976) observed that "anyone absentmindedly looking out the window during a lecture is experiencing trance with eyes wide open" (p. 47). The same is true of the person who is absorbed in a television program and does not hear the doorbell ring.

The everyday trance may be less intense and more fleeting than a formally structured trance, but it nonetheless appears to have the possibility of momentarily suspending habitual thinking, and it can provide those therapeutic moments during which suggestions may be more readily accepted. Drawing appears to have the potential for evoking everyday trance phenomena. As such, drawing is an effective medium for the application of Ericksonian principles.

DRAWING AS A THERAPEUTIC TOOL

As a therapeutic tool, drawing works well because it is technically within the grasp of virtually everyone. Any combination of marks on the paper, or in unusual cases no marks at all, can be labelled a drawing. Any drawing performance can constitute a starting point for a discussion of the subject's phenomenological perceptions of the effort. Naive, untutored renderings of drawings seem to express internal processing more directly than drawings by people who have been influenced by formal art techniques.

There may be some similarity between drawing in a waking state and automatic hypnotic writing in their potential for accessing unconscious processes. It may be the ideomotor quality of both waking drawing and automatic writing that enhances their effectiveness as a gateway to accessing intuitive thinking. In his work on ideomotor techniques, for example, Erickson (1932c/1980) concluded that their importance rested

> not in their elaborateness or novelty but simply in the initiation of motor activity, either real or hallucinated, as a means of fixating and focussing the subjects' attention upon inner experiential learnings and capabilities. (p. 138)

To capture this activity in nonautomatic drawing, the time element in performing the drawing task appears to be an important factor. The shorter the time allowed, apparently, the more likely a subject is to draw an image with freedom and without preconception, to "just let it happen." Luthe (1976) in his nonverbal, no-thought painting technique, for example, allowed the subject two minutes to complete a picture. Luthe reasoned that this time limit "minimizes the participation of left hemispheric functions" (p. 54) and opens access to the creative, symbolic processing of the right hemisphere. In practice, I have found that five minutes or so allowed the subject to complete more meaningful images.

Drawing is a highly phenomenological process that has the possibility in therapy of reflecting internal processing, which is outside the subject's immediate conscious awareness. Much remains to be known about the internal processing in the transformation of thoughts and/or emotions into a visual image on paper. Externally, the drawing performance is usually accompanied by a state of focused concentration and reduced awareness of external stimuli. Subjects often have the appearance of being "lost in thought" during this process.

In a phenomenological study of the art process (Bliss & Wilborn, 1992), subjects frequently experienced a sense of unknowingness in the drawing task, i.e., not knowing consciously what they were going to express in the drawing. Even when subjects had a general concept of the idea to be expressed, they were usually without a clear perception of how the drawing would develop on paper or in what order. There were also moments in the drawing task when subjects reported that the pastels seemed to have taken on a "life of their own."

Mills and Crowley (1986) noted that dissociation "naturally occurs as a result of the drawing process" (p. 174). The transfer of the image to paper separates it from the person, thereby objectifying it and making it easier for the subject to deal with its implications. Viewing the finished drawing at a distance also enhances the state of objectivity and offers the subject an opportunity to see the image/problem from another perspective, both psychologically and physiologically.

Drawings also represent personal metaphors that can be utilized therapeutically, in part or as a whole, to communicate with the subject on multiple levels. These images also serve as a resource for creating other metaphors in the subject's own language and perception of self and others. As more pictures are drawn in the course of therapy, each may add other perspectives to the subject's metaphorical view of the world. The content of the subsequent pictures may also indicate the degree to which therapeutic measures have been integrated into the life pattern.

Subjects generally accept that the content of a drawing mirrors a part of self. To enhance the exploration of the self, the therapist creates an accepting environment in which there are no "right" or "wrong" drawings. Whatever is put on paper is positively regarded as acceptable for what is being done at the time. Whatever the subject chooses to see in the drawing, which will in all probability be different from what is seen by the therapist, reveals that person's reality. That perspective gives important clues to that person's internal processing of events, which can then be redefined, with the help of the therapist, into a more therapeutic view.

THE ROLE OF THE THERAPIST

In the process of redefinition, a primary goal of the therapist is to create a favorable environment in which subjects can focus attention on inner experiential learnings. This kind of ambiance is intended to give subjects an opportunity to learn to cope with their difficulties in ways that are compatible with their inner view of reality.

To obtain a clearer focus of a subject's reality, the therapist shifts the primary role of the interpretation of the significance of the drawing to the subject. By so doing, the therapist indirectly conveys the idea that the subject has unique insights and consequently an active role in the therapy. This idea often transmits to the subject a sense of having untapped resources that can, in turn, be personally empowering.

After the content of the drawing has been thoroughly discussed, the therapist can expand the interpretation of the image to an exploration of what is *not* in the drawing. The technique of examining the nonexistent part tends to encourage the subject to focus inward in search of new meanings. If the drawing is a thematic problem task, e.g., where the subject is in coping with a specific situation, the therapist can ask the subject to sketch a mental imaginary drawing of what the next step might be in coping with the issue. Another imagined sketch could consist of what the picture would look like in a week, or at another date. The number of pertinent imaged sketches is limited primarily by time and their usefulness.

In each case the subject is asked to describe the imagined picture in some detail and is questioned about its content and possible significance. When a subject says, for example, "I want to find the real me that I know is there," the therapist can ask that person to draw a picture of the "real me" that *is* there. After that image has been mentally sketched, a number of drawings can be imagined about how the subject could achieve that goal. The utilization of such imaginative skills in therapy provides another pathway for bypassing the subject's habitual patterns of thinking and opening up new possibilities on an unconscious level.

If the subject is resistant, or simply unable to cooperate by seeing some personal significance in the drawing, that behavior is accepted and incorporated into the therapy. The subject can be told that people may not fully understand immediately the significance of what has been drawn, but when one thinks about it over the following week, new ideas may come to mind to give a more complete understanding of its meaning. This suggestion indirectly enhances the possibility that the subject will think about the drawing over the next week. Any additional ideas that occur will probably be different and may provide a broader understanding of the significance of the drawing.

When the subject is unable to relate to a problem situation, Erickson's My-Friend-John technique (Erickson & Rossi, 1932d/1980) is a useful approach to inspire a subject to explore possible solutions to a problem. In this technique, the subject is asked to imagine that a friend, who is invisible but present, has the problem. The subject is then asked to advise his/her friend on various ways the problem could be successfully resolved. Subjects are generally creative in suggesting to others solutions for resolving their own problems.

BASIC THERAPEUTIC STRATEGIES

The guiding strategies adapted for this Ericksonian model are *reframing* (Erickson & Rossi, 1979; Rossi & Ryan, 1985), *seeding* (Haley, 1973; Zeig, 1990), and *indirect forms of suggestion* (Erickson & Rossi, 1932e/1980). Reframing and seeding are natural extensions of the naturalistic and utilization concepts. Indirect suggestion is a complementary strategy in that it "permits the subject's individuality, previous life experiences, and unique potentials to become manifest" (Erickson & Rossi, 1932e/1980, p. 455) in the process of therapeutic change. These guiding strategies have been developed in detail in the literature on Erickson's work, and they are consequently presented here only in brief summary form.

The basic strategy of reframing or the creation of frames of reference is used primarily in this model as a tool in facilitating new therapeutic response patterns. Rossi (Rossi & Ryan, 1985) describes the reframing process as *"reorganizing and reinterpreting the significance and meaning in a person's life experience so that potentials and behavior could be utilized and expressed in a more felicitous manner"* (p. xiv). In this strategy it is important that the therapist accept the subject's view of any given situation to be reframed. The therapist then alters the context in which that situation is cast so that the subject perceives the same situation in a different and more positive perspective. In other words, reframing is an interpretation of the original situation in a way that provides the subject with new possibilities for more therapeutic responses.

The case of an injury of Erickson's son Robert, who at the age of three split his lower lip and had dental complications (Rossi & Ryan, 1985, pp. 7-10), offers a useful example of reframing. Erickson first acknowledged the pain of the immediate situation and then indicated that the pain would get better in a little while. In the next steps, Erickson reframed the distressing and frightening aspects of the situation into an intense focus of attention on counting the number of stitches Robert would have, in the hope of exceeding the number his older siblings had proudly displayed in their previous injuries. In Erickson's words, "so it became not a task in which he avoided feeling pain; it became a task in which he insisted on his right to as many stitches as possible" (Rossi & Ryan, 1985, p. 10).

A second basic strategy of the therapist is the "seeding" of ideas, which was noted by Haley (1973) and later elaborated by Zeig (1990). Seeding can be used in a number of different ways, but its underlying purpose is to introduce an idea at some point in therapy that will serve as a preparation or connecting bridge for a later intervention. The therapist gives the subject a direct or indirect reference at some prior time in therapy that prepares the subject for the presentation, if appropriate, of a later therapeutic response. Such ideas may be generated by the therapist, but they are more often gathered from clues presented by the subjects in their verbal and/or nonverbal behavior.

After the idea has been presented, the therapist can elaborate the concept as needed in succeeding sessions to bring about change in small successive steps. The seeding technique provides an opportunity to establish continuity in therapeutic themes from one session to another. In this context, seeding creates a sense of progression toward therapeutic goals. The seeding technique can be seen as a process of foreshadowing and is therefore most frequently future-oriented.

The case of a short, unattractive young woman who weighed 250-260 pounds and sought treatment for weight loss illustrates Erickson's use of seeding as an integral part of other interventions (Bliss & Erickson Klein, 1990). Initially Erickson agreed with the subject's negative self-evaluation, while seeding ideas of future improvement. Part of the treatment, which focused on the seeded ideas, involved a series of therapeutic homework assignments requiring extensive reading on the variety of human forms and the formulation of a personal metaphor of beauty. Over a 12-month period, the subject gradually reduced her weight to 150 pounds, improved her appearance generally, and adopted a more positive view of self.

The principal strategies of the therapist in this model are the indirect forms of suggestion that are, according to Erickson and Rossi (1979), the "semantic environments that facilitate the experience of new response possibilities" (p. 19; italics added). The forms of indirect suggestion discussed by Erickson and Rossi (1932e/1980) that have been incorporated into this model are: (1) indirect associative focusing; (2) truism; (3) implication; and (4) open-ended suggestion. Examples of these forms of suggestion are found in Table 1.

TABLE 1

Indirect Forms of Suggestion

Indirect Associative Focusing (About Drawing)

People are fascinated by the learnings they find in drawings.

One image recalls others that may be meaningful.

It is interesting the ways the inner self speaks on paper.

Each drawing may uncover new things that have not been seen before.

Looking at a drawing may bring other thoughts to mind, maybe now or later.

It is interesting how one learns from a drawing.

Drawings can relate to things that are about the past, present, and future.

Lines and shapes can be seen in different ways. A drawing might be one thing today and another tomorrow, or next week.

One image may add to another and give a better understanding.

A drawing may tell even more than can be immediately understood.

Implication

If you wonder about this over the next week, then you will find an answer that helps you to resolve this issue.

If you remember an experience, then you will also become aware of other thoughts that will be helpful.

If you explore any question further, then you will better know how to deal with it.

If you don't solve a problem one way, then you will know to use another.

If you choose to think in positive terms, then you will have some positive results.

If you think of yourself as worthwhile, then you will appreciate yourself more.

If you plant good seeds, then you will have taken an important step.

If you have done something once, then the experience will be a part of you.

If you choose a path of moderation, then you will walk in balance.

If you sow enough seeds, then some of them are sure to grow.

Truism

Believing in your potential is important.

Knowing you can do something can lead you to do it.

Keeping objectives in mind is a way to attain them.

Being able to forgive yourself and others promotes inner harmony and peace.

Learning as a step-by-step process can lead to new discoveries.

Practicing new habits makes them become old habits.

Dealing with issues one at a time can make problem solving more manageable.

Knowing which steps you need to take brings goals within reach.

If you have done something before, you may have some ideas about how to do it again.

Each time you solve a problem, the new learning becomes a part of you.

TABLE 1 *(Continued)*

Indirect Forms of Suggestion

Open-Ended Suggestion

It is always interesting to see where people begin to expand their self-confidence.

Sometimes difficulty is an opportunity to learn something new and exciting.

Something that may seem to be a mistake can really contain valuable lessons for the future.

Everyone has creative abilities that are useful in dealing with the everyday challenges of life.

Other ideas may come to you later today, tomorrow, or even next week.

As people begin to wonder about things, they may discover things that they didn't know that they knew.

Everyone can be interested in experiencing the new ways in which they become stronger.

As people do more things, they will become more aware of their abilities.

Every new experience can be a learning experience.

Becoming peaceful with the past can lead to contentment with the future.

One of the principal values of these forms lies in the ways they stimulate exploration of new pathways in thinking that go beyond the habitual patterns of conscious behavior. The everyday quality of these forms makes them seem like casual exchanges in therapy so that they are usually readily accepted by subjects.

The *indirect associative focusing* form of indirect suggestion raises a topic without direct reference to the subject, which generally has the effect of causing that person to begin thinking of the same topic in personal terms. When Erickson wanted someone to think about his/her mother, Erickson would talk about his mother. Although virtually any topic can be the basis of associative focusing, in this model, associative focusing has been used primarily to draw attention to the unconscious aspects of the drawing process. The therapist, for example, could say, "A drawing can give another perspective," which ideally would lead the subject to think about other possible considerations in the meaning of the image.

The underlying purpose of this kind of focusing suggestion is to encourage the subject to recognize that the drawings reflect valid aspects of self that can be transformed into available resources for coping with difficult situations. The associative focusing is also designed to provide a wide array of possibilities for the subject to explore. These suggestions are usually projections into the future to encourage the subject to think about the therapeutic meaning of the drawing beyond the session. If an image deals with the resolution of a specific problem, for example, the therapist could suggest that images in drawings often recall others that can be meaningful.

A *truism* is an observation of a simple, generally accepted fact, such as knowing you can do something can lead to doing it. Truisms are both disarming and reinforcing statements. The universality of such expressions usually make them readily recognized and accepted. Truisms tend to validate the subject's experiences as well as reinforce the credibility of the therapist's comments. The truism therefore contributes to greater trust in the therapeutic relationship. Truisms can also open the subject to other options if the therapist were to say, for example, "Learning is a step-by-step process that can lead to new discoveries."

Truisms furthermore never wear out; they can be used repeatedly in many variations. The "secret" is finding the truisms that facilitate the subject's inner search. If a truism is off mark, however, it simply becomes an interesting, valid statement in casual conversation. No harm is done, and an idea may have been planted that can be recalled at some future time.

The form of *implication* used in this model is constructed on the "if . . . then" clause. Such statements tie two actions together, and the second action flows from the first by implication. In the example, "If you explore a question further, *then* you will better understand how to deal with it," greater understanding results from further exploration.

When the subject accepts the first part of the statement as being true, it follows that the second part is also true. The latter part of the statement is designed to bypass usual frameworks of thinking and to facilitate a search of unconscious resources. In the example given immediately above, the subject ideally would achieve a broader understanding of the problem on an unconscious level that could lead to new ways of thinking about it.

The *open-ended suggestion* allows the subject a wide freedom of choice within a broad framework of ideas. Its effectiveness lies largely in its capacity to cover many contingencies in a general situation. If poor self-concept is an issue, the therapist can suggest that everyone has unused abilities that could be put into action when they are needed. An open-ended suggestion implies that the subject will do something, but what is done is of the subject's own choosing. The open-ended suggestion offers a range of unspecific possibilities from which the subject can select those responses that are the most useful.

Finally, in all of these forms of indirect suggestion, the therapist offers the subject a wide range of choice. It is important that the therapist keep in mind that the effectiveness of the indirect forms of suggestions is measured not by the complexity or simplicity of the ideas presented but by the degree to which the subject accepts and acts upon those ideas.

SUMMARY

In conclusion, this Ericksonian working model has shown promise as an effective method of using drawing in therapy in a naturalistic setting, i.e., without the induction of formal trance states. Research that is currently underway on this model may provide some light on the nature and process of this effectiveness.

REFERENCES

Beahrs, J. O. (1971). The hypnotic psychotherapy of Milton H. Erickson. *American Journal of Clinical Hypnosis,* 14, 73-90.

Bliss, S., & Erickson Klein, R. (1990), M. H. Erickson's interventions in an Adlerian context: Treatment of eating disorders. *Individual Psychology,* 14, 473-480.

Bliss, S., & Wilborn, B. (1992). The art process in therapy. *TCA Journal,* 20, 3-8.

Erickson, M. H. (1932a/1980). Naturalistic techniques of hypnosis. In E. L. Rossi (Ed.), *The collected papers of Milton H. Erickson on hypnosis. I. The nature of hypnosis and suggestion.* New York: Irvington, 168-176.

Erickson, M. H. (1932b/1980). Further clinical techniques of hypnosis: Utilization techniques. In E. L. Rossi (Ed.), *The collected papers of Milton H. Erickson on hypnosis. I. The nature of hypnosis and suggestion.* New York: Irvington, 177-205.

Erickson, M. H. (1932c/1980). Historical note on the hand levitation and other ideomotor techniques. In E. L. Rossi (Ed.), *The collected papers of Milton H. Erickson on hypnosis. I. The nature of hypnosis and suggestion.* New York: Irvington, 135-138.

Erickson, M. H., & Rossi, E. L. (1932d/1980). The "surprise" and "my-friend-John" techniques of hypnosis: Minimal cues and natural field experimentation. In E. L. Rossi (Ed.), *The collected papers of Milton H. Erickson on hypnosis. I. The nature of hypnosis and suggestion.* New York: Irvington, 340-359.

Erickson, M. H., & Rossi, E. L. (1932e/1980). The indirect forms of suggestion. In E. L. Rossi (Ed.), *The collected papers of Milton H. Erickson on hypnosis. I. The nature of hypnosis and suggestion.* New York: Irvington, 452-477.

Erickson, M. H., & Rossi, E. L. (1979). *Hypnotherapy: An exploratory casebook.* New York: Irvington.

Erickson, M. H., Rossi. E. L., & Rossi, S. (1976). *Hypnotic realities.* New York: Irvington.

Haley, J. (1973). *Uncommon therapy: the psychiatric techniques of Milton H. Erickson, M.D.* New York: W. W. Norton.

Luthe, W. (1976). *Creativity mobilization technique.* New York: Grune & Stratton.

Mills, J. C., & Crowley, R. J. (1986). *Therapeutic metaphors for children and the child within.* New York: Brunner/Mazel.

Rossi, E. L., & Ryan, M. O. (Eds.) (1985). *Life reframing in hypnosis: The seminars workshops, and lectures of Milton H. Erickson.* II. New York: Irvington.

Zeig, J. K. (1990). Seeding. In J. K. Zeig & S. G. Gilligan (Eds.), *Brief therapy: Myths, methods and metaphors.* New York: Brunner/Mazel, 221-246.

CHAPTER 25

Using Paradox in Hypnosis and Family Therapy

Camillo Loriedo & Gaspare Vella

INTRODUCTION

Despite the fact that paradox is one of the oldest and most central concepts in both hypnosis and family therapy, there is a striking absence of references to paradox in the current literature. To explain this decrease in interest, one could assume that the concept has lost its original validity professionally and is becoming an historical curiosity.

However, therapeutic paradox may be the most widely used intervention in both modern hypnosis and in family therapy. There is a possible explanation of the "paradox" of the therapeutic paradox being widely used but not referenced. In our opinion, it is not the concept that should be considered invalid, but the way in which the concept has been used historically. In particular, we posit that some aspects of paradox have not been explored while others have been overemphasized. For example, pathogenic and therapeutic paradox have not been sufficiently differentiated, and the reason for the efficacy of interventions never has been thoroughly clarified. On the contrary, the importance of paradox as a therapeutic technique and instrument of change probably has been overemphasized.

THE IMPACT OF THE ERICKSONIAN CONCEPT OF
RESISTANCE ON THE USE OF PARADOX

According to many authors (Anderson & Stewart, 1983; Haley, 1980; Madanes, 1984), therapeutic paradox should be used in the treatment of difficult, particularly resistant, families and patients. The traditional conception of resistance presupposes that patients and families resist therapeutic change and the therapist's exploration. The family/patient is seen as reluctant to change and unwilling to expose the material the cure requires: According to these premises, resistant patients and families are considered tricky and insincere.

In the traditional view of resistance, therapy was especially aimed to solve the patients' tricks and to unmask their insincerity. The initial success of therapeutic paradox was due to the fact that it appeared to be an elegant solution to these problems. For a long time paradox was considered the ultimate key to overcome patients' and families' tricks and insincerity.

Therapist's paradoxes primarily consisted of prescriptions suggesting symptomatic and other undesired behaviors; thereby, resistance would be defeated and patients would reach the desired change. Paradox was a sophisticated trick to defeat the patient's tricks.

The pioneering work of Milton H. Erickson, M.D., has deeply changed the concept of resistance and redefined it as a behavior that "should be respected rather than regarded as an active and deliberate, or even unconscious, intention to oppose the therapist ... resistance should be openly accepted, in fact graciously accepted, since it is a vitally important communication of part of their problems" (Erickson, 1964, p. 8).

In the Ericksonian model, resistance is considered a way in which patients and families collaborate with their own treatment according to their needs and interactive patterns. Also, resistance is connected to the symptom and, therefore, is not a deception by individuals and families, but an honest manifestation of their own distress.

As Erickson's concept of resistance took over, the old idea of therapeutic paradox gradually became outmoded. The rationale of using paradox as a trick to defeat individual and family tricks collapsed when it was clear that there was not a real opposition to therapy, but a particular form of collaboration that the therapist should respect and encourage. Hence, we should now have a more modern view of paradox coherent with the new concept of resistance proposed by Erickson. Next, we will provide a definition of paradox that provides a clear distinction between pathogenic and therapeutic paradox and explain the efficacy of paradox in psychotherapy.

DEFINITION OF PARADOX

In the initial descriptions (Bateson et al., 1956), pathogenic paradox was essentially considered a form of communicative dysfunction, an obscure and contradictory message able to create a bind in the receiver. This definition merely considers the sender's communication and does not really take into consideration the relationship between sender and receiver. In other words, one of the parents, almost always the mother, is usually blamed because of the incongruous messages sent to the child: Regardless of the relationship with his/her mother, the child who receives this kind of message and is not able to leave the field is expected to become crazy.

Most theorists are now convinced that a single message (even if repeated) is not enough to create dysfunctional behavior in a child. Pathogenic incongruence in the communicative pattern must be complex, since experience with families suggests that simple communicative incongruences are common and well tolerated by the family members.

In our opinion, pathogenic paradox derives from a particular incongruence concerning both the individual and other family members: the tendency of some human beings to think and act in terms of an illegitimate totality. According to this view, an incongruous message will not produce pathology unless it is illegitimately considered a totality.

The young boy who receives from his mother the message, "You should enjoy life," and goes to a party where he meets a nice and attractive young girl, may ask himself, "Did I enjoy my encounter because I like this girl or because of what my mother suggested to me?" Yet, if the boy does not consider the paradoxical message received from the mother as a totality, then he will simply enjoy the party and dismiss the implications of mother's instructions.

Therefore, in order to have a pathogenic paradox, one must concomitantly have a *paradoxical relationship;* that is, a relationship made of two or more persons who think and act in terms of illegitimate totalities. We will then have a *convergence of totalities:* People in the relationship believe that something is a total, an absolute.

This presence of totalities and absolutes is evident when we examine the language patterns of people in pathogenic paradoxes. It is abundant with such terms as "always," "never," "all," "nothing," "everybody," and "nobody." Also, these individuals frequently give suggestions regarding life as a whole (as the above-described mother), and they use absolute terms such as "autonomy," "spontaneity," and "others."

From this perspective, paradox is part of a peculiar type of relationship.

It is not merely a message that comes from one of the parents: If the totality introduced by the parents is not considered a totality by the child, it will not have the power to produce problems or symptoms in the relationship. When an illegitimate totality is shared, it produces an absence of distinctions, boundaries, and hierarchies in that particular relationship, and in so doing creates high risk for interactive dysfunctional patterns and symptomatic behaviors.

We may now define relational paradox as *an inappropriate totalization, shared by the people in the relationship, that tends to establish undecidable relational hierarchy and boundaries.* Therapeutic paradox should, of course, be different since it is supposed to be able to restore proper hierarchy and boundaries. Therapeutic paradox is *an intervention aimed to restore order in the incongruous hierarchy created by the pathogenic paradox.* Table 1 outlines differences between pathogenic and therapeutic paradox (Loriedo & Vella, 1992).

For purposes of this chapter, we emphasize that while pathogenic paradox prescribes an illegitimate totality (e.g., "Be spontaneous," "You should be autonomous," "You should be active"), which the receiver takes very seriously, therapeutic paradox is based, on the contrary, on the prescription of a circumscribed piece of behavior. The therapists's prescription does not suggest everything (a totality), but only what the subject or the family is already doing. The ongoing behavior is therefore prescribed, and the freedom to react to it in every possible way is left to the subject. In other

TABLE 1

Differences Between Pathogenic and Therapeutic Paradox Relationships

Paradoxical Pathogenic Relationship	Paradoxical Therapeutic Relationship
Meaningful and involving	Significant but not too involving
Totalizing	Partial
Repetitive and stereotyped interaction	Changes in the interaction according to the response
Absent or reduced limits: notable duration involves the entire relationship	Clear delimitation: limited duration involves only dysfunctional areas
Objective: change premises tendency to change others no availablity for personal change	Objective: resolve undecidability confirmation of other's behavior availability of the therapist for change

words, the paradoxical interventions *confirm* the individual's and family's behavior, not because they are directed to manipulate people by a therapeutic trick, but because they tend to restore the freedom to make choices in an undecidable relationship based on totalizing assumptions.

PARADOXICAL INTERVENTIONS AND THE ERICKSONIAN MODEL OF PSYCHOTHERAPY

Confirmation

In a previous work (Loriedo & Vella, 1992), we described therapeutic paradox as merely a form of confirmation and explained confirmation as the process of "observing, recognizing, respecting and validating the ongoing interactive behavior" (Loriedo & Vella, 1992, pp. 151-154). Confirmation is the way in which Erickson revolutionized the concept of resistance. Resistance is the right of a patient who wants to be correctly understood and helped, not an opposition to therapy that should be defeated. The supposed opposition will suddenly disappear as soon as the subject and family perceive the therapist as someone who is not trying to change their premises, but instead is collaborating with them.

The Ericksonian model, therefore, will confirm the individual's and family's ongoing patterns, yet will paradoxically require change and flexibility from the therapist. The therapist should, in fact, carefully observe the family and/or individual patterns to (1) have a genuine respect for these patterns; (2) be able to recognize individual and family potentialities; and (3) be ready to adapt to the peculiar individual or system. The therapist's readiness to change is the best possible modeling for the family or individual. It is "the anesthesia for change," as Carl Whitaker in Neill and Kniskern (1982) puts it: Change will not be considered painful by the patient if the therapist is not afraid to afford it.

Utilization

Utilization of symptoms and of other recurrent dysfunctional behaviors is the best way to confirm them. If dysfunctional behaviors are utilized by the therapist, they are, of course, confirmed and respected. They also are considered keys to the problems' solutions rather than difficult problems to be solved. When a dysfunctional behavior is utilized, it maintains its coherence but loses its formal characteristic as a symptom. These formal characteristics are:

a) stereotyped repetition
b) incomprehensibility

    c) involuntary nature

    d) tendency to produce social chaos

A dysfunctional behavior, when utilized, is no longer stereotyped and repetitive because it becomes something that will be utilized when needed, and will not be used when it is not necessary. When it is recognized that the behavior has a specific goal, it will make sense and not be incomprehensible. In order to be utilized, it will be under voluntary control and, therefore, not considered involuntary. Finally, if the dysfunctional behavior is useful, it will not cause social chaos; in fact, it may be a means to restore well being and order. Utilization, then, is respectful of the family and/or individual patterns, but it requires much effort on the part of the therapist, who should find a possible utilization for behaviors that previously appeared to be useless and disturbing.

The therapeutic transformation of symptoms from useless to useful should be convincing for the people who will have to apply the new framing to their lives. For these reasons, the most important part of a therapist's training should be to learn how to find possible useful meanings and applications for behaviors that are generally considered dysfunctional, not just to develop the ability to notice how distressful and destructive a certain behavior is. If the therapist really sees the positive part, the unknown side of the symptom, it will be easier to convince clients to comply with therapy with minimal resistance. A case example illustrates:

CASE ONE   Renata, a pleasant and gentle young woman, requested psychotherapy because of a generalized depressive attitude that made her see life as distressful. Her past experience of what she considered to be a miserable family life and the early loss of her mother convinced her that there was no chance for her to be happy. Even if she received consideration and consolation attempts from her sisters, sadness and dissatisfaction seemed to increase day after day. Some of her fellow college students called her and tried to invite her to dinner, but she unfailingly refused the invitation.

As she described the situation, "Every time someone invites me, I feel worse, and since for me it is difficult to refuse, I do not answer the telephone, or I tell my sister to say that I'm not at home. If I accept the invitation, I feel guilty; if I refuse, I also feel guilty. If for some reason I'm obliged to accept an invitation to a dinner or a party, then I remain silent and withdrawn for the entire evening: It is like I behave in a way that will induce people not to invite me anymore."

After a few sessions it was discovered that Renata's father was even more depressed than his daughter. After his wife died, he retired from work and gradually excluded himself from active life. A few close friends came to visit him, but he very rarely left home and spent his time lying in bed or sitting in his armchair in complete darkness.

Once he revealed to one of Renata's sisters that he would have "decided to die" if his three daughters were autonomous and able to live alone. The father's suicidal pronouncements were never subsequently discussed in the family. Instead, there was a secret agreement among the three sisters to take turns so he was not home alone. On his part, the father tried long and hard to convince his daughters to become independent. Nevertheless, for different reasons, none of the three sisters had serious plans to leave home. Renata, because of her symptoms, spent the greatest part of her time staying home with her father.

During hypnosis, she had an unpleasant dream of being trapped in a tomb together with her father. While she was trying to escape, he seemed to be resigned to his nap. She felt so discouraged by her father's resignation that she gave up, too.

Understanding the useful part of the symptom, the therapist implored Renata not be get rid of her depression because he was afraid that her father would commit suicide if she felt better and became autonomous. Not dating would be the best prevention against her father's suicide. She was acclimated to her secluded life, and to continue the same way would certainly be the safest solution.

Renata immediately disclosed that this appeared to be blackmail. She should be free to leave whenever she wanted. That same evening she openly confronted her father's suicidal ideas and invited him to be courageous enough to kill himself immediately. He became very upset and, for the first time in months, went out, slamming the door and screaming. He came back late in the night.

In the subsequent hypnotic session, she was asked to imagine herself alone in a small room. She commented that the room was closed and that her father was pushing on the outside of the door in order to keep her in.

Two days later, she had another fight with her father and she left home slamming the door. She went to visit a friend and made plans for a trip abroad. The therapist tried to convince her not to go on the trip because of her father's suicidal intentions, and she replied that her father was free to do what he wanted with his life. The therapist then asked if she was sure she would not feel guilty if, while she was abroad, her father committed suicide. She calmly replied that would be his decision and not dependent on her behavior.

Renata enjoyed her trip and when she came back, in her last hypnotic session, she again imaged the little room, but this time she was out of it. Then she looked carefully and saw her sisters inside. She was afraid they could be trapped and she was worried for a while. Then she concluded, "They too should find their way out by themselves."

THE UTILIZATION PARADOX

In the *Utilization Paradox*, as we call this particular form of therapeutic intervention, the behavior described as dysfunctional or symptomatic is observed and recognized in all its details. The therapist asks for a possible way to use it in order for the client to be undisturbed by the undesired consequences of that particular behavior; he does not try to stop or diminish it. It should be noticed that a therapist encouraging or prescribing a symptom will not suggest all possible forms of behavior (illegitimate totality), but only those particular behaviors (legitimate partiality) that clients and families consider the source of their distress and are unable to prevent.

The following clinical example will clarify the application of the utilization paradox to therapy:

CASE TWO   After the first two sessions with a resistant psychotic family, the therapist encountered a difficult problem: The 22-year-old identified patient, Alfredo, refused his appointments, and continued to be delusional and to speak an incomprehensible language. On their part, the family participated in the sessions but demonstrated an uncommon competence in speaking without expressing any clear meaning except in complaining about Alfredo's bizarre behavior.

Every attempt to convince Alfredo to participate in the therapy and to obtain from the family some meaningful interaction ended in failure. Being unable to work in that sort of vacuum, the therapist decided to accept the situation and adopt a utilization approach. In spite of their absurdity, Alfredo's crazy statements appeared more suitable for therapy than the family's logical nonsense.

Alfredo's father, Mr. B., was asked to contact Alfredo and to tell him that the therapist needed some help. If he would not come for the next session, would he send a phrase containing suggestions for the therapy. At the next session, the father reported a phrase pronounced by Alfredo in response to the therapist's request: "He should look in the pillow."

The family was surprised that the mysterious statement was taken seriously by the therapist, who literally accepted Alfredo's suggestion and devoted the entire session to the discussion of the family's pillows.

Mother had a strong preference for a soft pillow and she liked to sleep hugging it. Father's preference was a hard pillow and mattress. Yet, because his wife liked the soft mattress, he placed a wooden board under his part of the bed, which was thus divided into two parts: The hard side was the husband's domain and the soft side was the wife's territory. The division would have been satisfactory if Mr. B. had slept quietly during the night, but the strong anxiety he experienced during the day continued at night, and sometimes his sleep was so agitated that he frequently crossed the boundary and seized his wife's soft pillow. On these occasions, being deprived of her pillow, she could not sleep for the entire night.

Sometimes, she felt so miserable that she got up and took Alfredo's pillow, which was soft enough, and which he never used because he liked to sleep directly on the mattress. Alfredo's brother, Antonio, had his own pillow (not too hard, not too soft), but sometimes he was unable to sleep because he was afraid that someone would exchange pillows purposely or accidentally during the night. Because of this fear, Antonio spent the night trying to prevent an exchange of pillows, and every night before going to bed he inspected his pillow to check if it was someone else's. Alfredo's suggestion, which was initially considered bizarre, gave to the therapist the opportunity to explore, through the metaphor of the pillow, family dynamics previously considered not accessible.

In the next few sessions, therapy proceeded by utilization of Alfredo's "senseless" phrases. This proved to be much more revealing about the family than all the other members' statements obtained in the previous sessions. After some family-hidden feelings and secrets emerged, as if he had finished his indirect job, Alfredo appeared for the first time in a session.

The utilization approach usually centers on a symptom in order to make the symptom itself less absurd, and sometimes really useful for the development of therapy. In Case Two, the symptom also was utilized to overcome the family smokescreen and to obtain the identified patient's *indirect* participation in therapy.

In conclusion, therapeutic paradox respects behaviors that would traditionally be considered *resistance,* and gradually demonstrates that if the therapist is flexible enough to utilize symptoms as strengths and resources, they will prove the best keys to access strengths in individuals and families.

REFERENCES

Anderson, C. M., & Stewart, S. (1983). *Mastering resistance: A practical guide to family therapy.* New York: Guilford.

Bateson, G., Jackson, D. D., Haley, J., & Weakland, J. H. (1956). Toward a theory of schizophrenia. *Behavioral Science, 1,* 521-64.

Erickson, M. H. (1964). An hypnotic technique for resistant patients: The patient, the technique, and its rationale and field experiments. *American Journal of*

Clinical Hypnosis, 7, 8–32. Also found in Rossi, E. (Ed.), *The collected papers of Milton H. Erickson on hypnosis,* Vol. I. (pp. 299–330).

Haley, J. (1980). *Leaving home: The therapy of disturbed young people.* New York: McGraw-Hill.

Loriedo, C., & Vella, G. (1992). *Paradox and the family system.* New York: Brunner/Mazel.

Madanes, C. (1984). *Behind the one-way mirror.* San Francisco: Jossey-Bass.

Neill, J. R., & Kniskern, D. P. (Eds.) (1982). *From psyche to system: The evolving therapy of Carl Whitaker.* New York: Guilford.

CHAPTER 26

Writing Assignments in the Treatment of Grief and Traumas from the Past

Alfred Lange

INTRODUCTION

Mrs. Baum (48) presented for depression and couples therapy. She lived with her husband. Their (only) child had left the house last year. In the first sessions, it emerged that during the past 25 years she had developed a terrible grudge against her husband. Her husband revealed that there were many days that she barely spoke to him. Probing by the therapist revealed the following: Twenty five years ago Mrs. Baum gave birth to a child who lived for only one day. Mrs. Baum was not only upset by the death of the child but even more by what she called the "roughness" of her husband. He had not supported her at all and had even persuaded her to have sex with him on the day the child died. She never got over this and regularly observed that her husband had not changed and still reacted in a "rough" way.

Mr. Baum, the owner of a garage, did not give the impression of being someone who enjoyed hurting his wife or anyone else. He was a bit clumsy in expressing his feelings, but no more than that. He indicated that he did not know what his wife meant and that she had never mentioned this issue before.

The couple seldom fought, which they did not experience as being an asset. Mrs. Baum suppressed her feelings most of the time and expressed her negative feelings only when they were too overwhelming. The couple then fought and Mrs. Baum often threatened divorce. Notwithstanding these facts, there is still mutual affection, which explains why they sought therapy instead of a divorce.

Ann Mills (28) reported for therapy because of increasing social anxiety. Since the breakup a year ago with a boyfriend, she lived alone. She worked as a receptionist in a hotel but had increasing difficulties in doing her job. She was insecure, was unable to assert herself, and had problems maintaining relationships with partners.

After a couple of sessions, it became clear that she had had frightening experiences in her youth. Her father, whom she loved very much, had established an incestuous relationship with her when she was 12. After a year, he broke this relationship and focused his sexual attention on a 15-year-old niece who had come to live in their house. The mother was aware of the situation all along, but merely defended her husband. Both expressed a negative attitude toward young Ann, who tried to get a share of attention and love. This resulted in Ann's increasing withdrawal, the development of an aversion to sexuality, and growing feelings of insignificance.

In this chapter I will discuss how ritualized writing assignments can help patients to overcome traumatic experiences, including traumatic episodes such as those described above. Ritualized writing implies that patients write a letter to a central character about a traumatic situation, in a fixed place and time. Specific instructions as to themes should be included in the writing. First, a theoretical framework for the use of such assignments is discussed; subsequently, I will illustrate the method by means of clinical cases, and, finally, I will describe an experiment in which the method was systematically investigated.

THEORETICAL FRAME OF REFERENCE

Grief, which is classified in the DSM-III-R (APA, 1987) under posttraumatic stress, has become an important topic in psychiatry, clinical psychology, and psychotherapy. Initially, however, attention to the negative effects of grief or posttraumatic stress on psychological dysfunctioning, was found mainly in the psychodynamic literature (Averill, 1968; Bowlby, 1961; Bowlby & Parkes, 1970). Suppression of negative emotions was hypothesized to have negative consequences for the energetic equilibrium of the individual, causing psychological and somatic problems (Abdulla, 1985; Scheff, 1979; Scheff & Bushnell, 1984). Expressing negative emotions was supposed to result directly in a reduction of the intensity of the emotions and an enhancement of psychological functioning. This cathartic model was questioned by Hokanson (1970), whose criticism was taken up by many others, such as Frijda (1986) in his book *The Emotions.*

Further theoretical support for the effectiveness of expressing emotions is provided by learning theory. On the one hand, counterconditioning is supposed to play a role through central constructs such as "avoidance" and "confrontation" (exposure to the most feared stimuli). According to this theory, trauma and grief lead to painful and frightening images. The patient avoids stimuli that evoke these images and thus prevents the extinction of the negative emotions. Repeated exposure to the most frightening images supposedly leads to satiation. Many hypnotic and behavioral techniques are based on this principle (Rochkind & Conn, 1973).

On the other hand, many authors stress the importance of cognitive processes: Expressing emotions is supposed to lead to a "reappraisal" of the events, to a more realistic view, and to change in dysfunctional "automatic thoughts" (Janis, 1958, 1971; Beck, Freeman, et al., 1990; Lazarus, Kanner & Folkman, 1980; Rachman, 1980). This leads to an increase in control and concomitant decrease in helplessness. Inducing cognitive changes has been the main theme in the research by Meichenbaum and his co-authors. They systematically stimulated patients to change negative self-verbalizations to more positive self-verbalizations (Meichenbaum, 1979; Meichenbaum & Cameron, 1974). Frijda (1986), furthermore, stresses that negative emotions persist not only because of avoidance and a lack of self-confrontation, but because of reinforcement from the environment. The manner in which people express their emotions determines whether the emotions are extinguished or reinforced.

THE BEHAVIOR-THERAPEUTIC MODEL FOR OVERCOMING POSTTRAUMATIC STRESS AND GRIEF

In Figure 1 the most important elements of the behavior-therapeutic "confrontation model" for grief and posttraumatic stress are schematically shown.

In the first session, the patient is encouraged to tell his story about the past. By detailed probing, the therapist attempts to achieve two goals: gaining insight into what are experienced as the most painful elements and confronting the patients with these painful stimuli. With Ann Mills, probing by the therapist may have led to the discovery that it was not the incest itself that had been the most painful, but the fact that her father had rejected her when her niece came to live with them. Especially painful were the guilt feelings about this — the fact that she had wanted to continue the incestuous relationship with her father rather than be rejected so

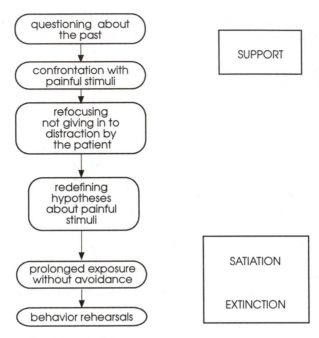

Fig. 1. Overview of the behavior-therapeutic model for overcoming grief and post-traumatic stress.

painfully. The therapy would then concentrate on confronting the patient with the frightening shame and guilt. The therapist would, for instance, ask, "What exactly did you feel and do when you discovered that your father had sexual intercourse with his niece?" In behavior therapy, as in many forums of hypnotherapy, no homework would be given; the confrontation and satiation would be sought entirely during the therapeutic sessions. It is very important in this confrontation model that the context of the sessions be positive and accepting; otherwise, the confrontations would only be unnecessarily difficult and probably unhelpful.

In the following sessions, which take place about twice a week, the behavioral therapist would continue to confront the patient with the most painful images by means of covert sensitization while preventing the patient from using strategies to divert the attention to less painful aspects. Such avoidance was, for instance, displayed by Ann Mills, who tried to avoid talking about the role her father played, how he had hurt her, and how it had affected her. Thus, the therapist tries to focus consistently on the most painful images (prolonged exposure, for example) by requiring

Ann to give a detailed description of the feelings she had experienced when she noticed that her father redirected his attention to his niece. Clearly, hypnotherapy may greatly assist this behavior therapeutic strategy.

In the last phase of the behavioral therapy, the therapist encourages the patient to adopt new behavior and to break with the past helplessness. For example, Ann Mills would have an "imaginary talk" with her father (behavior rehearsal) and tell him what he had done to her, what her feelings were, and how she would react to it in the future.

WRITING ASSIGNMENTS—A POWERFUL AND "FRIENDLY" TECHNIQUE FOR OVERCOMING GRIEF AND POSTTRAUMATIC STRESS

The elements of behavioral techniques are theoretically sound, but in practice they are very demanding for both patient and therapist. Since the process of confrontation is restricted to the duration of actual therapeutic sessions, it is time-consuming for the therapist. Furthermore, the patient has to adapt to the times of the therapy hours instead of working at his problems in his own time. Although ritualized writing assignments are based on the same concept (encouraging the patient to confront the painful images until satiation and extinction occur, followed by cognitive reappraisal), the method is much more flexible. The method is illustrated by the following two case studies, which were introduced above.

Rancor in Couples Therapy

I noted how the relationship of the Baums suffered from the rancor Mrs. Baum had developed toward her husband 25 years ago. After two sessions, in which the therapist diagnosed both individual pathology and characteristics of the relationship between the husband and wife, he shared his assessment with the couple. He stressed the fact that Mrs. Baum still suffered from a grief process that had started 25 years ago and had never been resolved. The therapist defined her rancor as being caused by grief that had never been worked through. This grief did not originate so much in the loss of her child, as in the discovery that her husband was not the man she thought she had married. She had suffered a serious disillusionment. This aspect of the past was very much part of her present and reflected on everything her husband did. As long as she did not come to terms with this, there was no solution to the interactional problems.

Reluctantly, Mrs. Baum accepted the therapist's view and wanted to hear what she could do about it. The therapist advised her to write a letter *to* her husband (not *about* her husband). In this letter, she should write uninhibitedly about the situations that had hurt her during the past 25 years. It was to be a *"rotten fish letter."* She could call her husband bad names, she could be verbally abusive. The main thing was that she should express her feelings as completely as possible. It was made clear that this letter was private and not to be mailed or given to her husband.

The writing was to be ritualized. It was agreed that she would write:

- three times a week, during daytime when her husband was not home,
- for a period of exactly three quarters of an hour,
- always in the same place (a table in her own study).

The next session was scheduled three weeks later. The therapist was careful to stress in advance that it was uncertain whether or not a period of this length would be sufficient. He did assure her that eventually she would experience changes in the intensity and direction of her emotions. Her writing assignment would then come to an end and important progress in working through her grief would be made.

In a subsequent session, it emerged that Mrs. Baum had reached this point of satiation. To her own surprise, she had experienced the writing as if it were a pill that had softened her feelings dramatically and greatly reduced her pain. The therapist then asked her to write a new letter to her husband. The topic was to be the same, but it would communicate her feelings in a worthy and dignified manner, without unnecessarily hurting her husband's feelings. It would describe the way her husband's behavior had affected her in the past, but also how she now had chosen to put the past behind her and start anew (the cognitive reappraisal). This letter would be written using the same ritualized procedure (i.e., the same place, established time, and frequency).

The therapist offered to read the letter before she handed it over to her husband. She accepted this offer and brought the letter to the third session. The therapist suggested different wording for certain parts in order to emphasize that she had left the troubling and painful aspects of their past behind her and would from now on "fight" her husband in a more sensible way. Furthermore, it was agreed that Mr. Baum would read the letter but not comment on it. The rational for this was that the letter should not become a "discussion paper," but a piece of work that Mrs. Baum now wanted to share with her husband.

In the next session, she reported the great relief both she and her husband had felt after she had handed over the letter. It was decided to end this phase of the therapy by having them visit the grave of their deceased child (which they had never visited) and have dinner at an exquisite restaurant in the city of Amsterdam.

After the three sessions devoted to the writing assignment, five more sessions followed in which communicational aspects of their interaction were addressed to facilitate their dealing with conflicts in a rational and constructive way. In this part of the therapy, monitoring assignments were given, social skills taught, and behavioral exchanges were encouraged (Becker, Heimberg & Bellack, 1987). A follow-up after two years indicated that the improvements they had made in this period were stable.

Overcoming Incest

The therapy with Ann Mills took 12 sessions. During the first sessions, the therapist succeeded in expressing the feelings that had most upset her in the period of incest and thereafter. He then advised her to write letters to both her father and her mother. As in Mrs. Baum's case, she was required to carry out her writing assignment in a ritualized way: a fixed frequency and amount of time, a fixed location, and without restriction on her use of language or choice of words.

She chose to start with the letter to her father. She was instructed to continue the writing assignment until she felt she had expressed her feelings completely and her emotions were extinguished. It was agreed upon that the letter would not be sent. Writing was not easy for the patient; it was upsetting and she found it difficult to determine what was really important to her. Between the sessions, the therapist read what she had written. The content of her letters, as well as the experience of the writing, provided the subject matter for the therapeutic sessions, which took place once a fortnight. During these sessions, the therapist directed the patient to express in her letters the role her father had played. After two months of writing, the patient started to experience a reduction of emotions. It became easier for her to write and she finished the letter. As in Mrs. Baum's case, the therapist then helped the patient to write a dignified letter, reappraising her position and confirming her restored self-respect.

The patient underwent the same process in regard to her mother. When both letters met her satisfaction, she sent them off. To her own surprise, her parents, especially her father, reacted positively. Her father had always felt that he had done her an injustice but had not dared to speak about it. Now his daugther's letter finally gave him the opportunity to do so.

Writing the letters was the basis for restoring self-esteem for Ann Mills. After this, the therapy required only a few sessions.

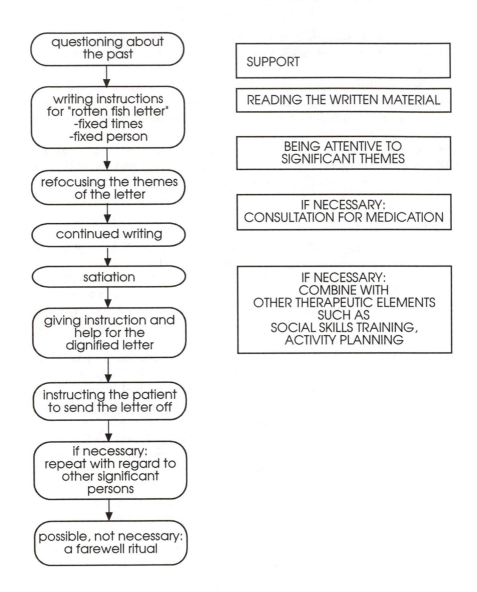

Fig. 2. Overview of the process of therapeutic writing assignments.

A MODEL FOR THE USE OF WRITING ASSIGNMENTS IN OVERCOMING GRIEF AND POSTTRAUMATIC STRESS

The essence of this model is the same as the behavior-therapeutic model. The difference is that it is more flexible and gives the patient the opportunity to work in her own time and pace. The various parts of this model are:

1. *Probing the past and giving instructions for writing.* Before the writing assignment is given, the therapist questions the patient about the traumatic experience to determine the most painful aspects of the experience.

2. *Refocusing.* During the process of writing, the therapist, who reads the letters, discusses the experiences of the patient and tries to refocus, if neccessary, on the painful elements. The importance of this is demonstrated by the therapy of Clara, a 30-year-old patient who applied for help because she could not relate to male friends. She soon told the therapist that she thought the incestuous suggestions her father used to make formed the basis of this. The therapist suggested that she write a letter to her father. She produced an enormous number of pages. In one of the sessions, during discussion of her experiences, she almost inaudibly whispered: "When I am alone with him, I am afraid I will go to bed with him." The therapist interrupted her and asked what exactly she meant. It emerged that she was not afraid of her father, but of herself. Fear and shame, associated with her own incestuous feelings, were such that she projected them on her father. This finding led to a significant change of the theme of the letter, which she eventually mailed to her father. The letter resulted in a great improvement in the relationship with her father and the therapy was soon concluded.

Important themes that often occur are feelings of helplessness and feelings of shame and guilt. There is a fair amount of literature in which feelings of helplessness are said to codetermine whether or not traumatic events lead to posttraumatic stress disorders (Op den Velde, 1989). There are also studies that indicate that the patients who consider themselves the ones to blame develop greater psychopathology following traumatic events than in the absence of such feelings of guilt (Morrow & Sorell, 1989). In discussing the writing experiences and the letters the therapist should keep these issues in mind.

3. *Ritualizing.* Therapist and patient agree on a fixed amount of time and frequency to which the patient strictly abides. Of course, these will depend on the situation of the patient and his/her motivation. The writing is always done in the same place.

4. *The "rotten fish" aspect.* The first letter is written without any restriction. The therapist should make clear that the patient should not worry about expressing negative feelings because the letter will not be mailed in this form.

5. *The dignified letter.* When it becomes clear that the patient has finished the "rotten fish" letter and indicates that the emotions are no longer painful and that he or she has nothing more to write, the therapist helps the patient to formulate a worthy letter. The phrasing of this letter is extremely important: It should express the patient's feelings appropriately in a respectful way. But it should also include new elements. It should convey the new appraisal of the situation and especially an improved self-esteem.

6. *Sending the letter off.* In both of our examples, the patients sent the dignified letter off. Usually patients are not willing to do so immediately because they fear that it will not do any good. Our experiences, however, are quite to the contrary. Many of the addressed react positively, and when they do not, little harm is done. Furthermore, patients usually feel better afterwards, having brought to a conclusion the work they started.

There are, of course, situations in which there is no one to send the letter to; for example, when the antagonist is deceased. In those cases, it is recommended that the letter be dispatched in a symbolic manner. It might be buried beside the grave of the deceased, burned, or kept in a special place.

7. *Ending the process with a ritual.* Sometimes, as we have seen with the Baum couple, the process is ended with a "farewell ritual," a symbolic farewell. This is not always necessary; if it is thought by both therapist and patient to consolidate the benefits of the therapy is it recommended. It is up to the patient to decide on the best symbolic way for a final reckoning with the past, but the therapist may give suggestions, such as visiting a grave, buying a present for oneself or another, or throwing a party.

8. *With or without the partner.* In both cases we have discussed, the partner was present throughout. Although this is not necessary, we encourage it, especially when the writing is addressed to the partner. The presence of the partner can be useful as it may help to avoid problems caused by treating one partner in the absence of the other. The partner who sees the therapist in action will understand the rationale of the writing assignment and will have less trouble taking a constructive attitude toward it. On the other hand, the presence of a spouse may inhibit the patient or reduce the willingness to write. The therapist should thus take a flexible approach, taking into account the needs of the patients.

9. *Brief or long therapy.* The two cases presented above were treated in relatively few sessions. However, the variation in length is quite large and does not seem to depend on the severity of the case. The therapist should avoid impatience if the desired effects are slow in coming. He should persist in focusing and motivating the patient till the process of saturation is completed.

10. *Combining with other elements of therapy.* The writing assignment

frequently is not the only element of the therapy. Often, it is combined with other interventions, such as social skills training or activity planning (with depressed patients).

11. *Support*. Directing grief-stricken patients or patients suffering post-traumatic stress to engage in self-confrontation, be it with or without writing assignments, requires from the therapist a certain robustness and attentiveness. Lacking these, she may fail to bring important themes to the fore. It is, therefore, extremely important that the therapeutic atmosphere be characterized by acceptance and support. It also may be desirable that the therapist remain accessible between the sessions.

12. *Medication*. Patients with pathological grief or related symptoms of posttraumatic stress are often on medication. A reduction of the medication, if feasible, is useful to increase the benefit of the writing process. If the medication is prescribed by someone else who is still treating the patient, consultation should be sought.

HISTORY AND RESEARCH ON WRITING ASSIGNMENTS

In transgenerational family therapy, writing letters to relatives as a means of dealing with the past was first described in a brilliant essay by Bowen (Anonymous, 1972). The emphasis, however, was less on self-confrontation than on restoring relationships with the relatives in question. Sending the letters was, therefore, the main goal. Ritualized writing as a means to self-confrontation was described by Van der Hart (1983) and by Lange and Van der Hart (1983). Later, several case studies showed the effectiveness of the writing technique for patients with pathological grief or with other symptoms of posttraumatic stress disorder (Lange, 1988). However, systematic and controlled research in this area is relatively scarce.

Using questionnaires, Lattanzi and Hale (1984) investigated 16 subjects who had lost a loved one and whose treatment included writing assignments. The researchers were mainly interested in the degree of structuredness of the writing, the degree of disclosure, and the timing of the intervention. Their conclusion was that even though the method is not suitable for everyone, in many cases it is of great value and gives people the opportunity to express and investigate their fear, hope, and fantasies. In addition, the writing can bring about changes in cognitions and coping mechanisms.

In a series of experiments, Pennebaker investigated the effects of writing about traumatic events compared to writing about trivial events on well-being and improved health of students (operationalized by the use of information concerning visits to the campus doctor and immunological processes) (Pennebaker, 1989; Pennebaker & Beall, 1986; Pennebaker, Kiecolt-Glaser & Glaser, 1988; Pennebaker, Colder & Sharp, 1990). Their results are encouraging. Using a "minimal" intervention, they found significant differences in the predicted direction. Most remarkable was the positive influence of the writing over a period of six weeks on the immune proliferation.

That writing is not the only way to stimulate disclosure was shown previously by Pennebaker, Hughes and O'Heeron (1987). They investigated the effect of "disclosure" and self-confrontation by requiring the subjects to talk into a microphone connected with a tape recorder. An interesting result of this study was that the immediate positive effects on physiological measures were smaller when the subject knew somebody was listening than in the experimental condition where this was not the case. This might imply that reading written material of patients obstructs the positive effects of writing. However, reading of the letters by a therapist differs from listening by an experimenter to disclosure at the moment it is spoken into a tape recorder by experimental subjects. Our clinical cases do indeed suggest that the patients benefit from the fact that the therapist reads the letters.

The Pennebaker experiments are open to various criticisms. Neale, Cox, Valdimarsdottir, and Stone (1990) question the validity of the psychophysiological measures and the methods used in the analysis. Furthermore, it is unclear exactly how the assignments were administered and supervised, and it is doubtful whether the results can be generalized from campus students to clinical practice. However, the results do encourage further research. Pennebaker, Barger, and Tiebout (1990) carried out a study with a more clinical character. They manipulated self-confrontation by encouraging 33 holocaust survivors to talk about their experiences during one or two hours. The content of the interviews was rated from minute to minute with respect to the degree of trauma expressed. As predicted, a positive correlation was observed between the degree of reported trauma and sympathical activation, operationalized by use of heartbeat and skin resistance. The authors interpret these results as support for the behavior-inhibition theory, which holds that inhibition in expressing emotions is unhealthy. In a follow-up 14 months later, it emerged that self-confrontation correlated positively with variables related to physical health. In another attempt to raise the clinical significance of the Pennebaker experiments, Murray, Lamnin, and Carver (1989) compared students who had been subjected to two sessions of writing with students who had received brief psychotherapy. They concluded that writing assignments are most effective when they result in cognitive restructuring.

In a recent study at our department by De Goederen and Sporry (1992), 34 students, who had reported that they suffered from traumatic experiences in the past, were given writing assignments. In a first session, they received explanation about writing assignments in general. Prior to this, they had completed the Dutch version of the Profile-of-Mood-States questionnaire (the POMS; Wald & Mellenbergh, 1990) and the Symptom Checklist (the SCL-90; Arrindell & Ettema, 1986). During one month, all of the subjects wrote a letter in the ritualized way described above. Every week during this period the same questionnaires were completed. The moods of the subjects also were assessed by daily monitoring at fixed times.

The data indicate that the minimal writing intervention resulted in significant improvement in mood as monitored daily. There was, furthermore, a significant and even dramatic reduction of fright, fatigue, and tension (as measured by subscales of the POMS) and depression and fear (as measured by the SCL-90). Posttreatment structured interviews indicated that the subjects considered both satiation and cognitive reappraisal to be important elements of their improvement.

A qualitative study was carried out by Duurland and Hagenbeek (1992) at the Amsterdam Post Office (PTT). Social workers were trained to use ritualized writing with multiproblem clients who had suffered from traumas, such as sexual abuse, physical abuse, divorce, severe illness, and problems in the work setting. Although only a limited number of patients (9) participated in this study, the results were very encouraging. The patients, whose problems can be characterized as severe, improved significantly on general psychopathology as measured by the SCL-90 and on mood, measured by weekly monitoring. Furthermore, the study demonstrated the importance of training the therapists before applying the method with regard to the instructions to the clients, the refocusing on important themes, and the timing.

SUMMARY AND DISCUSSION

The foundation of our model concerning writing assignments for patients with pathological grief and symptoms of posttraumatic stress disorder is based on learning theory with emphasis on the need for self-confrontation with stimuli the patient habitually avoids. We have described the similarities with and differences from our model and the behavior-therapeutic model. We have explicated how the process of ritualized writing should be introduced and supervised by the therapist. We have also stressed the importance of general therapist variables such as acceptance and support.

Two clinical case studies served to illustrate the method. Needless to say, these do not do justice to the wide variety of symptomatology in which ritualized writing might be useful. To name a few: pathological grief following death of a partner, a child, or other relatives; grief and/or rancor following divorce; posttraumatic stress symptoms following physical or sexual abuse; low self-esteem as a result of negative stimulation in the family context.

There are patients who are not able to write at all. With these patients other techniques, such as talking into a tape recorder in a ritualized way, can be considered. Also, patients may be able to write, but are not used to it. It should be made clear to such patients that the quality and amount of text is of no importance. Some patients do indeed benefit enormously from the procedure even though they have written only a few lines in several sessions. However, if patients show great reluctance, they should not be pushed. It is then preferable to suggest other methods of self-confrontation.

I have presented an overview of the sparse research in this area, including an uncontrolled trial we conducted at our department, which revealed very dramatic improvements after one month of ritualized writing in combination with minimal therapeutic support. Of course, there are still questions to be addressed. I cannot deal with all of them in the scope of this chapter, but some are of particular importance, such as the question of timing. In most cases it is "logical" to start the therapy with the writing assignments, because the traumatic experiences make it difficult to address any of the presenting symptoms in a fruitful way immediately. However, this is not always possible. For instance, the self-esteem of the patient may be so low that writing is too difficult a task. There are many reports that this is the case with victims of incest (Thiel, 1988). In those cases, it is necessary first to help the patient to gain some confidence. The writing assignment will be fruitful only in a later phase.

An issue of greater theoretical than clinical importance is the question of the effective elements of the writing assignment. Is it pure self-confrontation that brings about the benefit or is it the cognitive reappraisal of past experiences (or both)? How important is it that the therapist read the written material? In our department, we have recently embarked upon a long-term project in which several experiments will be carried out in order to gain insight into these questions. In our first experiment, we will vary the experimental conditions with regard to the instruction to write about the traumatic facts or about the feelings. In a second experiment, the instruction with regard to writing will be varied. In a third experiment, we will assess the effect of instructions to include new cognitions by means of positive self-statements in the writing. We hope to report on these experiments in the near future.

REFERENCES

Abdulla, A.K. (1985). *Catharsis in literature.* Bloomington: Indiana University Press.

American Psychiatric Association (1987). *Diagnostic and statistical manual of mental disorders* (3rd ed., rev.). Washington, DC: APA.

Anonymous, (1972). Toward the differentiation of the self in one's own family. In: J.L. Framo (Ed.), *Family interactions.* New York: Springer.

Arrindell, W.A., & Ettema, J.H.M. (1986). *SCL-90, Handleiding bij een multidimensionele psychopathologie-indicator (Manual for the SCL-90, a multidimensional psychopathology indicator).* Lisse: Swets & Zeitlinger.

Averill, J.R. (1968). Grief: It's nature and significance. *Psychological Bulletin,* 70 (6), 721-748.

Beck, A.T., Freeman, A., et al. (1990). *Cognitive therapy of personality disorders.* New York: Guilford.

Becker, R.E., Heimberg, R.G., & Bellack, A.S. (1987). *Social skills training treatment for depression.* New York: Pergamon.

Bowlby, J. (1961). Processes of mourning. *International Journal of Psychoanalysis,* 42(4-5), 317-340.

Bowlby, J., & Parkes, C.M.M. (1970). Separation and loss within the family. In: E.J. Anthony & C. Koupernik (Eds.), *The child and his family,* vol. I. Ann Arbor: Books Demand.

De Goederen, A., & Sporry, A. (1992). *Schrijfopdrachten; een experimenteel onderzoek naar de effecten en procedures. (Writing assignments: An interim report of an experimental study).* Amsterdam: Department of Clinical Psychology, University of Amsterdam.

Duurland, C.I.A., & Hagenbeek, H.P. (1992). *Schrijfopdrachten; een pilot studie bij getraumatiseerd PTT personeel (Writing assignments: A pilot study with traumatized PTT employees).* Amsterdam: Department of Clinical Psychology, University of Amsterdam.

Frijda, N. (1986). *The emotions.* Cambridge: Cambridge University Press.

Hokanson, J.E. (1970). Psychophysiological evaluation ot the catharsis hypothesis. In E.I. Megargee & J.E. Hokanson (Eds.), *The dynamics of aggression.* New York: Harper & Row.

Janis, I.L. (1958). *Psychological stress.* New York: Wiley.

Janis, I.L. (1971). *Stress and frustration.* New York: Harcourt Brace Jovanovitch.

Lange, A. (1988). Techniques and timing in directive family therapy with victims of the holocaust. In: E. Chigier (Ed.), *Grief and bereavement in contemporary society.* Vol. 2. Jerusalem: Freund.

Lange, A., & Van der Hart, O. (1983). *Directive family therapy.* New York: Brunner/Mazel.

Lattanzi, M., & Hale, M.E. (1984). Giving grief words: Writing during bereavement. *Omega Journal of Death and Dying,* 15 (1), 45-52.

Lazarus, R.S., Kanner, A.D., & Folkman, S. (1980). Emotions: A cognitive-phenomenological analysis. In: R. Plutchik & H. Kellerman (Eds.), *Emotion: Theory, research and practice.* New York: Academic Press.

Meichenbaum, D. (1979). *Cognitive-behavior modification: An integrative approach.* New York: Plenum.

Meichenbaum, D., & Cameron, R. (1974). The clinical potential of modifying what clients say to themselves. *Psychotherapy: Theory, Research and Practice,* 11, 103-117.

Morrow, K.B., & Sorell, G.T. (1989). Factors affecting self-esteem, depression, and negative behaviors in sexually abused female adolescents. *Journal of Marriage and the Family,* 51, 677-686.

Murray, E.J., Lamnin, A.D., & Carver, C.S. (1989). Emotional expression in written essays and psychotherapy. *Journal of Social and Clinical Psychology,* 8 (4), 414-429.

Neale, J.M., Cox, D.S., Valdimarsdottir, H., & Stone, A.A. (1990). The relation between immunity and health: Comment on Pennebaker, Kiecolt-Glaser, and Glaser. *Journal of Consulting and Clinical Psychology,* 56 (4), 636-637.

Op den Velde, W. (1989). Posttraumatische stress-stoornissen (Posttraumatic stress disorders). *Nederlands Tijdschrift voor Geneeskunde,* 133 (32), 1586-1593.

Pennebaker, J.W. (1989). Confession, inhibition and disease. In: L. Berkowitz (Ed.), *Advances in experimental social psychology,* Vol. 22. New York: Academic Press.

Pennebaker, J.W., Barger, S.D., & Tiebaut, J. (1990). Disclosure of traumas and health among holocaust survivors. *Psychosomatic Medicine,* 51, 577-589.

Pennebaker, J.W., & Beall, S.K. (1986). Confronting a traumatic event: Toward an understanding of inhibition and disease. *Journal of Abnormal Psychology,* 95, 274-281.

Pennebaker, J.W., Colder, M., & Sharp, L.K. (1990). Accelerating the coping process. *Journal of Personality and Social Psychology,* 58 (3), 528-537.

Pennebaker, J.W., Hughes, C.F., & O'Heeron, R.C. (1987). The psychophysiology of confession: Linking inhibitory and psychosomatic processes. *Journal of Personality and Social Psychology,* 52 (4), 781-793.

Pennebaker, J.W., Kiecolt-Glaser, J.K., & Glaser, R. (1988). Disclosure of traumas and immune function: Health implications for psychotherapy. *Journal of Consulting and Clinical Psychology,* 56 (2), 239-245.

Rachman, S.J. (1980). Emotional processing. *Behavior Research and Therapy,* 18, 51-60.

Rochkind, M., & Conn, J.H. (1973), Guided fantasy encounter. *American Journal of Psychotherapy,* 27, 516-528.

Scheff, T.J. (1979). *Catharsis in healing, ritual and drama.* Berkeley: University of California Press.

Scheff, T.J., & Bushnell, D.D. (1984). A theory of catharsis. *Journal of Research in Personality,* 18, 238-264.

Thiel, P. (1988). De behandeling van slachtoffers van verkrachting en incest (The treatment of victims of rape and incest). *Gedragstherapie,* 21 (4), 295-317.

Van der Hart, O. (1983). *Rituals in psychotherapy: Transition and continuity.* New York: Irvington.

Wald, F.D.M., & Mellenbergh, G.J. (1990). De verkorte versie van de Nederlandse vertaling van de Profile of Mood States (POMS) (The short version of the Dutch Profile of Mood States). *Nederlands Tijdschrift voor de Psychologie,* 45, 86-90.

PART VII

Specific Populations

CHAPTER 27

An Ericksonian Perspective on the Treatment of Sexual Abuse

Yvonne Dolan

INTRODUCTION

My purpose in this chapter is to offer an Ericksonian approach to the treatment of sexual abuse. I will first describe my own perspective toward treatment of sexual abuse, a perspective inspired in large part by the work of Milton Erickson and his students. I will then describe specific techniques stemming from Ericksonian principles of naturalistic trance states, elicitation and development of unconscious resources, and emphasis on positive future orientation.

A PERSONAL PERSPECTIVE

While I have been trained as an Ericksonian psychotherapist and hypnotherapist by various students of Milton Erickson, my perspective on sexual abuse is drawn from a personal as well as a professional context. In addition to being a therapist who specializes in treatment of Post-Traumatic Stress Disorders (PTSD), I am also a survivor of childhood sexual abuse. Between the ages of three and 10, I was sexually assaulted repeatedly, sometimes violently and by multiple perpetrators. When these memories first began to surface several years ago, I experienced acute symptoms of PTSD and learned more than I ever wanted to know firsthand about the experience of dissociation not in the "service of the ego." I share this information not because I believe that abuse survivors are intrinsically more qualified or even necessarily otherwise better suited to help others overcome PTSD symptoms, but for another reason: The experience of sexual abuse trauma is a powerful one that eludes verbal description and, therefore, there is the risk of well-intentioned therapists who are not experientially cognizant of the sexual abuse experience inadvertently minimizing or trivializing the degree of agony that accompanies the confrontation of previously repressed material.

Unless one has experienced a violent rape or assault, it may be difficult to grasp the level of terror and pain experienced by victims at the time of the abuse, and subsequently reexperienced through vivid and intrusive flashbacks and nightmares. The best way I can convey this is through the words of a recent client, who described her emerging memories of sexual abuse in the following way: "I remember sitting out in the sun and feeling safe and good, and then, I remember something happening and all the safety, all the good, was gone forever; and I felt myself disintegrating completely, terrifyingly. There was no longer a 'me' left to refer to . . . and I think at that point on some primitive level I had to make the choice of being completely destroyed as a personality or repressing this material. Every time I remember this, it is as if I were about to disintegrate all over again. It (the memory) is so intrusive, it eclipses everything else. All my strengths and resources, even the very sense of 'me,' start to disappear."

Imagine this experience happening to a young child; it would be a challenging psychological experience even for most adults to process and integrate!

The highly advanced dissociative skills, as evidenced by the above client who repressed the memory of her victimization for over 30 years, should not be viewed solely in the context of symptomatology. Rather, they should be appreciated as valuable hypnotic skills learned under severe duress (Dolan, 1991). It is my view that the naturally occurring dissociation needs to be worked with, therapeutically utilized for the client's benefit, rather than overridden by the therapist.

IATROGENIC EFFECTS OF INTENSIVE METHODS

In my role as a consultant to agencies and individual therapists who treat sexual abuse symptoms, I have sometimes been called in only after previous therapy has been unsuccessful or even worsened the client's PTSD symptoms. Repeatedly, I have seen misinformed good intentions on the part of therapists lead to personal hell for clients whose very real trauma is trivialized, minimized, and ultimately worsened. I have seen tragic examples of intrusive and debilitating symptoms such as anxiety, depression, suicidal ideation, self-mutilation, intrusive memories, and severe dissociation exacerbated rather than helped through therapists' misinformed or irresponsible use of abreactive techniques. Tragically, in such cases, the client is made to endure additional suffering with little or no resulting therapeutic gain.

While, as Hammond (1990, p. 524) notes, most trauma survivors are probably capable of "enduring" a "full abreaction," I question whether it is ethical or humane to routinely use such needlessly painful methods given the current level of technology regarding equally effective alternative methods currently available in our field.

To elicit repressed traumatic memory without simultaneously eliciting resources to provide a corrective emotional experience for the client is tantamount to a "rape of the unconscious" (Erickson & Rossi, 1989). In my workshops on the treatment of sexual abuse, a number of psychotherapists who were themselves treated for sexual abuse in the past have described the abreactive techniques used in their treatment as being "as bad as or sometimes worse" than the original victimization.

Would the fact that a patient could physically survive an excruciatingly painful medical or dental procedure without benefit of hypnotic or pharmacological anesthesia justify requesting or suggesting that she or he endure one? In my work with sexual abuse survivors during the past 10 years, I have consistently found that less intrusive, Ericksonian methods not only provide effective relief of PTSD symptoms and integration of sexual abuse trauma, but actually accelerate the course of therapy while maximizing clients' ability to continue to function in their everyday lives with reduced need for hospitalization. As one sexual abuse survivor said in requesting treatment:

> "I want to be able to still function in my life during treatment. I've already lost several years of my life to sexual abuse and suffering the effects of sexual abuse; I want to deal with it and resolve it, but I don't want to have to relive it in such a way that I fall apart and lose my ability to work and be a wife and a mother to my children. Living through it once was already too much."

Indeed.

Is it ethical for the therapist to implicitly demand that all sexual abuse clients repeatedly suffer the full pain of being assaulted all over again as the price of integration and resolution of the abuse? Often, clients I have seen who have previously been treated with flooding techniques evidence increased dissociation and numbing when talking about the experience of their abuse, but show little evidence of having regained the ability to live their life fully and joyfully. There is, perhaps, a fuller understanding and recall of all the ways they were tortured or otherwise sexually victimized, but little or no freedom from the psychological constrictions this abuse caused. In fact, in some cases the PTSD symptoms have actually worsened over time without ultimate relief. These clients resemble sexual abuse clients I have seen who seek therapy when they suffer a resurgence of symptoms following additional victimization such as rape or assault in adult life.

Proponents of the abreactive techniques would likely say to their clients and colleagues that in the treatment of sexual abuse the patients symptoms have to get worse before they get better. In some cases this may be true, but for how long should the already abused client be asked to endure additional suffering (from antiquated treatment methods) before experiencing symptomatic relief and a reasonable level of functioning in daily life? I worry that too much emphasis has been placed on creating exquisite insight and understanding of the excruciating details of the sexual victimization, and too little on empowering the client to move beyond the history of victimization to reclaim the birthright of living a satisfying life.

As a clinician, I have long worried about the risk of inadequately trained therapists creating pseudo memories of trauma in clients through sloppy or incompetent use of hypnotic techniques. Yapko (1992) does our field a service in cautioning therapists regarding the possibility of creating false traumatic memories. Yet, as a survivor of sexual abuse as well as a therapist who treats this population, I am now concerned about the pendulum swinging too far in the direction of the newly proposed "false memory symdrome" (Yapko, 1992). I am deeply concerned about the potential damaging effects sexual abuse victims will experience if upon confiding in their therapists they are further victimized by having their experience of abuse minimized or disbelieved because of therapists' skepticism about the veracity of memories. The focus of my clinical work over the past decade has stemmed from a desire to develop practical, but gentle and humane alternative techniques for sexual abuse survivors and the therapists who treat them.

USING ERICKSONIAN METHODS

My search for alternative treatment has led to my adaptation of Ericksonian principles for the resolution of sexual abuse. I feel the best way to communicate the resulting approach is to tell a story. While Erickson's work provided the language for me to understand clinical applications of dissociation, I first learned experientially about the naturalistic use of dissociation from my grandmother.

When I was a little girl, I lived in a small town in the Upper Peninsula of Michigan. It is an economically depressed area and has been at times compared with Appalachia in terms of poverty, illiteracy, and other problems. This was the town where my paternal grandmother lived.

At times throughout my childhood, I was lucky enough to live with my grandmother. The town we lived in had never been zoned, and it would be considered by some people to be quite ugly. Although there was a harbor, the area around the harbor was dotted with decrepit buildings and lots of gas stations. But the water itself was always a beautiful blue, and if you looked out into the middle of the harbor rather than at the town, that blue water was very pretty with the light shining on it. It was perhaps the town's one treasure, the only beautiful thing about that town.

My grandmother was a very positive woman. Every day she would look out the window into the middle of that harbor and say to me, "Just look at that view. Look at that light on the water. Isn't that beautiful?" And I would stop for a moment and look out and I would agree that it was quite beautiful.

But one day when I returned after being away for several months, I looked out to the middle of the harbor for a glimpse of that shining blue water and I was horrified. Now, even the water had been ruined! There were three immense grey oil drums placed right in the middle of the harbor in such a way as to ruin the view from all angles. I told my grandmother, "That looks terrible, those oil drums right in the middle of our harbor." She looked at me for a moment, and then she slowly replied, "I know, dear. But just look at the light on the water." Pretty soon, I could look out into the middle of the harbor and I did not even see the ugly oil drums. I would just see the light on the water, and to my mind it was beautiful again.

Finally, I grew up and went to college and I had a boyfriend. My grandmother met him when she came to see me at school. She told him about the wonderful view we had in front of her house looking out toward Lake Michigan. He was impressed with her description and the next summer he came to visit us. (I think he was expecting something like Cape Cod.) Anyway, the three of us went to the window and my grandmother said, "Isn't that beautiful?" He paused for a few seconds before he said, swallowing hard, " That's quite a view, Mrs. Dolan." As soon as she left the room he turned to me and said matter of factly, "Yvonne, that looks like hell." I looked at him for a moment before I answered with complete assurance, "I know. *But look at the light on the water.*"

The point I want to make is that in terms of treating sexual abuse, denial of the abuse is analogous to seeing *only* the light on the water; trauma and pathology are analogous to seeing *only* the oil drums. Resolution and integration can be understood as being able to see the oil drums *and* the light on the water *at the same time.*

And now I want to explore an Ericksonian perspective regarding the symptomatology traditionally associated with sexual abuse. A sexual abuse surivor is likely to experience some or all of the following symptoms (Courtois, 1988; Briere, 1989; Dolan, 1991): time distortion, eating disorders, anxiety, depression, substance abuse, self-mutilation, relationship difficulties, sexual dysfunction. pessimism or cynicism, difficulty trusting in intimate relationships, flashbacks, memory and concentration difficulties, and impaired ability to protect oneself or, even more tragically, later in life, one's children from further abuse.

Erickson claimed that trance was a naturalistic experience, part of everyday life. Trauma creates its own naturalistic trance state. The symptoms stemming from sexual abuse can be understood from a perspective of naturalistic trance, which initially occurs in response to the abuse trauma. This state can be reelicited spontaneously, sometimes without the victim's concious awareness, by internal or external stimuli, which are literally or symbolically reminiscent of the abuse. Most PTSD symptoms exist in this context.

Sexual abuse survivors, at the time of the abuse and subsequently, tend to spontaneously access a naturalistic hypnotic state when recalling the abuse. This state is characterized by partial or even full dissociation from external surroundings and internal resources. Full dissociation from external and internal resources is most likely to occur at times when the survivor is retrieving previously repressed or affectively dissociated traumatic experiences. This dissociative response can be traced back to the rigid associational compartmentalization that occurs as a defense in response to the original trauma.

In cases where only the affect but not the cognitive memory of the trauma has been repressed, the client will return to the above naturalistic hypnotic state of dissociation from internal and external resources when confronted with feelings reminiscent of those associated with the original trauma. The corrective emotional experience that is needed by sexual abuse survivors who suffer from recurrent PTSD symptoms in a context of separation from resources can be achieved by creating and connecting new associational bridges to the memory and perceived reexperiencing of the trauma.

TREATMENT ISSUES

Ironically, in the early stages of treatment, when victims most need the resources they have acquired, they are most likely, because of the phenomenon of rigid compartmentalization, to be unavailable. Associations to the abuse tend to be compartmentalized in such a way that they exist independently from associations to resources. The goal of treatment is to reestablish associational bridges so that the client can be aware of, for example, the existence of adult life resources, while experiencing intrusive memories linked to childhood sexual abuse. Once the client is able to simultaneously associate to current resources *and* to the memory of the abuse, psychological integration and emotional correction of the experience have begun and will continue. When trauma is truly resolved, the sexual abuse survivor is able to simultaneously be aware of the trauma and also of all the other experiences and resources that characterize his/her life.

Until this is accomplished, sexual abuse victims are likely to swing perceptually between overidealization and extreme cynicism, thus preventing healthy behavioral adaptation and healthy psychological integration of experiences.

When a client is cognizant of some resources and strengths, it is likely to be easier for her to summon awareness of her other resources and strengths. Evidence of hope for a survivor is likely to lead to more evidence of hope for a survivor. On the other hand, moments of hopelessness, in which the remembered experience of the trauma eclipses other emotions, are likely to trigger more associations to trauma and may even lead to suicide. A client described this associational compartmentalization in these words:

> "When I am in a relationship and things are going well, I can think about it, and all the other memories of good experiences with that person come to mind; like facial tissue, one association after another pops up, each apparently associationally connected to the previous one. On the other hand, when things are going badly, all I can think of is other times when things have gone badly, and one negative association after another pops up, each convincing me more and more that this relationship is hopeless. And this is just how it feels, these two polarities, in terms of my relationship with myself."

Another sexual abuse survivor client told me,

> "When I am in a good mood and thinking about good things in the present, I cannot imagine ever wanting to hurt myself. But when I am thinking about my past abuse, it seems that all I can remember are all the other bad things that have happened in my life and I can't remember any of the good things that make me want to go on living. And that is when I feel like cutting myself and abusing drugs; those are the times I have insomnia, depression, the worst anxiety, and those are the times I am most likely to do self-destructive things in relationships and at work."

The key for resolving this problem of rigid associational structures is to empower the client to create reliable associational bridges to resources that the client can utilize as needed to counterbalance the associational reliving of the trauma in a way that provides a corrective emotional experience. For many abuse survivors, initially, the present may be associationally the only undeniably safe place. The past contains the memory of the abuse and the future is uncertain, thereby allowing for the frightening possibility of further abuse. Given this, it is not surprising that in the beginning of treatment the therapist's presence often constitutes the first associational bridge between the trauma and the client's awareness of presently available psychological and relationship resources.

In my workshops on treating sexual abuse, psychotherapists frequently describe the phenomenon of sexual abuse clients telephoning initially in a state of acute distress, and then quickly shifting to a more resourceful state upon hearing the therapist's voice. In these cases, the therapist is probably one of the first if not the only associational bridge between the trauma and the client's resources.

ERICKSONIAN PERSPECTIVES

When working with rigid associational structures, because of the perspective Erickson provided in associationally eliciting and utilizing the client's existing perceptual and behavioral patterns, the Ericksonian therapist has a distinct advantage. The therapist's challenge is to assist the client in creating a bridge between these two, often rigidly separated associational polarities (trauma and nontrauma). An elegant example of a specific way that a client may be provided with a bridge to a much needed resource, drawn from Erickson's perspective on treatment of trauma, is described in *The February Man* (Erickson & Rossi, 1989).

In this example, Erickson worked to resolve symptoms stemming from repressed traumatic experience. Although the trauma was not sexual abuse, the frame he provides in this case is applicable to treatment of sexual abuse. Erickson arranged for a client, while working with traumatic material, to experience and be able to remain aware of ongoing feelings of comfort in her hand. He said, in describing this, "She might be miserable, but I wanted her hand in comfort" (Erickson & Rossi, 1989, p. 148). A client can be aware of an experience of comfort in the present even while working on the effects of an experience in the past.

For those who have trouble understanding how clients can be simultaneously aware of two psychological experiences at once, I offer the following story told to me by a colleague, a student of Erickson's, who once served as a subject for a demonstration by Erickson of hypnotic age regression.

The subject at this time was a man in his early 20s and he wore a moustache. Erickson age-regressed him to approximately five or six, and they had a pleasant conversation.

Eventually Erickson invited the subject to reach up and touch his own upper lip where the moustache was. As the subject touched his lip, Erickson asked, "What is that?" And without hesitation, the age-regressed subject answered congruently and innocently, "That is when I am older." He could be six years old and yet also be aware of the "older" moustache context. In a different context, for therapeutic purposes, the experience of the moustache presumably could be utilized as an associational bridge to an awareness that there are the potential resources of a more grown-up self available as well. This state of simultaneous awareness of more that one state is particularly valuable in treating sexual abuse victims. As Erickson said, "You don't alter the original experience, you alter the perception of it, and that becomes the memory of the perception" (Erickson & Rossi, 1989, p. 77).

It is important early on to provide the client with as much immediate relief, comfort, and symptom mitigation as possible. This will not prevent the client from processing the traumatic material necessary for resolution. Rather, it will strengthen him to face the material. In some cases, it will be an important factor in averting suicide attempts so that the client and therapist can, as one client put it, "buy enough time for [the client] to live long enough to work through the trauma and come out at the other end . . ."

EMPHASIZING THE POSITIVE

Techniques that provide symptomatic relief and stabilization, such as solution-focused therapy, immediately afford the client more control of the PTSD symptomatology. This will tend to accelerate the client's integration and eventual resolution of the trauma. In cases of repressed memories, placing emphasis on present resources and future goals will accomplish one or both of the following: It will either help restabilize the client long enough to accomplish much-needed developmental tasks and establish some of the inner resources needed in order to later psychologically survive conscious retrieval of the memories, or it will actually hasten the conscious emergence of the memories. Presumably, this is because repressed memories of trauma are rendered less frightening as the client stabilizes and progressively gains more control of the PTSD symptoms.

Frequently, in workshops, I have been asked by colleagues, "When working with sexual abuse survivors, how can you imply that the unconscious is benign and a resource when people have all these horrific symptoms of terrifying recurrent nightmares, flashbacks and intrusive memories of past trauma?" I view these intrusive unconscious reactions as originally being a protective unconscious response that has outlived its usefulness and instead become a symptom.

An example of the above is the flow of adrenaline that occurs when someone is badly frightened. It is a response that is valuable in that the increased energy available may enable the person to escape from danger. However, the same response may later be translated into pervasive and constricting symptoms such as anxiety attacks and panic disorders. Another example is the psychological numbing that originally occurred as a much needed escape from victimization. If it continues past the victimization experience and becomes chronic, it can prevent the client from recognizing and escaping from current danger. Recurrent flashbacks can be viewed as originating as unconscious attempts at desensitization. Flashbacks, however, are unlikely to provide sufficient desensitization in cases of severe trauma, just as retelling a story of victimization over and over again is often insufficient as the sole therapy on a conscious level.

Before moving on to specific descriptions of techniques, I want to emphasize that it is important for the therapist working with sexual abuse survivors to first take enough of a history of the client's abuse so as to allow the client to feel understood and supported and for the therapist to express compassion and empathy for what the client has endured. While solution-focused therapy is often associated with a diminished emphasis on the past, sexual abuse clients require special adjustments. To fail to take an adequate history from a client in this population risks inadvertently replicating the denial and trivialization that the client may have experienced from the abuser and in some cases from the client's family of origin where the abuse occurred.

I will now describe some of the techniques I have found especially helpful in empowering clients to build associational and, sometimes by extension, experiential bridges between the trauma and resources for purposes of integration of traumatic experiences and resolution of PTSD symptoms. I will begin with four techniques that are particularly useful for stabilizing clients in the earliest stages of treatment: A Symbol for the Present, the First Session Formula Task, the "Older, Wiser Self," and Solution-Focused Questions.

TECHNIQUES FOR CLIENT STABILIZATION

A Symbol for the Present

Ideally, the client should be asked, when she (or he) begins to tell the history of the victimization, to identify something in the room, a "symbol for the present" (Dolan, 1989), that can be used as a reminder of the here and now. Often, clients choose a personal item such as a wallet or purse, a picture of a spouse or partner or kids or other significant person, a piece of jewelry. Others might choose to simply focus on an object in the office that reminds them of the present.

In the spirit of Erickson's emphasis on the path of least resistance, it makes good sense to begin by offering clients, who by virtue of their sexual abuse victimization have already suffered severe intrusion, the least intrusive form of treatment. Solution-focused therapy provides the most advanced techniques currently available for building on clients' strengths rather than solely focusing on the sexual abuse survivors' vulnerabilities. While also serving the much needed purpose of counterbalancing the trauma (the "light on the water" while confronting the ugliness), a focus on what the client is doing that is right, good, and helpful provides the effect of much needed stabilization. It also provides a vehicle for increasing the likelihood that, once elicited, healthy behavior and perceptions will continue into the future.

The First Session Formula Task

A bridge between the trauma and the client's awareness of the present can also be provided by asking the client to make a written list of the things going on in her present life that she would like to have continue. This task, originally known as the First Session Formula Task (de Shazer, 1985) was developed at the Milwaukee Brief Family Center as an assignment after the first session to help clients who were initially vague in their description of what they wanted from therapy. In my work with sexual abuse survivors, I use it as a tangible reminder of the resources available in her present life that in most cases were not available at the time of the trauma.

Typically the list includes such items as:

1. my job
2. my relationship (with significant other)
3. my friends
4. my hobbies
5. self-care activities

The Symbol for the Present and the First Session Formula Task serve as associational bridges to the present that may be subsequently employed as needed within therapy sessions if the client begins to reexperience the trauma to a degree so overwhelming as to be countertherapeutic. These techniques may also be used as needed by the client at home as a way to self-soothe and reconnect to the safety of the present following experiencing of nightmares or intrusive memories and flashbacks. Each time this is done, there is less of a rigid compartmentalization of associations to the trauma; more of the awareness of the larger life context is available and the memory of the trauma gradually becomes less debilitating and terrifying.

Having a list to "hold onto" is particularly useful for clients during the early stages of treatment when a focus on past trauma can easily eclipse their much needed awareness of the comfort, safety, and support available in their everyday life in the here and now. Clients should be encouraged to make the list as long as they wish. Some clients choose to carry the list around in the early stages of treatment, even in some cases sleeping with it under their pillow, particularly if they are suffering from nightmares, flashbacks, and intrusive memories of their victimization. Carrying the list may serve to counteract the "spontaneous age regression" (Beahrs, 1982) that can occur in survivors of sexual abuse in response to events symbolically reminiscent of their abuse, particularly when long dissociated memories of the abuse are just coming into conscious awareness.

The "Older, Wiser Self"

Rather than only creating bridges between the trauma and the resources of the present, it is useful to also create resources from the perspective of the future and create a bridge between the past trauma and associations to a positive future. For example, I might say to a client,

> Imagine that you have grown to be a healthy, wise, nurturing, old woman (or man) and you are looking back on this time in your life in which you were integrating, processing, overcoming the effects of the past experience of sexual abuse. What do you think this wonderful, old, nurturing, wiser you would suggest to you to help you get through this current phase of your life? What would she/he tell you to remember? What would she/he suggest that would be most helpful in helping you heal from the past? What would she/he say to comfort you? And does she/he have any advice about how therapy could be most helpful and useful?

To enhance the therapeutic impact of these questions, the following homework assignment can be given: Ask the client to write a letter to the "older, wiser self" telling her/him what the client is struggling with right now. Then ask the client to take the role of the "older, wiser self" respond with as letter offering comfort, advice and helpful instructions based on what she/he has learned from old age. Another version of this exercise is to have the client imagine a presumably supportive but deceased "old, wise" friend or relative and write the letter from that perspective.

Solution-Focused Questions

Another way the future can be utilized as a bridge between the trauma and a resource state is through the use of solution-focused questions in reference to the trauma. Solution-focused questions (Lipchik, 1988; Lipchik & de Shazer, 1986) are questions asked by the therapist to help clients focus on what they are already doing that is working (even to a minor degree), on imagined solutions, and on ideas about how to make solutions occur. These questions are particularly useful in working with sexual abuse survivors because they tend to counterbalance the associational impact of focusing on the past trauma by giving a much needed emphasis to the present and future.

Constructive questions (Lipchik & de Shazer, 1986) are a specific form of solution-focused intervention that can be employed both individually and systemically. Individually oriented constructive questions help the client create an associational bridge to the future while identifying the specifics of his/her own solutions. Systemically oriented constructive questions evoke and utilize the client's associational resources of supportive family, friends, and meaningful others. These questions will serve to create an associational bridge between memories and reexperiencing of the trauma to a present- and future-oriented perspective of empowerment.

Here are some examples of constructive individual questions to help the therapist and the client identify what is needed to overcome the trauma and its constricting effects:

- What will be the first (smallest) sign that things are getting better, that the sexual abuse is having less of an effect on your current life?

- What will you be doing differently when the sexual abuse is less of a current problem in your life?

- What will you be doing differently with your time?

- What will you be thinking about or doing instead of thinking about the abuse?

- Are there times when this (the above) is happening already, to some (even a very small) extent? What is different about those times, and what is helpful about those differences?

- When the above healing changes have been present in your life over extended time (days, months, years), what differences will they make in how you experience your life?

These are some examples of constructive systemic questions for sexual abuse survivors:

- What do you think (your significant other) would say that would be a first sign that things are getting a little bit better? What do you think (your significant other) will notice first?

- What do you think (your significant other, friend, co-worker, boss, etc.) will notice about you as you heal even more?

- What positive differences will these changes make in your relationship with (above person) over time?

- What differences could these healing changes you've described make in future generations of your family?

Clients are asked to predict each "little sign" until they feel that if they did all of those things, they could say that they had overcome the effects of the abuse in that particular area of their life. "Overcoming the trauma," however, should be applied as a frame only to behaviors that clients are consciously able to influence and change.

A SAFE SELF-HYPNOSIS TECHNIQUE

I now offer an auto-hypnosis technique for mitigating symptoms of anxiety and insomnia. This technique also is frequently used by my clients to get back to sleep after disturbing nightmares reminiscent of the abuse, and to reconnect to the present when they are experiencing symptoms of post-traumatic stress.

In inducing self-hypnosis, sexual abuse survivors sometimes inadvertently move immediately into an anxiety attack or relive their victimization. This may occur because the relaxation inherent in many self-hypnosis techniques may be experientially associated with a lack of vigilance, control, and alertness, thereby eliciting feelings of vulnerability and fear reminiscent of victimization.

I first learned of the self-hypnosis technique while attending a workshop taught by Stephen Gilligan and Paul Carter, who referred to it as the "Betty Erickson Technique," respectfully named after Erickson's widow. I have adapted it to utilize the sexual abuse survivor's understandable tendency toward vigilance and awareness of external surrounding in order to feel comfort and relaxation. The focus is kept on present surroundings rather than utilizing associations to the past or more random associations that would carry a higher risk of traumatic material "bleeding through" into the experience. In using this technique with sexual abuse survivors, one should emphasize the external orientation, and also invite the client to use the option of keeping the eyes open, either the entire time or until experiencing a sense of comfort and security and a "pleasant" little urge to close the eyes.

The therapist first describes the general procedure and then models it for the client, answering any questions. The client is then guided through the following instructions:

1. "Find a comfortable position for your body and a pleasant place to focus your eyes, knowing that you can feel free, throughout this experience, to make any physical adjustments necessary for comfort and ease."

2. The therapist then makes the suggestion that "you can keep your eyes open throughout this experience, or perhaps you will choose to close them, but do not do this until you feel a pleasant little urge to close them."

3. A suggestion is then offered to enable the client to reorient at any time she wishes to do so. "If you want to reorient at any time, of course you can do so very easily just by moving around a bit, or perhaps you might like to count yourself to five, telling yourself that you will be progressively awake, alert, and refreshed with each number, e.g., one . . . more and more awake, two . . . a little more awake, three . . . beginning to feel refreshed and alert . . . four . . . even more awake, and five . . . all the way awake, alert and refreshed." This reorientation counting can be repeated should the client feel a need for more time to reorient.

4. The client then names aloud five sights, five sounds, five physical sensations, then proceeds to four sights, four sounds, four sensations, and so on until progressing downward to one of each category. At this point, the client can either stop and enjoy the comfort and peace of the present-oriented trance state she has created, or she can start again and deepen the level of this stage with the externally focused self-hypnosis (Zeig, 1992).

5. "Losing track of the category or number is actually a very good sign that you are doing well." Often, by virtue of going into a pleasant trance state with this technique, the client eventually becomes confused about what "number" or sensory category (sights, sounds, sensations) she is currently addressing. In this event, she should congratulate herself, since the confusion indicates that she has succeeded in creating a nice, present-oriented and relaxing trance

state. At this point, she can either stop and just enjoy the state for a while, or "guess" where she is and continue the technique for a pleasant deepening effect.

6. Other considerations: This technique can be used aloud or silently. The advantages of doing it aloud include the comforting familiarity of hearing one's own voice and the fact that it allows the therapist to monitor where the client is in the technique.

A TECHNIQUE FOR HELPING THE CLIENT END THE CYCLE OF VICTIMIZATION

This technique can be best explained by first providing a context for its use. It is a sad fact that untreated victims of childhood sexual abuse are at risk for choosing abusive partners in adult life. Perhaps even more tragic is the tendency for some sexual abuse victims to subsequently fail to protect the next generation of children, and in some cases, grandchildren from further sexual abuse. The inability to recognize danger and take action to protect oneself and others is due to a reoccurrence of the spontaneous dissociation and related rigid associational compartmentalization that occurred as an unconscious attempt at protection in the original victimization.

This experience of spontaneous dissociation is, as a result of the original victimization, subsequently powerfully linked to the victim's mental associations surrounding the abuse. This could be thought of as a form of classical conditioning. As a result, later in life, if the formerly abused person experiences a situation literally or symbolically reminiscent of the abuse, she or he will tend to spontaneously dissociate. Unfortunately, this dissociative response often results in a numbing of much needed feelings, awareness, and internal signals of danger.

The dissociative numbing produces further results in the victim, who, when confronted with the danger of further abuse in the present, becomes psychologically immobilized and passive instead of fleeing or taking other protective measures when in danger. This also can result in parents who are themselves untreated victims of sexual abuse failing to recognize or respond to signs that their own children are being abused. In this way, further abuse merely triggers a spontaneous dissociative response that may impair the victims' ability to end the cycle of victimization. The therapist is challenged to empower the sexual abuse survivor to overcome the numbing response so as to be able to appropriately recognize and respond to dangerous situations.

The most reliable way I have found for accomplishing the above is for the client to be asked to respond to one of the two following questions: 1) How will you respond to situations that portend danger when you are no longer feeling affected by your past abuse? 2) Think of someone you know who is already good at self-protection. On a scale of one to 10, how safe would that person rate the situation or person you are confronting at this point in your life? Some of my clients have gotten in the habit of mentally scaling potential partners before accepting dates. One woman told me,

> "It's funny but it was as if in the past I guess I got the message I wasn't allowed to do this, to assess whether or not someone was going to treat me respectfully. I guess I just had the feeling as a consequence of being abused that I had to go out with anyone who asked me and put up with his behavior indefinitely in the future regardless of how he treated me, or something terrible (even worse) would happen to me."

Scaling and borrowing the perspective of another person are two ways to reinstall the ability to respond to danger appropriately. Scaling (de Shazer, 1985) is the technique of assigning related numerical values to depict severity and comparative recovery from psychological problems. Colleagues sometimes ask: in having the client practice scaling safety or borrowing the perspective of another person regarding self-protection, wouldn't it be more effective if you first induced an altered state? However, I believe that when working with an abuse victim who has not yet resolved the effects of the trauma, asking the client to imagine a potentially abusive situation will in itself tend to elicit an altered state, usually a state of numbing and dissociation. The goal is to help the client learn to alter the resulting state into a more adaptive and functional one for purposes of safety and self-protection.

FOUR-STEP TECHNIQUE FOR MITIGATING FLASHBACKS, NIGHTMARES, INTRUSIVE MEMORIES

I will now descibe my Four-Step Technique for assisting clients in confronting memories of sexual abuse and resolving flashbacks. A thorough description of appropriate techniques for eliciting and reprocessing repressed traumatic material is beyond the scope of this chapter. I will therefore limit my discussion to techniques to be used in cases where the memories are already available or are currently emerging in the form of flashbacks, nightmares, or intrusive memories. This technique is used at first within the therapy session. Later the client can learn to use it independently as needed.

A flashback or intrusive memory may be understood as a spontaneously occurring visual, and sometimes auditory and kinesthetic, stream of vivid memories associationally triggered by an experience literally or symbolically reminiscent of the original trauma. These associations then trigger further traumatic associations until something occurs to interrupt or alter the associational pattern. This process tends to spontaneously and naturalistically occur and then continue to occur in a light or mixed naturalistic trance state.

In this state, typically the victim is simultaneously aware of the present and yet equally, or in cases of severe flashbacks, more vividly aware of experiences from the past than would be characteristic of a normal waking state. In the case of nightmares, there is a general theme of the victim being endlessly pursued and abused in ways that are literally or symbolically related to the original abuse.

While flashbacks may appear to be random, often they are triggered by a "traumatic associational cue" in the form of a sensory experience (sight, sound, smell, taste, touch) or an event that literally or symbolically resembles some aspect of the original trauma. This technique allows the client to experience a sense of control over flashbacks that can occur in social situations and when alone. Once mastered, the technique can be used by the client to depotentiate the effect of the flashback, to transform it into an integrative experience, and to make sense of it afterwards.

If used consistently, eventually this technique will come to mind at the first instance of a flashback, and each experience will end in further integration. Although this is not commonly reported, one client described spontaneously using this technique in a dream state when she was having a nightmare about the abuse!

The following four-step question technique will help the client experience more understanding, integration, and control of flashback experiences within and outside of the therapy setting:

1. What are you experiencing? When have you felt this way before?
2. In what ways are this current situation and the abuse situation similar? For example, is the setting, time of year, sights, sounds, sensations in any way similar to the past situation where you felt this way? If there is another person involved, is she or he similar in some way to a person from the past who elicited similar feelings?

   (The purpose of this question and of the previous question is to validate the client's experience and to help to identify the flashback trigger so it can't ambush her again. Flashback triggers, however, are sometimes so subtle that it is not possible to discern any specific, identifiable connection. If the client is unable to consciously identify any connection between questions 1 and 2, simply move on to question 3.)

3. How is your current situation *different* from the situation in the past in which you were abused? What is different about you, your sensory experience, your current life circumstances and life resources? What is different about the setting? If another person or persons are involved, how are they different from the person(s) in the past (abusive) situation?

4. What action, if any, do you want to take to feel better in the present?

   (For example, a flashback may indicate that a person is once again in a situation that is in some way unsafe. If this is the case, self-protective actions should be taken. On the other hand, a flashback sometimes merely means that an old memory has been triggered by an inconsequential resemblance to the past, such as a certain color or smell. In such cases, corrective messages of comfort and reassurance need to be given to the self to counteract old traumatic memories of trauma.)

SUMMARY AND CONCLUSION

In offering an Ericksonian perspective on treatment of sexual abuse, I have attempted to provide a way of looking at sexual abuse survivors that addresses the fact that they bring unique resources and skills to therapy just as they bring unique problems by virtue of their history of trauma. This perspective invites practical and respectful techniques that allow the therapist and client to work collaboratively to create new and more adaptive associational patterns that will overcome the constricting effects of the rigid associational compartmentalization that causes so many PTSD symptoms. Even though these new patterns will, in turn, provide the client increasing levels of control and mastery over the post-traumatic stress symptoms, the overall goal of therapy with sexual abuse survivors should not be merely symptom resolution, but that of living a satisfying, meaningful life.

REFERENCES

Beahrs, J.O. (1982). *Unity and multiplicity: Multi-level consciousness of self in hypnosis, psychiatric disorder and mental health.* New York: Brunner/Mazel.

Briere, J. (1989). *Therapy for adults molested as children.* New York: Springer.

Courtois, C. (1988). *Healing the incest wound.* New York: Norton.

de Shazer, S. (1985). *Keys to solution in brief therapy.* New York: Norton.

Dolan, Y. (1991). *Resolving sexual abuse: Solution-focused therapy and Ericksonian hypnosis for survivors.* New York: Norton.

Erickson, M.H., & Rossi, E.L. (1989). *The february man.* New York: Brunner/Mazel.

Hammond, C. (1990). *Handbook of hypnotic suggestion.* New York: Norton.

Lipchik, E. (1988). Purposeful sequences for beginning the solution-focused interview. In E. Lipchik (Ed.), *Interviewing* (pp. 105-117). Rockville, MD: Triangle.

Lipchik, E., & de Shazer, S. (1986). The purposeful interview. *Journal of Strategic and Systemic Therapies,* 5 (1-2):88-89.

Yapko, M. (1992). Address given at the Fifth International Congress on Ericksonian Approaches to Hypnosis and Psychotherapy.

Zeig, J. K. (1992). The virtues of our faults: A key concept of Ericksonian therapy. In J. K. Zeig (Ed.), *The Evolution of Psychotherapy: The Second Conference* (pp. 252-266). New York: Brunner/Mazel.

CHAPTER 28

Erickson's Approach to Multiple Personality: A Cross-Cultural Perspective

Madeleine Richeport

Milton H. Erickson, M.D., became interested in multiple personality in the 1940's when it was not as fashionable as it is today. He considered it an exceptional opportunity to learn about the development, organization, and structure of the human personality. He wondered how two separate personalities could develop within the same person when they had identical life experiences. Before he died, he had seen 23 cases. Although he wrote on the subject, he never wrote a definitive paper, and several of his writings were published posthumously (Erickson, circa 1940's/1980; Erickson & Kubie, 1939/1967; Erickson & Rapaport, circa 1940's/1980; Haley & Richeport, 1955/1991). Few of his students were interested in the subject at the time, although Beahrs (1982, 1986) and Haley most closely follow Erickson's approach.

This chapter will present Erickson's views on multiple personalities and their therapy. Because Erickson learned many of his techniques from observing naturalistic behaviors, including ritual trances, his therapy with multiple personalities may have been influenced by his knowledge of trances of spirit mediums because the behaviors are similar. Multiple personalities and mediums are typically excellent hypnotic subjects. The number of both alters and spirits seem to increase in therapy and during the development of mediumship. "Other selves" experience psychophysiological changes, and debates continue as to whether the behaviors are real or pretended, and whether they are normal or pathological (Richeport, 1992). I will show how Erickson utilized "other selves" as resources and draw parallels between his therapy and natural trance therapies cross-culturally.

Like many of Erickson's ideas, his view of multiple personalities departed from those commonly held. The most popular current view is that multiple personalities are dissociated states and a form of psychopathology. Erickson saw them as not necessarily pathological, but as a special type of person who, at times, gets into difficulties because of recurring periods of amnesia. He believed that there were primary and secondary personalities who were separate, distinct, and independent. Based on the same experiential lives, the dominant one had more of a reality orientation while the secondary one might have richer intellectual and emotional knowledge (Erickson, circa 1940's/1980).

Erickson was an extremely careful diagnostician. He took detailed histories, yet, a) he did not encounter the large number of personalities found by most researchers today, b) he did not find abuse as a major cause, c) he did not find that most personalities are vicious and malevolent, and d) he did not want to personify a hidden observer. Ross et al. (1989) found 15 personalities to be the mean number of personalities in 236 cases studied. In discussing the case of Sybil (Schreiber, 1974), for example, Erickson differed from the accepted view that she had 16 different personalities. Erickson believed she had three personalities, with twelve split-off parts. His cases are typically two or three personalities both before and during therapy.

Erickson did not regard secondary personalities as necessarily vicious or malevolent. On the contrary, they were helpful in two of the cases described below. Although abuse is considered the primary etiological factor to develop multiple personality disorder (MPD) (Putnam et al., 1989; Ross et al., 1989), Erickson never discussed abuse.

Erickson did not accept the concept of the "hidden observer" as an explanation in hypnosis or multiple personality. Hilgard (1977) in his neo-dissociation research likened the hidden observer to secondary personalities. He proposed that some part of the hypnotized person might experience things differently from the self that is hypnotized. This acted as a one-way amnesic barrier with the hypnotic subject as it does in the dual personality.

As an example, Erickson would suggest a negative hallucination. This would mean the person cannot see the object, yet to avoid it he must see it. Erickson referred to this as "unconscious awareness." Whether in a deep trance or in real life, you are not viewing yourself, you are just experiencing and not self-monitoring. According to Erickson, "you could be in a deep trance physically and a light trance mentally" (unpublished conversations between Erickson, Haley and Weakland, 1955). That is, trance is not uniformly experienced in the same individual.

Finally, Erickson differed from other therapists in that he did not usually bring family members into therapy with multiple personalities, nor did he inform them of the patient's condition. As in his therapy in general, he believed that the family would adjust to the patient's changes.

The general view is that multiple personalities show hysterical dynamics. Psychometric and projective tests of two of Erickson's cases, in collaboration with Rapaport (1940), countered the general view and were found to be of the obsessive-compulsive type. According to Rossi, "these important findings give the reports a significant place in line with the studies of dual personality by Azam, Mitchell, Prince, Sidis, Goodhart, and Janet "(1980, p. 230).

Researchers have claimed that hypnosis produces multiple personality (Harriman, 1942; Leavitt, 1947; Kampman, 1976). Others say that hypnosis does not produce multiples (Braun, 1984; Ross et al., 1989), but confusion arises because the switching process from ordinary wakefulness to trance is similar to the switching from one personality to the other in multiples (Bliss, 1983). Erickson helped to clarify this debate. According to Erickson (circa 1940's/1980), "Hypnosis is not a miracle worker. It is possible to build up in the subject pseudo personalities, but these are extremely limited in character and extent of development, and they obviously are temporary, superimposed manifestations. In addition, such personality constructions are restricted by the nature and origin of their development to the hypnotic situation" (p. 264). Erickson did not believe that hypnosis could produce an enduring personality. His unparalleled understanding of hypnosis enabled him to differentiate trance from the manifestations of secondary personalities.

Whereas most therapists today stress integration and postintegration adjustments, and might even consider it malpractice to settle for less, Erickson did not believe integration was a realistic or even desirable goal. In fact he viewed the secondary personality as a resource who, in many cases, could aid the primary personality and the therapist.

ERICKSON'S APPROACH TO MULTIPLE PERSONALITY

Erickson's approach with multiple personalities can be divided into three main steps: 1) Discovery, 2) Making Contact, and 3) Collaboration. Because his techniques were so similar to those found in other cross-cultural therapies, examples will also be offered to widen the view of multiplicity of the mind.

Discovering "Other Selves"

Erickson made intense observation in natural settings of conflicting responses, reactions, and patterns of behavior, and so was alert to unusual behaviors. He also tested for amnesia. This is illustrated in the case of Ellen (Haley & Richeport, 1991), a married woman in her early 20's when she began to work as a secretary in Erickson's office. Erickson was puzzled by changes in her walking, which was graceful at times and awkward at other times, and changes in the tempo of her typing. She was also forgetful. Erickson then discovered some cryptic writings that she denied doing.

> Finding on my table a note written in a juvenile script containing a comment about a red hat, I concealed it. Several days later, apropos of nothing, I addressed the general inquiry to nobody in particular, "Was it a black hat?" and then, without awaiting any answer, absorbed myself in my work. After an interval of a few days I found on my desk another note that said, "No, red," in a similar juvenile script. In this manner, I began a correspondence. Thus, upon finding a drawing or a note upon my desk, I would make some remark pertinent to it, but apparently silly, irrelevant, and meaningless. Within a few days I would find, concealed in my papers or on my desk, a reply bearing upon the previous note or drawing and my apparently meaningless comment.
>
> When shown these notes and drawings, Ellen evinced only a polite interest. However, I soon began to discover that if, when I found a note on my table, Ellen happened to be looking my way, there would appear momentarily on her face that peculiar alert, interested, and amused expression seen previously in different situations. I discovered further that Ellen was not aware that I had just picked up that note. After verifying these observations repeatedly and under varying conditions, the question arose as to what role Ellen played in this total situation despite her apparently unawareness of it.
>
> This question led rapidly to the discovery that her unusual behavior constituted a separate, complete, and consistent general pattern never in evidence at the same time as Ellen's usual behavior. In other words, there were two separate and distinct patterns of general behavior that did not overlap but, rather, alternated in appearance. (Erickson, 1940's/1980)

In his other published case (Erickson & Kubie, 1939/1967), Damon was a 20-year-old female psychology student who volunteered as a subject for hypnosis experiments. For more than a year she suffered from obsessive fears that doors had been left open, and of cats. Erickson induced trance in the first session and gave Damon a posthypnotic suggestion that her name would be "Miss Brown" in trance. She began practicing hand levitation and catalepsy. "In addition to the expression or dissociation there appeared a look of intense terror, . . . Soon these manifestations would disappear, quickly to be replaced by the previous look of eager, amused interest . . . and a disappearance of the catalepsy." Erickson then suggested that she try automatic writing at the same time that he had her read an article and make a summary of it. It took almost 12 hours to decipher her writing. When, finally, she asked, "Did I really write this nonsense?" her hand replied "No," of which Damon was unaware. Her hand replied to a series of questions that defined her dual personality. "When they showed Damon her answers, she remarked, 'Well that really must mean that I have a dual personality,' to which her hand wrote, 'Right.' Damon asked, 'Can I talk to you?' Brown replied, 'Sure' and gave her name as Jane Brown" (Erickson & Kubie, p. 344, 1939/1967).

Erickson presented the following additional but unpublished case at a teaching seminar:

> Vicki, a lesbian, walks and talks with all the manners of a lesbian. I noticed another pattern of behavior and discovered Marylee. Marylee was married with children. Her husband divorced her out of his confusion because sometimes Victoria would awaken and find a strange man in her bed and she would beat him up. Marylee would tell him she didn't beat him up. She didn't seem to be the same person, a seemingly alien type of behavior both to Vicki and to Marylee — seemingly hostile destructive behavior. I knew about that arson in Detroit — the bewilderment of the police. A girl had been identified as the arsonist. Vicki disclaimed that she had any knowledge of the arson. They later found out the girl named Marylee resembled Vicki. She seemed to wear the same clothes that Vicki did. Now they questioned her. They finally reached the conclusion that these were Vicki and Marylee. They could never get those two girls together despite many efforts. One might show up but the other failed to. And I knew about that. I couldn't put Vicki in a trance. I could hypnotize Marylee very easily.

Erickson used hypnosis with one personality to communicate with another.

> I put Marylee in a trance in the presence of another therapist and had Marylee become a bodyless mind leaving a frozen paralyzed body behind. I slowly slid her skirt up. All of a sudden a very

harsh voice profanely told me "Stop that and if I could get out of this frozen body, I'd kill you." That's how I learned about Christine. I knew I was in the presence of somebody awfully hostile. I could feel the hair on the back of my neck standing up. It was Christine who set the fire. Christine was a very antisocial person. (Unpublished teaching seminar, 1978)

SPIRITIST PARALLELS   In the Spiritist system adepts observe such behaviors as hallucinations, visions, and clairvoyant phenomena, and interpret them as signs of mediumship. The novices are encouraged to attend sessions where they practice going into trance and receiving their spirit guides, who often with great difficulty manifest the stereotyped behaviors characteristic of different entities. In both Erickson's therapy and in Spiritist therapy, people are encouraged to express "other selves" through automatic writing in a trance state. They are given names, and one self may be put in trance while the other selves are not in trance. Amnesia is investigated.

Making Contact with "Other Selves"

Erickson contacted "other selves" by accepting them as real people. He established cues to bring them forth and he taught them to write and talk. He used multiple meanings of words, puns, and ordeals to contact alters. As an example (Haley & Richeport, 1991), Erickson realized that Ellen was a dual personality, yet, it took 15 months for Ellen to accept it. The following communication techniques were used:

Then one day I found on my desk a note that bore the name Mary Anne Peters. I concealed it immediately. Several days later, on my next visit to the university, I remarked casually to Ellen upon the frequency of double meanings in apparently simple remarks. I suggested that she listen carefully to what I was about to say, since it would have a double meaning, and I urged her strongly to be sure to understand that second meaning. I then remarked that one may describe someone as having the "map of Dublin — M.A.P. — on his face." Ellen listened intently but in obvious bewilderment, incapable of realizing that in spelling the word map I had actually given three initial letters. At the same time, her hand was observed to pick up a pencil and to write, "Yes, Mary understand," in the script made familiar by the notes left on my table. This name "Mary" was later found to derive from the heroine of a novel read by Ellen in her childhood.

When Dr. Kubie, a noted psychoanalyst, arrived for a planned visit to meet a dual personality, Erickson talked with Ellen about a time for change and moved the furniture around. Then he told a story about a little girl. . . .

> She was tremendously delighted because she had learned to spell "cook"—C double o K, "look"—L double o K, and "book"—B double o K, and she was very proud of that, she never missed an opportunity to show her ability to spell. Then one day little Mary was reading a book and the sentence read "Up up Mary Ann," and so she read it (SPEAKING QUICKLY AND SHARPLY) "Double up, Mary Ann!" And there was Mary. (Haley & Richeport, 1991)

ESTABLISHING CUES   Once in contact, Erickson established cues to call the secondary personality, such as turning over a cigarette. Then he had to recognize the ways the alter communicated. For example, he received a letter from Ellen, and words would be interspersed forming a sentence by Mary.

With Christine, Erickson made it clear that if she ever dared to show up again without his permission,

> I'd get hold of Marylee, freeze her body, and send Marylee off into outer space. One thing that Christine couldn't tolerate was Vicki's lesbianism or Marylee's heterosexuality. The hostility seemed so general that I thought that type of exploration would elicit it. I had Christine remain within that body and not to feel that body at any time. In other words, I anesthetized her own sense of body. She did not want to touch that body she was confined in. She said she hated the body because it kept changing. I took her body away from her, not her mind. (Unpublished teaching seminar, 1978)

Teaching the Secondary Personality to Talk

> I told Mary that writing answers to questions was too difficult, that she had to learn to talk. She said, "I can't, I've never learned to talk." So I told Kubie to follow my lead and we started out bragging about our kids again, with Mary there. After we bragged awhile, I turned to Mary and told her she'd have to talk, we couldn't waste time letting her write her answers, and she wrote, "Can't," in very big letters. And I argued and pleaded and coaxed and begged, and then I began to lose my temper. And to Kubie's

horror, he saw one of the worst temper tantrums that any kid ever threw. And I was yelling and throwing books on the floor stamping my feet and pounding the desk, and finally I threw in the statement, "The least that you can do is when I ask you to talk you can say, 'No.' And now you talk! [and she said] 'No.' She looked at me and wrote, "You think you're smart, don't you." And I said, "We both do." So I said," You can talk, you said, 'No.' Do you think that you could say 'Yes' if you tried?" (Imitating her hestitant attempt) "Yes, yes yes." It was the most delightful thing. And I said," Well, You've said 'No,' you've said 'Yes' and you enjoyed saying 'Yes,' tell us your name." "Mary Ann." At first she was awfully slow in vocalizing, and then she picked up speed. (Haley & Richeport, 1991)

Mary was a well poised, self-confident, extremely capable woman, free from Ellen's neuroticisms and markedly different in every way, even giving the impression of being several years older than Ellen.

SPIRITIST PARALLELS   Erickson's colleague in Brazil, David Akstein, M.D., had several mediums as patients. He encouraged mediumship or the expression of "other selves" in his therapy. He believes that like hypnosis, spiritism is a subcultural way for the patient to attain autocontrol. His patient, Gladis, (Richeport, 1980) was an attractive 39-year-old married woman who presented symptoms of dizziness, nausea, and fear of going outside of her apartment alone. She was limited to the house unless accompanied by her husband, Fernando, or her 12-year-old daughter, Sonia. After consulting many specialists, she reluctantly agreed to see a psychiatrist; she did not believe that her symptoms were psychologically caused. Gladis was an Umbandista medium, and she talked about the Afro-Brazilian rituals she performed daily to protect herself and her family. However, when she entered therapy, she said that her Indian spirit guide advised her to give up her full-time mediumship practice, which she conducted in her own home, because it made her exhausted. Besides dizziness, the only other problem she expressed was her hostility toward her mother, who lived directly across the street and from her window supervised Gladis's life. Gladis behaved timidly, subordinating herself to her husband, and did not discipline her daughter, a spoiled, hyperactive girl, who continuously disrupted the therapy sessions.

    Akstein treated her with medication, psychotherapy, relaxation, and desensitization techniques. She improved, but the dizziness and street phobia did not disappear. He began to encourage her to return to mediumship. During one appointment, as he jokingly gyrated her (a typical trance induction technique employed in Umbanda), Gladis entered mediumship trance. During the subsequent sessions, Gladis was possessed by 11 of her 27 spiritual entities. Akstein called on her strong, aggressive Caboclo (Indian) guide, and asked him to aid the therapy and to protect Gladis when she went out on the street. Akstein saw parallels between his technique and the one applied by Pierre Janet. Akstein said, "It consists in the application of suggestive therapy in the second state, that is in deep hypnosis, preferably with spontaneous amnesia. It is as if applying suggestions to another person that had nothing to do with the subject" (Richeport, 1980).

Collaboration

Rather than trying to banish or integrate the alters, they are accepted and taught to collaborate with each other and to help Erickson deal with their problems.

When Erickson asked Ellen to write her autobiography, Mary also wrote to him about things that Ellen did not know. Mary helped Ellen recall an incident as a child when she saw an exhibitionist. Erickson elicited promises from Mary not to embarrass Ellen nor cause discord in their marriage. He made her promise never to go bed with Ellen's husband, Joe. When Joe returned from a four-year absence in World War II, Mary "slipped into bed with him" in the excitement. He knew he was in bed with a stranger and accused Ellen of being unfaithful and he wanted a divorce. Mary asked Erickson for advice and he wrote to Mary and told Mary, "Have Ellen become very seductive and seduce her husband and you keep out of it. After they have renewed their sex life, you start loaning one of your sex behaviors to Ellen, one of your body feelings to Ellen, one of your body responses, but do it very slowly and carefully so that the husband will think Ellen has just developed." Erickson commented: "My judgment is that Mary's orgasm was greatly different from Ellen's. The patterns of orgasm differ so greatly in women" (Haley & Richeport, 1991). Mary would not always help Ellen. When Erickson asked Mary to take over Ellen's pain, she refused.

In the case of Damon, described above, for 20 years Brown protected Damon from a painful, misunderstood childhood trauma related to her present fear of doors left open. Erickson and Kubie explain the function of Brown "that under the impulse of terror and anger, the young woman had made a very deep painful identification of herself with her grandfather. Somehow all of her later anxieties and cumpulsions stemmed from this momentous event. At some time she built up a protective companionate alter ego, Jane, who knew the things that she did not want to know and who was either unable or else forbidden to tell them to anyone but who exercised an almost continuous protective role toward the patient herself" (1939/1967), p. 360). She did this by shielding her, demanding special consideration for her, offering encouragement, distracting her attention, deliberately deceiving her, and employing various other protective measures. For example, Brown wrote automatically, "Won't let her feel scared, won't let her feel bad." One might say that a dual personality in this case was a decided advantage for the subject. When one personality was tired, the other did the work. When one had pain, the other took over.

"OTHER SELVES" AS THERAPISTS   Generally therapists treat secondary personalities as something to get rid of. Erickson utilized the secondary personality as a resource to aid the primary personality and to aid himself in the therapy. In the cases described, for example, Brown dictated the best ways that Erickson should proceed to uncover Damon's traumatic memory. Mary helped Erickson "put back the memory a little bit at a time into Ellen's mind" of the repressed childhood incident with an exhibitionist. As long as the secondary personality acted as protector, in keeping with his general "using what the patient brings," he utilized the protector. Since the personality was originally created to protect Damon from the trauma, through automatic writing, Erickson utilized the secondary personality to help uncover what it had been covering up.

Erickson's approach with multiple personalities stresses collaboration among the personalities. This is different from others who believe in banishing or integrating alters (Allison, 1985; Braun, 1986; Kluft, 1985). Erickson slowly and carefully confronted the primary personality with the realization that there were other personalities in the same body. Breaking down amnestic barriers seems to be a process of replacing the displacement of one personality by another with co-conscious mentation.

The positive way Erickson utilized the different personalties as resources is within the framework of his general therapeutic approach (Haley, 1967, p. 536). He treated each personality with respect and encouraged collaboration. He stressed the problem that in his cases the personalities feared death. He arranged ways they could retain their identity that would not disturb functioning. Rather than encouraging integration, Erickson channeled the dissociation in a socially acceptable way. He recommended living alternate weeks, he created cooperative arrangements between personalities so that the children would not see the secondary personality, thus avoiding confusion. As in his therapy in general, Erickson emphasized the smallest item amenable to change, which, when changed, would require that the entire system change around it. He achieved more by attempting less (Beahrs, 1983, p. 108). This is apparent in the immobilization of Marylee's body, teaching Mary to talk, and deciphering the automatic writing of Damon.

Erickson's hypnotic techniques were direct, not indirect, to clearly separate the involuntary switching in multiple personalities from the voluntary switching in hypnosis. Erickson was also the master of play in therapy. Once he got the personalities cooperating, he arranged for them to play tricks on people. Erickson arranged for another dual personality, for example, to have a date with a young male resident. They would switch while he was dancing with them. One minute he would be dancing with one girl and the next minute he would be dancing with another. It was the same girl, but also different. Erickson got them to have fun with each other like that, and that is how they could collaborate with each other. It made it an advantage to be two people (Grove & Haley, 1993; Haley & Richeport, 1992).

Many techniques, similar to those of Erickson, are illustrated in Akstein's case adapted from the cult groups. He called on the spirits for help in his therapy with Gladis. It was a play time with everyone enjoying the presence of Gladis's alters. Akstein summoned "Seven Arrows," the strongest entity that possessed Gladis, and asked for his help. The entity told the doctor that Gladis's dizziness was caused by the weight-reduction medication she was taking. Possessed by this entity, Gladis could better discipline her daughter and express dissatisfaction to her husband. She received other entities such as sexy pranksters, old wise slaves, and children, thus allowing a range of behaviors ordinarily unacceptable to a Latin American woman. In the family's discussions afterwards, Akstein reinforced the power of the strong Indian and other entities who manifested to cure Gladis and to help him. Through mediumship, Gladis practiced solutions to her problems, including her phobia and her relationship with her family. Her strength in the office as an "alternate self" seemed to act as as a rehearsal for behavior that was later translated into reality.

ADJUSTMENT TO CHANGE   Ellen and Mary and Damon and Brown moved from the primary personality having amnesia for the secondary to co-consciousness or awareness of the other's presence. In breaking down the amnesia, the pattern of alternating personalities is changed to coexisting personalities. This is not the horizontal split seen in repression. Instead the selves are placed side by side in a vertical split (Erickson & Kubie, 1939/1967). However, in the case of Marylee, Erickson was able to achieve collaboration among the alternating personalities, but they were not coexistent.

Mary and Ellen and Damon and Brown agreed never to let their children see the secondary personality so as not to confuse them. Over time, Brown became less interested in what Damon was doing. The amnesia was eliminated in these cases. However, in the case of Marylee, Vicki, and Christine, Erickson made them aware of each other. Neither one wanted to give up the self; Vicki is still homosexual. Marylee is still heterosexual, so he managed to have them compromise, each living alternate weeks. "Vicki has translated some of her lesbian tendencies into church work. Marylee was always devoted to the church. The work that Marylee does in church one week is torn down the next week by Vicki, who does it in a different way." They continue the pattern of alternating rather than being coexisting personalities.

In the case of Gladis, with the collaboration of her entities, she resumed her mediumship practice, became much less dependent, and her phobia was eliminated.

FOLLOWING ERICKSON'S APPROACH

Erickson's approach to multiple personality is being followed by Jay Haley in his supervision of therapists. In the following case, Haley was supervising a supervisor (Grove & Haley, 1993) who encountered difficulty in convincing the therapist to accept the client as having two or more real personalities, which would then lead to have them communicate with one another. The therapist believed the client was pretending. It also was difficult to convince the therapist that the goal was collaboration and not integration. Any evidence of personalities merging continued to be taken as a positive therapeutic response. Betty was a 37-year-old single parent of a 12-year-old boy. She sought therapy for her son, who was experimenting with drugs and disobeying at school. After several sessions. Betty began to complain of "sleepwalking" episodes in which she would find hickey marks on her body which she did not know how she received, and strange men's names on match boxes in her purse. One day, she "came to" in a bar without knowing how she got there or what she had done there. To prevent herself from "sleepwalking," she put bells on the doors to awaken her if she tried to leave the house at night; she also entrusted her keys and money to a neighbor.

Betty said these episodes were related to an imaginary persona that she invented when she was 12, called Candy, to help her cope with abuse by her alcoholic mother. Between the ages of 12 and 17, when Betty went out socially, she called herself Candy, an opposite of her usual inhibited self. She brought in letters written by Candy that showed a different handwriting. This began to convince the skeptical therapist that Betty was a dual personality.

Haley suggested acceptance of the two personalities who share the same body, and he established the goal of therapy to eliminate amnesia by having the two personalities communicate. Because Betty was so fearful of seeing Candy for the first time. Haley suggested that the therapist hypnotize Betty so that Candy could communicate through automatic writing. When the therapist attempted to wake up Betty, "I am Candy" was uttered. She then appeared to be a different person and reported her promiscuous episodes and told stories of childhood abuse. She also objected to Betty's ungainly appearance with her weight gain and eyeglasses. Haley suggested that they make an agreement that she would not break the law or harm the shared body or the son, and would not go out at night. During the fourth session, Betty appeared with makeup for the first time, her hair styled, and without glasses. She explained this change as the result of her communications with Candy. Rather than seeing Betty's behavior as pathological, Haley suggested seeing it as a "special ability."

Candy acted as a resource in several way to both Betty and the therapist. She insisted that Betty remember the traumatic experience of child abuse. She insisted that Betty lose weight and do things to make herself look more attractive. They collaborated in the decision to maintain only platonic relationships with men for awhile. Betty continued to lose weight and returned to school for her high school diploma. In follow-up sessions, Betty said that Candy was no longer taking over her body, but she could sense when Candy was "present" in her mind, especially in situations in which Betty was not facing up to things. There were no more episodes of amnesia. The collaboration led to patterns of co-consciousness rather than to alternation of the personalities.

Amnesia

The most important diagnostic criteria for multiples is amnesia. This can be considered pathological. Erickson (1939/1980) showed how we can employ in hypnosis the natural psychopathologies we experience in everyday life, like the normal forgetting we do. He utilized the natural phenomena of amnesia in his hypnotic techniques, such as creating hypnotic amnesia to break conscious waking patterns. These patterns, which disturb the linking or ordinary associative connections, can facilitate therapeutic work in hypnosis and cause dysfunction in multiple personalities. Erickson's understanding of many different kinds of hypnotic amnesia (Erickson & Rossi, 1974/1980) enabled him to break down the amnestic barriers in multiple personality. However, he noted, "No matter how rigid the boundaries, they are not absolute, the primary personality having some awareness of the secondary, however slight, and the secondary possibly having a degree of amnesia for the primary. Boundaries will shift from time to time as will barriers to information exchange" (Beahrs, 1982, p. 86).

Similarly in Spiritism, there is not total amnesia for all spirits. Some people are conscious of one spirit and unconscious of another. Although many people believe that true possession is indicated by total amnesia, in some Spiritist centers, as mediums become more adept, they become more conscious of the spirit.

Differentiating Trance from Pathology

In the 1950's, Erickson explored the relationship between schizophrenia and trance with Haley and Weakland (Unpublished audiotaped conversations, 1955). More than 50 percent of multiples receive a misdiagnosis of schizophrenia (Ross, 1989), as they share many of the same symptoms such as hallucinations and amnesia. Likewise, it is difficult to make a differential diagnosis between spirit mediumship and pschopathoplastic behavior that is colored by cultural beliefs.

According to Erickson, trance and schizophrenia look alike and have similar behaviors, but with different significance. In hypnosis, the subjective experience of trance is comfortable, for a legitimate purpose, with some control over it. In the schizophrenic, the subjective experience such as a hallucination is not part of self, has no purpose nor is it desired, and is out of control. In hypnosis, the experience is not permanent, but limited to the "now" in trance, whereas in schizophrenia there is an indefinite continuation in time in a vague way. In hypnosis, the subject loses contact with certain realities. The schizophrenic often is exceedingly aware even in a stuporous state and cannot limit attention to just one thing. Hypnotic subjects respond to the hypnotist. With the schizophrenic it is difficult to establish rapport. Catalepsy in trance is a response to the hypnotist, while the waxy flexibility of the catatonic is a response to the body part being moved. They are similar when they are doing automatic writing in that the subject in trance and the schizophrenic are not concerned with spacial arrangements or ordered sequences and will write anywhere on the paper. Although they are both literal, the hypnotic subject differentiates "is," and "as if," while the schizophrenic seems to confuse "as if" and "is."

Haley has described Erickson's playing with the metaphoric and literal communication of the trance subject. "He is floating or it is 'as if' he is floating." When Erickson accepted the metaphor of his psychotic patient who said he was Jesus, he took him literally and gave him employment as a carpenter (Haley, 1973). Erickson's approach with schizophrenics and multiples was similar in his acceptance and willingness to make pathological metaphors real. Erickson told a schizophrenic woman, when she had a psychotic episode, to deposit her hallucinations in manila envelopes in his office. She could examine them when she came to his office (Haley, 1973).

Just as he treated the hallucinations as real, he treated dual personalities as two real people. His approach was followed in a case supervised by

Haley. A therapist told a multiple personality that her child alter could stay in his office. The patient called from home saying that the child was afraid to stay in the office alone. The therapist said that he would go to the office and bring his daughter's teddy bear to stay with the child. The patient drove 40 miles and waited in the parking lot to verify that this was accomplished by the therapist. Just as Erickson took psychotic episodes seriously, this therapist took the metaphoric child seriously. As in his therapy in general, Erickson accepted the symptom, utilized it, and channeled it into a socially acceptable area that would improve the functioning of the patient.

In Spiritism, hallucinations are interpreted as signs of developing medium faculties. Learning to go into trance at prescribed times and settings brings unwanted behaviors under control. The behaviors are changed from symptoms to special abilities. According to Garrison (1978) and Akstein (1972), schizophrenics and multiple personalities do make up Spiritist clientele, and they are not seen as developed mediums. However, through practice they learn to control the appearance of "other selves" similar to Erickson's therapy with multiples. He controlled their behavior by giving them signals to appear. Like ritual behaviors, he established rules for conduct.

Symptomatic Dissociation to Hypnotic Dissociation

According to Erickson, mediumship trances and hypnosis are analogous states; this is, they are the same psychophysiological phenomena with different understandings (Erickson, personal communication, 1975). I do not know whether Erickson would have considered multiple personality an analogous state. However, in therapy, he used the dissociation of hypnosis to enable the dissociative personality to function. Likewise, spirit mediumship uses the possession trance experience to bring the negative experience of spirit possession under control. This is an example of the way Ericksonian therapy works. The symptomatic trance is turned into a therapeutic trance. The handicap becomes the asset. The symptom becomes the cure (Beahrs, 1986; Gilligan, 1987). Beahrs (1982, p. 175) sees the dissociative experience as one of the most positive in the psyche of mankind. It places primary thinking under secondary logic and leads to tertiary creativity.

Erickson's approach to multiple personalities may be considered a minority approach. However, worldwide it is the majority approach in utilizing "alternate selves" as resources to bring them under control. Cross-cultural studies clarify the ethnocentric medical paradigm that governs Western psychotherapy. MPD as a diagnostic category reflects this bias (Kenny,

1981). The worldview of most cultures favors the idea of multilevel consciousness and expression of "other selves." Erickson's strong interest in anthropology and naturalistic trance therapies may be one reason for his utilization of "alternate selves" as resources and for seeing them as positive. This seems all the more acceptable when we see how two of the cases, and many mediums, function fairly well for many years with multiple personality that was never even suspected nor was therapy sought.

For Erickson, there was no ethical dilemma in utilizing "other selves," whether in multiples or mediums. He used what the patient brought into therapy. A good example is the case of an Indian couple who said that a bad spirit followed them around and took control of them. They became obsessed with the idea that they could tip tables and that bad spirits were taking over. Erickson helped them tip a table in a way that disclosed a weak good spirit, and another, and another. When Erickson added up all the weak good spirits, their total strength exceeded the strength of the evil spirit. Erickson utilized the couple's belief system in order to change it. He was not able to change belief in spirits, but he changed the meaning from evil to good (Richeport, 1985). However, he objected to professionals who join the belief system and do not remain scientists. Elizabeth Erickson explained his view: "Milton respected David Akstein, M.D., highly for keeping the interpretation and control strictly scientific, while utilizing but not joining the belief system" (personal communication, August 19, 1986).

The cases discussed illustrate Erickson's interest in research and experimentation, which he viewed as important for understanding personality structure. Erickson's work and cross-cultural studies show that multiplicity of selves need not necessarily be seen as pathological, but can be an asset in enriching human life.

ACKNOWLEDGMENTS

I want to thank Jay Haley for allowing me to observe his supervision of two multiple personality cases. Although Haley had conversations about dual personalities with Erickson in the 1950's, it was not until the 1980's that he had the opportunity to work with this type of patient and to apply Erickson's approach. Haley differed from Erickson in bringing the family into the therapy in one of the cases. Appreciating the similarities between multiple personality and mediumship, he was also interested in trying out some mediumship techniques with these patients.

I am grateful to Elizabeth M. Erickson and Jay Haley for their stimulating interest and comments on this paper.

REFERENCES

Akstein, D. (1972). *Hipnologia.* Rio de Janeiro: Hypnos.

Allison, R. (1985). *Minds in many pieces.* New York: Rawson Wade.

Beahrs, J. O. (1982). *Unity and multiplicity: Multilevel consciousness of self in hypnosis, psychiatric disorder and mental health.* New York: Brunner/Mazel.

Beahrs, J. O. (1986). *Limits of scientific psychiatry: The role of uncertainty in mental health.* New York: Brunner/Mazel.

Bliss, E. (1983). Multiple personalities, related disorders and hypnosis. *American Journal of Clinical Hypnosis, 2,* 114–123.

Braun, B. G. (1984). Hypnosis creates multiple personality: Myth or reality? *International Journal of Clinical and Experimental Hypnosis, 32,* 191–197.

Braun, B. G. (1986). Issues in the psychotherapy of multiple personality disorder. In B. G. Bruan (Ed.), *Treatment of multiple personality disorder.* Washington, D. C.: American Psychiatric Press.

Erickson, M. H. (1939/1980). Experimental demonstration of the psychopathology of everyday life. In E. Rossi (Ed.), *The collected papers of Milton H. Erickson on hypnosis, Vol. III.* New York: Irvington Publishers.

Erickson, M. H. (circa 1940's/1980). The clinical discovery of a dual personality. In E. Rossi (Ed.), *The collected papers of Milton H. Erickson on hypnosis, Vol. III.* New York: Irvington Publishers.

Erickson, M. H., & Kubie, L. (1939/1967). Permanent relief of an obsessional phobia by means of communication with an unsuspected dual personality. In J. Haley (Ed.), *Advanced techniques of hypnosis and therapy: Selected papers of Milton H. Erickson, M. D.* New York: Grune & Stratton.

Erickson, M. H., & Rapaport, D. (circa 1940's). Findings on the nature of the personality structures in two different dual personalities by means of projective and psychometric tests. In E. Rossi (Ed.), *The collected papers of Milton H. Erickson on hypnosis, Vol. III.* New York: Irvington Publishers.

Erickson, M. H., & Rossi, E. L. (1974/1980). Varieties of hypnotic amnesia. In E. Rossi (Ed.), *The collected papers of Milton H. Erickson, Vol. III.* New York: Irvington Publishers.

Erickson, M. H., & Rossi, E. L. (1979). *Hypnotherapy: An exploratory casebook.* New York: Irvington Publishers.

Garrison, V. (1978). Support systems of schizophrenic and nonschizophrenic Puerto Rican migrant women in New York City. *Schizophrenia Bulletin, 4* (4), 561–596.

Gilligan, S. (1987). *Therapeutic trances: The cooperation principle in Ericksonian hypnotherapy.* New York: Brunner/Mazel.

Grove, D., & Haley, J. (1993). *Conversation in therapy: Popular problems and uncommon solutions.* New York: W. W. Norton.

Haley, J. (1967). Commentary. In J. Haley (Ed.), *Advanced techniques of hypnosis and therapy: Selected papers of Milton H. Erickson, M. D.* New York: Grune & Stratton.

Haley, J. (1973). *Uncommon therapy: The psychiatric techniques of Milton H. Erickson, M. D.* New York: W. W. Norton.

Haley, J., & Richeport, M. (Eds.) (1991). Erickson on multiple personality (audiotaped conversion). New York: W. W. Norton.

Harriman, P. L. (1942). The experimental production of some phenomena related to multiple personality. *Journal of Abnormal and Social Psychology, 37,* 244-256.

Hilgard, E. R. (1977). *Divided consciousness: Multiple controls in human thought and action.* New York: John Wiley & Sons.

Kampman, R. (1976). Hypnotically induced multiple personality: An experimental study. *International Journal of Clinical and Experimental Hypnosis, 24,* 215-227.

Kenny, M. G. (1981). Multiple personality and spirit possession. *Psychiatry, 44,* 337-358.

Kluft, R. P. (1985). Childhood multiple personality disorder: Predictors, clinical findings, and treatment results. In R. P. Kluft (Ed.), *Childhood antecedents of multiple personality.* Washington, D.C.: American Psychiatric Press.

Leavitt, H. C. (1947). The case of hypnotically produced secondary and tertiary personalities. *Psychoanalytic Review, 34,* 274-295.

Putnam, F. W. (1989). *Diagnosis and treatment of multiple personality disorder.* New York: Guilford Press.

Rapaport, D. (1942). *Emotions and memory.* (Menninger Clinic Monograph Series No. 2). Baltimore: Williams & Wilkins.

Richeport, M. (1980). El trance ritual como hipnoterapia clinica (Tres casos de psiquiatria transcultural), *Revista Ibero Americana de Sofrologia y Medicina Psicosomatica, 8*(4), 261-266.

Richeport, M. (1985). The importance of anthropology in psychotherapy: World view of Milton H. Erickson, M. D. In J. Zeig (Ed.), *Ericksonian psychotherapy: Vol. 1. Structures.* New York: Brunner/Mazel.

Richeport, M. (1992). The interface between multiple personality, spirit mediumship, and hypnosis. *American Journal of Clinical Hypnosis, 34,* 168-177.

Ross, C. A., Norton, R., & Wozney, K. (1989). Multiple personality disorder: An analysis of 236 cases. *Canadian Journal of Psychiatry, 34,* 413-417.

Rossi, E. R. (1980). Dual personality: Introduction. In E. Rossi (Ed.), *The collected papers of Milton H. Erickson on Hypnosis, Vol. III.* New York: Irvington Publishers.

Schreiber, F. R. (1974). *Sybil.* New York: Warner Paperbacks.

CHAPTER 29

Multiple Addictions, Multiple Personalities: An Erickson-Inspired View

John D. Lovern

AN ERICKSON-INSPIRED VIEW

The 1980s and early 1990s have witnessed a surge of interest in, and an abundance of treatment programs for, a wide range of addictions and addiction-like disorders, including alcoholism, drug dependence, eating disorders, sexual addiction, gambling, codependency, and others (Alcoholics Anonymous, 1976; Beattie, 1987; Lovern, 1990, 1991; Narcotics Anonymous, 1987; Overeaters Anonymous, 1980). Meanwhile, during roughly the same period of time, multiple personality disorder and related post-traumatic and dissociative disorders have received wider recognition, greater respectability, and heightened interest from professionals in the mental health field (Coons, 1984; Kluft, 1987; Putnam, 1989; Ross, 1989).

As the understanding of these two classes of disorders—addictive and dissociative—improves, it is becoming clear that they are much more intimately related than previously thought. Ross (1989) has proposed a new, broad diagnostic category, "Chronic Trauma Disorder," which encompasses both types of disorders (and others), and which traces their origins to early childhood trauma.

Although the connection between trauma, addictions, and multiple personality and other dissociative disorders is becoming more widely recognized, it is still too little understood. This chapter presents a model designed to facilitate an understanding of this connection and then examines treatment considerations from a point of view inspired by Milton Erickson.

EXPLANATORY MODEL

Memory Processing

Sensory information does not go directly or "raw" from the sense organs into memory. It is *processed,* that is, converted from patterns and rates of various types of nerve cell firings into retrievable code. Processing takes place in *stages,* of which there are at least two: (a) reception and temporary storage of incoming sensory information in component form (possibly conforming to Braun's "BASK" model (Braun, 1988a, 1988b, which postulates that the components are Behavior, Affect, Sensation, and Knowledge), and (b) assembly of the components into complete memories.

A useful analogy is to think of memory processing as equivalent to the flow of information in an office. First, information arrives in the *in-basket* (first stage). Then, it is moved to the *file room* where it is placed in a file according to a system designed to facilitate later retrieval (final stage). Under normal conditions, information is processed so quickly that the delay between the stages goes unnoticed.

It is crucial to point out that *conscious awareness* of the experience that is being processed does not take place until the final stage of processing, that is, while the memory is being assembled, or after it is inside the file room. Therefore, the entrance to the file room may be thought of as the *threshold of consciousness.*

Processing of Traumatic Material

The processing of traumatic experiences into memories is very different from routine memory processing. Traumatic experiences are so intense that they overwhelm a child's (and, later, an adult's) information processing system. They simply will not fit through the file room door. Therefore, they stay in the in-basket in component form, without ever registering as a conscious experience. In other words, they are *dissociated.* To the child, it is as if the experience had never happened. Certain drugs, such as powerful sedative-hypnotics, also can create dissociation that interrupts memory processing; they, in effect, shrink the file room door, forcing the experience to remain unconscious and in components in the in-basket.

Flashbacks

Traumatic material sometimes stays in temporary component storage for long periods of time with no apparent difficulty. Conversely, events may trigger one or more component pieces of partially processed traumatic experiences to escape from containment and resume processing. When processing resumes, the pieces cross the threshold of consciousness (into the file room) and become vivid, compelling experiences that feel like they are occurring in the present.

This intrusive recollection, or flashback, may consist of a single, short component piece (for example, a localized physical pain) or it may consist of a chain reaction in which one piece triggers others, and more and more components of the experience become conscious. When someone's flashback occurs as a chain reaction, the person typically becomes increasingly more uncomfortable and frightened, and seeks desperately to escape the mounting pain and terror. A person who suffers from flashbacks may be diagnosed with post-traumatic stress disorder (American Psychiatric Association, 1987).

Creation of Personalities

Dissociation protects young children from traumatic experiences by keeping the sensory information in component pieces and thereby preventing them from becoming conscious. A child's subjective experience during dissociation is often that of an "out of body experience" (Spiegel, 1984). In other words, the child "leaves" the body while the body is being traumatized, then "returns" after the trauma ends. While the child's consciousness is "away," the body is not completely unconscious. Rather, another, separate, consciousness is present during the trauma. If it is employed often enough to have a personal history, this new consciousness develops its own sense of identity by virtue of the child's creative imagination. It then becomes the first of what are likely to be a number of alternate personalities. From this beginning, the syndrome of multiple personality disorder (MPD) evolves.

STRATEGIES FOR WARDING OFF FLASHBACKS

When traumatic memories intrude, people experiencing them become extremely uncomfortable and want to escape from them as quickly as possible. They generally have only two options: either contain the memory by re-dissociating it or try to cope with it until it goes away by itself. They can re-dissociate a flashback by taking copious amounts of drugs or by using imagery techniques learned in therapy. Lacking this specific type of therapy, they really only have one drug-free option—to cope with the flashback until it goes away. Coping with a flashback means doing something to make it not hurt so much, or trying to distract oneself from it, and the urge to distract gives rise to driven relief-seeking behaviors, many of which are self-destructive.

The methods that traumatized people most often employ to ward off flashbacks involve one or more of the following: alcohol or drugs, eating and food-related behaviors, behavioral reenactment, self-mutilation, avoidance of triggers, and other distracting thoughts and behaviors, such as gambling and other risk-taking, crime, work, religion, shopping, sexual behavior, codependent relationships, and suicide. Each of these methods will be described in turn:

In sufficient doses, *alcohol* and certain other *drugs* can produce chemically induced dissociation, which facilitates re-dissociation of flashbacks. Milder drugs or dissociative drugs used in lesser doses can provide both distraction and analgesia. Drugs can take effect quickly and entail little effort on the user's part, so they tend to be one of the favorite methods employed for the purpose of escaping flashbacks.

Food use also can distract from flashbacks, softening their intensity and providing comfort to make them easier to tolerate. Binges and purging episodes provide more intense stimulation than simple overeating and, therefore, offer a more powerful form of distraction. Some forms of purging also allow for symbolic cleansing of aspects of some traumatic experiences (for example, vomiting to expel swallowed semen from the stomach or using laxatives to eject inserted objects from the rectum).

Behavioral reenactment consists of behaving as if what is happening in one's flashbacks is the actual, present reality. A less extreme form of reenactment consists of being influenced by feelings and urges that arise from flashbacks while retaining at least a partial conscious awareness of events taking place in the present. Behavioral reenactment may lead people to become victims repeatedly or to "turn the tables" and become perpetrators on others of what was done to them. Behavioral reenactment provides a sense of mastery and control; it allows people who were once in a completely powerless and helpless position to control a similar experience or to be the ones who both begin and end it. In addition, as with eating, the current behavior can help to distract from flashbacks by providing an experience rich in intense stimulation.

Self-mutilation may work because it provides an opportunity for either distraction or behavioral reenactment (or both). In addition, self-mutilation can activate the endogenous opioid system, providing self-created analgesia or, conceivably, chemically induced dissociation. Another, different, function served by self-mutilation is discussed in the section on ritual abuse.

One way to avoid the pain of flashbacks is to *avoid all situations that might trigger them.* The resulting lifestyle is likely to be severely inhibited and rigid, closely resembling that of phobics or persons with obsessive-compulsive disorder (American Psychiatric Association, 1987).

Many other behaviors can produce distraction, provided they are intense and involving enough. Examples of such behaviors are compulsive *gambling*, other *risk-taking* (from racing motorcycles to playing the stock market), *criminal behaviors* (which involve a high degree of risk and may also offer opportunities for behavioral reenactment), *work* (overdone, as a distraction), *religion* (practiced with an obsessive preoccupation or overinvolvement), *shopping* (as a distraction), *sexual behavior* (offering both distraction and behavioral reenactment), overinvolvement in relationships (*codependency*— mainly as a distraction), and preoccupation with *suicide* and suicide attempts (both distraction and risk).

DEFINITION OF ADDICTION

Addiction exists when the substance or activity that a person uses to *relieve* pain is also the *cause* of the pain that the person is trying to relieve. Generally, the addicted person fails to accurately perceive the connection between the substance or activity and the cause of the pain, in part because that connection is more remote and less immediate than the connection between the substance or activity and its ability to relieve pain.

Dependence on a sedative is an example of this dynamic. As people develop tolerance to the drug, they need more to achieve the same effect and they experience withdrawal symptoms upon cessation of use. Eventually, as the tolerance and withdrawal effects increase, people become completely addicted; they can barely consume enough of the drug to feel any effect at all, but they are forced to continue taking it in order to avoid the increasingly painful withdrawal syndrome. Solomon's work (Solomon, 1980; Solomon & Corbitt, 1974) demonstrates that tolerance and withdrawal effects (which he calls "opponent processes") can occur without any drug at all, but with any activity that is initially pleasurable (or, in some cases, painful). In other words, drug-free activities can be just as addictive as drugs.

This definition of addiction should help clarify the important differences between behaviors engaged in purely to ward off flashbacks and those that have taken on "a life of their own" as addictions. Addictions are perpetuated by rewards that go beyond the simple escape or avoidance of flashbacks. Like psychological "perpetual motion machines," they persist after the flashbacks have stopped, or in their complete absence, because they are needed to alleviate the pain that they themselves have caused. It is of vital importance that diagnosticians and therapists be alert to this distinction, because, once a flashback-escaping method has crossed over the line into addiction, it requires a different therapeutic approach.

COMPLEX COMBINATIONS OF
ADDICTIVE BEHAVIORS WITH MPD

Persons who have frequent flashbacks and numerous personalities have the potential to develop complex combinations of addictive behaviors. First of all, they are likely to employ a wide range of behavior patterns to help them distract from or avoid their flashbacks; each of these behaviors has the potential to become an addiction in its own right. Furthermore, each personality can develop one or more addictions, either separately from the other personalities or in common with them, and often in secret from the therapist and/or from each other. Finally, the addictions themselves can interact in such a way that one can exacerbate or activate another, creating an addictive chain reaction. For example, a patient's overeating can lead to feared or actual weight gain, which can trigger purging or amphetamine or cocaine use; the resulting anxiety and depression can then set off drinking or marijuana use.

Another important distinction for therapists to note is addiction proneness. Some patients are much more likely to develop addictions, and have more of them, than others, presumably due to a genetic predisposition. In addiction-prone patients, many or most alternate personalities (alters) have one or more addictions, while only a few, such as young child alters, are addiction-free. Other patients, who are less addiction-prone, tend to have only a small number of addicted alters, with fewer addictions per alter.

RITUAL ABUSE AND ADDICTIVE BEHAVIORS

Increasing numbers of MPD patients are reporting histories of abuse by organized groups of perpetrators, or cults. Such cults appear to abuse children and others in systematic ways with the goal of establishing and maintaining nearly complete control over their victims' behavior (Coons & Grier, 1990; Ganaway, 1989; Hassan, 1990; Hill & Goodwin, 1989; Kluft, 1989; Los Angeles County Commission for Women, 1989; Mayer, 1991).

They reportedly utilize sophisticated "programming" techniques (Connors, 1992; Neswald, Gould & Graham-Costain, 1991), many of which consist of administering powerful drugs and painful torture, to ensure that their victims dissociate, and then tell them that they can escape the pain if they carry out certain behaviors.

Later, programmers can expose their victims to information that is similar to information contained in dissociated memories of programming sessions, triggering flashbacks of one or more of them. As sensations of pain and terror begin to emerge, so too do the instructions about what the person must do in order to escape these feelings. The result is that the victim feels an overwhelming urge to engage in the programmed behavior.

Ritual abuse victims often suffer from both drug dependence and eating disorders, presumably due to the ways in which cults typically abuse and control their victims. If programming is done with drugs, victims often come to associate drugs with relief from torture and other pain, thereby making addiction to these substances more likely to occur. Many female victims are reportedly programmed to both overeat and undereat at times as a means of covering up their pregnancies when as young girls they are used as "breeders" (by having them gain weight during pregnancy so that it is not obviously visible, and then lose the weight afterward). In addition, shame and depression about excess weight make victims easier to control, so cults apparently foster these traits. The intense emotional pain about weight, combined with cult training to restrict food intake, or in many cases to purge, creates numerous instances of eating disorders.

Programmed behaviors resemble addictive behaviors. They possess a driven quality, and they are aimed at seeking relief from pain in what is often a self-destructive manner. Some programmed behaviors generalize and become true addictions. For example, cults often program victims to self-mutilate by cutting or burning their skin. Many victims learn that self-mutilation stops pain other than that contained in flashbacks, and this effect may be enhanced by activation of the endogenous opioid system. The result is an addiction to cutting, burning, or other types of self-mutilation.

Cult victimization or "membership," in general, also resembles addiction and may constitute actual addiction in many cases. The dynamics of addiction are definitely present: The cult administers pain and then relieves the pain that it administers, thereby placing the cult in the same position as that occupied by alcohol in alcoholism, or drugs in drug addiction. Programming and years of indoctrination obfuscate the connection between the pain and its origin in cult activities and stress the cult's ability to relieve pain. Leaving a cult is an extremely arduous undertaking, made difficult by countless programs and ongoing abuse, but this already immense difficulty is compounded even further by the phenomenon of addiction to the cult.

ERICKSON-INSPIRED THERAPEUTIC APPROACHES

Erickson's Unconscious

Erickson's concept of the unconscious mind was a "breath of fresh air" after decades during which the psychoanalytic concept held sway (Lovern, 1991). Erickson viewed the unconscious mind as something good, something smarter and more creative than the conscious mind, in contrast to the psychoanalytic view of the unconscious as a repository of unacceptable, repressed urges, which made it inferior to the conscious mind and ego. Any therapist who works with MPD patients needs a concept of the unconscious mind that is similar to Erickson's, since just about all of any MPD patient's personalities actually live inside the unconscious mind and employ imagination and creativity to a remarkable degree. Adopting Erickson's way of thinking makes it easy to meet, appreciate, and understand these fascinating entities.

Therapeutic Caveats

Some cautions are advised for therapists who might consider employing therapeutic techniques inspired by Erickson on a population of dissociative patients. These caveats are all the more important with dissociative patients who are also being treated for addictions, because addicted patients tend to be subjected to strong confrontation or "tough love," which could overwhelm an MPD patient or trigger disabling flashbacks.

Some of Erickson's techniques, such as the confusion technique or some forms of ordeal or paradox, may seem overly coercive, manipulative, or "tricky" to MPD patients, particularly those with a ritual abuse background. The same is true of many of the approaches to addiction treatment suggested by me (Lovern, 1991). MPD patients are people who have been subjected to the most extreme and ruthless forms of mind control imaginable. If their therapist uses techniques on them that resemble these abuse experiences, they will lose what little trust they may have been initially able to muster, and their therapy will stall or even come to a complete halt.

When working with patients who have both MPD and an addiction, at points where the customary approach to addiction treatment would differ markedly from the customary approach to MPD, therapists should choose the MPD approach over the addiction approach on the majority of occasions.

This advice is consistent with Ross's (1989) listing of MPD as the hierarchically highest disorder among those subsumed under chronic trauma disorder.

Utilization

With the caveats stated above, there remain many ways in which therapeutic approaches inspired by Erickson can be effective with MPD patients, with or without addictions. From the universe of possible approaches, I have selected *utilization*. Utilization (Erickson, 1967; Lovern, 1991) is essentially an attitude that therapists can adopt to stay attuned to behaviors and tendencies of their patients that they can use, instead of struggling with them, to help the patients make rapid therapeutic gains. Two characteristics of MPD patients that can be utilized are their dissociative abilities and their internal worlds.

MPD patients suffer many symptoms as the result of their use of dissociation as a protective strategy, including memory lapses, identity disturbances, and confusion. But dissociation is not just a problem creator; it can also be a powerful problem solver. A good example is the use of dissociation and visual imagery to contain flashbacks, which can be enhanced by a therapist who maintains an attitude of utilization.

Many patients can be taught quickly to either locate or create internal *containers* that hold component pieces of dissociated traumatic experiences. When a flashback occurs, they can re-dissociate it readily by closing or repairing the leaking containers. An alert therapist can help make this task even more effective and efficient by utilizing patients' own imagery styles and preferences. For example, one patient may prefer boxes, another may prefer steel drums, and a third may prefer Tupperware. Some patients may eschew containers altogether and form their memories into complex molecular structures. Then, depending on their preferred intellectual style, they can develop a unique, personal system for organizing and keeping track of the containers. Cooperation among the alters in devising these methods and systems enhances interpersonality communication and cooperation, an important therapeutic goal (Ross, 1989; Putman, 1989).

Since only one or a few alters can be "out" in the body at any given time, all the others remain, or live, inside (Bliss, 1984). Inquiry with most MPD patients reveals that the inside can be a remarkable place, an entire world or universe. The inside world is actually a *real* place. Its reality can be tested by consensual validation; all the alters who go there perceive the same features and aspects in a consistent fashion.

Obviously, the inside world differs from external reality in a number of ways. For example, neither the therapist nor any other "outside person" can see inside it. Another difference lies in how things or features come into being. In the inside world, imagination is all powerful. Alters can create almost anything they want there simply by imagining it into existence. What they can create ranges from small objects to houses to mountains or forests to planets, and beyond.

An alter of one adult female patient, a 10-year-old male who wanted to get drunk, listened in while I was explaining about how things could be created inside and he created alcohol, which he promptly drank to the point of intoxication. The entire personality system then became drunk and the patient staggered into my office seeking assistance. I utilized her ability to use imagination to create things in her inside world by suggesting that she create "sobering up pills" and pass them to everyone who wished to remain sober. She did so, and the problem was solved immediately.

SUMMARY

Multiple personality disorder (MPD) and addictive behaviors often share a common origin: early childhood trauma. Victims of child abuse typically develop coping mechanisms to help them survive experiences that would otherwise overwhelm or destroy them. These coping mechanisms include dissociation, creation of alternate personalities, and a host of behaviors designed to distract from or ward off intrusive recollections (flashbacks) of traumatic experiences. This chapter presented an explanatory model for the development of multiple personality, addictive behaviors, and other post-traumatic symptoms, and then examined the phenomena from a therapeutic perspective inspired by Milton Erickson. Some cautions about types of interventions that can backfire with addictive patients who also have MPD were offered. Some of the unique traits and talents of MPD patients that can be utilized to enhance their therapy were discussed.

REFERENCES

Alcoholics Anonymous. (1976). *Alcoholics anonymous.* New York: Alcoholics Anonymous World Services, Inc.

American Psychiatric Association. (1987). *Diagnostic and statistical manual of mental disorders* (3rd ed., rev.). Washington, D.C.: American Psychiatric Association.

Beattie, M. (1987). *Codependent no more.* New York: Harper/Hazelden.

Bliss, E.L. (1984). Spontaneous self-hypnosis in multiple personality disorder. *Psychiatric Clinics of North America, 7,* 135-149.

Braun, B.G. (1988a). The BASK (behavior, affect, sensation, knowledge) model of dissociation. *Dissociation, 1,* 4-23.

Braun, B.G. (1988b). The BASK model of dissociation: Clinical applications. *Dissociation, 1,* 16-23.

Connors, K.J. (1992, November). *Memory, trauma, and meaning: Treating ritualistically abused clients.* Paper presented at the Ninth International Conference on Multiple Personality and Dissociation, Chicago.

Coons, P.M. (1984). The differential diagnosis of multiple personality: A comprehensive review. *Psychiatric Clinics of North America, 7,* 51-67.

Coons, P.M., & Grier, F. (1990). Factitious disorder (Munchausen type) involving allegations of ritual Satanic abuse: A case report. *Dissociation, 3,* 177-178.

Erickson, M.H. (1967). Further techniques of hypnosis — Utilization techniques. In J. Haley (Ed.), *Advanced techniques of hypnosis and therapy* (pp. 32-50). New York: Grune & Stratton.

Ganaway, G.K. (1989). Historical truth versus narrative truth: Clarifying the role of exogenous trauma in the etiology of multiple personality disorder and its variants. *Dissociation, 2,* 205-220.

Hassan, A. (1990). *Combatting cult mind control.* Rochester, VT: Park Street Press.

Hill, S., & Goodwin, J. (1989). Satanism: Similarities between patient accounts and pre-inquisition historical sources. *Dissociation, 2,* 39-44.

Kluft, R.P. (1987). An update on multiple personality disorder. *Hospital and Community Psychiatry, 38,* 363-373.

Kluft, R.P. (1989). Editorial: Reflections on allegations of ritual abuse. *Dissociation, 2,* 191-193.

Los Angeles County Commission for Women. (1989, September). Report of the ritual abuse task force: Ritual abuse, definition, glossary, the use of mind control. Los Angeles: Author.

Lovern, J.D. (1990, April). *Food, drugs, and dissociation: Breaking the addictive cycle in multiple personality disorder.* Paper presented at the Third Annual Orange County Conference on Multiple Personality and Dissociation, Newport Beach, CA.

Lovern, J.D. (1991). *Pathways to reality: Erickson-inspired treatment approaches to chemical dependency.* New York: Brunner/Mazel.

Mayer, R.S. (1991). *Satan's children: Case studies in multiple personality.* New York: G.P. Putnam's Sons.

Narcotics Anonymous. (1987). *Narcotics anonymous.* Van Nuys, CA: Narcotics Anonymous World Service Office, Inc.

Neswald, D.W., Gould, C., & Graham-Costain, V. (1991, September/October). Common "programs" observed in survivors of satanic ritual abuse. *California Therapist,* 47-50.

Overeaters Anonymous. (1980). *Overeaters anonymous.* Torrance, CA: Overeaters Anonymous, Inc.

Putnam, F.W. (1989). *Diagnosis and treatment of multiple personality disorder.* New York: Guilford Press.

Ross, C. (1989). *Multiple personality disorder: Diagnosis, clinical features, and treatment.* New York: John Wiley & Sons.

Solomon, R.L. (1980). The opponent-process theory of acquired motivation. *American Psychologist, 35,* 691-712.

Solomon, R.L., & Corbit, J.D. (1974). An opponent-process theory of motivation: I. Temporal dynamics of affect. *Psychology Review, 81,* 119-145.

Spiegel, D. (1984). Multiple personality as a post-traumatic stress disorder. *Psychiatric Clinics of North America, 7,* 101-110.

Van Benschoten, S.C. (1990). Multiple personality disorder and satanic ritual abuse: The issue of credibility. *Dissociation, 3,* 22-30.

van der Kolk, B.A. (1989). The compulsion to repeat the trauma: Re-enactment, revictimization, and masochism. *Psychiatric Clinics of North America, 12,* 389-411.

CHAPTER 30

The Ericksonian Utilization Approach for the Rehabilitation of Paralyzed Patients

Bernhard Trenkle

INTRODUCTION

Milton Erickson's contributions to hypnosis and family therapy have been described in countless professional treatises. Less attention has been paid to his innovative contributions in the field of rehabilitation, which he developed intuitively while reestablishing his own mobility after contracting polio at age 17. As a professional, Erickson used his own experience to help patients who had suffered strokes or organic brain damage.

This chapter describes two components of Ericksonian approaches to rehabilitative work: (1) The utilization of a patient's real sense experiences and memories; and (2) the utilization of strong emotions, such as anger and rage. In addition, this chapter illustrates the way in which individual realities existing within unique therapeutic situations can be used to effectively apply these two components in promoting rehabilitation.

Parallels will also be drawn to centuries-old medical procedures from Ancient Persia, which exhibit some astonishing similarities to Erickson's methods. Also described is sports hypnosis, where similar techniques already have been employed for rehabilitative work with paralyzed people.

I will begin by briefly describing a case that shows my rather accidental introduction to the field of rehabilitation.

CASE ONE

At the time, I was working in the Department of Speech Pathology at the Heidelberg University Clinic. One of our speech therapists was a specialist in paralysis of the tongue and the swallowing reflex. Because one of her patients was suicidal, I was called in as a consulting psychologist.

The patient, in his mid-30's, had developed paralysis of the tongue and swallowing reflex after brain tumor surgery. After a few sessions of speech therapy, during which the patient related suicidal thoughts and bemoaned life changes that had resulted from his new physical situation, the speech therapist asked if I could use hypnosis to induce swallowing. Among other approaches, placing pieces of ice on the patient's throat had been successful several times. For me, this was a completely new field of work, but I remembered that Milton Erickson had successfully employed auto-hypnosis to improve his own physical condition after a severe attack of polio.

Case One Commentary: "Using Real Sense Memories Rather than Imagination"

There is an interesting passage under the heading of "Utilizing real sense memories . . ." in Erickson & Rossi (1980). Erickson told Rossi that he gradually learned to think so vividly about walking that he experienced the sense of walking. Subsequent fatigue and relaxation led to relief from pain. Rossi then summarized: "In your self-rehabilitative experiences between the ages of 17 and 19, you learned from your own experience that you could use your imagination to achieve the same effects as an actual physical effort" (Erickson & Rossi, 1980, pp. 112-113). Erickson answered:

> An intense memory rather than imagination. You remember how something tastes, how you get a certain tingle from peppermint. As a child I used to climb a tree in a wood lot and then jump from one tree to another like a monkey. I would recall the many different twists and turns I made in order to find out what are the movements you make when you have full muscles. . . . yes, you use real memories. At 18, I recalled all my childhood movements to help myself to relearn muscle coordination. (p. 113)

The Buster Keaton or Boris Becker Technique

In the same discussion with Rossi, Erickson says, "As you watch Buster Keaton in a movie teetering on the edge of a building, you can feel your own muscles tense up" (Erickson & Rossi, 1980, p. 113).

In this passage, Erickson mentioned a commonplace experience familiar to most of us. If our attention is focused sufficiently and there is a strong sense of identification with the object of our attention, we vividly experience the process taking place on the screen, and our muscles begin to react. It is this condition of intense focused attention that serves as the basis for rehabilitative work.

Steve and Carol Lankton (personal communication) once referred to Charles Tart's description of how in Sanskrit there are about 20 different concepts or terms for "consciousness" or "mind." Many Westerners are relatively unsophisticated about states of consciousness. In my own experience, we subsume many states of consciousness under the term "hypnosis." In the rehabilitative work described here, it is desirable to be in a state of consciousness with highly focused attention, akin to using a powerful telephoto lens to focus on one thing, thereby leaving everything else in the background. In contrast to this, there is another state of consciousness, consisting of a "wide-angle lens," which also can be named "hypnosis." This latter state, too, can be therapeutically valuable for patients during rehabilitation, both to aid regeneration and to promote relaxation.

To help patients recall a state of highly focused attention, I often use memories of watching Steffi Graf and Boris Becker on television at the Wimbledon tennis finals. For many patients, this provides a good example of the basic idea and of the potentials inherent in this state. The induction of hypnosis assists the ability to achieve a state of focused attention, even in the absence of a situation such as the Wimbledon finals. Stories of Buster Keaton or Boris Becker serve to "seed" (cf. Zeig, 1990) in the desired direction of a changed state of consciousness and its consequent therapeutic utilization.

Case One Continued

Once stimulated by the knowledge that Milton Erickson had reestablished physical mobility through the reactivation of sensory memories, I began to think about situations in which a person swallows more strongly, perhaps even more strongly than really desired.

After the induction of a focused hypnotic trance state, cues for situations where swallowing usually occurs were given in the form of various anecdotes or fragments of stories. I told the patient:

> Waiting for an oral exam or a job interview . . . thoroughly thinking over everything once again . . . looking through your notes . . . certain feeling and uncertain . . . nervousness . . . restlessly

> fidgeting to and fro . . . what will they ask . . . perhaps I should
> have still . . . this and that . . . suspense like that at a football
> match . . . catching a quick glance at the clock . . . 11 more minutes
> . . . the time is flying . . . tense . . . unbearable suspense . . . de-
> lays . . . or the opposing team is attacking, and time is moving
> much too slowly . . . lost possession of the ball again . . . dangerous
> situation . . . that makes you thirsty . . . like on a vacation . . . not
> a gas station in sight . . . almost out of gas . . . thirsty . . . dry, parched
> tongue sticking to the roof of your mouth . . . if only something
> would turn up soon . . . no gas and very thirsty. . . . Oh, for a beer
> right now . . . have another drink of beer again . . . or just a big
> sip of water . . . (the patient spoke of a similar situation during a
> vacation, of needing a beer, as well as of driving a race car on one
> of the big race tracks) . . . and that racing driver on the track
> before the start . . . the lure of danger . . . thinking over the track
> . . . new situation . . . the thrill of danger . . . tension . . . concen-
> tration . . . the mechanic almost finished . . . etc.

As I talked, the patient swallowed 20 or 30 times. Then I gave him a post-hypnotic suggestion to activate and use these and other memories stored in his unconscious mind, while daydreaming and while dreaming at night. This procedure was repeated during two subsequent sessions.

Activation of his tongue was attempted similarly. By means of a hypnotic age regression, activation of early memories of his infancy was attempted. I spoke of the approximately 600 sucking and swallowing movements an infant makes while drinking from a bottle, and of the different sucking and swallowing movements with various teats and pacifiers.

> . . . the difference between drinking from mother's breasts and
> from the bottle . . . a child's surprise when it tastes something for
> the first time . . . unknown taste and texture . . . chocolate pudding
> . . . strawberries . . . special smells and aromas . . . remembering
> the smell of food. . . .

During his next session, which was unfortunately his last due to a previously arranged date of discharge, the patient reported that during the past week he had eaten solid food again.

At a medical follow-up examination a few weeks later, he was able to press food up with the base of his tongue so he could finally choke it down. However, the swallowing movements possible in the trance state were not used during eating. It appeared, rather, that the patient managed to use the muscles of the floor of his mouth, thus making this progress possible.

(Afterwards, to my pleasant surprise, I was told that this was an excellent example of the patient using his own remembered responses. In the trance, we had concentrated on swallowing liquids, whereas the patient later used movements and reflexes of tongue and floor of mouth, typical of adults eating solid food.)

During the hypnotic session, I presented the patient visual and verbal cues to help him activate particular memories, so that these very memories would then evoke the desired physical swallowing reactions. I utilized my knowledge of my patient's hobbies and actual life incidents he had recounted — for example, driving in a car rally where, despite great thirst, he had to drive very slowly to conserve fuel in order to reach the next pit stop. Also, he once had the opportunity of test-driving a race car on a dangerous racetrack. All these situations, to my mind, could be associated with being keyed up and tense, full of suspense, and presumably feeling a strong urge to swallow.

The patient also was distressed by this hospital stay that separated him from his little daughter. Perhaps this fact helped him more easily to access and realize memories of small children's swallowing reflexes.

This principle of utilizing particular characteristics of the individual patient and his situation also will be demonstrated in the next case I will describe.

UTILIZATION OF INTENSE MEMORIES

Although Erickson obviously used this technique of "Utilization of Intense Memories" extensively for himself, there also are few reports in which he used the method in his clinical work. The case of "Dry Beds" (Rosen, 1982, pp. 113-117) presents the therapeutic procedure of using sensory memories as an element. The patient was an 11-year-old girl who, after years of frequent cystoscopies, could no longer control her urethral sphincter muscles and was incontinent during the night as well as during the day. During daytime, this happened especially when she laughed. When she told Erickson that she had been seen by numerous doctors and therapists without success, he responded that he was like all the others and wouldn't be able to help her either. In effect, he disrupted her conscious expectations and differentiated himself from the doctors. All the others had always said or implied, "I will help you," whereas none could. Erickson said, "I am like the others, and I can't help you either," implying, "I am different from the others." Then he added, "But you already know something but you don't know that you know. As soon as you find out what it is that you already know and don't know that you know, you can begin having a dry bed" (Rosen, 1982, p. 114).

This communication probably led to a trancelike state of consciousness and stimulated internal search processes. Erickson increasingly focused her attention by continuing, "I am going to ask you a very simple question and I want a very simple answer." As cited in Zeig (1980), Erickson deepened her state by having the girl focus on a paperweight before he posed the simple question: "If you were sitting in the bathroom urinating, and a strange man poked his head in the doorway, what would you do?" The girl answered, "I'd freeze" (Rosen, 1982, p. 115).

Erickson's interventions allowed the girl to experience physically and completely how this situation might affect the sphincter muscles. This is a variation of the above-mentioned "Buster Keaton Technique."

Erickson then expanded the experience in such a way that she could regain control of her sphincter through practice. Upon closer inspection, this case is an example of unusually innovative rehabilitative work rather than one of the customary therapeutic treatments of bedwetting.

CASE TWO

A few months later, the same speech therapist as in the previous case asked me whether or not I could support her treatment of a stroke patient with paralysis of tongue movements and swallowing mechanisms. According to the neurologists, the paralysis might be curable, but even after several weeks of treatment, no progress had been made. The patient was a self-made man, about 50 years old who had built a middle-size company.

One Monday I visited him in the neurological ward. His speech was slurred so he sometimes used pen and paper to communicate. He told me that he thought the use of hypnosis sounded like a good idea, but it would probably be of no avail. He explained that some of his comrades during the war had been hypnotized, but he was "too strong-willed." And indeed, various induction methods had brought about no change in his state of consciousness, as he noted with pride.

We began talking and I learned that he intended to turn his business over to his sons. He was waiting until one of his sons had obtained his industrial engineer's degree, so that this son could then assume management of the company. The other sons already held several positions within the business. The patient owned a yacht in the Mediterranean and now he intended to enjoy the fruits of his labors. Despite his incapacities, the patient was strong and highly dynamic. Through our discussion of university studies and of fathers and sons (I was just a little older than his sons), a strategy of how I could help him experience a hypnotic state began to develop—at first intuitively—in my mind.

I queried more and more whether or not he would manage to hand over the business to his sons in a really clean and clear-cut way. He was somewhat annoyed because I dared to doubt him. I countered with an example from my hometown, where I had studied with a son who was not given a promised directorship after graduation. Two years later, he surprised his father by announcing he had accepted a post in Africa. The patient resisted the implication that I might be putting him in the same category. I mentioned that I had, on the other hand, known people who had been able to relinquish their leadership and transfer it to the next generation in a clear, unambiguous way, but he just did not impress me as being that kind of man.

Finally, I suggested he try out the whole thing in his imagination as an experiment: He could feel free to imagine himself lying on his yacht, he could close his eyes briefly to test whether or not he really could simply relax on his yacht.

> Simply imagine yourself . . . you are lying on your yacht . . . your well-earned yacht . . . your sons are working at home . . . and you believe you can simply relax now . . . just relax . . . I simply can't quite believe that you can just relax . . . without having to think about whether or not your sons are doing this or that correctly . . . really believing . . . simply lying there, relaxed . . . the cry of the seagulls . . . the sun . . . the ship gently rocking . . . well deserved . . . just relaxing now . . . enjoying the peace . . .

(My rate of speech became slower as the ship rocked more and more calmly.)

After a few minutes, the patient began to breathe more peacefully and to relax more extensively. But as is often the case in a university clinic, sometimes the right hand does not know what the left is doing. A nurse who did not know me came into the room and ignored my nonverbal "stop" signals because vital signs simply had to be taken immediately. The patient reoriented himself and, once the nurse had left, I said:

> You are a self-made man and have always done everything in your life in your own way and according to your own will. I'll explain what the fundamental therapeutic idea is and then you can work on it yourself. You have enough time here in the clinic to carry everything out on your own.

I told him about Case One. I also told him that I knew from the speech therapist that he was a gourmet and often ate with his employees in good restaurants. He replied that the thought that he might never again to able to speak clearly didn't worry him particularly, but the idea that he might never again be able to enjoy a good beer was absolutely horrifying.

I explained that it had been my intention to hypnotize him so that he could remember the most intense sensations in his experience as a gourmet,

> . . . what was that special sauce like . . . how does the wine taste . . . the aromas . . . the tastes . . . what does the waitress look like . . . who is sitting opposite him . . . what do their faces look like . . . how do they sip the wine . . . what music is being played in the restaurant . . . the salad dressing . . . include all senses and experience them to the utmost . . . most intensely . . . and the beer . . .

Then I explained and demonstrated an easily learned method of self-hypnosis, intended to help him to concentrate on his therapeutic goal rapidly and in a relaxed state: He would be able to frequent the best restaurants in his thoughts.

Two days later, I visited him again and gave him some further ideas about how he could use self-hypnosis to facilitate his rehabilitation. I promised I would return the following Friday afternoon.

That Friday, I drove to the clinic on my day off, solely to keep my promise. After I had parked my car, I had a strong feeling: "Don't go in there today." Although I did not know what to make of that, I nevertheless decided to trust my intuition and drove home. On Monday afternoon I met my patient's wife first and she exclaimed, "My God, was he mad at you and the speech therapist! You had both promised to visit him on Friday, and neither of you came. He was so angry that he literally swept his mashed food off the table and ate a banana in a normal way again for the first time." During the following weeks his paralysis disappeared completely.

Here, again, the values, personality, hobbies, and personal history of a patient were utilized for his increased health and well-being. He was a dominant person and did not want to be doubted or questioned. Both his gourmet experiences and his ownership of the yacht were utilized. The "induction" of anger—that was at least consciously unintentional—and the resulting therapeutic "breakthrough" constitute an example of the second component of Ericksonian rehabilitative work, to which I shall return later.

COMPARABLE AND SUPPLEMENTARY PROCEDURES: A REVIEW OF THE LITERATURE

As I continued to work with and help a few more patients regain control of body functions through hypnotically retrieved memories, some doubts still remained: Was this a chance occurrence? Would the paralysis have improved spontaneously without hypnosis? Would the rehabilitative measures taken by the speech therapist have been successful without my aid? Why had Erickson written so little about an aspect that had been so helpful to him personally?

While preparing this chapter, I reviewed the literature to find references to this first aspect of "Ericksonian" rehabilitative work and was surprised to find that the history of the use of imaginative techniques and hypnosis for cases of paralysis goes back to the last century. In my review of the literature, I found such titles as "Die Erfolge der Suggestionstherapie (Hypnose) bei Nicht-hysterischen Laehmungen und Paralysen" (The Success of Suggestion Therapy [Hypnosis] with Non-Hysterogenic Lameness and Paralysis) (Grossmann, 1892), and "Die Erfolge der Suggestionstherapie (Hypnose) bei Organischen Laehmungen und Paralysen (The Success of Suggestive Therapy [Hypnosis] in Cases of Lameness and Paralysis) (Grossman, 1895).

In a survey article entitled "The Application of Imaginery Techniques to Special Populations" (Surburg, 1989), there were references to the literature of the last century. Many works were cited that show features parallel to the methods I have mentioned and which report several cases of successfully using hypnotherapeutic methods with paralyzed patients (Kroger, 1963; Crasilneck & Hall, 1970; Manganiello, 1986; Holroyd & Hill, 1989).

Unknown to me, a woman psychologist in a rehabilitation center not far from my office in the Heidelberg University Clinic was working much more intensively than I with hypnosis in the treatment of patients with brain damage. At the First European Conference for Ericksonian Hypnosis and Psychotherapy, she reported on the success of her work with, at that time, more than 30 patients (Goerz, 1990). In addition to other strategies, Goerz emphasizes the rehabilitative value of using hypnosis to orient the patients to a time before the illness, thereby reminding them of all the characteristics and capabilities of that earlier personality.

The utilization of hypnotherapeutic techniques, particularly for the recollection and reliving of previous experiences (including abilities and sequences in the motoric systems), appears to possess great potential, even in the case of patients otherwise difficult to treat. Also of interest in this respect are comparable methods adopted by sports psychology, where imaginative techniques as well as particular states of consciousness such as intense concentration are employed to optimize movement processes (Asken & Gooling, 1986).

Schlicht (1992) provided a topical survey of the efficiency of mental training for athletes and discussed the operant mechanism involved. He also discussed and evaluated the meta-analyses of Feltz and Landers

(1983), as well as those of Feltz, Landers, and Becker (1988), who analyzed more than 60 studies in order to evaluate mental training and its effect on learning and performance.

Schlicht (1992) summarized the results of these analyses as follows:

1. Mental training promotes the acquisition of an athletic skill. Performance of an already existing skill improves.

2. Mental training increases the learning and performance of cognitive tasks involving motor sequences more than in the case of tasks requiring purely motor-energetic efforts.

In other words, the positive effect of mental training is greater, for example, in maze solving, which requires cognitive performance, than in purely physical tasks such as balancing on a tilting board. According to this research, five or six repetitions are sufficient for an increase in the performance of cognitive tasks, whereas twice as many are necessary for purely motor-energetic performances.

3. The research of Feltz, Landers, and Becker (1988) refutes findings indicating that mental training can replace physical training. Their results showed that physical training alone was more efficient than the combination of physical and mental training, and this combination in its turn was more efficient than mental training alone.

Schlicht (1992) reanalyzed 35 random samples from the Feltz and Landers meta-analyses, but reclassified the samples, discriminating between the subjects who were experienced athletes and those who were beginners. The result was that experienced athletes benefit more from mental training than do beginners.

REAL SENSE MEMORIES AND THE UTILIZATION
OF SPECIFIC EXPERIENCE

The findings in sports psychology support, in my opinion, Erickson's advocacy of the use of real sense memories rather than imagination. Experienced athletes can rely on their own memories of physical movements, whereas beginners are dependent on imagination and/or they revive memories of their still-inefficient performance of motor sequences.

According to the utilization approach, it follows that the issue of how the patient had his/her experience or practice, and whether or not he/she is still a beginner, is of therapeutic significance.

Erickson was practiced in "jumping from one tree to another." For example, the patient in Case Two was a long-time gourmet. In light of the above research, therapeutic utilization of those areas of the patient's life that are practiced and well-trained should increase the efficacy of hypnotherapeutic mental training for rehabilitation. There remains to be mentioned that single, but particularly intense events often can contribute more to a state of being experienced than can numerous emotionally unimportant events. Such experiential highlights can be, in my opinion, of the greatest therapeutic value.

REHABILITATION THROUGH PROVOCATION AND UTILIZATION OF EVOKED EMOTIONS

The utilization of the intentionally provoked release of emotions, such as annoyance, is a second component of Ericksonian rehabilitation work.

Here, though, I would like to present a case from ancient Persia dating back more than a thousand years. It deals with treatment carried out by the famous Doctor Razi, who lived from A.D. 865 to 925.

A king suffered a severe illness of the joints and was too crippled to walk. The king had Razi captured and brought to him. Razi tried everything possible, but was unsuccessful. Finally, he explained that he wanted to begin a new therapy, but for this he would need the king's two fastest horses saddled and waiting outside the baths. Furthermore, he would need to be completely alone with the king in the baths, with neither servants nor guards. Then he put the king in the warm bath and gave him a potion to drink. This procedure was in keeping with the medical understanding of those times: "to liquefy the body's fluids and allow them to mature." Razi then got dressed and started to abuse and insult the king in order to frighten and enrage him. For instance, Razi told the king, "You ordered me to be bound, thrown on a ship, and brought here by force. Were I not to punish you, I would no longer be my father's son."

The king, in those days an inviolable personage, was left lying in the bath completely on his own and without any guard to punish the offender with death. Full of rage, the king pulled himself to his knees, but Razi went a step further to exacerbate his emotional state even more. He drew a dagger and the tension mounted. Spurred on by rage and terror, the sovereign rose to his feet. Razi ran to the horses and fled the kingdom as fast as he could. The king fainted. After he had regained consciousness and heard that Razi had escaped, he recognized the doctor's intentions. The king left the baths on foot, alone, without assistance. News of the cure spread and the king gave a feast in celebration. On the seventh day, Razi's servant brought the horses back along with a letter explaining the doctor's procedure. In gratitude, the king granted him a lifelong annuity (Zafari, 1989).

Therapeutic use of patients' feelings, such as rage and impatience, are found in most of Erickson's case reports where rehabilitation of patients with paralytic symptoms are concerned.

CASE THREE—FROM MILTON H. ERICKSON'S WORK

This is the case of a Prussian stroke patient (Erickson, 1980a, pp. 321-327; Haley, 1973, pp. 310-313) who was paralyzed after a severe stroke and was brought by his wife to see Erickson. The man had been lying helplessly in a university hospital for a year, with no hope for recovery. He was still unable to talk, but he could understand everything said to him or around him. He was a proud and stubborn man, accustomed to hard work and directing that everything be done *his* way. Now he was resentful, impatient, and disgusted, and did much grunting and snorting because of his inability to speak.

At the first session, Erickson insisted that the therapy be done at the office. Erickson made an appointment to see him again the next day, and he had his two older sons carry the patient out to the car. This angered the Prussian German very much, and he was uncooperative with his wife throughout the night.

The next morning when his wife drove the car up to their motel, she noticed that her husband, with the use of a cane, walked from the bedroom to the front door, and got into and out of the car on his own. At the office, Erickson told the man that he would have to follow his directions or he could go home and be rescheduled for the next day. The man was angered by this, but eventually nodded his head in assent. Erickson again told him that hypnosis would be used to help him and that the man would in no way interfere. Erickson then asked him to leave and to give his wife a rest, and if he grunted to his wife, she should tell him to shut up. The man walked out of the office and to the car, relying on his wife only for balance.

At the next session, Erickson spoke very roughly to the paralyzed man. He referred to Prussian Germans as Nazis, stupid, conceited, ignorant, and animal-like. He also accused the man of being lazy, of looking for charitable help, and acting like a mentally retarded criminal. This angered the man considerably and when Erickson asked him to come back tomorrow for another session, the man shouted, "No" (Haley, 1973, p. 312). Erickson then berated him for not talking for a year when, in actuality, he was able to talk after Erickson angered him. The man again responded, "No, no, no!" At this point, to the amazement of Erickson, the man managed to get to his feet, and made his way out of the office and to the car.

Erickson instructed the man's wife to drive him home and let him get some rest, and to bring him in the morning for another session. In the morning, the man walked to the car and into the office. He was restored to functioning on a satisfactory level and returned to his work. Ten years later, the man had another severe stroke, but could not be helped.

CASE FOUR—FROM MILTON H. ERICKSON'S WORK

Even more impressive is the lengthy case report of a 38-year-old woman (Erickson, 1980b, pp. 283–314), who suffered from aphasia, alexia, paralysis of the right side, and pain. In this case, too, Erickson worked consistently to arouse frustration, enlisting the assistance of the staff and the patient's nearest relatives and friends. For instance, they were required to speak for the woman, who was then unable to speak for herself, and to repeatedly give factually incorrect answers. As a result, the frustrated patient learned to utter single words again. Her "helpers" frustrated her further by systematically serving her the wrong food, until she finally told them what she wanted.

Another strategy was to send the patient to bed even though it was clearly an hour too early. What was so impressive in this case is the enormous engagement and creativity Erickson applied with the patient over many months to help her regain some of her ability to speak, read, and move.

CASE FIVE—FROM MILTON H. ERICKSON'S WORK

In this case (Haley, 1985, pp. 55–59), Erickson asked the husband of an aphasic patient to purchase a large aquarium with tropical fish. He protested, "But my wife doesn't like tropical fish" (Haley, 1985, p. 55). Erickson answered that he knew this and insisted that the man follow his directions. He told the patient,

> You hate tropical fish. You hate aquariums. All right, now I want you every night at 7 o'clock to take your husband in there and the two of you sit there and silently watch those fish for one-half hour. You don't know why. Your husband doesn't know why. Just spend one-half hour there, and keep absolutely silent; and you tell him that he is to remain absolutely silent. (pp. 55–56)

By means of this ploy, the woman began to speak again more and more.

In describing the case to Jay Haley, John Weakland, and Gregory Bateson, Erickson explained, "The woman spent that half hour desperately wishing she could ask her husband, 'What in hell goes on here? Why? What is Dr. Erickson trying to accomplish?' I wanted a tremendous motivation for talking" (Haley, 1985, p. 56).

Haley commented on Erickson's procedure by saying, "You punish her for silence. You punish her with silence." Milton Erickson answered, "Do you call it punishment, or do you say that you are using silence to create motivation? You are infecting speech with values" (Haley, 1985, p. 57).

INFECTING SPEECH WITH VALUES,
OR THE ETHICS OF UTILIZATION

I would like to conclude this series of case reports with one from medieval times, again a case history from ancient Persia (Zafari, 1989):

> A doctor was employed in the court of an Oriental king. The king granted him the favor of entering the harem and he was even allowed to take the pulse of any woman there. One day, they were sitting together in a section of the harem to which no other man had access. The king ordered food, and the women brought him his meal. One of the women took plates down from her head, bent down and placed them on the floor. As she tried to straighten up again, she found she was unable to. Because of thick mucous slime in her joints, she stayed stuck in this bent position. The king looked at the doctor and told him the woman must be cured immediately.
>
> Since the lack of medical supplies made a normal external treatment impossible, the doctor employed a psychological form of treatment. He ordered the woman's veil to be removed and her hair uncovered. To find herself unveiled in this situation made her feel ashamed. However, there was no change in her condition, so the doctor ordered something even more indecent. He had the woman's trousers pulled down. She was so ashamed that her body temperature increased and the mucous dissolved. She stood up and walked away erect and well. (pp. 19-21)

Obviously this case contains features similar to Erickson's procedures. These methods are found not only in rehabilitation, but also in other fields.

Some years ago, I was discussing with a colleague, who had some 10 years more experience in psychotherapy than I, my frequent unsuccessful efforts to convey the concept of utilization to other colleagues during training or supervision to enable them to detect and harness opportunities for utilization in therapy. My colleague expressed his opinion that most therapists would rather judge what is right or wrong than consider how the patient's values might be utilized (personal communication, Renartz, 1990).

This quote is an interesting supplement to Erickson's statement, "You are infecting speech with values." In the case of the harem girl, I can recognize only the use of her value system by the doctor—there is no mention of his. If I were to evaluate the Persian doctor's procedure, this would very probably reveal more about me than about him. The same holds true for many of Erickson's case descriptions. Time and time again, his therapeutic procedures are demonstrations of the utilization approach, and it is difficult to infer possible personal opinions or motives.

EVERY CLIENT AND EVERY THERAPIST IS AN INDIVIDUAL

One of the basic tenets of Milton Erickson is that every client is a unique individual who requires a unique therapeutic treatment. Conversely, this tenet applies to every therapist, too. For a while, I wondered how Erickson got the idea of intentionally evoking emotions of annoyance and rage in his patients. At first, I believed that he was already acquainted with the techniques of the ancient Persian doctor, since he had emphasized the importance of reading and knowing anthropology (Zeig, 1980). While working on this chapter, I was reminded of the events during his bout with polio at the age of 17, and I found the following passage consisting of a discussion between him and Rossi:

> As I lay in bed that night, I overheard the three doctors tell my parents in the other room that their boy would be dead in the morning. My mother then came in with as serene a face as can be. I asked her to arrange the dresser, push it up against the side of the bed at an angle. She did not understand why, she thought I was delirious. My speech was difficult. But at the angle by virtue of the mirror on the dresser I could see through the doorway, through the west window of the other room. I was damned if I would die without seeing one more sunset.

Rossi answered: "Your anger and wanting to see another sunset was a way you kept yourself alive through that critical day in spite of the doctor's predictions" (Erickson & Rossi, 1980, p. 111). Therefore, Erickson had experienced at an early age in his life, the therapeutic effects of intense annoyance on his own body. Presumably, with this background, it is easier to use congruently the "technique" of evoking vexation and rage.

I myself have never worked in a similar fashion, even though my not having visited the second patient described above likewise evoked anger and a consequent therapeutic breakthrough. For many years, I have been puzzled by that need to drive back home that I had unconsciously developed. And, at the moment, I cannot imagine myself working as Erickson did with that Prussian stroke patient. Of course, I have said that before about other therapeutic techniques. But then, when the corresponding therapeutic situation and the necessity arose, I suddenly found myself working with such techniques! Presumably, it is unethical to search for such therapeutic situations. If it did not sound so mystical, I would say it is preferable to let such situations seek the clinician, rather than seeking them oneself. In addition, the therapeutic situation should suit the individual personality of both the patient and the therapist.

CONCLUSION

The purpose of this chapter is to outline the Ericksonian utilization approach within the field of rehabilitation. Although I myself have worked only on the perimeter of this field, it was sufficient to stimulate interest in this area, which could, in my opinion, develop into one of the more important branches of hypnotherapy, comparable to the field of pain control.

In my chapter, I have dealt with two factors: (1) "real sense memories" in relation to imaginative processes and mental training; and (2) the provocation of intense emotions.

In closing, I would like to recall once more the fact that in one investigation in the field of sports psychology, physical training alone proved the most effective in enhancing performance. There can be no Olympic victor without intensive physical training. Neither the most brilliant hypnotherapeutic visualization nor trainers who can make an athlete's blood boil can induce performances that exceed the athlete's possibilities as based on physical training. Therefore, in many cases requiring rehabilitation, the priority must remain on physical training. Other procedures can act only to speed up and augment the process. In other cases, however, the reactivation and reacquisition of previously possessed abilities and skills can be achieved by hypnotherapeutic procedures alone.

REFERENCES

Asken, M. J., & Gooling, M. D. (1986). The use of sports psychology techniques in rehabilitation medicine. *International Journal of Sports Psychology, 17,* 156-161.

Crasilneck, H. B., & Hall, J. A. (1970). The use of hypnosis in the rehabilitation of complicated vascular and post-traumatic neurological patients. *International Journal of Clinical and Experimental Hypnosis, 18,* 145-159.

Erickson, M. H. (1980a). Provocation as a means of motivating recovery from a cerebrovascular accident. In E. L. Rossi (Ed.), *The collected papers of Milton H. Erickson on hypnosis, Vol. IV* (pp. 321-325). New York: Irvington.

Erickson, M. H. (1980b). Hypnotically oriented psychotherapy in organic brain damage *and* Hypnotically oriented psychotherapy in organic brain disease: An addendum. In E. L. Rossi (Ed.), *The collected papers of Milton H. Erickson on hypnosis, Vol. IV* (pp. 283-314). New York: Irvington.

Erickson, M. H., & Rossi, E. L. (1980). Autohypnotic experiences of Milton H. Erickson. In E. L. Rossi (Ed.), *The collected papers of Milton H. Erickson on hypnosis, Vol. I* (pp. 108–132). New York: Irvington.

Feltz, D. L., & Landers, D. M. (1983). The effects of mental practice on motor skill learning and performance: A meta-analysis. *Journal of Sports Psychology, 5,* 25–57.

Feltz, D. L., Landers, D. M., & Becker, B. J. (1988). A revised meta-analysis of the mental practice literature on motor skill learning. In D. Duckmann & J. Swets (Eds.), *Enhancing human performance: Issues, theories and techniques* (pp. 61–101). Washington, DC: National Academic Press.

Goerz, K. (1990). Rehabilitation von Schaedelhirnverletzten durch Hypnose. *Experimentelle und Klinische Hypnose, 6,* 137–156.

Grossman, J. (1892). *Die Erfolge der Suggestionstherapie (Hypnose) bei nicht-hysterischen Laehmungen und Paralysen* (The success of suggestion therapy [hypnosis] with non-hysterogenic lameness and paralysis). Berlin: Brieger.

Grossman, J. (1895). *Die Erfolge der Suggestionstherapie (Hypnose) bei organischen Laehmungen und Paralysen* (The success of suggestion therapy [hypnosis] in cases of lameness and paralysis). *Zeitschrift fur Hypnotismus, 3,* 54–64, 76–80.

Haley, J. (1973). *Uncommon therapy: The psychiatric techniques of Milton H. Erickson, M.D.* New York: W. W. Norton.

Haley, J. (1985). *Conversations with Milton H. Erickson, Vol II.* Rockville, MD: Triangle Press.

Holroyd, J., & Hill, A. (1989). Pushing the limits of recovery: Hypnotherapy with a stroke patient. *International Journal of Clinical and Experimental Hypnosis, 37,* (2) (April), 120–128.

Kroger, W. S. (1963). *Clinical and experimental hypnosis: In medicine, dentistry, and psychology* (2nd ed.). Philadelphia: Lippincott.

Manganiello, A. J. (1986). Hypnotherapy in the rehabilitation of a stroke victim: A case study. *American Journal of Clinical Hypnosis, 29* (1), 64–68.

Rosen, S. (1982). *My voice will go with you. The teaching tales of Milton H. Erickson, M.D.* New York: W. W. Norton.

Schlicht, W. (1992). Mentales training: Lern- und Leistungs-Gewinne durch Imagination? (Learning and performance gains through imagination?). *Sportpsychologie, 2,* 24–29.

Surburg, P. R. (1989). Application of imagery techniques to special populations. *Adapted Physical Activity Quarterly, 6,* 328–337.

Zafari, A. M. (1989). Psychosomatische Aspekte in der mittelalterlichen Medizin des Irans (Psychosomatic aspects of medieval medicine in Iran). *Dissertation,* Medical Faculty, University of Cologne.

Zeig, J. K. (Ed.) (1980). *A teaching seminar with Milton H. Erickson.* New York: Brunner/Mazel.

Zeig, J. K. (1990). Seeding. In J. K. Zeig & S. Gilligan (Eds.), *Brief therapy: Myths, methods, and metaphors* (pp. 221–246). New York: Brunner/Mazel.

PART VIII

Special Issues

A Five-Part Poetic Induction in Favor of Human Decency (Countering the Hate Movements)

Michele Klevens Ritterman

I. WHY TALK OF HATE MOVEMENTS AT AN HYPNOTHERAPY CONFERENCE?

Thoroughout the ages people have tried to believe that normal psychological behavior includes only that which is good at the social level . . . At times, man's inhumanity to man is given some euphemistic label, but no effort is made to investigate scientifi-

Note: While the views presented in this chapter may not conform to those of the Board of Directors of The Milton Erickson Foundation, the Board supports the right of Dr. Ritterman to express them.

cally the extremes to which the *normal, the good, the average, or the intellectual person or group* will go if given the opportunity: consider the Spanish Inquisition, the Salem witch trials, or the introduction of slavery into a country dedicated to the right of everyone to equality and freedom . . . How did it happen that noble purposes of the Pilgrims led to the position that "the only good Indian is a dead Indian"?

These words were written by Milton Erickson in 1968 (pp. 277, 278).

During our years of connection, Milton and I communicated about sanity, politics, and human rights. While he was still alive, I wrote much of my first book about a form of *hate that begins at home* in the intentional and unintentional abuse in families (Ritterman, 1983).

After Milton's death, I studied a case of *hate by the state,* in which General Augusto Pinochet, who had seized power in Chile, carried out a 16-year national ideological purge that included systematic torture (Ritterman, 1991). I described how families and communities resisted.

At the completion of my second book, Nelson Mandela had just taken his freedom walk in South Africa. In Chile, Pinochet was replaced by a Democrat and all of Europe, as if in a single gesture, shook off the chains of totalitarian communism. The cold war was miraculously ended and along with it our long nightmare of living under constant nuclear threat. Democratic capitalism blew in like a fresh wind, sweet with promises of *world peace.*

Before we could sigh with relief and *memorize this great historical moment,* violent nationalism, as if coming from under some dark, slimy rock, reared its head, feeding upon global economic unrest, hunger, and racial, religious, and ethnic differences.

Yugoslavia fractured into blood-thirsty rival peoples; East Germans turned against non-Aryan–looking immigrants; swastikas flew again in Rome, France, Austria, and Poland. These polluted tides threw up to the shores of North American public office David Duke, Patrick Buchanan, and others campaigning on a *reach out and hate someone* platform. Too many Americans accepted as justice the beating by a group of heavily armed white police of a defenseless black man, Rodney King.

Here we were on the vista overlooking the 21st century and sounding like World War II again, slipping linguistically to the level of racial epithets, discussing concepts like "ethnic cleansing," and letting people die in concentration camps. Here we were again, trampling in the garden of Eden.

Had not World War II, which lay waste cities, the genocidal war of the Holocaust, the nuclear bombing of Hiroshima and Nagasaki, the napalm burning of Vietnam sent humanity a wake-up call that *it is not the technol-*

ogies we have created but the violence in the nature of our species that is
the single most destructive force on earth?

To write now about a third form of hate—not familial or government-
sponsored, but organized civilian hate movements—I had to venture into
organized mean-spirited inductions. I quickly learned that in order to
study hateful suggestions, I needed first to confront and *discipline my own
mean spirits, animosities for people and not ideas, my own resentments of
relatives, of political candidates, of therapists who deviate from my line of
thinking about psychotherapy.*

I also had to find a way to *approach the baser passions without inciting
them.*

In this conference on therapeutic tale-telling I chose to invite poetry to
help me. To me, a story may imply invention, as though we could compose
a good life story, tell it to ourselves, and be done with what harm has been
perpetrated against us by a loved one or by an organized hate movement.

Human troubles are epitomized in their poetic distillation. *The poem
appeals to all the senses and to the intellect to trigger in the listener a
profound, even visceral, reaction.*

Naturally, to prepare this five-part *counterinduction to the hate movements,* I appealed to my muse for guidance.

When one thinks of the muse, one may imagine a frail poet consulting
with a Greek goddess. *The poet-warrior is as fundamental to the traditions
of the art as is the poet-lover.* In fact, the poet has at times been the inciter
of the mob spirit.

Listen to Tyrtaeus (1970) of 7th-century B.C. Sparta as he arouses his
defeated men to war, directly suggesting hate to do so:

> Each man should bear his shield straight at the foremost ranks
> and make his heart a thing full of hate,
> and hold the black flying spirits of death
> as dear as he holds the flash of the sun.

Another tough-talking poet and defender of civil rights, Yevgeny
Yevtushenko (1965), wrote:

> Poetry
> is no chapel of peace.
> Poetry
> is savage war . . .

The poet is no frail participant in the struggle for good or for evil,
because he is, according to John Donne, "involved in mankind." In fact,
there is no profession that cannot be abused for mean-spiritedness or

*constructed to cultivate human kindness, because these human capacities
naturally color our every endeavor.*

The muse I use today, by the way, is not a creature outside my mind but
the modern type, a state of mind I enter to *muse, to daydream, to waste
clock time, to enter into subjective time, and to creatively fathom this and
other passionate subjects from an unconscious and healing perspective.* I
invite you to muse along with me.

My hope for this synchronous daydreaming is to leave you with *a lasting
message, a time-release message, charming and valuable enough that you
may wish to keep it for a decade or two, or to use it in helping others for the
rest of your life: a poeticized induction in favor of human decency.*

II. THE COLLECTIVE MIND AS A NORMAL
AND NEUTRAL STATE: SYNCHRONOUS MUSING

The state of mind organized hate groups appeal to is, in reality, a neutral
state, *a readiness to care for*

> or to hate,
> a kind of mental slate
> engraved upon,
> by those who monger hate
> *and peace lovers,*
> poets and hypnotherapists.

*Caring and hate take us as their scribe and witness, writing on our
minds.*

William Carlos Williams (1969), the physician and poet, helps us to
visualize the swayable group brain that submerges our individuality and
allows us to follow the leader or the group mood, for better or worse, in a
grand game of Simon Says:

> *At the Ball Game*
>
> The crowd at the ball game
> is moved uniformly
>
> by a spirit of uselessness
> which delights them —
>
> all the exciting detail
> of the chase

and the escape, the error,
the flash of genius —

all to no end save beauty
the eternal.

So in detail they, the crowd,
are beautiful

for this
to be warned against,

saluted and defied —
It is alive, venomous,

it smiles grimly,
its words cut.

The flashy female with her
mother, gets it —

The Jew gets it straight.
It is deadly, terrifying.

It is the Inquisition, the
Revolution.

It is beauty itself
that lives

day by day in them
idly . . . without thought.

Lewis Thomas, M.D. (1992), the biology watcher and essayist, suggests that "when we humans are collected together at close quarters all over the face of the earth, in angry mobs or in orderly but folly-prone nation states or in auditoriums listening carefully and silently to the Late Quartets," we are immersed in a kind of group mind, a unique collective entity, a human equivalent of the ant community. Each ant singly, with a life span of a few weeks, seems smart enough only to pick up a fecal pellet. Yet the fact that, collectively, ants are able to build tall termite anthills in Africa, lasting a hundred years, each with unique architecture and airconditioning systems, has led scientists (Thomas, 1992) to speak of a super organism.

That this *collective mind is affected differently by suggestions to care and invitations to hate* gives us some decision-making power in its absorption.

Social hate is the destructive use of this state of collective reverie. *Decent social suggestion* can be creatively employed *to slow down invitations that one group makes to another group to entice them to harm a third group.*

May not one *invoke,* as readily as the warrior for hate, *the muse of love?*

III. SOCIAL SUGGESTIONS:
WORDS THAT HARM, WORDS THAT HEAL

Organized Hate (Nongovernmental)

Where do hate inductions come from? Any holier-than-thou religious pulpit espousing a defaming theology, violence-prone youth identity group, correct-line professional organization, or gender-biased group, or any nongovernment entity may intentionally or inadvertently adopt this destructive inductive posture. Organized hate is epitomized by what I call Hate-While-You-Wait groups. These racially oriented, paramilitary organizations keep their members pent-up, but ready to take power in an orgy of violence.

Hate groups feed on *family values* about Us vs. Them: *We* are good, smart, clean, strong, and have better genes. *They* are bad, dangerous, smelly, materialistic, ignorant, or primitive. Social hate is also nourished by individual animosities, fears, ignorance, lack of self-discipline, and an attraction to blaming someone else for one's troubles. Even scientific detachment can provide hate groups with something personal to sink their teeth into. Severed from unconscious understandings and affect, scientific analysis leaves us cynical and indifferent to the plight of others. Hate loves indifference to others' pain. *Do not be afraid to shed a tear in the name of science.*

The Three Targets of Social Hate Inductions

Social hate groups need three different kinds of inductions because they must uniquely affect three distinct social categories: *haters-in-training, victims-to-be, and witnesses.*

1. *Goals for Haters-in-training:* For this group, *hate must be passionate and obsessive.* Haters-in-training must be made to feel threatened by their victims-to-be. The inducers of mob hate must debase, dehumanize, and depotentiate the victims-to-be. The instinct to identify with the victims-to-be must be shut off in the haters-in-training, lest they weaken at the moment of harming.

This summer in Israel, Miriam Druch, a holocaust survivor in her sixties, told me of the Nazi soldier who came to her home in Poland when she was five years old. He stormed into the house, informed Miriam's parents and the three children that he was under orders to kill them, cocked his gun, and then lowered it. "I have a family and children just like yours," he said to Miriam's parents, breaking down. "I can't do this." Others better desensitized to the humanity of the victims did carry out their orders, but this soldier gave the Druch family the chance to shelter Miriam, who was raised by a priest as his daughter.

For risks they will take toward harassing the enemy, Haters-in-training must be offered rewards such as financial benefits, special uniforms, and status within the hate group, a chance to be a somebody by hurting someone else.

It is rare that a hate group proclaims itself such. Usually, words like identity, patriotism, defense, and freedom appear in the group name. The Christian Patriot Defense League is the name of a group that, since 1979, has held conferences called freedom festivals, which combine weapons training with bigotry. In 1981 their workshops included guns and reloading; demolition and camouflage; anti-aircraft, anti-tank, and knife fighting (Anti-Defamation League, 1987).

Hate, effectively suggested directly or indirectly to this group of persons, will trigger *seemingly automatic* behavioral responses, from cross-burnings and lynchings to wife-beating and murder.

2. *Hate Inductive Goals for the Victims-to-be:* The hated must be made to feel isolated or ghetto-ized and then exhausted with fear, humiliation, inferiority, and shame so that they are weakened and rendered at least emotionally defenseless. They are to remain uncertain or confused about the actual extent of danger posed to them, so that they seem at first paranoid, then spineless.

Whether or not a victim defends against it, hate hurts. It produces a sympathetic nervous system reaction of danger or threat, which, when constant, keeps the target of choice keyed up most of the time. Hate often refers to body and identity: women's or mens' genitalia, skin color, distinctive features. Whether victims ignore or fight them, as suggestions get more detailed and body-focused, the suggestions are harder to resist.

Paradoxically, the hate group ties the hated to itself. Hate binds. Think how inextricably and passionately hate binds Klansman to Afro-American, Turk to Armenian, Israeli to Palestinian, Serb to Croat, Chinese to Tibetan, Irish Protestant to Irish Catholic, North American settler to Native American. On an individual level, think of the rapist who stalks his unwitting victim, obsessed with the details of her life.

3. *Witnesses in Training.* The third group hate movements must affect suggestively: those reluctant to associate with either the haters or the hated. As a wife is asked by her husband only to look away when her daughter is sexually abused by him, so a third sector of society is asked by the haters just to look the other way, to not hear, not empathize, not see while they do the dirty work of abusing the victims.

But most importantly the witness group—typically the majority of any population—must be induced to silence.

Poetically, in sum thus far:

> Hate loves a uniform
> when it is not wartime.
> It has a name for everyone:
> kraut, honkey, wop, injun, broad, faggot, gimp—
> *names I utter*
> *for you to feel*
> *the effect of a single hateful word.*

> For hate,
> nothing is sacred
> holy,
> unspeakable.

> Hate waits
> coiled
> for the signal
> to release,
> which is pleasing,
> orgasmic,
> frenzied,
> bloody,
> ecstatic.

> Hate is humorless,
> but mocking.
> It creates
> only enemies.
> It fantasizes
> only in differentnesses.
> It hallucinates
> animals, viruses, cancers and madmen—
> where ordinary people stand.

Hate works best
when it aims at its target
with a single arrow
or a half sentence,
in a tone of fury,
with its finger angled for accusation
using a phrase like
"tired of talk."

Hate would electrify to silence
anyone who has seen the shadow fall
and would otherwise cry out:
Beware, hate is in the room.

Hate is in a hurry.
All the molecules in the great social beaker
must be speeded up.
There must be
no time to think
or feel.
Action!
Only Action.
Follow orders.

Like the sexual abuser
hate may boast in public,
but hides
its dirtiest deeds,
if not in shame,
then in fear that
a passing wind
will catch the victims' stiffled cries
and carry them to
the conscience of others.

Hate is passionate, obsessive.
It is the rapist who stalks his victim.
It is the worst of us ungirdled
the most destructive force on earth.
What if we try to bury hate
with other obsolete
weapons of mass destruction?

Untended,
it lies, coiling up again,
building up its great
frustration,
waiting for its next chance
to thrust.

Can we not render hate
something momentary?
Can not this momentary hate
be used somehow
to trigger
love . . .

IV. WHY PROMOTE HUMAN DECENCY?

To prepare against the likelihood of natural disasters—earthquakes, forest fires, diseases—we tirelessly work in high-risk areas to construct earthquake resilient and fireproof buildings, to improve social hygiene, and to make vaccinations mandatory. Is it not also *important to shore up human resources against the storm troopers of hate?*

Moral and Biological Imperative: Excessive and prolonged hatred threatens our biological imperative as a single species programmed linguistically and otherwise for interdependent living *to cooperate, feed the hungry, clothe the naked, house the homeless, care for the special needs of the disabled, and employ those who can work.*

Hating the haters will not do! As the Israeli peace activist and poet Jehuda Amichai reminds us: *"Even a fist was once an open palm with fingers"* (1991).

Likewise, Alice Miller (1990) reminds us that adults who commit hate crimes have often themselves been victims of child abuse—as were Hitler and Saddam Hussein. Cutting down on domestic violence is imperative. A recent National Public Radio program cited a Michigan-based study on domestic violence showing that when police stop men in the act of abusing their wives and tell them to take a walk and cool down, 70 percent of them will not abuse again. When police give abusers advice, 81 percent will not abuse again. When abusers are arrested, 90 percent of the men will not physically harm their wives again. I believe there is a social analogy to these figures: Hate, unchallenged, accumulates. Hate, pushed back, can be dissuaded.

Socially: Often in the tenor of recent political life, resonating with polarities and antagonisms between Us and Them, each of us receives an invitation to hate: at home, school, church; from the detached observations of the press, violence on television, racist radio sermons; from politicians, neighbors, shopkeepers, other therapists. What about abuses of feminist values that led, according to an NPR report, to the banning of the writing of the provocative Camille Paglia as "anti-woman" at a Connecticut women's college? Where do we draw the line? What are the First Amendment rights of the Ku Klux Klan? Has our threshhold for scapegoating descended or our tolerance for intolerance ascended to virtue? Do we conceive of the common interest at least as often as we use the word *hate?*

Professionally: Those of us who know that the *unconscious mind is more than a receptacle for hate and pain* bear some proud responsibility for delivering that message. Our message must be more effective than that of intolerance, because *our message is privileged to draw its vision from a broader range of human emotions and to be more farsighted biologically.* In order to be effective with the public, we need to rule out pettiness, grudges, and needless dichotomizing in our own field. Do we show real concern for the well-being of our clients or go through the motions, refining technique but neglecting the heart of the approach?

> *Even as we defend against it,*
> *hatefulness takes us as its scribe and witness.*
> *Therefore, decency becomes a tool*
> *to transform this sad poem*
> *into a song of hope*
> *a prayer for love.*

We can better defend ourselves against socially hateful invectives with *Self-discipline:*

> Neither a victim nor an oppressor be.
> Do not bear witness silently.

and *Education:*

If you are biased against a culture, gender identity, or religion, educate yourself about it. Farley Mowat (1988), grappling with his own ignorance of wolves, learned that it is humans who "eat like wolves," not wolves, who save their food to regurgitate it for their young.

V. HOW TO DAILY CELEBRATE ALL OUR SENSES AND OUR CONSTRUCTIVE STRENGTHS

When I first met Milton Erickson, I was an intern at Philadelphia Child Guidance Clinic with Salvador Minuchin and Jay Haley. I told Milton that we studied videotapes of initial family interviews to train ourselves to quickly track long sequences of interaction. I said that I had a habit of listening with my eyes closed and was often quick at assessing what was going on.

"All right," he said, *"but why wouldn't you want to use all of your senses?"*

In my experience, an effective countering of internal hate, besides the *outward-focused* activities already mentioned, requires *the disciplined enjoyment of all our senses.*

Fill Your Eyes With Natural Beauty:

I was in Venice recently. There I was reminded how context etches itself visually onto our brain cells, how the life around us writes itself onto our minds.

Far from the urban streets of North America, on a gondola, returning from the Lido island back to Venezia, I allowed the circling dark waters of the Adriatic Sea to *hypnotize me.*

I let the water have its way with my mind, asking only that I be able *to recall, refeel, relive this moment of natural beauty,* this sense of going back in time to the 14th century.

Enchanted by ancientness, I allowed my mind to memorize the drops of sunlight bouncing on the water's deep blue surface. Having surrounded myself with great works of art, I at last entered into an imagist painting, myself a wind-brushed receptacle for light and peacefulness, aglow with a pastel *tenderness for the human* endeavor and all that nature so gracefully provides.

Even as we defend against beauty, it takes us as its scribe and witness.

I visited in Florence the Keats-Shelley House and saw in Keats' own handwriting, the original manuscript of "A Thing of Beauty Is a Joy Forever."

> "A thing of beauty is a joy forever:
> Its loveliness increases; it will never
> Pass into nothingness; but still will keep
> A bower quiet for us, and a sleep
> Full of sweet dreams, and health, and quiet breathing."

It is important, not trivial, to concentrate on natural beauty.

> At home,
> my husband and I
> were hypnotized
> by our Bonsai.
> I stared at the little tree
> given to me as a gift,

feeling myself to be
in a beautiful Japanese garden
communing with a giant stone
feeling not lonliness but alone
in an atmosphere of holiness.

I did not hear the roar of highway traffic,
but only the birds,
the wind,
my own spirit rustling.

It is Important, Not Trivial to Allow Your Ears
to receive beautiful and pleasing sounds
and not ugly rumorings
but music which exalts
the happy, longing songs of birds ready to mate,
the crickets singing with their feet
about the temperature of the night.
In sound alone
we can perceive
the harmony possible
for all that lives.

We Can Celebrate Our Sense of Synchronicity

Lewis Thomas (1992) writes:

> The oxygen in the air is not placed there at random, any old way;
> it is maintained at precisely the optimal concentration for the
> place to be livable. A few percentage points more than the present
> level and the forests would burst into flames, a few less and most
> life would strangle. It is held there, constant, by feedback loops of
> information from *the conjoined life of the planet.* (p. 22)

We can observe intelligence in the interrelatedness of all forms of life
from the complex relations between the cricket and the bat to the match-
ing up of the medicinal properties of a rare plant that grows in the Brazilian
rain forest with the ailment of a city dweller in New York.
As Individuals Need To Use All of the Senses, so the Species Needs To
Use All its Peoples, and Synchronously.
Ought not each culture be regarded like an endangered or threatened
species, a one-of-a-kind mixture, a unique experiment? Just as each individual is as unique as his fingerprints and optic and dental nerve x-rays, so

all of the peoples of the earth are unique in terms of the niche they inhabit, food, clothing, color, language, discoveries and inventions.

What is More Powerful More Primitive Than Our Senses of Taste and Smell and Feel which carry us on the currents of our sweetest memories of lilac, honeysuckle, fruit of the vine?

>I hypnotized a group of Salvadorans.
>They had escaped the death squads
>that killed tens of thousands of Salvadorans in just ten years.
>These Salvadorans lived the life of exiles
>in Costa Rica.
>In trance,
>to heal from hate which had displaced them,
>they all traveled home
>to the poor communities they had come from.
>They went back in time before the terror
>and home to smell the streets, the schoolyard,
>to smell the courtyard air around the church,
>and most of all to smell the food
>being prepared by mother,
>still steaming from the big pot, stirred by mother
>being prepared by mother with them beside her
>now
>as if it really was happening.

❀   ❀   ❀

>The world is
>not with us enough,
>O taste and see . . .
>living in the orchard and being
>hungry, and plucking
>the fruit (Levertov, 1962, p. 53)

And What of the Physical Sensations and Passions?

>There is a comfort in the strength of love;
>'Twill make a thing endurable, which else
>Would overset the brain, or break the heart . . .
>(Wordsworth 1965, p. 134).

>I sing the body electric,
>. . . And if the body does not do fully as much as the soul?

And if the body were not the soul, what is the soul?
(Whitman, 1931, p. 97).

The river in its abundance
many-voiced
all about us as we stood
on a warm rock to wash

slowly
smoothing in long
sliding strokes
our soapy hands along each other's
slippery cool bodies

quiet and slow in the midst of
the quick of the
sounding river (Levertov, 1962, p. 55)

I ask the most important thing of you
you there listening to my voice today
enjoying as much as I hope
and more than I can know
all your faculties and senses,
that you *REMEMBER me when you are packing your suitcase*
as you put the clothes you brought back into the suitcase,
that you put your own ideas of beauty
into the folds,
that you fill the sensuous corners with humor,
and your shoes
with an expanding compassion
to lengthen your gait.

When you return home and are unpacking,
won't you remember me,
my message to you?
And when you wake up
the next morning,
will you not allow your eyes and ears
to fill with beauty
so that you will have,
let's say in five years, little room for hate,
in a decade, no time or space to waste on hate.

When we talk about the heart of Erickson,
is not the bottom line

that we *have the courage*
to stand up
for the best that human nature is capable of,
whether or not we see that best around us.

For Milton the limits of the imaginable were discovered in working hard
to attain it.

Human decency remains
an unfinished business.
We are a neonatal
even foetal
species . . .
perhaps that is why
we sometimes care more
for the unborn
than the living.

I end my talk today
with *this photo*
of a statue from Michelangelo's prisoner series.
It shows that we
are struggling to
extricate ourselves from
what we are made of,
still prisoners to our nature,
an uninished work
a work in progress,
which leaves much to the imagination.

For those of you
who like to travel light,
five words:
Hate harms.
Caring can repair.

REFERENCES

Amichai, Jehuda. *Even a Fist Was Once an Open Palm With Fingers.* New York:
     HarperCollins, 1991.
Erickson, Milton. "The Inhumanity of Ordinary People," *International Journal
     of Psychiatry,* October 1968, pp. 277-279.
Anti-Defamation League of B'nai Brith. *The Hate Movement Today: A Chronicle
     of Violence and Disarray.* New York: Anti-Defamation League, 1987.

Hillesum, Eity. *An Interrupted Life*. New York: Washington Square Press, 1983.

Levertov, Denise. "Eros at Temple Stream," in *O Taste and See*. New York: New Directions, 1962, p. 55.

Levertov, Denise. "O Taste and See," in *O Taste and See*. New York: New Directions, 1962, p. 53.

Miller, Alice. *For Your Own Good: Hidden Cruelty in Child Rearing and The Roots of Violence*. New York: Noonday Press, 1990.

Mowat, Farley. *Never Cry Wolf*. Toronto: Bantam, 1988.

Ritterman, Michele Klevens. *Using Hypnosis in Family Therapy*. San Francisco: Jossey-Bass, 1983. (Available through author)

Ritterman, Michele Klevens. *Hope Under Siege: Terror and Family Support in Chile*. Norwood, NJ: Ablex, 1991. (Available through author)

Thomas, Lewis. *The Fragile Species*. New York: Charles Scribner's Sons, 1992, pp. 112-113

Tyrtaeus. "To the Soldiers, after a Defeat," in *Greek Lyrics* (Trans. Richmond Lattimore), Chicago: University of Chicago Press, 1970, p. 15.

Williams, William Carlos. "At the Ball Game," in *William Carlos Williams Selected Poems*. New York: New Directions, 1969, pp. 31-32.

Wordsworth, William. *The Prelude, Selected Poems and Sonnets*. New York: Holt, Rinehart and Winston, 1965, pp. 134-235.

Yevtushenko, Yevgeny. "Poetry," in *The Poetry of Yevgeny Yevtushenko 1953-1965*, New York: October House, 1965, p. 153.

CHAPTER 32

Memories of the Future: Regression and Suggestions of Abuse

Michael D. Yapko

He told his wife that he simply couldn't deal with the scars remaining from his horrible experiences in Vietnam. Married more than 20 years, she'd seen plenty of strange episodes that led her to believe him. One night, he went berserk in an apparent reaction to the sneakers she happened to be wearing. After he calmed down, he told her that his Vietcong captors wore similar sneakers when they would come to the bamboo cage in which he was kept prisoner. He was regularly beaten and degraded by their urinating on him, helpless to do anything about it. He told her he had been a prisoner for 15 days after a carrier-based F-4 jet fighter on which he was navigator was shot down. He said he escaped after strangling a guard, who, incidentally, was also wearing the same kind of sneakers.

He finally went to see a therapist for his problems. He was diagnosed as suffering post-traumatic stress syndrome, and was treated for his severe symptoms of depression, guilt, and explosive anger. Treatment did not help quickly enough, however, for he finally took his own troubled life through carbon monoxide poisoning.

After his death, his wife attempted to get his name placed on the state Vietnam War Memorial. His therapist wrote a letter on his behalf encouraging that his name be included among those of the other war casualties. Only then was his background researched.

How could anyone have known that he had never been to Vietnam?

This is a true story, involving one of my most highly esteemed professional colleagues. How could this happen? How could this patient have such severe symptoms associated with such specific memories for events that had never actually occurred? His wife believed him. His therapist believed him. And why not?

Now, let's change the patient's gender and the content of his Vietnam story. Let's substitute a woman as the patient who reports terrifying flashbacks, horrific nightmares, panic attacks, and a marked fear of men and sexual victimization. Let's change one aspect of her narrative, though. Let's say she has no idea what causes her symptoms, but her therapist directly suggests to her that her symptoms indicate that she must have been sexually abused. Soon, with the therapist's help, she recovers memories of sexual abuse. Did these episodes of abuse actually happen? Or were they manufactured *unintentionally* in order to accommodate the expectations and suggestions of the therapist?

AN EPIDEMIC OF ABUSE

Roseanne Arnold, Oprah Winfrey, a former Miss America, and scores of other celebrities and role models have publicly announced their private shame, being victims of childhood sexual abuse. It seems the entire country is in an uproar over the almost daily allegations surfacing of sexual abuse occurring somewhere to someone, famous or otherwise. In fact, on September 4, 1992, television history was made by three major networks (PBS, CBS, NBC) simultaneously running a special program on child abuse ("Scared Silent") produced by Oprah Winfrey. Consciousness about the problem is greater than ever, and is still growing. Child abuse is considered one of the most heinous crimes one could commit, and no proven child abuser gets much in the way of sympathy.

It is currently estimated, probably incorrectly since exact figures are impossible to obtain, that about one in four women was abused as a child, and one in six men (*Newsweek*, October 7, 1991). It is further estimated that there are countless abuse survivors who don't yet know it because their memories are still repressed. Thus, experts in depression, eating disorders, panic disorders, substance abuse, and countless other problem areas routinely suggest to many troubled people that they may best explain their terrible symptoms by recognizing that they were sexually abused. And, if they still can't remember it, then abuse is often considered to be all the more likely since repression is so powerful a defense mechanism (Bass & Davis, 1988).

As a clinical psychologist, I am all too aware of the enormous pain suffered by survivors of incest and sexual abuse, and my concern for them is deep and genuine. It is a profoundly moving experience to share in a survivor's anguish and in the painfully slow rebuilding of his or her life. I am appreciative that we as a profession and we as a society have finally created the avenues for survivors to come forward and proclaim their freedom from the shackles of shame and self-blame by directly or indirectly confronting their abusers. It is a huge step forward for us to take seriously the sanctity of the family and the terrible aftermath suffered by survivors when that sanctity is violated.

SURVIVING ABUSE THAT NEVER HAPPENED?

With the outpouring of sympathy and feelings of protectiveness for incest and sexual abuse survivors, it seems a critical issue has been overlooked. Can we believe *every* allegation of abuse? Can a memory of abuse be suggested and integrated as if true? How do we distinguish a real survivor from one who made up (confabulated) a story of abuse?

It seems naive to believe that *every* reported episode of abuse happened. Yet, how can we possibly discount a report that has such great potential to ruin a genuine abuse survivor's life by ignoring or refuting it? More specifically, how should we treat reports of abuse that surface in therapy that were "repressed memories," i.e., forgotten memories that too often arise in response to a therapist's suggestions and influence?

Therapy necessarily involves influence. A fundamental reality of clinical practice is that whatever has the capacity to be therapeutic has an equal capacity to be antitherapeutic. Can people be convinced to adopt beliefs that ultimately harm them? Yes. Can people be convinced or convince themselves that something happened that never really happened? Yes.

FALSE MEMORY SYNDROME

In the second edition of my textbook on clinical hypnosis, *Trancework: An Introduction to the Practice of Clinical Hypnosis* (Yapko, 1990), I included a short but significant section called "Focal Point: Creating False Memories." I believe the following paragraphs taken from that section can do much to highlight the problems I wish to address in this chapter.

> Consider this letter advertising a workshop I received a short while ago. It is reproduced here in edited form in order to protect those responsible.
> "*Dr. Yapko, Director:*
> *As bizarre as the following question seems, please take the time to read further and give serious consideration to the subject discussed.*

During a hypnosis session, have you ever had a client that believes that he/she had an alien (extraterrestrial) abduction or encounter? Has this person experienced missing time or repetitive dreams about unusual night visitors? In the last four years there has been a 65% increase in reported abduction cases. Many of these reports have surfaced during hypnosis sessions.

What would you do if information similar to this was revealed by one of your clients during a hypnotic session? How do you help this person?

. . . Some of the people have had conscious recall of the event. However, the majority of them recalled the encounter while under hypnosis—which many had sought out to help them with other problems . . ."

One fact the letter doesn't mention is that a popular book called *Communion,* by Whitley Strieber, came out a few years ago. The book is an intelligent and articulate description of the author's belief he has had repeated experiences of being abducted by extraterrestrials. Prior to becoming aware of the abductions, all Strieber had were periods of time he was amnesic for, and unusual dreams of abductions in which he served as a human guinea pig for extraterrestrials' experiments. Is it coincidence that there is a 65% increase in reported abduction cases following the release of Strieber's book? Obviously not. If so many people can be convinced so easily of "trance channelers" (people who go into trance and become the medium through which other entities, perhaps as old as 35,000 years according to one, can share their "wisdom"), thanks to popular books like Shirley MacLaine's *Out on a Limb,* then you can convince a percentage of the population of *anything.* Hypnotic past-life regression, hypnotic ESP, hypnotic aura-reading, and countless other "applications" of hypnosis are offered to those who are open to or already have beliefs in such phenomena.

So what's the problem? The serious problem is that a clinician can suggest an experience that the individual accepts as "true." With extraterrestrial abductions, it is easy to dismiss the problem lightly.

However, consider what happens if what is suggested instead is that, "You may have been molested as a child. Let's do hypnosis to find out" (pp. 254–256)

This section of my book served as a lightning rod for attracting people from literally all over the world who had been accused of horrendous acts of sexual abuse by grown children with whom they previously had enjoyed what they thought was a "normal" relationship. What happened?

The names and faces differed from case to case, but the stories were surprisingly similar. A daughter, typically, went to therapy for her problems, e.g., depression, anxiety, or relationship problems. The therapist would suggest childhood sexual abuse as an explanation for her symptoms. Denial of abuse by the patient was framed as evidence of "repression," and suggestive methods like guided imagery or hypnosis were then used to attempt to lift the repression. The result: Memories of abuse surfaced that would fit suspiciously well with the therapist's expectations, and the client would, over time, come to genuinely believe in their validity. This is what has come to be known in some circles as "False Memory Syndrome."

I must now make a very, very important distinction for you to consider as you read on. I must distinguish those cases where someone *now knows and has known all along* that he or she was abused from those cases where someone *"discovered" the abuse through the suggestions of a therapist.* The heart of this chapter relates to the latter scenario exclusively, namely, the abuse being discovered or remembered through the directions provided by a therapist.

How often does this happen? No one can know for certain, but anecdotal evidence suggests the above scenario happens more frequently than we might like to believe. I can think of many times in just my own clinical experience when the unthinkable has happened. For example, a woman called me and asked if I would hypnotize her in order to determine whether or not she had been molested as a child. I asked where she first got the idea that she might have been. She told me she called another therapist about her self-esteem problems, and the therapist suggested to her — a woman the therapist had never met — over the telephone that she must have been abused and should be hypnotized to find out. *That* level of professional incompetence should be considered abuse!

What about the not uncommon scenario in which someone is hypnotized who has a single image, ostensibly from six months old, that involves some kind of abuse? Should it be considered real? Should she go home and allege abuse and tear apart the family on the basis of such an image? Those therapists who believe such memories are valid will say "Yes," and those who don't will say "No." And, that's the essence of the problem I am addressing here: A client's fate is placed at the mercy of a therapist's seemingly arbitrary belief system about the nature of memory. It is vital that we as a profession take a clearer stand on this issue and at the very least discourage therapists from imposing their arbitrary beliefs on clients when the stakes are so very high.

As one who is knowledgeable about patterns of suggestion and hypnosis, I am keenly aware that suggestion is powerful in influencing perceptions, including perceptions of memory. Formal hypnosis, i.e., an hypnotic procedure overtly identified as such, does *not* need to be utilized in order for an individual to respond to suggestions that are either directly stated or merely implied. How easily can this be done? Consider one abuse guru, who, with a series of television programs and books, influenced a large segment of Americans into believing they have an "inner child." People now literally talk to their inner child, comfort it, give it a name and a personality, defend its right to exist, and find ways to continually get to know it better. *There is no inner child: it is simply a metaphor!* But, to millions its existence is now a "fact" and dictates their way of life. This expert suggested to people a new identity, a new perspective, and detailed memories for an inner child's entire life that didn't even exist before his programs were aired! That is *very* effective use of suggestion.

SUGGESTION AND MEMORY

The notion that a memory is stored accurately as if the mind were a computer is a commonly held but inaccurate metaphor (Loftus, 1980). Memories can*not* simply be plucked from the brain through hypnosis or any other "memory enhancing" tool without the use of suggestions of one sort or another that *alter the memory in some way* (Zelig & Beidelman, 1981). Memory is influenced by many factors, ranging from physical and psychological factors to situational variables (Loftus, 1980). Memory is, in part, a constructive process in which new details or ideas may be added to old images and other such memory fragments, potentially changing the meaning or emotional value of a memory (Loftus & Hoffman, 1989). In fact, this is the basis for much of what happens in psychotherapy. We can't change what actually happened to someone, but we can, and do, change how they interpret it, feel about it, and subsequently remember it. What was first remembered as emotional abandonment, for example, can become remembered instead as Mom being pitifully overworked trying desperately to keep the family together (Yapko, 1990).

In a more relevant example, consider a memory of your mom or dad giving you a bath when you were very young. Where did he/she wash you? Did he/she touch your "private parts?" Did you give your mother or father permission to touch you there? Was it more of a touch or more of a caress? Now, pause. Can you see how quickly suggestive or leading questioning can turn a simple bath into a sexually tainted experience? If done seriously in the context of therapy with a client who is desperate to understand his or her symptoms, the bath could be permanently remembered as a sexually inappropriate or even abusive experience even though it had never previously been defined in that way (Doris, 1991). Memory is malleable, and can be influenced unintentionally by the asking of leading questions and the suggestion of implications (Spiegel, 1980; Putnam, 1979).

A DELICATE MATTER

Families are in crisis. Imagine your adult daughter going to therapy and coming home and accusing you of sexually molesting her once when she was only three months old. How horrible to have to face such a situation, yet that is precisely what can happen in cases of suggested memories of abuse.

The delicacy of the situation is evident in the double bind associated with it: If we validate the memory, as if a memory from three months old were valid, we then condemn the individual to a life in which her main identity is that of an abuse survivor. If we invalidate the memory, we isolate her and make her doubt her own mind and sanity. It is a terrible bind to be in, and even as a psychologist who is especially "tuned in" to these issues, I have found it difficult to find ways to walk the line between validating and invalidating such sensitive issues in people's lives.

HYPNOSIS AND MEMORY

Hypnosis can alter perceptions—that is one of the principal reasons behind its widespread clinical use. Medical hypnosis involves altering sensory and physiological perceptions, while psychological hypnosis may involve altering perceptions of personal traits, relational patterns, expectations, mood, and other such dimensions of experience (Yapko, 1990). The presupposition in all cases where hypnosis is attempted is that there is some element of the client's experience that is malleable, and, therefore, changeable. Is memory a negotiable phenomenon? Is it responsive to suggestion and subject to the principles that govern human perception? The answer to both questions is "Yes."

A memory is not the experience. Memory involves a representation of experience. Simply put, remembering your high school graduation is not the same as being there. What you will remember, if anything, about your high school graduation is a composite of many variables (Loftus, 1980; Bower, 1981; Dywan & Bowers, 1983). These variables are listed in Table 1.

With some few exceptions, experts in the field of clinical hypnosis have

TABLE 1

Factors Influencing the Accuracy of Memory

Motivation to Attend to Stimulus
Competing Stimuli
Sensory Acuity
Mood
Expectation
Intensity of Stimulus
Novelty of Stimulus
Meaningfulness of Stimulus
Elapsed Time

been noticeably silent about the role of suggestion in influencing memories relative to the issues of child abuse. The professional hypnosis community has, through our passivity, allowed practitioners to continue to use the analogy of the mind as a computer that accurately records experiences even though we already know that analogy is specious. We have, through our passivity, let people continue to believe that hypnosis is some sort of lie detector, a truth serum of sorts that permits people to undergo hypnotic procedures to "find out" if they were abused. I see this as tragic and irresponsible on the part of our profession. Prior to the issues of child abuse becoming so prominent, considerable research was done on hypnosis as a memory enhancing tool (Spiegel, 1980; Pettinati, 1988). In particular, hypnosis was examined as it related to law enforcement investigations (Putnam, 1979; Orne, 1979; Watkins, 1989). Could hypnosis be used to obtain information that was apparently "recorded" but "repressed?" Could hypnosis permit greater and more accurate recall by eyewitnesses to crime? A host of studies reached similar conclusions: Hypnosis is generally an unreliable investigative tool. Thus, the California Supreme Court, followed by most other states, ruled that hypnotically obtained testimony was inadmissible in court. Forensic hypnosis was dealt an all but fatal blow by this decision. Why is this so, and what does it have to do with the issues of abuse under consideration in this chapter?

The Council on Scientific Affairs of the American Medical Association (1985) issued the following statement to help close the door on investigative hypnosis:

> *Recollections obtained under hypnosis can involve confabulations and pseudomemories and not only fail to be more accurate, but actually appear to be less reliable than non-hypnotic recall.*

The use of hypnosis with witnesses and victims may have serious consequences for the legal process when testimony is based on material that is elicited from a witness who has been hypnotized for the purposes of refreshing recollection.

The above statement says in no uncertain terms what I have come to believe to be true on the basis of my experience: Hypnosis can work in a destructive manner relative to memory. *It can increase the inaccuracy* of recall, and *it can increase the level of certainty* about the recall (Orne, 1979; Sheehan, Statham & Jamieson, 1991). In essence, a person remembers incorrectly, and yet feels very sure that the memory is accurate

Isn't it for the very properties of hypnosis to facilitate shifts in perception that we use it in clinical contexts? I recall speaking at length about hypnosis with Ernest Hilgard, professor emeritus from Stanford University (personal communication, 1988). Dr. Hilgard had a simple yet most insightful way of characterizing hypnotic experience. He called it "believed-in imagination." I think that phrase captures well the spirit and essence of hypnosis. We encourage people to alter their realities and accept frameworks for living (believed-in imaginations) that we think will help. So, we lead people to believe in their imagination that they each have a wise inner sage they can talk to, or that seeing white lights in their body can heal them of cancer. These suggested experiences can and do become "believed-in imaginations," and they can forever change a person's life.

Hypnosis is powerful, especially the self-hypnosis that shapes one's reality. Once the premise is accepted that an inner child exists, then and only then can it be found. Once you accept the premise of reincarnation, only then can you recover and relive past lives in hypnosis. In the reincarnation example, people will "recover memories" in vivid detail of past lives and then cite as evidence for their validity the voluminous details they conjure up. Clearly, more detail does not mean more truth. Likewise, once the premise is accepted that you have a wise inner sage, only then can you go find and commune with him or her. Hypnosis is most widely used to gain acceptance for the initial premise, for once that is accepted, the other suggested experiences naturally follow (Hilgard, 1979; Laurence & Perry, 1983).

The literature of social psychology describes well the phenomenon of cognitive dissonance (Aronson, 1992). Once a belief is established, contradictory input is filtered out. Experience then becomes self-confirming. For example, if I believe I am unlovable, then I will not accept love from anyone, leaving me feeling unloved and thereby confirming that I am unlovable. The self-confirming distortions of experience represent the greatest hazard of adopting *any* belief system. This is why the premise of

sexual abuse, in particular, is one that must be imparted to our clients only
with a great deal of care and discretion.

SUGGESTIONS OF ABUSE

Once the premise of abuse has been accepted by the client at the therapist's direction, he or she can easily recover vivid details that would seem
to support the premise. The suggestions of abuse need not be direct. After
all, as Watzlawick (1985) pointed out, hypnosis is possible without trance,
and as Zeig (1988) has described, hypnosis is the language of injunction. A
business card that says "Abuse Specialist" is injunctive. It says, "Consider
that you may have been abused before you call me." A leading question
like, "How were you abused as a child" is injunctive. It suggests that you
ought to consider abuse as an explanation for your symptoms. An indirect
statement like, "People with your symptoms were typically sexually abused
as children" is injunctive. It suggests that you fit an established profile that
can redefine your identity.

QUESTIONS, NOT ANSWERS

When does memory begin? When can someone know directly that his or
her memory represents something that really happened, rather than the
memory being the result of just having been told about it, after which it
was incorporated as a memory? How old is someone before memory is
realistic? When can we trust that when someone says something happened
it really did? These are very difficult questions to answer. The evidence, to
date, suggests the answer is between two and three years of age (Loftus,
personal communication, 1992).

I have one specific goal in presenting this material. It is to highlight that
it is all too possible to lead people to believe that which seems plausible,
yet may not be accurate. In the case of suggested sexual abuse, the falsely
accused suffer the virtual destruction of their lives, the newly identified
survivor is placed on a long, laborious path that is fraught with danger, and
the therapist is the unwitting catalyst for the devastation.

We cannot realistically believe every allegation of abuse, despite the
emotional accusation that we are "in denial" if we don't. Nor can we
responsibly dismiss every allegation of abuse. What is true in such cases, in
all likelihood, lies somewhere between total believing and total disbelieving.
Therefore, the key question is this: How do we distinguish a real memory
from a confabulated one? I wish a valid answer could be forthcoming, but
no such answer currently exists.

TABLE 2

Errors to Avoid Regarding Suggestions of Abuse

Do Not:
- Jump quickly to the molestation conclusion simply because it is plausible
- Suggest molestation directly or indirectly out of a therapeutic context
- Refer out for a quick hypnotic confirmation/disconfirmation as if hypnosis were a lie detector
- Ask leading questions (involving presuppositions)
  - When were you abused?
  - How did he/she molest you?
- Assume repression is in force when someone has little memory of childhood
  - Consider primary temporal orientation
- Rely on your memory of interaction
  - Use videotape, audiotape to review to make certain no suggestions were made

SUGGESTED THERAPIST GUIDELINES

Since there is no reliable means for determining whether or not a memory is authentic or confabulated, I want to offer some specific guidelines to help assure that therapists are less likely to be the problem and more likely to be the solution. In light of everything I have stated about the role of suggestion in making the "diagnosis" to a client that he or she may have been abused when that was not a presenting problem, the following guidelines in Table 2 seem like useful precautions to observe.

By following guidelines such as the above, and by being aware of the suggestibility of help-seeking clients in general and their memories in particular, it is my hope that therapists will come to appreciate the considerable power they wield in the explanations they offer for their clients' symptoms. Abuse is simply too volatile an issue with too many dramatic implications to offer it as a casual suggestion to someone.

So, what do I mean when I speak of "Memories of the Future?" I refer to the consequences of suggesting memories of abuse that, once accepted, come to govern the rest of that person's life. His or her future is created at the moment the suggested memories of abuse are accepted.

REFERENCES

Aronson, E. (1992). *The social animal* (6th ed.). San Francisco: W.H. Freeman.
Bass, E., & Davis, L. (1988). *The courage to heal: Women healing from sexual abuse.* New York: Harper & Row.

Bower, G. (1981). Mood and memory. *American Psychologist, 36,* 129-148.

Council on Scientific Affairs (1985). Scientific status of refreshing recollection by the use of hypnosis: A council report. *Journal of the American Medical Association, 253,* 1918-1923.

Doris, J. (Ed.). (1991). *The suggestibility of children's recollections.* Washington, D.C.: American Psychological Assn.

Dywan, J., & Bowers, K. (1983). The use of hypnosis to enhance recall. *Science, 222,* 184-185.

Hilgard, J. (1979). *Personality and hypnosis: A study of imaginative involvement (2nd ed.).* Chicago: University of Chicago Press.

Kihlstrom, J., & Evans, F. (1979). Memory retrieval processes during post-hypnotic amnesia. In J. Kihlstrom & F. Evans (Eds.), *Functional Disorders of Memory* (pp. 179-218). Hillsdale, N.J.: Erlbaum.

Klatzky, R., & Erderly, M. (1985). The response criterion problem in tests of hypnosis and memory. *International Journal of Clinical and Experimental Hypnosis, 33,* 3, 246-257.

Labelle, L., Laurence, J-R., Nadon, R., & Perry, C. (1990). Hypnotizability, preference for an imagic cognitive style and memory creation in hypnosis. *Journal of Abnormal Psychology, 99,* 222-228.

Laurence, J-R., Nadon, R., Nogrady, H., & Perry, C. (1986). Duality, dissociation, and memory creation in highly hypnotizable subjects. *International Journal of Clinical and Experimental Hypnosis, 34,* 4, 295-310.

Laurence, J-R., & Perry, C. (1983). Hypnotically created memory among highly hypnotizable subjects. *Science, 222,* 523-524.

Lindberg, M. (1991). An interactive approach to assessing the suggestibility and testimony of eyewitnesses. In J. Doris (Ed.), *The Suggestibility of Children's Recollections* (pp. 47-55). Washington, D.C.: American Psychological Assn.

Loftus, E. (1980). *Memory.* Reading, Mass.: Addison-Wesley.

Loftus, E. (1991). Commentary: When words speak louder than actions. In J. Doris (Ed.), *The Suggestibility of Children's Recollections* (pp. 56-59). Washington, D.C.: American Psychological Assn.

Loftus, E. (1992). The reality of repressed memories. Paper presented at the 100th Annual Convention of the American Psychological Association, Washington, D.C.

Loftus, E., & Hoffman, H. (1989). Misinformation and memory: The creation of new memories. *Journal of Experimental Psychology: General, 118,* 100-104.

Loftus, E., & Ketcham, K. (1991). *Witness for the defense.* New York: St. Martin's Press.

Lynn, S., Weekes, J., & Milano, M. (1989). Reality vs. suggestion: Pseudomemory in hypnotizable and simulating subjects. *Journal of Abnormal Psychology, 98,* 137-44.

McConkey, K., & Sheehan, P. (1980). Inconsistency in hypnotic age regression and cue structure as supplied by the hypnotist. *International Journal of Clinical and Experimental Hypnosis, 28,* 394-408.

Newsweek (October 7, 1991). The pain of the last taboo, 70-72.

Orne, M.T. (1979). The use and misuse of hypnosis in court. *International Journal of Clinical and Experimental Hypnosis, 27,* 311-341.

Pettinati, H. (Ed.). (1988). *Hypnosis and memory.* New York: Guilford.

Putnam, W. (1979). Hypnosis and distortions in eyewitness memory. *International Journal of Clinical Hypnosis, 27,* 437-448.

Sheehan, P., & Grigg, L. (1985). Hypnosis, memory, and the acceptance of an implausible cognitive set. *British Journal of Clinical and Experimental Hypnosis, 3,* 5-12.

Sheehan, P., Statham, D., & Jamieson, G. (1991). Pseudomemory effects over time in the hypnotic setting. *Journal of Abnormal Psychology, 100,* 1, 39-44.

Spiegel, H. (1980). Hypnosis and evidence: Help or hindrance. *Annals of the New York Academy of Science, 347,* 73-85.

Spiegel, D., & Cardena, E. (1991). Disintegrated experience: The dissociative disorders revisited. *Journal of Abnormal Psychology, 100,* 3, 366-378.

Strieber, W. (1987). *Communion.* New York: Avon Books.

Watkins, J. (1989). Hypnotic hyperamnesia and forensic hypnosis: A cross-examination. *American Journal of Clinical Hypnosis, 32,* 71-83.

Watzlawick, P. (1985). Hypnotherapy without trance. In J. Zeig (Ed.), *Ericksonian Psychotherapy* (Vol. I) (pp. 5-14). New York: Brunner/Mazel.

Yapko, M. (1990). *Trancework: An introduction to the practice of clinical hypnosis* (2nd ed.). New York: Brunner/Mazel.

Zeig, J. (1988). An Ericksonian phenomenological approach to therapeutic hypnotic induction and symptom utilization. In J. Zeig & S. Lankton (Eds.), *Developing Ericksonian Therapy: State of the Art* (pp. 353-379). New York: Brunner/Mazel.

Zelig, M., & Beidelman, W. (1981). The investigative use of hypnosis: A word of caution. *International Journal of Clinical and Experimental Hypnosis, 29,* 401-412.

About The Milton H. Erickson Foundation, Inc.

The Milton H. Erickson Foundation, Inc., is a federal nonprofit corporation. It was formed to promote and advance the contributions made to the health sciences by the late Milton H. Erickson, M.D., during his long and distinguished career. The Foundation is dedicated to training health and mental health professionals.

Strict eligibility requirements are maintained for attendance at our training events or to receive our educational materials. The Milton H. Erickson Foundation, Inc., does not discriminate on the basis of race, color, national or ethnic origin, religion, age, sex, or physical challenge. Directors of The Milton H. Erickson Foundation, Inc., are Jeffrey K. Zeig, Ph.D., Kristina K. Erickson, M.S., M.D., Elizabeth M. Erickson, B.A., and J. Charles Theisen, M.A., M.B.A., J.D.

ELIGIBILITY

Training programs, the newsletter, audiotapes, and videotapes are available to professionals in health-related fields, including physicians, doctoral level psychologists, podiatrists, and dentists who are qualified for membership in, or are members of, their respective professional organizations (e.g., AMA, APA, ADA). Activities of the Foundation also are open to professionals with graduate degrees from accredited institutions in areas related to mental health (e.g., M.A., M.S., M.S.N., M.S.W.). Full-time graduate students in accredited programs in the above fields must supply a letter from their department, certifying their student status, if they wish to attend events, subscribe to the newsletter, or purchase tapes.

TRAINING OPPORTUNITIES

The Erickson Foundation organizes International Congresses on Ericksonian Approaches to Hypnosis and Psychotherapy. These meetings have been held in Phoenix in 1980, 1983, and 1986, and in San Francisco in 1988. In 1992, The Foundation held its Fifth International Congress in Phoenix on the subject "Ericksonian Methods: The Essence of the Story." Each was attended by 1700-2200 professionals.

In the intervening years, the Foundation organizes national seminars. The four-day seminars are limited to approximately 450 attendees, and they emphasize skill development in hypnotherapy. The 1981, 1982, and 1984 seminars were held in San Francisco, Dallas, and Los Angeles, respectively. In 1989, the Foundation celebrated its 10th anniversary with a training seminar in Phoenix.

The Milton H. Erickson Foundation organized The Evolution of Psychotherapy Conference in 1985, in Phoenix. It was hailed as a landmark conference in the history of psychotherapy. Faculty included Beck, the late Bruno Bettelheim, the late Murray Bowen, Ellis, M. Goulding, the late Robert Goulding, Haley, the late Ronald D. Laing, Lazarus, Madanes, Marmor, Masterson, May, Minuchin, Moreno, E. Polster, M. Polster, the late Carl Rogers, Rossi, the late Virginia Satir, Szasz, Watzlawick, Whitaker, the late Lewis Wolberg, Wolpe, and Zeig. This conference was repeated in 1990 in Anaheim, California, with a similar faculty including Bugental, Glasser, Hillman, H. S. Kaplan, Lowen, Meichenbaum, and Selvini Palazzoli. Keynote addresses were given by Viktor Frankl and Betty Friedan. In 1994, a European Evolution Conference is scheduled for Hamburg, Germany, in July. The Third Evolution Conference is scheduled for December 1995 in Las Vegas.

The Milton H. Erickson Foundation organized a special conference on Brief Therapy. In December 1993, this multidisciplinary conference was held in Orlando, Florida.

Regional workshops are held regularly in various locations. Training programs are announced in the Foundation's newsletter.

The Foundation provides both training and supervision for professionals. The Foundation is equipped with observation rooms and audio/video recording capabilities. Inquiries regarding services should be made directly to the Erickson Foundation.

ERICKSON ARCHIVES

In December 1980, the Foundation began collecting audiotapes, videotapes, and historical material on Dr. Erickson for the Erickson Archives. The goal is to have a central repository of historical material on Erickson. More than

300 hours of videotape and audiotape have been donated to the Foundation. The Erickson Archives are available to interested and qualified professionals who wish to come to Phoenix to independently study the audiotapes and videotapes that are housed at the Foundation. There is a nominal charge for use of the Archives. Please call or write for further details and to make advance arrangements to view the Archives.

AUDIO AND VIDEO TRAINING TAPES

The Milton H. Erickson Foundation has available for purchase professionally recorded audiotapes from its meetings. Professionally produced video-cassettes of one-hour clinical demonstrations by members of the faculty of the 1981, 1982, 1984, and 1989 Erickson Foundation Seminars and the 1983, 1986, 1988, and 1992 Erickson Congresses also can be purchased from the Foundation. Audio- and videocassettes from the 1985 and 1990 Evolution of Psychotherapy Conferences and the 1993 Brief Therapy Conference also are available from the Foundation.

The Erickson Foundation distributes tapes of lectures by Milton Erickson from the 1950s and 1960s when his voice was strong. Releases in our audiotape series are announced in the newsletter.

In *The Process of Hypnotic Induction: A Training Videotape Featuring Inductions Conducted by Milton H. Erickson in 1964*, Jeffrey K. Zeig, Ph.D., discusses the process of hypnotic induction and describes the microdynamics of techniques that Erickson used in his 1964 inductions.

In *Symbolic Hypnotherapy*, Jeffrey K. Zeig, Ph.D., presents information on using symbols in psychotherapy and hypnosis. Segments of hypnotherapy conducted by Milton Erickson with the same subject on two consecutive days in 1978 are shown. Zeig discusses the microdynamics of Erickson's symbolic technique.

Videotapes are available in all U.S. formats, as well as in the European standard. For information on purchasing tapes, contact the Erickson Foundation.

PUBLICATIONS OF THE MILTON H. ERICKSON FOUNDATION

The following books are published by and can be ordered through Brunner/Mazel Publishers, Inc., 19 Union Square West, New York, NY 10003:

A Teaching Seminar with Milton H. Erickson (J. Zeig, Ed. & Commentary) is a transcript, with commentary, of a one-week teaching seminar held for professionals by Dr. Erickson in his home in August 1979.

Ericksonian Approaches to Hypnosis and Psychotherapy (J. Zeig, Ed.) contains the edited proceedings of the First International Erickson Congress.

Ericksonian Psychotherapy, Volume I: Structures; Volume II: Clinical Applications (J. Zeig, Ed.) contain the edited proceedings of the Second International Erickson Congress.

The Evolution of Psychotherapy (J. Zeig, Ed.) contains the edited proceedings of the 1985 Evolution of Psychotherapy Conference.

Developing Ericksonian Therapy: State of the Art (J. Zeig & S. Lankton, Eds.) contains the edited proceedings of the Third International Erickson Congress.

Brief Therapy: Myths, Methods & Metaphors (J. Zeig & S. Gilligan, Eds.) contains the edited proceedings of the Fourth International Erickson Congress.

The Evolution of Psychotherapy: The Second Conference (J. Zeig, Ed.) contains the edited proceedings of the 1990 Evolution of Psychotherapy Conference.

The following book is published by and can be ordered through Jossey-Bass Inc., Publishers, 350 Sansome Street, San Francisco, CA 94104: *What is Psychotherapy? Contemporary Perspectives* (J. Zeig & W. M. Munion, Eds.) contains the edited commentaries of 81 eminent clinicians.

The Ericksonian Monographs

The Foundation sponsors *The Erickson Monographs*, published on an irregular basis, up to three times per year. Edited by Stephen Lankton, M.S.W.; only the highest quality articles on Ericksonian hypnosis and psychotherapy (including technique, theory, and research) are selected for *The Monographs*. Nine issues have been published since 1985. Manuscripts should be sent to Stephen Lankton, M.S.W., P.O. Box 958, Gulf Breeze, FL 32562. For subscription information, contact Brunner/Mazel Publishers.

Newsletter

The Milton H. Erickson Foundation publishes a newsletter for professionals three times per year to inform its readers of the activities of the

Foundation. Articles and notices that relate to Ericksonian approaches to hypnosis and psychotherapy are included and should be sent to the coeditors, Roxanna Erickson Klein, R.N., M.S., and Betty Alice Erickson, M.S., L.P.C., 3516 Euclid, Dallas, TX 75205. Business and subscription matters should be directed to the Erickson Foundation at 3606 North 24th Street, Phoenix, AZ 85016-6500.

MILTON H. ERICKSON INSTITUTES

There are more than 50 Milton H. Erickson Institutes/Societies in the United States and abroad that have applied to the Foundation for permission to use Dr. Erickson's name in the title of their organization. Institutes provide clinical services and professional training. There are institutes in major cities in North America, South America, Europe, and Australia. For information contact the Erickson Foundation.

Faculty of the 1992 International Congress on Ericksonian Approaches to Hypnosis and Psychotherapy

KEYNOTE PRESENTERS

Jay Haley, M.A.
  Rockville, MD
Cloé Madanes, Lic. Psychol.
  Rockville, MD

Ernest L. Rossi, Ph.D.
  Malibu, CA

FACULTY PRESENTING INVITED ADDRESSES

*Joseph Barber, Ph.D.
  Seattle, WA
*Philip Barker, M.B., B.S.
  Calgary, Alberta, Canada
Shirley Bliss, Ph.D.
  Denton, TX
*Gene Combs, M.D. &
Jill Freedman, M.S.W.
  Evanston, IL

*Steve de Shazer, M.S.S.W.
  Milwaukee, WI
*Yvonne Dolan, M.A.
  Golden, CO
*Betty Alice Erickson, M.S.,
L.P.C.
  Dallas, TX
*Richard Fisch, M.D.
  Palo Alto, CA

---

*Indicates faculty who also presented invited workshops

Brent Geary, Ph.D.
Phoenix, AZ
*Stephen Gilligan, Ph.D.
Encinitas, CA
Jean Godin, M.D., Ph.D.
Paris, France
Jean-Michel Oughourlian, M.D., Ph.D.
Paris, France
*Ronald Havens, Ph.D. &
Catherine Walters, M.A., M.S.W.
Springfield, IL
*Carol Kershaw, Ed.D.
Houston, TX
Alfred Lange, Ph.D.
Amsterdam, Netherlands
*Carol Lankton, M.A.
Gulf Breeze, FL
*Stephen Lankton, M.S.W.
Gulf Breeze, FL
*Camillo Loriedo, M.D.
Rome, Italy
John Lovern, Ph.D.
Orange, CA
*Herbert Lustig, M.D.
Wynnewood, PA

*Robert Pearson, M.D.
Houston, TX
Madeleine Richeport, Ph.D.
Rockville, MD
*Michele K. Ritterman, Ph.D.
Oakland, CA
*Sidney Rosen, M.D.
New York, NY
*Olga Silverstein, M.S.W.
New York, NY
*Sandra Sylvester, Ph.D.
Cedar Crest, NM
*Kay Thompson, D.D.S.
Carnegie, PA
Bernhard Trenkle, Dipl. Psych.
Rottweil, Germany
*John Weakland, Ch.E., M.F.C.C.
Palo Alto, CA
*Andre Weitzenhoffer, Ph.D.
Nathrop, CO
*Michael Yapko, Ph.D.
San Diego, CA
*Jeffrey K. Zeig, Ph.D.
Phoenix, AZ

FACULTY PRESENTING WORKSHOPS ONLY

Brian Alman, Ph.D.
Leucadia, CA
Norma Barretta, Ph.D. &
Philip Baretta, M.A.
Lomita, CA
John Beahrs, M.D.
Portland, OR
Philip Booth, Cert. P.S.W.
Oxford, England
John Edgette, Psy. D. &
Janet Edgette, Psy.D.
Rosemont, PA

Michael Elkin, M.A.
Wellesley, MA
Linda Epstein-Graval, M.A., M.F.C.C.
Encino, CA
Helen Erickson, R.N, Ph.D.
Austin, TX
Carl Hammerschlag, M.D.
Phoenix, AZ
D. Corydon Hammond, Ph.D., A.B.P.H.
Salt Lake City, UT

Marlene Hunter, M.D.
West Vancouver, British Columbia, Canada

Tad James, M.S.
Honolulu, HI

Lynn Johnson, Ph.D.
Salt Lake City, UT

Norman Katz, Ph.D. & Marc Lehrer, Ph.D.
Albuquerque, NM

William Matthews, Jr., Ph.D.
Amherst, MA

Robert McNeilly, M.B.B.S.
Brighton, Victoria, Australia

Scott Miller, Ph.D.
Milwaukee, WI

Joyce Mills, Ph.D.
Kekaha, Kauai, HI

Nancy Napier, M.A., M.F.C.C.
New York, NY

Jane Parsons-Fein, C.S.W.
New York, NY

Burkhard Peter, Dipl. Psych.
Munich, Germany

Noelle Poncelet, Ph.D.
Menlo Park, CA

Deborah Ross, Ph.D.
Los Gatos, CA

Gary Ruelas, Ph.D., Richard Lanc Ph.D. & Terry Argast, Ph.D.
Santa Ana, CA

Alan Scheflin, J.D.
San Francisco, CA

Gunther Schmidt, M.D.
Heidelberg, Germany

Robert Schwarz, Psy.D.
Villanova, PA

Francine Shapiro, Ph.D.
Palo Alto, CA

Olga Silverstein, M.S.W.
New York, NY

Donna Spencer, Ph.D.
St. Louis, MO

Charles Stern, Ph.D.
Royal Oak, MI

Terry Tafoya, Ph.D.
San Francisco, CA

Moshe Talmon, Ph.D.
Kefar Shemariahu, Israel

Lars-Eric Unestahl, Ph.D.
Orebro, Sweden

Paul Watzlawick, Ph.D.
Palo Alto, CA

R. Reid Wilson, Ph.D.
Chapel Hill, NC

ACCEPTED PAPERS

Susan Lee Bady, M.S.W.
Brooklyn, NY

Keith L. Buescher, Ph.D.
Springfield, IL

Richard E. Dimond, Ph.D.
Springfield, IL

Hansjorg Ebell, M.D.
Munich, Germany

J. Ricardo Figueroa Quiroga, M.S.
Guadalajara, Jalisco, Mexico

Eric Greenleaf, Ph.D.
Berkeley, CA

Paula J. Haymond, Ed.D.
Houston, TX

Jan Henley, Ph.D.
Johnson City, TN

Michael Hoyt, Ph.D.
Hayward, CA

Wendy Hurley, M.A.
Santa Cruz, CA

Tommaso Longobardi, M.D.
  Naples, Italy
Don Malon, Ph.D.
  St. Louis, MO
Keiichi Miyata, M.A.
  Niigata-Shi, Japan
Sandra Roscoe, M.S.
  Ft. Lauderdale, FL
Mary J. Sant'Eufemia, M.S.W.
  New York, NY

Harry Vincenzi, Ed.D.
  Philadelphia, PA
Marc Weiss, Ph.D.
  Chicago, IL
Dawn M. White, Ph.D.
  Cornville, AZ
Hugh R. Willbourn, M.A.
  London, England

ACCEPTED SHORT COURSES AND SYMPOSIA

Jorge Abia, M.D. & Teresa Robles, Ph.D.
  Mexico City, Mexico
Jeffrey E. Auerbach, Ph.D.
  Sherman Oaks, CA
James M. Auld, B.D.S., Dipl. Soc. Sc., MSc.
  Inverell, New South Wales, Australia
Rubin Battino, M.S.
  Yellow Springs, OH
Cheryl Bell-Gadsby, M.A. &
Anne Siegenberg, M.S.W., M.A.
  North Vancouver, British Columbia, Canada
Betty Blue, Ph.D.
  Long Beach, CA
Russell A. Bourne, Jr., Ph.D.
  Ashland, VA
William R. Boyd, Jr., Ph.D.
  Dayton, TN
Heinrich Breuer, Dipl. Psych.
  Cologne, Germany
Sky Chaney, M.A., M.F.C.C.,
Marcia Anton, M.A., M.F.C.C.,
Nicholas Anton, M.D., &
Bobbie Chaney, M.A.
  Santa Rosa, CA

Theresa Eytalis, M.S.W.
  St. Louis, MO
Jeffery B. Feldman, Ph.D.
  Charlotte, NC
Steven Feldman, M.A.
  Seattle, WA
Douglas G. Flemons, Ph.D.
  Fort Lauderdale, FL
Bill Forey, M.A.
  Vermillion, SD with
    Dayton Vogel, M.A.
      Rock Valley, IA
Brent Geary, Ph.D.
  Phoenix, AZ
Steven Friedman, Ph.D.
  Hingham, MA
Richard J. Gellerman, Ph.D.
  Tucson, AZ
H. L. (Lee) Gillis, Ph.D.
  Milledgevile, GA with
    Christian Itin, M.S.W.
      Boulder, CO
Michael A. Gass, Ph.D.
  Durham, NH
George Glaser, M.S.W.
  Austin, TX
Bruce Gregory, Ph.D.
  Van Nuys, CA

Brian Grodner, Ph.D., A.B.P.P.
  Albuquerque, NM
Steven Hassan, M.Ed.
  Boston, MA
Richard Hatten, Ph.D.
  Sacramento, CA
Harriet E. Hollander, Ph.D.
  Princeton, NJ with
  David Mandelbaum, M.D., Ph.D.
    Highland Park, NJ
Gail Isenberg, M.S.
  Middlebury, VT
Charles E. Johnson, M.S.W.
  Denver, CO
Leeann Jorgensen, Ph.D. &
Anita Klassen
  Marshall, MN
Rodger S. Kessler, Ph.D.
  Stowe, VT
Carolyn K. Kinney, Ph.D.
  Austin, TX
Suzanne I. Lerner, Ph.D.
  Berkeley, CA
Brian M. Lippincott, Ph.D.
  Hollister, CA with
  Peter Brown, M.D.
    Toronto, Ontario, Canada
  Carol Sommer, M.S.
    Downers Grove, IL
  Ernest L. Rossi, Ph.D.
    Malibu, CA
  Shirley Sanders, Ph.D.
    Chapel Hill, NC
Julien Mercure, M.A.
  Ottawa, Ontario, Canada
William A. Miller, Jr., Ph.D.
  Absecon, NJ
Joyce Mills, Ph.D.
  Kekaha, Kauai, HI
Donald Miretsky, M.Ed.
  Tucson, AZ
Susan H. Mullarky, M.A.
  Tucson, AZ

W. Michael Munion, M.A.
  Mesa, AZ
Doris B. Murphy, M.A.
  Solana Beach, CA
Patricia F. Newton, M.D. &
Lusijah Marx, M.N., Psy.D.
  Portland, OR
Michaela M. Ozelsel, Ph.D.
  Obernburg, Germany
Maggie Phillips, Ph.D.
  Oakland, CA with
  Claire Frederick, M.D.
    Tahoe City, CA
Rick Pipkin, M.S.
  Dallas, TX
Iris A. Ramos, ACSW
  Austin, TX
Mark Reese, M.A.
  Cardiff by the Sea, CA
Michael Samko, Ph.D.
  Solana Beach, CA with
  John R. Windle, M.A.
    Hood River, OR
Lee G. Shilts, Ph.D. &
James Rudes, M.S.W.
  Fort Lauderdale, FL
Barbara Sinclair, Ph.D.
  Los Angeles, CA
Douglas A. Sue, Ph.D.
  Stratford, CT
Iona Marsaa Teeguarden, M.A.
  Palo Alto, CA
John L. Walter, M.S.W. &
Jane E. Peller, M.S.W.
  Chicago, IL
Neil Weiner, Ph.D.
  Mesa, AZ
Nancy Winston, M.S.W. &
Paul Lounsbury, M.A.
  New York, NY
Christian Ziegler, M.D.
  Faulensee, Switzerland

MODERATORS

Sandra Zoe Brown, Ph.D.
    Torrance, CA
Seyma Calihman, M.S.S.W.
    Austin, TX
Sally Franek, Ph.D.
    Moscow, ID
Brent Geary, Ph.D.
    Phoenix, AZ

Joseph Hicks, M.Ed.
    Dover, DE
Susan Mirow, Ph.D., M.D.
    Salt Lake City, UT
Marian Richetta, M.A.
    Solana Beach, CA
Hillel Zeitlin, L.C.S.W.
    Baltimore, MD

EDITORIAL REVIEW BOARD

Sandra Zoe Brown, Ph.D.
Seyma Calihman, M.S.S.W.
Kristina K. Erickson, M.S., M.D.
Sally Franek, Ph.D.
Brent B. Geary, Ph.D.

Joseph Hicks, M.Ed.
Susan Mirow, Ph.D., M.D.
Marian Richetta, M.A.
Hillel Zeitlin, L.C.S.W.